A Handbook for the Study of Mental Health

Social Contexts, Theories, and Systems

Edited by

ALLAN V. HORWITZ   TERESA L. SCHEID

CAMBRIDGE
UNIVERSITY PRESS

PUBLISHED BY THE PRESS SYNDICATE OF THE UNIVERSITY OF CAMBRIDGE
The Pitt Building, Trumpington Street, Cambridge, United Kingdom

CAMBRIDGE UNIVERSITY PRESS
The Edinburgh Building, Cambridge CB2 2RU, UK   http://www.cup.cam.ac.uk
40 West 20th Street, New York, NY 10011-4211, USA   http://www.cup.org
10 Stamford Road, Oakleigh, Melbourne 3166, Australia

© Cambridge University Press 1999

First published 1999

Printed in the United States of America

Typeface Times 10/12.5 pt.   *System* AMS-T$_E$X   [FH]

A catalog record for this book is available from the British Library

Library of Congress Cataloging in Publication Data
The sociology of mental health and illness / edited by Allan
V. Horwitz, Teresa L. Scheid.
p.   cm.
Includes bibliographical references and index.
1. Social psychiatry.   I. Horwitz, Allan V.   II. Scheid, Teresa L.
RC455.S643   1999
616.89 – dc21   98-11638
                                                                  CIP

ISBN 0 521 56133 7 hardback
ISBN 0 521 56763 7 paperback

A Handbook for the Study of Mental Health
Social Contexts, Theories, and Systems

This study of mental health offers an interdisciplinary approach to analyzing mental health and mental disorder in their social contexts. Researchers examine such issues as the social factors that shape psychiatric diagnosis and thus affect the definition and treatment of mental disorders; the effects of sociodemographic variables on mental health and illness experience; the role of various forms of social stress and social support; the organization, delivery, and evaluation of mental health services; and mental health–care policy.

This book offers the first comprehensive presentation of the sociology of mental health and illness – one that includes original, contemporary contributions by experts in the relevant aspects of the field. Divided into three sections, the chapters cover the general perspectives in the field, the social determinants of mental health, and current policy areas affecting mental health services.

A Handbook for the Study of Mental Health is designed for classroom use in the fields of sociology, social work, human relations, human services, and psychology. With its nontechnical style and comprehensive overview of the historical, social, and institutional frameworks for understanding mental health and illness, the text is suitable for advanced undergraduate or lower-level graduate students.

Allan V. Horwitz is Professor and Chair of the Department of Sociology at Rutgers University. He is the author of *The Social Control of Mental Illness* and *The Logic of Social Control,* as well as numerous articles on various aspects of mental disorder.

Teresa L. Scheid is Associate Professor of Sociology at the University of North Carolina at Charlotte. Her research focuses primarily on the organization of mental health services and the work of mental health–care providers, and her articles have been published in a variety of academic journals.

We dedicate this volume to James R. Greenley, who devoted his professional life to improving mental health services.

Contents

Contributors

Carol S. Aneshensel, Ph.D.
Professor
Department of Community Health Sciences
School of Public Health
University of California, Los Angeles

Joanne E. Atay, M.A.
Statistician
Survey and Analysis Branch
U.S. Center for Mental Health Services

William R. Avison, Ph.D.
Professor of Sociology, Psychiatry, and
    Epidemiology and Biostatistics
Director, Centre for Health and Well-Being
University of Western Ontario

Carol A. Boyer, Ph.D.
Associate Director
Institute for Health, Health Care Policy,
    and Aging Research
Rutgers University

Judith A. Cook, Ph.D.
Professor of Sociology in Psychiatry
Department of Psychiatry
University of Illinois at Chicago

Stephen Crystal, Ph.D.
Research Professor
Chair, Division on Aging and Director,
    AIDS Research Group
Institute for Health, Health Care Policy,
    and Aging Research
School of Social Work
Rutgers University

Bruce P. Dohrenwend, Ph.D.
Foundations' Fund for Research in
    Psychiatry Professor
Department of Psychiatry
Columbia University

William W. Eaton, Ph.D.
Professor
Department of Mental Hygiene
School of Hygiene and Public Health
Johns Hopkins University

Bradford Gray, Ph.D.
Director
Division of Health and Science Policy
New York Academy of Medicine

Michelle Harris-Reid, Ph.D.
Department of Sociology
University of Michigan

Marilyn J. Henderson, M.P.A.
Assistant Chief
Survey and Analysis Branch
U.S. Center for Mental Health Services

Virginia Aldigé Hiday, Ph.D.
Professor of Sociology
Department of Sociology and Anthropology
North Carolina State University

Allan V. Horwitz, Ph.D.
Professor of Sociology
Department of Sociology
Institute for Health, Health Care Policy,
    and Aging Research
Rutgers University

Caroline L. Kaufmann, Ph.D.
Director of Research
Kentucky Center for Mental Health Studies

Ronald C. Kessler, Ph.D.
Professor
Department of Health Care Policy
Harvard Medical School

Harriet P. Lefley, Ph.D.
Professor of Psychiatry and Behavioral
    Sciences
Department of Psychiatry
University of Miami School of Medicine

Mary Clare Lennon, Ph.D.
Associate Professor of Clinical Public
    Health
School of Public Health
Columbia University

Nan Lin, Ph.D.
Professor of Sociology
Department of Sociology
Duke University

Bruce G. Link, Ph.D.
Mailman Professor of Public Health
School of Public Health
Columbia University

Ronald W. Manderscheid, Ph.D.
Chief
Survey and Analysis Branch
U.S. Center for Mental Health Services

Gloria Maramba
Department of Psychology
Penn State University

David Mechanic, Ph.D.
René Dubos Professor of Behavioral
    Science
Director, Institute for Health, Health Care
    Policy, and Aging Research
Rutgers University

Elizabeth G. Menaghan, Ph.D.
Professor of Sociology
Department of Sociology
Ohio State University

John Mirowsky, Ph.D.
Professor of Sociology
Department of Sociology
Ohio State University

Joseph P. Morrissey, Ph.D.
Professor of Social Medicine, Psychiatry,
    and Health Policy
Deputy Director for Research
Cecil G. Sheps Center for Health Services
    Research
University of North Carolina –
    Chapel Hill

Carles Muntaner, M.D.
Assistant Professor
Institute of Occupational and
    Environmental Health
West Virginia School of Medicine

Leonard I. Pearlin, Ph.D.
Graduate Professor of Sociology
Department of Sociology
University of Maryland – College Park

M. Kristen Peek, Ph.D.
Assistant Professor
Department of Health Promotion and
    Gerontology
University of Texas Medical Branch

Bernice A. Pescosolido, Ph.D.
Professor of Sociology
Department of Sociology
Indiana University

Christopher Peterson, Ph.D.
Professor of Psychology
Department of Psychology
University of Michigan

Jo C. Phelan, Ph.D.
Assistant Professor of Public Health
School of Public Health
Columbia University

Susan A. Pickett, Ph.D.
Assistant Professor of Psychology in
    Psychiatry
Department of Psychiatry
University of Illinois at Chicago

Lisa Razzano, Ph.D.
Assistant Professor of Psychology in
   Psychiatry
Department of Psychiatry
University of Illinois at Chicago

David A. Rochefort, Ph.D.
Professor of Political Science and Public
   Administration
Department of Political Science
Northeastern University

Sarah Rosenfield, Ph.D.
Associate Professor of Sociology
Department of Sociology
Institute for Health, Health Care Policy,
   and Aging Research
Rutgers University

Catherine E. Ross, Ph.D.
Professor of Sociology
Department of Sociology
Ohio State University

Mark Schlesinger, Ph.D.
Associate Professor
School of Public Health
Yale University

Teresa L. Scheid, Ph.D.
Associate Professor
Department of Sociology
University of North Carolina – Charlotte

Lori R. Schlosser, M.S.W.
Research Assistant
Institute for Health, Health Care Policy,
   and Aging Research
Rutgers University

Sharon Schwartz, Ph.D.
Assistant Professor
School of Public Health
Columbia University

David T. Takeuchi, Ph.D.
Professor of Sociology
Department of Sociology
Indiana University

Peggy A. Thoits, Ph.D.
Professor of Sociology
Department of Sociology
Vanderbilt University

R. Jay Turner, Ph.D.
Professor of Sociology
Department of Sociology
University of Miami

Edwina Uehara, Ph.D.
Associate Professor
School of Social Work
University of Washington

Jerome C. Wakefield, D.S.W.
Professor
School of Social Work
Institute for Health, Health Care Policy,
   and Aging Research
Rutgers University

Blair Wheaton, Ph.D.
Professor of Sociology
Department of Sociology
University of Toronto

David R. Williams, Ph.D.
Professor
Department of Sociology
Senior Research Scientist
Institute for Survey Research
University of Michigan

Michael J. Witkin, M.A., C.P.A.
Statistician
Survey and Analysis Branch
U.S. Center for Mental Health Services

Shanyang Zhao, Ph.D.
Assistant Professor
Department of Sociology
Temple University

Preface

Bruce P. Dohrenwend

This volume is sponsored by the Mental Health Section of the American Sociological Association and is intended for classroom use by upper-level undergraduates and lower-level graduate students. In its broad focus on social factors in mental health and mental illness, it contrasts with and usefully complements more psychologically and biologically oriented textbooks.

Chapters have been contributed by most of the major sociological investigators of the kinds of psychological distress, irrational thinking, and bizarre behaviors that have come to be called "mental illnesses." Various definitions of these problematic affects, cognitions, and actions are discussed, and data are presented on the prevalence and distribution of some of the most important ones (as classified in the diagnostic manual of the American Psychiatric Association). Although the emphasis is on the role of social factors, psychological and biological factors are not ignored, and more than one author points to the need for interdisciplinary bridges if we are to understand the cause of these problems.

If there is a central theme, it is a concern with the nature and importance of social stress processes. But the variations on this theme are so rich and complex as to constitute fully developed subtopics in their own right. For example, several chapters introduce a life-span perspective and give careful consideration to the role of family structure. There are chapters on the social statuses related to gender, ethnic/racial background, and socioeconomic position.

Much of this handbook is concerned with social factors that are likely to increase the risk of impairing mental health and developing mental disorders, as well as with how these risks might be prevented or reduced. The book finishes with a series of chapters on social factors in the organization and delivery of mental health care. These chapters are wide-ranging and include descriptions and analyses of the relation of mental health systems to criminal justice systems, the particular problems posed by severe, chronic disorders such as schizophrenia, and cross-national and cross-cultural comparisons of different types of mental health care.

This volume brings together, for the first time, the wealth and variety of socio-logical theory and research that has been developing concurrently with advances being made by more psychologically and biologically oriented investigators over the past few decades. It will stimulate students to think and ask questions about the role of social factors in the development, course, and treatment of problems of mental health and mental illness. It should do no less for mental health researchers from other disciplines in psychiatry, psychology, and the social sciences.

Acknowledgments

All books are collective efforts, but a work of this sort is especially so. It grew out of the general feeling of members of the Mental Health Section of the American Sociological Association that no existing book aimed at a student audience adequately dealt with the range of issues covered by the sociology of mental health and illness. This volume thus reflects the thinking of a community that shares many of the same assumptions about the nature of this field. In particular, the sociology of mental health and illness seeks to link broad, macro-level structural phenomena to micro-level, individual experiences. In addition, it is concerned with the most vital policy issues concerning the organization of mental health services and the treatment of persons who are mentally ill. The editors approached leading experts in each area, most of whom are also active members of the Mental Health Section, and nearly all agreed to contribute chapters.

The effort in coordinating thirty-one contributions went well beyond our expectations. We could not have completed this endeavor without the efforts of Ivana Brierova, who served as research assistant, copyeditor, computer specialist, and indexer, among other roles. Ruth Kranes provided secretarial assistance of many sorts. We are also grateful for the support of Leonard Pearlin, Carol Aneshensel, Bruce Link, and Mary Clare Lennon, the chairs of the Mental Health Section while this book was being completed. Our editors at Cambridge University Press – first Elizabeth Neal and then Mary Child – have also been unfailingly helpful in all aspects of the publication process. Matt Darnell, our production editor, did an extraordinary job in bringing this volume to publication.

If this work stimulates a new generation of mental health sociologists to form their own collective understanding of how social arrangements affect mental health and mental illness, it will have fulfilled the major purpose that stimulated its creation.

Part I

Approaches to Mental Health and Illness: Conflicting Definitions and Emphases

Allan V. Horwitz & Teresa L. Scheid

The sociology of mental health and illness is a very diverse field that encompasses many different approaches to its subject matter. Some researchers focus on social and cultural factors that define what is normal and abnormal in societies, while others consider how social environments are more or less likely to cause psychiatric disorders. Another difference is between research into the social causes of specific types of psychiatric disorders and research that emphasizes how social factors are related to why some people are distressed and others happy. A third difference in approach is whether sociologists are interested primarily in understanding the social aspects of mental health and illness or rather in developing and changing social policies regarding mental disorders. The chapters in the first section of this volume provide general introductions to these and other core issues that provide the basic framework for the sociology of mental health and illness.

Mental Health and Illness as Continuous or Discrete

An essential starting point for the study of mental health and illness is understanding this question: What is mental health and illness? As David Mechanic indicates in his overview of this area, there are many diverse definitions of mental health and illness. Through the 1970s, a *continuous model* of mental health and illness dominated research and practice in the mental health field. In this model, mental health and illness are seen as opposite poles of a continuum, with most people falling somewhere in between the extremes. Mental illness is not a distinctly different category from mental health; instead, there are varying degrees of health and sickness, of normal and abnormal behaviors. The boundary between health and illness is not rigid but is fluid and subject to social and environmental influences. In the continuous model of health and illness, anyone can become "sick" if subjected to enough stress in their psychosocial environment.

Since the 1980s there has been a shift away from the notion of mental health and illness as points on a continuum toward an increased emphasis on a *discrete,* or dichotomous, model of mental illness. This medical model rejects the idea that mental health and illness form a continuum and instead views health and illness as opposites that form a dichotomy, so that one is either sick or well. In this view, people who are mentally ill are placed into specific disease categories by the identification of specific symptoms. One either has, or does not have, types of mental disorders such as schizophrenia, depression, or anxiety disorders. This discrete model stems from biomedical research emphasizing more organic, biological approaches to mental illness and postulating that mental illnesses have genetic, biological, biochemical, or neurological causes (Michels & Marzuk 1993; Wilson 1993).

Whether mental illnesses should be viewed as a continuum with mental health or as specific disease entities is a controversy that has not been resolved. In this volume, some chapters take the former view, some the latter view, and some combine both approaches. It is probably best not to look at this question as one that has an absolute answer but rather as one where the most appropriate view of mental disorder depends on the research question being addressed.

One question that proponents of both the continuous and discrete perspectives often overlook is: What is mental health? Although researchers generally examine various aspects of mental disorder, they rarely delineate the aspects of mental health. Mental health includes a number of dimensions: self-esteem; realization of one's potential; the ability to maintain fulfilling, meaningful relationships; and psychological well-being. Ryff's (1989) overview of psychological well-being draws upon Allport's conception of maturity, Jung's formulation of individuation, Maslow's conception of self-actualization, and Rogers's view of the fully functioning person. She conceptualizes and measures well-being as including self-acceptance, positive relations with others, autonomy, environmental mastery (i.e., a sense of competence and ability to manage the world one is confronted with), purpose in life, and personal growth. It is clear that such a view of mental health constitutes far more than the mere absence of illness or disorder. Most people would probably fall far short of optimum mental health, indicating that mental health is not a statistical norm but a goal toward which to strive. Consequently, advocates of mental health focus on a broad delivery of mental health services to the general population – not just to the most seriously disturbed people. They also emphasize prevention and education, as well as interventions that aid people who have already developed particular types of mental illnesses.

Psychiatric Symptoms as Illness or as Deviance

One divergence in the field is whether mental health and mental illness are dichotomies or rather points on a continuum. Another is whether psychiatric symptoms are best viewed as indicators of illness or as forms of deviant behavior. Most psychiatrists and other mental health professionals regard the various forms of mental illness as indicators of disease. They focus on people whose illnesses are persistent and dysfunctional and use the definition of mental illness that is found in the most recent official manual of psychiatric disorders: the fourth edition of the American Psychiatric Association's *Diagnostic and Statistical Manual* (DSM-IV). The DSM-IV defines mental illness as follows.

> In DSM-IV, each of the mental disorders is conceptualized as a clinically significant behavioral or psychological syndrome or pattern that occurs in an individual and that is associated with present distress (e.g., a painful symptom) or disability (i.e., impairment in one or more important areas of functioning) or with a significantly increased risk of suffering death, pain, disability, or an important loss of freedom. In addition, this syndrome or pattern must not be merely an expectable and culturally sanctioned response to a particular event, for example, the death of a loved one. Whatever its original cause, it must currently be considered a manifestation of a behavioral, psychological, or biological dysfunction in the individual. Neither deviant behavior (e.g., political, religious, or sexual) nor conflicts that are primarily between the individual and society are mental disorders unless the deviance or conflict is a symptom of a dysfunction in the individual, as described above. (APA 1994: xxi–xxii)

According to DSM-IV, the major types of mental illnesses are discrete groups of symptoms that indicate some kind of psychopathology within the individual. Chart I shows the nine major categories of disorders in DSM-IV. Mental health clinicians and researchers use these categories as a basis for the diagnosis of what sort of problem an individual has, the likely cause of the problem, the expected course of the disorder, and the appropriate treatment to apply. The DSM was a significant factor in making psychiatric diagnoses more comparable to diagnoses in medical specialities. It is a purely descriptive document that does not posit any specific causes of mental illness. However, its emphasis upon classification legitimates a medical model that assumes mental illness is a disease as opposed to a form of deviance.

In contrast to the view taken in DSM-IV, many sociologists view mental illness as a type of deviant behavior, that is, behavior that does not indicate an intrapsychic disorder but that is a violation of social rules. According to this view, those who are called "mentally ill" are people who do not act in socially appropriate ways. They may talk too much or too little, display bad manners or unusual patterns of speech, drink or take drugs, or otherwise act in ways that displease those around them. The ones who obtain the label of "mentally ill" are those who are not powerful enough to resist the definitions of mental health professionals, family members, teachers, and others who apply these labels. The definition of mental illness in DSM-IV (just quoted) explicitly excludes these types of behavior; nonetheless, the definitions of a number of particular disorders in the DSM – such as drug and alcohol disorders, conduct disorder, antisocial personality disorder, and many others – do in fact encompass a wide range of deviant behaviors that need not indicate intrapsychic pathology (see also Chapter 2).

Chart I. *DSM-IV categories of disorder*

Schizophrenia and other psychotic disorders
These severe disorders are characterized by the presence of psychotic symptoms (delusions and/or hallucinations) leading to impairments that interfere with the capacity of an individual to meet the ordinary demands of life. The types of schizophrenia include paranoid, disorganized, catatonic, undifferentiated, and residual.

Mood disorders
These are characterized by disturbances in mood – either markedly depressed, elevated, or both. Included in the mood disorders are major depressive disorder (with changes in appetite, sleep, energy level, feelings of worthlessness or guilt, and suicidal thoughts), dysthymic disorder (chronic depressed mood), and bipolar disorder (with movement back and forth between extreme depression and extreme mood elevation).

Anxiety disorders
All the anxiety disorders deal with the presence of an intense fear and with subsequent avoidance of what is feared or other maladaptive coping strategies. Included in the anxiety disorders are panic attacks (sudden onset of intense fear, shortness of breath, and feelings of "loss of control"), agoraphobia (anxiety and avoidance of places that are felt to be "threatening"), specific phobias, social phobia, posttraumatic stress disorder, generalized anxiety disorder (six months of excessive general anxiety and worry), and obsessive-compulsive disorder.

Dissociative disorders
This category is characterized by a disassociation from the self as well as by periods of lost time too extensive to be explained by normal forgetfulness. This includes dissociative amnesia (inability to recall important personal information), dissociative fugue (sudden travel away from one's home and the embodiment of a new identity that is not a conscious decision), and dissociative identity disorder (formerly "multiple personality disorder," involving the presence of two or more distinct identities or statuses that reflects a failure to integrate the self and accompanied by an extensive loss of time).

Disorder usually first diagnosed in infancy, childhood, or adolescence
Many of these disorders are found both in children and adults, but they are often diagnosed early in life. This category includes mental retardation, development disorders (autism), attention deficit disorder (or ADD, involving symptoms of inattention and/or hyperactivity), conduct disorder (patterns of behavior that violate societal norms), and oppositional-defiant disorder (patterns of hostile and defiant behavior).

Delirium, dementia, amnestic, and other cognitive disorders
These disorders are characterized by deficits in cognition and/or memory that represent a significant change from a previous level of functioning. This DSM-IV category includes dementia (multiple cognitive impairment, i.e. Alzheimer's) and amnestic disorder (memory impairment only).

Somatoform disorders
Somatoform disorders are diagnosed when there are physical symptoms that cannot be fully explained by a medical condition. This category includes somatization disorder (with many physical symptoms, formerly referred to as "hysteria"), conversion disorder (symptoms affecting voluntary motor or sensory functions, i.e. blindness), and hypochondriasis (the preoccupation with the fear of having a disease despite medical reassurance). All of these disorders are *not* under voluntary control, and all cause significant distress and social impairment (affect one's ability to function in society).

Chart I *(cont.)*

Eating disorders
Problems with eating behavior associated with a disturbance in perception of body weight and shape. Includes anorexia nervosa (refusal to maintain a minimally normal weight) and bulimia nervosa (binge eating following by self-induced vomiting).

Personality disorders
This category is characterized by enduring patterns of inner experience and behavior that deviates markedly from cultural expectations and leads to distress. The personality disorders include paranoid (distrustful of the motives of others), schizoid (detached from social relationships), schizotypal (discomfort in close relationships, eccentricities of behavior), histrionic (excessive attention-seeking behavior), narcissistic (grandiosity and the need for admiration, lack of empathy), borderline (unstable personal relationships and self-image, impulsive), antisocial (disregard for and violation of the rights of others), dependent (submissive and "clinging," excessive need to be taken care of) and obsessive-compulsive (preoccupation with orderliness, perfection, and control).

The DSM-IV contains five axes, each of which refers to a different realm for clinical attention (APA 1994). Axis I refers to the symptoms of the clinical disorders in the manual; Axis II is used to classify the personality disorders as well as mental retardation. Axis III is used to report general medical conditions that may be relevant to understanding and treating an individual's mental disorder. Axis IV is used to record psychosocial and environment problems (such as negative life events, environmental deficiencies, or family and interpersonal stressors) that will affect treatment and prognosis of the mental disorders. Axis V is used to report the clinician's evaluation of the individual's overall level of functioning (i.e., ability to manage life) and is referred to as the global assessment of functioning.

Sociologists who regard mental illness as a form of deviant behavior usually study the processes and rules used to define mental illness rather than symptoms within individuals. For sociologists in this tradition, the work of the French philosopher, Michel Foucault (1965) has been influential. Foucault postulates that the view of "madness" as a disease and the corresponding dread of "unreason" grew together in the eighteenth century. He links this to the development of civilization, which enabled abstract contemplation without any corresponding exercise of the body. Beginning around this time, people who had lost their reason were removed from society, lest they contaminate others. Madness became increasingly individualized, as well as associated with crime. Psychiatry, as the science of mental disease, and the asylum developed as a result of the need to differentiate the madman from other suspect populations such as criminals and the poor (Foucault 1975).

In addition to Foucault, the work of the psychiatrist Thomas Szasz has been an important influence in the debate over whether mental illness is a genuine individual pathology or a socially invented category of deviant behavior. Szasz (1963, 1984) has argued that mental illness is not a disease (because there are no physical lesions associated with it) but instead is a label placed on willful behavior that is socially disvalued. Calling people "mentally ill" is, for Szasz, a way of denying the fact that human beings freely choose their actions. Szasz believes that involuntary treatment in mental institutions does not differ from incarceration in penal institutions in any fundamental way. Another well-known study that questions the validity of the medical view of mental illness is Rosenhan's (1973) study of the failure of psychiatrists and medical personal to detect "sanity" in pseudo-patients who, once admitted to a psychiatric unit, behaved normally. Rosenhan's work is widely cited by those who argue that mental illnesses are not in fact diseases and cannot be diagnosed accurately by medical personal.

Chapter 1, by David Mechanic, examines many of the issues and controversies involved in the debate between those who view mental illness as intrapsychic pathology and as deviant behavior. It serves as a general introduction to the chapters that follow.

Measuring Mental Illness in Community Populations

How can such an illusive phenomenon as mental illness be measured? The next two chapters in Part I deal with the ways in which sociologists measure and count mental illness. In Chapter 2, Jerome Wakefield discusses some of the important conceptual issues involved with determining whether somebody is mentally ill and with measuring mental illness in community populations. The measurement of mental illness is one way in which the sociological approach is clearly differentiated from the clinical approach to mental disorders. Sociologists are less interested in studying people who enter clinical settings than in understanding the development of mental illness in community settings. Sociologists believe that people who enter clinical treatment are a biased sample of all people who develop mental disorders. This is because most people who develop mental disorders do not seek help from mental health professionals but instead seek no professional help at all or enter general medical practice, religious settings, or alternative healing contexts. The need to study untreated individuals in the community raises many important conceptual issues regarding the definition and measurement of mental illness. Wakefield's chapter indicates the great difficulties facing researchers who wish to study and measure mental illness in community populations.

In assessing mental illness in the community, there are a variety of terms with which the student needs to be familiar. *Epidemiology* refers to the study of the distribution of illness in a population. Epidemiological research not only assesses overall rates of disease but, by identifying who is susceptible to particular conditions, can also lead to a better understanding of the specific causes of a disorder. *Morbidity* is the prevalence of diseases in a population, and *comorbidity* is the occurrence of more than one disease in the same individual. *Point prevalence* refers to the percentage of the population affected with an illness at a given point in time; *lifetime prevalence* refers to the percentage of the population *ever* affected with an illness. *Incidence rate* is the rate at which new cases of an illness or disorder form in the population within a specific time period.

Beginning in the 1970s, the epidemiological study of psychiatric disorder began to shift away from the use of continuous measures of distress toward the use of diagnostic categories of disorder that parallel those found in the DSM (see Chart I). The first such study was the Epidemiologic Catchment Area (ECA) project (Robins et al. 1981). This study trained lay people to administer interviews to thousands of community members in five areas of the United States. Computer-generated psychiatric diagnoses serve as the basis for comparing the rates of particular types of psychiatric disorder in different demographic groups in the community (e.g., men vs. women, young vs. old, married vs. unmarried).

The third chapter in this part, by Ronald Kessler and Shanyang Zhao, reports the results of the most recent large epidemiological study of psychiatric disorder in the United States, the National Comorbidity Survey (NCS) that was conducted in the early 1990s. The NCS is the only study of particular psychiatric disorders in a nationally representative community population. Although the use of categorical measures of psychiatric diagnoses in community populations has been criticized (Mirowsky & Ross 1989a), the field of psychiatric epidemiology has moved away from the use of continuous measures of distress toward the use of diagnostic categories that more closely parallel the categories used in clinical practice by mental health professionals. Kessler and Zhao show how the prevalence of psychiatric disorders differs across a variety of groups with respect to sex, age, social class, ethnicity, marital status, and so on. This kind of descriptive data forms the basis for explanations of these differences that are the focus of subsequent chapters in Part II of this book.

In addition to the studies of psychiatric disorders in the United States that are the focus of these chapters, a good deal of research examines the prevalence and types of mental illness in many other cultures. All cultures characterize some forms of behavior as mental illness, but there is disagreement over whether the specific categories of mental illness found in official manuals such as the DSM-IV are universal (Patel & Winston 1994). This question is very difficult to answer because it involves many complicated issues. One is whether mental illness is a biological disease, a form of psychological disorder, a product of the social environment, or a label applied to abnormal behavior. Another is that definitions of "normality" and "abnormality" are culturally specific: definitions of mental health that involve concepts such as self-esteem, self-actualization, or psychological well-being reflect the biases of modern Western cultures (Draguns 1984). The distinction between mental health and physical health (the mind–body dichotomy) is not found in many cultures. For example, Native Americans and many Asian cultures take a more holistic approach to health and illness, one that views mental and physical health as intrinsically intertwined. Consequently, it is very difficult to transplant instruments created to measure mental health and illness from one culture to another. This is especially true because mental health measures usually ask respondents to describe their emotional or subjective feelings and experiences. Measures that would adequately compare disorders across cultures would have to take into account varying culturally influenced understandings of mental health and illness. Even within a large, complex, and heterogeneous modern society such as the contemporary United States, adequate comparison of different ethnic and cultural groups requires an understanding of how these groups develop and manifest various types of psychiatric disorders.

Biological, Psychological, and Sociological Perspectives on Mental Illness

The fourth and fifth chapters in this section review the major theories in the two disciplines that are central to the mental health professions: biology and psychology. Nearly all who work in the mental health professions adhere to one of these two perspectives or to some combination of them. The biological and psychological views are critical for understanding how mental health professionals view mental disorder. In addition, they have dominated the study of psychiatric disorder over the course of the twentieth century. Nearly all treatment for psychiatric disorders is also based on biological and/or psychotherapeutic models. It is impossible to understand sociological perspectives on mental disorder without knowing the key tenets of the biological and psychological approaches.

Sharon Schwartz's Chapter 4 provides an overview of current biomedical research. She shows how knowledge of mental disorders has improved over the past decade as a result of new technologies that have begun to unlock the structure and functioning of the brain. These technologies, which allow researchers to directly examine brain activity and to locate different types of mental functioning in different particular regions of the brain, have led to enhanced understanding of the complex systems that underlie some forms of mental disorder. In addition, greater knowledge about how the brain operates has generated drug treatments that are more effective than previous therapies in alleviating many types of psychiatric symptoms. Schwartz's chapter also gives an overview of research underlying biological approaches – including adoption studies, twin studies, and studies of the brain – that indicate some genetic component to many serious forms of mental disorders. As she indicates in her conclusion, the results of biologically oriented research need not conflict with a sociologically informed understanding of this topic, but both types of approaches are necessary for a full understanding of psychiatric disorder.

The fifth chapter, by the psychologist Christopher Peterson, provides an overview of a second prevalent type of understanding of mental disorders: psychological approaches. Until recently, psychological approaches were the dominant mode of studying and treating the mentally ill. Peterson shows that there is not a single psychological approach but rather at least four major traditions in psychological thinking about psychiatric disorders. He describes the psychoanalytic, cognitive-behavioral, phenomenological, and family approaches to the study of mental disorder. As with biological approaches, psychological approaches do not contradict sociological approaches to mental health and illness but can complement them.

Both the biological and psychological approaches see the primary causes of psychiatric disorder as *intraindividual*. From the biological perspective, people become mentally ill because of genetic, neurochemical, viral, and other factors that are largely independent of the social environment. For the psychologist, the critical determinants of psychiatric disorder lie in early patterns of socialization, cognitive styles, personal identities, and other factors that are essential aspects of individual personalities. The biological and psychological approaches emphasize different forces that can lead people to develop psychiatric disorders, yet both pay only scant attention to the social environment. Sociological approaches, in contrast, indicate what sorts of circumstances that are external to particular individuals are conducive to the development of mental disorders.

The sixth chapter in this section, by Peggy Thoits, clearly indicates the differences in the way sociologists approach the study of mental illness from that of the biological and psychological models. The sociological study of mental illness focuses on how factors external to individuals in their social environments can explain why some people develop mental disorders. These factors include chronic strains in their environment, such as poverty, poor living conditions, dangerous neighborhoods, and overwhelming role responsibilities, as well as more acute negative life events, such as natural disasters, sporadic unemployment, social relocation, and adjusting to new social environments and roles. Thoits shows how structural and stress theories can explain why members of different social groups have such varying rates of mental disorder. She also indicates that the social factors related to the treatment and adaptations of people who are labeled mentally ill are not always the same factors that cause psychiatric disorders. Her chapter, which many subsequent chapters will amplify, shows how factors in the social environment influence both how people come to develop psychiatric disorders and how they come to enter certain social roles because of their psychiatric disabilities.

The Labeling of Mental Disorders

While most sociologists examine how social factors make various groups more or less likely to develop psychiatric disorders and distress, others study a different kind of question: How do social factors affect the way that people who are called mentally ill are treated in society? These researchers argue that definitions of what is considered normal and abnormal behavior are socially constructed. The sociologist Thomas Scheff, for example, uses labeling theory to describe mental illness as deviance from social norms: "Psychiatric symptoms as withdrawal, hallucinations, continual muttering, posturing etc., may be categorized as violations of certain social norms – these norms are so taken-for-granted that they are not explicitly verbalized, which we have called residual rules" (Scheff [1966a] 1984: 40).

Researchers who use the tradition of labeling theory study how definitions of normal and abnormal behavior are developed and sustained in social interaction. The construction of mental illness involves identifying "anomalous" behavior for which no rule or set of instructions can be found (Smith 1978: 35). Mental illness is thus determined by the incomprehensibility, irrationality, or unintelligibility of an individual's behavior (Coulter 1973; Foucault 1965; Horwitz 1982a; Ingleby 1982).

An important consequence of the argument that definitions of health and illness are culturally defined is a focus on the social control (rather than treatment) of those identified as mentally ill. To the extent that psychiatric disorders are violations of social norms rather than intrapsychic disturbances, psychiatrists and other mental health–care providers serve to control abnormal or disruptive behavior. As Friedson (1988: 346) points out: "Medicine is not merely neutral, like theoretical physics . . . . As a moral enterprise it is an instrument of social control which should be scrutinized as such." The moralization of mental illness or disorder is evident in the degree of stigma attached to the individual so labeled or defined. A stigma is a discrediting attribute, one that involves stereotypes that can result in active discrimination. Unlike most medical diagnoses, which do not stigmatize the person who is ill, labels of mental illness are widely viewed as stigmatizing the person who receives them.

Many surveys show that people typically believe those with mental illnesses are dangerous, unpredictable, abnormal, unreasonable, and dysfunctional. Those with mental illnesses are often feared and shunned. Williams (1987) states that mental illness is the most stigmatizing of all medical conditions. Consequently, there is a long research tradition that examines the course and consequences of stigma for persons who are labeled mentally ill. Portrayals of mental illness in the media often contribute to the stigma that surrounds this condition. Feature films, television programs, cartoons, and novels characterize people with mental illness as fundamentally different, as well as violent and dangerous (Wahl 1995). Disparaging labels and slang (crazy, loony, nutty, etc.) are used to refer to those with mental illnesses. Moreover, psychiatric labels such as schizophrenia are often used incorrectly, contributing to misunderstandings and misconceptions about mental illness. These characterizations can have many harmful consequences and contribute to public fear and avoidance of those with mental illnesses.

In Chapter 7, Bruce Link and Jo Phelan provide an overview of the effects that labeling has on people who are considered to be mentally ill. Link and Phelan's chapter shows not only that the stigma of mental illness carries negative moral connotations but also that it can result in social isolation, withdrawal, a devalued sense of self, and lower self-esteem in the stigmatized individual. In addition, labeling and stigma can have negative effects on social interactions and employment prospects, which further isolates individuals labeled as mentally ill.

Studies of the impact of labeling on mental disorder indicate that social conditions lead to different amounts of disorder and also that cultural attitudes toward mental illness lead to varying courses of disorder. This is illustrated by one of the best-known studies of serious mental illness, the World Health Organization's comparative study of schizophrenia in ten nations. This study obtained the surprising result that people with schizophrenia in less-developed countries had better outcomes than their counterparts in more-developed societies. Their illnesses lasted for shorter periods of time and were less likely to recur, and the affected individuals were more able to assume normal social roles. These findings contrasted with the initial expectations of the researchers that more sophisticated understanding of mental disorders and treatment technologies in developed nations would lead to a better prognosis. One explanation for these findings is that technologically less-developed societies place less stigma on mental illness and allow people with these illnesses to assume normal social roles more quickly. Thus, cultural attitudes toward the mentally ill, in addition to the nature of psychiatric symptoms, can have a powerful impact on the course of mental illnesses.

Summary

The chapters in Part I of this book show that mental disorders exist at the intersection of genetic and biological influences, individual life experiences, and social context. It is difficult to separate the influences of these diverse sets of variables on mental health and illness. These chapters provide overviews of the most critical issues in the field and lay the groundwork for the chapters that follow, which deal with more particular themes. Our goal is for students to understand both the distinctively social contribution to the development and response to mental disorders as well as the way that social factors interrelate with biological and psychological influences on mental health and illness.

1

Mental Health and Mental Illness: Definitions and Perspectives

David Mechanic

David Mechanic defines mental illness as a form of deviant behavior that is bizarre, irrational, or unusually distressful. Yet there are different models and approaches to understanding the etiology (or causes) of mental illness. The medical model views mental illness as a disease with a physical cause and an identifiable course. The problem with this model is that criteria for making a psychiatric diagnosis are not theoretically based, and people experiencing the same "illness" may display very different kinds of symptoms. Calling mental conditions "diseases" has helped to destigmatize mental illness, but there is still little understanding of the causes and appropriate treatment for most mental illnesses. Mechanic also describes how (a) the recognition and identification of mental illness involves judgments about normal and abnormal behavior and (b) how such judgments are related to one's cultural and social position. This has led to much debate over whether people who violate accepted norms are more or less healthy than those who conform to the norms of their social group. Although psychiatrists cannot define healthy behavior, they do seek universal patterns that characterize unhealthy behavior, or psychopathology. These universal patterns (such as the complex of symptoms in schizophrenia) are more likely to be representative of biological as opposed to cultural systems. Mechanic concludes his chapter with a general overview of the different orientations to the study of mental illness: the biological, epidemiological, developmental, and sociological perspectives. Students should ask where their own views of mental illness fit and what they can learn from the other approaches to understanding mental illness.

Mental illness is a form of deviant behavior. It arises when the individual's thought processes, feelings, or behaviors deviate from usual expectations or experience and the person affected or others in the community define it as a problem that requires intervention. Typically, the concept has two aspects. First, the thoughts, feelings, and behaviors that are said to stem from mental illness are distressing or disruptive in some fashion. Second, the problem is believed to arise from some dysfunction in the person, some aspect of his or her mind and body that is not functioning as it should. Embodied in this relatively simple statement are great complexities and many uncertainties.

From a lay point of view, mental illness is usually recognized by highly bizarre behavior that makes no sense to the observer. From a sociological point of view, the observer takes the role of the "other" and tries to understand the motives underlying what the actor says and does. Behavior that departs radically from expected patterns and for which the observer can identify no reasonable motive is said to be "crazy." Such behavior may include bizarre and meaningless talk, having visions and seeing and hearing things that others do not see or hear, and behaving in ways that are bizarre for no apparent purpose. People readily distinguish between behavior they think is "bad" and behavior they think of as "sick." To the extent that they perceive a self-interested motive in the behavior, they are likely to think of it as bad. Behavior that seems to make no sense, in contrast, is more likely to be characterized as sick. For example, a poor person repeatedly caught shoplifting would typically be seen as bad, reflecting the fact that we have no difficulty ascribing a motive to the person. In contrast, we are puzzled by the motivation of a very wealthy person engaged in the same behavior and are more likely to conceive of the behavior as sick.

Mental health professionals often appraise behavior in ways similar to the appraisals of lay people. Professionals identify mental illness through reports or observations of deviant behavior, bizarre speech and expressions of affect, and indications that the person is feeling unusual degrees of pain as in severe depression or anxiety. Like the general public, they try to differentiate deviance that results from rational motives and uncommon life stresses (such as bereavement) from deviance that arises from mental functions that have gone wrong in some way. The difficulty is that there are few clear criteria or objective tests for making this distinction. Like the general lay public, mental health professionals can be misled by their own limited social and cultural background. A person reporting extreme distress because a neighbor has performed witchcraft on her would certainly seem bizarre and irrational if she were a middle-class white Protestant raised in Columbus, Ohio. It would be more problematic if she had been raised in some African and Caribbean cultures.

These problems are not as formidable as they may seem for the practicing mental health professional. Most professionals do not go into the general population looking for mentally ill people to treat. They practice in offices, clinics, hospitals, and agencies, and they wait for patients who refer themselves (because they feel distressed) or patients who are referred by doctors, family members, and others because of some manifest problem. To the extent that the consultation is voluntary and the therapist is dedicated to helping in a manner that is consistent with the patient's wishes, ambiguity about definitions is no major problem because both patient and professional share a common goal. However, definition becomes a serious problem in the case of involuntary treatment, in deciding whether treatment will be covered under insurance coverage for mental illness, in litigation and the judicial process, and in carrying out mental health research in community populations. Thus, it becomes essential to delve into definitional matters more thoroughly. We begin by considering disease models.

The Medical Model and Concepts of Disease

Human populations exhibit extraordinary diversity, and most human traits and characteristics are distributed over a wide range. Generally, societies will become concerned with certain characteristics of people when their functioning, on the one hand, causes pain and distress or, on the other hand, has implications for future function and longevity. When distress or inappropriate behavior is thought to be a consequence of a bodily dysfunction, it is called a "disease." Dysfunction in medicine is commonly documented by objective laboratory tests and body imaging, but it is also commonly inferred from taking a medical history or doing a physical examination.

Doctors are trained to use a disease diagnostic model that builds on the accumulated body of medical knowledge. Over time, we have learned that certain patterns of symptoms and signs are syndromes representative of particular dysfunctions. In evaluating a patient with specific complaints, the physician seeks to identify the underlying syndrome that explains the patient's distress. This process of diagnosis follows a particular logic that all young physicians learn. Each diagnosis is part of a body of knowledge about the syndrome – this can be called a *disease theory*. Depending on the state of medical knowledge, disease theories can be confirmed, partially confirmed, or unconfirmed. In the case of a confirmed theory, once the diagnosis is made, the doctor immediately knows the causes of the problem, the likely progression of the disease, and the most effective treatment (Mechanic 1978). Thus, making the correct diagnosis substantially provides the solution to the problem. In partially confirmed theories, the doctor may know how the disease will progress and how to treat it yet not know its causes. In other instances, causes may be known but no effective treatments are available. In the case of mental illness, most disease theories are either partially confirmed or unconfirmed.

A further word is needed on the arbitrariness of disease definitions. There are many bodily dysfunctions that are seen as nuisances but are not sufficiently important for medical concern. Dandruff is as much a disease as cancer, but few patients will endear themselves by consulting their physicians about it. Some human characteristics (like blood pressure) have wide distributions, with some societies having higher average values than others. Generally, research on blood pressure shows that it is a linear function, so that lower blood pressure is associated with less risk of heart disease and stroke. Medicine arbitrarily defines hypertension (high blood pressure) in terms of a specific value (140/90), though achieving ever-lower levels continues to reduce risk. In recent years physicians have been debating the advisability of treating blood pressure closer to the norm (borderline hypertension). The establishment of the threshold that is called a disease is a matter of arbitrary judgment. For example, physicians in some countries (e.g. Germany) commonly treat low blood pressure as a disease, despite its protective features (Payer 1988).

Are Mental Illnesses Like Other Diseases?

Some critics (Szasz 1961) have argued that mental illnesses – because they are typically identified by deviant behavior and are not validated by objective tests that demonstrate lesions or dysfunctions – are not real diseases. It should be clear from the prior discussion that the theory of disease as used in medicine can be applied to mental as well as physical disorders. The issue is not whether the disease is real in the sense of demonstrating a visible bodily defect but rather the extent to which disease theory is sufficiently confirmed to assist the therapist in helping the patient.

The diagnostic bible of American psychiatrists is the *Diagnostic and Statistical Manual* (DSM) of the American Psychiatric Association, which is now in its fourth edition. The manual provides empirical descriptions of what are believed to be psychiatric conditions and specific criteria for making diagnoses. The DSM is a menu of disorders that psychiatrists treat, where the classifications and criteria have been established by a committee process seeking broad professional consensus. The inclusion and exclusion of some entities such as homosexuality, neurosis, and defeatist personality occurred via processes that were more political than scientific (Bayer & Spitzer 1985).

The DSM has both strengths and weaknesses. Its strengths lie in the attempt to codify systematically the problems faced by mental health professionals with specific criteria for making diagnoses. Thus, it provides a tool that allows clinicians to communicate more meaningfully with one another and researchers to define clinical groups in reasonably consistent ways. It is also a useful tool in the practical world because it offers a consistent set of definitions and criteria to insurers, courts, and other agencies that deal with persons with mental illnesses.

The weaknesses of DSM are primarily scientific. The diagnostic manual presents a descriptive rather than a theoretically validated approach to diagnostic entities and thus provides limited reliable information about causes, course, and appropriate treatments. In most cases the causes of the conditions are unknown (or disputed) and the treatments uncertain. Diagnoses are grouped empirically in terms of their manifest similarities, but even those diagnoses (like schizophrenia) that are based on much research and experience probably include many different specific entities that lead to similar types of bizarre behavior. Although some drugs in psychiatry are now used in more specific ways than in the past, treatments for many psychiatric disorders remain unspecific, and a great variety of treatment approaches are used with comparable patients. These problems are also found in respect to some physical illnesses in general medicine, but psychiatric knowledge is still far short of medical knowledge for most of the problems it encompasses.

Conceptions of the Causes of Mental Illness

Human beings are biosocial animals, and all behavior has origins in complex and continuing interactions between individuals and the environments in which they live. Individuals are a product of their genes, biosocial developmental processes, and life experiences. Thus, it is pointless to argue whether illnesses are biological or social. They all represent interactions among biological potentialities, individual vulnerabilities, environmental conditions, social stressors, social networks and supports, psychological orientations, and learned behavior. Genetic background is important in many disorders, including schizophrenia and bipolar affective disorders, but genes rarely determine specific behavioral outcomes (Mechanic 1999). The difficulty is that, while most professionals in the field agree that the major mental disorders involve an interaction between biological vulnerabilities and environmental events, neither the biogenetic processes nor the psychosocial events can be specified precisely enough to be informative in designing effective interventions.

Disease Models and Continuum Conceptions

The diagnostic disease model embodied in the DSM is based on the idea that disorders are discrete entities distinguishable from related symptoms that do not meet clinical diagnostic criteria for a disease. Therapists coming from a psychoanalytic or psychodevelopmental background are more likely to conceive of many disorders as continua varying from mild to severe. These alternative conceptions have different implications. Within the disease model, people either have a disease or not; we do not talk about mild and severe cancer, for example, although we classify cancers by their developmental stages. Diseases might vary in their stage or severity, but the diagnosis is a discrete judgment. Thus, deciding whether the person meets the necessary clinical threshold is important. Therapists who see disorder as a continuum are much less concerned about making a definitive diagnosis, since their treatment approaches are unlikely to differ on the basis of meeting diagnostic criteria.

As noted previously, the criteria for making a psychiatric diagnosis under DSM are not theoretically based; thus, in many instances it remains unclear whether the dividing line is a useful distinction. Major depression, for example, is a significant psychiatric disorder, yet people can meet the criteria by a variety of different symptoms that are not comparable. To meet the definition of disorder, patients must have five of a possible nine symptoms (during the same two-week period) that signify a change from previous function. At least one of these symptoms must be either "depressed mood" or "loss of interest or pleasure." The other symptoms cover a wide range, varying from a suicide attempt or a specific plan for suicide to such symptoms as insomnia or a significant weight loss or gain.

A valid disease model would supply a strong basis for diagnostic judgments and would not simply choose an arbitrary cutoff number of symptoms. Studies often show that persons who have symptoms of depression but do not meet diagnostic criteria experience similar distress, life disruptions, and loss of ability to function (Wells et al. 1989b). Moreover, studies also show that the same risk factors seem to have comparable effects in community and treated clinical samples. The cutoff for diagnosis of depression has no theoretical basis, and it is unclear whether those who do versus do not meet the criteria are different in any fundamental way.

Those who adhere to a continuum conception believe that depression ranges from mild to extremely severe and that individuals can move back and forth on this continuum, depending on their biological vulnerability, life stressors, social supports, coping capacities, and treatment interventions. They also believe that early interventions to reduce stressors, provide supports, and teach effective coping can protect the person from developing more serious and complicated depressions. Those who hold this view tend to believe that the risk factors for depression are similar regardless of one's location on the continuum. Those with a disease conception, in contrast, believe that causal factors for a major depressive illness are different from those for less severe depressive states.

Some types of affective illness appear to fit a disease model better than others. Bipolar affective conditions characterized by both depressed affect and manic states appear to have a stronger biological basis than major depression, and they seem to be triggered independently of environmental stressors. Major depression, in contrast, typically follows humiliating life difficulties in individuals who lack social supports and other protective environments (Brown, Harris, & Hepworth 1995). Persons who have suffered abuse as children and those who come from families with depressed parents are more vulnerable.

Many psychiatric disorders are defined primarily on the basis of behaviors that are widespread but become extreme and troublesome in a small proportion of cases. Examples include alcohol abuse and dependence, drug abuse and dependence, and conduct disorders in children. It is well known that each of these problems can be destructive to a person's life – affecting family life, work, school, and community functioning. Such persons often have devastating life trajectories that do great harm to themselves and others. The DSM develops arbitrary criteria for designating these as disorders, but it remains unclear how useful such diagnostic definitions are for understanding and treating them. Making the diagnosis offers little information on causes or the course of the disorder or on how to intervene effectively. Calling these conditions "diseases" has helped destigmatize them and has facilitated ushering the affected individuals into treatment; it has also helped justify health-insurance coverage for treating these conditions. But it remains unclear whether much is gained by conceiving of them as diseases in contrast to problems in living.

Public Definitions of Mental Illness

Most people enter treatment voluntarily because of personal distress and seek help in reducing their pain and improving their life adjustments. The help-seeking and illness behavior of the patient is a social phenomenon influenced by a variety of psychosocial and organizational factors. Thus, there is no one-to-one correspondence between those with greatest mental health need and those who seek help for psychological or emotional problems. Community studies repeatedly show that most people who meet DSM criteria for mental illness do not seek help and that many help seekers do not meet criteria for disorder (Leaf et al. 1985). For patients, the major issue is the distress and disability they experience and their capacity to tolerate it. Yet the amount of pain and disability does not itself meet the formal criteria of a disorder.

Problems multiply when persons come to treatment not because they seek help but because their disruptive behavior has induced family members, employers, or public authorities to insist they seek assistance. Conflicts sometimes develop between a person who insists that nothing is wrong and others who regard that person's behavior as intolerable and indicative of illness. Making judgments in such adversarial situations is difficult because the bases for these judgments are more likely to be contested.

Typically, the client in such situations behaves in ways that others find deviant and incomprehensible. The clinician in such instances must first establish that the behavior is not merely deviant as judged in terms of subculture, age group, and other aspects of the social context. Increasingly, populations encompass mixtures of persons of many races, ethnicities, cultures, religions, and national origins. Culture is also stratified by age group, with young people behaving in ways that often shock their elders who may see their behavior as "sick." Thus, there can be major differences of perspective in a context of cultural mix, and a determination must be made that the behavior is deviant. If a child of a conventional family declares that he or she is gay, joins the Moonies, converts to another religion, or engages in promiscuous sexual activity, is the person behaving in a psychologically deviant fashion? Certainly, there is room for disagreement.

In any free society there is much room for deviant behavior, and only some types of deviance are illegal. Thus, deviant behavior in itself is a basis for neither condemnation nor treatment. Persons who make extraordinary sacrifices for their friends and communities are as deviant as those who violate its most basic precepts. Indeed, we reward many kinds of deviance while condemning others. From a clinical point of view, good deeds as well as bad ones may arise from psychopathology. But we don't typically seek to explain "what went wrong" when we approve of the individual's behavior.

Behavior we find intolerable or bizarre may arise from normal patterns of socialization. People may steal or cheat because they learned to do so and believe that such behavior is in their interests. Individuals may behave in seemingly peculiar ways because they identify with particular groups or subcultures that value these behaviors. Young people may dress and act in offbeat ways because they are testing the limits of permissible behavior or because they enjoy shocking their parents or friends. Many deviant types of behavior can result from normal socialization processes and peer-group influences or from abusive parenting, deprivation, and disorganized family life.

In order to establish that a person is mentally ill, the clinician must determine that the troubling behavior at issue arises from a failure of physical, mental, or developmental mechanisms – but here is where things get murky. There are no objective tests for establishing psychopathology, so much depends on clinical judgment. If people feel sad in a context where they should feel happy, we infer something wrong with the affective mechanism. If a person talks in a jumbled fashion, making no sense, and the person is sober and not on drugs, we infer something wrong with cognitive functioning. If people report delusions and hallucinations that have no connection with their culture, we infer pathology. Extreme cases are relatively easy, but it is often unclear whether the person's difficulties are due to a breakdown in function, problems in living, selfishness, or some other personal orientation.

When someone commits a brutal murder for no apparent purpose or is more vicious in criminal behavior than required to meet criminal objectives, the lay public is likely to believe that the person must be sick. Although certain behaviors lead to strong inferences of sickness, sickness logically can never be inferred from acts themselves without also assessing mental function. But in real life we typically do regard some behavior as so extraordinarily crazy as to leave no other interpretation.

Psychiatrists have always treated some subgroups of patients for whom it has been difficult to demonstrate psychopathology. One such group of patients are called psychopaths or sociopaths – individuals who commit repeated abhorrent acts without evidence of remorse. Some clinicians regard lack of remorse itself as a sign of psychopathology and attribute sickness solely on this basis. Others would argue that there is no evidence of a breakdown in mental function and that such people are simply bad. Trying to make sense of the difference between the bad and the mad takes us into deeper philosophical issues of free will and determinism.

The Distinction between Mad and Bad

We live our lives on the assumption that individuals can distinguish between right and wrong and can decide to behave in accordance with the legal and other norms of the community; in other words, we assume they have "free will." The social and behavioral sciences, in contrast, are based on the assumption that behavior is determined by prior events and by the various forces that act on the individual at any given point in time. From a behavioral perspective, psychological orientations and function are shaped by genetic endowments, social development, and environmental influences. Thus all behavior – good and bad, sick and healthy – is predetermined by preceding events and influences. In this sense all behavior is a result of biological endowments, individual psychodynamics, and social context. We live our lives with an uneasy compromise between free will and determination. We cling to both sets of ideas despite the incongruity. Of course, a society that assumes free will and the capacity to choose also influences behavioral responses through the expectations and sanctions it establishes. In a sense, our value system and what we believe about human capacities is a crucial influence on the trajectories people follow, even though the trajectories may be determined. Our belief in free will allows us to hold individuals responsible, to make attributions of blame and worthiness, and to bind individuals to the norms of the community.

The Role of Values

Evaluations of the presence of mental illness are typically made by judging behavior, and the values of the observer substantially influence these judgments. Assessments of social adjustment and evaluations of nonconformity with respect to community and family expectations are dependent on what individuals regard as right and proper, which is shaped by culture and the social context in which people live. Differences in religious, social, and political values lead people to different commitments, and priorities and behavior that may seem bizarre from one cultural perspective can be perfectly acceptable from another.

There have been many debates about whether people who struggle against the accepted norms of their community are more or less healthy than those who conform comfortably. Were Germans who fought against their Nazi government at the risk of their lives, or Americans who engaged in civil disobedience to protest the Vietnam War, more or less healthy than those who comfortably adjusted to the social milieu and went on living their lives in ordinary ways? Some psychoanalysts have argued that people who struggle against tyranny are more psychologically healthy than those who are docile and simply conform to current ways of thinking (Fromm 1941). Moreover, there is much evidence that some of the most creative people in history were driven individuals who were terribly unhappy and out of sync with their social context. Creativity itself is a form of deviant behavior that requires individuals to break from usual assumptions and understandings in developing entirely new perspectives and approaches.

In short, there is no scientific way to adjudicate among different value systems and to identify healthy responses. These definitions are a product of particular cultures, social contexts, and times in history. This explains the attractiveness to psychiatrists of the disease model and disease theories. Although they recognize the futility of defining health, they believe it possible to identify underlying conditions that would be pathologies in any culture or any time in history, whether recognized or not. By focusing on underlying pathology, they seek to establish universal generalizations.

The diagnosis of schizophrenia offers an example of how the logic of disease theories would proceed. Schizophrenia is seen as a disturbance in processes of attention and perception, changes in motility and body awareness, and changes in thinking and affective processes (McGhie & Chapman 1961). Such patients give the impression that they are retreating from reality and are suffering from unpredictable disturbances in their streams of thought. Although persons with this diagnosis may be very deviant in their social behavior, the diagnosis is made on the basis of the subject's hearing voices, having delusions, and giving other indications of pathological cognitive and affective processes. These varying symptoms and signs constitute a pattern, or syndrome, suggesting an underlying disorder of the mental apparatus. There are various biological theories about what goes wrong in the brain of schizophrenic patients, but none have been confirmed.

The pattern of symptoms (e.g. hallucinations and delusions) known as schizophrenia is found in every culture, although persons with these symptoms may behave in different ways and be regarded with varying levels of tolerance (Murphy 1976). There is now considerable cross-cultural evidence that the social behavior of persons with schizophrenia is to some degree a response to how these people are treated and not an inevitable consequence of the condition. For example, cultures that treat schizophrenia patients in highly critical and coercive ways increase the probability of violence and agitation. Such patients do better in social contexts that are less critical and more tolerant (Leff & Vaughn 1985). Thus, psychiatry seeks to identify mental illnesses by those characteristics that are most universal and most likely to be representative of the biological as contrasted with the cultural system. Psychiatrists recognize that culture may affect how people experience, define, attribute meaning, report, and behave in response to the symptoms, but the symptoms themselves are found everywhere.

The impossibility of arriving scientifically at a definition of mental health does not stop professionals from searching for this holy grail, and there is no lack of criteria suggested for differentiating the healthy from the unhealthy. People who pursue this venture seek to define aspects of social character and personality that could conceivably be viewed as independent of social context. Among the themes emphasized are social sensitivity, the capacity for environmental mastery, a unifying outlook on life, self-actualization, self-acceptance, a sense of humor, empathy with others, and the like (Jahoda 1958). However attractive these traits may be, they remain cultural judgments and not universal characteristics of mental mechanisms. Why should self-acceptance be healthy? It is through self-criticism and striving to improve ourselves that we often make progress. Too ready self-acceptance inhibits motivation and makes us complacent. We can agree that social sensitivity is an attractive trait, but often insensitivity and single-mindedness contribute to extraordinary achievements. And so on for the rest.

People vary a great deal in their internal dispositions. Some are highly introspective, very much concerned with their own thoughts and feelings. As a result they may know themselves better but also experience more psychological distress (Hansell & Mechanic 1991). Others are relatively uninterested in their inner states and direct most of their attention to external events. Persons with these contrasting orientations seek different occupational outlets. Persons in engineering tend to be low on introspectiveness whereas artists, poets, novelists, and others in the arts tend to be much higher. Persons who make good astronauts, and who readily tolerate the risks and loneliness of space travel, tend to be low on introspectiveness. Their focus on the outer environment assists in task completion and limits diversions. The point here is that people have many types of traits and dispositions and generally try to sort themselves into social contexts compatible with their needs and dispositions. Persons who do well in one context often do less well in others. It is difficult to imagine human behavior that is completely independent of social context.

General Orientations to the Study of Mental Illness

Much of this volume is devoted to examining specific conceptions of mental health and mental illness. My purpose here is not to discuss specific theories or research results but rather to sketch in broad strokes how different behavioral disciplines think about mental illness and how they go about investigating it. Since this book is devoted to the sociology of the area, I give this discipline's view the most attention, but sociology cannot be oblivious to important developments in genetics and the neurosciences. After briefly reviewing some biological perspectives, I focus on the logic of some of the major psychosocial approaches.

Biological Perspectives

The body and mind constitute a biological system that evolves in a social context. The biological and social are inseparable, and both are essential to understanding mental illness. Researchers attempt to understand how families transmit psychological vulnerabilities and how various intrauterine, congenital physical illness, trauma, and other environmental events result in biological vulnerabilities or dysfunctions. There is a long tradition in psychiatry of studying families, twins, and adoptees. Most major mental disorders are found to occur disproportionately more in some families than others, suggesting genetic transmission, although social causes cannot be eliminated as possible explanations in such studies. However, studies of identical and fraternal twins (and adoptees of mentally ill parents) make a persuasive case that many major mental disorders are in part genetically transmitted (Mechanic 1999). These studies show that identical twins have a higher probability of illness if the other twin becomes ill than do fraternal twins, and that children of schizophrenic mothers adopted at birth have risks of future illness more characteristic of their natural than their adopted mothers. Most scientists believe this genetic vulnerability is a product of several genes – that the vulnerability is *polygenetic*. In the case of bipolar affective disease (commonly known as manic depressive illness), researchers on various occasions believed they were on the threshold of identifying specific genes, but these efforts generally resulted in disappointment.

The genetic studies show that genes affect vulnerabilities to mental illness, but they also support the proposition that – even in the most serious mental disorders – such vulnerabilities are translated into illness only under specific social and environmental circumstances. Social scientists seek to understand social vulnerability factors and how they interact with genetic vulnerabilities.

Advances in science depend on developing new technologies and methodologies that allow researchers to probe more deeply into basic mechanisms. Developments in genetic investigation hold much promise for the future as we proceed to describe the human genome. Advances in molecular biology made it possible to develop molecular probes to identify markers for genes that increase susceptibility to specific diseases. Similarly new tools in the neurosciences have stimulated a great many new investigations of brain function and of how drugs affect different transmitter systems. Such imaging technologies as positron emission technology (PET) and nuclear magnetic resonance (NMR) allow us to image the brain directly and observe how it responds to various stimuli, including drugs.

Many sociologists tend to be skeptical of biological interpretations and the reductionism they imply in understanding highly complex response patterns. But scientific developments in genetics and the neurosciences have demonstrated a considerable role for biological substrates of schizophrenia and other major mental illnesses. It is now established that chemical neurotransmitters operate at most brain synapses and that, although genetically endowed, they are multidimensional and are influenced by a variety of environmental factors (Kety 1986). There is a tendency toward a parochial silliness and oversimplification in both disciplines, and there is a need for biologists and social scientists to work together to help unravel the extraordinary complexity of individual functioning.

The Epidemiological Perspective

Many of the results reported in the various chapters of this book are derived from epidemiological studies. Epidemiology is a method of investigation, but it is also a powerful perspective for thinking about how diseases occur in populations and the various factors that influence their occurrence and persistence. As August Hollingshead noted, "The triumph ... has been its utility in helping researchers trace out, step by step, interdependencies between the life ways of individuals and the appearance and nonappearance of disease in a population" (1961: 6). The researcher using the epidemiological method seeks to ascertain who in a population develops a disease, on what occasions, and under what influences. By learning who is affected and under what conditions, epidemiological studies lead to more focused questions and possibly to practical interventions. In one of the great historical examples, John Snow traced the pattern of occurrence of cholera in London and was able to demonstrate in 1854 that the epidemic was due to a contaminated water source. Thus it was possible to control the epidemic by closing the source of bacterial contamination.

Epidemiology is a useful approach to describe the pattern of mental illness in a community and also to study various causal hypotheses. Two major studies discussed in later chapters, the Epidemiologic Catchment Area project (Robbins & Regier 1991) and the National Comorbidity Survey (Kessler et al. 1994) provide many examples of how this approach is used to show the prevalence of mental illness and how this prevalence varies by age, sex, geographic area, ethnicity, social class, and many other characteristics. But epidemiology also offers a handy way to conceptualize and test various theoretical ideas about how such factors as stress, social support, and coping affect the occurrence of disorder. Epidemiology is also an excellent vehicle for studying the interactions between various biological and social variables.

Developmental Perspectives

The developmental perspective seeks to develop a biographical–historical perspective of the individual's personality and functioning. Many psychologists, social psychologists, and psychoanalysts adopt this perspective, which is based on the view that there is a logical continuity in personality and behavior, whether normal or abnormal. Thus, the same principles of behavior govern an understanding of both normal and abnormal behavior. Because disturbed behavior is seen as an adaptation in response to early experience, developmental factors, and social stressors, it would seem logical to study such behavior from the same perspectives used to study adaptation in general.

Developmental researchers have different points of view. Some stress early developmental influences, whereas others focus on more contemporary stresses and coping. Some emphasize psychodynamic processes; others focus on social learning and social reinforcement. Some stress cognitive processes and ways of thinking while others focus on behavior. But they all believe that a person's past experience contributes in important ways to patterns of functioning and present difficulties.

Developmentalists seek to understand the various factors that influence personality and behavioral trajectories. They focus on such variables as child abuse and neglect, quality of parenting, family communication, peer group experience, role conflict, and the like. They give major attention to the quality of relationships and the emotional attachments that develop in the family and later. There is an increased emphasis on self-confidence and sense of personal control, social networks and attachments, life difficulties and adversities, social supports, and coping capacities. Developmental models are increasingly highly complex and probabilistic in seeking to understand how personality trajectories develop and change over time (Brown 1986).

The implications of developmental perspectives are very different from those of disease models. Development is seen as continuous, and the line between normality and illness becomes just a matter of degree. Disease models, in contrast, are discrete and discontinuous. Developmental models assume that the same predictors affect undisturbed and disordered behavior. In contrast, disease models assume that disorders are explained by unique pathological processes.

Research on gender and mental illness illustrates some of the varying implications of these two approaches. Many epidemiological and clinical studies have observed a much higher incidence and prevalence of depressive disorders among women than men (Cleary 1987). Gender seems to be unrelated to the prevalence of schizophrenia. However, substance abuse and dependence, personality disorder, and antisocial patterns predominate among males. A disease framework will treat each of these diagnoses as discrete entities with unique causes, courses, and outcomes. If one looks at the aggregate picture, however, the excess prevalence in diagnoses associated with acting-out behavior in men seem to balance the excess prevalence of depression among women.

A developmental perspective might suggest that these patterns are more closely linked than they may first appear. Men and women with comparable biological vulnerabilities facing various developmental adversities and situational pressures may express their difficulties in different types of adaptations. Women who are socialized to be attuned to emotional issues and to acknowledge distress may manifest distress internally, with explicit acknowledgment of their pain and desperation. Men, who in contrast are socialized to deny pain and to stigmatize its expression, may be more likely to express their distress through drink, drugs, fights, and other interpersonal disputes. These different reaction patterns can be seen as unfolding from a prior biography in which biology, psychosocial development, social norms, and social stressors interact in complex ways.

The disease and developmental models are two different ways of looking at the world; neither is wrong. For scientists and clinicians, the issue is the utility of these different perspectives in helping us understand mental illness and helping people overcome such disorders. With respect to examining gender differences, it is difficult to resolve at this time which is the more useful approach. Many clinicians are quite eclectic in their thinking, moving back and forth between perspectives depending on their utility at the moment. Thus, a clinician may use a disease model in deciding the most appropriate medication but shift to a developmental model in counseling the patient.

Sociological Conceptions

There are many sociological conceptions of mental illness. Most important are the perspectives of stress and coping, labeling, and collective mobilization. These concepts are not necessarily in conflict with disease and developmental perspectives and can even supplement them, although some exaggerated statements seek to suggest an alternative interpretation of mental illness. These viewpoints will receive detailed coverage in the chapters that follow. Here I simply introduce the ideas underlying the various perspectives and relate them to alternative conceptions of the nature of mental illness.

The *stress and coping* model falls neatly within the developmental perspective. Psychological distress and some mental illnesses are seen as resulting from failures in coping with stressful life events. Stress within such models is seen as an imbalance between the demands on persons and their capacities to deal with them. Coping is generally seen as the needed resources for dealing with demanding situations. Coping is typically divided into instrumental efforts to deal with stressors and efforts to deal with the emotions elicited by the situation (emotion-focused coping). The developmental model relates to coping in many ways. Prior experiences and social situations affect what demands individuals will have to face, the types and quality of attachments and supports they have, their skills in dealing with adverse events and feelings, and so forth. Similarly, biological vulnerabilities and earlier personality affect how people cope – as well as their capacities to elicit support and assistance from others.

The *labeling* perspective argues in essence that processes of social definition and response shape the behavior of persons under stress. Labeling processes often stigmatize and isolate them, closing certain opportunities and so forcing them into particular life trajectories. There are both "hard" and "soft" versions of the labeling conception. The hard version, popular in the 1960s, argued that social processes of definition and exclusion of persons believed to be mentally ill reinforce their aberrant behavior and push them into mentally ill roles, reinforcing self-conceptions as a mentally ill person and subsequent aberrant behavior (Scheff 1966a). In general, investigation of this perspective could not sustain its contention that labeling itself was powerful enough to produce the behavior we call mental illness (Robins 1975).

The soft version of the labeling perspective maintains not that labeling can cause illness but rather that it can have important effects on both the course of the disorder and how persons with mental illness respond to their situations over time. Thus, this version gives special attention to the effects of stigma, discrimination, and social exclusion.

The *collective mobilization* perspective follows from the soft version of the labeling perspective and argues that social definitions and social and environmental structures can either exaggerate or minimize the importance of personal impairments. This perspective is also developmental in its focus, but it gives greatest attention to the social and political factors that affect the life of individuals with particular impairments. Within this perspective, society produces disabilities by the way it defines persons with impairments, limits their access to community facilities and employment, discriminates against them, and in other ways inhibits their potential to be productive participants in their communities. An example is the success of the gay community in redefining homosexuality as a personal life-style choice and in making inroads against discrimination. Psychiatry (in a clearly political context) has dropped homosexuality as a disorder (Bayer 1981), but it is not unreasonable to conceptualize homosexuality as a deviation from how the human organism ordinarily functions.

Another example is the political success of the disability movement in opening access to physical facilities, transportation, and employment. Arguing that their disabilities are as much a product of discrimination and prejudice as they are of the impairments per se, they have successfully lobbied for major national legislation (The Americans with Disabilities Act) that increases public access to many types of opportunities. The basic argument is that any impairment may become either a major aspect or a more subsidiary characteristic of an individual's identity or function. The social and governmental response to persons with impairments, and the degree of physical and social accessibility to opportunities, can either facilitate or limit their productivity and level of independence.

Conclusions

In this chapter I have tried to illustrate that mental illness is a far more difficult and slippery concept than it may seem. It is certainly biological, but then so is all human behavior because the mind is part of our biological system. The definition of mental illness is arbitrary and culturally conditioned, but all societies recognize persons with serious mental illness as being different and treat them in special ways. However, the manifestations of psychological pathology are socially defined, and societal meaning systems and social definitions very much shape the course of these conditions.

In Western society we have a number of different views of mental illness, some complementary and others in conflict. Predominant among them is the disease model of mental illness, which has gained distinction with the development of new drugs, advances in molecular genetics, and breakthroughs in brain imaging. But the fact remains that the disease conception is simply a theory, at best only partially confirmed. In recent years psychiatry as a profession has moved substantially into the biological camp, separating itself from its psychodynamic roots.

The disease model has many uses and may indeed turn out to be the most productive approach to mental disorder. There are dangers, however, in closing options too quickly and defining research efforts and treatment too narrowly. There are many instances in the history of psychiatry where enthusiasm for biological theories brought no gains but helped denigrate other approaches for helping patients. Sociological research has much to contribute to developmental and disease perspectives both, because human biology and development must occur in a social context.

2

The Measurement of Mental Disorder

Jerome C. Wakefield

This chapter examines the assessment and measurement of mental disorders. Researchers must distinguish between clinical prevalence (people who are currently being treated for mental disorder) and true prevalence (the actual rate of disorder in a community, including those not in treatment). The measurement of mental illness must be conceptually valid; that is, there must be criteria that successfully distinguish cases of disorder from cases of nondisorder. In the past, researchers relied upon symptom checklists, which identify a threshold above which an individual is considered disordered. An alternative to checklists is provided by the American Psychiatric Association's *Diagnostic and Statistical Manual* (DSM) of mental disorders. The assumption behind the DSM is that mental disorders result from internal problems, a presumption that Wakefield demonstrates is often violated by the DSM's own criteria for mental disorder. His critique of the DSM is illustrated with several DSM diagnoses. In addition to thoroughly discussing the conceptual basis of the DSM, Wakefield provides examples of the attempts to use DSM-derived criteria to measure the prevalence of mental disorder in the community. These examples demonstrate the recurrent problems with conceptual validity that plague the measurement of mental illness. It is unclear whether these problems can be overcome or circumvented with methodological innovations. The student should consider why it is so difficult to determine who is mentally disordered. Is a conceptually valid resolution of these problems likely?

How many people in the United States suffer from mental disorder in general and from each specific mental disorder, and what characteristics are correlated with each disorder? The answers to such questions are important in formulating mental health policy, in evaluating theories of the causes of disorder, in planning efficient distribution of mental health care, and in justifying funding for mental health services and research. Thus, there have long been efforts to measure the rate, or *prevalence,* of mental disorder both in the population as a whole and in various segments of the population. *Psychiatric epidemiology,* the discipline that pursues such studies, is logically part of medical epidemiology, the study of the occurrence and correlates of medical disorders in various populations. However, psychiatric epidemiology has remained as much within the province of sociologists as of physicians and psychiatrists because many of the questions that psychiatric epidemiologists attempt to answer – such as those concerning the effects of social stress on mental health or the prevalence of mental disorder in various socioeconomic, gender, racial, and ethnic groups, as well as the survey methodology often used in this field – traditionally fall within the domain of sociology.

Good clinicians, with the help of an adequately detailed history and diagnostic interview, can generally recognize a case of mental disorder when they see it. It is a very different matter to measure how many people in the general population – most of whom have never seen a clinician – suffer from mental disorder. Epidemiological surveys lack many of the safeguards and corrective mechanisms available in a clinical evaluation and, generally speaking, are more prone to diagnostic error. This chapter will explore the special problems that have arisen in epidemiologists' attempts to transfer diagnostic criteria from the domain of clinical evaluation to the much different epidemiological arena, where surveys measure disorder in the general population.

The Current Crisis in Psychiatric Epidemiology

It is usually too costly for clinicians to perform full diagnostic interviews with large samples of the general population, so psychiatric epidemiologists have come to rely on structured interviews administered by lay interviewers in order to distinguish disordered from nondisordered individuals. Two major studies using such instruments, both well funded and using the best methodological resources available, have been mounted in recent years in an attempt to obtain valid, definitive answers to psychiatric epidemiologists' questions. The first is the Epidemiologic Catchment Area (ECA) project (Robins & Regier 1991), which surveyed samples of the general population at five sites (or "catchment areas," as they were called in community mental health legislation) across America, from New Haven to Los Angeles. The second is the National Comorbidity Survey (NCS; Kessler et al. 1994), so named because it focused on establishing the degree to which different disorders occur in the same individuals (or are "comorbid").

Rather than resolving the challenges of psychiatric epidemiology, these two studies have instead thrown the field into something of a crisis. The studies have run into two basic difficulties. First, the estimated prevalence rates of mental disorder seem, to many observers, to be too high; for example, the ECA project found that about a third of all Americans suffer from a mental disorder at some point in their lives, and the NCS indicated that the figure is closer to a half. The prevalence rates for many specific disorders also seem high; for example, the ECA study claims that about 14% of Americans suffer from an alcohol abuse or dependence disorder at some point in their lives. The second difficulty is that – although they use very similar instruments and other research technology – the studies yield surprisingly different results in many instances. To take one extreme example, the ECA project found that about 6% of Americans suffer at some time in their lives from a depressive disorder, whereas the comparable NCS figure is about 17%. We have noted as well that the two studies' overall lifetime prevalence rates for all psychiatric disorders differ quite substantially (one third versus one half of the population).

There are many possible reasons for these problematic results, and no clear agreement on the explanation has yet emerged. However, it appears that the way in which mental disorder was measured in these studies had something to do both with the high absolute magnitudes of the rates and the differences in the rates. When two such state-of-the-art studies yield such troubling and divergent results with no clear explanation, one might consider the field to be in a scientific crisis. This crisis situation with respect to current measures led me to take a rather different approach to this chapter than I otherwise might. Rather than surveying the measurement of mental disorder in psychiatric epidemiological studies as if such measures were an accomplished fact, I approach the measurement of mental disorder as an ongoing challenge that has yet to be satisfactorily resolved. This chapter provides glimpses of aspects of this problem using specific examples that represent broader issues.

True Prevalence versus Clinical Prevalence

One obvious way to try to measure the rate of mental disorder in a community is to take a census of how many mental patients are being treated (in hospitals, psychiatric clinics, mental health professionals' offices, and general medical practices) or are being dealt with by other community authorities. Such surveys of patients yield what might be called the *clinical prevalence* of mental disorder. For purposes of scientific theory and social policy, however, epidemiologists are mainly interested not in the apparent, clinical prevalence of disorder but rather in its *true prevalence* – that is, the actual rate of mental disorder in a community, whether treated or not.

Some early psychiatric epidemiological studies were based on the assumption that clinical prevalence could validly be used to infer the community population's true prevalence. Unfortunately, using clinical prevalence to measure true prevalence begs one of the central questions of psychiatric epidemiology – namely, to what degree mental disorders in the general population go untreated. It is the rate of *untreated* mental disorder that most forcefully argues for the need for greater funding of mental health services, and it has long been an article of faith – and more recently an empirically demonstrated fact – that large numbers of people who are classified as disordered do not have access to or do not make use of mental health services. Thus, clinical surveys cannot be used to measure true prevalence rates.

Moreover, the characteristics of a community's patient population may not be a valid guide to the characteristics of a community's overall disordered population. There are many possible reasons (e.g., availability or mix of community services) why the clinical population might diverge in make-up from the overall disordered population. For example, Ruesch (1949) studied clinic populations in New Haven and concluded: "We can state that the lower class culture favors conduct disorders and rebellion, the middle class culture physical symptom formations and psychosomatic reactions" (cited in Srole et al. [1962] 1978: 294). But Srole and colleagues, in their community population study of midtown Manhattan (the "Midtown Study"), did not find this to be the case.

> The data . . . do not support that generalization. A more plausible interpretation of Ruesch's observation is that (1) rebellious lower class individuals with "acting out" character disorders tend to be shunted to psychiatric facilities by action of community authorities or agencies; (2) their status peers with psychosomatic reactions get strictly medical or no attention; (3) middle-class individuals with psychosomatic disorders tend to be referred to psychiatric outpatient services, generally on the advice of their own physician. (Srole et al. [1962] 1978: 294)

Thus, social factors that determine how a problem is dealt with in the community can dramatically affect how frequently a given problem shows up in mental health clinics in different subpopulations.

Another example of how service structure can affect the results of studies based on clinical samples can be found in the seemingly contradictory clinical prevalence estimates of Hollingshead and Redlich's (1958) study of New Haven and Srole et al.'s (1962) study of midtown Manhattan. Hollingshead and Redlich's clinical data, based on a census of New Haven mental treatment centers (including public and private hospitals and outpatient offices and facilities), indicated dramatically higher disorder prevalence rates among those of lower socioeconomic status (SES), whereas Srole et al.'s clinical data indicated higher rates of disorder in the upper classes. Hollingshead and Redlich claimed that their finding of more psychiatric patients among the lower classes supported the etiological hypothesis that social stress is a primary cause of mental illness. They found the following clinical prevalence rates per 100,000 population in various socioeconomic classes: I–II (highest), 556; III, 538; IV, 642; and V (lowest), 1,659.

These findings are in stark contrast to the results of the Midtown Study of clinical venues, which found the following total patient rate per 100,000 in three SES classes: upper, 1,703; middle, 1,178; lower, 1,060. Aside from the fact that the rate is overall much higher, there is also the striking fact that the direction of the relationship between SES and treatment rate is reversed. It seems that in New Haven the poor become ill more frequently, whereas in Manhattan it is the rich who do so. Do these data reflect an actual difference in the relationship between SES and mental disorder in the two locations?

Almost certainly they do not, because Srole and associates also did a community study, and their population statistics (as opposed to their clinical prevalence rates) indicated that lower socioeconomic classes do have higher rates of disorder. How, then, did it happen that Srole et al.'s clinical prevalence rates indicated the opposite of both their own community study and the results of Hollingshead and Redlich?

The answer seems to have more to do with treatment availability than with a correlation between SES and disorder. When the Midtown SES data are broken down by treament site, the patients are distributed as follows: public hospitals – 98 (upper), 383 (middle), and 646 (lower); private hospitals – 104, 39, and 18; clinics – 61, 160, and 218; office therapists – 1,440, 596, and 178. These dramatic differences in direction of relationship between SES and patient population in different settings exist also in the New Haven data, as a reanalysis by Srole et al. revealed. In fact, the direction of the relationship between SES and patient population is the same for each category in both studies; in both cases, more poor people use public hospitals and more middle- or upper-SES people use office therapists. The difference in the overall prevalence rates is due to the fact that the mix of available services is different in the two locations. New Haven's services are oriented more toward public hospitals, which are used disproportionately by the poor, whereas Manhattan's services (at least at the time of the Srole et al. study) contain a much greater proportion of private outpatient therapists, who are used by the better off. It appears that different SES segments of the population use different types of services, and that the mix of services offered in a given locale may substantially affect the rates at which individuals from given SES categories use the services.

In sum, a patient census cannot tell us the true prevalence of mental disorder in a population or the relative rates of disorder across such critical variables in psychiatric epidemiology as SES and other subgroups of the population. Psychiatric epidemiologists have therefore largely rejected patient surveys for these purposes and focused instead on using direct surveys of community populations to establish true prevalence. This strategy entails considerable methodological demands and costs. Mental health professionals have already screened clinical populations and have observed them over a period of time in order to confirm the validity of their diagnoses. Thus, the patients that are counted in clinical surveys are to a large extent already "validated" as patients with specific disorders. Clinical prevalence can thus be ascertained simply by obtaining summary statistics from each community setting. However, community populations have not been pre-screened, so each individual must be surveyed directly. Moreover, the rates of some specific mental disorders are quite low, so one must interview a very large number of individuals to obtain a sample sufficient to establish the population prevalence. There are many other problems that arise in such surveys; for example, in the space of a short interview, individuals may not accurately remember symptoms that may have occurred some time before, they may be reluctant to reveal such symptoms to a lay interviewer, or they may misinterpret the meaning of symptom questions that ask about unusual and subtle matters of subjective experience. But the most difficult and fundamental problem in community surveys – and the one on which I focus here – is constructing an instrument that validly distinguishes disordered from nondisordered individuals.

Conceptual Validity and Symptom Checklists

It has often been observed that there is no "gold standard" by which the presence of a mental disorder can be conclusively inferred, as there is in the case of certain physical disorders that can be conclusively identified through laboratory tests. In the absence of such markers, we must judge as best we can from apparent symptoms and other available information whether a condition is or is not a disorder.

Criteria for a specific disorder that successfully distinguish cases of disorder from cases of nondisorder are *conceptually valid* criteria (Wakefield 1992a,b, 1993). Owing to the high cost of using professionals to diagnose or even to administer survey instruments to large samples, epidemiologists have turned to structured questionnaires that (a) can be administered by a lay person and analyzed by computer and (b) contain all the questions necessary to make a diagnosis. At no point does clinical or professional expertise enter into the administration and analysis of such structured survey instruments. Thus, the entire diagnostic process must be based on explicit, rigid rules about how the answers to a fixed set of questions determine whether a diagnosis is appropriate. The challenge of community studies, then, is to construct conceptually valid rules for diagnosing specific mental disorders.

It cannot be overemphasized that diagnostic criteria play a uniquely important role in an epidemiological study. The logical structure of such studies is like an upside-down pyramid: the wide base of the pyramid consists of a vast array of activities, from sample selection and data collection to instrument development and data analysis; the usefulness of all this rests upon the narrow point of the pyramid, which consists of a handful of diagnostic criteria for the disorders that are being studied. The entire enterprise has its foundation in – and its potential for success depends on – these few definitions of disorder. No matter how sophisticated and flawless the instrument development, sampling procedures, data collection techniques, and methods of data analysis may be, if the diagnostic criteria used to identify disorders are invalid then all the other efforts will be to no avail in achieving the goal of accurately estimating true prevalence. Conceptual validity, then, is critical to the epidemiological enterprise.

Before the development of the new wave of instruments used in most recent epidemiological studies (which I will consider shortly), most studies used symptom checklists and defined some number of symptoms as the threshold above which an individual is considered disordered. These instruments generally consisted of sets of questions about symptoms that yielded an overall, unidimensional score of disordered status. A prominent example is the Langner (1962) scale.

Langner Scale Questions

1. I feel weak all over much of the time.
2. I have had periods of days, weeks, or months when I couldn't take care of things because I couldn't "get going."
3. In general, would you say that most of the time you are in high (very good) spirits, good spirits, low spirits, or very low spirits?
4. Every so often I suddenly feel hot all over.

5. Have you ever been bothered by your heart beating hard? Would you say: often, sometimes, or never?

6. Would you say your appetite is poor, fair, good, or too good?

7. I have periods of such great restlessness that I cannot sit long in a chair (cannot sit still very long).

8. Are you the worrying type (a worrier)?

9. Have you ever been bothered by shortness of breath when you were *not* exercising or working hard? Would you say: often, sometimes, or never?

10. Are you ever bothered by nervousness (irritable, fidgety, tense)? Would you say: often, sometimes, or never?

11. Have you ever had any fainting spells (lost consciousness)? Would you say: never, a few times, or more than a few times?

12. Do you ever have any trouble in getting to sleep or staying asleep? Would you say: often, sometimes, or never?

13. I am bothered by acid (sour) stomach several times a week.

14. My memory seems to be all right (good).

15. Have you ever been bothered by "cold sweats"? Would you say: often, sometimes, or never?

16. Do your hands ever tremble enough to bother you? Would you say: often, sometimes, or never?

17. There seems to be a fullness (clogging) in my head or nose much of the time.

18. I have personal worries that get me down physically (make me physically ill).

19. Do you feel somewhat apart even among friends (apart, isolated, alone)?

20. Nothing ever turns out for me the way I want it to (turns out, happens, comes about, i.e., my wishes aren't fulfilled).

21. Are you ever troubled with headaches or pains in the head? Would you say: often, sometimes, or never?

22. You sometimes can't help wondering if anything is worthwhile anymore.

In general, a score of four or more positive answers to questions on the Langner scale was considered to indicate disorder. Looking at the scale's questions, one immediately sees two weaknesses. First, one might easily answer four or more questions positively for reasons other than that one has a mental disorder. Many of the listed symptoms could be normal reactions to misfortunes in life, or even symptoms of physical disorder. It has been commonly observed that many of the listed symptoms in this and comparable instruments – from feeling alone or that one's wishes are not fulfilled to feelings of worry, nervousness, or low spirits – could easily indicate a normal response of demoralization to negative life events. If one is reacting normally to a difficult environment then one is not disordered, yet the Langner scale and other symptom scales might classify one as disordered.

The second important weakness is that general scales such as Langner's do not distinguish among different types of disorders.

It turns out that the number of false positives – that is, people whom the scale finds to be disordered but who actually have no disorder – with the Langner scale is considerable (Dohrenwend & Dohrenwend 1982). Based on statistics provided by Langner (1962) himself, one can calculate that, in a community sample diagnosed by mental health professionals – and using these professionals' diagnoses (which may themselves contain false positives) as the criterion against which Langner's scale is tested – the scale substantially overreported the rate of mental disorder. Professionals diagnosed 23% of the sample with mental disorder compared to 31% as measured by the Langner scale. The challenge of the false positives problem is also brought out by the fact that, in Srole et al.'s (1962) study, fully 82% of the surveyed population reported some psychiatric symptomatology. The 82% estimate of the prevalence of psychiatric symptoms has often been cited in critiques as a reductio ad absurdum of the validity of psychiatric epidemiological estimates based on symptom checklists. All it really shows, though, is that a useful epidemiological instrument must pay extremely careful attention to the problem of false positives and must distinguish true disorders from normal distress.

In more recently devised instruments, the problems of symptom checklists are dealt with in a variety of ways. First, separate sets of symptoms are presented for each disorder, so that disorders can be discriminated from each other. Second, each disorder is tapped by a large number of possible symptoms, with diagnosis triggered only when the individual has a certain number of listed typical symptoms. Third, exclusion clauses are used to eliminate the possibility that symptoms are caused by problems (such as physical disease) other than the target disorder. For example, the criteria for depressive disorder might include an exclusion clause such as the following: "The symptoms are not due to the direct physiological effects of a substance (e.g., a drug abuse, a medication) or a general medical condition (e.g., hypothyroidism)" (APA 1994: 327). Some of these features are illustrated in examples presented later. As we shall see, even using all these strategies, false positives remain a challenging problem.

DSM and the Concept of Mental Disorder

Psychiatric epidemiology's need for rules to determine whether someone has specific mental disorders converged in the 1980s with the attempt to provide operationalized, theory-neutral, reliable criteria for mental disorders in the third edition of the American Psychiatric Association's *Diagnostic and Statistical Manual* (DSM-III; APA 1980). The project of refining such criteria was carried forward in DSM-III-R (APA 1987) and DSM-IV (APA 1994), and I will refer to these collective efforts as "DSM."

The DSM is much more than a list of mental disorders. It is an attempt to use symptom lists to create necessary and sufficient rules for diagnosing all major mental disorders. The basic idea is that a disorder can be recognized by its specific symptomatic effects (Spitzer & Williams 1982). For example, alcohol dependence can be recognized by patterns of behavior that indicate inability to control alcohol use, anxiety disorders can be recognized by certain patterns of excessive anxiety, and depressive disorders can be recognized by certain symptoms that indicate excessive sadness and despair.

There are several goals of DSM's symptom-based diagnostic system. First, the construction of DSM is an attempt to respond to antipsychiatric critics who argued that the unreliability of psychiatric diagnosis (i.e., the tendency for different professionals to assign different diagnoses to the same case based on the same data) shows that mental disorder does not really exist and that psychiatry is just a legitimation of social control of conditions that are socially undesirable but not really disorders. In order to undercut this criticism and show that diagnosis can be reliable, DSM criteria are framed in terms of explicit symptoms and use explicit rules for diagnosing disorders on the basis of those symptoms. Reliability is supposed to be achieved through the formulation of operationalized criteria that focus on observable behaviors or reportable experiences that are relatively unambiguous and noninferential. (Whether reliability has actually been substantially improved using this strategy remains controversial; see Kirk & Kutchins 1992.)

Second, DSM is a response to the theoretical fragmentation of psychiatry. The idea here is that all mental health professionals can agree that certain symptoms indicate a disorder, even if they cannot agree on the explanation for the symptoms. Hence a symptom-based system of diagnosis can be a common, theory-neutral foundation for all mental health professionals. Theory neutrality is supposed to be accomplished via criteria that make no reference to etiology and instead focus on observable behaviors and reportable experiences; psychiatric schools of thought differ in their theories of the causes of disorder, but they can agree on the presence of manifest symptoms and on the disorders such symptoms imply. Thus, diagnostic rules based on quasi-behavioral, operationalized criteria that consist essentially of symptom lists are DSM's vehicle for achieving both reliability and theory neutrality.

Researchers soon observed that DSM offers exactly the kind of diagnostic system that could provide psychiatric epidemiology with the sort of criteria needed to survey large populations and identify disorders through diagnostic algorithms (rules) that do not require professional judgment. Consequently, all important recent psychiatric epidemiological studies have derived their criteria directly from DSM, and only these kinds of criteria will be examined here.

The DSM criteria are supposed to distinguish true mental disorders in the medical sense from the vast array of problematic but nondisordered human conditions often referred to as "problems in living." But how does one know if DSM's theory-neutral criteria define genuine mental disorders? To know whether one is validly measuring mental disorder, one must be clear about the object of measurement. Thus, the question of how to measure mental disorder quickly brings one face-to-face with perhaps the most fundamental of all questions about mental disorder: What, exactly, is mental disorder, and how does mental disorder differ from the "normal suffering of everyday life" of which Freud spoke or from the normal reactions to stress that sociologists refer to as "problems in living"?

Because the criteria used in epidemiological studies are generally derived from DSM, it seems appropriate to look at what DSM itself has to say about the nature of disorder. The definition of mental disorder in the manual's introduction (APA 1994: xxi–xxii), which "helped guide decisions regarding which conditions . . . should be included in DSM-IV" (p. xxi), has remained essentially the same from DSM-III to DSM-IV and is based on earlier work by Robert Spitzer (the editor of DSM-III and DSM-III-R) and colleagues (Spitzer & Endicott 1978). Note that the point of the definition is not to establish sharp boundaries along the continuum between disorder and nondisorder – almost all concepts are fuzzy and have somewhat arbitrary boundaries – but rather to show, contrary to antipsychiatric accusations, that a coherent and valid distinction can be drawn between clear cases of mental disorder and nondisorder in a way consistent with the use of "disorder" in the broader medical sciences. The DSM definition is as follows.

> In DSM-III each of the mental disorders is conceptualized as a clinically significant behavioral or psychological syndrome or pattern that occurs in an individual and that is typically associated with either a painful symptom (distress) or impairment in one or more important areas of functioning (disability). In addition, there is an inference that there is a behavioral, psychological, or biological dysfunction, and that the disturbance is not only in the relationship between the individual and society. (When the disturbance is limited to a conflict between an individual and society, this may represent social deviance, which may or may not be commendable, but is not by itself a mental disorder.) (APA 1980: 6)

The definition makes four useful points. First, disorder is something in the individual; it is not an unfortunate environmental stress to which a person responds with proportionate emotional pain but rather a condition in which something has gone wrong inside the person. Second, the internal condition, which must be inferred from manifest symptoms, is a dysfunction; that is, something must have gone wrong with the way the internal mechanism normally functions. Not all problematic internal states are disorders; for example, ignorance and appropriate sadness over a loss are problematic internal states but not disorders. Only those problematic internal states that are also dysfunctions are disorders in the medical sense. In the case of mental disorders, the dysfunctional mechanism must be a cognitive, motivational, behavioral, emotional, or other psychological mechanism. Of course, "dysfunction" is itself an obscure concept and requires its own analysis. Wakefield (1992a,b, 1993) provides an analysis according to which a dysfunction, in the sense relevant to both physical and mental medical disorder, is a failure of some internal (mental or physical) mechanism to perform a natural function for which it was designed by natural selection.

Third, a dysfunction of some internal mechanism is not enough to imply disorder. Many things that go wrong with various mental and physical mechanisms – breakdowns in the functioning of specific mechanisms that constitute what Donald Klein (1978) has called "part dysfunctions" – do not deserve to be called "disorders" because they do not have sufficiently negative implications for the individual's overall well-being. The difference between dysfunctions that can be classified as disorders and those that cannot be so classified thus lies in whether the dysfunction causes real harm to the person. In DSM's definition, the harms that generally occur as a result of dysfunctions and are diagnostically useful are divided into two kinds, distresses and disabilities. Finally, it is noted that the distress, disability, or other harm must come about as a direct result of the dysfunction and not just because society disapproves of the person's condition or for other reasons originating in interpersonal conflicts or in conflict between the individual and society. This last condition is meant to preclude the misuse of psychiatry sheerly for purposes of social control, as occurred in Soviet psychiatry. But the critical insight in DSM's definition is that mental disorders, like all medical disorders, are distresses or disabilities resulting from internal dysfunctions: "Whatever its original cause, it must currently be considered a manifestation of a . . . dysfunction in the individual" (APA 1994: xxi–xxii). A disorder is more than just appropriate unhappiness or distress or reduced functioning because of unfortunate circumstances.

In sum, the concept of disorder, as it applies to both physical and mental conditions, is that of a "harmful dysfunction" (Wakefield 1992a,b, 1993, in press). The harm can be any negatively evaluated or undesirable outcome; the dysfunction must involve something gone wrong with some internal mechanism, so that the mechanism is no longer performing one of the functions for which it was "designed" by natural selection.

Specificity and the Problem of False Positives

Conceptual validity is not easy to attain, for one basic reason: The same symptoms that can indicate mental disorders can also be normal when they occur in response to certain kinds of stressful environments. For example, deep sadness can indicate a major depressive disorder, or it can indicate a normal reaction to loss; intense anxiety can be a symptom of generalized anxiety disorder, or it can be a normal response to an unusually stressful set of circumstances. Likewise, antisocial behavior can represent a breakdown in the ability to function according to social rules and thus be a conduct disorder, or it can represent a decision to join a gang and go along with gang activities in a dangerous neighborhood where one's life is otherwise in danger; excessive alcohol intake can be a manifestation of an addiction that is a disorder, or it can be a youthful attempt to be exuberantly excessive, having no long-lasting negative implications and involving no addiction. In these and many other instances, criteria that use symptoms to pick out disorders might also pick out large numbers of normal conditions that have the same "symptoms" as the disorders. This is the problem of *false positives,* and it is a serious challenge to the conceptual validity of epidemiological surveys.

Mental disorders are relatively rare, whereas normal misery in response to problems in the environment is relatively common. Consequently, if an instrument does not successfully distinguish problems in living from true disorders, the estimate of the prevalence of disorder in the population could easily be greatly inflated by a large number of false positive diagnoses.

In epidemiology, it is common to distinguish sensitivity and specificity of criteria as two aspects of conceptual validity. Criteria must be *sensitive* so that, when they are applied correctly, no false negatives arise; that is, no genuine disorders are mistakenly classified as nondisorders. Criteria must be *specific* so that, when applied, they generate no false positives; that is, no nondisorders are mistakenly classified as disorders. If criteria lack specificity, then nondisordered individuals may be falsely classified as disordered and the criteria are said to be "overinclusive." In sum, criteria are sensitive to the degree that they identify as disorders *all* the true disorders and do not miss any disorders; criteria are specific to the extent that they identify as disorders *only* the true disorders and do not classify any nondisorders as disorders.

I will be concerned in this chapter only with the conceptual specificity of criteria for mental disorder. Although there are many important problems that could be addressed regarding sensitivity, specificity is by far the more difficult and important issue of the two.

Specificity is generally more difficult to achieve than sensitivity. There are atypical instances of each disorder, but most disorders are accompanied by certain predictable kinds of behaviors and so reasonably high levels of sensitivity are not hard to attain. For example, all phobias involve intense and irrational fears, all alcoholic disorders involve heavy drinking, and all depressions and anxiety disorders involve inordinate sadness and anxiety. Therefore, it is generally not hard to find criteria that apply to most or all instances of a disorder. The harder problem is to make the criteria specific enough to pick out only disorders from among the broader realm of problems in living. In some disorders, such as schizophrenia, the typical symptoms are far enough from the normal that there is relatively little problem with specificity, though even here the variations in the normal – including dissociative and even hallucinatory experiences that are not pathological (such as hallucinations of seeing a deceased spouse during some normal grief reactions) – can lead to false positives. But with many disorders (e.g., depression, anxiety, phobias, and alcohol or drug abuse and dependence), the same or very similar kinds of behaviors typically manifested by disordered people are also manifested by nondisordered people, so specificity becomes a very challenging problem.

Within psychiatric epidemiology, specificity is of particularly critical importance because of the well-known fact that even small problems with specificity can devastate the validity of epidemiological prevalence estimates. The reason for the disproportionate power of specificity is that, with respect to any given disorder, the samples in epidemiological studies of the general population generally contain many more people who do not have than do have the disorder. Indeed, it is common to have 10 to 100 times as many nondisordered as disordered individuals (with respect to a given disorder) in such a sample. Consequently, failures of specificity that yield small percentages of errors can still lead to many incorrect diagnoses.

The following example illustrates the point. Suppose a disorder has an actual prevalence of 1% of the general population. Suppose further that a set of diagnostic criteria for identifying the disorder has identical 10% rates of error for false positives and false negatives. That is, of all those who actually have the disorder, the criteria correctly identify 90% of them as disordered and incorrectly classify 10% as nondisordered; and, of all those who actually do not have the disorder, the criteria correctly identify 90% of them as nondisordered and incorrectly classify 10% of them as disordered. Although the error rates for false negatives and false positives are the same, the two error rates have very different impacts on the resulting prevalence estimates because the populations involved – the normal and the disordered – are of such different sizes. The rate of false negatives means that 10% of the disordered 1% of the population, or 0.1%, are misdiagnosed as nondisordered. In contrast, the rate of false positives means that 10% of the nondisordered 99% of the population, or 9.9% of the population, are misdiagnosed as having the disorder. In this example, the 10% false positive rate has an effect on the prevalence estimate that is 99 times as large as the effect of the 10% false negative rate. Together, both 10% error rates change the prevalence estimate from a true 1% to 10.8%, an increase of about 1,000% over true prevalence. The power of small errors in specificity to yield such large prevalence errors is the central challenge of measurement in any psychiatric epidemiological study aimed at establishing true prevalence in community samples.

The implication is clear: To accurately measure the prevalence of disorder in community samples, diagnostic criteria must, if anything, err on the side of specificity. Unfortunately, as we shall see, specificity has not been the highest priority in formulating such criteria.

DSM-IV and the Problem of False Positives

As noted earlier, contemporary psychiatric epidemiological studies take their diagnostic criteria from DSM, generally without substantial change. The extreme importance of specificity to epidemiology raises the question of whether DSM, a manual designed to be used primarily with a clinical population, adequately addressed specificity in the construction of its diagnostic criteria. Although in principle the goal of diagnosis in DSM and epidemiological instruments is the same (viz., valid diagnoses using operationalized criteria for specific mental disorders), there are divergent features of clinical and epidemiological contexts that entail different implicit emphases when constructing diagnostic criteria. For several reasons, these different emphases lead DSM criteria to be weaker with respect to specificity than is desirable for epidemiological criteria.

First, clinical interviewing and treatment extend over time and allow the clinician the luxury of correcting a mistaken initial diagnosis based on later findings. As new information emerges, the clinician might even conclude that there were extenuating circumstances and that the individual does not genuinely suffer from a disorder after all. The clinician can even countermand the official DSM criteria when the context of symptoms warrants such an exception. For these and other reasons, the cost of an initial false positive diagnosis in a clinical setting is not as great as the cost of a false negative, where an individual may not get the treatment that is needed. Even if there is a false positive, some purpose may be served because treatment may still be useful with subclinical conditions. In contrast, epidemiological diagnoses are almost always based on one contact, and there are no feedback loops or corrective mechanisms by which diagnostic evaluations can be reconsidered in light of emerging information. Nor is there second-guessing the criteria; epidemiological surveys rely exclusively on the diagnostic criteria in the epidemiological instrument in an algorithmic all-or-none fashion. Thus, false positives remain false positives. And false positives defeat the essential point of an epidemiological study, which is to count disorders.

Second, clinical populations are highly self-selected and consist of individuals who have been willing to undergo considerable inconvenience to obtain help with their problems. The psychological and institutional obstacles that help seekers must overcome mean that members of the clinical population are likely to be suffering from very high levels of distress, disability, or other harm, which may be indicative of a genuine disorder. This tends to make the issue of conceptual specificity superfluous. Diagnosis becomes a matter of choosing the category of disorder that best applies to the patient. This is a very different kind of problem from the one facing epidemiologists. Epidemiological surveys encompass many people who report problems similar to those of clinical populations but who have never sought out a mental health professional. In such cases, the seriousness of the condition, and thus its disorder status, is more questionable. Consequently, there is a much greater danger that the epidemiological survey will incorrectly diagnose nondisordered people as disordered. These divergent features of clinical and epidemiological contexts should make one wary about uncritically transposing clinically derived criteria into the epidemiological domain.

It turns out (Wakefield 1993, 1996) that many DSM criteria are conceptually inconsistent with DSM's own definition of disorder and consequently can give rise to false positives. In particular, two of DSM's definitional requirements for disorder are frequently violated by its own criteria. The first is that the condition must be due to a psychological or biological dysfunction, yet many of the criteria describe human states and behaviors (e.g., intense anxiety, excessive use of alcohol) that need not originate in dysfunctions. The second requirement that is often violated is the stipulation that the harm cannot be the result of social conflict or the attempt by society to control disapproved behavior; many of the criteria, however, involve "symptoms" that are clearly manifestations of social conflict (e.g., arrest for use of illegal drugs, family disapproval of one's alcohol use) and are not harms directly caused by dysfunctions. The following are just a few examples of how DSM's rules for diagnosis diverge from the concept of disorder to encompass nondisordered problems of living. (I thank the American Psychological Association for permission to use here some material previously published in Wakefield 1996.)

Major Depressive Disorder

A diagnosis of major depressive disorder is based on having several out of a set of symptoms typical of an extreme sadness response – for example, sadness, emptiness, lack of enjoyment in one's usual activities, loss of appetite, lack of concentration, trouble sleeping, and so on. The criteria correctly contain an exclusion for uncomplicated bereavement (i.e., one is not diagnosed as disordered if the symptoms are due to a normal-range response to having recently lost a loved one, with up to two months of symptoms allowed as normal), but they contain no exclusions for equally normal reactions to other losses, such as a terminal medical diagnosis in oneself or a loved one, separation from one's spouse, or losing one's job. If, in grappling with such a loss, one's reaction includes just two weeks of depressed mood, diminished pleasure in usual activities, insomnia, fatigue, and diminished ability to concentrate on work tasks, then one satisfies DSM criteria for major depressive disorder even though such a reaction need not imply pathology any more than it does in bereavement.

Separation Anxiety Disorder

Separation anxiety disorder is diagnosed in children on the basis of symptoms indicating age-inappropriate, excessive anxiety concerning separation from home or from those to whom the individual is attached, lasting at least four weeks. The symptoms (e.g., excessive distress when separation occurs, worry that some event will lead to separation, refusal to go to school because of fear of separation, reluctance to be alone or without major attachment figure) are just the sorts of things children experience when they have a normal, intense separation anxiety response. The criteria do not adequately distinguish between a true disorder, in which separation responses are triggered inappropriately, and normal responses to perceived threats to the child's primary bond due to an unreliable caregiver or other serious disruptions. For example, in a study of children of military personnel at three bases that happened to occur at the time of Desert Storm – when many parents of the children were in fact leaving for the Middle East and where children knew that a parent could be killed or injured – the level of separation anxiety was high enough among many of the children for them to qualify as having separation anxiety disorder according to DSM standards. In fact, they were responding with a normal-range separation response to an unusual environment in which they had realistic concerns that the parent would not come back (A. M. Brannan, pers. commun.).

Substance Abuse

Diagnosis of substance abuse requires any one of four criteria: poor role performance at work or home due to substance use; substance use in hazardous circumstances, such as driving under the influence of alcohol; recurrent substance-related legal problems; or social or interpersonal problems due to substance use, such as arguments with family members about substance use. Contrary to DSM's definition of mental disorder, these criteria allow diagnosis on the basis of conflict between the individual and social institutions such as police or family. Arguments with one's spouse about alcohol or drug use, or between a child and his or her parent, is sufficient for DSM-based diagnosis, as is being arrested more than once for driving while under the influence of alcohol or for possession of marijuana. These social problems and interpersonal conflicts need not be due to mental disorders.

Disorder of Written Expression

An op-ed piece on DSM-IV in the *New York Times* by Stuart Kirk and Herb Kutchins (1994) – which the *Times* titled "Is Bad Writing a Mental Disorder?" – used disorder of written expression from the category of learning disorders as an example of the "nonsense" in the manual. Because DSM-IV criteria for this and other learning disorders require only that the child's achievement level be substantially below average, the criteria do not distinguish very bad penmanship from disorder. Clearly, a distinction is needed here: bad penmanship is not a disorder in itself, but bad penmanship caused by a dysfunction in one of the mechanisms that enable children to learn to write is a disorder (Kirk and Kutchins acknowledged that this distinction could be made). This sort of distinction has been common in the learning disorders community for decades and requires that, before diagnosing a child with a learning disorder, one must attempt to eliminate possible normal causes of the lack of achievement, such as family distractions, lack of motivation, or inability to understand the language of instruction. The DSM-IV criteria fail to make this distinction.

Antisocial Personality Disorder

Criminal behavior must be distinguished from antisocial disorders of personality. Traditionally, this distinction was made by requiring that an antisocial mental disorder must involve a dysfunction in one of the mechanisms that usually inhibit such behavior, such as those that provide the capacity for guilt, anxiety, remorse, learning from mistakes, or capacity for loyalty. The DSM-IV criteria for antisocial personality disorder require that, in addition to having been conduct-disordered before age 15, the adult must meet three or more of the following criteria: inconsistent work history or failure to honor financial obligations, breaking the law, irritability and aggressiveness, impulsivity, deceitfulness, recklessness, and lack of remorse. These criteria do not adequately distinguish between career criminals and the mentally disordered. The criminal certainly meets the illegal activity criterion and may well meet the work/finance criterion (criminal activity is not "work" as intended in this criterion), the deceit criterion (criminal careers often involve substantial deceit), and one or more of the impulsivity, irritability/aggressiveness, or recklessness criteria (by the very nature of criminal activity). The "remorse" criterion was added as a concession to the traditional approach to validity, but because only three criteria are necessary for diagnosis, the inclusion of a seventh "remorse" criterion does nothing to prevent false positives on the basis of three out of the other six criteria.

ECA: Lifetime versus Active Prevalence

In the final sections of this chapter, I present three extended examples of attempts to use DSM-derived criteria in an epidemiological study to measure the prevalence of particular mental disorders – namely, generalized anxiety disorder, major depressive disorder, and alcohol abuse. I selected these examples because they are among the disorders with the highest prevalence rates, and so their defining criteria warrant special attention for specificity.

The advantages of using carefully delineated, operationalized criteria are obvious, and such criteria generally lead to excellent sensitivity. I will focus my comments on the kinds of problems that can occur with false positives and lack of specificity when such DSM-style criteria are used. The examples are drawn from the ECA project (Robins & Regier 1991), and the criteria are part of the Diagnostic Interview Schedule (DIS; Robins et al. 1985) developed specifically for that study. The DIS is essentially a translation of DSM-III criteria into the format of an epidemiological instrument. Note that in some instances the validity of certain DSM criteria may have improved in DSM-III-R or DSM-IV. The NCS (Kessler et al. 1994), a later study that is still in the process of publishing its results, uses criteria from DSM-III-R as the basis of its instrument. However, the general kinds of problems illustrated here appear to be endemic to current DSM-derived criteria. No systematic cure for these problems has yet been identified.

The ECA, like many epidemiological studies, presents estimates for both "lifetime" and "active" (current) prevalence of disorders. Lifetime prevalence refers to the percentage of people who have ever had a given disorder in their lives. Active prevalence, in the context of the ECA study, refers to the percentage of people who have had a given disorder at any time in the past year. I will be concerned here only with lifetime prevalence (note that lifetime prevalence *includes* "active" people who currently have the disorder).

Before looking at lifetime rates, however, a brief comment on special problems of measuring active rates is in order. In establishing whether individuals have ever had a disorder, one simply wants to know whether the subjects met the diagnostic criteria for the disorder at any point in their lives. But, in deciding whether an individual still actively has the disorder – as well as when the person acquired the disorder ("onset") or when the disorder ended ("remitted") – a new problem arises. The problem is whether having the disorder at a given time requires that all the diagnostic criteria for the disorder be met at that time, or whether instead it is enough for some of the symptoms of the disorder to be present while assuming that all the criteria are met later or earlier. For example, does schizophrenia or depression start when the first symptom appears, even if the entire set of criteria for the disorder are not met until later, or does it not start until the full set of required criteria are met? Does the disorder end when the full set of criteria is no longer present, or does it not end until the last symptom goes away, even if that is long after the required set is no longer fully present? Any answer one chooses to these questions leads to difficulties.

The ECA study calculated active prevalence rates as follows: "*Active* illnesses [are] defined as disorders that meet two conditions: (1) criteria have been met at some time in the person's life, and (2) there has been some sign of the disorder within the year before interview" (Leaf, Myers, & McEvoy 1991: 13). When ECA researchers say that "some sign" of the disorder must have occurred within the last year, they mean only that "at least one symptom (or one episode) has been present in the year prior to interview" (Robins, Locke, & Regier 1991: 329–30). So, contrary to intuition, an "active" disorder did not mean that the individual actively (i.e., within the past year) met the diagnostic criteria for the disorder. Rather, it meant that the individual met criteria for the disorder at *some* time in the past and had at least one symptom in the past year (in a few cases, more than one symptom was necessary; the criteria varied to some extent from disorder to disorder).

This method of measuring active rates leads to serious validity problems. Even if a symptom is related to an earlier disorder, it may not be of sufficient weight by itself to warrant continued attribution of a disorder, and most of the symptoms used in DIS criteria are not good indicators by themselves of the presence of disorder; that is why the full set of criteria exists in the first place. Moreover, the very notion that the active symptom is connected to the previously diagnosed disorder involves a possibly invalid inference; many of the symptoms used by the DIS have high baseline rates in the general population independent of their relation to any specific disorder. The ECA definition of "active" is based on the assumption that, whenever a symptom that is part of the criteria for a disorder occurs *after* the individual meets full criteria for the disorder, one can infer that the underlying disorder must still exist and is manifesting itself in the symptom. Imagine applying this premise to physical disorder. For example, if I had whooping cough when I was a child, and if one symptom used to diagnose the disorder was a cough, and if I had a cough within the past year, then by ECA logic I can be diagnosed as having an active case of whooping cough!

Those who constructed the DIS were aware that the ECA definition of an active disorder leads to validity problems:

> Do we consider the date at which the person last had enough symptoms to meet criteria or the date of the very last symptom? . . . For the most part, we chose the simpler rule, the date of the last symptom. . . . We reasoned that clinicians would hesitate to consider a person who emerged from a depressive episode as recovered if some symptoms persisted, even if enough symptoms had remitted to prevent meeting diagnostic criteria on a cross-sectional basis. Yet, it is easy to cite situations where our decision seems awkward. Relatives may complain about a single drink taken by someone with a history of alcohol abuse even after he has stopped drinking heavily, for fear that the problems will reemerge. That person is then diagnosed as current alcohol abuse because he has a single alcohol problem [i.e., he has the problem of family members disapproving of his drinking], although he is not drinking excessively. (Robins et al. 1985: 155–6)

In part because of these special problems that attach to the measure of active disorder, I shall focus entirely on lifetime prevalence, which measures how many people reached full criteria for disorder at some time in their lives.

ECA: Generalized Anxiety Disorder

Generalized anxiety disorder (GAD) is a disorder of chronic anxiety arousal. Based on ECA data, Blazer and colleagues conclude that "generalized anxiety is clearly a common disorder" (1991: 188). Lifetime prevalence in the general population is estimated by the ECA to be 8.5% (Robins et al. 1991: 343, Table 13-7). The commonness of GAD, combined with other features of the data to be explored shortly, led Blazer et al. to question whether the conditions diagnosed as GAD by the DIS are really disorders: "Generalized anxiety disorder is a common condition, even among people not suffering from any other disorder. Its association with a number of social risk factors makes us wonder whether it is a disorder in the ordinary sense of the word. Could it be a residual of symptoms reflecting poor life satisfaction or generalized stress?" (1991: 199). In other words, given all the stresses in our environment, there is a question of whether the ECA criteria correctly distinguish disordered anxiety reactions from normal reactions to stressful environments.

The ECA diagnoses are made on the basis of the following criteria (Blazer et al. 1991: 183).

DIS–ECA Criteria for Generalized Anxiety Disorder

A. "Yes" answer to the following "gate" question:
   "Now I want to ask you about longer periods of feeling anxious or afraid. Have you ever had a period of a month or more when most of the time you felt worried or anxious (perhaps afraid that something bad was going to happen either to you yourself or to someone you cared about)?"
B. At least one symptom from each of the following three categories:
   1. Motor tension: eyelids twitched, jittery or fidgety, body trembled, tired very easily, restless, tense or jumpy, easily startled, trouble relaxing.
   2. Autonomic hyperactivity: sweating a lot, heart pounding, dizziness or light-headedness, tingling in hands/feet, upset stomach, diarrhea, frequent urination, face flushing or turning pale, mouth dry, breathing too fast, hands cold or clammy.
   3. Vigilance and scanning: trouble sleeping; trouble concentrating; irritable, impatient, or on edge.

The central problem in inferring an anxiety dysfunction is that anxiety reactions are a natural part of life. Human beings are designed to experience anxious arousal in the face of various kinds of threats and stressors, from momentary dangers to chronically overwhelming demands. Thus, the sheer occurrence of anxiety, even intense anxiety, is an insufficient basis on which to infer internal dysfunction. Moreover, there is no natural limit to the length of time during which people can appropriately respond with anxiety to an ongoing environmental stressor, so the persistence of anxiety is not in itself a good indicator of dysfunction. Because chronic anxiety is a normal response to some situations, more than just chronic anxiety is needed to warrant diagnosis of an anxiety disorder. Perhaps the best circumstantial evidence for the existence of an anxiety dysfunction is intense, persistent anxiety that is not in any coherent or proportional way related to environmental stressors.

Unfortunately, the DIS–ECA criteria for GAD simply assess anxiety and do not address the problem of distinguishing normal anxiety from pathological anxiety. The gate question makes no reference at all to the relation of the anxiety to situational stressors; it simply asks if the respondent has ever been worried, anxious, or afraid for a period of two weeks or longer (at the Los Angeles site) or for one month or longer (at the Durham and St. Louis sites; GAD was studied at only three of five ECA sites). The examples that are used in the gate question to guide the respondent's answer ("perhaps you were afraid that something bad was going to happen either to you yourself or to someone you cared about?") do not help matters much; certainly we can be legitimately worried that something bad might happen to ourselves or to our loved ones, and nothing in the wording of the example suggests that the respondent is being asked to identify only excessive or unreasonable instances of worry. Thus, the gate queston provides no basis whatever for sorting dysfunction from normal anxiety responses.

As noted, the gate question asks whether the anxious mood was experienced over a period of two weeks (at the Los Angeles site) or one month (at two other GAD sites). This time criterion, which aims to ensure that the anxiety response is not a normal transient emotional response to an immediate threat or danger, nevertheless fails to distinguish dysfunction from normality. A person could easily experience intense anxiety over a period of two weeks or a month due to stressful life circumstances, such as the ups and downs of a life-threatening illness in a loved one; the ongoing threat of losing one's job; the process of preparing for doctoral examinations, bar exams, or some other school or occupational challenge; or watching one's savings evaporate in a stock market plunge. The time criterion does not distinguish chronic anxiety that is a normal response to chronic stressors from chronic anxiety that results from a malfunction of anxiety-regulating mechanisms.

If the gate question is answered positively, then the respondent is asked a series of questions about specific symptoms. To meet diagnostic criteria, at least one symptom in each of three categories must be reported as having occurred during the same period as the anxious mood described in the gate question. However, the symptoms are just the components of any intense anxiety response, and such responses can be either normal or pathological. The symptom questions therefore add nothing to the conceptual validity of the criteria because they fail to distinguish anxiety caused by a dysfunction from normal anxiety.

The overall inadequacy of the DIS criteria for GAD is illustrated in a study by Breslau and Davis (1985). When these researchers evaluated 357 mothers of chronically ill children using DIS criteria, they found an astonishingly high lifetime GAD rate of 45%. It seems plausible to suggest that, rather than all of the diagnosed women being disordered, most of these women were reacting normally to an extremely stressful situation. Breslau and Davis themselves interpreted their findings to mean that the criteria lacked specificity. The results of their study suggest that DIS GAD criteria are easily met by normal people facing a chronic stressor.

The ECA results are in certain respects reminiscent of Breslau and Davis's findings. For example, Blazer and colleagues find that those who are dependent on unemployment compensation, disability payments, social security, the Veteran's

Administration, or welfare, and who are therefore more likely to be in a financially precarious situation, experience a prevalence of generalized anxiety disorder about four times as high as those who are not dependent in this way. Moreover, GAD decreases with increasing income (Blazer et al. 1991: 196). It is possible that those with anxiety disorders have fared worse in life owing to the disorder, but the most plausible interpretation of these findings is that the stress of financial and related problems causes anxiety symptoms. However, such people are not necessarily any more disordered than the mothers of chronically ill children in the Breslau and Davis study. The upshot of this analysis is that it appears that the ECA data provide no grounds for making even a rough guess of the true prevalence of GAD as a genuine disorder of anxiety arousal.

ECA: Major Depressive Disorder

According to Robins et al. (1991: 343, Table 13-7), the lifetime prevalence of major depressive episodes in the general population is 6.4%. The DIS–ECA criteria for major depressive disorder require that the individual report a major depressive episode that is neither part of a bipolar disorder nor an instance of uncomplicated grief after the death of a loved one. Thus, at the heart of the definition of major depressive disorder is the notion of a major depressive episode, which is defined essentially as a two-week period of dysphoric mood accompanied by four or more of the following symptoms: sleep disturbance, changes in psychomotor activity, loss of ability to experience pleasure and interest, fatigue, feelings of worthlessness or guilt, difficulty in concentrating, and preoccupation with death or a wish to die.

An individual is classified as having a major depressive episode if that individual answers "yes" to question A and "yes" to four or more symptom questions under B (criteria adapted from Robins et al. 1991: 410–11 and Table 4-1).

DIS–ECA Criteria for Major Depressive Episode

A. In your lifetime, have you ever had two weeks or more during which you felt sad, blue, depressed, or when you lost all interest and pleasure in things that you usually cared about?

B. During the period indicated in A:
   1. Did you lose your appetite? Or, did you lose weight without trying to – as much as two pounds a week for several weeks? Or, did your eating increase so much that you gained as much as two pounds a week for several weeks?
   2. Did you have trouble falling asleep, staying asleep, or with waking up too early? Or, were you sleeping too much?
   3. Did you talk or move more slowly than is normal for you? Or, did you have to be moving all the time – that is, you couldn't sit still and paced up and down?

4. Was your interest in sex a lot less than usual?
5. Did you feel tired out all the time?
6. Did you feel worthless, sinful, or guilty?
7. Did you have a lot more trouble concentrating than is normal for you? Or, did your thoughts come slower than usual or seem mixed up?
8. Did you think a lot about death – either your own, someone else's, or death in general? Or, did you feel like you wanted to die? Or, did you feel so low you thought of committing suicide? Or, did you attempt suicide?

The central validity problem for any definition of depressive disorder, analogous to the problem with anxiety disorders considered earlier, is to distinguish pathological depression from the common and normal depressive reactions that occur in response to significant losses or failures of all kinds. As Weissman and associates note, the ECA study is concerned only with pathological reactions: "Transient moods of sadness or elation occur frequently in the general population and are considered normal. . . . However, here we are concerned with affective disorders as clinical syndromes codified in DSM-III" (1991: 53). Unfortunately, as we saw earlier, DSM criteria themselves do not validly distinguish normal sadness responses from disorders, and the DIS inherits this shortcoming.

To appreciate the basic validity problem with DSM-III criteria for major depressive disorder, it is useful to start by reflecting on why grief reactions are justifiably excluded from the category of disorder even though such reactions can contain all the symptoms characteristic of a pathological depression. The exclusion is justified because such grief reactions appear to be normal-range responses that play an adaptive role in coming to terms with loss and so are presumed to be part of how human beings are designed to react to such losses. The occurrence of such loss responses, however painful they may be, does not represent a psychological mechanism failing to perform its function; rather, it represents the proper workings of emotional mechanisms. In fact, the *lack* of such a response may be indicative of dysfunction. Hence the exclusion of grief reactions from the category of disorder is essential to validity. Obviously, only those grief reactions that are "uncomplicated," meaning that they do not involve excessive persistence or severity of symptoms given the nature of the loss, are excluded from disorder status; grief reactions can be pathological when unduly persistent or severe.

From the viewpoint of validity, it is entirely arbitrary to exclude grief reactions to loss of a loved one from the category of disorder and yet *not* exclude all the other uncomplicated, normal sadness reactions to life's losses and failures that are comparable to grief in the nature of the experienced symptoms. There are many circumstances of loss or failure when people normally and appropriately experience sadness that meets the listed criteria for a depressive episode. Consider, for example, the following vignettes, taken from Wakefield (in press; I thank the American Psychological Association for permission to use this material here).

Vignette 1 (Reaction to a life-threatening medical diagnosis).

The patient, a 35-year-old physician, had been diagnosed three weeks before with a malignant brain tumor and was told by his physician that there is no effective treatment. He came to a research medical center for a second opinion, and was given some hope that an experimental treatment might give him five to ten more years of life. Referred by the neurosurgical staff for a psychiatric assessment, he reports that since his diagnosis he has experienced chronic feelings of sadness over the loss of his health and the implications for his wife and child, markedly diminished interest or pleasure in usual activities as he focused on possible treatments, insomnia due to thinking about his illness and his prospects, lack of energy due to sadness and insomnia, diminished ability to concentrate on everyday tasks due to his attempting to come to terms with the possibility that he might soon die, and some suicidal ideation when he earlier thought the course of his illness would be more rapid and hopeless and he considered whether it would be better for him and his family to end his life before the occurrence of deterioration due to the disease.

This patient's response qualifies him for a DSM-IV diagnosis of major depressive disorder. However, once one takes into account the subjective meanings that are causing the loss response – namely, his discovery that he is suffering from an imminently life-threatening illness – his reaction appears to be consistent with a normal-range, nondisordered response. This is perhaps especially so because he is a physician and fully understands the implications of the diagnosis. Note that although he has stopped functioning in his normal routines – which is entirely understandable given his prognosis – he has continued to assertively seek out the best available medical care. The failure to distinguish normal from pathological sadness responses to threatening medical diagnoses could be seriously counterproductive in this case; if the clinician had followed DSM and offered a diagnosis of major depressive disorder, that could have placed this normal individual outside the parameters of the research prototcol governing the experimental treatment he is seeking.

It is not only the patient but also the patient's family and other loved ones who may experience severe sadness reactions to news of a life-threatening medical diagnosis.

Vignette 2 (Reaction to a medical diagnosis in a loved one).

A woman who is visiting a medical center distant from her home consults a psychiatrist at the center, asking for medication to help her sleep. In the diagnostic interview it emerges that the woman's son, a physician to whom she is very close and who is the pride of her life, has just three weeks before been diagnosed with a malignant brain tumor. The woman has traveled to the medical center to be with her son for an evaluation and possible immediate operation. After the news of her son's diagnosis, the patient was devastated by feelings of sadness and despair and was unable to function at work or socially. She did, however, devote herself to helping her son arrange for a visit to the medical research center for further evaluation and possible treatment, and she offered him and his wife emotional support. Although she kept up a brave front for her son, the patient has been in a state of great distress since the diagnosis: crying intermittently, unable to sleep, lacking the ability to concentrate, and feeling fatigued and uninterested in her usual activities as she attempted to come to terms with the news of her son's diagnosis.

This woman satisfies the ECA and DSM criteria for diagnosis with a major depressive disorder, yet her reaction appears to be within normal range for a loving parent in such a situation. The horror of such an illness in a beloved child who is still young, who carries one's hopes for the future and thus one's sense of life's meaningfulness, and to whom one has devoted much of one's life, appropriately causes an extreme and enduring emotional reaction. Once the subjective meaning to the mother of her son's diagnosis is taken into account, her reaction is consistent with a nondisordered response.

Vignette 3 (Ending of a passionate romantic relationship).

The patient, a male professor in the social sciences, comes to the consultation seeking antidepressant medication and medicine for insomnia. He must present a paper in another city as part of a job interview and is afraid he cannot function adequately to do so. He reports that for the past month he has experienced depressed mood and extreme feelings of sadness and emptiness, as well as lack of interest in his usual activities (in fact, when not with friends, he has largely lain in bed or watched television). His appetite has diminished, and he lies awake long into the night unable to fall asleep owing to the pain of his sadness. He is fatigued and lacking in energy during the day, and does not have the ability to concentrate on his work. There is no suicidal ideation; nor are there feelings of guilt or worthlessness. However, there is functional impairment: the patient is barely managing to meet minimal occupational obligations (e.g., he has shown up at class relatively unprepared and has not attended the monthly faculty meeting or worked on his research). He has also avoided social obligations, except to be with close friends to lessen his pain.

When asked what event might have precipitated these distressing feelings, he reports, holding back tears as he speaks, that about a month before, an extremely intense and passionate five-year love affair with a married woman (the patient is single) to whom he had been completely devoted had been ended by the woman after she made a final decision that she could not leave her husband. Both lovers had perceived this relationship as a unique, once-in-a-lifetime romance in which they had met their "soulmate" and experienced an extraordinary combination of emotional and intellectual intimacy.

If one is abandoned by a lover whom one believes (perhaps with good reason) was a once-in-a-lifetime "soulmate," it is not abnormal or inappropriate to feel extreme sadness and even despair, with all the associated depressive symptoms. The meaning to the patient of this relationship reveals that the reaction is not necessarily disordered, despite its intensity. Similarly, loss of a partner due to separation or divorce may also cause a normal loss response of great and enduring intensity. In general, the end of a serious relationship can cause a feeling that the world is drained of meaning as the person grapples to no longer see the world partly through the eyes of the other. The associated feelings may satisfy DSM criteria without actually being a major depressive disorder.

All the patients described in these vignettes satisfy DSM criteria for major depressive disorder. Had they been subjects in the ECA study, they would have correctly answered the questions in a way that qualified them for diagnosis under DIS–ECA criteria as well. Yet, none of them need be disordered. Of course, the suffering experienced by these patients could trigger a genuine depressive disorder, but there is no evidence in these cases of such a pathological reaction. The ECA criteria do not allow such circumstances to be taken into account in diagnosis. Neither the DSM-III nor the DIS draws an adequate distinction between nonpathological and pathological depression; without such a distinction, there is no way to tell how many of the depressive episodes reported by the ECA study are actually disorders.

ECA: Alcohol Abuse

The use of alcohol is common in our culture, both as an individual preference and as a coping method. The culture often implicitly endorses or idealizes even excessive use of alcohol. Thus, there is a heavy burden of proof on whoever claims that an individual who uses alcohol to excess is disordered.

Nevertheless, the ECA project claims to demonstrate that alcoholism is "one of the most prevalent psychiatric disorders in America" (Helzer, Burnam, & McEvoy 1991: 115), concluding that 13.8% of the American population suffers from an alcoholic disorder. (Relying on this figure, *U.S. News & World Report* asserted in 1994 that "sooner or later, alcoholism affects 14 percent of all adults.") Moreover, as Helzer and colleagues note, "Lifetime prevalence for men is even more dramatic, with almost one-quarter (23.8%) meeting the criteria" (1991: 84). Even Helzer et al. must admit that "the huge lifetime prevalence for men strains credibility" (p. 84), but they offer no analysis of why the ECA study might have gone wrong in its quest for the true prevalence of alcohol disorders. These statistics represent the combined prevalence of two alcohol disorders identified by the ECA project, alcohol abuse disorder and alcohol dependence disorder; I focus here on alcohol abuse disorder. The ECA criteria for these alcohol disorders are an attempt to translate into diagnostic terms the condition commonly called "alcoholism." However, alcoholism is a vague concept applied to a broad range of behaviors, not all of which necessarily indicate disorder in the medical sense.

Alcohol abuse disorder is diagnosed if an individual reports one symptom from A and one from B. (Symptoms are listed in the order of reported frequency in both the general population and those diagnosed as disordered; illustrative questions from the DIS are presented after some symptoms.)

DIS–ECA Criteria for Alcohol Abuse Disorder

A. Pattern of pathological alcohol use
   1. Drank a fifth (or equivalent) in one day.
   2. Blackouts. ("Have you ever had blackouts while drinking, that is, where you drank enough so that you couldn't remember the next day what you had said or done?")
   3. Alcohol binges or benders. ("Have you ever gone on binges or benders, where you keep drinking for a couple of days or more without sobering up?")
   4. Wanted to stop but couldn't. ("Have you ever wanted to stop drinking but couldn't?")
   5. Set rules to control drinking.
   6. Drank despite serious health problems.
   7. Couldn't do daily work without alcohol. ("Has there ever been a period in your life when you could not do your ordinary daily work well unless you had had something to drink?")

B. Impairment in social or occupational functioning due to alcohol
   1. Family objects that respondent drinks too much. ("Has your family ever objected because you were drinking too much?")
   2. Physical fights while drinking. ("Have you ever gotten into physical fights while drinking?")
   3. Trouble driving due to drinking. ("Have you ever gotten into trouble driving because of drinking – like having an accident or being arrested for drunk driving?")
   4. Arrested for drinking. ("Have you ever been arrested or held at the police station because of drinking or for disturbing the peace while drinking?")
   5. Friends, doctor, clergyman, or other professionals said drinking too much.
   6. Job (or school) troubles from drinking. ("Have you ever had job or school troubles because of drinking – like missing too much work or drinking on the job or at school?")
   7. Lost job (or expelled from school) because of drinking.

The criteria for alcohol abuse disorder suffer from problems of conceptual validity. Consider the following counterexamples.

(1) A female college freshman, who rarely drinks, attends a fraternity party marking the end of finals and drinks until she passes out; the next day, she does not remember what happened toward the end of the evening. When she mentions this to her parents, they become angry about her drinking. On this basis alone, the student could be diagnosed with alcohol abuse disorder (criteria A2 and B1).

(2) A young woman, who grew up in a Mormon family that prohibited alcohol consumption, hangs out with a crowd where moderate drinking is expected on the weekends. Although she feels guilty and wants to stop her moderate drinking, her desire to be socially accepted is such that she is not able to stop. A clergyman she consults urges her to stop drinking. On this basis alone, she could be diagnosed with alcohol abuse disorder (criteria A4 and B5).

(3) A young man reacts to being rejected by his girlfriend by going on a drinking binge and acting rowdy in public, which leads to his arrest. On this basis alone, he could be diagnosed as having alcohol abuse disorder (criteria A3 and B4).

(4) A man loses his job (for reasons unrelated to alcohol consumption) and takes a few drinks to deal with his despair, despite the fact that he has a serious health problem that might be exacerbated by drinking. A friend, knowing about the health problem, criticizes his drinking. On this basis alone, the man could be classified as having alcohol abuse disorder (criteria A6 and B5).

However, none of these people is necessarily disordered. The DIS–ECA criteria for alcohol abuse disorder simply do not distinguish excessive use from disordered abuse. The criteria in some cases may indicate "abuse" (that is, bad use) of alcohol, but using something badly and using it pathologically are not the same thing. We can "abuse" anything, from library borrowing privileges to sick leave, without being disordered. The mere bad use of alcohol is no more intrinsically a disorder than are other negative behaviors, and society's desire to control drinking does not transform the behavior into a disorder.

Obviously, many people who satisfy the ECA criteria for generalized anxiety disorder, major depressive disorder, or alcohol abuse disorder are indeed suffering from the respective mental disorder. The problem, as our analyses demonstrate, is that many who satisfy those same criteria may not be disordered. Thus, we cannot know to what degree ECA prevalence estimates accurately reflect true prevalence of mental disorder.

Conclusion

When the United States some years ago launched the Hubble space telescope at a cost of over one billion dollars, it was discovered after the launch that the mirror suffered from a degree of distortion, yielding fuzzy images that could not provide the new view of the universe that was the goal of the project. As a result, the many other aspects of the program – the rest of the telescope, the computers and motors that aimed the telescope with extreme precision, the solar panels providing power, the telemetry that allowed the telescope's readings to be transmitted to earth, and even the successful launch itself – all became relatively worthless. The value of every other aspect of the enterprise depended on the expectation that the mirror could yield clear images. Fortunately, a later repair mission was able to fix the mirrors and allow the entire project to go forward and fulfill its mission of providing sharp images of our universe.

We find ourselves today in a somewhat similar position with respect to psychiatric epidemiology and its measuring instruments. The entire, extremely expensive apparatus of such studies – from instrument development, sample selection, and data collection to statistical analysis of data – depend for their meaningfulness on the validity of a few definitions of mental disorders, generally taken from DSM. Yet, if the foregoing argument is correct, there is reason to believe that these definitions do not give a clear and valid picture of the domain of disorder. Instead, they seem to fuzzily encompass a broad range of abnormal and normal situations in which human beings feel distress or are impaired in their usual functioning. For all their innovation and sophistication, and despite the genuine progress they represent, DSM-derived criteria do not overcome the problems in distinguishing disorder from nondisorder that beset the earlier symptom checklists. The question that faces psychiatric epidemiology is whether some kind of "repair mission" can succeed in fixing these criteria or, alternatively, whether some methodological innovation can circumvent these validity problems.

There is reason to hope that refined criteria and tailored methodologies can finally overcome the problem of false positives. For example, future epidemiological studies may use a two-stage process in which subjects are first screened using DSM or comparable criteria and then those meeting DSM criteria for disorder are interviewed by a professional to distinguish genuine cases from false positives. Criteria may be refined to take the situational context of the symptoms into account and thus reduce the magnitude of the problem (Wakefield 1996). In any event, current studies, though flawed, do provide large amounts of valuable data on the prevalence of disorder, distress, and impairment. However, for now, the question remains open as to when (or whether) psychiatric epidemiology will reach its goal of accurately measuring the true prevalence of mental disorder in community populations.

3

The Prevalence of Mental Illness

Ronald C. Kessler & Shanyang Zhao

Ronald Kessler is the Principal Investigator for the National Comorbidity Survey (NCS), which is the only nationally representative survey in the United States to assess the prevalence, causes, and consequences of mental illnesses. The NCS is based upon a household survey of over 8,000 respondents aged 15 to 54 and a supplemental sample of students living in group housing. Kessler and Zhao begin their chapter by describing how mental illness is measured and provide background information about two of the most commonly utilized classification schemes: the *Diagnostic and Statistical Manual* (DSM) and the International Classification of Diseases (ICD). Kessler and Zhao also provide an overview of the earlier attempt to determine the prevalence of mental illness in the population in the Epidemiologic Catchment Area (ECA) study, which interviewed over 20,000 respondents in five epidemiological communities using the Diagnostic Interview Schedule (DIS). Limitations in the ECA study led to the NCS, which relied upon a modified version of the DIS to make psychiatric diagnoses. After describing the DSM-III-R conditions that the NCS assessed, the authors provide an overview of the findings of the NCS. They describe the estimated prevalence of all the disorders assessed in both the ECA and NCS surveys; they then provide more detailed results about comorbidity among these disorders and about major depression and posttraumatic stress disorder. Their findings show that mental disorder is widely prevalent in the United States and that many of those suffering from one mental illness are also experiencing other disorders (usually some combination of mental illness and substance abuse). Kessler and Zhao point out that the major burden of mental illness falls on a small group of individuals who are highly comorbid, and these individuals comprise the bulk of those with serious mental illness. The chapter concludes with a discussion of future research directions in the study of the prevalence of psychiatric disorders. Students should discuss the overall prevalence rates: Were they surprised by the data presented in this chapter? Do they think the public is generally aware of the widespread prevalence of mental illness?

Introduction

Background

As readers of the chapter by Professor Wakefield will know, the answer to the question "How many people have a mental illness?" depends on how one conceptualizes and measures mental illness. For purposes of the present chapter, the focus will be on measures of psychiatric disorder – as assessed in the *Diagnostic and Statistical Manual* (DSM) of the American Psychiatric Association (APA) or the World Health Organization's (WHO) International Classification of Diseases (ICD) and as operationalized in lay administered fully structured diagnostic interviews like the Diagnostic Interview Schedule (DIS; Robins et al. 1981) or the Composite International Diagnostic Interview (CIDI; Robins et al. 1988). Although a number of versions of the DSM and ICD classification schemes exist, most of the results reported here are based on the DSM-III-R (APA 1987) because this is the system that has been the basis for most recent general population research on the prevalence of psychiatric disorders.

It is worth noting at the onset that most of the research by sociologists on the prevalence of mental illness has not focused on DSM or ICD disorders. Measures of nonspecific psychological distress have been much more commonly used as outcomes. (For a review, see Link & Dohrenwend 1980a.) Research based on these continuous measures of distress has an advantage over research based on the assessment of dichotomous measures of psychiatric disorder in that the former deals much more directly with the actual constellations of signs and symptoms that exist in the population and with less reliance on the classification schemes imposed on these constellations by the committees that created the DSM and ICD diagnoses. However, there is also a disadvantage of working with distress measures; there is nothing in these measures themselves that allows us to discriminate between people who do and do not have clinically significant psychiatric problems. This discrimination is important for purposes of making social policy decisions regarding such things as the number of people in need of mental health services. Researchers who work with measures of nonspecific psychological distress often deal with this problem by developing rules for classifying people who score above a certain threshold as psychiatric "cases" (e.g., Radloff 1977). The precise cutoff points are sometimes arbitrary, but they are usually based on statistical analyses that attempt to discriminate optimally between the scores of patients in psychiatric treatment and those of people in a community sample. Dichotomous diagnostic measures, in comparison, allow this sort of discrimination to be made directly based on an evaluation of diagnostic criteria. We prefer them for analyses when "case" issues are involved.

It is important to recognize that there is an inherent ambiguity in making the dichotomous decision that is required to define some people as cases and others as noncases. This ambiguity is recognized by the clinicians involved in work to establish diagnostic criteria (Frances, Widiger, & Fyer 1990). It is an ambiguity that is more difficult in the study of mental illness than other areas because of the absence of medical tests to make diagnoses and the inherent political nature of some distinctions regarding the types of behaviors that are socially normative. As a result, prevalence estimates should be interpreted cautiously. There are some ways in which this ambiguity is not different from the situation in areas of physical medicine where yes–no treatment decisions must be made based on continuous data, such as the decision of where to draw the line in blood pressure readings to define hypertension. Decisions of this sort are usually made on the basis of actuarial evidence regarding subsequent risk of some fairly well-defined outcome (e.g., stroke) associated with the continuous measure, but there is certainly no expectation that 100% of the people on one side of the line will experience the outcome or that 0% on the other side of the line will do so. However, the situation is more difficult in the area of psychiatric assessment because there are no relatively unequivocal dichotomous outcomes equivalent to having a heart attack or developing cancer that can be used as a "gold standard." Despite this ambiguity, it is still necessary for treatment as well as for social policy purposes to make dichotomous diagnostic distinctions of this sort. That is why we do so here.

Data Sources

The need for general population data on the prevalence of mental illness was noted two decades ago in a report commissioned by President Carter (President's Commission on Mental Health and Illness 1978). It was impossible to undertake such a survey at that time because there was no structured research diagnostic interview capable of generating reliable psychiatric diagnoses in general population samples. Recognizing this need, the National Institute of Mental Health (NIMH) funded the development of the Diagnostic Interview Schedule (Robins et al. 1981), a research diagnostic interview that can be administered by trained interviewers who are not clinicians. The DIS was first used in the Epidemiologic Catchment Area (ECA) study, a landmark project that interviewed over 20,000 respondents in a series of five community epidemiologic surveys (Robins & Regier 1991). The ECA study has been the main source of data on the U.S. prevalence of psychiatric disorders and utilization of services for these disorders for the past decade (Bourdon et al. 1992; Regier et al. 1993; Robins, Locke, & Regier 1991) and is a major source of data for the review presented in this chapter.

It is important to note that general population reliability and validity studies of the DIS were not carried out until after the completion of the ECA data collection (Anthony et al. 1985; Helzer et al. 1985). The results of these methodological studies showed generally low agreement between DIS classifications and the classifications independently made by clinical reinterviewers. Questions have been raised about the accuracy of the ECA results based on these methodological studies (see e.g. Parker 1987; Rogler, Malgady, & Tryon 1992). However, others have noted that the validity problems in the DIS are concentrated among respondents who either fall just short of meeting criteria or just barely meet criteria and that the errors due to false positives and false negatives tend to balance out to produce fairly accurate total population prevalence estimates (Robins 1985). Although this observation provides no assurance that the different errors are counterbalanced in all important segments of the population (Dohrenwend 1995), the documentation that this pattern is true in the population as a whole suggests that the ECA results yield useful overall prevalence data.

Another important limitation of the ECA study – in terms of providing representative data – is that it was carried out in only five localities around the country:

New Haven, Baltimore, Durham, St. Louis, and Los Angeles. Although the ECA investigators used after-the-fact weighting procedures to combine these local data into a consolidated data file that was representative of the country as a whole with respect to the distribution of age, sex, and race, no attempt was made to adjust the sample for the distributions of such important variables as socioeconomic status or health-insurance coverage. Furthermore, it was impossible to apply any type of weighting or adjustment procedure to compensate for the fact that the five ECA sites were all in urban areas that contained large university-based hospitals. As the interviews were conducted entirely within the metropolitan areas containing these hospitals, the results can tell us nothing about areas of the country that have low access to speciality mental and addictive services, including rural areas that are not contiguous to a major metropolitan area. Twenty percent of the U.S. population live in such rural areas.

This problem was subsequently addressed when the NIMH funded the National Comorbidity Survey (NCS; Kessler et al. 1994), a household survey of over 8,000 respondents in the age range 15–54 that was carried out in a widely dispersed (174 counties in 34 states) sample designed to be representative of the entire United States. The NCS interview used a modified version of the DIS known as the Composite International Diagnostic Interview (Robins et al. 1988). The CIDI expands the DIS to include diagnoses based on DSM-III-R (APA 1987) criteria as well as the ICD, version 1.0 (WHO 1990). World Health Organization field trials of the CIDI have documented adequate reliability and validity for all diagnoses. (For a review, see Wittchen 1994.) However, it is important to recognize that most of the WHO field trials were carried out in clinical samples. Previous research has shown that the estimated accuracy of diagnostic interviews is greater in clinical samples than in general population samples (Dohrenwend et al. 1978b). Therefore, the same caution regarding diagnostic accuracy as noted in our discussion of the ECA is needed in interpreting the results of the NCS.

Some assistance in evaluating the magnitude of the potential problems with diagnoses based on structured lay interviews in the ECA and NCS can be obtained by comparing results with those based on the small number of modern epidemiologic surveys that have used semistructured research diagnostic interviews, such as the Structured Clinical Interview for DSM-III-R (SCID; Spitzer et al. 1990) administered by clinical interviewers either in an entire community sample or in a second-stage subsample of a larger community sample that was selected to overrepresent possible cases. Given the enormous expense of carrying out clinician-based epidemiologic surveys of this sort, it is not surprising that only a handful of such studies have been assayed and that these studies are either quite small (e.g., Weissman & Myers 1978) or based on samples that are not representative of the general population (e.g., the sample of twins interviewed by Kendler et al. 1992a) or have been carried out elsewhere than the United States (e.g., Dohrenwend et al. 1992). As a result, it is impossible to aggregate the results of these studies and so generate an accurate portrait of the prevalence of mental illness in the U.S. population.

Nonetheless, we refer to these studies in several places in the following review in an effort to provide a rough external comparison with the results based on the lay interview diagnoses obtained in the ECA and NCS surveys.

A final point regarding data sources that needs to be mentioned here concerns diagnostic coverage. Almost all of the diagnoses are Axis I disorders in the DSM-III and DSM-III-R diagnostic systems. Not all Axis I disorders are covered in these surveys. However, the most commonly assessed Axis I disorders are mood disorders (major depression, dysthymia, mania), anxiety disorders (generalized anxiety disorder, panic disorder, phobia, obsessive-compulsive disorder, posttraumatic stress disorder), addictive disorders (alcohol abuse and dependence, drug abuse and dependence), and nonaffective psychoses (schizophrenia, schizophreniform disorder, schizoaffective disorder, delusional disorder, brief psychotic reaction). Axis II disorders, which include the personality disorders and mental retardation, are generally not covered, although antisocial personality disorder (ASPD) and some measures of cognitive impairment are often assessed. The absence of information on personality disorders other than ASPD is a major omission, but it was necessitated by the fact that valid structured diagnostic interview methods to assess personality disorders did not exist at the time these surveys were carried out. This situation is changing rapidly, however, as several groups are working to develop measures of personality disorders that are appropriate for use in general population surveys (Lenzenweger et al. 1997; Pilkonis et al. 1995); we can anticipate, based on this work, that future large-scale epidemiologic surveys will include comprehensive evaluations of personality disorders. For now, though, our review of evidence regarding the prevalence of personality disorders other than ASPD must rely on the results of a small number of surveys from around the world that have been carried out using one of the recently developed assessment methods.

Plan of the Chapter

This chapter is organized into sections defined by particular disorders and combinations of disorders. We begin with a broad overview of results concerning the estimated prevalence of all the disorders assessed in the ECA and NCS. Then we turn to separate sections, reviewing more detailed results concerning comorbidity among these disorders and two of the most important and common of the individual disorders assessed in these surveys: major depression and posttraumatic stress disorder. The final section reviews the small literature on general population surveys of personality disorders. The chapter closes with a discussion of future directions in the investigation of the prevalence of psychiatric disorders.

Lifetime and Recent Prevalence of Axis I DSM-III-R Disorders

We focus initially on results from the NCS, as this is the only nationally representative survey in the United States to have assessed the prevalence of a broad range of DSM-III-R disorders. As described in more detail elsewhere (Kessler et al. 1994), the NCS is based on a national household sample of respondents in the age range 15–54. The NCS also includes a supplemental sample of students living in group housing, the largest segment of the population that is not in the household population. Table 3.1 shows NCS/DSM-III-R prevalence estimates for the 14 lifetime and 12-month disorders assessed in the core NCS interview. Lifetime prevalence is the proportion of the sample who *ever* experienced a disorder, whereas 12-month prevalence is the proportion who experienced the disorder at some time in their lives and *also* reported an episode of the disorder in the 12 months prior to the interview. The prevalence estimates in Table 3.1 are presented without exclusions for DSM-III-R hierarchy rules. Standard errors are reported in parentheses.

The most common psychiatric disorders assessed in the NCS are major depression and alcohol dependence. Seventeen percent (17.1%) of respondents reported a history of a major depressive episode in their lifetime, and 10.3% had an episode in the previous 12 months. Fourteen percent (14.1%) of respondents had a lifetime history of alcohol dependence and 7.2% continued to be dependent in the past 12 months. The next most common disorders are social and simple phobias, with life-time prevalences of 13.3% and 11.3% (respectively) and 12-month prevalences of 7.9% and 8.8% (respectively). As a group, addictive disorders and anxiety disorders are somewhat more prevalent than affective disorders. Approximately one in every four respondents reported a lifetime history of at least one addictive disorder and a similar number reported a lifetime history of at least one anxiety disorder. Approximately one in every five respondents reported a lifetime history of at least one affective disorder. Anxiety disorders, as a group, are considerably more likely to occur in the 12 months prior to interview (19.3%) than either addictive disorders (11.3%) or affective disorders (11.3%), suggesting that anxiety disorders are more chronic than either addictive or affective disorders. The prevalence of other NCS disorders is quite low. Antisocial personality disorder, which was assessed only on a lifetime basis, was reported by 2.8% of respondents, and schizophrenia and other nonaffective psychoses (NAPs) were found among only 0.5% of respondents. It is important to note that the diagnosis of NAP was based on clinical reinterviews using the SCID rather than on the lay CIDI interviews. As documented elsewhere (Kendler et al. 1996), the prevalence estimates for NAPs based on the CIDI were considerably higher but were found to have low validity when judged in comparison to the clinical reappraisals.

As shown in the last row of Table 3.1, 49.7% of the sample reported a life-time history of at least one NCS/DSM-III-R disorder and 30.9% had one or more disorders in the 12 months prior to the interview. Although there is no meaningful sex difference in these overall prevalence rates, there are sex differences in the prevalence of specific disorders. Consistent with previous research (Bourdon et al. 1992; Robins et al. 1981, 1991), men are much more likely to have addictive disorders and ASPD than women, whereas women are much more likely to have

Table 3.1. *Lifetime and 12-month prevalence of CIDI/DSM-III-R disorders in the National Comorbidity Survey NCS*

Disorders	Male Lifetime %	(SE)	Male 12-month %	(SE)	Female Lifetime %	(SE)	Female 12-month %	(SE)	Total Lifetime %	(SE)	Total 12-month %	(SE)
Affective disorders												
Major depressive episode	12.7	(0.9)	7.7	(0.8)	21.3	(0.9)	12.9	(0.8)	17.1	(0.7)	10.3	(0.6)
Manic episode	1.6	(0.3)	1.4	(0.3)	1.7	(0.3)	1.3	(0.3)	1.6	(0.3)	1.3	(0.2)
Dysthymia	4.8	(0.4)	2.1	(0.3)	8.0	(0.6)	3.0	(0.4)	6.4	(0.4)	2.5	(0.2)
Any affective disorder	14.7	(0.8)	8.5	(0.8)	23.9	(0.9)	14.1	(0.9)	19.3	(0.7)	11.3	(0.7)
Anxiety disorders												
Panic disorder	2.0	(0.3)	1.3	(0.3)	5.0	(1.4)	3.2	(0.4)	3.5	(0.3)	2.3	(0.3)
Agoraphobia without panic	3.5	(0.4)	1.7	(0.3)	7.0	(0.6)	3.8	(0.4)	5.3	(0.4)	2.8	(0.3)
Social phobia	11.1	(0.8)	6.6	(0.4)	15.5	(1.0)	9.1	(0.7)	13.3	(0.7)	7.9	(0.4)
Simple phobia	6.7	(0.5)	4.4	(0.5)	15.7	(1.1)	13.2	(0.9)	11.3	(0.6)	8.8	(0.5)
Generalized anxiety disorder	3.6	(0.5)	2.0	(0.3)	6.6	(0.5)	4.3	(0.4)	5.1	(0.3)	3.1	(0.3)
Posttraumatic stress disorder	4.8	(0.6)	2.3	(0.3)	10.1	(0.8)	5.4	(0.7)	7.6	(0.5)	3.9	(0.4)
Any anxiety disorder	22.6	(1.2)	13.4	(0.7)	34.3	(1.8)	24.7	(1.5)	28.7	(0.9)	19.3	(0.8)
Addictive disorders												
Alcohol abuse	12.5	(0.8)	3.4	(0.4)	6.4	(0.6)	1.6	(0.2)	9.4	(0.5)	2.5	(0.2)
Alcohol dependence	20.1	(1.0)	10.7	(0.9)	8.2	(0.7)	3.7	(0.4)	14.1	(0.7)	7.2	(0.5)
Drug abuse	5.4	(0.5)	1.3	(0.2)	3.5	(0.4)	0.3	(0.1)	4.4	(0.3)	0.8	(0.1)
Drug dependence	9.2	(0.7)	3.8	(0.4)	5.9	(0.5)	1.9	(0.3)	7.5	(0.4)	2.8	(0.3)
Any substance abuse/dependence	35.4	(1.2)	16.1	(0.7)	17.9	(1.1)	6.6	(0.4)	26.6	(1.0)	11.3	(0.5)

Table 3.1 (cont.)

Disorders	Male				Female				Total			
	Lifetime		12-month		Lifetime		12-month		Lifetime		12-month	
	%	(SE)	%	(SE)	%	(SE)	%	(SE)	%	(SE)	%	(SE)
Other disorders												
Antisocial personality	4.8	(0.5)	—	—	1.0	(0.2)	—	—	2.8	(0.2)	—	—
Nonaffective psychosis[a]	0.3	(0.1)	0.2	(0.1)	0.7	(0.2)	0.4	(0.1)	0.5	(0.1)	0.3	(0.1)
Any NCS disorder	51.2	(1.6)	29.4	(1.0)	48.5	(2.0)	32.3	(1.6)	49.7	(1.2)	30.9	(1.0)

Note: SE = standard error.
[a]Nonaffective psychoses include schizophrenia, schizophreniform disorder, schizoaffective disorder, delusional disorder, and atypical psychosis.
Source: Kessler et al. (1994), *Archives of General Psychiatry* 51: 8–19. Copyright 1994, American Medical Association.

affective disorders (with the exception of mania, for which there is no sex difference) and anxiety disorders than men. The data also show, consistent with a trend
found in the ECA study (Keith, Regier, & Rae 1991), that women in the household
population are more likely to have nonaffective psychoses than men.

It is instructive to compare these NCS results with the results of the earlier ECA
study. As noted previously, the ECA project was carried out in five communities around the country, and the results were subsequently combined and weighted
to the population distribution of the United States on the cross-classification of
age, sex, and race in an effort to make national estimates (Regier et al. 1993).
To the extent that this "poststratification" succeeded in adjusting for the lack of
representativeness of the local samples, it should be possible to make valid comparisons between the ECA and NCS results. One problem with doing so is that
the ECA study was based on an unrestricted age range of adults whereas the NCS
was based on the 15–54 age range. Another problem is that the ECA diagnoses
were based on DSM-III criteria (APA 1980), while the NCS diagnoses were based
on DSM-III-R criteria (APA 1987). These two diagnostic systems differ substantially in a number of respects. In order to resolve these problems, collaborative
ECA–NCS comparative analyses have been carried out in which subsamples in
the 18-54 age range in both samples were compared using common measures that
operationalize DSM-III criteria (which can be reconstructed from the NCS data,
although DSM-III-R criteria cannot be reconstructed from the ECA data). The as
yet unpublished results show a great deal of consistency between the two surveys,
both in the prevalence of individual disorders and in overall prevalence of having
any disorder.

Comorbidity among Axis I Disorders

An important observation about the results in Table 3.1 is that the sum of the individual prevalence estimates across the disorders in each row consistently exceeds
the prevalence of having any disorder in the last row. This means that there is
considerable comorbidity among these disorders. For example, though the 49.7%
lifetime prevalence in the total NCS sample means that 50 respondents out of every
100 in the sample reported a lifetime history of at least one disorder, a summa-
tion of lifetime prevalence estimates for the separate disorders shows that these 50
individuals reported a total of 102 lifetime disorders (2.0 per person). This comorbidity is quite important for understanding the distribution of psychiatric disorders
in the United States (Kessler 1995). Although it is beyond the scope of this chapter
to delve into the many different types of comorbidity that exist in the population,
some aggregate results are important to review.

Table 3.2 documents that these patterns are very important in understanding the
distribution of psychiatric disorders among persons aged 15–54 in the United States
and provides an empirical rationale for more detailed examination of particular

Table 3.2. *Concentration of lifetime and 12-month CIDI/DSM-III-R disorders among persons with lifetime comorbidity in the NCS*

Number of lifetime disorders	Proportion of sample		Proportion of lifetime disorders		Proportion of 12-month disorders		Proportion of respondents with severe 12-month disorders[a]	
	%	(SE)	%	(SE)	%	(SE)	%	(SE)
0	52.0	(1.1)	—	—	—	—	—	—
1	21.0	(0.6)	20.6	(0.6)	17.4	(0.8)	2.6	(1.7)
2	13.0	(0.5)	25.5	(1.0)	23.1	(1.0)	7.9	(2.1)
3 or more	14.0	(0.7)	53.9	(2.7)	58.9	(1.8)	89.5	(2.8)

Note: SE = standard error.
[a] Severe 12-month disorders include active mania, nonaffective psychoses, or active disorders of other types that either required hospitalization or created severe role impairment.
Source: Kessler et al. (1994), *Archives of General Psychiatry* 51: 8–19. Copyright 1994, American Medical Association.

types of comorbidity. The four rows of the table represent the number of lifetime disorders reported by respondents. As shown in the first column, 52% of respondents never had an NCS/DSM-III-R disorder, 21% had one, 13% had two, and 14% had three or more disorders. Only 21% of all the lifetime disorders occurred to respondents with a lifetime history of just one disorder. This means that the vast majority of lifetime disorders in this sample (79%) are comorbid disorders. Furthermore, an even greater proportion of 12-month disorders occurred to respondents with a lifetime history of comorbidity. It is particularly striking that close to six of every ten (58.9%) 12-month disorders and nearly nine of ten (89.5%) severe 12-month disorders occurred to the 14% of the sample with a lifetime history of three or more disorders. These results show that, although a history of some psychiatric disorder is quite common among persons 15–54 in the United States, the major burden of psychiatric disorder in this age segment of our society is concentrated in a group of highly comorbid people who constitute about one sixth of the population.

Given this evidence, it is of some interest to learn more about detailed patterns of comorbidity. The ECA investigators were the first to do this in a community sample. They documented that comorbidity is widespread. Over 54% of ECA respondents with a lifetime history of at least one DSM-III psychiatric disorder were found to have a second diagnosis as well. Of lifetime alcohol abusers, 52% received a second diagnosis, and 75% of lifetime drug abusers had a second diagnosis (Robins et al. 1991). Respondents with a lifetime history of at least one mental disorder, when compared to respondents with no mental disorder, had a relative odds of 2.3 of having a lifetime history of alcohol abuse or dependence and a relative odds of 4.5 of some other drug-use disorder (Regier et al. 1990). Similar results were found in the NCS. Among respondents with a lifetime history of at least one DSM-III-R disorder, 56% also had one or more other disorders (Kessler et al. 1996). Of respondents with lifetime alcohol abuse or dependence, 52% also had a lifetime mental disorder and 36% had a lifetime illicit drug-use disorder. Among respondents with a lifetime history of illicit drug abuse or dependence, 59% also had a lifetime mental disorder and 71% had a lifetime alcohol-use disorder.

Major Depression

Although it is impossible to discuss these disorders in depth in a brief overview chapter such as this, it is of some interest to examine more detailed results concerning some of these disorders. This section focuses on major depression (MD). The overall prevalence estimates of MD in the NCS – 17.1% lifetime and 10.3% 12-month – are considerably higher than those reported in the first wave of the ECA study (Weissman et al. 1991) and in other epidemiologic studies based on the ECA methodology (Bland, Newman, & Orn 1988a; Bland, Orn, & Newman 1988b; Canino et al. 1987b; Chen et al. 1993; Hwu, Yen, & Chang 1989; Wells et al. 1989a). However, as noted previously, the ECA and NCS estimates are more similar when the two waves of ECA data are combined. We believe that this result stems from an underestimation of disorders in the ECA due to recall failure, a problem that was addressed in the NCS by using special recall enhancement strategies (Kessler, Mroczek, & Belli in press b). In comparison, the NCS prevalence estimates are quite similar to those found in smaller epidemiologic studies based on clinical interviews (Boyd & Weissman 1981; Kendler et al. 1992; Weissman & Myers 1978).

Epidemiologic research has documented a number of consistently significant correlates of MD, including stressful life events, low social support, personality, and a range of demographic variables such as low socioeconomic status and being female and young. (For a review, see Horwath & Weissman 1995.) The higher prevalence of MD among women than men has been of special interest to sociologists, so we focus on it in this section. This sex difference has been found consistently in community epidemiologic studies throughout the world using a variety of diagnostic schemes and interview methods. (For reviews see Bebbington 1988; Nolen-Hoeksema 1987; Weissman & Klerman 1985, 1992.) The prevalence of MD among women has typically been between one and a half to three times that found among men.

Sociological research on the sex difference in MD has emphasized the importance of stresses associated with adult sex roles (e.g., Barnett & Baruch 1987; Gove & Geerken 1977; Wilhelm & Parker 1989). This emphasis is based on the observation that the sex difference is most pronounced among middle-aged married

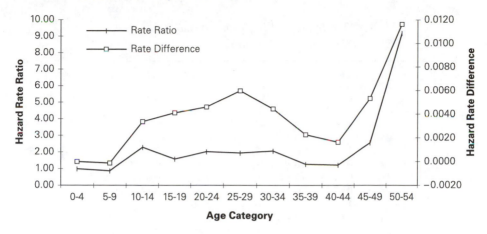

Figure 3.1. CIDI/DSM-III-R hazard rate ratios (female : male) and rate differences (female − male) for major depressive episodes in the NCS. *Source:* Reprinted from *Journal of Affective Disorders,* vol. 29, R. Kessler et al., "Sex and depression in the National Comorbidity Survey I: Lifetime prevalence, chronicity, and recurrence," pp. 85–96, 1993, with kind permission from Elsevier Science − NL, Sara Burgerhartstraat 25, 1055 KV Amsterdam, The Netherlands.

men and women, especially when the wife is a homemaker. However, analysis of epidemiologic data shows that this is an inadequate explanation because sex differences in onset risk emerge first in early adolescence, prior to full adult sex-role differentiation. It is instructive to emphasize several patterns in the data that need to be taken into consideration in future theorizing. The first concerns age of onset. Epidemiologic studies find no significant sex difference in the age of onset of MD (Kessler et al. 1993; Weissman et al. 1993), but they do show that the sex difference emerges most consistently after the onset of puberty (Brooks-Gunn & Petersen 1991; Petersen et al. in press) and decreases near the end of mid-life (Kessler et al. 1993; Weissman et al. 1993). Figure 3.1 shows this general pattern for the NCS data by presenting comparative data on the age-specific rates of the first onset of depression. We show both the female/male ratio as well as female–male differences in these rates.

These results show clearly that women are more likely than men to become depressed, but do they remain depressed longer than men once onset has occurred? This has been a relatively neglected question in the literature on sex and depression, even though sociological sex-role theories strongly imply that chronicity should be greater for women than men (see the reviews in Gilbert 1992; Gotlib & Hammen 1992; Hammen 1982; Nolen-Hoeksema 1987). However, contrary to this expectation, the results in Table 3.3 (from the NCS) show that there is no evidence for a sex difference in the persistence of MD. Furthermore, separate studies

Table 3.3. *Sex difference[a] in chronicity and recurrence of CIDI/DSM-III-R major depression*

Age	Chronicity		Acute recurrence	
	OR[a]	(95% CI)	OR[a]	(95% CI)
15–19	1.06	(0.23, 4.90)	0.83	—[b]
20–24	1.14	(0.22, 5.85)	0.31	(0.09, 1.07)
25–29	1.04	(0.22, 4.89)	0.80	(0.25, 2.52)
30–34	0.72	(0.30, 1.71)	1.36	(0.59, 3.11)
35–39	0.71	(0.18, 2.76)	2.20	(0.69, 6.94)
40–44	0.51	(0.07, 3.52)	0.46	(0.19, 1.09)
45–49	1.09	—[b]	5.10	—[b]
50–54	0.60	(0.10, 3.49)	35.88	—[b]
Total	0.81	(0.53, 1.25)	1.06	(0.71, 1.60)

Notes: CI = confidence interval; OR = odds ratio.
[a] Effect of female.   [b] Low precision.
Source: Reprinted from *Journal of Affective Disorders*, vol. 29, R. Kessler et al., "Sex and depression in the National Comorbidity Survey I: Lifetime prevalence, chronicity, and recurrence," pp. 85–96, 1993, with kind permission from Elsevier Science – NL, Sara Burgerhartstraat 25, 1055 KV Amsterdam, The Netherlands.

of the three processes that contribute to the size of these ratios – the probability of a first episode becoming chronic, the probability of episode recurrence among people who are not chronically depressed, and speed of episode recovery among people with recurrent episodes – fail to find evidence of a sex difference (Kessler et al. 1993; McLeod, Kessler, & Landis 1992).

These results must be interpreted with caution, because most are based either on retrospective reports in cross-sectional surveys or on short-term longitudinal surveys. There is evidence that men are more likely than women to forget past episodes of depression (Ernst & Angst 1992), and this could distort these results. However, arguing against this possibility is recent research showing that women are not much more likely than men to recall the lifetime occurrence of a two-week episode of dysphoria and that the higher prevalence of lifetime MD among women is due primarily to the fact that women are more likely than men to report symptoms occurring in their worst two-week episode that meet diagnostic criteria for MD (Kessler et al. 1993; Young et al. 1990). A higher level of recall failure among men than women is unlikely to explain this pattern. Nor is this pattern consistent with the possibility that men are less willing to admit depression than women, as the results show that men do not so much report lower rates of depressive episodes as associated symptoms. Based on these results, we believe that the observed sex difference in lifetime MD is genuine and not a methodological artifact, that it is due largely to a higher rate of first onset among women than men beginning in the early teenage years and persisting through mid-life, and that there is no substantial sex difference in the course of depression once it starts. These results argue for the necessity of rethinking adult sex-role theories in order to account for (a) the beginning of elevated MD among women prior to the time adult sex roles begin and (b) the fact that depressed women are not more chronic than depressed men.

Posttraumatic Stress Disorder

It has long been known that pathological stress response syndromes can result from exposure to war (Freud 1919), sexual assault (Burgess & Holstrum 1974), and other types of trauma (Burgess & Holstrum 1974; Freud 1919; Grinker & Spiegel 1945). However, research on the prevalence of these disorders was unsystematic prior to the codification of diagnostic criteria in DSM-III (APA 1980) under the diagnosis of posttraumatic stress disorder (PTSD). A number of traumas have been studied in detail since that time, including criminal victimization (Kilpatrick et al. 1987; Kilpatrick & Resnick 1992), sexual assault (Frank & Anderson 1987; Pynoos & Nader 1988), exposure to natural disaster (Green, Grace, & Gleser 1985; Madakasira & O'Brien 1987; Wilkinson 1983), and combat exposure (Blanchard et al. 1982; Egendorf et al. 1981; Keane, Malloy, & Fairbank 1984; Kulka et al. 1990). The empirical information and conceptual refinements (Brett & Ostroff 1985) generated by this research have importantly advanced our understanding of posttraumatic stress responses and have led to revisions of the diagnostic criteria for PTSD in DSM-III-R. These now include: (i) exposure to a traumatic event that is "outside the range of usual human experience"; (ii) reliving the experience in either nightmares, flashbacks, or intrusive thoughts; (iii) numbing or avoidant symptoms; and (iv) hypersensitivity, as indicated either by general signs and symptoms of autonomic arousal or by hypersensitivity to cues reminiscent of the trauma. These symptoms must persist for at least one month (APA 1987).

Despite a growing body of work on the extent to which PTSD is associated with specific traumas, limited epidemiologic data are available describing the population prevalence of PTSD or the kinds of traumas most strongly associated with PTSD. Three recent studies, however, have reported data of this sort. In a national telephone survey of women, Resnick and colleagues (1993) found that 12.3% of respondents (equivalent to 17.9% of those exposed to trauma) had a lifetime history of PTSD. In a study of young adults, Breslau and associates (1991) found that 11.3% of women (30.7% of those exposed to trauma) and 6.0% of men (14.0% of those exposed to trauma) had a lifetime history of PTSD. And the NCS estimated that 10.4% of women (20.4% of those exposed to trauma) and 5.0% of men (8.1% of those exposed to trauma) had PTSD at some point in their lives.

Only limited information is available on the types of traumatic experiences most strongly associated with PTSD. The NCS has the most comprehensive data

Table 3.4. *Lifetime prevalence of trauma experience in the NCS*

	Men ($n = 2812$)			Women ($n = 3065$)		
	% (1)	(SE) (2)	n (3)	% (4)	(SE) (5)	n (6)
Trauma						
Rape	0.7*	(0.2)	19	9.2	(0.8)	281
Sexual molestation	2.8*	(0.5)	78	12.3	(1.0)	376
Physical attack	11.1*	(1.0)	313	6.9	(0.9)	210
Combat	6.4*	(0.9)	179	0.0	—	0
Shock	11.4	(1.1)	320	12.4	(1.1)	381
Threat with weapon	19.0*	(1.3)	535	6.8	(0.6)	208
Accident	25.0*	(1.2)	703	13.8	(1.1)	422
Natural disaster with fire	18.9*	(1.4)	532	15.2	(1.2)	467
Witness	35.6*	(2.0)	1,002	14.5	(0.7)	445
Childhood neglect	2.1*	(0.4)	58	3.4	(0.5)	105
Physical abuse	3.2*	(0.4)	91	4.8	(0.6)	146
Other qualifying trauma	2.2	(0.5)	61	2.7	(0.4)	83
Any trauma	60.7*	(1.9)	1,707	51.2	(1.9)	1,570
Number of traumas						
1	26.5	(1.5)	745	26.3	(1.7)	806
2	14.5	(0.9)	407	13.5	(0.9)	415
3	9.5*	(0.9)	268	5.0	(0.6)	154
4 or more	10.2*	(0.8)	287	6.4	(0.6)	195

Notes: Sample distributions reflect the weighted number of respondents rounded to the nearest whole number. SE = standard error.
* Sex difference significant at the .05 level, two-tailed test.
Source: Kessler et al. (1995d), *Archives of General Psychiatry* 52: 1048–60. Copyright 1995, American Medical Association.

on this issue (Kessler et al. 1995d). Estimates of the lifetime prevalence of trauma exposure in the NCS are presented in Table 3.4. Sixty percent (60.7%) of men and 51.2% of women reported at least one traumatic event in their lives, and the majority of people with some type of lifetime trauma actually experienced two or more traumas. This existence of multiple traumas in the lives of many people has been found in other research as well (Kilpatrick & Resnick 1992). The types experienced by the most people are witnessing someone being badly injured or killed; being involved in a fire, flood, or natural disaster; and being involved in a life-threatening accident. A significantly higher proportion of men than women reported experiencing each of these three as well as physical attacks, combat experience, and being threatened with a weapon, held captive, or kidnapped. In contrast, a significantly higher proportion of women than men reported rape, sexual molestation, childhood parental neglect, and childhood physical abuse.

Table 3.5. *Conditional probabilities of specific traumas in the NCS being the basis for the assessment of CIDI/DSM-III and, once selected for assessment, for being associated with PTSD in the NCS*

	Lifetime prevalence of PTSD									
	Men					Women				
Trauma type	P1 (1)	(SE) (2)	P2 (3)	(SE) (4)	n_t (5)	P1 (6)	(SE) (7)	P2 (8)	(SE) (9)	n_t (10)
Rape	62.1	(11.6)	65.0	(15.6)	12	74.4	(4.1)	45.9	(5.9)	209
Sexual molestation	26.9	(6.2)	12.2*	(5.3)	21	61.4	(2.8)	26.5	(4.0)	231
Physical attack	35.7	(5.1)	1.8*	(0.9)	112	42.0	(7.7)	21.3	(7.3)	88
Combat	57.7	(6.7)	38.8*	(9.9)	103	—	—	—	—	0
Shock	44.8	(4.7)	4.4*	(1.4)	144	55.4	(4.0)	10.4	(2.0)	211
Threat with weapon	32.9	(3.0)	1.9*	(0.8)	176	36.4	(4.8)	32.6	(7.8)	76
Accident	44.6	(3.6)	6.3	(1.8)	314	44.5	(4.1)	8.8	(4.3)	188
Natural disaster with fire	35.9	(2.8)	3.7	(1.8)	191	44.4	(4.4)	5.4	(3.8)	207
Witness	52.4	(2.7)	6.4	(1.2)	524	47.1	(4.2)	7.5	(1.7)	209
Childhood neglect	27.8	(5.8)	23.9	(10.3)	16	28.1	(5.8)	19.7	(7.7)	30
Physical abuse	50.4	(4.7)	22.3*	(5.2)	46	37.0	(5.0)	48.5	(9.5)	54
Other qualifying trauma	77.6	(7.8)	12.7*	(4.8)	48	80.8	(5.0)	33.4	(8.0)	67
Any trauma	—	—	8.1	(1.0)	1,707	—	—	20.4	(1.5)	1,570

Notes: P1 = probability that a respondent who reported the lifetime occurrence of a particular trauma type will have this be the basis for the assessment of PTSD (i.e. that this trauma will either be the respondent's only lifetime trauma or be nominated the "most upsetting" trauma). P2 = probability that a particular trauma type, once selected as the basis for the assessment of PTSD, will be associated with PTSD. n_t = weighted number of respondents (rounded to the nearest whole number) with a particular "only or most upsetting" trauma type who were diagnosed as having lifetime PTSD. SE = standard error.
* Sex difference significant at the .05 level, two-tailed test.
Source: Kessler et al. (1995d), *Archives of General Psychiatry* 52: 1048–60. Copyright 1995, American Medical Association.

The NCS evaluated PTSD for only the one trauma nominated as most upsetting by each respondent. As shown in columns 1 (men) and 6 (women) in Table 3.5, the probability of a trauma being the basis for an assessment of PTSD varies substantially across trauma types. This variation is a complex function of differences in the distribution of the joint occurrences of multiple traumas and the likelihood that some types of trauma are generally more distressing than others. Among men and women alike, rape is the listed trauma with the highest conditional probability of being the basis for the assessment of PTSD, while sexual molestation and childhood neglect have the lowest conditional probabilities for men and women, respectively. Consistent with previous research reviewed by March (1992) and by Kilpatrick and Resnick (1992), columns 3 (men) and 8 (women) of Table 3.5 show that the proportion of respondents with a trauma who meet criteria for PTSD varies significantly by type of most upsetting trauma, with rape most likely to provoke PTSD.

Table 3.6. *Percentage of those with CIDI/DSM-III-R PTSD reporting each most upsetting trauma by sex in the NCS*

Trauma	Men (n = 139)			Women (n = 320)		
	% (2)	(SE) (3)	n (1)	% (5)	(SE) (6)	n (4)
Rape	5.4*	(2.8)	8	29.9	(3.4)	96
Sexual molestation	1.8*	(0.7)	3	19.1	(3.1)	61
Physical attack	1.4*	(0.6)	2	5.9	(1.6)	19
Combat	28.8	(6.1)	40	—	—	0
Shock	4.5	(1.4)	6	6.8	(1.2)	22
Threat with weapon	2.5*	(1.1)	3	7.7	(2.2)	25
Accident	12.1	(3.4)	20	5.1	(2.4)	16
Natural disaster with fire	5.2	(2.5)	7	3.5	(2.3)	11
Witness	24.3*	(4.8)	30	4.9	(1.1)	16
Childhood neglect	2.8	(1.1)	4	1.8	(0.7)	6
Physical abuse	7.4	(2.0)	10	8.2	(2.9)	26
Other qualifying trauma	3.8	(1.6)	6	7.0	(2.1)	22
Any trauma	100.0	—	139	100.0	—	320

Notes: Sample distributions reflect the weighted number of respondents rounded to the nearest whole number. SE = standard error.
* Sex difference significant at the .05 level, two-tailed test.
Source: Kessler et al. (1995d), *Archives of General Psychiatry* 52: 1048–60. Copyright 1995, American Medical Association.

A comparison of Table 3.4 and Table 3.5 shows that, although men are more likely to experience at least one trauma overall, women are more likely to experience a trauma associated with a high probability of PTSD. Whereas 44.6% of men with a lifetime trauma reported that their most upsetting trauma was one of those associated with high probability of PTSD among men (i.e., rape, combat exposure, childhood neglect, or childhood physical abuse), a significantly higher 67.6% of women with a lifetime trauma reported that their most distressing trauma was one of those associated with high probability of PTSD among women (i.e., rape, sexual molestation, physical attack, being threatened with a weapon, or childhood physical abuse). Furthermore, for all "most upsetting" traumas other than rape and childhood neglect, a higher proportion of women than men meet criteria for PTSD. The combination of these influences – greater exposure to high-impact traumas and greater likelihood of developing PTSD once exposed – lead to the finding that women exposed to a trauma are more than twice as likely as men to develop PTSD (20.4% of women compared to 8.1% of men).

The probabilities of having each type of "most upsetting" trauma in the subsample of NCS respondents with lifetime PTSD are presented in Table 3.6. The traumas most commonly associated with PTSD among men are combat exposure

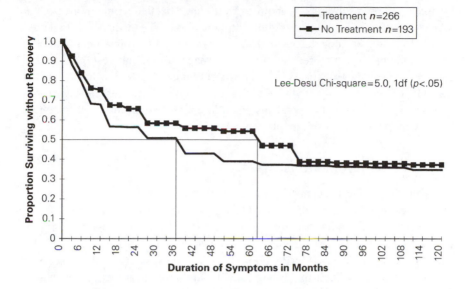

Figure 3.2. Duration of CIDI/DSM-III-R posttraumatic stress disorder in the NCS. *Source:* Kessler et al. (1995d), *Archives of General Psychiatry* 52: 1048–60. Copyright 1995, American Medical Association.

(nominated by 28.8% of men with PTSD) and witnessing someone being badly injured or killed (nominated by 24.3%). As shown in Tables 3.4 and 3.5, combat exposure is a fairly uncommon event (6.4% lifetime prevalence among men) that is associated with a high probability (38.8%) of PTSD when nominated as the most upsetting trauma. In comparison, witnessing is a much more common event (35.6% lifetime prevalence among men) but is associated with a low probability (6.4%) of PTSD when it is nominated as the most upsetting trauma. Among women, the events most commonly associated with PTSD are rape (nominated as the most upsetting trauma by 29.9% of women with PTSD) and sexual molestation (nominated by 19.1%). Together, rape and molestation were the nominated events for 49.0% of women with PTSD. These events are both common in the general population of women (9.2% of women in the NCS reported lifetime rape and 12.3% molestation) and associated with high probabilities of PTSD when nominated as "most upsetting" (45.9% for rape and 26.5% for molestation).

Finally, we consider the issue of chronicity. The NCS respondents who met criteria for PTSD were asked how long after onset of their index episode they continued to have symptoms at least a few times a week. Survival curves based on these retrospective reports are presented in Figure 3.2 separately for respondents who ever sought professional treatment for a mental problem and those who did not. The curves decrease most steeply in the first 12 months after the onset of symptoms in both subsamples, and they continue to decline with a more gradual slope for approximately six years after symptom onset. The median time to remission is 36 months among the respondents who ever sought professional treatment and 64 months among those who did not. Perhaps of more interest than the difference between the two curves is the consistent finding that somewhat more than one third of persons with PTSD fail to remit even after many years; this holds not only in the subsample of respondents who did not receive professional treatment but also in the treatment subsample.

Personality Disorders

As with PTSD, the concept of personality disorder can be traced back to the beginnings of nineteenth-century psychiatry (for a review, see Tyrer, Casey & Ferguson 1991), but it has become the subject of epidemiologic research only recently because standardized diagnostic criteria were unavailable prior to the ICD-9 (WHO 1977) and DSM-III (APA 1980) classification systems. Unfortunately, it has proven to be difficult to develop reliable and valid measures of personality disorder (Perry 1992; Zimmerman 1994). Furthermore, there are a number of differences between the ICD and DSM systems (Blashfield 1991) as well as substantial changes within each of these systems in recent revisions (Morey 1988), all of which adds to the complexity of synthesizing the available epidemiologic evidence.

All classification schemes recognize three broad clusters of personality disorder, each defined by a series of traits that must be manifest habitually in a number of life domains to qualify as a disorder. These three are the *odd* (e.g., paranoid or schizoid personality disorders), the *dramatic* (e.g., histrionic or borderline personality disorders), and the *anxious* (e.g., avoidant or dependent personality disorders) clusters. A comprehensive international review of the epidemiology of personality disorder (de Girolamo & Reich 1993) found only four fairly small community studies that assessed personality disorder in all three of these clusters using valid assessment methods. These four studies yielded very consistent lifetime prevalence estimates for overall personality disorder ranging from 10.3% to 13.5%. A prevalence of 11.0% was found in a more recent nonpatient survey of personality disorder (Lenzenweger et al. 1997). Caution is needed in interpreting these results, however, since previous research has shown that prevalence estimates vary substantially depending on whether (as in these surveys) full diagnostic criteria for personality disorder are required or instead respondents are counted if they simply manifest some traits of personality disorder on dimensional scales (Kass 1985).

There have also been a number of community surveys that included assessments of one or more specific personality disorders without attempting to assess the full range of personality disturbances. By far the most commonly studied of these has been antisocial personality disorder, a disorder characterized by persistent evidence of "irresponsible and antisocial behavior beginning in childhood or early adolescence and continuing into adulthood" (APA 1987). Irritability, aggressiveness, persistent reckless behavior, promiscuity, and the absence of remorse about the effects of this behavior on others are cardinal features of antisocial personality disorder. A number of epidemiologic surveys, including both the ECA and NCS, have found lifetime prevalences of antisocial personality disorder averaging about 1% among women and 4–5% among men (de Girolamo & Reich 1993; Merikangas 1989). Much less is known about the prevalence of other individual personality disorders, although the available evidence suggests that none of them alone has a prevalence greater than about 2% in the general population (de Girolamo & Reich 1993; Merikangas 1989; Weissman 1993).

Overview

The results reviewed here show that psychiatric disorders are highly prevalent in the general population. Although no truly comprehensive assessment of all Axis I and Axis II disorders has ever been carried out in a general population sample, it is almost certainly the case that such a study would find that the majority of the population met criteria for at least one of these disorders at some time in their life. Although such a result might initially seem remarkable, it is actually quite easy to understand. The DSM and ICD classification systems are very broad. They each include a number of disorders that are usually self-limiting and not severely impairing. It should be no more surprising to find that half the population has met criteria for one or more of these disorders in their life than to find that the vast majority of the population has had the flu or measles or some other common physical malady at some time in their life.

The more surprising result is that, although many people have been touched by mental illness at some time in their life, the major burden of psychiatric disorder in the population is concentrated in the relatively small subset of people who are highly comorbid. This means that a pile-up of multiple disorders is the most important defining characteristic of serious mental illness, a result that points to the previously underappreciated importance of research on the primary prevention of secondary disorders (Kessler & Price 1993). It also means that epidemiologic information about the prevalence of individual disorders is much less important than information on the prevalence of functional impairment, comorbidity, and chronicity. This realization has led to a recent interest in functional impairment and to changes in diagnostic criteria in DSM-IV (APA 1994). This can also be seen in the emphasis of the National Advisory Mental Health Council (1993) on what they defined as "severe and persistent mental illness" (SPMI) and of the Substance Abuse and Mental Health Service Administration (1993) on what they defined as "serious mental illness" (SMI). Joint methodological analyses of the ECA and NCS data suggest that the one-year prevalence of DSM-III-R SPMI and

SMI is approximately 3% and 6% (respectively); the one-year prevalence of having *any* DSM-III-R disorder exceeds 30% (Kessler et al. 1995a). It is likely that epidemiological research on adult mental disorders over the next decade will focus on these serious and severe disorders rather than on overall prevalence. To the extent that the prevalence of particular disorders is emphasized in such work, it will likely be to study the underlying pathologies associated with ongoing impairment in functioning. An increased interest in the part played by personality disorders in the creation of ongoing role impairment is likely to emerge over the next decade in light of recent advances in conceptualization and measurement (Loranger, Sartorius, & Janca 1996). There will also be a considerable expansion of research on the epidemiology of child and adolescent disorders, a topic that has not been covered in this chapter, owing to new initiatives that have not yet advanced far enough to be reviewed here.

4

Biological Approaches to Psychiatric Disorders

Sharon Schwartz

From a biological point of view, mental illness is a disease of the brain. The biological revolution in psychiatry was sparked by evidence for a genetic component to psychiatric disorders and by pharmaceutical advances in drug therapies that added to our understanding of the chemistry of the brain and neuronal communication (neurochemistry). Moreover, advances in neuroscience or neuroanatomy have furthered our understanding of the relationship between the structure of the brain and human behavior. Schwartz provides an overview of what biological psychiatrists know about the brain, limiting her discussion to schizophrenia and depression. While most claim that the evidence is incontrovertible for viewing schizophrenia as a brain disease, some disagree and point to inconsistencies in the data. Schizophrenia has been hypothesized to result from an excess of dopamine, and its symptoms are often reduced with the administration of medications that block specific dopamine receptors. Yet this evidence does not demonstrate that the cause of schizophrenia is a chemical imbalance because not all people respond to medications, the medications only affect some of the symptoms of schizophrenia, and studies report inconsistent responses. Contradictory findings and gaps also exist in our knowledge of the role of neurotransmitter dysfunctions in depression. Although the evidence for a genetic link to schizophrenia and depression is compelling, Schwartz describes a variety of methodological problems that make heritability estimates questionable. Also, the specific mode of transmission and complex interactions among genetic and environmental factors need further examination. Schwartz concludes by outlining the role that sociologists can play in researching factors that affect the etiology and course of mental disorder and by using the findings from biological psychiatrists to further understand the relationship between social and biological factors. Students will want to read this chapter carefully and recognize that information they might have considered incontrovertible (i.e., that schizophrenia is caused by a particular gene) is in fact not yet verified.

Introduction

Psychiatry has undergone a biological revolution in recent decades. The Presidential proclamation that the 1990s are "The Decade of the Brain," the frequent newspaper headlines announcing the location of yet another gene for some psychiatric or behavioral condition, an advertising campaign pronouncing "Depression: A Flaw in Chemistry, Not Character," and T-shirts and greeting cards with one-liners about medication for a psychiatric disorder (e.g., "Don't Worry, Take Prozac") all suggest that the biological revolution has become entrenched in our culture.

This revolution was sparked by two achievements in biological psychiatry: the compelling evidence from twin and adoptee studies for a genetic component to psychiatric disorders, and pharmaceutical advancements in the development of drugs that target specific symptom constellations (Chua & McKenna 1995). It has gained momentum from technological advances in molecular genetics and in the ability to visualize the structure and functioning of the brain. Stunning victories in understanding the biological mechanisms of some disorders, such as Huntington's disease, have also fanned the hopes for the future of this revolution in psychiatry.

However, as Nancy Andreasen (a prominent biological psychiatrist) notes, this revolution was not based on breakthroughs in knowledge about the etiology of psychiatric disorders; rather, it was based on new conceptualizations of where to look for etiologic factors.

> It is a revolution not so much in terms of what we know as in how we perceive what we know. This shift in perception suggests that we need not look to theoretical constructs of the "mind" or to influences from the external environment in order to understand how people feel, why they behave as they do, or what becomes disturbed when people develop mental illness. Instead, we can look directly to the brain and try to understand both normal behavior and mental illness in terms of how the brain works and how the brain breaks down. The new mode of perception has created the exciting feeling that we can understand the causes of mental illness in terms of basic biological mechanisms. (Andreasen 1984: 138)

But what is this revolutionary shift in perspective all about? How do biologically oriented researchers approach the search for the causes of psychiatric disorders? What constructs, tools, and paradigms do they employ and what have they concluded about the development of mental illness? And, indeed, why should sociologists care? Is there a place for sociologists in a revolution that seems to dismiss the need to consider "impacts from the external environment," or is our only recourse to become counterrevolutionaries?

Given the huge and complex literature in biological psychiatry, addressing these questions, even in a very preliminary way, is a daunting task. Nonetheless, in this chapter we will attempt to: (1) provide a general overview of some of the main biological approaches in psychiatry; (2) illustrate some of the main findings regarding two psychiatric disorders – schizophrenia (the disorder most frequently studied from a biological perspective) and depression (the disorder most frequently studied in sociology); and (3) discuss some of the implications of this approach for sociologists interested in mental health.

Biological Approaches to Psychiatric Disorders

From a biological perspective, psychiatric disorders are illnesses like any other; they are diseases of the body – specifically, diseases of the brain. The goal of a biological approach to psychiatric disorders, therefore, is to understand how disruptions in brain functioning lead to the development of psychiatric disorders (Andreasen 1984; Andreasen & Black 1995).

The constructs of interest are "disease entities." The ultimate goal is to define diseases by their particular biological mechanisms (pathophysiology) and, if possible, distinct cause. However, since the pathophysiology of most psychiatric disorders is virtually unknown, diagnoses are currently defined by clinical symptoms, which seem to cluster and form similar patterns that may help predict course and treatment response (Robins & Guze 1970).

The relationship between diagnosis and etiology or pathophysiology is therefore reciprocal: current diagnostic categories are used to search for pathophysiology, and knowledge of pathophysiology will be used to refine diagnostic categories. For example, many biological psychiatrists speak of "schiozphrenias" rather than schizophrenia, suggesting that the category as currently defined is heterogeneous – that is, the symptoms may have different etiologies and/or biological pathways. There may be more than one genetic form of schizophrenia, or there may be a genetic and an environmental form. Schizophrenia may be the result of injury to different brain systems causing somewhat different symptom patterns. The definitions of the outcomes of interest – specific psychiatric diseases – are therefore dynamic. As knowledge about cause and mechanisms increases, so too will diagnostic precision. This current lack of precision in diagnosis is a great challenge to biological psychiatry and, as we shall see, is frequently invoked as an impediment to advancement and as a cause of inconsistent and unreplicated research findings.

There are many different approaches to understanding the biology of psychiatric disorders, using the tools and paradigms of many different disciplines. We will focus on three: brain structure and function (neuroanatomy), neuronal communication (neurochemistry), and gene effects (genetics). In the optimum, information from each of these strategies would integrate with and inform the others to provide a satisfactory understanding of the biological disease process. To understand how this interrelationship works, we need at least a crude (extremely oversimplified) understanding of what biological psychiatrists mean by the brain and its function and dysfunction.

A common metaphor used to understand the brain and its functioning is that of neural networks. The brain is conceptualized as an integrated system of command centers composed of bodies of nerve cells (grey matter) connected to each other by branches (white matter) that communicate through electrical impulses and chemical and molecular exchanges. Instructions for the synthesis and metabolism of these chemical and molecular messengers (neurotransmitters) and complex proteins that form other components of this communication system are coded in DNA. These chemical exchanges are conceptualized as the biological substrate of thought, emotion, memory, judgments, and feelings – the components of what we think of as our inner life and the arenas that are affected in psychiatric disorders (Andreasen & Black 1995; Lickey & Gordon 1991).

The brain can be "broken" at many points in this system, as when the neural command centers malfunction, the connections are disrupted, the chemical balances and feedback loops are not working, the proteins are not synthesized in appropriate quantities, or the implicated genes are mutated (Andreasen 1984). Biologically oriented researchers look for brain dysfunctions in all of these areas. We will discuss the approaches to this search from the most macro level (anatomy and function) to the most micro level (genetics). The goal of such research is to provide a coherent picture of the pathophysiology of the disorder. For example, a genetic defect may be related to the synthesis of a protein involved in a particular type of chemical communicator that is present in the area of the brain producing the symptoms of the disorder where damage has been located (Deakin 1996). Such a picture has yet to materialize, but the field seems alternatively excited and cautious about the prospects (see e.g. Andreasen 1984; Bogerts & Lieberman 1989).

Brain Structure and Function: Neuroanatomy

Szasz (1961) has long argued that psychiatric disorders do not deserve the appellation "disease" because they are not associated with any lesions (pathological alterations in body tissue). Research on anomalous brain structure and function is the most direct search for such lesions. Central to this search is the premise that the brain is composed of highly specialized and differentiated areas. Although there is redundancy and plasticity in the system, different parts of the brain perform different functions. Here we will give a brief overview of the brain structures thought to be important in psychiatric disorders.

The brain's surface consists of ridges (*gyri*) and fissures (*sulci*), as if a lot of material were bent and folded to fit into a relatively small container. It is divided by a deep crease into right and left hemispheres, which are connected by a large number of fibers called the *corpus callosum*. As you look "through" the brain, from the top of the head downward, the forebrain, the midbrain, and the hindbrain come into view sequentially. The complexity of the functions performed by these brain components declines from the top to bottom of the brain. The higher, more uniquely human functions (e.g., thought, speech) are performed in the forebrain. The midbrain controls sleep, alertness, and pain, while the hindbrain takes care of vegetative functions such as respiration and heart rate. The spinal cord is connected to the bottom of the brain and receives sensory information from the rest of the body and gives commands to the muscles (Lickey & Gordon 1991).

The forebrain is the brain area most implicated in psychiatric symptoms, so we will discuss this in somewhat more detail. The entire forebrain closest to the skull is covered by the cerebral cortex, which has a grayish hue because it is densely packed with neuronal cell bodies. Each half of the cerebral cortex is divided into four lobes – the frontal, parietal, occipital, and temporal lobes. The frontal lobe is thought to perform functions related to various aspects of thinking, feeling,

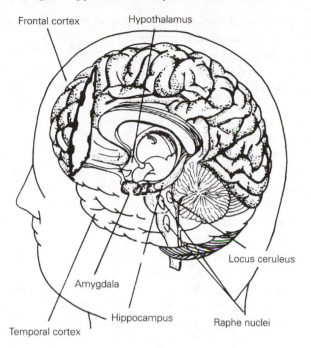

Figure 4.1. Brain structures involved in mental disorders. *Source:* Adapted from Lewis E. Calver, University of Texas, Southwestern Medical Center, Dallas, Texas; reproduced in U.S. Congress (1992).

imagining, and decision making. The parietal lobe controls information about bodily sensations, movement, and spatial orientation; the occipital lobe, information related to vision; and the temporal lobe, auditory information, memory, and language. Underneath the cerebral cortex, deeper within the forebrain, is a group of control centers that form the limbic system. These structures – the thalamus, hypothalamus, hippocampus, and amygdala – are of great interest to psychiatry since they relate to cognition, emotion, learning, memory, and hormonal functioning (Andreasen 1984; Lickey & Gordon 1991).

At approximately the same level in the brain is the basal ganglia. Although the function of this area is mainly movement and the integration of sensory information, it is of interest because two disorders with symptoms related to depression and schizophrenia (Huntington's and Parkinson's disease) both evidence lesions in this area. The *locus cerrilius* (regulating stress response) and the *raphe nuclei* (connected to the limbic system) are two structures, lower in the brain, that are implicated in psychiatric disorders (U.S. Congress 1992). See Figure 4.1.

The ventricular system is also of interest because it can index brain damage. This system is composed of four cavities, filled with cerebral spinal fluid, that project into the cerebral cortex. When cells of the brain are damaged, the ventricles enlarge to fill the space. Ventricular enlargement may therefore be an indicator of brain atrophy (Andreasen 1984).

The functional mapping of the brain is an ongoing process. What is known about normal brain functioning provides hypotheses about where to look for damage that would be likely to produce the specific symptoms of the disorders of interest. For example, in schizophrenia, where integrative problems seem central, frontal lobe involvement is a reasonable hypothesis. In turn, knowledge gained from observing the effects of brain lesions informs brain mapping.

Because the brain cannot be biopsied, early knowledge about brain function was based on autopsies and serendipitous situations – the correlation between obvious brain damage and symptom patterns. A famous example in psychiatry is that of Phinneaus Gage, an efficient and capable railroad worker who had a stake driven through his frontal lobe in an explosion accident. Gage survived the accident but experienced a dramatic change in personality, becoming capricious, impatient, irresponsible, and socially inappropriate (Plotnik 1993). The changes in his behavior led to deductions about the tasks performed by the frontal lobe. Serendipity, being serendipitous, is of limited utility as the basis for brain mapping. Autopsy results also have limitations, since brain structures can change owing to cause of death and postmortem delays (Chua & McKenna 1995). In addition, the usual long time lag between disorder onset and death makes it difficult to determine if the brain damage was the cause of the symptoms or if the symptoms (or treatment of the symptoms) caused the brain damage.

The search for anatomical and functional brain deficits has gained new impetus from technological advances in brain imaging that enable the examination of brain structure and function in living persons. The main imaging techniques for brain *structure* are CAT (computer aided tomography) and MRI (magnetic resonance imaging) scans. In CAT scans, low-level radiation is emitted and its absorption in different parts of the brain is measured. The denser the brain area through which the radiation passes, the more radiation is absorbed. This absorption is mapped onto a grid. A computer assigns numbers to these differences in absorption and translates them into a visual picture with levels of absorption indicated by different colors. In MRI scans, the head is placed in a magnetic field that disturbs brain cells. Their relaxation time is differentiated by structural density, which is again translated by computer into pictures of brain structures indicated in different colors. Although MRI scans are clearer and more detailed than CAT scans, both can image the size and shape of various brain structures and can therefore reveal evidence of atrophy, damage, and tumors (Andreasen & Swayze 1989).

Two methods have also been developed to visualize brain *functioning:* PET (positron emission tomography) and SPECT (single-photon emission computed tomography) scans. In both technologies, radioactive tracers are injected that localize differentially in the brain based on activity level. This differential activity –

indexing blood flow and metabolic or chemical activity (such as changes in protein and neurotransmitter synthesis) – is again translated into images depicting different rates of brain activation (Malaspina, Kegeles, & Van Heertum 1996). The amount and location of brain activity among people with and without the disorder of interest can be compared when the subjects are either resting or participating in different cognitive tasks.

Since the first CAT scan in psychiatric research in 1976 and the first MRI study in 1983, there have been dozens of brain imaging studies of schizophrenia and a few of depression (Chua & McKenna 1995). The search for lesions in schizophrenia has produced sporadic findings of diminished area and volume in various parts of the brain and anomalies in the *corpus callosum* (Lieberman, Brown, & Gorman 1994). The most replicated finding has been evidence of enlargement of the third ventricle, which is surrounded by the thalamus, basal ganglia, and hippocampus (Bradbury & Miller 1985; Pfefferbaum et al. 1990; Raz & Raz 1990). However, this ventricular enlargement has been found only in some people with schizophrenia. In addition, the mean differences between cases and controls tend to be small and within normal ranges (Chua & McKenna 1995; Lewis 1990). Efforts to correlate ventricular enlargement with specific symptom patterns, course, and treatment outcomes have been inconclusive (Andreasen & Swayze 1989). Any etiological role of ventricular enlargement is unknown and uncertain, although it apparently occurs early in the development of the disorder and seems to be nonprogressive and independent of medication history (Deakin 1996; Dwork 1996). If ventricular enlargement indexes an etiologic component then these factors suggest that schizophrenia may be a neurodevelopmental disorder, lending credence to the potential etiological significance of early developmental assaults such as maternal viral infections, nutritional deficits, and obstetric complications (Bradbury & Miller 1985; Crow 1994; Susser & Lin 1992). Findings of anatomic anomalies are less frequent and less consistent in depressive disorders. However, there are some findings of ventricular enlargement, similar to the finding for schizophrenia. This may indicate that ventricular enlargement is not a specific deficit in schizophrenia (Andreasen & Swayze 1989; Anisman & Zacharko 1982; Bogerts & Lieberman 1989; Jeste, Lohr, & Goodwin 1988).

There have also been a large number of functional brain imaging studies of schizophrenia, as well as a smaller number of studies of affective disorders, using PET and SPECT scans. Results here are less consistent than are the CAT and MRI results. There is some suggestion of hypofrontality (i.e., less activation of the frontal lobe) among people with schizophrenia, particularly during cognitive tasks. These results have not been consistent (Lieberman et al. 1994). Some not very well replicated studies have also shown hypofrontality in depressive disorders (Andreasen & Swayze 1989).

So what have biologically oriented researchers concluded about the search for a lesion in psychiatric disorders, particularly for schizophrenia? Most have concluded, despite the inconsistencies and lack of specificity, that the evidence is incontrovertible that schizophrenia is a brain disease. Others conclude that, despite tremendous advances in understanding the brain, uncertainties warrant caution – and the recognition that the historical path toward understanding schizophrenia is strewn with unsubstantiated breakthroughs (Chua & McKenna 1995).

Many researchers lay the blame for research inconsistencies at the door of numerous methodological problems in brain imaging research – in particular, small sample sizes and inadequate control groups (Buckley et al. 1992; Deakin 1996). As research methods employing these new technologies advance, many of these problems should be rectified. Heterogeneity may also account for some inconsistencies, with different subtypes of schizophrenia (as yet unsuccessfully categorized) related to different structural and functional abnormalities. It is also possible to conclude that schizophrenia and other psychiatric disorders (except for dementia) may be related to subtle brain anomalies for which there is no unique anatomical lesion (Bogerts & Lieberman 1989). Indeed, the early models of brain dysfunction in terms of single lesions has been abandoned in favor of more dynamic models (Heinrichs 1993). Brain pathology in schizophrenia may be qualitative rather than quantitative, making it difficult to assess given the large variation in normal samples (Chua & McKenna 1995). It seems in some ways that the most startling finding of brain imaging studies is that a disease such as schizophrenia can so severely compromise presumed brain functions without evidence of gross anatomical abnormalities (Malaspina et al. 1996).

Neuronal Communication: Neurochemistry

When we train a microscope on particular brain structures, we see that the brain is composed of millions of nerve cells of different sizes and shapes. Nerve cells are of two main types – *glial cells* (the most numerous) and *neurons.* The glial cells serve as supporting, connecting, and nourishing structures for the neurons. We will focus attention on the neurons because their functioning is the basis of theories of psychiatric disorders at this level of organization (Plotnik 1993). In order to understand these theories, we need some basic outline of the neuronal communication system.

Neurons have three basic components (see Figure 4.2): (1) the *cell body,* which fuels the communication process and provides the DNA instructions for the production of the chemicals involved in neuronal communication; (2) *dendrites,* branch-like structures that protrude from the cell body and receive information from other neurons; and (3) *axons,* longer extensions from the cell body (insulated by a covering called the myelin sheath) through which messages are sent (Plotnik 1993). Neurons that are in close proximity send messages to each other. However, they never actually touch. Rather, they are separated by a tiny space called the *synapse* (or synaptic cleft). Communication between neurotransmitters occurs via chemical exchanges through this synapse (Lickey & Gordon 1991).

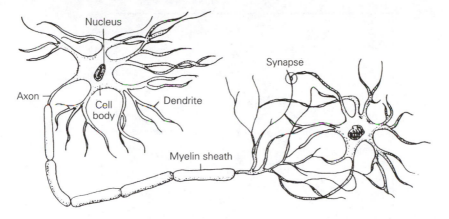

Figure 4.2. Two neurons in synaptic contact. *Source: The Brain* by Richard Restak, M.D. Copyright © 1984 by Educational Broadcasting Corporation and Richard M. Restak, M.D. Used by permission of Bantam Books, a division of Bantam Doubleday Dell Publishing Group, Inc.; reproduced in U.S. Congress (1992).

When a neuron is activated, an electrical impulse (an "action potential") flows down to the end of the axon to hundreds of bulblike swellings called axon terminals. In these axon terminals are numerous saclike structures (synaptic vesicles) that contain chemical substances called *neurotransmitters*. When the electric charge reaches these synaptic vesicles in the axon terminal (in this instance called the presynaptic terminal, since it is sending the message), the sacs burst and release neurotransmitters into the synapse (Plotnik 1993). See Figure 4.3.

These neurotransmitters react with receptors on adjacent neurons (the postsynaptic neuron in this case, because it is receiving a message). These receptors are highly specialized and respond only to specific types of neurotransmitters. Indeed, specific subtypes of receptors for the same neurotransmitters have been discovered. When a neurotransmitter is of the type to which the particular receptor can respond, it binds to the receptor. This binding either encourages an action potential in the postsynaptic neuron (if the message is excitatory) or discourages an action potential (if the message is inhibitory) (Plotnik 1993). The sensitivity of the receptors can be influenced by the number of receptors for a particular neurotransmitter, the affinity of the receptor for the neurotransmitter, and the efficiency with which the binding is translated into a message to the receiving neuron ("second messenger" system) (Kaplan, Sadock, & Grebb 1994).

Each neuron receives messages from dozens of other neurons and must therefore have receptors for many of the different neurotransmitters (Andreasen 1984). The postsynaptic neuron will send a message (or "fire") only if the excitatory messages exceed the inhibitory ones. Some inhibition and excitation messages

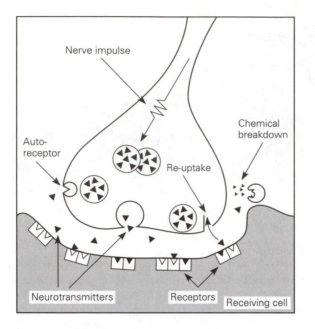

Figure 4.3. The synapse and associated structures. *Source:*
U.S. Congress (1992).

work directly through the receptors and are therefore instantaneous. Other neurotransmitters (including many that are important in psychiatry) work indirectly by
activating enzymes that cause biochemical changes in the postsynaptic cell that
can influence the action potential after a delay of minutes or hours (Lickey & Gordon 1991). Whether or not a neuron fires is therefore extremely complicated and
involves the integration of many different messages.

The binding of the neurotransmitter to the receptor prevents the receptor from
receiving new messages until the neurotransmitter of this message is removed from
the receptor and the synapse. The neurotransmitter is removed from the synapse
either through enzyme action in the synapse that decomposes the neurotransmitter
(metabolism) or through re-entry into the presynaptic membrane, a process known
as *re-uptake.* It then either re-enters the vesicle, to be released again at a later date,
or is destroyed by enzymes in the presynaptic terminal (Lickey & Gordon 1991).

An adequate supply of neurotransmitters is maintained in synaptic vesicles
through several regulatory mechanisms. In the short term, enzymes may prevent
the activity of neurotransmitter precursors (the substances from which neurotransmitters are synthesized) if there is a sufficient supply of neurotransmitters; on the
other hand, if the neuron has been very active and there is neurotransmitter depletion then the production of these precursors can be increased. If there is long-term

hyperactivity and synaptic depletion, the DNA of the neuron can cause increased production of neurotransmitter precursors. In addition, some neurons have receptors (called autoreceptors) in the presynaptic membrane that – when bound by released neurotransmitters – can decrease the amount of neurotransmitters released (Andreasen & Black 1995).

There are three main groupings of classic neurotransmitters: cholinergic (acetylcholine), biogenic amines (dopamine, norepinephrine, serotonin), and amino acids (GABA, glycine, and glutamate). Different parts of the brain use different neurotransmitters, but brain locations using the same neurotransmitters perform different functions. The basal ganglia and motor cortex have high concentrations of acetylcholine, but acetylcholine is also used diffusely throughout the brain. Dopamine is concentrated in the midbrain and hypothalamus, but it also projects to the limbic system and the cerebral cortex. Norepinephrine (also called noradrenaline) and serotonin begin in the brainstem (norepinephrine in the *locus ceruleus* and serotonin in the *raphe nuclei*) and project throughout the cerebral cortex. These neurotransmitter systems therefore overlap with the sections of the brain that seem to be involved in producing the symptoms of schizophrenia and depression (Andreasen 1984).

There are several methods that researchers have used to test the hypothesis that psychiatric disorders reflect dysfunctions in neuronal communication systems. These include examining the mechanism of psychiatric medications and responses to drug challenges; measuring the level of neurotransmitters and their metabolites (i.e., the substances into which they are broken down) in cerebral spinal fluid, blood, and urine; and examining postmortem brain tissue to check the density of receptors in different parts of the brain. More recently, researchers have begun to use such functional brain imaging techniques as PET scans to examine neurotransmitter activity (Anisman & Zacharko 1982; Nathan & Schatzberg 1994).

The hypothesis that schizophrenia is related to an excess of dopamine is probably the most researched and viable current theory in the neurochemistry of this disorder. The best evidence for this hypothesis comes from the mechanism of antipsychotic medications that block the transmission of dopamine between neurons. Medication effectiveness is correlated with the drug's ability to block a specific dopamine receptor (Andreasen & Black 1995). In addition, amphetamine – a dopamine agonist (i.e., a substance that increases dopaminergic activity) – when taken over an extended period can cause hallucinations and delusions, the primary symptoms of schizophrenia (Sharif 1996). However, this pharmaceutical evidence does not support a simple excess of dopamine as a necessary and sufficient cause of schizophrenia, because (a) not all people with schizophrenia respond to these medications, (b) the medications seem to affect the positive symptoms of schizophrenia (e.g. hallucinations) but not the negative ones (e.g. asociality and lack of motivation), and (c) the effect of neurotransmitter production occurs within hours whereas the effect on symptoms occurs only after weeks of treatment (Heinrichs 1993).

There have been numerous investigations of the major metabolite of dopamine (homovanillic acid) in cerebral spinal fluid, blood, and urine. The results from these studies have been inconsistent, and the metabolite levels do not correlate with specific symptoms of schizophrenia. Pharmacologic "challenges" have also been used to study this hypothesis, with mixed results. In these studies, drugs that are known to increase dopaminergic activity are given to people with schizophrenia and to control subjects. The logic behind these studies is that people with schizophrenia should have an increased vulnerability to psychotic symptoms induced by levels of these drugs that would not cause such symptoms in controls. A review article of 36 such studies found that the drug challenges produced inconsistent responses in people with schizophrenia (Lieberman et al. 1994).

The hypothesis that abnormalities in the dopamine system are the primary neurochemical problem in schizophrenia has been challenged by the arrival of newer drugs that influence the serotonin as well as the dopamine system and are more effective for both positive and negative symptoms of schizophrenia. These drugs (known as "atypical" antipsychotics) include clozapine, risperidone, olanzapine, and sertindole (Kinon & Lieberman 1996). However, studies of serotonin metabolites in blood and cerebral spinal fluid have yielded mixed results. Norepinephrine has also been studied, with some research suggesting that people with schizophrenia have increased levels of norepinephrine in their cerebral spinal fluid. However, there is substantial overlap in the levels of cases and controls (Lieberman et al. 1994).

In depression, norepinephrine and serotonin have been the neurotransmitters most widely implicated and studied. The original hypothesis derived from a serendipitous finding that 15% of people treated for hypertension with reserpine (which depletes norepinephrine) became depressed (Kaplan et al. 1994). Here too, the best evidence for the role in depression of a deficit in these neurotransmitters comes from the effects of antidepressant medications. Trycyclics (one class of antidepressant medication) prevent the re-uptake of norepinephrine. This has the effect of allowing this neurotransmitter to remain in the synapse longer and to bind to receptors several times. Monoamine oxidase (MAO) inhibitors, another type of antidepressant, inhibits the action of MAO, which is an enzyme that breaks down norepinephrine and serotonin (Sapolsky 1994). The serotonin hypothesis has gained from the success of a new class of antidepressants, serotonin specific re-uptake inhibitors (SSRIs); as their name suggests, these specifically inhibit serotonin re-uptake and thus leave more serotonin in the synapse for a longer time. However, there is a discrepancy between the short time within which the drugs affect neurotransmitter levels and the longer time frame for symptom relief (Kaplan et al. 1994), and studies of norepinephrine and serotonin metabolites have yielded uneven results. The interrelationship between norepinephrine and serotonin is ill-defined (Gershon & Nurnberger 1995). There is also some evidence implicating GABA and acetylcholine in depression.

A role for norepinephrine in depression is indirectly supported by evidence suggesting a relationship between depression and dysfunctions in the endocrine system (i.e., disregulation of the hypothalamic–pituitary–adrenal axis). A role for this system is suggested by symptom similarity between adrenal gland disorders and depression (i.e., fatigue and appetite/sleep disturbance). The most compelling evidence for such a connection comes from drug challenges with dexamethasone. When the brain perceives a stressful situation, the hypothalamus releases CRT (corticotrophin releasing factor), which stimulates the pituitary to release ACTH (adrenocorticotropic hormone), which in turn stimulates the adrenal glands to release cortisol, a substance released in response to stress. To test the hypothesis that this system is dysfunctional in people with depression, cases and controls are given dexamethasone, a synthetic substance that resembles cortisol. When dexamethasone levels increase in the blood, the hypothalamus stops producing CRT, just as it would when the levels of cortisol increase. In some people with depression, this suppression of cortisol production does not occur. Other endocrine problems have also been found with other drug challenges. The pattern of endocrine results suggests that the problem may lie with the regulation of the hypothalamus, which uses norepinephrine as its main neurotransmitter (Andreasen 1984). It was originally hoped the dexamethasone suppression test could be used to diagnose depression. However, only a minority of people with depression test positive, and a similar effect is found with other disorders (Gold, Goodwin, & Chrousos 1988b).

As was the case with studies of brain structure and function, studies of neurotransmitter dysfunctions in schizophrenia and depression have met with many nonreplications and inconsistencies. There is no lack of methodological reasons for these problems. In many studies, control group selection was not optimal. Many factors that can influence the level of metabolites – such as age, sex, and dietary intake – were not controlled. In addition, measures of metabolites in urine, blood, and cerebral spinal fluid are poor proxy measures for neurotransmitter levels in the brain. Perhaps more problematic for etiologic theories is that most positive findings are for a "state" effect of neurotransmitter excess or deficit, rather than for a "trait" effect, so that there is no evidence for neurotransmitter deficits temporally prior to active symptom formation (Nathan & Schatzberg 1994). This leaves open the interpretation that the symptoms cause the neurotransmitter abnormalities, or that they are the neurotransmitter expression of the symptoms. Improved techniques allowing for expanded use of PET scans in neurotransmitter functioning should provide better evidence about these hypotheses (Sharif 1996).

Our vastly increased understanding of neuronal communication suggests another reason for inconsistent findings: etiological hypotheses based on an excess or deficit in a specific neurotransmitter are too simplistic. The number of neurotransmitters (and neurotransmitterlike substances) discovered in the brain has multiplied rapidly. Complex interactions among neurotransmitters, the specification of multiple receptors for the same neurotransmitters, and complexities in second messenger systems all require more sophisticated explanations (Gold, Goodwin, & Chrouses 1988a; Kaplan et al. 1994). Progress has come not in the specification of the neurochemical processes underlying schizophrenia and depression, but rather in a fuller understanding of the systems of neuronal communication in general.

Genetics

The genetic component of the biological revolution in psychiatry has had perhaps the greatest influence on the popular imagination. Faraone and Santangelo (1992) have described a series of four hierarchical questions, the "chain of genetic epidemiologic research," which summarizes the genetic approach.

(1) Is there evidence that the disorder is familial?
(2) If the disorder is familial, what are the relative magnitudes of the genetic and environmental components?
(3) What is the mode of transmission?
(4) On which chromosome and where on that chromosome is the implicated gene(s) located?

Each of these questions is addressed by different methodologies; respectively: (1) familial aggregation, (2) twin and adoptee studies, (3) segregation analysis, and (4) linkage and association studies. Although each study design has many different permutations, we will discuss just the basics of each category.

Familial Aggregation. The most fundamental requirement for a disorder to be considered genetic is that it aggregate in families. Familial aggregation is evidenced by higher disorder rates for the biological relatives of probands (persons with the disorder) than for the biological relatives of controls (people without the disorder). Furthermore, the disorder rates should correlate with the degree of biological relationship (Faraone & Tsuang 1995).

Early studies of familial aggregation of schizophrenia found rates averaging 6% for parents, 10% for siblings, and 13% for children, compared with general population rates of around 1%. However, these early studies were fraught with methodological difficulties. Often there was no specific control group (rates in relatives were compared with general population rates), diagnostic criteria were often not explicit, and researchers were not blind to proband disorder status when examining relatives, leading to the potential for interviewer bias (Kendler 1988). More recent studies using more rigorous methods generally find increased risk for family members, but the risks are lower than in earlier studies (Lyons et al. 1991).

There have been fewer studies of familial aggregation in depression, and some of these do not differentiate bipolar depression (i.e., depression alternating with mania) from unipolar depression (depression without manic episodes). However, a number of studies have demonstrated an increased risk of depression for off-spring of depressed women (Beardslee et al. 1983; Downey & Coyne 1990). The strongest evidence comes from a number of well-controlled double-blind studies (Gershon et al. 1975, 1982; Tsuang, Winokur, & Crowe 1980; Weissman, Gershon, & Kidd 1984) that find elevated rates of unipolar depression in the biological relatives of depressed probands, providing strong evidence of familial aggregation (Tsuang, Faraone, & Lyons 1989).

It should be noted, however, that familial aggregation is not consistently specific; that is, probands with one type of disorder may have biological relatives with an excess of many different types of disorders. For example, there seems to be overlap in the heritability of bipolar depression, unipolar depression, schizoaffective disorder, anorexia, bulimia, and alcoholism (Gershon & Nurnberger 1995). Although it is reasonably clear from these studies that both schizophrenia and depression aggregate in families, the source of the familial aggregation is left unaddressed because families share many potential risk factors (e.g., socioeconomic status, exposure to viruses, coping mechanisms) for disorder in addition to genes (von Knorring et al. 1983). The next step, therefore, is to test the hypothesis that this familial aggregation has a genetic component.

Twin and Adoptee Studies. Twin and adoptee studies capitalize on special circumstances that allow for the separation of genetic and social inheritance. The basic assumption underlying these designs is that variance in any disorder can be divided into three general categories: genetic factors; shared environmental factors (i.e., aspects of the environment – like childhood socioeconomic status and exposure to household toxins and parenting style – that siblings have in common); and unique environmental factors (i.e., risk factors – like peers, accidents, different family roles – that siblings do *not* share). Shared risk factors for disease (whether environmental or genetic) increase concordance – that is, similarity in disease status for twin pairs. Unique risk factors (environmental or genetic) to which only one twin is exposed increase discordance or *dis*similarity in disease status for twin pairs.

Because they are the source of considerable confusion, I will go into some detail about how twin studies assess the relative magnitudes of these genetic and environmental contributions. Twin studies capitalize on the fact that whereas monozygotic (MZ) twins share 100% of their genes, dizygotic (DZ) twins, like any other sibling pair, share on average only 50% of their genes. For this reason, the factors that lead to concordance and discordance differ for MZ and DZ twins. For MZ twins, the concordance rate reflects 100% of the genetic component of the variance in the disorder plus 100% of the shared environmental component. For DZ twins, the concordance rate reflects 50% of the genetic component (the proportion of genes that, on average, DZ twins share) and 100% of the shared environment. As seen in Table 4.1, these differences can be mathematically modeled to estimate

Table 4.1. *Heritability estimates from twin studies*

Disorder Variance = Genes + Shared Environment + Unique Environment
MZ Concordance = (100% Genetic + 100% Shared Environment)/Total
DZ Concordance = (50% Genetic + 100% Shared Environment)/Total
MZ Discordance = (100% Unique Environment)/Total
DZ Discordance = (50% Genetic + 100% Unique Environment)/Total

Therefore: MZ Concordance − DZ Concordance = 50% of the genetic effect

Example: MZ Concordance = 90%, DZ Concordance = 50%
    90% − 50% = 40% = Half of the Genetic portion of the total variance
    40% × 2 = 80% = Genetic portion of the total variance
    90% − 80% = 10% = Shared Environment portion of the total variance
    100% − 90% = 10% = Unique Environment portion of the total variance
Variance in the Example: 80% Genetic, 10% Shared Environment, 10% Unique Environment

Source: Adapted from Plomin (1990).

the proportion of the variance in an outcome that is due to genetic factors, shared familial environment, and unique environmental factors (Plomin 1990).

In adoptee studies, social and genetic inheritance are separated in a different way. Since adopted children are reared by parents with whom they do not share genes, any correlation between their disorder and that of their adopted parents is due to shared environmental factors. Conversely, because adoptees are not reared by their biologic parents, any concordance with their biological parents is due solely to genetic components rather than shared environments.

Twin and adoptee studies of schizophrenia provide strong evidence for a genetic component to this disorder. Based on data from eight twin studies of schizophrenia reviewed by Torrey (1992), the concordance rates for MZ twins is between 30% and 40% (depending on the specific method used to estimate concordance), and the concordance for DZ twins is between 6% and 15%. Kendler (1983) concludes from twin studies that the (genetic) heritability for schizophrenia is about 70%.

Results of adoptee studies that use several different designs are also fairly consistent. Some studies compare rates of disorder for the biological and adoptive relatives of adoptees exhibiting schizophrenia with the rates in relatives of control adoptees. Others compare disorder rates in adoptees whose birth mother had schizophrenia with adoptees whose mothers did not have schizophrenia. Most of these studies show a higher concordance for biological than adoptive relatives (Heston 1966; Kety et al. 1975; Wender et al. 1974).

Although fewer in number than studies of schizophrenia, twin studies support a genetic component to depressive disorders; concordance rates for MZ twins are about 40% and for DZ twins abount 18% (Tsuang & Faraone 1990). Adoptee studies are less consistent: some support a genetic component (Mendelwicz & Rainer 1977; Wender et al. 1986), whereas others do not (Cadoret et al. 1978; Cadoret, O'Gorman, & Heywood 1985).

Twin and adoptee studies and heritability estimation are appealing methods for separating genetic and environmental effects, but they are based on assumptions that warrant discussion. One basic assumption is that twinship and adoption per se are not correlated with risk factors (or protective factors) for the disorder of interest. For example, if MZ twins have problems developing individuated identities then they may also have elevated rates of schizophrenia. If so, results from twin studies would not be generalizable. In schizophrenia research, at least, this complication has been recognized; the rates of schizophrenia among twins has been estimated, and it appears to approximate general population rates (Rose 1991). However, this assumption is probably less well grounded in adoptee studies. Because adoptive parents usually are carefully screened, they may have a low rate of social and psychological risk factors for disorder. For example, divorce (a factor hypothesized to be important in depression) is markedly low among adoptive parents (Cadoret 1991).

The most contested assumption of twin studies is the "equality of environmental covariance" for MZ and DZ twins (see e.g. Lewontin, Rose, & Kamin 1984). Monozygotic twins clearly experience greater environmental similarity than DZ twins. For example, they are more likely to dress alike, play together, share a room, and have frequent contact. However, it is less clear if MZ twins experience greater environmental similarity on factors that relate to psychiatric disorders (Rose 1991). This assumption can also be contested from the other direction: certain aspects of the environment of MZ twins may not be as similar as was once thought (e.g., the *in utero* environment; see Torrey et al. 1994).

Additivity is another problematic assumption. Heritability estimates assume an additive relationship among genetic, shared environmental, and unique environmental risk factors. This assumption is almost certainly unjustified. Indeed, most theories of depression and schizophrenia assume gene–environment *interactions,* with certain genes sensitizing people to environmental risk factors or with environmental risk factors activating dormant genes (Kendler, Lyons, & Tsuang 1991b). In addition, gene–environment *correlations,* where certain genotypes influence the types of environments to which individuals are exposed, are ubiquitous (Scarr & McCartney 1983). Gene–gene interactions have been hypothesized that would also violate the assumption of additivity. It is almost certain that these assumptions are violated in the study of schizophrenia and depression, since the DZ concordance rate is frequently less than half the MZ concordance rate – which should not happen if the assumptions of additivity hold. Although twin and adoptee studies provide compelling evidence for a genetic component to depression and schizophrenia, these methodological problems make heritability estimates questionable, an issue to which we shall return.

Segregation Analysis. These studies attempt to ascertain familial patterns of disorder to obtain clues about the mode of genetic transmission. Simple Mendelian transmission (dominant, recessive, and X-linked) yields recognizable patterns in the distributions of disorders across generations. It is unlikely that psychiatric disorders fit these patterns, as Mendelian disorders tend to be much rarer than most psychiatric disorders. Among the complex modes of transmission being studied are: single major locus with incomplete penetrance (one major gene where not everyone with the genotype acquires the disease); oliogenetic (several genes involved); polygenetic (many genes involved); and multifactorial (gene and environmental effects). It is also possible that the disorders may be divided into numerous subtypes, each of which relates to different genes (Faraone & Tsuang 1995). Mathematical models have been developed to assess the mode of transmission that best fits the disorder pattern. Such analyses have not yet been successful in illuminating the modes of transmission for either depression or schizophrenia (Tsuang, Faraone, & Lyons 1989).

Linkage Studies. Linkage studies have produced numerous headlines in recent years with the discovery of the location of the genes associated with Huntington's disease, Alzheimer's, and breast cancer (to name just a few). Once located, the genes can be isolated and their functions identified; thus the pathophysiology of the disorder could be specified (Risch 1991).

Linkage analyses are based on estimations of the probability that, within a family, a genetic propensity for a particular disease is inherited along with a genetic marker (a gene with a known location on a particular chromosome). If the probability is high, it is assumed that a gene making a major contribution to the appearance of the disease under study is in close physical proximity to the genetic marker. Recent advances in molecular genetics have led to the discovery of new types of genetic markers, including RFLPs (restriction fragment length polymorphisms). This has greatly enhanced the utility of linkage studies, since these markers cover the entire human genome and so enable a full search for a gene's location (U.S. Congress 1992).

Linkage analyses have met with tremendous success in the location of genes associated with many disorders, but they have been a disappointment in psychiatry (Risch 1991). Numerous studies suggesting linkage have failed replication attempts or have been disconfirmed after longer observation of the pedigrees (see Bassett et al. 1988; Gershon et al. 1979; Hallmayer et al. 1992; Kennedy et al. 1988; Sherrington et al. 1988). The characteristics of psychiatric disorders make them less than optimal for the application of linkage methods. Linkage studies are best suited for detecting disorders with Mendelian traits – rare disorders with relatively discrete symptom patterns and known modes of inheritance. As discussed previously, psychiatric disorders do not have these attributes. However, linkage has been successful in locating genes implicated in other complex diseases such as breast cancer. Other approaches to gene location – such as association studies (looking for genes that are linked in the population), the use of candidate genes (genes with known pathogenic effects), and mutation screening (searching for genetic mutations that differentiate people with and without the disorder of interest) – are also being employed. The utility of these methods should increase with a fuller understanding of the pathophysiology of psychiatric disorders.

Status of the Revolution

In each of the areas we have discussed (and summarized in Table 4.2) – brain structure and function, neuronal communication, and genetic effects – it would appear that, instead of answering existing questions, methodological breakthroughs have given rise to new questions of greater complexity. The pathophysiology and etiology of psychiatric disorders are not likely to be as straightforward as early hypotheses suggested. It is unlikely that a single lesion will be found for most psychiatric disorders; rather, the presence of subtle, diffuse, qualitative brain representations is more probable. Likewise, deficits or excesses of single neurotransmitters are not likely to yield compelling explanations for psychiatric disorders. Instead, symptoms are probably explained by interactions among neurotransmitters, specific receptors, and complex second messenger systems. Evidence for a genetic component to many disorders is substantial, but single genes are probably not responsible. The specific mode of transmission, as well as the interactions among genetic and environmental factors, remain to be explicated. In the biological revolution, as in most revolutions, maturity brings complexity. Although clinical practice has been dramatically altered – with advances in psychopharmacology offering new hope to many people with severe psychiatric disorders – the shift from mind to brain in the search for etiology is likely to advance slowly, with frequent setbacks that increase the sophistication of the paradigm.

Implications of This Revolution for Sociology

Do participants in the biological revolution see a place for sociologists? Some clearly do. As they eagerly point out, a concordance rate of less than 100% for MZ twins indicates an environmental component to psychiatric disorders. Indeed, some see genetic research in particular as providing the best evidence that environmental factors do play a role (Lyons et al. 1991; Reiss, Plomin, & Hetherington 1991). Others demur (Heston 1992; Klein & Wender 1993). They argue that a concordance rate of less than 100% could still imply only biological causes since MZ twins may not be as alike as we once assumed (e.g., there could be DNA-to-RNA transcription errors, effects of placental differences, phenotyping errors) (see McGuffin et al. 1994; Torrey et al. 1994). In addition, "environmental" does not imply psychological or sociological factors; "environmental" just means "not

Table 4.2. *Summary of key research findings for schizophrenia*

Model	Research techniques	Key findings for schizophrenia	Reviews of topic
Neuroanatomy	Brain imaging techniques		Chua and McKenna (1995)
	CAT and MRI	Ventricular enlargement	Malaspina et al. (1996)
	PET and SPECT	Decreased activity in frontal lobe	
Neurochemistry	Pharmacologic models		Sharif (1996)
	Dopamine hypothesis	Amphetamine mimics dopamine and causes psychotic symptoms; conventional antipsychotic drugs block dopamine receptors	
	Serotonin hypothesis	LSD mimics serotonin and causes psychotic symptoms; newer "atypical antipsychotic" drugs block serotonin receptors	
Genetics	Familial aggregation studies	Schizophrenia aggregates in families	Lyons et al. (1991)
	Twin and adoption studies	A genetic component in schizophrenia is supported	
	Segregation analyses		
	Linkage analyses		

Source: Peter Weiden.

genetic." Such influences could still be biological (e.g., viral infection, brain damage). Sociology may have a place in understanding "normal" depression, but depressive disorder is a biological phenomenon for which psychological (and surely sociological) explanations are largely irrelevant.

And how have sociologists responded? Some have argued, much like their biological counterparts, for a separatist position. Sociologists should not concern themselves with psychiatric phenomena, such as schizophrenia, that have a powerful genetic etiology and fit well within the medical paradigm. Rather, sociologists should focus on mental phenomena – such as anxiety and subclinical depression – that are likely to have a powerful social etiology (Pearlin 1989).

The separatist position seems to be based on a distinction between mental illness that is largely genetic and that which is largely environmental in origin. This distinction itself is problematic on several grounds. It seems to imply an acceptance of heritability estimates as providing limits on the importance of social etiological factors. That is, if schizophrenia is 70% heritable then, barring methodological errors, the environment is of minimal importance in the etiology of this disorder. This treats the heritability estimate as if it were inherent in the disorder – a dubious proposition. The parceling of nature and nurture influences is environment-specific. If you change the environment, the heritability estimate may change as well. The more environmentally homogenous the study population, the larger the heritability estimate, all other things being equal (Tucker 1994). Furthermore, there is a disjuncture between apparent causal importance and appropriate intervention. Even when a heritability estimate is huge, a successful intervention may be entirely environmental (Jencks 1980). A commonly cited example of this is phenylketonuria, a genetic disorder leading to an inability to metabolize phenoalynine that has a heritability estimate of virtually 100%. The successful intervention for this disorder – a diet without phenoalynines – is environmental. A high heritability estimate tells you nothing about either the importance of environmental causal factors or the potential efficacy of environmental interventions.

In addition, when we try to identify the cause of a condition, we usually begin by examining how the factor varies in a population. If you want to know the causes of depression you look at how depression is distributed in the population. However, as Lieberson (1985) points out, the distribution may reveal the cause of this factor's *variation* in a population but not necessarily the cause of the factor *itself* or of its magnitude. What causes the distribution of a factor within a population may not be what causes the rate of the factor. For example, depression appears to be a disorder with a genetic component. However, there is also evidence for a cohort effect in depression, with rates increasing and age of onset decreasing in recent cohorts. The causes of any increase in the rate of depression is likely to be environmental. But even if the cause of the rate increase is environmental, the proportion of the variance explained by genetic factors in any population may be unaffected. Sociological explanations could account entirely for the rate of disorder, whereas genetic influences explain who within a population is more likely to get the disorder.

Finally, as discussed in the section on genetic approaches, heritability estimates do not take interactions into account. Twin studies are modeled in such a way that any gene interaction with shared familial environment (which include most powerful sociological variables) is included in the genetic effect. Advances in molecular genetics itself point to the futility of trying to proportion gene–environment interactions into their contributory components. Gene–environment interactions are dynamic, with the brain responding in a continuous way to environmental phenomena (Sharif 1996). Genes are inherited at conception and are basically unchangeable, but what is inherited are genes – not disease outcomes. Genes do not cause disease or behavior, they only create proteins that interact in minute and ongoing ways with the environment, which feeds back to the body to change the proteins and their products. Genes are constantly turned on and off. Though a separatist position has appeal, declaring that mental phenomena with large genetic components are "off limits" to sociologists renders too much unto biology.

But if we reject a separatist position, how can sociologists relate to this revolution? There are many possible options, depending on the particular questions that sociologists wish to address. We'll briefly outline three options: active participation in the revolution, cooptation, and counterrevolution.

Active Participation. Sociologists can participate in and advance research that is conducted from within the biological paradigm, an approach congruent with what Aneshensel, Rutter, and Lachenbruch (1991) refer to as the "sociomedical" paradigm. In this paradigm, the focus is on the disorder; factors influencing the etiology and course of the disorder are of primary interest. Sociologists can delineate the types of environmental factors that are implicated in the cause and course of these disorders. The interactions between biological vulnerability and sociological factors are central to such work. This approach is exemplified by the collaboration of Kendler and Kessler (see e.g. Kendler et al. 1991a, 1992b, 1993a,b, 1995), where sociological phenomena are explicitly measured and included in twin studies.

In such analyses, sociology plays a supporting role. The focus of interest, diagnostic categories, are defined and refined by criteria that are unique to the disorder. This specificity increases the importance of individual-level variables over social-level variables. As knowledge about the pathophysiology of psychiatric disorders increases – and with it, diagnostic precision – biological factors will, by definition, be seen as the necessary if not sufficient causes of the disorder. Within this paradigm, sociology can identify factors that trigger these biological dysfunctions as well as social factors that influence the course of these disorders. In this way, sociology can play an important (albeit secondary) role in advancing the biological revolution.

Cooptation. Another possibility is to use biological explanations to advance the cause of sociology. Several recent review articles have identified the examination of multiple outcomes as a promising new direction for stress research, a prominent paradigm within the sociology of mental health (Aneshensel et al. 1991; McLean & Link 1994; Thoits 1995a). They argue that, since sociological factors influence a broad range of both physical and psychiatric disorders, we underestimate the effects of such factors if we examine only a limited number of outcomes. Research deriving from the biological perspective can help advance this agenda by encouraging the search for unifying theories that encompass both physical and psychiatric disorders. There has been a tendency in sociological research to create an artificial separation between mental and physical disorders, emphasizing different social risk factors in each area (Thoits 1995a). In part, I think, this happens because mental disorders are considered basically psychological phenomena, ending in the mind rather than in the body. Our theories of how social factors influence mental health have therefore been derived from and often (one can argue) reduced to psychological factors such as self-esteem, locus of control, learned helplessness, and mastery. In physical disorders the pathway ends in the body, implying different sets of causal variables. Biological explanations of psychiatric disorders suggest there may be more unifying sociological theories, since psychiatric disorders also have biological representations.

Yet as McLean and Link (1994) point out, even though multiple outcomes need to be examined, it is not fruitful to simply clump all socially relevant risk factors with all health outcomes to which they may be linked. We need to develop theories that would suggest boundaries for both risk factors and outcomes. Ideas deriving from biological psychiatry can serve as a useful supplement to our repertoire of theoretical ideas. Biological theory may suggest novel approaches to deciding which outcomes to examine in the same study. Currently, when multiple outcomes are examined, this usually means the combination of several psychiatric disorders in one study (e.g., Dohrenwend et al. 1992; Kessler, Turner, & House 1989; Thoits 1995a). The implied commonality between disorders such as antisocial personality and schizophrenia is that they are conceptualized as psychological phenomena. But once we see psychiatric disorders also as biological phenomena, new combinations are suggested. For example, coronary artery disease and depression are comorbid, and at least one social factor has been suggested as being etiologically significant for both: jobs lacking direction, control, and planning (Karasek, Gardell, & Windell 1987; Link, Lennon, & Dohrenwend 1993). Is this occupational phenomenon related to bodily changes that are common to both disorders? Can this help explain their comorbidity? In more general terms, the physiology of stress may suggest the types of social risk factors that may be most fruitfully explored for specific constellations of disorders. For example, chronic strain and life events have very different effects on the body. Understanding the biological substrate of physical and psychiatric disorders may suggest which types of stress may be more important for which types of outcomes (Sapolsky 1994). Biological theories may also suggest the stage of development at which sociological phenomena of different types may have their effects. For example, if schizophrenia is a neurodevelopmental disorder then social factors influencing early development may have the greatest salience.

Examining the biological substrate of psychiatric disorders may also broaden the types of linkages we examine between social factors and psychiatric disorders. Instead of limiting ourselves to linkages through psychological phenomena, we can also examine nonpsychological phenomena. For example, social class may be related to psychiatric disorder not only through its effect on stressful life events, coping, and so forth, but also through increased exposure to viral infections, head injuries, birth trauma, and other physical phenomena. The influence of social structure is no less important if it works through the disparate and unequal distribution of physical risk factors than through psychological ones.

Biological linkages may also strengthen the need for investigations of psychiatric disorders outside the framework of survey research. Sociological phenomena may influence disorder through direct effects on the body that are not consciously recognized by the individual. For example, the effects of unrecognized and unnamed racial discrimination has been implicated in high blood pressure (Krieger 1990). It may be that such factors also have connections with depression, where bodily responses to stress are intimately tied to the neurotransmitters identified in biological theories as implicated in the etiology of depression. Such theories may suggest linkages – between social phenomena and biological expressions of stress – that can be exploited.

Anomalous findings from a biological perspective may also suggest fruitful avenues for sociological examination. At the anatomical, neurochemical, and genetic levels, there are often biological deficits that are common for disparate disorders. For example, there is some evidence for a shared biological vulnerability to depression and alcoholism. Yet these disorders have very different distributions. Indeed, whereas depression and alcoholism are comorbid on the individual level, there are social groupings that have high rates of one and low rates of the other (i.e., gender groupings and some ethnic groupings). This may suggest a venue for examining the relationship between biological substrate and disease expression. These are just a few ideas of how the biological approach can be used to inform sociological understandings of the relationship between the social world and mental health.

Counterrevolution. An understanding of the biological perspective of psychiatric disorders is important for sociology as the basis for advancing the social component in biological theories of psychiatric disorders and for using such theories to advance the sociology of mental health. However, it is also important to provide the basis of a sociological critique of the biological approach. The biological revolution in psychiatry carries – along with its promise – the danger of biological reductionism, biological determinism, and the hegemony of biological explanations for psychiatric disorders and other social problems. There are many fronts on which this counterrevolution must be fought; I'll outline just a few.

The dominance of the biological perspective in psychiatry was reinforced by the scientific successes of genetic and pharmaceutical research, but that is clearly only a part of the story. Sociologists do and should examine the interrelationships between social and political phenomena and the rise of the biological revolution. Why does this paradigm have such appeal in the current social context? Who are the beneficiaries of this revolution and who are the losers? Proponents of a biological perspective suggest that it decreases the stigma associated with psychiatric disorders. Has it decreased stigma? For whom?

Sociological analyses of the social construction of psychiatric disorders are also important, particularly at this juncture when the number of disorders officially recognized in psychiatry is growing at an unprecedented rate. All behaviors have biological, psychological, and sociological components. The question is: On which level of organization is the phenomenon defined, and why? Deciding to define a phenomenon in terms of its biological component and call it a "disease" is a political issue, one that demands sociological analysis. The medicalization of social phenomena and the labeling of biological differences as "defects" needs to be discussed. What phenomena should be defined based on their biological representations, and which should not? How are these decisions being made, and by whom? What are the consequences of these decisions? Should phenomena with similar biological representations be considered the same thing, regardless of contextual differences? Advances in biological psychiatry itself point to the problem of diagnosis; what may be a unitary phenomenon from a genetic perspective may be diverse phenomena from a neurochemical perspective. Which definitions will be most useful depends on the discipline involved.

Sociologists also need to examine the types of questions that a biological perspective can and cannot address. For example, questions about the causes of an increase in the rate of a disorder, or about differences between disorder rates in different areas, are generally not answerable from a biological perspective. In addition, studies designed to examine biological phenomena, which benefit from socially and psychologically homogenous samples, are ill-suited for examining the causes of disease rates. Yet biological studies are often used to address such questions. Sociology needs to critique such analyses and to delineate the types of questions for which biological approaches are unsuitable. However, this counterrevolution cannot be waged without first understanding the basis for biological explanations of psychiatric disorders.

5

Psychological Approaches to Mental Illness

Christopher Peterson

Psychologists focus attention on the individual factors that produce abnormal thoughts, feelings, and behaviors. Psychologists also provide therapies that try to alleviate the distress caused by mental illness. Peterson provides an overview of the views of human nature, abnormality, and treatment found in four psychological models of mental illness. The psychoanalytic model, which originated with Freud, assumes that people are closed energy systems motivated by a variety of drives. Abnormality can be understood developmentally in that early childhood events affect adult functioning. Psychoanalytic treatment generally involves helping the individual to achieve insight and to free energy from unhealthy purposes through catharsis. A second model is the cognitive-behavioral, which emphasizes cognition and learning. People are viewed as information processing systems who attempt to maximize pleasure and minimize pain. All types of learning (classic conditioning, operant conditioning, and modeling) must be placed in a cognitive context – that is, learning takes place within a thinking context. Abnormalities arise when individuals are placed in highly unusual situations or have unusual ways of thinking. Interventions encourage adaptive habits and teach individuals to perceive the world more accurately and to solve problems more efficiently. The third psychological model of mental illness is the humanist-existential-phenomenological approach, represented by such psychologists as Abraham Maslow and Carl Rogers. It emphasizes the need for self-actualization rather than diagnosis of mental illness. The focus lies in the individual's experience of the world and in the creation of a supportive atmosphere characterized by genuineness, empathy, and unconditional positive reward. A final model is the family systems approach, which sees most problems as originating in the family. Accordingly, couples or family therapy is undertaken, where the therapist intervenes to develop healthy ways of relating to one another. Each model works well with some types of problems and falls short with others. An integrated approach may be best, where one identifies the purposes best suited for a particular model. In comparing the different psychological approaches to mental illness, students should examine the potential conflict between intervention strategies.

Psychology is but one of several disciplines concerned with abnormality. Although psychologists throughout much of the twentieth century have pursued theoretically focused strategies, recent years have seen a recognition that the topic demands a broader approach (Castonguay & Goldfried 1994; Omer 1993). The biochemical underpinnings of particular types of abnormality need to be specified, along with the possible contribution of genetic influences (see Chapter 4 of this volume). At the same time, abnormality must be placed in its larger social context – that provided by history, society, and culture (see Chapter 6).

Engel's (1980) "biopsychosocial" model, which calls for theorists to consider the biological mechanisms, psychological processes, and social influences on abnormality, is widely endorsed by many psychologists today. However, this model remains just a slogan until one can fill in its details for specific instances of abnormality – anxiety, depression, substance abuse, schizophrenia, and so on – and much work remains to be done before this vision is achieved.

The purpose of this chapter is to discuss the major psychological perspectives on mental illness. In terms of the biopsychosocial model, the unique contribution of psychology lies in its attention to the intraindividual mechanisms that produce abnormal thoughts, feelings, and behaviors (Persons 1986). Although psychologists today take diagnosis seriously, most are not satisfied with simply showing that individuals whose problems fall into different diagnostic categories are different. Their goal is to explain why these differences exist. Usually, psychological theorists assume that abnormality and normality are continuous; because the same psychological mechanisms presumably produce both abnormal and normal behavior, there is no discrete break between the two.

Another contribution of psychology to the field of mental illness has been the development of individual therapies that try to undo or neutralize the psychological mechanisms specified by various theories of abnormality, thereby alleviating distress. Research testifies to the effectiveness of a variety of psychological therapies (Lambert & Bergin 1994; Lipsey & Wilson 1993).

Psychological Models of Abnormality

All useful psychological models of abnormality share a common form. At the core of each is a set of assumptions about human nature. Each model takes a stance on the nature of behavior (general psychology), on how behavior can go awry (psychopathology), and on how abnormality can be prevented and/or corrected (intervention). Although there are a number of popular psychological models of abnormality, the present chapter focuses on the psychoanalytic approach, the cognitive-behavioral approach, the existential-humanistic-phenomenological approach, and the family systems approach (see Table 5.1).

Psychoanalytic Model

The psychoanalytic model of abnormality originated in Sigmund Freud's influential theorizing. At its core, this model implies that people are closed energy systems. Freud (1950) seemed to regard psychological energy (or *libido,* to use his term) as an actual thing, one that neurologists would eventually discover. Subsequent versions of psychoanalytic theory use the notion of energy in a more metaphorical way, but common to all these theories are assumptions stemming from the view of people as engaged in the transformation and redirection of psychological energy.

Table 5.1. *Psychological models of abnormality*

Model	Assumptions
Psychoanalytic	People are energy systems. Problems result from the investment of energy in symptoms. Treatment releases energy by encouraging insight.
Cognitive-behavioral	People are information processing systems. Problems result from inappropriate learning and/or thinking. Treatment changes the environment and/or thoughts.
Humanistic-existential- phenomenological	People choose and define their own existence. Problems result from the failure of self-actualization. Treatment encourages authentic living.
Family systems	People are products of their family. Problems result from family dynamics and the creation of an unhealthy homeostasis. Treatment changes the family status quo.

Key Concepts. One of the overarching ideas of psychoanalytic theorizing is that behavior is *overdetermined*, meaning that even the most simple of our actions has numerous causes. The assumption of overdetermined behavior helps explain why the psychoanalytic model has been controversial. On the one hand, psychoanalytic theorizing about abnormality does justice to the complexity of the subject. On the other hand, because so many theoretical notions must be brought to bear in a single psychoanalytic explanation, the process may become unwieldy and appear arbitrary (Rapaport 1959).

Another important aspect of the psychoanalytic model is that it takes a *developmental* approach to abnormality, stressing events and occurrences early in life that affect adult functioning. This emphasis stems from Freud's original medical training in neurology, where it is a truism that early structures form the foundation that underlie later structures. Put another way, the behavioral styles that children develop early in life become the ingredients of their adult personalities.

Freud believed that children develop by passing through a fixed sequence of psychosexual stages, discrete periods defined by the part of the body that provides gratification of the sexual drive. The child who passes through these stages – oral, anal, phallic, latency, and genital – in satisfactory fashion becomes a normal adult. But frustration or indulgence at any stage may leave the child with a fixation at that stage, which influences adult character. An orally fixated person, for example, might drink too much or eat too much as an adult, creating such problems as alcoholism or obesity.

Yet another noteworthy psychoanalytic idea is that of the dynamic *unconscious*. According to Freud and subsequent psychoanalytic theorists, there exists important mental activity of which we are not aware. The unconscious is not just a deficit in knowledge but an active process that motivates us to keep threatening material from our conscious minds. Chief among these threatening contents are the sexual and aggressive motives that underlie our every action.

Where does psychological energy originate? Freud's answer is that we have certain innate drives, in particular sexuality and aggression, that demand discharge. The term for the sexual drive is Eros (after the Greek god of love). Eros is manifest not just in the narrow sense of genital activity culminating in orgasm, but also more broadly in any and all activities that involve bodily pleasure. The aggressive drive is sometimes called Thanatos (after the Greek god of death). This drive is presumably behind the destructive acts we direct against ourselves and others: suicide, drug abuse, murder, and war.

Another important concern is the struggle between individuals and their drives and the restrictions imposed by the larger social groups to which they belong. According to Freud (1930), civilization would not be possible if people directly satisfied all their sexual and aggressive drives as they arose. Who would raise children, harvest crops, or pay taxes? For society to exist, people's drives must be curbed.

Freud held that drives could not be eliminated. But people could be induced to compromise, to delay their gratification or to find indirect or symbolic means of satisfying them. In the course of socialization, children are transformed from bundles of drives – literally, wild animals – into creatures capable of modifying their impulses or holding them in check. Socialization is never fully achieved, and it produces casualties: people who never learn to control their drives and those who control them too well.

When infants are born, their only mental structure is what Freud termed the *id*, responsible for our irrational and emotional aspects. The id operates according to the pleasure principle: gratification without delay. In the course of socialization, the infant develops an *ego*, which operates according to the reality principle: adaptation to external constraints. The internalization of parental dictates – mainly "thou shalt nots" – is accomplished by the development of yet a third mental structure, the *superego*. In the adult, these three systems (the id, ego, and superego) interact continually. Their dynamic balance determines an individual's personality in general and his or her problems in particular.

How does the mind defend itself? One of Freud's most important contributions to psychological thought is the notion of *defense mechanisms*. These are mostly unconscious strategies that the ego uses to protect itself from anxiety. All people presumably use defense mechanisms, but they may show considerable variation in those they habitually favor (Vaillant 1977). Some people rely mainly on primitive defenses, such as denial or repression, that distort or deny reality. Other people use more subtle ones, such as humor or sublimation. People with severe problems tend to use particularly immature or exaggerated defenses. Indeed, the psychoanalytic model gives us a rich vocabulary for describing various disorders in terms of the defense mechanisms that people typically use. For example, paranoid individuals use projection, phobic individuals use displacement, and so forth.

Psychopathology. Psychoanalytic theorists see problems as resulting from defects in the transformation and use of psychological energy. These ideas explain both circumscribed and pervasive problems. So, in *dysphoria* – that is, general anxiety or depression – a person invests too much energy in defenses, thus having less available energy for more gratifying activities. In severe forms of abnormality such as schizophrenia, a person may not invest enough energy in defenses and as a result become overwhelmed by drives.

Defenses can end up being problems in their own right. Consider multiple personality disorder: the existence within the same individual of discrete personalities with little awareness of one another. Some research implicates sexual or physical abuse in the childhood of most people with this disorder (Putnam et al. 1986). One interpretation is that individuals who later develop multiple personality disorder create in childhood an alternative personality as a defense against abuse. It is a way to escape an intolerable situation, psychologically if not physically. This strategy, although useful at the time, creates obvious problems for those who continue its use.

Intervention. The first modern "talking cure" was Freud's psychoanalysis, and subsequent psychological therapies have often used it as a model (Luborsky 1984). Even psychotherapists who take issue with psychoanalysis have been influenced by it. Many believe that talking about problems in a special way is curative, that insight into the source of one's own problems is a critical ingredient in improvement, and that a nonjudgmental relationship between client and therapist is crucial.

Psychoanalytic treatment usually involves releasing energy, freeing it from investments in unhealthy purposes so that it is available for use elsewhere. The process by which energy is freed is termed *catharsis*, which is accompanied by sudden emotional relief. As noted, attaining insight is a major strategy in this kind of intervention, thus bringing conflicts and motives into conscious awareness. If people become conscious of ideas and impulses heretofore repressed, then they have taken a major step toward helping themselves because psychological energy is thereby made available for pursuits more gratifying than the maintenance of defenses.

Psychoanalysts have developed a host of strategies for revealing unconscious conflicts. The technique of *free association* is one example. Here the person is instructed and encouraged to say anything that comes to mind, one idea leading to another and then another. The hope is that the train of emotional associations will lead eventually back to unconscious memories. Dream interpretation is another strategy for accomplishing the same purpose. According to Freud (1900), dreams are "the royal road to the unconscious," and he theorized extensively about how dreams may represent disguises of our unconscious wishes and fears. We can gain insight once these disguises are stripped away. Just like defense mechanisms, dreams disguise conflicts, yet dreams hint of them via symbolism.

Another strategy emerging from psychoanalytic theory is the analysis of the *transference* relationship between therapist and client. By this view, clients in therapy inevitably react to therapists as they reacted earlier to those people with whom their conflicts originated. If the therapist and client can recreate these conflicts, then they have clues about how conflicts operated in the past. Again, insight is the goal. To help this process along, the therapist deliberately cultivates a pose of neutrality, a so-called blank screen.

It is quite difficult to say, fully one century after Freud first began to treat hysterical patients by asking them to free associate, whether or not this type of treatment is effective (Henry et al. 1994). Its terms are ambiguous, the duration of psychoanalytic therapy is typically years, the clients are highly select, and some psychoanalytic therapists are reluctant to subject their efforts to scientific investigation. Few if any methodologically sound investigations of psychoanalysis have been conducted.

Psychodynamic Approaches. Throughout his long career, Freud attracted a number of followers. Many of these individuals proposed their own versions of psychoanalysis, and what we have today is a large number of such approaches, each with somewhat different emphases. It is customary to refer to Freud's original theory as psychoanalysis, and the family of related approaches as psychodynamic theories, because they are concerned with the dynamic workings of the mind. These theories in general assume that people's problems result from inner conflicts that overwhelm their defenses.

Contemporary psychodynamic theorists often follow the lead of Alfred Adler (1927), Carl Jung (1924), and the neo-Freudians – such as Karen Horney (1937), Erich Fromm (1947), Harry Stack Sullivan (1947), and Erik Erikson (1963), among others – by placing less emphasis on the purely biological or sexual aspects of personality. They are more likely to be interested in social determinants. Along these lines, they tend to downplay or even eliminate reference to psychological energy and drives.

Contemporary psychodynamic theorists have also followed the lead of the "ego psychologists" – such as Anna Freud (1937), Heinz Hartmann (1939), and Robert White (1959) – by placing less emphasis on the conflict between id and superego and more stress on the ego as an active (not reactive) agent. Sometimes these theorists refer to defense mechanisms as "coping" mechanisms in order to emphasize their active nature.

Many psychodynamic theorists today are particularly interested in the mental representations that people have of themselves and others. These representations are called *object relations* (Greenberg & Mitchell 1983). "Object" was Freud's term for people or things, and the term "relations" refers to the perceived link between these objects and the individual. In one sense, this emphasis on object relations reflects the trend in recent decades for psychology to be more interested in cognition (Gardner 1985). But object relations theories maintain the traditional psychoanalytic emphases on unconscious, irrational, and emotional processes.

Cognitive-Behavioral Model

A second psychological perspective on abnormality combines approaches that emphasize cognition on the one hand and processes of learning on the other. Early theories of learning stemmed from behaviorism and thus made no use of cognitive explanations. Indeed, throughout most of the twentieth century, learning theories and cognitive theories were clearly distinct and often antagonistic (Sweet & Loizeaux 1991). Although some contemporary therapists regard themselves as strictly behavioral or strictly cognitive, recent years have seen many other therapists successfully combine these approaches (Peterson 1992, 1996). The resulting cognitive-behavioral model of abnormality views people as information processing systems that attempt to predict and understand events in the world with the goal of maximizing pleasure and minimizing pain. Stated another way, the cognitive-behavioral model regards people as thinking hedonists.

Explicit in this view of human nature is the assumption that people constantly interact with the world. Bandura (1986) termed this give and take between a person and the world "reciprocal determinism." Each of us is influenced by prevailing patterns of rewards and punishments in the environment, and our actions in turn influence these patterns. Furthermore, this transaction is mediated cognitively. We react to the world in terms of how we interpret events. The reality in which our behavior takes place is a *perceived* reality.

Forms of Learning. Cognitive-behavioral theorists emphasize several psychological processes, especially several basic forms of learning. *Classical* conditioning – remember Pavlov's salivating dogs? – is the process by which people come to associate particular emotional reactions to previously neutral stimuli. Imagine people who have had a series of traumatic experiences with dogs, or with airplane travel or sexual relations. They may well develop fears or aversions to these.

Operant conditioning is the process by which we come to associate responses with their consequences. If the consequences are reinforcing, we are more likely to repeat the actions that preceded them. Children might throw tantrums when doing so is the only way they can get attention from their parents or teachers. If the consequences of responses are painful, then we tend to refrain from repeating these actions.

Modeling – or vicarious conditioning – is the process by which we learn new behaviors by watching others perform them. If the person we watch (the model) meets with reward, then we are more likely to follow his or her example, even in problematic directions. Any of a number of psychological difficulties can be produced by modeling.

Cognitive Contents and Processes. Cognitive-behavioral theorists believe that all of these types of learning (classical conditioning, operant conditioning, and modeling) must be placed in a cognitive context. Learning does not automatically occur just because certain environmental events take place. It occurs most readily for a thinking organism. Even the simplest examples of learning may reflect the influence of expectations (Schwartz 1984). Theorists have accordingly introduced a host of cognitive constructs.

One way to bring some order to cognitive theorizing is by distinguishing the content of thought from its process. Cognitive contents are mental representations: particular thoughts and beliefs. We transform and utilize these representations by using cognitive processes: judging, decision making, and problem solving. Our cognitive contents are organized. A *schema* refers to an organized set of beliefs about some subject, for example, your sense of who you are: your strengths, weaknesses, hopes, dreams, and fears. The key characteristic of a schema is that it has a structure.

Various principles have been suggested as a way of describing the organization of our different schemas (Taylor 1981). One guiding principle is consistency (Festinger 1957). People often seek out balance and harmony among their thoughts (Heider 1958). They want their ideas to be consistent with one another. Consistency can take an insidious turn if individuals happen to have a negative view of themselves. Consistency may lead them to notice only events that confirm their negative views and to ignore disconfirming ones (Mischel, Ebbesen, & Zeiss 1973). Another guiding principle is accuracy. People try to understand the facts of the world. In particular, they notice very quickly what makes them feel good or bad. A third guiding principle is self-aggrandizement. Many individuals put a positive spin on their experiences whenever possible (Taylor 1989). Depression is a notable exception.

The needs for consistency, accuracy, and self-aggrandizement influence our thoughts, and they may push us in different directions. What we think is always a compromise among them. Sometimes consistency or self-aggrandizement wins out, in which cases we change our perceptions of reality to fit how we think. Other times accuracy wins out, and we change how we think to fit the available evidence.

Psychopathology. According to the cognitive-behavioral model, people's problems are not intrinsically different from their normal behavior; rather, all actions are produced by the same processes of learning and thinking. People encounter difficulties either when they are placed in situations that encourage problems or when they happen to be ignorant, confused, or mistaken.

General dysphoria is often explained by cognitive-behavioral theorists in terms of exposure to unpredictable and uncontrollable events coupled with exaggerated beliefs about vulnerability and loss. Severe mental illness is seen in similar terms, presumably brought out by highly unusual experiences and/or ways of thinking. For example, schizophrenic individuals have difficulties in the psychological mechanisms responsible for selective attention. Too much information is available to them, and they think in overly inclusive terms. The hallucinations and delusions that characterize schizophrenia are derived from these attentional problems.

Intervention. To treat problems from the cognitive-behavioral view, the therapist encourages adaptive habits, behavioral or cognitive or both. Clients are helped to see the world more accurately and to solve problems more efficiently. Therapists equate their treatment with education, because they conceive of it as learning or relearning.

In the last few decades, a host of cognitive-behavior therapies have been developed. First was *behavior therapy,* which applied ideas of classical conditioning and operant conditioning to people's problems. Joseph Wolpe's (1958) systematic desensitization was one of the first such therapies to be widely used. A person is asked to imagine a series of increasingly disturbing images while deeply relaxed. This process is repeated until the images no longer elicit fear. Systematic desensitization continues to be one of the most effective treatments for specific phobias.

Next was the development of strategies based on modeling (Bandura 1969). Behavior change need not occur through trial and error. Sometimes people can shed old habits and acquire new ones by watching other individuals behave in adaptive ways. A person who is afraid of spiders or snakes is helped by watching someone else approach them without fear.

At the same time there appeared therapies assuming that people's problems are brought about by the thoughts and beliefs they entertain. An effective way to treat problems would thus involve changing these thoughts and beliefs. These cognitive interventions were foreshadowed by the approaches of George Kelly (1955), whose fixed-role therapy encouraged people to try out specific roles in order to experience the perspectives that went along with them, and Albert Ellis (1962), whose rational-emotive therapy identified and challenged people's irrational beliefs, chiefly those that were rigid and absolutist: "I must make $125,000 a year in order to be happy."

Today, one of the best-known cognitive interventions is *cognitive therapy*, which targets for change the negative thoughts that depressed people hold about themselves (Beck et al. 1979). They are encouraged to evaluate their ideas against relevant evidence, testing the "reality" of their beliefs. Cognitive therapy has also been used to treat anxiety disorders characterized by exaggerated beliefs about vulnerability.

In cognitive therapy, a client may be told to carry out experiments that allow the gathering of pertinent evidence. Clients who regard themselves as social losers might be instructed to invite ten different people to share a cup of coffee during a break at work. What is the anticipated versus actual result? Of course, if a therapist suggests such experiments, they should not be overly stringent. Then they will fail and confirm the client's negative views. If there is reason to suspect that all ten people will refuse to have coffee with the client, this experiment is best left on the drawing board. Perhaps the person should be instructed on *how* to ask somebody to have a cup of coffee.

In this example, you see how cognitive treatment slides into behavioral treatment, hence the growing trend to combine these approaches to abnormality and its remediation. This combination is called *cognitive-behavior therapy*. Indeed, one good way to change how people think is to change how they behave, and vice versa (Bandura 1986).

Today it makes sense to speak of a cognitive-behavioral model of abnormality; we can subsume the various techniques of behavior therapy and cognitive therapy under this umbrella and call them cognitive-behavior therapy (Mahoney 1974; Meichenbaum 1977). Many "behavioral" techniques pay attention to mental occurrences; even the epitome of behavior therapy, systematic desensitization, employs mental images to bring about behavioral change. And many cognitive therapies take into account rewards and punishments.

Cognitive-behavioral techniques have been used with a variety of problems, often with very good success (Emmelkamp 1994; Engels, Garnefski, & Diekstra 1993; Hollon & Beck 1994). In some cases, like infantile autism or organic brain disorder, the problem is not eradicated so much as the individual is helped to compensate or cope. In other cases, such as a specific phobia or sexual dysfunction, the problem indeed goes away. These techniques are presumably effective in eliminating problems when they can undo basic causes. They may also be effective in helping an individual cope by providing an alternative way of reaching some goal.

Cognitive-behavioral approaches also have their share of difficulties. They seem to work best when problems fit their formula – that is, when the problem is circumscribed, behavioral, and associated with immediately accessible thoughts. When problems do not readily fit this framework, cognitive-behavior therapy is apt to be misdirected.

Some advocates regard cognitive-behavioral approaches as superior to drug-based therapies because they effect long-lasting changes in behavior or cognition, as opposed to temporary changes in biochemistry (Rush et al. 1977). But the facts do not support the conclusion that cognitive-behavioral changes are always permanent. In many cases, they are not. Nor are they as general across situations as we might want.

This failure represents not only a practical problem but also a theoretical one. Part of the rationale for cognitive-behavioral approaches is the assumption that people have problems because they have not learned "appropriate" ways of being happy and winning rewards. Therapy facilitates this new learning. The person without social skills should find a whole new world opened up once these skills have been acquired. Depression or anxiety stemming from this lack of knowledge about social skills should be permanently precluded. But this is not always so. Short-term benefits are simply that. Why do the new skills not lead to a dramatically different life?

One possible answer is that the environment did not change, and thus it cannot sustain the changes in behavior. If a person lives in an objectively distressing world then any therapy, no matter how successful, is likely to appear ineffective when he or she returns home. Treatment cannot make someone oblivious to the world. Another possible answer is that the changes brought about by cognitive-behavior therapy are not always sufficiently deep. If these changes take place on only a superficial level then they can be dislodged. This criticism points, perhaps, to the need for these approaches to address the physiological, emotional, and unconscious levels of problems.

Humanistic-Existential-Phenomenological Model

The psychodynamic and cognitive-behavioral models try to specify the causes of problems. Their approach to behavior very much characterizes twentieth-century psychology, especially in the United States. But there have been voices of dissent that gave rise to several important strands of thought. These dissenting traditions regard human behavior as freely chosen and inappropriately explained in terms of cause and effect. These traditions also have something to say about the nature of abnormality and its treatment.

Key Concepts. *Humanism* is the doctrine that the needs and values of human beings take precedence over material things, and further that people cannot be studied simply as part of the material world. Humanists argue that psychologists may miss what is most important about people by focusing on the supposed causes of behavior, as if people were simply billiard balls, doing poorly or well depending on whatever happens to ricochet into them. Many psychologists are in turn impatient with humanistic theories, which seem vague and impossible to test.

Well-known psychologists within the humanist tradition include Abraham Maslow (1954) and Carl Rogers (1961). Both emphasized that people strive to make the most of their potential in a process called self-actualization, which can be thwarted by various conditions. But if these conditions are changed then the potential within each individual will necessarily unfold.

This approach is a very different way of thinking about human nature, one that stresses the goals for which people strive, their conscious awareness of this striving, the importance of their own choices, and their rationality. Hence the focus is directed away from mechanical causes and toward fundamental questions about existence and meaning.

The humanistic models often overlap with another viewpoint, termed *existentialism*. The critical idea of existentialism is that a person's experience is primary. To understand any individual is to understand him or her subjectively, from the inside out. Existentialists see people as products of their own choices, which are freely undertaken. To use their phrase, existence precedes essence, with essence understood to mean a person's particular characteristics. They also stress that there is no fixed human nature, only the sort of person that each unique individual becomes by the self-definition he or she chooses.

As applied specifically to psychology, these humanistic and existential viewpoints have several emphases (Urban 1983):

- the significance of the individual,
- the complex organization of the individual,
- the capacity for change inherent in the individual,
- the significance of conscious experience,
- the self-regulatory nature of human activity.

Implicit here is a criticism of scientific psychology as typically conducted, because it does not deal with what is most important about people (Maslow 1966).

Humanists and existential theorists believe that psychologists must pay more attention to an individual's way of seeing the world, and here they join ranks with yet another intellectual movement, *phenomenology,* which attempts to describe a person's conscious experience in terms meaningful for that individual. Phenomenology has a superficial resemblance to cognitive approaches in that both are concerned with thoughts and thinking, but this similarity is misleading. Cognitive approaches start by specifying the terms with which to describe "cognition" and then use this theoretical language to describe the thoughts of all people. In contrast, phenomenologists start with the experience of a specific individual and then attempt to describe it.

Many models of abnormality are antithetical to the phenomenological goal of describing experience, because the theoretical terms introduced by these models turn people into objects, denying them – by implication – any experience. Scottish psychiatrist Ronald D. Laing (1959) has eloquently phrased this critique. He points out that psychologists and psychiatrists describe schizophrenic symptoms with colorful terms like word salad, loose associations, and poverty of speech; this makes schizophrenic individuals seem like broken machines. Laing advised us to listen to what "abnormal" people communicate, because their experience – even when at odds with our own – is still their defining characteristic, just as our own experience defines us.

Psychopathology. Humanistic, existential, and phenomenological psychologists are not much concerned with traditional diagnosis. Although they recognize that people have problems, their view of them is quite different. Problems ensue when people experience a discrepancy between their sense of who they are and the way the world treats them. Sometimes the world is to blame, in the sense of creating circumstances that lead individuals to doubt their own choices (Rogers 1942). Sometimes people have made poor choices by not declaring to themselves their true intentions. Simply put, problems are seen as derailments along the way to self-actualization.

People have a central fear, according to many theorists in this tradition, and this fear is one of nonexistence – death. Needless to say, all of us will die, but many of us fail to confront this eventuality. In denying death, we fail to live in an authentic way and fall short of actualizing our potential. Fear of death and our failure to deal with this fear may figure in cases of general dysphoria characterized by anxiety and depression.

Severe mental illness must similarly be examined from the inside out. In a well-known case study, Laing (1959) recounted the story of Peter, a young man diagnosed as schizophrenic. Among his symptoms was smelling something rotten that no one else could detect. We could simply call this an olfactory hallucination and be done with it, but Laing delved into Peter's experience. He discovered that Peter had been raised in a family where he was not exactly abused but rather ignored – in a profound way. His parents fed him and clothed him, but otherwise paid him absolutely no heed. They went about their business in their small apartment as if their son did not exist.

Peter came to experience the world in a highly idiosyncratic way. He never developed a sense of intersubjective reality: the convention that certain experiences are "public" because other people treat them as real, whereas other experiences are "private" because other people do not acknowledge them. Peter never regarded his experiences as public versus private because his parents never validated or invalidated any of them. So what if other people did not experience smells in the way that Peter did? None of his experiences had intersubjective reality. To call his experience a "hallucination" is to disregard its significance. Simply diagnosing Peter as a schizophrenic is inadequate if our goal is to understand and eventually help another human being.

Intervention. Most humanistic, existential, and phenomenological approaches to treatment were proposed by therapists originally trained in the psychoanalytic tradition. Disenchanted, these therapists articulated their own views of human nature, problems, and treatments. They described people's problems with terms like angst, despair, crisis, and failure to take responsibility. These problems are aspects of the human experience, and they can be changed only by encouraging the person to confront them and choose to act more forthrightly (Greenberg, Elliott, & Lietar 1994).

Viktor Frankl (1975), a well-known existential theorist and therapist, devised strategies that illustrate this point. For example, in dereflection, people are encouraged to turn from their own problems to those of others. An insecure and depressed individual might be told to do volunteer work in a hospice. An aggressive and hostile person might be asked to undertake relief work for victims of famine. The purpose of dereflection is not to distract oneself but rather to cultivate self-understanding and to provide meaning to one's own life.

Among the best-known humanistic therapies is the client-centered therapy developed by Carl Rogers (1951). Although originally trained in psychoanalytic therapy, Rogers found it less than useful for many of the problems he encountered among his clients. He proposed his own view of human nature, one in which people know their own problems and also how to solve them if only they could be placed in a setting that encouraged their natural wisdom. And thus his therapy emphasized the creation of a supportive atmosphere – one characterized by genuineness, empathy, and unconditional positive regard. As in psychoanalysis, there is an emphasis on the characteristics of the therapist, but in contrast to a carefully cultivated neutrality we see warmth and concern. Such therapists try not to judge or evaluate what clients say. Rather, they repeat disclosures back to them in order to convey understanding and positive regard. When clients can speak openly and without hesitation about their problems, solutions may follow.

Unlike many therapists in this tradition, Rogers believed that the effectiveness of therapy was an open question that could be investigated scientifically. He conducted pioneering investigations of psychotherapy effectiveness. Several conclusions emerged from his studies (Beutler, Crago, & Arizmendi 1986). First, personal qualities of the therapist such as warmth, genuineness, and empathy are important ingredients in effective therapy, but in themselves they are not enough. Second, therapy works to the extent that people's perceptions of themselves become more consistent. Third, client-centered therapy is effective in treating milder forms of anxiety and depressive disorders, in which problems with self-esteem and self-perception predominate, but it is of more limited use when problems are more severe. Rogers conducted a well-known investigation of client-centered therapy with schizophrenia but found little evidence for its effectiveness (Rogers et al. 1967).

Family Systems Model

Some problems can be described as existing between and among people. This perspective is embodied in the family systems model, which takes the position that most problems – depression, anxiety, and substance abuse – are manifestations of disturbances in the family (Jacobson & Addis 1993).

Key Concepts. Family systems theories usually agree on several points (Haley 1976; Minuchin 1974; Stanton 1981). Most basically, individuals must be located in their immediate social context, and usually this means their family. Each family has a unique style or character which shows itself in repetitive patterns of interactions among family members. Also, each family is regarded as a complex system, with every person's behavior simultaneously a cause and an effect of everyone else's behavior. It is therefore difficult, if not impossible, to specify simple cause–effect relationships within the family. This model instead focuses on the factors existing among family members that maintain the behavioral status quo. The status quo is called *homeostasis:* balance among the behaviors of the family members. Conflicts in one aspect of the system are counteracted by changes elsewhere in an attempt to restore homeostasis.

Psychopathology. In a healthy family, the status quo is one in which the individuals can thrive as individuals as well as family members. But in other families, the status quo is achieved at a cost. An individual might develop symptoms as a way of compensating for problems elsewhere in the family. Family systems theorists call the family member with symptoms the "identified patient," making the point that this person is merely the one who shows family problems most blatantly.

Stanton (1981: 364) provides the following example of how a disturbed family takes its obvious toll on one family member:

> Spouse A is driving and Spouse B is in a hurry to get to their destination. . . . A accelerates through a yellow light, B . . . criticizes A, who retorts and steps on the gas. B protests more loudly, A shouts back, and the child, C, starts to cry. At this point the argument stops, while B attends to C and A slows down.

If this pattern repeats itself over and over, then the child runs the risk of being seen as having an emotional problem, although the child's "problem" obviously serves a purpose. It reduces the tension between the parents and restores homeostasis.

The family systems approach often places great emphasis on triangles like the one just described, regarding these as the basic unit of family interaction. When there is tension between two people in the family, a third person will often diffuse or eliminate it. Appreciate the complexity involved here, because all sorts of possible triangles exist even within a small family.

The general problem with the family systems approach is that it may be circular. Given a family member with a problem, it is often assumed without independent verification that family dynamics must be responsible. Other family members may be blamed for enabling the difficulty rather than seen simply as bystanders or indeed as victims themselves.

Different psychological problems are explained in terms of the particular ways in which a family achieves homeostasis. A family member may develop a circumscribed symptom – such as a phobia about traveling – if this is a way to distract the family as a whole from fighting about how to spend summer vacations. More severe problems reflect gross difficulties in family styles of communication. Several theories of schizophrenia, for example, propose that the disorder is most likely to occur in families where messages are consistently disguised, contradictory, or accompanied by strong criticism (Bateson et al. 1956; Lidz 1975). Research does not support the hypothesis that such family styles cause schizophrenia, but there is good evidence that the family environment plays a role in maintaining or exacerbating schizophrenia once present (Leff & Vaughn 1985).

Intervention. Family systems theorists, not surprisingly, feel that problems are best dealt with by treating the family as a whole. Couples therapy or family therapy accordingly is undertaken. The goal of the therapist is to intervene so that a new equilibrium can be established in the couple or the family, one without victims.

The idea of homeostasis leads the family systems therapist to expect resistance by the family to change. The family's style of relating, however unhealthy, is the status quo, and it maintains itself. Therefore, the therapist must be a strategist, planning treatments that create change (Haley 1973). One way of conducting this strategic form of therapy is with reframing interventions: techniques that encourage a more benign interpretation of what is going on. Also part of the repertoire of family systems therapists are so-called paradoxical interventions, suggestions that subtly communicate the message "don't change." In resisting these sorts of interventions, the family ends up changing (Haley 1973, 1976).

On the average, couples who go through couples therapy fare better than those who do not, tending to resolve conflicts more satisfactorily and staying together longer (Alexander, Holtzworth-Monroe, & Jameson 1994; Dunn & Schwebel 1995). It seems to work better for younger couples and for those who have not begun divorce proceedings. In any event, this kind of therapy proves more effective in solving marital problems than does individual therapy undertaken with only one spouse.

Couples therapy can also be of help as a treatment for ostensibly "individual" problems, including depression, substance abuse, and obesity (Black, Gleser, & Kooyers 1990; Jacobson, Holtzworth-Munroe, & Schmaling 1989; O'Farrell 1989). Although each of these problems has numerous determinants, among the important influences may be interpersonal processes that couples therapy can address.

In family therapy, the therapist attempts to establish a healthy equilibrium within the family. Studies show that this kind of therapy is often effective for reducing conflicts and resolving specific problems such as bulimia (Cox & Merkel 1989); it sometimes exceeds individual therapy in effectiveness (DeWitt 1978). Family therapy also has proven to be of value as an adjunct to individual treatment of problems like substance abuse, bipolar disorder, and schizophrenia (Lebow & Gurman 1995). This kind of therapy can also help individuals and their families adjust to life-threatening and chronic physical illnesses such as cancer, AIDS, or Alzheimer's disease.

Conclusions

Psychologists have long hoped that a given approach would answer all of the questions we might pose about each and every disorder. This hope has not been realized for any of the existing models. Rather, each model has what Kelly (1955) termed a "focus of convenience," a domain of the world (in this case, abnormality) where it works particularly well. And each model certainly encounters aspects of abnormality where it falls short. Put another way, there is no best psychological model of abnormality. Indeed, it may be impossible to evaluate any of these models as a whole, much less to make across-the-board comparisons. The task of the theorist and the practitioner is to identify those purposes for which a given model is best suited. For a given disorder, which model best accounts for its risk factors and mechanisms? Which model generates the most demonstrably effective treatments?

As noted in the introduction to this chapter, many contemporary psychologists try to integrate the insights of the different models of abnormality, along with the contributions of biological and sociocultural perspectives (Peterson 1996). *All* problems, circumscribed or severe, are profitably viewed as having a biological basis and as residing in a social context. The psychological mechanisms specified by the theories described in this chapter play critical roles as well. Adding to the complexity of a fully integrated perspective on abnormality is the mutual influence among all of these factors.

6

Sociological Approaches to Mental Illness

Peggy A. Thoits

The sociological approach focuses on factors external to the individual – the environmental or social context – and views mental illness as a breakdown in the face of overwhelming environmental stress. Thoits provides an overview of three dominant social theories and describes their basic assumptions, advantages and limitations, and implications for treating or preventing mental illness. Stress theory assumes that accumulations of social stressors can precipitate mental health problems. However, the relationship between stress exposure and psychiatric symptoms is not strong because individuals have extensive coping resources to help them handle stress. Stress researchers focus on the relationship between stress and coping mechanisms, and also on the unequal distribution of chronic strains and a variety of coping resources in the population. In order to treat mental illness, one needs to eliminate or reduce stressors, teach the affected individuals different coping strategies, and bolster their personal resources. Structural strain theory locates the origins of disorder and distress in the broader organization of society. For example, structural conditions such as hard economic times can cause people to experience major stressors and can provoke mental illness. In order to prevent or reduce mental illness, society should be restructured to reduce levels of stressors or to enhance coping capacities. A third approach to mental illness is labeling, or societal reaction theory (to be described in detail in Chapter 7). The logic behind labeling theory is that treatment of mental illness may exacerbate the conditions of people called mentally ill. Symptoms of mental illness are viewed as violations of the normative order whereby individuals violate taken-for-granted rules about how one should think, feel, and behave. One way to reduce or prevent mental illness is to change the standards that define what is normal and what is abnormal behavior. The student should think about the various ways the three sociological approaches to mental illness complement each other as well as how they complement the biological and psychological understandings of mental disorder.

The three general approaches to mental illness that are discussed in this volume can be broadly characterized by their underlying metaphors. The biological or medical approach views mental illness as if it were a disease or physical defect in the brain or body. The psychological approach treats it as if it were a sickness or abnormality in the mind or psyche (i.e., the soul). Finally, the sociological approach views mental illness as if it were a breakdown in the face of overwhelming environmental stress. The key distinction between the biological and psychological perspectives, on the one hand, and the sociological perspective, on the other, is the location of the primary cause of mental illness. From the biological and psychological approaches, the determinants of mental illness are internal – "in" the person (in the physical body or in the person's mind). From a sociological approach, the cause is external – in the environment or in the person's social situation. Although obviously oversimplifying the differences among the three approaches, this characterization helps clarify the focus of this chapter: the social (rather than biological and psychological) origins of mental illness.

Within the social approach, there are three dominant theories of mental illness etiology, the study of the origins or causes of a disorder. These are stress theory, structural strain theory, and labeling theory. This chapter reviews each theory's basic concepts and assumptions, theoretical limitations and advantages, and implications for treating or preventing mental illness.

Stress Theory

Hans Selye, a physiological researcher, introduced the term "stress" into scientific discourse in the mid-1930s. By stress or "stressors" he meant anything that puts wear and tear on the body, usually noxious environmental stimuli. Because he experimented with laboratory animals, stressors meant such conditions as extreme heat or cold, overcrowded cages, and repeated electric shocks. Selye (1956) showed that animals progress through three physical stages of reaction when exposed to prolonged noxious stimuli. He called these three stages the general adaptation syndrome (G.A.S.).

In the first stage, the alarm reaction, the animal responds to stress with what others have called the "fight or flight" syndrome (Cannon 1929). Briefly, the animal becomes physiologically aroused and thus physically ready to fight aggressively or to flee from threat. Selye showed that all laboratory animals respond with similar states of physiological readiness, marked by increased production of adrenocortical hormones (adrenaline, for example, which increases heart rate, blood pressure, and perspiration), decreased immune functioning (because of changes in the lymph glands), weight loss, and irritation of the stomach lining. In the second stage, the stage of resistance, the body returns to equilibrium but at a higher than usual level of aroused readiness to continue combatting the effects of stress or threat. In the final stage of exhaustion, the body's physical defenses become depleted and the animal is likely to succumb to disease or infection. Selye showed that prolonged or repeated exposure to noxious stressors would almost inevitably produce illness in laboratory animals.

Because laboratory studies convincingly showed a relationship between prolonged or repeated stress exposure and disease in animals, speculation turned to the effects of stress on human beings. Researchers began to focus on *social* stressors – in particular, on major life events (Holmes & Rahe 1967). Thomas Holmes and Richard Rahe defined life events as major changes in people's lives that require extensive behavioral readjustments. They hypothesized that extensive readjustment of behavior could overtax a person's ability to cope or adapt, thus leaving the person more vulnerable to physical illness, injury, or even death. To test this hypothesis, Holmes and Rahe first went through the medical records of Navy personnel, recording the most common life events that preceded Navy men's doctor visits and hospitalizations, abstracting a list of 43 major life events. Next they asked groups of people to judge (independently of one another) how much behavioral readjustment each event on their list required. They assigned a readjustment score of 500 units to "getting married" and asked their judges to assign scores ranging from 0 to 1,000 to other events with marriage as their comparison or standard. For each event, Holmes and Rahe averaged the judges' scores and divided the result by 100 (to simplify the scores), obtaining what they called "life change units" or LCU scores. Table 6.1 shows the resulting Social Readjustment Rating Scale (SRRS), with Holmes and Rahe's 43 events ordered by their average LCU scores (i.e., by the amounts of behavioral readjustment that people believe they require).

This life events checklist gave social researchers an easy way to assess whether exposure to social stressors would have health consequences for human beings. The answer was clear: The more life events that individuals experienced in a given period of time (say, during six months or a year) and the higher their LCU scores, the more likely they would have an injury, an illness, or even die (Cohen & Williamson 1991; Kessler, Price, & Wortman 1985b; Lin & Ensel 1989; Rodin & Salovey 1989). Literally thousands of studies showed a significant relationship between the amount of life change that one experienced and illness, including heart attacks, strokes, tuberculosis, ulcers, asthma attacks, flu, and even the common cold (Cohen 1996). More exciting to mental health researchers was that major life changes and LCU scores were significantly associated with the onset of anxiety, depression, schizophrenia, and generalized states of psychological distress. An accumulation of social stressors, then, could precipitate mental health problems.

You may notice that there are several problems with the Holmes and Rahe SRRS. For example, there are many important life events missing from the list (e.g., losing custody of one's children, "coming out of the closet," gaining a stepparent); in fact, subsequent life events checklists have been expanded to include anywhere from 100 to 200 events (Dohrenwend et al. 1978a). Another problem is that the events on the SRRS tend to be ones that happen primarily to males and whites; events that are experienced more by women or minority group members are underrepresented. Also, many items on the SRRS are possible symptoms of psychological problems rather than life events in themselves (e.g., change in eating habits, change in sleeping habits, sexual difficulties). Researchers have since gone to extensive lengths to eliminate these and other problems (Wethington, Brown, & Kessler 1995). With improved life events measurement, the same basic relationships reported in this volume are still found.

Soon after the discovery of these basic relationships, investigators' attention turned to the types of stressors that were most likely to precede the onset of mental

Table 6.1. *The Social Readjustment Rating Scale*

Rank	Event	Life change units
1	Death of spouse	100
2	Divorce	73
3	Marital separation	65
4	Jail term	63
5	Death of close family member	63
6	Personal injury or illness	53
7	Marriage	50
8	Fired at work	47
9	Marital reconciliation	45
10	Retirement	45
11	Change in health of family member	44
12	Pregnancy	39
13	Sex difficulties	39
14	Gain of new family member	39
15	Business readjustment	39
16	Change in financial state	38
17	Death of close friend	37
18	Change to different line of work	36
19	Change in number of arguments with spouse	35
20	Mortgage or loan over $10,000	31
21	Foreclosure of mortgage or loan	30
22	Change in responsibilities at work	29
23	Son or daughter leaving home	29
24	Trouble with in-laws	29
25	Outstanding personal achievement	28
26	Wife begins or stops work	26
27	Begin or end school	26
28	Change in living conditions	25
29	Revision of personal habits	24
30	Trouble with boss	23
31	Change in work hours or conditions	20
32	Change in residence	20
33	Change in schools	20
34	Change in recreation	19
35	Change in church	19
36	Change in social activities	18
37	Mortgage or loan less than $10,000	17
38	Change in sleeping habits	16
39	Change in number of family get-togethers	15
40	Change in eating habits	15
41	Vacation	13
42	Christmas	12
43	Minor violations of the law	11

Source: Reprinted from T. A. Holmes and R. H. Rahe, "The Social Readjustment Rating Scale," *Journal of Psychosomatic Research* 11 (1967), with permission from Elsevier Science.

illness. It is important to understand that people often use the term "stress" ambiguously: it can refer to the cause of psychological problems or it can describe one's subjective emotional experience (e.g., "I feel so stressed"). To avoid this ambiguity, researchers usually restrict the terms "stress" and "stressor" to refer to major life events and chronic strains – the environmental causes of emotional problems. The phrases "stress reaction" or "stress response" are used to distinguish emotional consequences from their environmental causes. In this book, psychological distress and mental disorder are the stress reactions of primary concern, and major life events and chronic strains are the causal agents.

Notice that Holmes and Rahe's scale implicitly assumes that *all* life events, both positive and negative, can require behavioral readjustment and thus overtax individuals' coping resources and leave them physically or emotionally vulnerable. However, researchers next found that when events were subdivided into culturally desirable (or positive) and culturally undesirable (or negative) types, undesirable events were more strongly associated with psychological problems than were desirable ones (Brown & Harris 1978; Ross & Mirowsky 1979). George Brown and Tirril Harris's pathbreaking sociological study of life events and depression offers compelling evidence.

Brown and Harris randomly selected about 460 women in the Camberwell district of London for in-depth interviews. Through the interviews they established whether any of the women met the clinical criteria for major depression and, if so, the month when the depression had begun. About 15% of the women were found to be clinically depressed at the time of the study. A central part of the interview canvassed all of the major life changes and chronic difficulties the women had experienced over the past year or up to the time of depression onset. This was not a simple checklist type of assessment but instead an in-depth, probing discussion of the various changes and difficulties the women had been through in the past year.

Brown and Harris defined "severe" life events as negative events that most people would agree are serious long-term threats to personal well-being. They found that severe events predicted the onset of major depression much better than nonsevere events (i.e., minor negative events and positive events). Among the Camberwell women who were clinically depressed, 68% had had at least one severe negative event in the previous nine months; among those who were not depressed, only 20% had had one or more severe events in the prior nine months. Virtually equal percentages of the depressed and nondepressed women had had at least one nonsevere event in the past nine months (about 15%). Brown and Harris concluded that major negative life events precede – and make individuals vulnerable to – clinical depression.

These researchers discovered, too, that ongoing difficulties (also called "chronic strains" in the stress literature) were almost as important as severe negative events in predicting depression (see also Pearlin et al. 1981). Examples of ongoing difficulties are living in overcrowded conditions, having persistent family arguments, and having too little money to buy necessary food, clothes, or medicine. Among the clinically depressed women, 49% had had at least one major difficulty in their lives which had lasted at least two years and which was rated by independent judges as severe (very threatening to well-being); among the nondepressed women, only 17% had had a major difficulty during the same time period. When severe events and long-term major difficulties were considered together, Brown and Harris found that, overall, 89% of the depressed women had experienced one or the other or both in the past nine months; only 30% of the nondepressed women had had events or difficulties or both during the same time period. In short, acute negative events and chronic strains put individuals at much higher risk of developing major depression. Not *all* changes (positive and negative) but only negative changes in people's lives are causes of psychological problems.

Subsequent research showed that negative events and chronic strains also predicted the onset of schizophrenia, anxiety attacks, and milder states of depression and generalized distress (Aneshensel 1992; Avison & Turner 1988; Brown & Harris 1989; Pearlin et al. 1981; Thoits 1983; Turner 1995). In other words, acute events and chronic strains (the latter defined as environmental demands that require repeated or daily readjustments in behavior over long periods of time) are causally implicated in a variety of forms of mental illness, from mild to marked. Research also pinpointed the types of events – those that are nonnormative, unexpected, uncontrollable, and clustered in time – that more often precede psychological disorder. You will learn more about these various types of stressors and their effects in Part II of this volume.

As findings on the psychological effects of stress mounted, researchers began to turn their attention to a related problem: Although there clearly is a relationship between exposure to stressors and the subsequent development of psychological problems, this relationship is not strong. The strength of a relationship is measured as a correlation. A *correlation* between two variables ranges in value from 0.0 (no relationship at all) to 1.0 (a perfect positive relationship – i.e., for each negative event experienced there is an accompanying unit increase in psychological symptoms). Most studies report correlations around 0.3, which is a modest correlation between stressors and symptoms of psychological distress or disorder. In other words, many people who experience severe stressors do *not* become disturbed, while others who experience few or minor stressors *do*. Why is this?

According to elaborations of stress theory (Lazarus & Folkman 1984; Pearlin 1989; Pearlin et al. 1981), the modest correlation between stress exposure and symptoms occurs because many individuals have extensive coping resources and use effective coping strategies when handling stressful demands, thus buffering the negative psychological impacts of those demands. "Coping resources" refer to social and personal characteristics that people rely on when dealing with stressors (Pearlin & Schooler 1978). A key *social* resource is one's social network, from which one can obtain emotional and practical support when facing stressors (social support is emotional or practical assistance received from significant others such as family or friends). Two important *personal* (or personality) resources for coping are self-esteem and a sense of control or mastery over life. People who have high self-esteem and those who strongly believe that they are in control of their lives are more likely to engage in active problem-solving efforts to overcome difficulties (Folkman 1984; Pearlin et al. 1981) or to use a variety of coping strategies flexibly to meet stressful demands (Mattlin, Wethington, & Kessler 1990; Pearlin & Schooler 1978).

Coping strategies are usually defined as behavioral or cognitive attempts to manage situational demands that one perceives as taxing or exceeding one's ability to adapt (Lazarus & Folkman 1984). Coping strategies are typically subdivided into two types: problem-focused and emotion-focused. Problem-focused coping efforts are directed at changing or eliminating the stressful demands themselves, whereas emotion-focused strategies are attempts to alter one's emotional reactions to stressful demands. In most stressful episodes, people use both types of strategies (Folkman & Lazarus 1980). For example, when facing a major exam, students may attack the problem by studying an hour or two each day and practicing answers to possible test questions. They also may control their anxiety by telling themselves that they understand more of the material than other students do, reminding themselves that they have done well before on these kinds of tests, and perhaps engaging in some strenuous exercise to ease physical tension.

As Chapters 8 and 10 will show in more detail, coping resources (social support, self-esteem, a strong sense of control) and coping strategies "buffer," or reduce, the negative psychological impacts of stressors. This is why the relationship between stress exposure and psychological problems is far from perfect: in essence, some people are able to protect themselves from being overwhelmed by stressful demands (conversely, some people are poorly equipped to protect themselves because they lack social support or a sense of control over their lives or have not acquired efficacious coping strategies). Of crucial importance to sociologists of mental health is the finding that life events and chronic strains – as well as social support, self-esteem, and a sense of mastery – are *unequally distributed* in the population, leaving some groups of people (e.g., women, the elderly, the very young, the unmarried, those of low socioeconomic status) both more likely to experience certain stressors and more vulnerable to the effects of stressors in general (Turner 1995; Turner & Marino 1994; Turner & Roszell 1994). These key findings (discussed in more detail throughout Part II) point very clearly to the important role that social factors can play in the etiology of mental illness and psychological distress. Moreover, they suggest an explanation for the higher rates of mental disorder and psychological distress found in lower-status, disadvantaged groups (see Chapter 14) – these are the groups that are more likely to be exposed to stressors and less likely to have important coping resources.

The advantages of stress theory are several. First, the theory focuses on aspects of the individual's current social situation, which the biological and psychological approaches tend to de-emphasize or ignore. Second, it helps to explain why psychological distress and disorder occur more frequently in lower-status groups than in higher-status groups, patterns that the biological and psychological perspectives have difficulty explaining parsimoniously. Third, stress theory allows for more direct empirical testing than the biological and psychological approaches do. Conventional survey and interview methods allow researchers to measure key concepts (e.g., stress, coping, social support) and to test relationships among them explicitly, unlike biological studies where researchers can only infer an association between (say) serotonin uptake and major depression from the effects of specific drugs. Similarly, psychological researchers must assume a relationship between childhood traumatic experiences and mental illness from the effects of psychotherapy, which often unearths such past experiences. Finally, as you will see in later chapters, there is considerable empirical evidence that supports the stress explanation of psychological disturbance. Despite these advantages, however, the limitations of the theory should not be ignored.

One key limitation is that stress theory cannot explain why this person and not that one became mentally ill; in other words, it cannot explain individual cases of psychological disorder. Stress theory is better suited to explaining group differences in psychological problems – for example, why lower-class people are more likely to have a mental disorder in their lifetimes than middle- and upper-class people are, or why people without social support are more vulnerable to stressors than people who have it. Second, stress theory is *nonspecific* with respect to outcomes: it does not explain why some groups are more prone to certain disorders while other groups develop different disorders (e.g., why women become depressed and anxious, why men develop antisocial personality disorder and more often abuse drugs and alcohol – for more on this see Chapter 19). Finally, the theory does not apply equally well to all types of mental disorders. Stress theory is very relevant to what used to be called neuroses (now called affective and anxiety disorders) and to adjustment disorders – people clearly can become depressed or anxious or have trouble adjusting in response to stressors. It is more difficult to explain the etiology of psychoses with stress theory; psychoses by their very seriousness and complexity seem to require additional explanatory factors, such as genetic predisposition, imbalances of certain chemicals in the brain, faulty childhood socialization, or early traumatic experiences. In short, to explain psychoses and perhaps most clinical disorders adequately, one might better employ diathesis-stress theory (Rosenthal 1970), which argues that disorder is the result of a *diathesis* (technically, a constitutional or genetic weakness, but more generally used to mean "vulnerability") combined with exposure to stress. Diathesis-stress theory suggests that stress experience alone is not sufficient to cause mental disorder; instead, stressors may cause disorder when they occur along with other vulnerability factors in a person's body, psyche, or circumstances.

The treatment implications of stress theory are straightforward and quite different from biological and psychological approaches. To treat or prevent mental illness one needs to change the individual's situation (eliminating or reducing stressors), teach the person different coping responses (allowing better management of stressors), or bolster personal and social resources (e.g., by increasing available social support, raising self-esteem, or empowering a stronger sense of control). Because directly changing people's life situations can be intrusive and expensive, interventions aimed at people's actual sources of stress are less frequently attempted than efforts aimed at their coping strategies or their personal and social resources. Some well-crafted experiments (see e.g. Price et al. 1988) show quite clearly that interventions which change people's coping strategies and which bolster their social support do, in fact, reduce their emotional reactions in response to major life events (e.g., a diagnosis of cancer, major surgery, divorce, unemployment). Thus, stress theory offers real promise for devising preventive mental health interventions.

Structural Strain Theory

"Structural strain theory" is an umbrella term that covers a number of more specific sociological hypotheses about mental illness etiology. In contrast to stress theory, which focuses on specific events and strains as the causal factors in people's mental health, structural strain theory locates the origins of distress and disorder in the broader organization of society, where some social groups are disadvantaged in comparison to others. Merton's (1938) anomie theory of deviance provides a useful example of a structural strain theory.

Merton's anomie theory attempts to explain not only mental illness but the occurrence of deviant behavior in general (including criminal, addictive, and rebellious behaviors). Merton argues that American culture emphasizes success and wealth as important values; Americans are taught to desire and strive for economic success virtually above all other goals. American society also views educational attainment as one key means, if not *the* key means, to economic success. Merton assumes that most people view the educational system as a legitimate route to the widely shared goal of financial success. Unfortunately, large segments of society also perceive (correctly) that their means to success are systematically blocked. The poor and many minority group members live in neighborhoods with inadequate school facilities and poorly trained teachers; they lack the preparation, encouragement, and financial assistance to pursue higher education; and they experience class-based and race-based discrimination in schools and in the labor force, which defeats their efforts to succeed when following legitimate paths.

Merton uses the term *anomie* to describe the gap between cultural goals (desires for financial success) and the structural means to those goals (access to adequate education and employment). He argues that people who experience anomie adapt to that dilemma in one of several possible ways: by changing their goals, pursuing alternative means, or both. Merton described five adaptive responses, which are displayed in Table 6.2.

Table 6.2. *Merton's anomie theory of deviance: Responses to anomie*

Response	Adherence to cultural goal of economic success	Seek legitimate means to success
Conformity	+	+
Ritualism	−	+
Innovation	+	−
Retreatism	−	−
Rebellion	+/−	+/−

Notes: + = acceptance; − = rejection; +/− = rejection and substitution of new goals and means.

"Conformists" are people who continue to adhere to culturally shared goals and to pursue legitimate means to those goals, despite awareness that these efforts are unlikely to pay off. "Ritualists" are those who reduce their aspirations (give up the possibility of ever achieving success) yet continue to behave in socially acceptable ways (they perhaps finish high school and work steadily at some low-paying, low-prestige job). Neither conformist nor ritualist responses create major social problems. However, the remaining three adaptive responses are generally viewed as behaviorally deviant and hence socially problematic. "Innovators" are people who continue to desire and seek wealth but resort to illegitimate means to reach that goal; innovators are essentially society's criminals, from simple thieves to executives engaged in fraud and tax evasion. "Retreatists" are those who give up the goal of success *and* do not attempt to follow legitimate avenues. Instead, they retreat from the world into substance abuse or mental disorder. Finally, "rebels" are people who reject both the goals and the socially acceptable means to those goals, substituting both new goals and new avenues; these are people who lead or participate in social movements or, more threateningly, riots and rebellions. Although it is clear that Merton could have generated additional adaptive responses (e.g., a person could substitute new goals while following legitimate avenues), the central point of his analysis is this: Mental illness is an adaptive response to structural strain; more specifically, it is a response to finding one's legitimate roads to valued rewards irrevocably blocked. It is important to note that this blockage is due not to one's own inadequacies but to the structure or hierarchical organization of society, which unfairly privileges the desires and efforts of some social groups over others.

Like Merton's more general theory of deviance, most structural strain explanations of mental illness suggest that strains in macro (large-scale) social and economic systems cause higher rates of mental disorder or mental hospitalization for certain groups. Before Merton, the French sociologist Emile Durkheim (1897) analyzed the social causes of suicide, a behavior that on the surface seems highly psychological and individual in nature. Durkheim found unequal distributions of suicide within and across societies. For example, Protestants had higher rates of suicide than either Catholics or Jews; unmarried people, especially those without children, had higher rates than married people or parents; military men committed suicide at higher rates than civilians; and suicide rates were higher during times of rapid economic expansion and depression than during more stable economic periods, among many other patterns.

Searching for an underlying explanatory factor, Durkheim eventually argued that groups and societies differ in their social integration, which he defined as the degree to which people are bound together and regulated by shared norms. He maintained that norms (rules that guide appropriate behavior in specific situations) serve to moderate our passions and sustain our ties to others, preventing our desires and emotional impulses from spiraling out of control. Hence members of groups that are weakly integrated suffer from disappointment and misery because their escalating passions, unregulated by norms or relations with others, inevitably go unfulfilled. Durkheim called this kind of suicide "egoistic suicide," because individuals in poorly integrated groups are more likely to succumb to despair caused by unchecked and unfulfilled personal desires. On the other hand, Durkheim recognized that social integration can be too strong, leading some to commit what he called "altruistic suicide." In overly integrated groups, individuals subordinate their passions and impulses for the good of the group, adhering to strong rules that guide almost all aspects of daily experience (military life is a good example). When the group or society is threatened, its members are therefore more likely to sacrifice themselves for the community. Finally, Durkheim described "anomic suicide," a condition induced by rapid changes in social structure and breakdowns in norms. Durkheim's concept of anomie refers to a state of normlessness or normative confusion (notice that Merton's use of the term "anomie" is somewhat different, although related). Societies or groups undergoing rapid social or economic change (e.g., sudden increases in the divorce rate, sudden changes in the unemployment rate) frequently find that traditional rules for behavior no longer apply. The resulting sense of confusion or normlessness causes individuals' passions once again to become unregulated, plunging them into disappointment and despair.

In short, according to Durkheim, the cause of suicide resides in the degree to which a society's members are tied tightly or loosely together through shared normative expectations for behavior. A too weakly or too strongly integrated society, or a society undergoing rapid change, induces conditions of structural (in this case, system-level) strain, manifested in noticeably higher rates of suicide in its members relative to groups with moderate degrees of integration.

Evidence for Durkheim's structural theory of suicide has accumulated over the years. In a classic study, Faris and Dunham (1939) plotted the previous residences of all patients admitted to hospitals for schizophrenia and other psychoses in Chicago during the mid-1930s. They found clear patterns: schizophrenic patients lived in poor areas of the city, concentrated in the inner urban core, with high population turnover, a high percentage of rental apartments and boardinghouses, and a high percentage of foreign-born (probably immigrant) residents – thus, in neighborhoods where few people knew one another or formed lasting ties. Faris and Dunham concluded that schizophrenia was caused, in part, by prolonged social isolation. Schizophrenic patients' lack of stable, organizing ties to others is reflected not only in the isolating aspects of their residences but also in their frequent lack of employment and their tendency to be unmarried or formerly married (Braginsky, Braginsky, & Ring 1969). These are all conditions that reflect a lack of social integration.

Harvey Brenner's (1973) well-known study of the relationship between employment rates and mental hospitalization also offers some support for Durkheim's notion of anomic suicide. Brenner plotted mental hospitalization rates for new cases of psychosis against employment rates in New York from 1910 to 1960. He found that the lower the employment rate, the more new admissions to treatment for psychosis – especially for men, the young and the old, and those with less than high school education. In contrast, economic upturns were associated with lower mental hospitalization. (There was a lag of about three years between a change in the economy and a subsequent change in hospitalization rates.) Most theorists, including Brenner, interpreted these findings in terms of structural strain: hard economic times (a structural condition) probably caused people to experience major stressors in their lives, which in turn provoked mental illness and thus hospitalization for illness. It is important to note that Brenner did not show that rapid economic *expansion* was associated with increased hospitalization (as Durkheim's theory would predict). Other studies examining the relationship between sudden economic good fortune and psychological well-being have also produced mixed findings (Abrahamson 1980; Pierce 1967). The most consistent finding is that economic misfortune is psychologically disturbing, both for individuals and in large social groups.

As a careful researcher, Brenner suggested an alternative to his economic "provocation" hypothesis. His "uncovering" hypothesis was that economic recessions might have uncovered cases of psychosis already existing in the population. Under conditions of economic recession or depression, individuals who are already disturbed but still managing to work are likely to be those who are laid off first and who find it most difficult to acquire new jobs. These individuals (or their financially overtaxed families) may turn to the mental hospital as an economic safety net. Dooley and Catalano (1984a,b) identified still a third possibility, which they termed the "contextual" hypothesis: a high unemployment rate may create a context or climate of uncertainty and insecurity for everyone, thus exacerbating people's worries and difficulties in general and leading to increased mental hospitalization for psychological problems among the most vulnerable. The studies by Dooley and Catalano (1984a,b; Catalano, Dooley, & Jackson 1981) generally supported the provocation and contextual hypotheses over the uncovering hypothesis. Once again, a structural condition (here, a change in the unemployment rate) was shown to be a major cause or facilitator of psychological problems.

Underlying most of these examples of structural strain theories are two assumptions. First, a society's organization, especially its economic organization, puts some groups (minority group members, women, the unmarried, the elderly, the poor) at a social or economic disadvantage. Second, socioeconomic disadvantage is a strain that in turn leads to higher rates of emotional or psychological breakdown. Note that stress theory implicitly underlies most structural strain arguments. Structural theorists usually do not spell out these implications clearly because their thinking and empirical research stay at the aggregate or group level (i.e., their research looks at percentages of all adult men who are unmarried or rates of unemployment, for example, rather than examining individual people as cases). But it is fairly easy to see the implications of, say, high unemployment rates for the life experiences of specific persons: individuals are more likely to lose their jobs, lose income, and experience persistent financial difficulties (which may lead to marital conflict), all of which are chronic strains that may overwhelm their abilities to cope.

That stress theory is necessary to make structural strain theory sensible is one of the weaknesses of structural approaches. Structural theorists generally do not elaborate the ways in which broad social structures and broad socioeconomic trends become actualized in the lives of specific individuals, and thus they do not clarify how or why macro social trends can produce psychological distress or disorder. Structural approaches also tend to emphasize economic factors as etiologically crucial while neglecting the effects of other large-scale changes on mental health. Particularly important may be changing trends in the organization and quality of family relationships (e.g., increasing rates of divorce, absentee fathers, and child and spouse abuse). Structural theorists tend to forget that not only socioeconomic disadvantages but also interpersonal relationships are primary sources of stress and strain in people's lives, or they tend to explain macro changes in such relationships in terms of changes in the economic system.

On the other hand, structural strain theories have advantages. The most important is the unique contribution they make to theories of mental illness etiology. As you have seen earlier, mental illness is not randomly distributed in society; it is concentrated in several demographic groups that are socially and economically disadvantaged. The theory suggests that the very structure or organization of society may itself play a role in mental illness epidemiology and causality, which is an idea that stress theory does not capture and that psychological and biological theories miss altogether. (Stress theorists may recognize but usually do not capitalize on the idea that stressors may themselves be a product of the way our society is organized.) If our goal is to understand thoroughly the complex and multiple causes of mental illness, then social systems, social organizations, and the strains induced by them surely must be taken into account.

Structural strain theory suggests that, in order to prevent or reduce mental illness in society, one must intervene in fairly large-scale ways – for example, by creating guaranteed income programs to eliminate the strains of unemployment or by instituting voucher systems to equalize access to educational opportunities. Because structural solutions to the problem of mental illness require massive (and usually expensive) social programs that are difficult for policymakers to legislate and fund, the preventative implications of structural strain theory usually go untested. One exception deserves mention, however. During the early 1970s, the federal government funded a major social policy study called the Seattle and Denver Income Maintenance Experiments (SIME/DIME). Five thousand low-income families in Seattle and Denver were selected for the study, with half of the families randomly assigned to a guaranteed-income condition and the other half assigned to a control condition. Experimental families received guaranteed incomes pegged at the official poverty line ($3,800 for a family of four in 1971), at about 25% above, or nearly 50% above poverty level for a period of three to five years. The major purpose of the experiment was to determine the effects of unconditional economic support on adults' work behavior and family stability. Fortunately, the study also included repeated measures of subjects' symptoms of psychological distress. Unexpectedly, when the distress symptoms of experimental and control subjects were compared over time, there were minimal differences found between them (Thoits 1982a), suggesting that guaranteeing a stable income to working-class and poor families may not be an efficacious mental health intervention. (The experiment did have major effects on labor-force participation, divorce rates, and birth rates, often in unexpected ways – see Robins et al. 1980.) Other evidence, however, suggested that relatives and friends of the experimental families may have increased their requests or demands for help (since the experimental subjects were in relatively better economic circumstances), and these requests may have counteracted the beneficial mental health effects of receiving a guaranteed income. Such findings should remind us that social behavior is enormously complicated and that even well-planned interventions may have unintended consequences arising from a failure to anticipate or take those complexities into account.

Labeling Theory

Like structural strain theory, labeling theory (also called *societal reaction theory*) offers a uniquely sociological explanation of the causes of mental illness; some have described it as a radical sociological explanation. The theory has had enormous intellectual impact and has played an important role in the movement to deinstitutionalize the mentally ill (for further information about deinstitutionalization, see Part III).

Labeling theory is based on one key idea: *People who are labeled as deviant and treated as deviant become deviant. Deviance* refers to rule breaking or violation of norms. In the case of mental illness, symptoms of psychiatric disorder are themselves viewed as normative violations. Symptoms essentially break taken-for-granted rules (Scheff 1966a) about how people should think, feel, and behave (e.g., it is not appropriate to believe that the CIA is tapping your phones; you should not constantly feel anxious or depressed; you should not run naked and screaming through the streets).

Labeling theorists (Becker 1973; Lemert 1951; Scheff 1966a) assume that every-one violates norms at some time in their lives for any of a multitude of reasons. Reasons for rule breaking can include biological causes (fatigue, undernourish-ment, genetic abnormalities, illness), psychological causes (unhappy childhood, a need for attention, internal conflicts, low self-esteem, antisocial personality), sociological causes (role conflict, peer pressure, exposure to stressors), cultural causes (following subcultural norms that differ from those of the dominant soci-ety), economic causes (a need for money, buying prestige in the eyes of others), and even miscellaneous reasons (carelessness, accidents, sheer ignorance of the rules). Labeling theorists regard these various causes of "primary deviance" (initial rule-breaking acts – in this case, psychological symptoms) as relatively unimportant. What matters is how the social group reacts to an individual's primary deviance. This is why the theory is often called societal reaction theory.

Most often, rule-breaking acts are ignored, denied, or rationalized away by family, friends, and the rule breakers themselves; according to the theory, those primary acts are then rarely repeated. However, when individuals' norm violations are frequent, severe, or highly visible, or when rule breakers are low in power and status relative to agents of social control (i.e., police, social workers, judges, psy-chiatrists), rule breakers are much more likely to be publicly and formally labeled as deviant (in this case, mentally ill) and forced into treatment.

Why is public, official labeling so important? Once labeled and in psychiatric care, rule breakers begin to experience differential treatment on the basis of their label (Rosenhan 1973). People labeled mentally ill or disturbed are stereotypically viewed as unpredictable, dangerous to themselves or others, unable to engage in self-care, and likely to behave in bizarre ways (Scheff 1966a). These stereotypes cause others, even mental hospital staff, to treat patients as though they were ir-responsible children (Goffman 1961; Rosenhan 1973). Mental patients hear jokes about crazy people, are reminded of their past failures or inadequacies, and are pre-vented from resuming conventional adult activities (leaving the hospital grounds without permission, using the showers or a razor without staff present, making pri-vate phone calls, driving a car, returning to work, voting, seeing family or friends at will, etc.). One consequence of differential treatment, then, is blocked access to normal activities. Differential treatment also leads to association with similar deviants. In hospitals or treatment centers, patients spend more time in the com-pany of other mental patients than nonpatients. This in turn allows socialization into the mental patients' subculture; one learns a deviant world view, or a deviant set of values, which reinforces adopting a simple life within the safe, protective walls of the hospital (Braginsky et al. 1969; Goffman 1961).

The unfortunate outcome of differential treatment, according to labeling theory, is identification with the mental patient role: one takes on the identity of a mentally ill person. And because this identity becomes "who I am," mental patients continue to expect psychiatric symptoms from themselves and to exhibit symptoms. In labeling-theory terms, patients display "secondary deviance" – continued rule breaking (i.e., continued abnormal behavior or symptoms) *because* they have internalized and identified with the mental patient role. This process is an example of a self-fulfilling prophecy (Merton 1956). In short, people who are labeled as deviant and treated as deviant become deviant. Mental illness becomes the issue around which one's identity and life become organized – a "deviant career."

Why the theory has sometimes been described as radically sociological may now be clear: it turns our usual causal thinking about mental illness on its head. Deviance or mental illness is not "in" the person's biology or psyche nor even primarily caused by the individual's life situation. Instead, mental illness is created and sustained by society itself. In his book *Outsiders,* Becker (1973: 9) sums it up this way:

> Social groups create deviance by making rules whose infraction constitutes deviance, and by applying those rules to particular people and labeling them as outsiders. From this point of view, deviance is not a quality of the act the person commits, but rather a consequence of the application by others of rules and sanctions to an "offender." The deviant is one to whom that label has been successfully applied; deviant behavior is behavior that people so label.

Essentially, then, chronic mental patients are victims of labeling and differential treatment by others, and they would not be chronic patients otherwise. Chapter 7 elaborates this theory further and will examine the evidence both for and against its tenets. For now it is sufficient simply to point out that there are a number of problems with the theory, at least as it was originally formulated (for solutions to some of these problems, see Link 1987 and Link et al. 1987). Clearly, the theory best applies to patients who have been involuntarily committed to treatment and to those who have become chronically ill. Because a majority (about 70%) of patients seek treatment voluntarily (NIMH 1987) and since most episodes of disorder are short-lived, the theory has limited explanatory power. The theory tends to ignore the crucial role of informal labeling by family members and neighbors; mental patients are usually brought to psychiatric attention through the tentative preliminary labeling of these unofficial "agents of social control." Also problematic are two implicit assumptions of the theory. One is that a behavior or symptom will usually stop if it is not labeled. This is an assumption that flies in the face of both casual observation and considerable evidence, as you will see. The other problematic assumption is that labeling and differential treatment are the key causes of continued psychiatric symptoms (Scheff 1966a); this implies that the initial causes of psychological symptoms (biological, psychological, sociological, and so on) cease to have major influences on the individual's thoughts, feelings, or behaviors after labeling has occurred – which, of course, is not a sensible implication. In short, the theory probably overestimates considerably the importance of labeling as a cause of sustained mental disorder.

Although flawed, the theory still has major advantages. Perhaps most important, it has sensitized psychiatric social workers, psychiatrists, and judges to the potential for bias or error in diagnostic judgments, especially when patients are poor, female, elderly, or minority group members (i.e., low in power and status). Moreover, state laws have been revised to make involuntary commitments more difficult, giving the accused access to legal representation and ensuring that involuntary hospitalization lasts no longer than so many days without a review (Gove 1982). Labeling theory has also made policymakers and hospital administrators more aware of the problem of "institutional syndrome," where long-term patients become overly dependent on hospital staff, unable to care for themselves, and passive and compliant as a result of their hospital experience. (One of the goals of the deinstitutionalization movement is to prevent institutional syndrome by moving patients back into the community before they can become overly dependent on the hospital.) Labeling theory is especially valuable because it reminds us that mental illness is to some extent socially created and sustained, and that there are risks to accepting psychiatrists' judgments as invariably valid and reliable assessments of mental disorder. Wrongful commitments can occur, and societal reactions based on stereotypes can make the experience of disturbance more severe and potentially more long-lasting.

The treatment implications of labeling theory are quite different from those of stress and structural strain approaches. Potential ways to reduce or prevent mental illness include changing social conventions that define "normal" thoughts, feelings, and behaviors; attacking widely held misperceptions of the mentally ill; avoiding the formal diagnosis and hospitalization of individuals for aberrant behavior; and reducing the length of stay of hospitalized individuals to prevent them from acquiring a deviant identity. Although many of the treatment and preventative implications of labeling theory seem overly idealistic – the student will learn more about the (mostly negative) consequences of deinstitutionalization in Part III – the theory remains important for its sensitizing, critical perspective on psychiatric diagnosis and the effects of mental hospital life.

Integrating the Three Sociological Theories

By this point, the careful reader might see that the three dominant sociological explanations of mental illness could be integrated. Structural strain theories suggest that the ways in which societies are organized create general patterns of opportunity or risk for particular social groups. Stress theory could help bridge the gap between macro structure and micro (individual-level) experience by explaining how structured risks become actualized in the lives of individuals as stressful experiences. According to stress theory, when events and strains accumulate in people's lives, they can overwhelm people's psychosocial resources and abilities to cope and so generate symptoms of psychological disorder (primary deviance, in labeling theory's terms). Labeling theory picks up at this point and suggests that frequent, severe, or highly visible symptoms – or symptoms exhibited by those with little social prestige or power – can launch a victimizing process. Societal reactions to symptoms may result in the person receiving a formal psychiatric diagnosis, becoming hospitalized, and ultimately accepting the mental patient identity. As mentioned earlier, however, evidence shows that chronic patienthood is not an inevitable consequence of the labeling process, despite assertions of labeling theorists to the contrary (e.g., Scheff 1966a). Explaining how and why the majority of people who have been diagnosed and hospitalized do *not* become chronically mentally ill is the next theoretical task for sociologists to tackle.

Final Commentary

It is important for the student to remember that sociological theories of etiology do not claim to explain fully the causes of mental illness. No one approach to mental illness – biological, psychological, or sociological – can completely explain its origins. For example, even if deficits of certain neurotransmitters in the brain were shown to be directly responsible for major depression (a biological explanation), the onset of a depressive episode is probably due to multiple factors operating simultaneously: a person's gender, age, social class, number of current stressful experiences, past unresolved psychological conflicts, and perhaps a lack of social support. Each broad theoretical approach to mental illness tends to focus on only certain kinds of causes (biological, psychological, or sociological ones) and thus each approach inadvertently de-emphasizes the importance of other causes. Although we will continue to focus on sociological approaches in this volume, the reader should remember that it is not our intention to downplay the importance of other causal factors.

We seek to deepen and elaborate the student's appreciation of sociological factors involved in the causes, consequences, treatment, and prevention of mental illness because these sociological factors are the most likely to be ignored or neglected in the field of mental health. Mental illness is not randomly distributed in the population, but is socially patterned. Patients in treatment are not a random set of individuals, but once again are socially patterned. Effective treatments, excellent hospitals, and beneficial community services are not equally available, but yet again are socially patterned. Grasping the impact of these social inequalities in the experience of mental disorder, in the quest for treatment, and in the availability of mental health services is crucial for a well-rounded understanding of the causes and consequences of mental disorder.

7

The Labeling Theory of Mental Disorder (I): The Role of Social Contingencies in the Application of Psychiatric Labels

Jo C. Phelan & Bruce G. Link

Phelan and Link provide an overview of the research concerning the social factors that influence the labeling of mental illness. A label is a definition that is applied to a person and specifies what type of person that individual is. Many of the signs and symptoms of mental illness are violations of taken-for-granted rules or norms. One result of the label of mental illness is stigma, whereby an individual is characterized as undesirable and is avoided or rejected. There has been a long-standing debate over labeling, centered on the question of whether it is the behavior or rather the label that results in the rejection and isolation of individuals. Two pivotal points of the debate – the importance of social factors in determining who is labeled, and the importance of the label in inducing stigma – remain central sociological questions. The social characteristics of the rule breaker and of those responding to the rule breaker, an interaction between the two, and contextual factors all impinge on the labeling process. Data from "true prevalence" studies of mental disorder, which assess the psychiatric status of individuals independently of whether or not they have sought treatment from the mental health system, demonstrate that the severity of symptoms has a strong relationship to the probability of seeking treatment. Yet, it is also clear that social factors independent of symptomatology influence who is labeled and who is not. Behavior is more likely to be viewed as incomprehensible when the observer is relationally and culturally different from the person displaying the behavior. That is, those who are close to (or similar to) the person who exhibits unusual behavior are less likely to label that behavior as mental illness. Social processes also affect the kinds of labels that professionals apply and the kinds of treatment a labeled person experiences. Furthermore, the cultural distance – between clinicians and those whom they diagnose and treat – affects the accuracy of the labels conferred. Students should consider their own systems of interpretation: What kinds of behavior and what sort of people do you consider incomprehensible, weird, or unusual? Under what kinds of circumstances is such behavior tolerated, and when is it unacceptable? Why are such people stigmatized?

When we ask who is labeled mentally ill and what the consequences of such labeling are, we ask questions that are central to the sociological understanding of mental disorder. Such questions are relevant to mental health professionals who bemoan the fact that so many people with serious mental disorder go unlabeled and untreated (Regier et al. 1993). Such questions are also relevant to people attempting to recover from mental illness who may feel that they suffer as much from being labeled mentally ill as they do from mental illness itself (Deegan 1993).

As a society, we have created specific professions (including psychiatry, clinical psychology, psychiatric social work, and psychiatric nursing) upon whose members we confer the authority to define, label, and treat mental disorder. Social processes determine who is brought to these professionals and the types of labels that are applied to them when they arrive. Once labels are assigned, social processes further determine what sorts of consequences the labels will have. This chapter reviews the evidence concerning the social factors that influence labeling – how, to whom, by whom, and on what basis are such labels applied? Chapter 20 considers the consequences of such labels for the lives of the people to whom they become attached. We begin our review of the labeling process with some important conceptual distinctions.

Conceptual Distinctions

A label is a definition. When applied to a person, it identifies or defines what type of a person he or she is. A label can be either deviant (when it designates the violation of a social norm) or "normal" (when it makes a distinction that does not involve the violation of norms). Many of the signs and symptoms of mental illness violate taken-for-granted rules or normative standards. This is most obvious with some symptoms of psychotic disorders, which involve bizarre delusions such as believing that one's thoughts are being broadcast on the radio or that one is the reincarnated Christ. However, as Thoits (1985) points out, it applies also to anxiety and depressive disorders because these violate taken-for-granted "feeling rules" that dictate the kinds of emotions considered appropriate to given situations.

Labeling is a starting point for societal responses – it suggests possibilities for how the labeled person should be managed by calling up preexisting sentiments and beliefs about the type of person who receives such a label. The social response that ensues may lead to revulsion and avoidance, compassion and caring, or apathy and indifference. It can involve the ministrations of professionals, the actions of lay people, or the labeled person's own responses. It can be restitutive and inclusionary or punitive and exclusionary (Braithwaite 1989). Perhaps the core concept for understanding the consequences of labeling is that of *stigma*. Stigma, as conceptualized by Jones and colleagues (1984), is a process in which individuals are "marked" by a label that sets them apart from others and links them to undesirable characteristics. The individual is then avoided and rejected as a consequence of this linkage to undesirable characteristics. (See Chapter 20 for a review of the evidence concerning stigma and other consequences of labeling.)

Although labels can be informal as well as formal, in this review our main focus (as in most of the research literature) will be the determinants of official labels, by which we mean labels that are acquired through contact with treatment systems. Although specific diagnostic labels may be applied in such settings, our concern rests with the mark conferred by the simple fact of being in a mental hospital or being treated by a psychiatrist or other mental health professional. Official labels are of special interest to us because they (1) carry potent cultural meanings; (2) can activate these meanings in diverse settings in a way that informal labels cannot; and (3) are far more difficult to effectively dispute, ignore, or hide than are informal labels.

The Labeling Debate

Scheff's *Being Mentally Ill* (1966a) opened a long-standing debate about the importance of labeling as it applies to mental disorder. Scheff conceptualizes mental illness as a form of "residual deviance." He points out that, for many types of deviant or rule-breaking behavior, there are relatively explicit and concrete definitions of the proscribed behavior and equally explicit prescriptions for societal responses to those behaviors. For example, burglary, prostitution, and treason refer to specific acts, and specific responses to them are codified into the law. But not all rule-breaking behavior fits easily into such recipes. Scheff points out that there are "numerous and unnameable" acts that do not fall into such clear-cut categories but rather violate taken-for-granted, unspoken rules of social interaction. Such acts constitute a set of "left-over" or residual forms of deviant behavior. Most manifestations of mental illness, he argues, belong to this residual category. For instance, if a person is extremely withdrawn, holds conversations with persons others cannot see, or speaks in a way that does not seem logical to the listener, then an observer may make the judgment that "something is wrong" with the person even though the behavior does not violate explicitly stated social rules.

Scheff claims that acts of residual deviance are extremely common but that usually they are transitory, are not considered particularly noteworthy by others, and do not develop into enduring problems. Only under certain circumstances are such acts publicly recognized. These circumstances often involve the social characteristics of rule breakers and of those reacting to them. When an act of residual deviance does elicit a strong societal reaction and becomes labeled, particularly by treatment professionals, powerful social forces work to stabilize the residual rule breaking and further shape the individual's behavior, creating a stable pattern of behavior referred to as "mental illness." Key aspects of Scheff's theory are captured in the following quotation.

> In a crisis, when the deviance of an individual becomes a public issue, the traditional stereotype of insanity becomes the guiding imagery for action, both for those reacting to the deviant and at times the deviant himself. When societal agents and people around the deviant react to him uniformly in terms of the

traditional stereotypes of insanity, his amorphous and unstructured rule breaking tends to crystallize in conformity to those expectations, thus becoming similar to the behavior of other deviants classified as mentally ill, and stable over time. The process of becoming uniform and stable is completed when the traditional imagery becomes a part of the deviant's orientation for guiding his own behavior. (Scheff 1966a: 82)

Walter Gove (1970, 1975, 1980, 1982), Scheff's most persistent critic, takes sharp issue with Scheff's characterization of the labeling process. He argues that labels are applied much less capriciously and with much less pernicious consequences than the labeling perspective suggests. In Gove's view, existing research supports the idea that, if ex-mental patients are rejected, it is because their behavior is disturbed and not because they have been labeled. Moreover, he argues, labeling is not an important cause of further deviant behavior. "The available evidence," Gove concludes, "indicates that deviant labels are primarily a consequence of deviant behavior and that deviant labels are not a prime cause of deviant careers" (1975: 296).

Although subsequent research has shown that neither Scheff's nor Gove's position is tenable in its entirety (Link & Cullen 1990), their sharply opposed stances have inspired and provided a framework for the elaboration of theory and empirical investigations that refine our understanding of the issues they addressed. Consequently, the two pivotal points of the debate – the importance of social factors in determining who is labeled, and the importance of label-induced stigma – remain central questions for our field. In the remainder of this chapter, we review evidence concerning the first of these two questions: the importance of social factors in the application of labels. Chapter 20 takes up new theory and research relevant to the second major question: the consequences of mental illness labeling.

Evidence Concerning the Importance of Societal Reaction in Determining Who Gets Labeled

A core proposition of labeling theory is that social and contextual factors are critical in determining who is or is not officially labeled. Stated in its most general form, labeling theory says that factors unrelated to the rule-breaking behavior influence the application of labels. These factors include the social characteristics of the rule breaker, the social characteristics of those responding to the rule breaker, an interaction between the two, and contextual factors that impinge on the actors in a holistic way. Gove's emphasis is diametrically opposed to this one. He says that "deviant labels are primarily a consequence of deviant behavior" (1975: 296). Do the social factors suggested by labeling theorists affect the application of official labels, or can official labeling be accounted for primarily by deviant behavior alone? To address this question, we review evidence concerning the importance of psychiatric symptoms in determining whether people will be labeled as mentally ill. We then review evidence on the labeling proclivities of lay persons, professionals, and the labeled individuals themselves.

Symptoms of Mental Illness and Labeling

True prevalence studies of mental disorder are a useful starting point for an inquiry into labeling processes, since they assess the psychiatric status of community residents independently of whether they have sought treatment from a mental health professional. As such, these studies can tell us something about the relationship between the symptoms of mental illness and the probability of official labeling through treatment contact. In a review of eleven true prevalence studies, Link and Dohrenwend (1980b) found that the median proportion in treatment for all types of mental disorder combined was 26.7%. For the seven studies that reported results for psychotic disorders, the median proportion in treatment was 59.7%; for the six studies reporting results for persons with a diagnosis of schizophrenia, the median proportion was 83.3%. More recently, two large-scale true prevalence studies – the Epidemiologic Catchment Area (ECA) study and the National Comorbidity Survey (NCS) – have provided results that are consistent with the earlier Link and Dohrenwend review (Kessler et al. 1994, 1996; Shapiro et al. 1984). For example, the NCS reports that only 26.2% of those who had experienced a mental disorder and only 41.0% of those who had experienced three or more such disorders had *ever* received treatment from a mental health professional (Kessler et al. 1994). Both studies also show that the vast majority of people who have experienced a recent disorder have not received mental health treatment (or any professional treatment) for that disorder (Kessler et al. 1994; Shapiro et al. 1984). According to Shapiro et al.'s (1984) findings from three ECA sites, there is no diagnostic category for which a majority of people with a current diagnosis have seen a mental health professional in the previous six months. The highest proportion currently in treatment was among those diagnosed with schizophrenia, but even for that most severe psychiatric diagnosis the highest figure across the three sites reached only 48.1% (Shapiro et al. 1984).

If one examines the mental health status of those who report current treatment, one finds equally startling results. In one of the ground-breaking true prevalence studies, the Midtown Manhattan study, only 52.5% of those currently in treatment were clinically impaired according to that study's classification scheme (Srole et al. 1975). Almost as dramatic are findings from the ECA and NCS studies showing that about one third of those reporting mental health treatment in the recent past (six months for ECA and twelve months for NCS) had no diagnosable disorder during the same period (Kessler et al. 1994; Shapiro et al. 1984). Efforts to understand this finding as reflecting treatment for past disorder or subclinical symptoms fail to fully account for it (Regier et al. 1993). Given that the disorders assessed in these studies represent the major disorders believed to need official labeling and treatment, it is surprising, to say the least, that such a large proportion of our treatment effort goes to people who exhibit none of them.

These findings show that the severity of the symptoms of mental illness have a strong relationship to the probability of seeking treatment, indicating that psychiatric status is important in influencing whether one receives a label of mental illness. It is equally clear, however, that factors other than mental disorder influence whether a person will become involved in treatment. If mental disorder alone were a sufficient explanation for labeling, why have about two in five persons diagnosed as having a psychotic disorder never been a mental patient? Even more puzzling, why would a third of those currently in treatment have none of the major psychiatric diagnoses assessed in the true prevalence studies? In and of themselves, these findings do not confirm the labeling perspective, since factors that have little to do with social responses may be responsible for some of the discrepancies between who has symptoms of mental illness and who is officially labeled. Invalidity in the assessment of mental disorder in true prevalence studies is one possibility, while barriers such as distance from a treatment setting (Commission on Lunacy 1855), language differences, and inconvenient hours are others. Still, because these striking findings suggest that the symptoms of mental illness cannot fully explain official labeling, they allow the possibility that factors identified by labeling theory may be important. Is there, then, any convincing evidence to suggest that differential societal reaction influences the likelihood of official labeling? To answer this question, we review evidence concerning labeling by lay persons, self-labeling, and labeling by professionals.

Evidence Concerning Labeling by Lay Persons

There is now extensive evidence to suggest that social factors independent of the deviant behavior itself influence who is labeled and who is not. As far back as Hollingshead and Redlich (1958) there was recognition of the power of the public's labeling behavior, conceptualized as "lay appraisal." Hollingshead and Redlich observed that nonprofessionals are involved in a first and crucial step in the process that determines whether someone is labeled and what the nature of the label will be. Horwitz (1982a; see also Rosenberg 1984) points out that, in large measure, mental illness labeling by lay persons derives from what he calls *incomprehensibility.* Thus, according to Horwitz, labeling occurs when the "categories observers use to comprehend behavior do not yield any socially understandable reasons for the behavior" (1982a: 16). This observation leads to predictions about the conditions under which mental illness labeling is more or less likely. Specifically, behavior is more likely to be perceived as incomprehensible when the observer is relationally and culturally different from the person exhibiting the behavior. This reasoning is consistent with two formal propositions set forth by Horwitz: First, "the tendency to label an individual mentally ill varies directly with the relational distance between the observer and the actor" (1982a: 36); second, "the tendency to label an individual mentally ill varies directly with the cultural distance between the observer and the actor" (p. 47). In addition, Horwitz used existing literature on labeling processes to generate a third proposition: "The recognition of mental illness varies directly with the social class of the labeler" (p. 64). Evidence for the first and third of these propositions is considered in this section. Evidence for the second proposition is reserved for a subsequent section on labeling by mental health professionals.

Horwitz's first proposition – that labeling is more likely among those who are relationally distant – is supported by studies showing that husbands (Sampson, Messinger, & Towne 1964) and wives (Yarrow et al. 1955) are often extremely reluctant to label their spouses' deviant behavior as "mental illness." Although more recent studies indicate that the public has become somewhat more medically oriented in their views of mental illness, these studies continue to document extremely long periods before official labeling occurs (Perrucci & Targ 1982). Kadushin's (1969) and Horwitz's (1977b) research on the steps that lead patients into treatment indicates that friends and employers are more likely to label than spouses. Moreover, recent data show that police remain major actors in bringing people with mental illness to psychiatric emergency rooms (Sales 1991; Way, Evans, & Banks 1993). Finally, strangers, although they can often ignore deviant behavior, are perhaps the most ready to apply mental illness labels. A good example of this is the apparent public perception that most homeless people are deinstitutionalized psychiatric patients, when the facts suggest otherwise (Phelan & Link 1995; Shlay & Rossi 1992; Snow et al. 1986).

The proposition that higher-status persons are more likely to use mental illness labels is supported by the epidemiological true prevalence studies referred to earlier. At least in the United States, higher-status persons with or without psychiatric problems are more likely to have entered treatment and received an official label (Katz et al. in press; Link & Dohrenwend 1980b; Srole et al. 1975). Moreover, in their responses to vignettes depicting mental disorders, higher-status persons are more likely to attribute the behaviors described to mental illness and are more likely to recommend psychiatric treatment for the problem (Hall et al. 1993; see also Dohrenwend & Chin Shong 1967). Again, these findings suggest that factors other than deviant behavior influence labeling decisions. At the same time, however, they seem to contradict some aspects of labeling theory. Specifically, Scheff (1966a: 100) indicates that *less* powerful rule breakers are more likely to be labeled. Yet, as we have seen, higher-status persons, who presumably have more power, are actually more likely to receive an official label. Other data, however, suggest that the power prediction may simply need to be specified further – power may have more to do with the patient's treatment career than with the simple fact of whether an official label is applied. For example, Hollingshead and Redlich (1958) found that lower-class patients were more likely than higher-class patients to receive lobotomies (see also Gallagher, Levinson, & Erlich 1957; Kandel 1966; Link 1983; Link & Milcarek 1980; Schofield 1964). Other research has shown that less powerful groups (e.g., racial minorities and the less educated) are more likely to be restrained, secluded, and involuntarily committed than more powerful groups, even after controlling for illness severity and other relevant characteristics (Flaherty & Meagher 1980; Rosenfield 1984; Rushing 1978; Snowden & Holschuh 1992). And, of course, poor people are much more likely to be treated in state mental hospitals and public health clinics where staff are overworked, where employee turnover is high, and where many staff are employed because they cannot find work elsewhere. Thus the power hypothesis may be more effective in explaining how people are sifted and sorted into desirable or undesirable niches within the treatment system than it is in explaining whether mental illness labeling occurs.

Self-Labeling

Much of the emphasis in labeling theory, as the term "societal reaction" implies, has been on the influence of other people's responses in determining who is labeled mentally ill. Thoits (1985) faults this emphasis by pointing out that most mental illness labeling, though socially influenced, involves voluntary self-labeling. Drawing on the literature of the sociology of emotions (e.g. Hochschild 1979), Thoits argues that there are "feeling rules" concerning the appropriateness of emotional expression in the context of social circumstances. She points out that people learn to apply these rules to their own circumstances and to monitor themselves for signs of what she calls "emotional deviance." When emotions seem deviant to them (i.e., when emotions are inexplicable given what has been happening to them), they enlist the opinions of others and seek to manage their emotions through social support. Sometimes these efforts reveal that their feelings are not really deviant but can be explained by some aspect of their circumstance of which they were unaware or had discounted. But if nonnormative emotions persist and cannot be accounted for or ameliorated by efforts to manage them, the probability of self-labeling increases.

Thoits's formulation grew out of weaknesses she identified in labeling theory – its inability to explain voluntary seeking of treatment and its overemphasis on the coercive responses of others – but her approach is supportive of the more general proposition that social factors influence the probability of labeling. This is so for two reasons. First, her formulation is deeply social in that it indicates that one is socialized to learn feeling rules and then to imaginatively compare oneself to others experiencing similar situations in evaluating one's emotional deviance. Second, others' opinions about the appropriateness of the emotions are crucial in determining whether one arrives at a self-label of mental illness or concludes that the emotions are appropriate to the situation. Thus social factors shape the labeling process even in the absence of coercive responses from others.

Labeling by Professionals

If the labeling orientation is correct, then social processes will affect the kinds of labels that professionals apply and thus the kinds of treatment a labeled person encounters. Again, there is considerable evidence to suggest that this is so. Studies have shown that factors unrelated to psychiatric condition – such as the suggestion of a diagnosis by a "prestigious colleague" (Temerlin 1968), the side taken in a legal proceeding (Simon & Zusman 1983), insurance coverage (Kirk & Kutchins 1988), and the presence of housing and caregiving resources (Holstein 1993) – can all affect clinical decision making. In addition to these factors, a particularly powerful form of social influence on labeling decisions is suggested by Horwitz's proposition concerning the effects of cultural distance.

Numerous studies have demonstrated how cultural distance – between clinicians and those they diagnose and treat – affects the accuracy of the labels conferred. This has obvious applications for cross-cultural encounters (Weiss, Raguram, & Channabasavanna 1995) but can also affect diagnostic practice when subcultures within the United States are considered. One study (Rosenbaum & Prinsky 1991) highlights the effect of cultural distance between adult and youth culture and its effect on mental illness labeling. The authors note the existence of a "punk" and "heavy metal" music subculture that conflicts with adult culture and has led to programs designed to "depunk" and "demetal" young people. To determine whether mental health treatment programs would label and treat youths on the basis of their involvement in punk and heavy metal music, the authors constructed a hypothetical situation in which parents were concerned about their child's choice of music, clothes, and posters. No symptoms of mental illness were mentioned, and drugs, alcohol, depression, violence, and suicide were explicitly mentioned as *not* being a problem in the described case. When a male research assistant posing as the youth's father called intake supervisors at six public and six private inpatient facilities, 83% (ten supervisors) indicated that they believed the described youth's problems required psychiatric hospitalization – even though the only problems mentioned were those involving participation in a youth subculture.

Other important sources of subcultural division are race, gender, and religion. In one study, Pavkov, Lewis, and Lyons (1989) selected a random sample of 313 people with severe mental illnesses and recorded the diagnoses they were given by four hospitals in the Chicago metropolitan area. Meanwhile, the respondents were interviewed with an established research instrument, the Schedule for Affective Disorders and Schizophrenia (SADS). Because it provides an explicit guide to diagnosis with suggested probes, this instrument is arguably less subject to bias than are standard clinical diagnostic procedures. Pavkov and colleagues found that, controlling for the SADS research diagnosis, African Americans were more likely to receive a hospital diagnosis of schizophrenia. This finding coheres with theory suggesting that distrust of white institutions, normative in the African-American community, is sometimes misinterpreted as indicating paranoid delusions consistent with a diagnosis of schizophrenia (Ridley 1984). Another demonstration of the impact of subcultural factors on official labeling is provided by Loring and Powell (1988). These authors conducted a vignette experiment in which psychiatrists were asked to diagnose a hypothetical individual whose description included a fixed array of psychiatric symptoms, but whose race and gender varied. Most of the psychiatrists diagnosed the individual with undifferentiated schizophrenia; however, the race and gender of both the diagnosing psychiatrist and the vignette subject – and, crucially, the interaction between the two – dramatically influenced the diagnosis assigned. For example, black male vignette subjects were most likely to be assigned the more severe diagnosis of paranoid schizophrenia, and female vignette subjects were more likely to be diagnosed with a depressive disorder by male than by female psychiatrists. (Also see Hamilton, Rothbart, & Dawes 1986 for evidence of bias in assigning histrionic characteristics to women.)

Summary of the Evidence Concerning Who Gets Labeled

As the true prevalence studies show, symptoms of mental illness are important determinants of mental illness labeling. People with symptoms of mental illness are much more likely to have been officially labeled than those who do not have such symptoms, and those who have more severe symptoms are more likely to have an official label than those with less severe symptoms. Still, by themselves, the symptoms of mental illness are poor predictors of who is labeled and who is not. Labeling theory called for a shift in emphasis – from the rule-breaking behavior to the social context – in explaining mental illness labeling. Although specific propositions of labeling theory were not always confirmed by our review, the utility of the general thrust of this approach was supported. There is extensive evidence suggesting that social factors unrelated to the symptoms of mental illness have a strong influence on the labeling proclivities of the general public, on rule breakers themselves, and on the mental health professionals who confer official labels.

The evidence does not necessarily confirm, yet is consistent with, the following formulation. Social, psychological, and biological factors are involved initially in producing psychopathology (see Chapters 4, 5, and 6). These symptoms of mental illness are then evaluated, interpreted, and responded to by the affected individual and by others in his or her social context. Together, the severity of the symptomatology and the nature of responses to it determine whether formal mental illness labeling, and thus treatment contact, takes place. If it does, then social and clinical factors shape the professional response determining the nature and the quality of the treatment received.

We believe the trajectory of research in this area of sociological concern has evolved in a reasonable fashion from the strongly stated opposing viewpoints of Scheff and Gove to more refined theory and research (Horwitz 1982a; Thoits 1985) that sheds light on the important questions framed by the labeling debate. We believe that the continued accumulation of sociologically inspired work – maintaining labeling theory's emphasis on the social interpretation of behavior in context – is essential if we are to achieve a broad understanding of labeling processes that can lead people into treatment. Absent this breadth of understanding, we run the risk of misconstruing people's labeling and self-labeling proclivities by interpreting behavior within a narrow framework of individual decision making.

Part II

The Social Context of Mental Health and Illness

Teresa L. Scheid & Allan V. Horwitz

Stress and Social Support

Betsy is 28 years old, white, and wears a shade of lipstick that strikes one as a bit too red; her clothes are a few years out of style. She has been married for three years. She met her husband at a group home where they used to reside (they now live with his mother, which is a source of ongoing strain for Betsy). Betsy is looking for work as a secretary; she has three years of college at a nearby state university, where she majored in French. She dropped out of college when she became pregnant, entering a residential home for pregnant teens in a city far from her family, who were disgraced and embarrassed by her condition. After putting the baby up for adoption, Betsy moved into the group home and began outpatient therapy for severe depression. Yet Betsy's problems began before the pregnancy, in high school. As she recalls, "I got real depressed, feeling suicidal, crying all day long, I just couldn't stop crying. At night I'd stay awake, walk around the house, make phone calls, disturb everybody, call my pastor at 2 in the morning. Did bizarre things like that." She was hospitalized in high school – taken to a university medical school in a program for adolescent girls. "I had a lot of fun there, we played a lot of games." Despite her depression and hospitalization, Betsy was able to finish high school (thanks to a tutor at the hospital and correspondence courses) and was fine until her pregnancy and forced isolation from her family ("I had to get out of . . ., my mother's friends, she didn't want her friends talking about me, gossiping). Betsy was very much on her own and recalls difficulty finding employment. After the adoption, Betsy became psychotic. Again, she recalls in a factual manner: "I had a psychotic episode and had to get back on medication. I kept threatening, saying I was going to kill myself, and I kept repeating it and repeating it. I was telling people I didn't want to live any longer; I didn't want to give the baby up."

Betsy's story illustrates the importance of stress and social support in understanding mental health and illness. As she herself states, "a major event and a lot of stress" affect when she gets "sick." Adolescence, college, pregnancy, relationships with others – all are stressful life events that can precipitate periods of mental instability, depression, or even schizophrenia.

The study of stress and social support has predominated sociological research in mental health and illness since the 1960s. The initial studies of life stressors relied on a checklist method, where respondents would indicate whether or not they experienced a variety of stressful events such as the death of a close relative, divorce, unemployment, and the like (Holmes & Rahe 1967). Over thirty years of research have demonstrated a consistent relationship between the occurrence of stressors and the development of psychological distress (Turner, Wheaton, & Lloyd 1995). Yet this relationship, though consistent, is modest: many people who experience stressors do not become distressed.

The modest relationship between the occurrence of life stressors and the development of distress led researchers to search for factors that could account for why life stressors had such variable impacts on different individuals. Because stress does not affect everyone the same way, researchers must also take into account *vulnerability* to stress. Vulnerability was originally conceived as a purely psychological concept that depended upon individual resources and personality traits. Sociologists view vulnerability as a group concept as well. For example, membership in some social categories (e.g., ethnicity, gender, or age) provides people with differential access to resources and different socialization experiences that may structure their reactions to stressful experiences. Differential access to resources can influence both exposure to various risk factors and the ability to either avoid or cope with psychological distress (Link & Phelan 1995).

Beginning in the 1970s, researchers modified the life stress model to take into account the important role played by social support and other resources that assist individuals in coping with the stressful events in their lives. A prominent theme became how external sources of social support as well as internal coping resources, such as self-esteem and mastery, could help prevent stressors from occuring in the first place and help limit the resulting amount of distress after the stressful event.

Supportive family and friends may help people both to cope with stress and to avoid exposure to additional stressors. These supporters may provide emotional support such as love, empathy, and understanding, as well as more instrumental forms of support such as money, a place to live, or help with child care. Although much theoretical attention is given to how social support can reduce mental disturbance, researchers still know relatively little about the precise mechanisms by which social support influences coping abilities such as feelings of self-esteem and mastery (Thoits 1995a). Furthermore, we do not fully understand how social networks influence help seeking from both lay and professional sources. Often a family's shame or ignorance of the reality of mental illness can prohibit someone from seeking out professional help or therapy. Alternatively, a family that has had positive experiences with professional care providers may routinely access mental health services. Another issue that has not been sufficiently explored is the negative impact of social network members: interactions with spouses, parents, children, lovers, and friends can benefit mental health but can also lead to serious mental health problems. Yet most research focuses solely on the positive side of social interactions.

In addition to the development of models of stress that include vulnerability, coping, social support, and exposure to stressors, researchers are increasingly concerned with the measurability of stress and major life events: what one person may find stressful can actually bring relief to someone else experiencing the same type of event (Aneshensel et al. 1991). For example, one person might find a divorce psychologically and socially devastating. Such an individual might suffer severe depression as an outcome of the divorce as that individual experiences grief, guilt, and the painful necessity of reconstructing a shattered sense of self. Another person, however, may find divorce to be a liberating experience accompanied by a sense of freedom, autonomy, and mastery. This reaction is especially likely if the marriage was especially stressful or marked by emotional or physical abuse (Wheaton 1990). Scales of life events that simply add up the number of stressful life events fail to consider how the same type of event can be experienced in different ways by different individuals and groups. Newer methods of measuring life events use more sophisticated measures that attempt to capture more contextual aspects of these events (Turner et al. 1995).

The first four chapters in this part of the book examine the general aspects of the stress paradigm that has dominated research in the sociology of mental health. In Chapter 8, Len Pearlin provides an overview of the stress process and its key elements. The following chapter, by Blair Wheaton, provides an overview of the major models and descriptions of the most important stressors that people face. Next, Jay Turner focuses on the relationships between social support, coping, and distress. In Chapter 11, Carol Aneshensel discusses the outcomes of the stress–support–coping model. The subsequent chapters in this part examine how particular social characteristics and social processes are related to various aspects of the sociology of mental health and illness.

Family and Social Networks

One general aspect of social life that is related to mental health and illness lies in one's social involvement and investment in meaningful role relationships. A long tradition of sociological research that began with Emile Durkheim's (1897) work on suicide relates the strength and type of peoples' social relationships with mental health and illness. Durkheim postulated that people who had strong social relationships had low suicide rates because of their greater social integration, protection from life strains, and sense of security, meaningfulness, and purpose. Thus, he found that married people were less likely to commit suicide than unmarried people, married people with children had lower suicide rates than those without children, people who had lost important social relationships such as the widowed or divorced had higher rates of suicide, and so forth. Indeed, it would not be an exaggeration to say that, for Durkheim, people find meaning in life through their social relationships.

To this day, sociologists continue to find that people with strong social ties have better mental health and lower rates of distress and mental illness than those who are more isolated (Horwitz, White, & Howell-White 1996a; Ross 1995; Waite 1995). The correlation between the presence of strong social ties and better mental health to some degree represents the fact that people with good mental health are better able to form social ties in the first place. But even taking into account states of mental health that preceded social relationships, social ties themselves appear to have mental health benefits (Horwitz et al. 1996a). In general, strong social relationships promote a sense of belonging and security and lead to more opportunities to develop a sense of efficacy and mastery. The more of these ties people have, the greater their opportunities to receive social support.

The institution that is perhaps most strongly related to social ties is the family. Family interactions affect mental health in all periods of the life course – from the impact of parents on the mental health of children, to spouses' effects on each other and on their children, to the relationships of one's adult children and grandchildren on mental health. Whereas many psychologists, particularly those influenced by Freudian thought (see Chapter 5), emphasize the influence of early childhood experience on mental health in adulthood, sociologists have been more concerned with how family life in the present affects mental health and illness. Experiences such as growing up in a two- or one-parent family, being a single parent or part of a married couple, or having children or remaining childless can all affect psychological well-being. Further, family life is not isolated from other social processes but indeed is profoundly structured by socioeconomic, ethnic, and gender considerations. William Avison discusses the impact of the family on mental health in Chapter 12.

Although family ties are a critical type of social relationship, many other relationships have important impacts on mental health and illness. Sociologists often refer to the total number of connections between people as their *social network*. In Chapter 13, Nan Lin and Kristin Peek discuss research on how various characteristics of social networks – including size, density, and degree of interconnectedness – influence mental health. Studies do not provide a consistent picture of how social networks affect psychological well-being, but the social network perspective does hold great promise of illuminating how one aspect of the social environment influences mental health and illness.

Social Class, Race, and Ethnicity

James is a well-dressed, articulate, 32-year-old black man. He now lives with his girlfriend in an apartment and visits his son from a previous marriage every week- end. After graduating from high school he enlisted in the army, where he first got sick. While in Panama for jungle training, the "guys in my platoon put something in my drink and it got me real sick, I lost my mind, I couldn't remember nobody, my daddy's name, my momma's name. I lost my memory." Consequently he was hospitalized for some time. James now takes prolixin for his schizophrenia and does not hear the voices if he remembers to take his medicine. If he forgets, or stops taking it because he "gets to feeling real good, feeling normal," then he again hears voices and has had several other short hospitalizations. Despite these disruptions to his life, James has always worked: as a dishwasher in high school, for his father's flour mill after the military hospitalization, and most recently as a janitor.

James's story illustrates the importance of social conditions – such as socioeconomic status, race, and ethnicity – that place some individuals at greater risk for disease and illness. One of the most consistent findings of research has been the inverse relationship between social class and various types of mental disorder (Dohrenwend 1990). Epidemiological studies consistently find that those in the lower social classes have higher levels of schizophrenia, depression, alcohol abuse, and general mental impairment (Dohrenwend et al. 1980; Kessler et al. 1994; Robins et al. 1984). Blacks also are considerably more likely than members of other ethnic groups to be admitted to state and county inpatient units of mental hospitals (Snowden & Cheung 1990). Furthermore, James's social position as a working-class black male is associated with his decision to enter the military, where "something" happened to trigger a psychotic episode.

Social class is generally referred to by sociologists as socioeconomic status (SES) and is commonly measured by three factors. First is economic position, reflecting one's income and wealth (including inheritence, property, and savings). Second is status, or prestige, which generally reflects the type of occupation and education an individual possesses. Economic position is fairly objective, but prestige is subjective and is determined by society's ranking of the prestige of various occupations. A third determinant of one's SES is the amount of power an individual possesses. This may refer to political power (i.e., the ability to influence the political process) as well as having power over other people. In *The Power Elite,* C. W. Mills defines the powerful as those "whose positions enable [them] to transcend the ordinary environments of ordinary men and women; they are in positions to make decisions having major consequences" (1956: 5).

Those in lower-SES groups are subject to higher levels of chronic stress; that is, their social environments subject them to more stressful conditions and also limit the available coping resources for dealing with chronic stressors such as unemployment or poverty. Social class can also affect one's sense of control over the conditions in life and thereby self-esteem and mastery. Long-term exposure to stress, often called chronic stress, can erode one's sense of self-efficacy; furthermore, if stressors are uncontrollable then otherwise beneficial personal traits (such as belief in personal control) may even be detrimental to mental health (Aneshensel 1992).

There are two general explanations for the inverse relationship between SES and mental disorder: social causation and social selection. *Social causation* models postulate that lower-status groups are subject to more stressors such as poverty, unemployment, discrimination, or residence in dangerous neighborhoods than members of higher-status groups, and that the elevated level of exposure to these stressors accounts for higher levels of mental disorder in lower-SES groups. In contrast, *social selection* models focus on how characteristics of individuals, such as their psychological and genetic propensities, lead them to positions in the lower stratum of society. Such individuals may be unable to hold a job or sustain meaningful relationships with others because of their mental disorders, and they may "drift" down the social-class ladder. Others, who are born into the lower class, may not be able to rise above lower-class status because of their disorders. In Chapter 14, Eaton and Muntaner provide a more in-depth and detailed explanation of the relationship between socioeconomic status and mental health and illness.

Work, as well as the lack of work, is one aspect of the social environment that has major implications for mental health and illness. Work can be a major source of stress, especially when work decreases individual opportunities for autonomy and self-control or when work is a source of anxiety. Job stress has been rising in the United States, and some economic trends such as downsizing, downward mobility, and declining individual wages can compound the experience of job-related distress. Karasek and Theorell (1990) find that high-strain jobs (those with high levels of psychological demands and low degrees of autonomy) result in moderately severe rates of depression and exhaustion as well as in higher levels of pill consumption. Workers in jobs with little discretion, autonomy, or control over their work experience higher rates of physical illness and depression, as well as loss of self-esteem. These job experiences are more common among the lower and working classes. On the other hand, jobs that are more common among higher-SES people usually involve more control and decision latitude and so contribute to esteem and mastery, which are important to mental health.

Work can be stressful, but not having a job at all is one of the most powerful social sources of distress. In an extensive review of the literature, Perrucci and Perrucci (1990) conclude that there is strong aggregate support for the positive relationship between unemployment and decreased mental health. Reynolds and Gilbert (1991) find that unemployment contributes to psychological distress among individuals. Warner (1994) argues that the effects of extended unemployment – isolation, withdrawal, anxiety, and depression – are similar to the symptoms commonly associated with schizophrenia. Mary Clare Lennon focuses on work and unemployment as stressors in Chapter 15.

Chronic stressors – including poverty, unemployment, marital and family disruption, discrimination, and poor physical health – fall disproportionately on minority groups (Williams, Takeuchi, & Adair 1992a). Members of minority groups also face higher levels of stigma and conflicting cultural messages, as they are expected to conform to the values and standards of the dominant "white" culture. Racism and discrimination can be significant sources of stress. However, because members of many ethnic minorities (particularly blacks and some Hispanic groups) are also disproportionately concentrated in lower-class positions, it is difficult to untangle the separate effects of class and race on mental health. Ethnicity is also associated with differential access to and attitudes toward social support networks. Traditional values and strong family support networks may explain the relatively low prevalence of mental illness among Hispanics as well as their infrequent use of mental health professionals (Vega & Rumbaut 1991). It is possible that stronger coping resources exist among disadvantaged minorities, so they might develop less distress than we would expect based on the number of stressors that they face. In addition, cultural factors might lead members of different ethnic groups to express mental distress in different ways. For example, some clinicians have observed that young black males are more likely to act out and engage in high-risk behaviors (Stiffman & Davies 1990) whereas Native American youth may be more likely to become alcoholic or suicidal. The many ways that ethnicity can affect mental health and illness influence both the development of mental disorder and how individuals seek to ameliorate and cope with stress and mental disability. David Williams and Michele Harris-Reid discuss the relationship between ethnicity and mental health in Chapter 16.

Age and Gender

Elizabeth Wurtzel, author of *Prozac Nation,* describes the experience of being young and depressed (1995: 60–1).

That summer, I am just thirteen, everything sucks and I am stuck at camp wondering about the Olympics . . . . I sit on the porch of my bunk listening to Bruce Springsteen's first album. Paris, a girl I also go to school with, comes outside to sit with me. Paris is, I guess, what I would call a friend. I've known her since kindergarten, and like everyone else who's been in my life for a while, she's just kind of waiting for me to snap out of this funk so we can have play dates and polish our nails in baby pink like we used to do when we were seven. She lives across the street from me so we still walk home from school together sometimes, which can't be any fun for her because all I want to talk about is the oncoming apocalypse in my brain . . . . That's me, I say to Paris. I'm the girl who is lost in space, the girl who is disappearing always, forever fading away and receding farther and farther into the background. Just like the Cheshire cat, someday I will suddenly leave, but the artificial warmth of my smile, that phony, clownish curve, the kind you see on miserably sad people and villians in Disney movies, will remain behind as an ironic remnant. I am the girl you see in the photograph from some party someplace or some picnic in the park, the one who looks so very vibrant and shimmery, but who is in fact soon going to be gone. I will no longer be there. I will be erased from history, like a traitor in the Soviet Union. Because with every day that goes by, I feel myself becoming more and more invisible, getting covered over more thickly with darkness, coats and coats of darkness that are going to suffocate me in the sweltering heat of the summer sun that I can't even see anymore, even though I can feel it burn.

In addition to social class and ethnicity, one's social position is structured by age and gender. Studies generally find that people in mid-life – between 40 and 60 – have the highest levels of well-being. Some studies find that both younger and older people have more distress than the middle-aged (Mirowsky & Ross 1989b). Many studies, however, find that mental disorders are especially prevalent among young people (Kessler et al. 1994; Robins et al. 1984). It is also possible that rates of mental illness, especially depression, have been growing among the young in recent decades (Klerman 1988).

In Chapter 17, Menaghan surveys the major determinants of child and adolescent mental health. As she indicates, one crucial issue lies in the permanency of childhood mental disorders. Although the most severe disorders in childhood may persist throughout life, many milder forms of distress and antisocial behavior are transitory and short-lived. Understanding the most appropriate response to disturbances in children and adolescents requires knowledge about whether problems are likely to go away on their own or whether professional intervention is required. Menaghan also indicates how interconnected are the factors we have mentioned – SES, work, ethnicity, and family composition – with the development of mentally healthy or distressed children and adolescents.

In Chapter 18, Mirowsky and Ross focus on mental health among adults through the life course. As they point out, age reflects a number of other statuses, including social integration, material resources, physical health, and psychological qualities. In addition, age also interacts with SES and minority status. For example, younger members of disadvantaged minorities may be particularly vulnerable to stress and mental disorder. Vega and Rumbaut (1991) report that American Indian children (aged between 10 and 19) are three times more likely to commit suicide than members of other ethnic groups. Aneshensel and Sucoff (1996a) find that youth growing up in lower-SES neighborhoods in Los Angeles perceived greater hazards such as crime, violence, and drug use than youth in high-SES neighborhoods, and that the perception of a neighborhood as dangerous damages mental health. Children who live in dangerous and threatening neighborhoods have more symptoms of internalizing disorders such as anxiety and depression, as well as more symptoms of externalizing disorders such as conduct disorder and oppositional-defiant disorder. The fact that approximately three of five black children grow up in poverty, and in neighborhoods considered less than desirable, obviously has serious mental health implications.

Gender also has a major impact on many aspects of mental health and illness. Men and women exhibit different types of mental illness and disorder; women have higher levels of mood disorder, anxiety, and depression, whereas men have higher rates of personality disorder and substance abuse (Kessler et al. 1994; Robins et al. 1984). Rates of most psychotic disorders, on the other hand, are roughly equivalent for men and women. From the late 1800s until recently, women's higher levels of mood disorder were felt to result from either their biological or psychological differences from men. Over the past 20 years, in contrast, sociologists have actively studied social factors that influence the mental health and illness of men and women.

One sociological theory about how social factors differentially influence the mental health of men and women is the *social role* hypothesis. The social role explanation posits that women experience higher levels of mental distress than men because their roles entail more stress (Gove & Tudor 1973). In particular, role stress theory explains the higher rates of depression among housewives by arguing that the single occupational role of housewife provides few sources of gratification and reward, requires little skill, and lacks social prestige. Married women who work may experience less distress than housewives but still have higher levels of distress than working men, because they typically have jobs that are lower in pay and status and also face role overload from caring for their homes and children in addition to their work. Elevated levels of distress among working women can stem from the role strain and role conflict that results from attempts to meet obligations at work as well as family commitments.

Another sociological theory of sex differences argues that men and women respond to the stress in their lives in different ways. Drawing on the theories of Durkheim, Schwartz (1991) focuses on the social context of depression and differentiates between levels of integration and regulation in society. Altruism (value preferences that are oriented toward other people) is associated with high levels of group integration, whereas fatalism (beliefs that one has little control over what happens in life) is associated with high degrees of regulation over choices and actions. Girls are socialized to be "other oriented" and to accept strong normative controls over their behavior – especially sexual behavior. These dual conditions of high integration and high regulation produce both altruism and fatalism, which in turn lead girls to feel helpless and powerless and to have lower self-esteem. Because of their altruistic orientation, girls may also direct anger at themselves rather than at others. All of these social conditions are consistent with the etiology of internalizing mental disorders, especially depression (Schwartz 1991).

Boys, on the other hand, are socialized in contexts that place less emphasis on group membership and that have lower levels of normative regulation on behavior. Consequently, males are less likely to develop internalizing disorders but more likely to display antisocial behaviors in response to stress. That is, they are more likely to act out, display aggressive or hostile behavior, or resist normative authority. Hence, the gender-based social conditions just described could account for the elevated levels of internalized disorders among women and externalized disorders among men. Chapter 19, by Sarah Rosenfield, discusses the impact of gender on mental health and illness.

A final stressor that can influence mental health and illness is the labeling of mental illness itself. In Chapter 7, Phelan and Link showed how various social factors influence what kinds of people are labeled as mentally ill. In Chapter 20, Link and Phelan look at the other end of this process: how the labeling of mental illnesses affects the self-conceptions of people who receive these labels. They show how labeling has both positive aspects (bringing people into beneficial treatments) and negative aspects (generating degrading stereotypes that can lead to isolation and rejection). Although labeling is not often thought of as a stressor, the stereotypes invoked by labeling can be one of the most stressful aspects of being mentally ill.

Conclusion

As a group, these chapters develop the various aspects of the most common sociological model that explains mental health and illness: the stress process. They also show how different social groups experience varying amounts and types of stress and display divergent reactions to the stressors they face. Taken together, they illustrate how the process of developing mental disorders – and of maintaining mental health – is profoundly shaped not only by biological and psychological factors but also by the social environment.

8

Stress and Mental Health: A Conceptual Overview

Leonard I. Pearlin

Pearlin begins his chapter by describing the ways in which a sociological approach to stress and mental health is distinct from other perspectives and why an understanding of social stress is central to the etiology of psychological disorder. The "stress process" has three components: stressors, moderators, and outcomes. Stressors refer to any type of condition which can upset the adaptive capacity of the individual. There are many types of events and strains that generate stress, and serious stressors usually generate additional stress – a process referred to as "stress proliferation." In their responses to stress, individuals use the resources of coping, social support, and mastery. These three resources have all been given considerable research attention, and they have been found to mediate the effects of stress. Outcomes refer to mental health and well being, or to the degree of mental illness and disorder. Social researchers are more interested in the social origins of disorder; consequently, they use scales that measure the intensity of a disorder. One important issue Pearlin discusses is that people exposed to the same stressors are not necessarily affected in the same manner. Students may want to consider the sources of stress unique to the student role, observe how their friends and classmates respond differently to stress, and note which resources help them cope with such stress.

Sociologists have multiple stakes in the study of mental health. First, they may be drawn to the field out of humanistic concerns and the wish to contribute to the alleviation of suffering, not unlike the concerns of those in the healing professions. However, although the interests of sociologists may overlap with those of clinicians and representatives of other disciplines, a sociological approach to mental health is distinctly different. In particular, social scientists are more likely to be concerned with the social and environmental conditions that broadly contribute to mental health problems and less likely than clinicians to be concerned with the amelioration of specific disorders by direct intervention in the lives of individuals.

These perspectives and strategies are not mutually exclusive, of course, but they historically stem from different theoretical orientations and applications. The intellectual roots of sociological orientations can be traced to the distant past of the discipline, long before such constructs as stress and mental health were created. In fact, contributions to contemporary thinking about social stress and mental health were unknowingly made by theoreticians to whom these concepts would have been quite foreign. Examples can be detected in the writings of Marx, especially in his treatment of class conflict and alienation (see e.g. Bendix & Lipset 1966). They can be observed even more clearly in the work of Durkheim (1897). His search for the causes of suicide led him to examine the strength of people's social attachments and the stability and disruption of normative orders, the very conditions a contemporary sociologist might consider in attempting to account for suicide. The same may be said of Robert Merton's (1938) treatment of anomie, which focused on the inability of opportunity structures to satisfy the socially and culturally stimulated aspirations for achievement and advancement. The concern with social causation, a distinctive hallmark of sociological inquiry into mental health, has an established history.

The sociological study of mental health and mental disorder is distinguished from other disciplines in still another way. In the course of studying social influences on the mental health of individuals, sociologists also stand in a position to learn more about the societies of which the individuals are a part; as we identify individuals at risk for mental illness, we are better able to identify critical features of social life and its organization. In particular, the variations in mental health among social and economic groups help to guide our attention to the conditions that underlie these variations. The sociological study of mental health, therefore, can be employed as a reflecting surface that illuminates relevant aspects of the surrounding society and its organization.

Thus, the sociology of mental health is very much a two-way street. On the one hand it has the potential to inform us about the nature of mental disorder and its social and economic epidemiology; on the other hand, the identification of the social structural locations of people who are susceptible to mental disorders can help to illuminate those aspects of society, interpersonal relationships, and normative activities that affect well-being. Thus, sociologically oriented research into mental health can both enlarge our understanding of the causes of psychological disorder and, at the same time, highlight critical features of the larger society and the patterned experiences of people within it. Whichever the direction sociologists travel on this two-way street, they are bound to encounter terrain that is both interesting and challenging.

The present chapter cannot traverse all of this terrain; to do so is far beyond its scope. Instead, it explores the part played by social stress in the etiology of psychological disorder. This exploration will be guided by what has come to be referred to as the stress process. This process has three major components: stressors, moderators, and outcomes. As will be described, these components are closely interrelated, so that changes in one result in changes in the others. Consequently, the stress process provides a framework in which stress is viewed not simply as something that erupts and then dissipates but as a dynamic and ongoing set of interrelationships that surface and change across time. Each of the three components is described in turn.

Stressors

Stressors refer to any condition having the potential to arouse the adaptive machinery of the individual (Pearlin & Schooler 1978). The number and variety of conditions fitting this definition are, of course, enormous. However, the task of identifying stressors is simplified by the fact that not all types of stressors are of equal sociological interest. Specifically, stressors whose occurrence is unrelated to the social or economic characteristics of the people exposed to the stressor hold little interest for the sociologist. These would include stressors that surface in a random fashion or are unique or idiosyncratic to an individual. Such stressors may exert a powerful impact on the lives of people, but their very randomness indicates that they are not social in origin, making them of greater interest to clinicians than to social scientists. It should be recognized, however, that stressors that randomly surface may have nonrandom consequences. Thus, being struck by lightning would hardly be considered a social stressor, yet the disruptions of life resulting from the injuries may very well be influenced by social factors. Although the number and variety of specific stressors are vast, most fall into two fairly clear types or categories: eventful and chronic.

Eventful Stressors

A large class of potential stressors are those that surface abruptly at particular points of time; that is, they are events having discrete temporal origins. When research into the mental health effects of events began about 25 years ago, it was generally assumed that all events acted as stressors (Holmes & Masuda 1974; Holmes & Rahe 1967). Some events, it was thought, may demand less adjustment than others, but all events impose the need for at least some adjustment. It was reasoned that regardless of whether an event is good or bad, desired or undesired, the life change bound up in an event creates an inner disequilibrium capable of undermining well-being. Before the healthy functioning of the organism can be restored, an equilibrium must be reestablished through adaptive activities. Since those early studies, however, it has generally come to be recognized that only particular kinds of events are likely to act as stressors (Gersten et al. 1974; Thoits 1983). Events that are stressful are, for the most part, what have come to be described as "unscheduled," as differentiated from those that are "scheduled" (Pearlin & Radabaugh 1985).

Unscheduled events, as the term implies, are those that are unexpected within the projection of the life course. Thus, conventional marriage is a scheduled event because it is a normatively expected life-course occurrence. By contrast, divorce is considered to represent an unscheduled event: we are usually not wed with the expectation of later divorce, nor are we socialized for divorce as we are for marriage. Events of the unscheduled type – such as the death or injury of a child, premature death of a spouse, or involuntary job loss – are quite capable of having deleterious effects. By contrast, scheduled events, those that are built into the unfolding of the life course, typically do not have negative consequences for mental health (Pearlin & Lieberman 1979).

People exposed to the same eruptive event are not necessarily affected by it in the same way. Some may experience divorce, for example, as a release from an onerous life while their former spouses may view it as nothing short of a calamity (Wheaton 1990). In attempting to explain such variability, researchers have tried codifying the intra-event conditions that result in the variant impacts of a single event type (Brown 1974; Dohrenwend et al. 1978a). Essentially, these efforts place events in the meaning-shaping contexts in which they appear. For example, the death of a loved one might be examined to determine if the death was preceded by a slow and painful decline, by the quality of the relationship between the deceased and the survivor, and so on. These kinds of intra-event conditions, presumably, have a potentially useful role in clarifying the observed relationships between exposure to an event and indicators of health.

It is interesting that chronic or persistent stressors are frequently and misleadingly treated as life events. This can be seen in virtually all lists of life events; increased conflicts with spouses or job supervisors, for example, are treated as events rather than as changes in the intensity of ongoing stressors. This kind of slippage is not simply a definitional problem. More seriously, it represents a conceptual confusion that stands in the way both of accurately identifying the social sources of the stressors and of the accurate attribution of their observed effects.

Chronic Stressors

Persistent or chronic stressors usually arise more insidiously than events. Indeed, because many chronic stressors are rooted in social structures, roles, and relationships that tend to persist over time, the stressors themselves may be as enduring as the social arrangements from which they stem. For purposes of this chapter, three classes of chronic stressors can be identified: status strains, role strains, and contextual strains.

Status strains are stressors that arise directly from one's position in social systems having unequal distributions of resources, opportunities and life chances, power, and prestige. It will be recognized that such systems are collectively referred to as socially "stratified" systems. Examples include economic classes, occupational statuses, race and ethnicity, gender, and, some have argued (Riley, Johnson, & Foner 1972), age. Depending on people's standing within these stratified orders, of course, they may experience a variety of severe material deprivations, as well as personal devaluation and damage to their self-esteem (Rosenberg & Pearlin 1978). Status strains are as ubiquitous and persistent as the systems from which they grow; consequently, they can become chronic fixtures of people's lives that are capable of directly exerting deleterious health effects.

Status characteristics may also have indirect effects on health outcomes by influencing exposure to other kinds of stressors, such as *role strains.* As indicated by the name, role strains are stressors that arise within the context of institutionalized social roles; family and occupational roles are prominent among them (Pearlin 1983). One type of role strain entails conflicts among those with whom one interacts in the course of enacting the role – for example, conflicts between parents and children, husbands and wives, employees and employers, and so on. The very notion of role implies the presence of others within what is called a "role set" (Merton 1957). Not infrequently, members of the same role set come together with different agendas and interests and with different expectations of and obligations to one another. These differences can elevate considerably the potential for conflict; indeed, it is surprising this does not occur more often. When such conflict does occur, however, its effects are likely to be pronounced. First, because roles in major social institutions are important to their incumbents and to the society both, problems that arise within them cannot easily be treated with indifference. Second, the roles and the troubled relationships within these institutions tend to be continuous, with the result being that the troubles are also continuous.

Other role strains are similarly enduring. For example, strains may arise where people are unable to satisfy the simultaneous demands of their multiple roles. Such interrole conflict has been observed in a variety of circumstances, such as the difficulties of people in meeting both the requirements of their jobs and those of child rearing – a problem for many mothers, married as well as single (Parcel & Menaghan 1994).

In addition to strains arising from intra- and interrole conflicts, other strains may reflect the fact that the demands of the role exceed the energies and stamina of its incumbent. This is apparent in roles that develop around long-term caregiving to impaired relatives, as in the case of those stricken with Alzheimer's disease, where one can easily experience role overload (Aneshensel et al. 1995). A related concept is what has been described as "role captivity," where one assumes or retains a role without wanting it (Pearlin 1975). Among the many examples of role captives are the involuntarily retired who prefer to be employed, those in the labor force (because of economic constraints) who prefer to be at home, grandparents who are surrogate parents, or people who become caregivers to older relatives by default.

Finally, role strains may stem from changes in the expectations or composition of role sets. Some of these changes are driven simply by the aging process. For example, as children become adults and procreate their own families, parents (now grandparents) must constantly fine-tune their expectations and actions in a way that corresponds to the changed status of their children. Similarly, one's occupation or work setting will undergo change as one changes jobs or as people leave and newcomers enter the role set. Roles are constantly being restructured and, just as constantly, the incumbents of roles are called upon to make adjustments. The necessity to change one's ways may itself be a role strain; moreover, refusing to change as one's role circumstances are altered will most certainly be stressful as well.

Let us now consider briefly a final type of strain, *contextual strains.* These refer to the hardships and problems that derive from one's proximal environments, such as neighborhood and community. As in the case of role strains, exposure to those that are contextual may vary with the social and economic characteristics of people. They also appear to vary with age. Thus, very young people, whose lives are substantially confined to the boundaries of a community and its schools, may be more sensitive to strains within this context than those less confined. The contextual conditions of particular salience concern: level of violence and threats to safety, educational climate, organization of social life, availability of leisure and cultural facilities, quality of housing, access to health care, and so on. To think that young people, because of the innocence of their years, are exempt from stress processes goes against the grain of our knowledge. Namely, in addition to their immediate families, there is a host of conditions surrounding their everyday lives that can have a profound impact on their mental health.

The same may be said of community elders. Frailty and physical limitations may heighten their exposure and sensitivity to threats to their safety. Moreover, if they have resided in a community for a sufficiently long period, they are likely to have experienced considerable turnover among their neighbors, leaving them with the sense that they are living in isolation among strangers. Where resources that support social life are limited, this sense might be further heightened. The ease or difficulty in accessing health care, shopping, and transportation are also among the community-based daily stressors that many older people experience (Pearlin & Skaff 1995).

The Proliferation of Stressors

It is important to specify as accurately as possible the different types of eventful and chronic stressors that people experience. Such specification helps both to trace the origins of stressors and to target efforts at prevention and amelioration. However, when we examine people's actual experiences at a given time, it is highly unlikely that we shall find but a single stressor of a clearly defined type. On the contrary, single stressors rarely remain isolated over time. Instead, multiple stressors typically configure around the lives of people, and these configurations will include a variety of eventful and chronic stressors. Serious stressors usually generate additional stressors, a phenomenon referred to as "stress proliferation."

Stress proliferation can theoretically involve any combination of eventful and chronic stressors. Thus, one event may lead to another, as where divorce necessitates a residential move (Wertlieb 1991). Events commonly also create chronic strains of one kind or another, as when divorce results in economic hardship

(Pearlin & Johnson 1977). Certainly, too, chronic strains may contribute to exposure to negative events (e.g., where spousal conflict leads to divorce) and to other chronic strains, as when the demands of caregiving at home create problems on the job (Aneshensel et al. 1995). In addition, a structural feature of people's lives that substantially contributes to the proliferation of hardships – and so to the development of constellations of stressors – is that people are the incumbents of multiple roles and statuses. This, in turn, means that the events and circumstances present in one role or activity are interrelated to experiences in another role or area of activity. Spousal relationships are related to parental relationships; what happens on the job may be reflected in what goes on in the family; economic strains may have an erosive affect on network ties; and so on.

Suppose we wish to study the consequences of a serious life event, such as involuntary job loss. We would treat this loss as a *primary* stressor as a way of emphasizing its temporal priority. If we return to observe the same individual at a later time (see e.g. Pearlin et al. 1981) and discover, as we have, that since the job loss there has been an increase in his or her marital strife, then we might consider marital problems as a *secondary* stressor, calling attention to the possibility that job loss has exacerbated marital tensions. At this point, the mental health of the individual would potentially be affected both by the job loss and by the intensified marital conflict. If we looked at many people who experienced job loss – the primary stressor – it would probably be found that there is considerable variability among them in the relationship of this stressor to changes in mental health. One reason for this variability is that some of those exposed to the primary stressor will not have been exposed to the secondary stressor. Consequently, if we seek a comprehensive understanding of the connections between stress and mental health, it is necessary to cast a sufficiently wide net to account for both the primary and secondary stressors that may be present in the lives of individuals.

Strategies for the Study of Stressors

For someone learning for the first time about research into social stress, it might be a mystery as to how stressors are identified and assessed. These matters can also be mysterious to those of us with more experience. Obviously, the complex procedures that have been employed cannot be reviewed here in detail, but a brief overview might be useful.

At the risk of being overly simplistic, three research strategies can be distinguished: that which targets groups of people exposed to a particular event or strain; research that targets groups enmeshed in the same difficult situation; and studies involving large-scale samples representative of communities, where no assumptions are made with regard to the stressors to which people are exposed. Each of these strategies will be described in turn.

In the first, researchers know beforehand the events or chronic stressors they wish to observe, and they select groups for study in which the particular stressors of interest either have occurred or have a high likelihood of occurring. For example, the researcher might want to study the effects of involuntary job loss from individual plant closings (Hamilton et al. 1990; Perucci et al. 1988) or how parental divorce affects children (Wertlieb 1991). In order to pursue this kind of preestablished interest in a defined event and its consequences, it is necessary to target the people who have experienced or are expected to experience the event. Depending upon the event, this can be done with such documents as death records, newspapers, court records, clinic populations, union or industrial information, or any other source of information appropriate to the stressor of interest. It can be noted that longitudinal inquiries that start out by targeting those who have been exposed to a particular event may easily become studies of secondary stressors, both eventful and chronic. This happens when the inquiry is expanded to include the stressors that stem from the initial event.

The second research strategy involves groups embedded in persistent and inherently difficult situations known to be capable of giving rise to a host of stressors. Prime examples of this type of strategy are studies of long-term caregivers to relatives or partners impaired by progressive ailments, as in Alzheimer's disease and AIDS (e.g., Pearlin et al. 1990). People facing the same situational demands do not necessarily become exposed to the same stressors, nor do they necessarily experience stressors with the same intensity. The targeting of demanding situations rather than of specific stressors, therefore, enables the researcher to identify the conditions whereby people enmeshed in similar situational contexts may become exposed to very different configurations of stressors over time. These kinds of differences, it can be noted, often correspond to variations in the social and economic characteristics and to the resources of people caught up in the situation.

Finally, the community model has probably the most sociological merit, particularly when longitudinally designed. However, because of costs and funding priorities, the approach is underutilized. In effect, this strategy can sample different locations within such social structural systems as economic class, occupational and educational status, age, gender, race and ethnicity, and so on. It also attempts to gather information across a wide swath of stressors that may be present in the multiple domains of individuals' roles and activities. This research approach is thus able to fashion a social epidemiology of stress by looking at the distribution of different types of stressors across major social and economic groups who are engaged in a variety of roles (see e.g. Aneshensel & Frerichs 1982; Pearlin & Lieberman 1979). Unlike other strategies, it can yield a comprehensive view of stressors, their interrelations, and their place in the larger organization of people's lives.

Resources

Individuals are usually not passive objects, unresponsive to the problems and hardships that they may face. Even without necessarily being aware of what they are doing, they react to such circumstances in ways that often (but not always) help to protect them from their harmful consequences. The beliefs, actions, and interactions in which people engage in response to hardships and threats are collectively called resources. Three among them are particularly prominent in stress research: coping, social support, and mastery.

Coping involves things that individuals do on their own behalf to avoid stressors or to minimize the stress resulting from exposure to them. *Social support* pertains to the assistance or emotional uplift individuals are able to draw from their networks. *Mastery* refers to individuals' sense of control over the forces impinging on their lives. A vast literature has grown up around each of these resources, but in this chapter they will be treated collectively, highlighting their functions within the stress process. We first consider how these resources may exercise moderating effects on the process.

The Moderating Functions of Resources

The term "moderating resources" suggests that they are able to moderate or reduce the negative impact of stressors. Thus, if two people were exposed to similar stressors but possessed different resources, the negative effects of the stressors could be expected to be less for the person with greater resources. There are several ways in which moderators exercise this function (Ensel & Lin 1991; Wheaton 1985). One is known as *buffering*. With stress buffering, the resource has its greatest moderating effects among those who are exposed to the most intense stressors. That is, the very people who are at greatest risk for deleterious outcomes are those who are most protected by coping, social support, or mastery. Those who need resources less gain less from their possession. Thus buffering capabilities of resources are potential equalizers in the stress process, and for this reason they have drawn considerable research attention.

However, buffering is not the only way resources are found to moderate or contain the effects of stressors. A second mode of their moderating effects, more commonly observed than buffering, is referred to as additive or *main effects* (La Rocco, House, & French 1980). Main effects are those in which there is a reduction or suppression of the intensity of the stressor. Briefly: If people are good copers, have access to generative support, and entertain a high level of mastery, then they are likely to demonstrate positive mental health regardless of stressors they might experience. Thus, whereas the magnitude of buffering effects depends on the scope and intensity of stressors, the additive or main effects are independent of these conditions. Moreover, both buffering and main effects can occur within the same situation of stress.

The earlier distinction drawn between primary and secondary stressors is crucial in identifying the junctures in the stress process at which the moderating functions of resources can be observed. For example, one's coping responses to a difficult demand might help to reduce the intensity of the primary stressors and, in so doing, reduce the chances of secondary stressors surfacing and thereby minimize negative mental health outcomes. Or, perhaps, these responses function to block the proliferation of secondary stressors without reducing the intensity of those that are primary. Still another intervention hypothesis is that coping responses function to prevent damage to mental health while facing stressors that remain intense. Finally, the coping might function to restore mental health that has been damaged.

Interestingly, it is the last two functions that research usually targets. This practice can be recognized when the efficacy of the moderating resource is evaluated only by its observed ability to control negative outcomes, such as depression, or to improve the mental health of people under severe stressors. Indeed, there is a "stress industry" that promises – for a fee – to relieve people of symptoms of distress by a variety of means. It should not be inferred that the relief of distress is a trivial function. However, if attention is confined to the latter stages of the stress process, the full power of the moderators in governing the outcomes cannot be appreciated.

The Mediating Functions of Resources

The place of resources in the stress process is not limited to their moderating functions; they may also act as mediators (Wheaton 1985). To understand this function, it is necessary to recognize that resources do not exist in some fixed state but are subject to change over time: people adopt different coping strategies, turn to different people or look for different forms of support, or reappraise their mastery. One of the conditions that can change resources in these ways is exposure to stressors, especially where exposure is chronic. Thus, while resources moderate the effects of stressors on mental health outcomes, they may be changed by the very stressors whose effects they are moderating.

The mediating function of resources is reflected in situations where stressors affect outcomes through their effects on the resources. In other words, mediation occurs when stressors do not have a direct impact on mental health but instead act indirectly through their effects on resources. There is typically a negative effect of stressors on resources. That is, stressors undermine coping dispositions, adversely affect support systems, or erode the sense of mastery (see e.g. Mullan 1992). When stressors undermine resources, the depleted resources contribute to decreased mental health. In this manner, the impact of stressors on mental health is mediated by the diminished circumstances of the resources.

However, it can be pointed out that the effects of stressors on resources may entail more than their diminishment. Specifically, they might also function to mobilize resources that are dormant in the absence of stressors (Wheaton 1985). For example, divorce might lead a housewife to find a job she finds stimulating. Although empirical evidence for resource mobilization is yet to be produced, there is at least the suggestion that unfavorable circumstances may have favorable consequences.

Although coping, social support, and mastery are distinctly different resources, they are interdependent. Thus, people may turn to their social support systems for guidance in coping with difficult situations; coping, in turn, may involve the mobilization of appropriate social support; and, finally, we know that the maintenance of mastery depends to some extent on the amount and nature of one's social support (Skaff, Pearlin, & Mullan 1996). Because of these kinds of interconnections, resources tend to come in packages. Thus, if people are limited in one resource then they are likely to be limited in the possession of the others as well; conversely, if they have access to one then they are likely also to command the others.

The Limits of Resources

There is no doubt that coping, social support, and mastery have a critical role in the stress process, both individually and collectively. However, it is necessary to exercise some caution in drawing conclusions about the power of these resources in blunting the effects of stressful life conditions. Some situations, such as noxious conditions in a formally organized job setting, are highly resistant to individual coping efforts (Pearlin & Schooler 1978). Similarly, there are circumstances where emotional support does not make life easier, as in caring for a close relative with Alzheimer's disease (Pearlin et al. 1995). Mastery also has its limits, as in altering the course of an irreversible fatal disease that has stricken a loved one.

Thus, when we speak of the functions of resources in the stress process, we do not mean to suggest that such functions are universal – exercised without regard to the nature of the stressors with which people are grappling. In looking for stress-reducing functions it is necessary to keep in mind that there is a crucial specificity in the relationships of stressors and resources: certain kinds of resources when activated in the face of certain kinds of exigencies will have certain kinds of effects. Thus, there is no standard way of coping that is uniformly effective in dealing with different types of problems; there is neither a form nor source of support that can govern the effects of stressors of all kinds; and similarly, mastery is most certainly not a cure-all. In order to assess most clearly the efficacy of a resource, therefore, it is necessary to assess as well the particular nature of the stressors that are involved.

Outcomes

Health and well-being are the general outcomes usually evaluated in stress research, particularly as reflected in psychological functioning. Despite its common usage, the construct of mental health has resisted clear definition. Moreover, the social contexts from which mental health might arise have generally been overlooked. Thus, attempts to specify the indicators of mental health have traditionally emphasized such individual qualities as self-actualization, maximization of potential, the possession of self-esteem, and so on (Allport 1955; Jahoda 1958; Maslow

1954). It would be difficult to argue about the desirability of such qualities or their appropriateness as indicators of mental health. However, these qualities should not be regarded as somehow resulting solely from the efforts, motivations, and circumstances of the individuals in whose personalities they reside. The attributes that serve as markers of mental health do not develop within a social vacuum.

Although ultimately such attributes must be viewed as properties of individuals, it is necessary to take into consideration the social conditions that constrain or enhance their development. From a sociological perspective, it is not likely that mentally healthy individuals will emerge from social and economic conditions that fail to support or that go against the grain of qualities such as self-actualization or self-esteem.

It is no easier to define and measure mental illness than to define mental health. To begin with, illness is not the opposite of health, nor can one be assumed to exist in the absence of the other. Although one who is mentally ill can hardly be judged as simultaneously healthy, one who is not ill is not necessarily healthy, and someone who is not healthy is not necessarily ill. Partly because of the multiple perspectives of the various disciplines that are concerned with mental illness, it has been difficult to resolve the ambiguities surrounding the meaning and nature of mental illness. Three such perspectives are distinguished here: those brought to bear by clinicians, including but not limited to psychiatrists; those employed by researchers into social stress; and those found among those whose work is oriented toward symbolic interaction and social construction.

Clinical Perspectives of Mental Health

Although clinicians certainly may be interested in the social causes of mental illness, their immediate concerns are with its treatment. From a public health perspective, the treatment of mental illness requires the identification of people in the community who need treatment and of the particular disorders for which treatment is needed. Just as in other clinical specialties, mental health workers seek to distinguish cases from noncases. Cases are represented by those whose mental problems meet the criteria of distinct diagnostic categories, which serve as the basis for deciding on a treatment regimen. For example, the regimen for people diagnosed as schizophrenic would not be employed for those classified as having bipolar depression. Thus, the categorization of patients is entirely in keeping with the treatment imperatives that operate in psychiatry as a medical specialty.

As will be discussed shortly, there is considerable difference of opinion concerning the usefulness of diagnostic categories for defining cases of mental illness. For example, often a person cannot be categorized as simply being mentally ill or not, because doing so ignores the degree to which mental illness might be present (Mirowsky & Ross 1989a). Thus, people who do not qualify as cases of mental illness may nevertheless lead their lives in emotional troughs and with psychological dysfunction. Moreover, it is sometimes contended that the notions of mental illness in general and of diagnostic categories in particular have no intrinsic validity but are, instead, social inventions that function to control behavior by applying labels to those whose actions are socially deviant (Horwitz 1982a; Scheff 1966a). Whatever the merits of such arguments, it can be recognized that the operant imperatives for psychiatrists and other clinicians who conform to the medical model stem from their serious responsibility for therapeutically intervening in the lives of individuals. They are guided in this effort by the use of categorical nosologies and the clinical treatments presumed to be efficacious for people in that category.

The Perspectives of Social Stress Research

Researchers into social stress also have a serious responsibility, but of a different order: it is to identify the environmental and experiential conditions that may contribute to psychological dysfunctions and to the prevention or relief of such dysfunctions. An overriding interest of social researchers, therefore, is the identification of the social origins of disorder. The use of diagnostic categories does not serve these purposes as well as do scales measuring variations in the intensity of different types of dysfunction. Thus, although a scale of depression would not substitute for the diagnosis of depression for a clinician, such a scale might be very useful to the researcher seeking to ascertain whether and to what extent environmental conditions are inimical to the mental health of people. This purpose is best served by scales that distinguish degrees of distress, not by categories that draw the line between cases and noncases.

Social Constructionist Perspectives

Whereas stress researchers are likely to accept the reality of mental illness, questioning only how it is best defined and measured, another perspective questions the very reality of mental illness. There is a tradition of sociological inquiry more oriented to pondering the social meaning and functions of the concept of mental illness than to validating and measuring its presence (for a discussion, see Horwitz 1982a). Within this tradition, as noted, mental illness is viewed as a socially constructed label attached to people as a mechanism for controlling behavior that is considered deviant or otherwise unacceptable. From this perspective, if mental illness is a real state of being, it may be caused by the labeling rather than the other way around.

Other social constructionists, primarily symbolic interactionists, argue that mental illness is a construct invented not to control unacceptable behavior but to explain its incomprehensibility (Horwitz 1982a; Rosenberg 1992). When the actions of those with whom we interact defy our ability to explain or plausibly interpret them, we are likely to define them as mentally ill. For example, Rosenberg (1992) argues that it is when one is unable to place oneself in the role of the other that the other is thought to be disordered. The ability to take the role of another, it can be noted, may depend as much on the structural and cultural distance separating the observed from the observer as on the inherent nature of the behavior displayed by the observed.

The central point is that conceptions and measures of mental well-being cannot easily be judged as right or wrong. Rather, they are evaluated in terms of how appropriate they are to the purposes of the social scientists or practitioners using them. There is nothing intrinsic to mental health or illness that dictates the definition and meaning of these constructs. The way they are conceived depends on such considerations as (a) whether those who have a stake in mental health are involved in therapeutic interventions or research and (b) the clinical, behavioral, or social theories that guide their work.

Despite the many questions, uncertainties, and disputes that swirl around the study of mental health and illness, the practices usually adopted by research into social stress and mental health largely sidestep these problems. Thus, the research typically avoids diagnostic categories as outcomes and relies instead on symptom scales measuring a variety of general disorders, such as depression and anxiety. Moreover, it usually takes at face value the information provided by individuals about their own mental health or disorder. In doing so, usual research practices in effect view mental status as real rather than as a social construction without intrinsic substance. By and large, these strategic procedural decisions do not answer questions about the nature of mental health and illness, how these constructs are perceived by researchers and practitioners, or about the social influences on their recognition and meaning.

A final issue concerns the diversity of outcomes. Mental disorder is not a unitary phenomenon; on the contrary, it can be manifested in many ways and can assume many forms. What is of sociological interest about the multiplicity of outcomes is the possibility that different social and economic groups selectively manifest them. For example, it has been observed that – upon exposure to stressors – women are more disposed than men to react by becoming depressed and men more than women by alcohol abuse and aggressivity (Aneshensel et al. 1991).

Such selective manifestations of disorder pose a potential problem for interpretation of the stress process and its outcomes. Suppose, for example, that only depression were included in our study of the effects of stressors. What would be found in this instance is that women were more depressed than men who experience the same stressors. Such a finding, in turn, might tempt the interpretation that women are more vulnerable than men to the stressors and less able to deal with them in an efficacious manner. However, if multiple outcomes of the stress process were observed, including alcohol abuse and indicators of antisocial behavior, the conclusion about women's vulnerability would probably be different because the effects of the stressors on men would be just as severe but manifested in different ways. Thus, to avoid the misinterpretion of outcomes that can stem from their selective manifestations, a useful strategy is to observe outcomes sufficiently varied as to reveal the different effects of the same set of stressors on people occupying different segments of the social system.

Summary Observations

Several conclusions can be drawn from this chapter. Most apparent, of course, is the contention that the stress process offers a productive set of guidelines in looking for the origins of mental health and illness. It should be equally apparent that the stress process itself might be quite complex, entailing much more than a stroke of misfortune that leads to mental disorder. The misfortunes one can encounter include highly varied specific events as well as ongoing conditions of life. Moreover, one misfortune often leads to others, a phenomenon known as stress proliferation. Hence, in order to understand the way in which social stress may contribute to mental health problems, it is necessary first to capture the array of proliferated stressors that may impinge on people's lives. In turn, this requires that people be observed over a span of time in order to discern the developing configurations of the proliferated stressors. The stress process is primarily useful as a conceptual framework that unfolds over time.

A consistent finding in research into stress and mental health is that people exposed to the same stressors are not necessarily affected in the same ways. Some may be devastated, others seemingly untouched. There are several explanations for this variability, including the legacy of accumulated experience people bring with them into each new situation. The variable effects of stressors may also reflect differences in the possession of moderating resources – particularly coping repertoires, social support, and the sense of mastery or control. These kinds of resources may enter into the stress process at multiple points, alleviating the intensity of stressors, blocking their proliferation, or cushioning their impact on mental health.

The causal pathways leading to mental disorder, then, may not always be direct and clear. Nor do these pathways necessarily begin with the individuals who experience the disorder. Instead, the origins of health and disorder may reside deeply in the larger structures of the society and in the individual's position within them. These social and economic statuses may regulate the stressors to which people are likely to be exposed and their proliferation, the moderating and ameliorative resources to which they have access, and the ways in which they manifest disorder. Although genetic and biological forces may drive some mental health problems, broadly distributed mental health problems are inseparable from social and economic circumstances.

9

The Nature of Stressors

Blair Wheaton

This chapter focuses upon extending our understanding of stressors – the sorts of conditions that lead to distress. Wheaton begins by distinguishing stress from stressors (which are both different than distress) and then examines models that have shaped our understanding of the stress concept: the biological stress model, the life-change events model, and the engineering stress model. Wheaton then turns to a consideration of the varieties of stress, and he draws from the engineering model to develop a stress continuum along which different types of stressors can be arrayed. Described in an elaboration of this continuum are sudden traumas, life-change events, daily hassles, nonevents (when something anticipated did not happen, such as graduating from college), and chronic stressors. Wheaton also distinguishes micro stressors (which occur at the junctures of daily life) from macro stressors (which occur at the level of social system above the individual). Daily hassles are micro stressors, whereas economic recession or the divorce rate are macro stressors. Wheaton then considers the impact of stressors on mental health outcomes, asking whether stressors have independent effects or are the effects of other stressors. He concludes that different types of stressors have distinct and cumulative effects on mental health. Chronic stressors have the greatest impact, although childhood traumas also have an important effect. Hence we cannot understand the role of stress unless we assess a number of sources of stress over an individual's life-span. The chapter concludes by addressing a number of misconceptions about stress; students may want to explore these misconceptions and discuss their own experiences of stress and stressors.

Introduction

It is difficult to write about something that everyone already feels they understand. Stress is "in the air" these days, mostly as a residual and rather vague explanation of all that goes wrong. When a mental health problem does not yet have a clearly delineated cause (meaning, primarily, a biological or genetic cause), the reasoning is that it *could* be stress. This term is used presuming we all have the same impression of what stress is – but we do not.

"Stress" is a term used regularly in popular books, in the media, and in daily life. From the perspective of someone who studies stress, it is difficult not to notice the differences in meaning and understandings of stress, as well as a wide array of reactions to the topic of stress. Inevitably, the assumptions made about stress are wrong in some respect. There are themes in these misconceptions. For example, when others learn that I study stress, the responses fall into one or more of the following paraphrased types:

- "I have so much stress, I'm sure you could study me."
- "I feel stressed all the time."
- "Oh, they blame stress for just about everything these days."
- "But life is inherently stressful, so if it's always there, how can it make any difference?"
- "But doesn't it help to do relaxation exercises?"
- "Stress is just an excuse. Giving in to it is just a sign someone isn't strong enough."
- "But isn't depression basically genetic?"
- "Stress only happens to people who ask for it."

These responses reveal a strange mixture of overgeneralized skepticism and overgeneralized embracing of stress as an explanation of life problems. This chapter will explicate the underlying misconceptions and confusion in these responses by addressing the following issues:

(1) defining and distinguishing different types of stress;
(2) anchoring the concept of stress in an underlying model that allows for the necessary distinctions among concepts in a stress process;
(3) investigating the empirical distinctiveness of different types of stress;
(4) discussing misconceptions or confusion about what stress is and is not.

It is helpul to begin with a definition of stress that states the common elements of its various manifestations. In order to provide focus in the *psychosocial* approach to stress, I argue that we need to define stressors more than we need to define stress (see Wheaton 1996). Given that stress itself is usually defined in terms of a biological state of the body – a generalized physiological alert, if you will – in response to threatening agents, it is the realm of stressors that we must define yet have never been able to define adequately. As a reference point, then, I define stressors as *conditions of threat, demands, or structural constraints that, by their very occurrence or existence, call into question the operating integrity of the organism*. In this definition, a threat refers to any challenge to the person that implies personal harm or damage. Demands stand for the "load" component of stressors, indicating the level of current expectations, duties, and responsibilities that either accrue in social roles or are precipitated by specific life events. Terms like "work overload" and "work–family strain" imply excessive demands. Finally, structural constraints arise from social locations (i.e., places in the social structure) defined by serious, perhaps even severe, non–self-limiting social disadvantage. These structural constraints are especially manifest either as a restriction of choice or opportunity, or as persistent underreward in social exchange. In addition, we can think of reduced returns on efforts, qualifications, and contributions – such as lower income than others in the same position – as forms of underreward defined by a social relationship.

Origins of the Stress Concept

The Biological Stress Model

The foregoing definition is based on certain assumptions about the underlying model of stress that most clearly apply to the study of psychosocial stressors. In effect, parts of two different stress models – the biological model and the engineering model – apply to the study of stressors.

Selye's (1956) classic work on biological stress is a useful starting point. Selye's stress model included four stages: (1) stressors – in Selye's approach, a wide variety of events and conditions that represented threat or insult to the organism; (2) conditioning factors that alter the impact of the stressor on the organism, as in coping resources in the psychosocial model; (3) the general adaptation syndrome, an intervening state of stress in the organism; and (4) responses, adaptive or maladaptive. This conceptual model informs the study of stress to this day, since it incorporates essential distinctions in an overall process from stimulus problem to response. For example, we still see coping resources (such as social support) as fulfilling the conditioning factor role noted in this model. The separation of stress from coping capacity is an important contribution to the study of stress, since it allows us to discover how the two combine to produce healthful or nonhealthful outcomes. Further, the biological model makes the point, albeit implicitly, that the occurrence of stress is separate from more general behavioral responses (such as distress or depression) that form and stabilize over time.

For Selye, the heart of the matter of stress was the *general adaptation syndrome* itself. This syndrome was defined in terms of physiological indications of a three-stage response sequence to "noxious agents": the alarm reaction, the stage of resistance, and the stage of exhaustion (Selye 1956). Thus, Selye's primary interest was in identifying and describing a biologically based and generalized response syndrome to threatening agents. To help with the metaphor, he adds that stress could be defined as the "state of wear and tear of the body" (1956: 55). Having identified stress as a physiological response state of the body, Selye then proceeds to define a stressor as "that which produces stress" (1956: 64). The issue of defining stressors is thus inexorably tied to whether they produce stress or (in the psychosocial approach) distress or disorder. There are two fundamental problems with this. First, a stressor is simply a putative problem whose actual threat value is still to be defined by contextual circumstances. A stressor cannot be defined purely (and retrospectively) by its consequences, because in so doing we preclude, or seriously impair, the identification of classes or types of social environments that are problematic to mental health in the population. Second, exposure to stressors has other consequences than changes in health that may bypass the actual occurrence of stress, biologically defined. Stressors may undermine educational performance, lead to marrying earlier, cause interruptions in labor-force activity, lower income, and so forth. It simply is not necessary that biological stress occur for stressors to have important consequences.

The biological model clearly gives little guidance on bounding or delimiting what stressors are or, for that matter, are not. If we conceptualize what we are trying to accomplish in stress research as, in part, the identification of highest risk experiences for the largest part of the population, then we want a definition of stressors that leads us to a set of the most virulent experiences, at the same time being careful not to exclude sources of stress simply because they are difficult to measure or detect. This lack of guidance in the biological model implies, I believe, that one cannot use the biological stress model as a basis for derivation of any particular psychosocial stress model; yet that is precisely what we have done.

Life-Change Events: The Model Stressor. When the word "stress" is used in research circles, the most common operational link that gives expression to this word is the life-change event: a discrete, observable, and "objectively" reportable event that requires some social and/or psychological adjustment on the part of the individual – the operant word here being *event*. Early research on important life changes included positive events, but over the last two decades the usual approach has been to focus on negative events in particular, since those events have been found to be much more harmful to mental health than positive events have been found to be either harmful or helpful (Ross & Mirowsky 1979). To give some flesh to the kinds of events studied, issues include being fired from a job, getting a divorce, the death of a spouse or loved one, having an abortion or miscarriage, being assaulted or robbed, and ending a romantic relationship. The lists of such events range from about 30 items to well over 100 in attempting to capture the essential set of stressful life changes (Dohrenwend et al. 1978a; Holmes & Rahe 1967). In the development of these inventories we see the opportunity to study stress using a set of objectively verifiable occurrences.

If we look to Selye's work for clues as to what stressors are, we find examples that are quite instructive. The noxious agents cited include things such as toxic substances, noise, extreme heat or cold, injury, and weight (Selye 1956). Although some of these agents qualify as "events," it is clear that some should be viewed instead as conditions or continuous states. In fact, it has never been the case that biological stressors were restricted to the notion of an event (Hinkle 1987). Thus, it is something of a mystery in the first place as to why – other than expedience of measurement – the concept of life-change events was assumed to be closer to the core of what is stressful than other life problems. Of course, the idea was that change is a challenge, but then so is dealing with unremitting sameness. The problem in defining continuous states as stressors seemed to be that it was difficult to designate at what point or level they become stressful. But the problems in measuring more continuous, ongoing problems as stressors should not distract attention from them, especially if they are important in terms of mental health risk.

Probably because life events could be self-reported and therefore measured more straightforwardly, and even then with a number of cautionary attendant problems, the measurement of other forms of stress waited while the life events tradition flourished. But our intuitions and our experience tell us that a stressor can also exist as a "state," a continuous and persistent problem. Another stress model explicitly distinguishes between such types of stressors and includes as well a broader – and, in some ways, more flexible – metaphor for how stress affects humans. Ironically, this model is derived from the stress model of physical mechanics.

The Engineering Stress Model

The "original" stress model was formulated to understand the effects of external forces on the integrity of metals. In fact, it was the 1984 collapse of a bridge over a river on Interstate 95 in Connecticut that first drew my attention to the engineering stress model. The main span of this bridge collapsed in the night without the slightest provocation of an "event" – no high winds, no unusual rate of traffic that day. It occurred to me then that breakdown often occurs in both the physical and social world without an observable precipitating event. In these cases, breakdowns require explanations that use concepts beyond the very notion of an event. Basically, the continual stress to the bridge of unobserved rusting had simply reached a critical structural limit, and the bridge collapsed.

In the engineering model, stress is essentially an external force acting against a resisting body (Smith 1987). One could say that stress also becomes a stressor when the level of force exceeds limits defining structural integrity. It appears that stressors and stress are not distinct phases in the engineering model – both refer to the external force or threat. As a metaphor, this makes the engineering model more amenable to translation into the psychosocial model.

More precisely, stress is defined in the engineering model as the load exerted by a force divided by the capacity of the material to resist (Smith 1987). The capacity of the material to resist is analogous to the concept of coping capacity in the psychosocial stress model. I have argued elsewhere (Wheaton 1996) that it is best to consider the stressor and the resistance posed by coping as separate issues in order to study what levels of each are optimally health protective or carry the greatest health risk. The engineering model, in this area at least, is less conceptually flexible than the biological model.

Figure 9.1 reproduces from Smith (1987) the curve showing the relationship between stress and strain according to the engineering model. In the engineering model, strain is the response state of the material – specifically, the state of the elongation and compression of the material. Obviously, strain is the distress side of the model. The level of stress is shown on the Y axis, the level of strain on the X axis. The material, in a pristine healthy state, starts at zero. As long as the stress

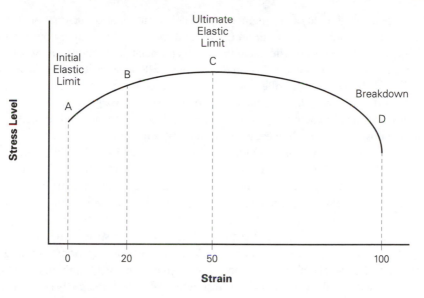

Figure 9.1. The stress-versus-strain curve in the engineering stress model. *Source:* Adapted from Smith (1987).

applied does not exceed point A on the stress scale, the material will not exceed its elastic limit, and it will return to its original shape after the stress is removed. The model does allow for changes in the elastic limit of the material, however. When stress exceeds A, say to level B, the material is able to adjust by elongation or compression and, in the process, achieve a new, greater elastic limit. In other words, it is stronger. This feature of the engineering model offers greater flexibility than the biological stress model of Selye in that the engineering model allows for the enhancement of coping capacity, rather than just the minimization of damage to existing capacity, as a result of facing stressful situations.

The model also allows for deterioration of capacity to resist, since the material has a finite elastic limit. The psychosocial implication is that, at some point, an individual's ability to respond with adjustments that enhance strength will no longer be possible. The size and force of the stressor will overwhelm the human capacity to withstand. Point C in Figure 9.1 represents the ultimate elastic limit of the material: the point of maximum strength. If stress is applied beyond point C then the amount of stress that the material can resist will actually decrease until point D, known in the engineering model as fracture or breakdown. The curve in Figure 9.1 can be considered a representative curve; materials (and people) will differ in the amount of rise and fall of the curve, and in the left-to-right distance for enhancements versus deteriorations in strength.

A fundamental point of the engineering model is that stress occurs in more than one form, sometimes as a catastrophic event and sometimes as a continuous force. This distinction has been articulated in the psychosocial stress model in the work of Pearlin and his colleagues (Pearlin & Schooler 1978; Pearlin et al. 1981; Pearlin 1983) and Brown and his colleagues (e.g., Brown & Harris 1978), emphasizing the importance of what have come to be known as *chronic* rather than *event* stressors. The distinction between catastrophic and continuous forces maps directly in the psychosocial approach to event versus chronic stressors.

Why is this distinction useful in the engineering model? In effect, the types of adjustments possible on the part of the material are defined by whether the force is a trauma or a continuous force. Thus, we expect that the model showing how (i.e., via mediating variables) chronic stress affects mental health will be quite distinct from the model showing how life events affect mental health. For example, one can imagine that dealing with life event stress may involve a stronger role for coping resources that can be easily mobilized but exist over short periods only (e.g., unusually high levels of social support after a spouse dies). On the other hand, chronic stress may demand more stable resources that are automatically rather than conditionally activated.

Varieties of Stress

Whether or not the engineering model is invoked, the importance of continuous and ongoing sources of stress can be argued from a psychosocial perspective per se (Pearlin 1989). This argument includes the notion that chronic forms of stress are likely to result from stable features of differences in position in a social structure. Pearlin has also made consistently clear in his work that stressors should be distinguished because they are involved in a dynamic interplay of causation over time, leading to either the spread or containment of stress experience over people's lives depending on the sequence and types of stressors involved. Earlier stressors may change the level of threat resulting from later stressors, as when exposure to an earlier stressor, such as parental divorce, changes both the likelihood and the mental health consequences of a personal divorce (Roszell 1996). In this approach, earlier stress in the life course can be part of the context of the meaning of later stress. Thus, distinguishing types of stressors is a necessary condition of understanding the complex interrelationships among distinct stress experiences over the life course, as well as the collective and cumulative impacts of stress on mental health.

The Stress Continuum

Contrasting the idea of an event with the idea of a continuous force allows us to anchor two ends of what I call a "stress continuum," along which a number of other types of stressors discussed in the literature can be arrayed.

Event versus Chronic Stressors. As stressors, *life events* have the following characteristics: they are discrete, observable events standing for significant life changes with a relatively clear onset and offset; once in motion, they are made up of a relatively well-defined set of subevents describing the normal progress of the event. Of course, some life events (such as the death of a pet) have little internal structure, but most others actually involve a process, often a partially ritualized process. Divorce, job loss, and death of a spouse are classic examples. The defining issue in a life event is its discreteness: its onset, typical time course, and offset. Life events do not typically emerge slowly as an issue; rather, they usually begin with the announcement of unfortunate news that begins the life change. As stressors, life events typically have a clear offset, a point at which the stressor ends – for example, court settlement of the divorce or actual death of the spouse. That life events take time to unfold is well documented by Avison and Turner (1988).

Taking such events as a point of departure, then, we can define a very different class of stressors, referred to as *chronic stressors,* that (1) do not necessarily start as an event, but develop slowly and insidiously as continuing and problematic conditions in our social environments or roles; (2) typically have a longer time course than life events, from onset to resolution; and (3) are usually less self-limiting than life events. The crux of the distinction between event stressors and chronic stressors is the time course of the stressor, but more is involved – including differences in the ways that the stressor develops, exists, and ends.

There is, of course, the inevitable fact that some life events will be more chronic than others and some chronic stressors will act more like discrete problems. This overlap in phenomenology is not at issue. Event stressors and chronic stressors represent two large and distinct classes of how stressors occur. Some stressors will begin like an event, with sudden news or a clear change, but then become open-ended and protracted. This situation describes what could be considered a borderline case, a hybrid. But in many cases such as this, it is likely that not one but two stressors have occurred and in effect have been spliced together. The distinction between event and chronic stressors allows us to distinguish, for example, the effects of *getting* divorced from those of *being* divorced. Keeping the stressors separate allows us to distinguish between the problems of identity threat and identity adjustment, on the one hand, and the problems of continual vigilance and pressure, on the other. Put another way, we can correspondingly distinguish the loss of another and the absence of another as two stressors.

Forms of Chronic Stress. Chronic stress can occur in a number of ways. Wheaton (1997) distinguishes seven kinds of problems that suggest chronic stress, including:

(1) threats – as in the threat of regular physical abuse, or the threat of living in a high-crime area, where the threat itself is the chronic stressor;

(2) demands – as in facing levels of expectation or duty that cannot be met with current resources, including overload due to cross-role and within-role expectations;

(3) structural constraints – including lack of access to opportunity or necessary means to achieve ends as well as any structured reduction in available alternatives or choices;

(4) underreward – literally, reduced outputs from a relationship relative to inputs, as in lower pay for a job than others with the same qualifications;

(5) complexity – as in the number of sources of demands, or direct conflict of responsibilities across roles, or constant contingency and instability in life arrangements, or complex content in role responsibilities;

(6) uncertainty – a problem only when one desires or needs resolution of an ongoing issue; in effect, unwanted waiting for an outcome; and

(7) conflict – when regularly re-enacted and thus institutionalized in relationships, without apparent resolution, as embodied by fundamental differences over goals or values.

It should be clear that the concept of chronic stress is not coextensive with the concept of role strain. Pearlin (1989) explicitly uses the term chronic stress to include not only role-based or role-defined stressors but also what he calls "ambient stressors" that cannot be attached to any one role situation. The importance of this point cannot be overstated. If chronic stress is tied exclusively to occupancy in major social roles – spouse, worker, parent – then role occupancy becomes conceptually confounded with the experience of chronic stress because it becomes a necessary condition for reporting that type of stress. This is especially unfortunate when one realizes that selection into these roles is based partly on whatever is taken for social competence, and this component could suppress relationships between chronic stress and mental health indicators. Thus, we need to be mindful, in measuring stressors of this kind, that we must target stressors that accompany not only role occupancy (e.g., work overload, marital conflict) but role inoccupancy as well (e.g., not having children when you want to, not having a partner when you want to be in a relationship) as well as a range of ambient stressors not directly related to roles (e.g., time pressure, financial problems, or living in a place that is too noisy).

Figure 9.2 shows the stress continuum formed by considering the distinction between discrete and continuous stressors, with different types of stressors placed on the continuum from most discrete to most continuous. As we shall see, some stressors are inherently more variable than others in terms of their typical position on this continuum. Life events are near the discrete end of the continuum, based on a typical profile of the clear onset of an event and its defined course until resolution. At the other end of the continuum is chronic stress, characterized by its slow and sometimes imperceptible onset ("I don't know how I got here") and its

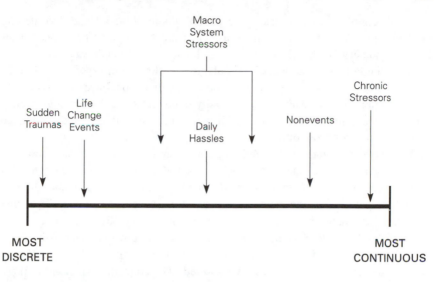

Figure 9.2. The stress continuum.

open-ended recurring character as a problem. The fact that some stressors are indeed chronic is suggested by findings using a recent 90-item measure of chronic stress (Wheaton 1991), which asked respondents how long each problem had been present in their lives. The average time was five years, suggesting that some stressors do have a typically chronic course.

The stress continuum in Figure 9.2 includes a number of other types of stress that are typically distinguished in current approaches. I now turn to a discussion of these distinctions.

Daily Hassles. A concept that is often mistaken for chronic stress is that of daily hassles (Kanner et al. 1981). Daily hassles are defined as "the irritating, frustrating, distressing demands that to some degree characterize everyday transactions with the environment" (1981: 3). In fact, there is considerable variability in the degree to which the daily hassles used in measures are regular features of daily life. It is interesting to note that some examples of daily hassles given by Kanner and colleagues – work overload, status incongruity between spouses, noise – are chronic stressors, but more importantly, these examples are not at all typical of what is measured in the daily hassles scale.

The daily hassles scale has been the subject of some controversy. Complaints that a significant number of items are really measures of other concepts in the stress process model, including outcomes such as distress, seem all too valid (Dohrenwend et al. 1984). For example, items such as "thoughts about death," "use of alcohol," "trouble making decisions," "being lonely," and "not getting enough sleep" are very clearly measures of distress or related concepts. Other items sound very much like life events and should not be included as daily hassles per se – "laid off or out of work"; "problems with divorce or separation" – and a large number indeed reflect standard chronic stress items but have little to do with the stated definition of daily hassles as daily minor stresses: "not enough money for basic necessities," "overloaded with family responsibilities," and "prejudice and discrimination from others."

At the core, daily hassles do stand for a unique area of stress that is not tapped by the more general conceptualization of chronic and event stressors. Daily hassles include such issues as: "troublesome neighbors," "misplacing or losing things," "care for a pet," "planning meals," "repairing things around the house ," "having to wait," "too many interruptions," "preparing meals," "filling out forms," "the weather," and "traffic problems." What is unique about this concept is the focus on insidious aspects of the mundane, the specification of a level of social reality at which other stressors are not usually specified. The concerns expressed in these types of items on the daily hassles scale – grocery shopping, traffic jams, caring for a pet, misplacing things, the weather – nicely express the mundane realities of daily life that, when experienced cumulatively, may be annoying and stressful. But note that they do not consistently refer only to *regular* features of daily life, though some items (e.g., troublesome neighbors, preparing meals) clearly do refer to the almost automatic or ritualized concerns of daily life and thus may be more chronic in their manifestations. Such issues are defined as chronic by the unavoidability of their enactment. At the same time, a number of these items refer to more episodic and irregular events that cannot be anticipated daily and occur only contingently, for example, "misplacing or losing things," "having to wait," or "the weather." For each of these items, the usual scenario would be that the problem occurs at some times but not others, and usually unpredictably.

Thus, daily hassles span the realm of both discrete events and chronic problems. In general, daily hassles tap something that would be better termed "micro events," at the border between quasi-regular events and continuous life conditions that suggest chronic stress per se. Because of this, Figure 9.2 shows daily hassles as occupying a middle point on the stress continuum. Daily hassles are the true borderline stressors in this classificatory scheme. Most daily hassles occur in the range of "episodic but recurring" to "ritualized and regular but as a series of distinct occurrences."

Daily Diary Studies. A closely related approach to stress comes under the rubric of "daily diary" studies (Bolger et al. 1989; Stone & Neale 1984). Here stresses are observed daily as part of a diary regimen. Stone and Neale (1984) identify a set of severe daily events, some of which are purely events (such as a child getting sick or injured) and some of which can be enactments of more general chronic stressors (such as an argument with a spouse). Bolger and associates (1989), on the other hand, focus primarily on manifestations of more chronic stressors – specifically, conflicts, arguments, and role overloads.

Thus, daily diary studies also do not specify a particular type of stressor along the stress continuum. What they offer is a unique research design that allows a more micro assessment of the stress process than most other research designs used in this field.

Macro Stressors. If there are such things as micro stressors, then there must be macro stressors as well. In the previous section, I refer to micro stressors based on a time referent for dividing up the concerns of life – starting from "daily" and implying other stressors that are conceived of in larger time chunks (e.g., a bad work situation). Units of analysis can also be divided by level of social reality. Daily hassles refer to stressors that occur at the experienced juncture of daily life and microsocial routines. At the other extreme, we have what may be called system stressors or, in other words, macro stressors. These stressors occur at the macrosocial system level, or at least at a level of social system above the individual and the interpersonal.

The predominant focus in this approach has been the issue of economic recessions, usually embodied in studies of the unemployment rate (Brenner 1973; Dooley & Catalano 1984b). However, a number of other macro system stressors qualify and can be included, such as the divorce rate, infant deaths, high school dropout rate, and disasters (Linsky, Colby, & Straus 1987). Recent work also points to neighborhood-level contextual factors – such as the configurational demographics of the neighborhood, the crime rate, pollution and other ambient physical stressors, segregation, and collective economic pressures, to name a few examples – as potential stressors that operate to affect individual mental health either directly or indirectly in conjunction with individual-level factors (Aneshensel & Sucoff 1996b).

Like daily hassles, this group of stressors contains both event and chronic concerns. The point here is generally the same as for micro stressors, with this proviso: macro stressors span a broader range of discrete occurrences (disasters) to chronic conditions (recessions, crime). Accordingly, macro stressors are represented in Figure 9.2 as a particularly variable type, occupying a range on the stress continuum. At the same time, Figure 9.2 centers their manifestation at an average level of discreteness. This reflects the fact that for every macro event stressor there seems to be a corresponding chronic version. Consider, for example, war and recession. Wars may be chronic, as in the Vietnam War, and recessions may also be chronic, as in the Great Depression. But some military and economic events at the macro level are very acute in nature. A military coup is a system-level traumatic event, as is a stock market crash in the economic sphere.

Nonevents. Gersten and colleagues (1974) use arousal theory to point out that lack of change can be as stressful as change. They use this point to suggest the importance of a kind of stressor that they term "nonevents." A nonevent is defined as an "event that is desired or anticipated and does not occur . . . . Alternatively, a nonevent could be seen as something desirable which does not occur when its occurrence is normative for people of a certain group" (1974: 169). Thus, an anticipated promotion that does not occur, or not being married by a certain age, can be considered nonevents. These examples raise the clear possibility that nonevents are a form of chronic stressor. Yet nonevents additionally have the ironic quality of seeming like events; this is clear even in the foregoing definition. This quality is clearest in the case of nonevents that reflect the absence of specific expected events, such as a scheduled promotion or not having a child by a given age.

On the other hand, nonevents that derive from nontransitions to desired roles and are not tied to normative timing seem more clearly like classic chronic stressors. Even the absence of promotion can be seen as "role captivity," the inability to leave or alter a given role situation. In such cases it is the unwanted waiting for an outcome or the very lack of change that becomes the problem. Seen from this perspective, such nonevents look very much like a type of chronic stressor. In a recent study, I asked respondents to report any expected things that didn't happen in the last year that they wanted to happen. They gave a wide array of answers, many of which qualified as classic nonevents: "hoping for a loan for low-income housing but didn't get one," "wanted a relationship with parent to improve but it didn't," "planned a trip that didn't happen," "expected higher marks in school," and so on. Many of these issues also reflect chronic ongoing problems in which an individual takes issue with the current state of affairs and wants change; in this case, a lack of change is stressful.

Figure 9.2 appropriately shows nonevents as close to the continuous end of the stress continuum, with a small qualifier. Even if we interpret nonevents as the conjunction of ongoing chronic conditions and passing markers in time, they do show one characteristic of events: because they *refer to* expected or desired events, the nonevent is itself like an event. Thus nonevents are placed closer to the discrete end of the continuum than chronic stressors.

Traumas. There are stressors that are thought to be so serious, so overwhelming in their impact, that we must give them separate status to distinguish them from the usual class of events that we designate as stressful. The most applicable term for these stressors is traumas.

It is necessary to clarify what is meant by this term when contrasted with, for instance, the usual stressful life event. The DSM-III-R manual defines a traumatic event as one "that is outside the range of usual human experience and . . . would be markedly distressing to almost anyone" (APA 1987: 250). This definition emphasizes one of the essential characteristics distinguishing traumas from the kinds of life events commonly used in life event inventories: the magnitude of the stressor. Norris (1992) defines traumas in terms of a population of events marked by a sudden or extreme force and denoting "violent encounters with nature, technology, or humankind" (1992: 409). Both this and the APA definition point to important classes of traumas, but they are incomplete. First, not all traumas occur only as events. For example, a single rape would be considered a traumatic event, but repeated, regular, and therefore expected sexual abuse is best thought of as a chronic traumatic *situation*. Including chronic situations allows us to broaden the definition to include Terr's consideration both of events and of situations marked by "prolonged and sickening anticipation" (1991: 11). Second, and obviously, not all traumas need be violent; some, like a life-threatening illness or a partner's ending an important and valued romantic relationship, may well not involve violence at all.

Thus, a number of elements of traumas are important: (1) they must be more severe in level of threat than the usual life change event; (2) they may occur either as isolated events or as long-term chronic problems; and (3) because of their severity, they are thought to have greater potential for long-term impacts than most other types of stressors.

Traumas include a potentially wide range of severe situations and events, such as war stress (Laufer, Gallops, & Frey-Wouters 1984), natural disasters (Erikson 1976), sexual abuse or assault during childhood or adulthood (Burnam et al. 1988; Kendall-Tackett, Williams, & Finkelhor 1993), physical violence and abuse (Bryer et al. 1987; Gelles & Conte 1990; Kessler & Magee 1994a), parental death (Brown, Harris, & Bifulco 1986b; McLeod 1991; Saler 1992), and parental divorce (Amato & Keith 1991; Glenn & Kramer 1985).

The most distinguishing feature of traumas is the level of imputed seriousness of the stressor – an order of magnitude beyond what is included on life event or chronic stress scales. Some items on life event inventories, such as the death of a child, would in fact qualify as traumas. There is no clear-cut division, only the obvious fact that many traumatic experiences are not measured in life event approaches, presumably because they are too rare. Using an inventory of 20 lifetime traumas, Wheaton, Roszell, and Hall (1997) report that the prevalence rates of these experiences in a general population range from a low of 3.5% for being sent away from home in childhood to nearly 50% for experiencing the death of a spouse, child, or other loved one. In general, these stressors are not that rare: the average prevalence is close to 20%.

One prevalent and typical form of trauma – the sudden onset form – is represented at the most discrete end of the stress continuum in Figure 9.2. Although traumas come in many forms and with a variety of natural histories, this subtype of trauma comes closest to the archetype of an unanticipated, sudden, dramatic, one-time experience that is often associated with the term "trauma." The experience of living through, without warning, a destructive tornado is a prime example of this type of trauma. Other examples include sexual assault, the unexpected and sudden death of a partner, victimization in a violent crime, and severe accidents.

The Empirical Distinctiveness of Stressors

The discussion to this point suggests that stressors come in a variety of manifestations yet share the qualities of a significant threat, demand, or constraint. Beyond the conceptual distinctions, a basic issue is whether there is empirical support for the idea that different types of stressors have independent effects on mental health, or rather are part of a larger "stress package" that does not require these distinctions. This section makes two simple, but essential, points. First, there are no "fundamental" stressors that absorb and express the impacts of all other sources of stress. Second, the types of stress distinguished here have independent effects on mental health, so that proper assessment of the total impact of stress *requires* consideration of multiple sources of stress.

In considering the impact of stressors, we must remember that stressors are also related to each other – that is, they occur in some sequence, so that some act as the foundation for others. This is important because the true overall impact of a type of stress includes not only its unique, independent effect on mental health (controlling for other stress experiences) but also its indirect effects on mental health via its impact on the risk of experiencing later stressors, which then in turn also affect mental health. In what follows, I therefore distinguish the "unique" effects of each stressor (i.e., its net effect on mental health after controlling for other stressors) from its "total" effect on mental health (i.e., the unique effect plus all indirect effects through other stressors).

In order to operationalize this distinction when studying an array of stressors, we must make some assumptions about the probable causal sequence in which different types of stressors typically occur. The causal sequence among types of stressors is likely to be complex, but guidelines are available. Using assumptions or findings reported in the literature (Pearlin et al. 1981; Wheaton 1994), I assume that life events are more likely to set in motion chronic stressors than vice versa, that both nonevents and daily hassles are basically epiphenomenal outcomes of current chronic stress and recent life events, and that childhood traumas (or early adult life traumas in some samples) temporally precede all other forms of current or recent stress experience. Finally, I make no assumptions about the relationship between hassles and nonevents. Of course, these assumptions are all made more difficult by the fact that we are talking about overall classes of stressors rather than individual stressors. Some nonevents may lead to chronic stress, and some chronic stressors may increase the risk of life events. The assumptions used here reflect only the modal reality for the causal sequences involved among different types of stress.

Table 9.1. *Standardized effects of stressors on distress in three studies: Unique and total effects*

	Stress Measurement Study		Toronto Mental Health and Stress Study		National Population Health Survey	
	Unique	Total	Unique	Total	Unique	Total
Childhood traumas	.145**	.387**			.105**	.273**
Earlier adult life events	.128*	.191**				
Lifetime traumas			−.002	.209**		
Recent life events	.215**	.289**	.184**	.270**	.122**	.242**
Chronic stressors	.396**	.425**	.406**	.406**	.374**	.374**
Nonevents	−.062	−.054				
Daily hassles	.133*	.128*				
R^2	.43		.25		.23	

* $p < .01$.   ** $p < .001$.

Table 9.1 presents results from three different studies: the Stress Measurement Study, based on randomly selected households in three Canadian cities ($N = 530$); the Toronto Mental Health and Stress Study, a longitudinal study of 1,393 randomly selected adults in Toronto between the ages of 18 and 55 (Turner et al. 1995); and the National Population Health Survey (NPHS) of Canada, conducted in 1994–95 with a sample of 16,291 adults. This last study is among the few to attempt to measure systematically a range of stressors in a national population. Each of these studies included measures of multiple sources of stress.

The measures used in these studies had much in common. The Stress Measurement Study included a 90-item version of a chronic stress index (Wheaton 1997), the Toronto study a 51-item version, and the NPHS a 16-item version. Life events were taken from a standard list (Turner et al. 1995), and the trauma measure was developed as part of the Toronto study (Wheaton et al. 1997). To enhance comparison across studies, I used distress as the standard mental health outcome in each analysis. The Stress Measurement Study also included measures of daily hassles (in a 25-item reduced form), nonevents, and earlier adult life events reported after leaving home but before the last two years.

Table 9.1 shows standardized regression coefficients, meaning that the relative size of effect can be compared within each study. The first two columns (under the Stress Measurement Study) document five important findings. First, five out of six of the stressors measured in this study have independent effects on distress. In fact, the level of explained variance in distress is 43%, indicating that the overall impact of stressors is strong. The obvious implication is that, unless we measure a variety of stressors, we will underestimate their impacts on mental health. Second, looking at the unique impacts, it appears that chronic stressors have the greatest importance as predictors of distress ($\beta = 0.396$). However, even childhood traumas that occurred as many as 20 to 50 years earlier have a distinct impact. Third, among current stressors, daily hassles do have some influence but nonevents have little, at least when controlling for other chronic stressors. Fourth, the effects of other stressors do not replace the role of life events; rather, they supplant this role. In fact, the size of the effects for life events in these findings are very close to what is reported in the life events literature when other stressors are not measured. Thus, we cannot conclude that life events are less important than they have seemed; it is simply that other stressors also matter. Finally, focusing on the total effects of each stressor, we see that childhood traumas indeed have a considerable influence on later mental health as measured by distress, second only to current chronic stressors.

Only three types of stress were measured in the Toronto study and the NPHS. Looking in particular at the total effects in the Toronto study, again we see that three sources of stress have independent influences and thus distinct roles to play, with chronic stress again having the largest impact. It should be noted here that the total impact of lifetime trauma is much larger than the unique influence because most of its impact is indirect – that is, due to the fact that trauma increases the risk of both stressful events and chronic stressors later in life. In the NPHS, we see a similar pattern for these three stressors. The chronic stress index used was much shorter than in the other studies, so its slightly smaller impact may simply reflect the fact that not all of the most important chronic stressors were included in this survey. Again, as in the Stress Measurement Study, childhood traumas have the second largest total effect on distress.

I present these results to demonstrate the stability of findings across studies and to underline a fundamental point: stress comes in a number of forms, and we cannot understand its role without measuring a number of sources of stress over the entire life course. The stress literature has been plagued by the idea that stress has more modest impacts on mental health than originally hoped or expected. There have been many answers to this, including the invocation of coping resources as crucial specifiers of who is most and least affected by stress exposure. In a sense, broadening the content of stressors provides another answer: once stressors are specified more fully, we may observe overall impacts on mental health that more straightforwardly justify a focus on environmental – as opposed to biological – risk factors for mental illness.

Misconceptions about Stress

I began this chapter with a list of typical misconceptions about stress. With a conceptual framework and some evidence in place, we can consider these misconceptions more fully.

The Illusion of Personal Stress. It is difficult to avoid the assumption that the stress in one's own life is worse than others; individuals actually feel their own stress but not the stress experienced by others. But in fact, a majority of individuals experience only average amounts of stress. At the same time, when we measure stress by asking people specific questions about problems or events that have occurred to them, we do find clear variability in terms of stress in their lives. An important point is that some lives are indeed characterized by low stress, and this fact must be remembered when considering the specific problems posed by high amounts of stress.

The Illusion of Constant Stress. A related illusion reported by many is that they are always stressed, as if life never ebbs and flows in terms of demands, threats, and constraints. Obviously, this cannot be so, but it does suggest that people are forgetting about or not noticing when things improve, as in "good news is no news at all." The bias toward perception of problems but not their relief leaves the impression that stress acts as a constant over time and thus cannot be causally involved in the development of mental health problems. On second thought, however, it should be clear that there are periods of greater stress and and of lesser stress in most lives. In order to understand the role of stress properly, it is necessary to see that the periods of greater stress could have an impact only if there is a contrast to periods of lesser stress.

The Illusion of Useful Vagueness. Stress is indeed cited all too easily as a cause of all sorts of ills in life, especially when it is not clear exactly what the cause is. This kind of substitution of stress for uncertainty leaves the impression that stress is a vague concept best suited to a residual role in the explanation of mental health problems. "When in doubt, it must be stress." The standard response – of medical experts and the lay public alike – to an unexplained or sudden illness is to imagine stress as an invisible, amorphous, but powerful force that somehow accounts for the problem. But in this role, all sorts of things are cited as stress that do not necessarily qualify. Retrospectively, once a maladaptive response has occurred, anything that preceded the illness can be seen as "stressful." Thus, even relatively benign experiences for many can be transformed into stressors, given the knowledge of what resulted. The problem with this approach is that it assumes that practically anything can be stressful and so begs the viability of the whole concept. In this chapter, I have argued that stressors must qualify on one of three grounds: as an excessive threat, demand, or constraint. If one gets shingles, everyone will certainly feel that stress is somehow involved. Thus, a workload that was seen at the time as manageable though demanding (because one has previously had similar periods of work) becomes unmanageable in retrospect. The problem with this reasoning is that factors that undermine coping capacity can make normal stress seem more virulent. However, this should be conceptualized as the effect of low resources in coping rather than as a high amount of stress.

The Illusion of Ubiquitous Stress. If there is one most prevalent illusion about stress, it is that stress is everywhere, inherent in every life experience. This is not, essentially, an illusion of the self but rather an illusion that stress is a built-in quality to all striving. When we measure stress in surveys and ask about the occurrence of hundreds of stressors of various types, my experience in general populations has been that *not one stressor occurs in even a majority of the population*. Even the most common of assumed stressors, "taking on too many things at once," was reported by only 44% of the sample in the Stress Measurement Study. Of course, some traumas are prevalent because they measure built-in life-course events, such as the death of a loved one. Even this stressor is reported by just under 50% of an adult general population (Wheaton et al. 1997), since age is a major factor explaining exposure to this event. Most traumas and chronic stressors are actually much less prevalent than this, affecting 10–20% of the population. Life events measured within the last year are by necessity much rarer.

It is necessary to understand that stress is not as omnipresent as is commonly assumed. If it were, its influence on most life outcomes would surely be trivial, since prevalent experiences are by definition assumed to be less dangerous or threatening.

The Illusion of Simple Solutions. The market for quick solutions to stress has spawned a major industry. The basic premise is that stress can be counteracted by "magic bullet" solutions, including relaxation exercises, massage therapy, cultist social isolation, ideological commitment, returns to nature, and the simple assumption that all stress is ultimately an opportunity for growth. Hidden in all of these approaches is the idea that one must reduce the consquential power of stress but cannot make it go away. In short, there is a fatalistic element in the underlying theory of coping that drives many of these approaches. Three things are misunderstood in these "philosophies": (1) temporary respite from the stress problem does nothing to prevent it from returning as soon as one returns to normal social roles; (2) cognitive reinterpretation of the stressor may be a valid approach, by whatever means, but it does nothing to address issues in the structuring of life that may well regenerate either the stressor or other related stressors; (3) stress is a complex issue that may require a multifaceted approach.

What is particularly misleading in these approaches is the fact that they implicitly deny or mask the importance of social structure as the foundation of the stress exposure in the first place. Thus, the *basis* of the stressor is often a situation in one's life that is not easily changeable. On the other hand, active coping attempts – attempts to remove or alter the stressor itself – are usually undermined by magic-bullet thinking. The resulting irony is that one may actually increase the power of the stressor because of inherently fatalistic assumptions, allowing it to grow or maintain itself owing to the absence of effort to change its course. The fundamental value of active coping, whether the situation is difficult to change or not, is the very process of not giving up, of continuing to try to change the situation.

The Illusion That Stress Is an Illusion. Some believe that stress is just an excuse for people with weak coping skills – in effect, that stress is "not real." The underlying but false presumptions in this attitude are that everyone has about the same amount of stress and that there is no stress powerful enough to overwhelm some people. It would be wiser to assume that we all have a stress-defined "Achilles heel" but that some of us manage to avoid those stressors over our lifetime.

The claim that stress is not real often implies that some people are just weak copers. Coping certainly makes a difference, but findings such as those in the previous section, as well as myriad other findings, suggest that stress is indeed real. In general, it is wise to urge caution in committing oneself to the proposition that stress is not real, because this belief may induce, ironically, a particularly vulnerable response in the face of truly important and difficult stressors.

The Illusion of Biological Determinism. I hesitate to raise this large issue in such a small space, but a simple point can be made. Our current understanding of the role of biological or genetic factors in mental illness suggests, at best, a partial and contingent role for these factors. When the media report that an illness has been found to be genetic, what is usually lost in the report is the probabilistic nature of this influence – it does not nearly explain every case. There is usually unexplained variation, which is explicitly stated in the original research as possibly due to environmental causation.

The stress hypothesis is a central alternative to genetic or biological explanation. I do not deny that stress can act in conjunction with these factors; in fact, I think this hypothesis is very likely – for example, in helping to explain why some manifest cases of an illness while others do not, given a common genetic component. What we forget, however, is that stress may plausibly play roles other than this kind of synergistic function with biology. It may play an independent role, as follows: social location determines chances of exposure to important stressors, and these stressors in turn set off other social processes that lead to depression, with possibly biological concomitants. Another version posits that stress actually shifts the biological functioning that forms the basis of the depression. In either case, stress plays an indirect causal role that needs to be recognized.

The Illusion That People Cause Their Own Stress. The self-selection hypothesis has plagued serious interpretation of findings in the stress literature. This notion is a version of the "stress is not real" hypothesis. The idea that people get themselves into trouble is convenient, and it is certainly consistent with conservative philosophies about social life, but evidence nonetheless suggests that (to paraphrase a famous saying) "stress happens." Many stressors are in fact randomly patterned with respect to whom they affect (Aneshensel 1992), and even when patterned by social status and social location there is still a large undetermined component to their occurrence.

Some examples may help. If the economy goes bad and someone loses his job, it is difficult to attribute this to self-selection. If a drunk driver hits your car on the way home and you end up paralyzed, there is obviously no self-selection. If a woman is sexually assaulted when jogging through a park when the last 5,000 women jogging in the park were not, it would be absurd to claim this was her fault.

It is impossible here to address all misconceptions about stress – worthy cause though it is. However, it is important to address the most prevalent and most damaging misconceptions, precisely because this is a subject that forms a part of day-to-day life, and opinions have already been based on *some* source of information. The problem is that little of the public discourse about stress reflects how it is actually understood or used in a very large research and theoretical literature on stress.

Conclusions

It may be useful to review some fundamental points in this chapter.

(1) Stressors are not the same thing as stress, in either the biological or the engineering model, for different reasons.
(2) Stressors need to be defined independently of their specific consequences, because they lead to more than merely changes in the risk of illness.
(3) Stressors come in multiple forms, which should be treated separately so that we can discover how they combine in affecting health.
(4) Stressors differ in terms of their discreteness versus continuity as a problem, and also in terms of the level of social reality at which they occur.
(5) There are no "fundamental" stressors: some are more important than others, but evidence suggests that many different sources of stress independently predict mental health differences.

In a recent commentary on stress research, Kaplan (1996a) questions the necessity and wisdom of using the term "stressor" at all. This kind of reaction may be due to the unwieldy nature of the concept. However, the consequences of forsaking this term and this framework should be considered carefully. First, the separation of variables into roles in a conceptual framework – the stress process – helps us to understand how to avoid confounding and misspecifying the overall impact of the set of variables we choose to include under "stress" and "coping." Otherwise, we invite chaos and ambiguity as to even what the issues are. Second, it is a mistake to assume that the term "stressor" means "stressful to everybody in every circumstance." This issue has unnecessarily plagued much of stress research. In fact, a stressor need only have the *potential* to be stressful in most instances – that's why we measure it. We must distinguish between a realm of potential stressors (the starting point in what we measure) and stressful stressors, which are defined by features of context and life history that render the stressor threatening to that person. We need not specify context in order to designate a class of potential stressors, only to define the stressfulness of stressors as a subset of the total.

In defining a class of potential stressors, what are we trying to do? Basically, we must use the vague referent of what is challenging for "most people." This is unfortunately imprecise, but it does imply the point of measuring stressors in the first place: we are trying to capture the most important threats to mental health in the population in the broadest terms, so that the largest sources of mental health risk are identified. We cannot make it the goal of research to capture every stress story at the individual level; we know that there will always be someone, somewhere, who will find practically any situation stressful. But such specificity does not deny the existence of stressors that are difficult in a broad range of situations in many lives.

Finally, we need not specify a priori the level a stressor must attain in order to exceed elastic limits in general – this is not what is done in either the engineering or the psychosocial model. All we need to do is measure the current level of coping capacity that applies to individuals, so that we can detect when the combination of a certain level of stress and weak resources exceeds *their* elastic limit. We must also measure contextual factors that help determine the meaning (and hence the threat value) of the stressor, but this is not part of measuring stress itself.

Perhaps the most general theme of this chapter is the safety, wisdom, and clarity afforded by disaggregation of stress concepts and of other concepts in the stress process, even if we must reaggregate concepts to understand the full power of stress. In the case of specifying context, in extricating coping from its dependence on stress, disaggregation is the key to understanding. In a differentiated and disaggregated stress process model, no single form of stress is sufficient to capture all that is stressful. If we are ultimately interested in a full representation and a fair evaluation of the relevance of stress to mental and physical health, or to a range of life outcomes, then we must consider a range of types of stressors that vary in their typical time course and that occur at different stages in the life course and at different levels of social reality. We must specify the social and biographical context of each stressor; we must investigate the buffering effects of coping resources for stressors defined as contextually threatening; we must specify the foundations of stress; and we must be sensitive to the full range of possible outcomes and the level at which these outcomes are specified. This may seem to be an impossible task, but at least now the task is much better defined than it was a quarter of a century ago.

10

Social Support and Coping

R. Jay Turner

Social support refers to one's social bonds, social integration, and primary group relations – all concepts central to sociological theory and research. Social bonds and supportive relationships with others are essential to mental health; furthermore, social support can protect people from the effects of stressors. Turner demonstrates how social support is a multidimensional concept that involves perceived, structural, and received support. The major hypothesis in this research is that low levels of social support increase risk for depressive symptomatology. Studies consistently find support for this hypothesis, but the models that explain how social support affects mental health differ. The degree to which social support affects one's mental health (main effect) and the degree to which it buffers the effects of stress (moderating effect) also vary across different social status groups of the population. Social status (gender, SES, marital status) affect the availability of social support as well as exposure to stress. It is also probable that mental health status and personality influence the availability and perception of social support. Students might ask themselves whom they have available for support in their networks and whom they would actually approach for support in a variety of different situations such as getting sick, doing poorly in school, unwanted pregnancies, and so forth.

The *Oxford Illustrated Dictionary* defines support, in part, as to "keep from failing or giving way, give courage, confidence, or power of endurance to . . . . Supply with necessities . . . . Lend assistance or countenance to" (1975: 850). What distinguishes *social* support from the broader concept is that it always involves either the presence or implication of stable human relationships. The domain of social support has been addressed under a variety of labels, including "social bonds" (Henderson 1977), "social networks" (Wellman & Wortley 1989), "meaningful social contact" (Cassel 1976), "availability of confidants" (Brown, Bhrolchain, & Harris 1975), and "human companionship" (Lynch 1977), as well as social support. Although these concepts are not identical, they are similar and share a focus on the relevance and significance of human relationships.

This focus has been the subject of considerable attention and research effort, particularly during the 1980s but continuing to the present. As Veil and Baumann (1992a: 1) remark, "measured by both its impact on current thinking concerning the social etiology of mental and physical disorders, and by the sheer volume of publications, social support has joined stress and coping as one of the three most important constructs in current mental health research." However, this intense recent interest hardly signals the discovery of a new idea. In Genesis (2:18) the Lord judges that "It is not good that [one] be alone," and philosophers from Aristotle to Martin Buber have emphasized that the essence of human existence is expressed in our relation with others.

Social bonds, social integration, and primary group relations in general are central constructs in sociological theory and have long been prime considerations within sociological analyses. As Hammer, Makiesky-Barrow, and Gutwirth (1978: 523) observe, social linkages "may be thought of as the basic building blocks of social structure; and their formation, maintenance, and severance are universal and fundamental social processes." A central hypothesis of primary group theory "holds that our morale, our sense of well-being is sustained by membership in primary groups, and that without any primary group affiliations we would become despairing .... Withdrawal from primary contacts would be seen as dangerous to an individual's cognitive and emotional states" (Weiss 1974: 18). Focusing on heart disease rather than mental health, Lynch (1977: xv) concludes from wide-ranging evidence that "there is a biological basis for our need to form loving human relationships. If we fail to fulfill that need, our health is in peril."

Perhaps nowhere has the significance of human associations been more dramatically demonstrated than with respect to child development. The profound negative consequences of maternal deprivation observed by Spitz (1946) among institutionalized infants, the implications of unresponsive mothering suggested by Harlow's (1959) research with baby monkeys, and Bowlby's (1969, 1973) dissertations on the indispensability of attachment for healthy human development are prominent among countless examples that illustrate this point. As Pierce and associates (1996) note, developmentalists and family researchers have long viewed social support, particularly that provided by parents, as a crucial contributor to personality and social development (Rollins & Thomas 1979; Symonds 1939).

From evidence of the significance of social support as a developmental contingency, it was only a minor leap of faith to the now pervasive assumption that this important developmental factor must also be significant with respect to personal functioning and psychological well-being throughout the life course. This view – that social bonds and supportive interactions are important for maintaining mental health – seems to have a long history, but specific research evidence on the connection has accumulated mostly over the past 20 years. The immense growth in research on (and evidence for) the significance of social support was stimulated by the publication of seminal review articles by John Cassel (1976) and Sidney Cobb (1976). These papers set forth preliminary evidence for a hypothesis that remains a dominant issue within current theory and research – that social support may represent an important moderator of the impact of life stress and thereby constitute a protective factor.

R. Jay Turner

Concepts of Social Support

The diversity of opinion with respect to how social support should be conceptualized and measured has been widely commented on in the literature for more than a dozen years (see e.g. Gottlieb 1983; Turner, Frankel, & Levin 1983), and this diversity remains apparent today. When the full range of offered definitions and potentially relevant elements are considered together, a kind of conceptual imperialism seems apparent. That is, social support has been used to refer to an ever-widening domain of content that seems almost coextensive with the structural and social aspects of all human relationships and interactions.

In seeking to delimit the meaning of social support, a number of researchers have concluded that social support is a multifactorial construct. They have described different types or categories of social support that should be considered and that may have differing consequences (Dean & Lin 1977; Funch & Mettlin 1982; Hirsch 1980; House 1981). Vaux (1988: 28) argues that social support is best viewed as a metaconstruct, "comprised of several legitimate and distinguishable theoretical constructs." Three such constructs are specified: support network resources, supportive behavior, and subjective appraisals of support. These dimensions or constructs correspond closely with Barrera's (1986) distinction between social embeddedness (the connection individuals have to significant others or their social environment), enacted support (actions that others perform in rendering assistance), and perceived social support.

Perhaps the best-known and most influential conceptualization of social support is that offered by Cobb (1976: 300). He views social support as "information belonging to one or more of the following three classes: (1) information leading the subject to believe that he is cared for and loved; (2) information leading the subject to believe that he is esteemed and valued; and (3) information leading the subject to believe that he belongs to a network of communication and mutual obligation." In other words, social support refers to the clarity or certainty with which the individual experiences being loved, valued, and able to count on others should the need arise.

Cobb (1979: 94) argues the importance of distinguishing social support from support that is instrumental (counseling, assisting), active (mothering), or material (providing goods or services). However, he does not suggest that these other forms of support are not important or that they lack relevance for health and well-being. His point is simply that we should distinguish social support as self-relevant information from various support resources and support activities.

This perspective was prominent in focusing the interests of many on social support as a social psychological variable – an interest consistent with W. I. Thomas's (Thomas & Thomas 1928) familiar admonition that situations defined as real are real in their consequences. It is an axiom of social psychology that events or circumstances in the real world affect the individual only to the extent and in the form that they are perceived. As Ausubel (1958: 277) points out, "This does not imply that the perceived world is the real world but that perceptual reality is psychological reality and the actual (mediating) variable that influences behavior and development."

Accumulated evidence is highly consistent with this latter point. Indeed, it was pointed out long ago by House (1981) that the great bulk of evidence pointing to the significance of social support for health and well-being comes from studies focused on "emotional support" – his term for perceived support. He further acknowledged that emotional support was the common element across most conceptualizations, that it was what most people meant when they spoke of being supportive, and that, indeed, it seemed to be the most important dimension. Since that time, studies have repeatedly demonstrated that the strongest correlations between measures that purport to assess social support and indices of psychological distress or well-being are found with measures of perceived social support. For example, Wethington and Kessler (1986: 85) have presented specific evidence for the primacy of perceived over received support. They documented "not only that perceptions of support availability are more important than actual support transactions but that the latter promotes psychological adjustment through the former, as much as by practical resolutions of situational demands." This finding further supports House's (1981: 27) suggestion that "social support is likely to be effective only to the extent perceived."

Notwithstanding the apparent mental health significance of perceived social support, the dominant view among sociologists and psychologists is that social support is best understood as a multidimensional construct. Descriptions of relevant elements vary somewhat, but most include, along with emotional or perceived support, the dimensions of structural support and received support or supportive behaviors. *Structural support* refers to the organization of individuals' ties to one another, involving the frequency of contact with network members and the structural characteristics of social ties. Relevant structural characteristics include degree of reciprocity of exchanges between provider and receiver, the strength of the bonds involved, the degree of similarity among network members, and the density of relationships among network members (Wellman 1981, 1990). As Thoits (1995a) notes, network measures often reflect the individual's level of social isolation or social embeddedness. Received support simply refers to the help that helpers extend in providing either instrumental or informational assistance.

There does seem to be ample basis for concluding that social support phenomena involve objective elements (relational connections and helping behaviors) as well as subjective ones. Indeed, as Pearlin (1989) argues, an understanding of the significance of social institutions and contexts will ultimately require the consideration of social networks and resources along with perceived support. However, the grounds for according primary importance to perceived support seem equally clear. The twin facts – (i) that perceived social support is most persistently and powerfully associated with mental health and (ii) that other elements apparently exert their effects by influencing this perception – focus attention on perceived social support as an outcome or dependent variable. That is, it represents the most direct criterion for assessing the role and significance of network characteristics, of other social resources, and of potentially supportive actions generally. The importance of this is that perceived social support appears to provide a basis for identifying behaviors and circumstances that may constitute promising targets for intervention efforts to prevent or ameliorate mental health problems.

The Nature of Perceived Social Support

Two general views have been offered to explain the protective benefits of perceived social support: (1) a situation-specific model in which perceived support performs as a coping resource in relation to particular stressful events or circumstances, and (2) a developmental perspective that sees social support as a crucial factor in social and personality development (Cohen 1992; Pierce et al. 1996). These views are not contradictory but reflect the probability that social support has both short- and long-term consequences for psychological well-being (Pierce et al. 1996). Although both of these perspectives view the social environment as the primary source of supportive experiences (and hence of the perception or belief that one is supported by others), the first focuses largely on the contemporary social environment. The second view, in contrast, emphasizes the effects of the social environmental context on personality over time, attaching special significance to the developmental years.

That the tendency to perceive others as supportive may partially be a reflection of stable personality characteristics makes intuitive sense in the context of Cobb's (1976) conceptualization of social support described earlier. This definition describes social support as information that one is loved and wanted, valued and esteemed, and able to count on others should the need arise. Thus, reflected appraisal, which is a central component of self-esteem (Rosenberg 1965, 1979, 1985), also represents an element of perceived social support, and experiences that foster or challenge one of these constructs must also be relevant to the other. Moreover, there is basis for assuming a degree of reciprocal causation. Surely, the experience of being supported by others contributes to more stable and positive self-esteem, and one's level of self-esteem must set at least broad limits on the perceived level of social support. It is clear that individuals vary in their tendency or capacity to derive meaning and emotional sustenance from a given amount of evidence of positive regard and affection. Everyone has encountered individuals who cannot seem to incorporate messages of social and emotional support no matter how frequently or clearly they are delivered. Self-esteem presumably contributes to such differences in receptiveness, because one's capacity to experience the esteem of others must require some minimal level of esteem of self.

Other grounds for assuming that personality factors are implicated in perceptions of support include evidence that such perceptions tend (a) to be consistent over time and reasonably consistent across situations (Sarason, Pierce, & Sarason 1990a) and (b) to be related to various personality characteristics such as social competence and personal control (Lakey & Cassady 1990). It has been hypothesized that appraisals of the supportiveness of the social environment reflect, at least in part, "support schemata" – referring to "knowledge structures whose content include information about the likelihood that others, in general, will be able or willing to meet one's needs for support. Support schemata encompass one's expectations about the forthcomingness of the social environment in providing aid should one need it" (Pierce et al. 1996: 5). The origins of such schemata are seen as substantially rooted in early experience with attachments, especially attachments to parents (Sarason et al. 1990a).

From this perspective, an important part of the linkage between perceived social support and the objective supportiveness of the environment derives from the tendency for those high in perceived support to be more effective at developing and maintaining supportive relationships, on the one hand, and to interpret ambiguous actions and statements as supportive in nature, on the other (Lakey & Dickinson 1994). As Pierce et al. (1996: 6) note, those with the firm expectation that others will be supportive "create supportive relationships in new social settings, thereby further confirming their expectation that others are likely to be supportive."

However, the evidence seems compelling that expectations, beliefs, or confidence about the availability of social support cannot be independent of one's history (including recent history) of real-world experiences of being supported by others (Cutrona 1986; Sarason et al. 1990a; Vinokur, Schul, & Caplan 1987). Thus, expressions of support and supportive actions may be seen as important in the short term for the coping assistance provided and, in the long term, for the contribution made to the receiver's expectation or confidence that such support will be available in the future. Although early attachment experiences may well influence the individual's tendency to foster and perceive environmental supportiveness, there seems good basis for concluding that later experiences can profoundly shape and modify these tendencies. The perception of being loved and wanted, valued and esteemed, and able to count on others must be a function of one's history of supportive and unsupportive experiences, with both early life and recent experiences representing major influences.

Social Support and Mental Health

An ever-growing number of volumes and reviews document the apparent significance of perceived social support for emotional health and well-being (Cohen & Wills 1985; Cohen & Syme 1985; Dean & Lin 1977; Gottlieb 1981a; Kessler et al. 1985b; Sarason & Sarason 1985; Sarason, Sarason, & Pierce 1990b; Turner

1983; Turner et al. 1983; Vaux 1988; Veil & Baumann 1992). Perhaps the largest portion of this very substantial research effort has been focused on the hypothesis that low levels of social support increase risk for depressive symptomatology. Taking note of this, Henderson (1992) identified and evaluated 35 separate studies that have addressed the social support–depression relationship. These studies utilized measures of depression that varied from very brief self-report inventories to standardized interviews based on accepted diagnostic criteria. Similarly, procedures for indexing social support differed widely, varying from the use of a single item on the presence or absence of a confidant to sophisticated multi-item interviews or interviewer-based methods. Despite such variable assessments of both social support and depression, Henderson observed remarkable consistency across studies. Virtually all reported a clear inverse association between social support and depression, with studies employing more brief measures of one or both variables demonstrating just as strong relationships as studies employing more elaborate methods. The connection between perceived social support and mental health status generally, and depression in particular, appears to be highly robust.

Main versus Buffering Effects

Much of the strong interest in social support effects on mental health has been associated with the hypothesis, strongly articulated in the influential papers by Cassel (1976) and Cobb (1976), that social support may act to buffer or moderate the effects of life stress. From this perspective, social support tends to be of mental health significance only within stressful circumstances. As Cobb (1976: 502) argues, "social support facilitates coping with crises and adaptation to change. Therefore, one should not expect dramatic main effects from social support. There are, of course, some main effects simply because life is full of changes and crises. The theory says that it is in moderating the effects of the major transitions in life and of the unexpected crises that the effects should be found." Here "main effects" refers to the idea that social support is of relevance in all circumstances, whether or not significant stress is present.

In an influential study, Brown and his colleagues (1975; Brown & Harris 1978) considered factors that might influence vulnerability to depression in the face of adversity. Specifically, they examined the influence of a close, confiding relationship in reducing the risk of depression following a major life event or long-term difficulty. Among those women who lacked a confiding relationship with a husband or boyfriend, 38% developed depression following life stress or major difficulties, compared with only 4% of women who did have such a confiding relationship. Consistent with this result, Henderson's (1992) review of 35 social support–depression studies revealed only four that did not report such a buffering or protective effect.

However, it is also clear from Henderson's review and from the wider literature that a number of studies have found that a low level of support increases risk for depression, or for mental health problems generally, whether or not exposure to unusual stressors had also taken place. Whether these findings allow the conclusion that social support can be of importance in the absence of social stress – that there is a main effect of social support – cannot be easily answered. Antonovsky (1979: 77) forcefully argues that "all of us . . . even in the most benign and sheltered environments, are fairly continuously exposed to what we define as stressors . . . . We are able to get low scores on stress experience [only] because we do not ask the right questions or do not ask patiently enough and not because there really are any low scorers." He insists that "even the most fortunate of people . . . know life as stressful to a considerable extent" (1979: 79). If this constancy-of-stress argument is accepted, then both the main and interactive effects that have been observed would be theoretically interpretable in terms of the buffering hypothesis.

From this perspective, it might seem to follow that the debate over buffering versus main effects is not worth worrying about. However, even if what look like main effects are really buffering effects, it would remain important to determine whether social support is of greater significance when stress is relatively high than when relatively low. Given the inevitability of limited resources, it would be useful to identify those who most need and who might most benefit from a social support intervention. In other words, while all might benefit from enhanced social support, the issues of relative need and relative benefit with respect to psychological distress and disorder remain salient.

Evidence from a study of young mothers may shed some additional light on the inconsistency of findings relating to the buffering hypothesis (Turner 1981; Turner & Noh 1983). In initial analyses, social support was related to psychological distress independent of stress level. The "life stress by social support" interaction term was not significant when the main effect of social support was controlled, suggesting an absence of buffering effects. This finding was consistent with the hypothesis of "main" or direct social support effects and with the significant minority of other studies that have reported no evidence for a stress-buffering role.

Further analyses of these same data, however, indicated that the question – of whether social support is an influence in its own right or is important wholly (or largely) as a buffer against unusual stress – may not be so simply answered. With young mothers of lower socioeconomic status distinguished from middle-class study participants, Turner and Noh (1983) regressed psychological distress on perceived social support within each of three stress-level categories. Within the lower-class grouping, the significance of social support varied substantially by level of stress. No significant relationship was observed among the lower-class group in either the low- or medium-stress circumstance; however, perceived social support was of dramatic significance in the high-stress circumstance.

Results for the middle-class group contrasted sharply with these findings. Clear and quite consistent social support effects were observed regardless of stress level. Thus, the answer to the question of whether social support has main or buffering effects is both conditional and complex. The significant associations observed among the middle class at all three stress levels demonstrated a main effect. In sharp contrast, no main effects were observed among the lower class, as evidenced by small and nonsignificant associations observed within the low- and medium-stress conditions. Social support was found to matter, and matter importantly, only among those lower-class individuals experiencing a high level of stress. This finding provides clear support for the buffering hypothesis. Thus, the significance of social support appears to vary with both social class position and stress level.

At this point, available evidence suggests the appropriateness of three working hypotheses with respect to the main effects–buffering debate: (1) social support tends to matter for psychological well-being in general, and for depression in particular, independent of stressor level; (2) social support appears to matter more where level of stress exposure is relatively high; and (3) the extent to which (1) and (2) hold varies across population subgroups defined by class level and, perhaps, by other variables.

Social Status and Social Support

The starting point for a great deal of research on the sociology of mental health has been findings connecting certain social statuses with mental health problems. The most persistently observed and provocative of these linked low socioeconomic status or SES (Gurin, Veroff, & Feld 1960; Hollingshead & Redlich 1958; Srole et al. 1961), being unmarried (Gurin et al. 1960), and being female (Al-Issa 1982; Nolen-Hoeksema 1987) with increased risk for psychological distress and depression. As noted previously and argued elsewhere (Pearlin 1989; Turner & Marino 1994), variations in the perceived availability of social support arise out of developmental (and contemporary) life conditions to which individuals have been (and are being) exposed. To the extent that significant differences in such life conditions are importantly influenced or defined by one's gender and one's socioeconomic and marital status, it may be that the observed relationships between these statuses and mental health arise, at least in part, from associated differences in level of perceived social support.

For this hypothesis to be tenable, variations in social support across social statuses must show a pattern that is the inverse of the known distributions of mental health problems across these statuses. That is, low levels of perceived social support should be found where rates of psychological distress or depression are highest, and vice versa. This is precisely what has been reported with respect to socioeconomic and marital status by the limited number of studies that have examined the issue. Married individuals quite consistently report higher levels of perceived social support than do the unmarried, and social support appears to increase with levels of socioeconomic status (Ross & Mirowsky 1989; Thoits 1984, 1995a; Turner & Marino 1994). In contrast, observed sex differences in social support do not turn out to be the inverse of differences in distress and depression. Although some studies have reported no gender difference in social support, most have found substantially higher levels of perceived support among women (Flaherty & Richman 1986; Leavy 1983; Ross & Mirowsky 1989; Turner & Marino 1994). Because women appear to experience higher levels of social support than do men, social support can provide little assistance in understanding the tendency for women to experience higher levels of psychological distress and depression. In this connection it should be borne in mind that, among women (as among men), higher levels of social support are clearly associated with lower levels of distress and depression. It thus follows that, without the advantage of higher social support, distress and depression levels among women could be even more elevated relative to men.

The findings on the SES and marital status distributions of social support are consistent with the hypothesis that social support differences contribute to status differences in mental health. Turner and Marino (1994) present results assessing the magnitude of the contribution of social support in explaining SES and marital status differences in depression. Their findings indicate that social support differences account for only about 15% of observed SES differences in depressive symptomatology but for more than 50% of marital status differences. Thus, social support is an important mental health contingency that accounts for a small part of the SES–depression association as well as a substantial portion of the connection between depression and marital status.

That the level of perceived social support varies systematically with one's gender, SES, and marital status supports the argument that social support is importantly conditioned by differences in social experience and/or contemporaneous life circumstances. These findings thus illuminate ways in which social structures affect the processes relevant to social support. Specifically, they suggest the appropriateness of two assumptions: (1) that variations in the availability of social support arise, as do differences in exposure to social stress, substantially out of developmental and contemporaneous conditions of life (Aneshensel 1992; Pearlin 1989); and (2) that one's gender, SES, and marital status effectively define significant differences in such conditions of life. House, Umberson, and Landis (1988) suggest that these status differences are associated with variable exposure to structural barriers and opportunities in society, which tend to shape social relationship structures and processes and hence the availability of social support.

Causal Interpretation

A fundamental assumption among those who investigate the social correlates of psychological distress and depression is that there is an etiologic message to be found within these well-demonstrated linkages. However, in the case of social support, as with other social variables, there has been difficulty in reaching a clear conclusion about the nature of this message. Most of the studies reporting this relationship have been cross-sectional or epidemiological in character, and they consequently confront the classic dilemma of whether the finding should be interpreted from the perspective of social causation or social selection. Does perceived support operate (directly or indirectly) to make psychological distress and depression less likely? Do high levels of distress or depression limit the likelihood that the individual will secure and maintain social relationships or experience the social support that is, in fact, available? The first of these questions is a social causation hypothesis, whereas the second points to social selection processes.

A second form of selection interpretation proposes that the observed connection between social support and mental health may simply be an artifact deriving from the personal inadequacies of those who later become distressed or depressed – inadequacies that also limit the ability to secure and maintain supportive relationships. One version of this latter form of social selection hypothesis proposes that dispositional characteristics, as opposed to the nature of the social environment, largely account for differences in perceived social support (Heller 1979; Sarason, Sarason, & Shearin 1986) – characteristics that may also be associated with increased risk for distress and depression.

As noted earlier, it is clear that supportive experiences in the family context represent crucial early developmental contingencies that importantly influence personality. Thus, social support is causally relevant to personality processes and, by extension, to psychological well-being. However, the question remains of whether social support represents a promising intervention target throughout the life course or only during early developmental phases. To answer this question in the affirmative requires that some part of the causal flow involved in the social support–mental health connection go from social support to distress and depression, and that the level of perceived support be at least partially a function of contemporary processes and circumstances.

At this point it seems clear that no single study provides persuasive evidence on these matters. However, more than 15 years ago House (1981: 51) reached the conclusion that much of the causal flow is from social relationships to health, rather than vice versa. Although much of the evidence supporting this conclusion involved physical rather than mental health outcomes, its applicability to phenomena such as psychological distress and depression seems apparent. John Cassel's (1974, 1976) early argument on the health significance of social support was substantially based on evidence derived from animal studies on the effects of laboratory-induced stress. Examples include Liddell's (1950) finding that suggested the presence of the mother protects young goats from experimental neurosis; the Conger, Sawrey, and Turrell (1958) observation of the relevance of isolation for the occurrence of ulceration in rats; and the Henry and Cassel (1969) report on the significance of littermate presence for the prevention of persistent hypertension in mice. Other kinds of studies reviewed by House (1981, 1987) and others (e.g. Turner 1983) – including laboratory analog studies with humans, intervention studies, and longitudinal and panel studies – strongly suggest that some important portion of the causation involved in the well-established link between perceived social support and mental health status goes from social support to mental health.

In considering the issue of causation, it is useful to acknowledge that neither human development or functioning is likely to proceed in terms of linear or clear-cut causes and effects. Rather, most causes and effects in human affairs are likely to be reciprocal in nature. As Smith (1968: 277) argued long ago, development is a matter of benign circles or vicious ones, and causation in personal and social development is "inherently circular or spiral, rather than linear, in terms of neatly isolable causes and effects." In the present case, evidence suggests that the perceived availability of social support has important consequences for distress and depression. At the same time, it is probable that one's mental health status and personality characteristics affect the availability of social support and the ability or tendency to experience the support that is available. Accumulated evidence from diverse sources appears to constitute a compelling case for the causal impact of social support. It thus also follows that social support represents a promising target for intervention efforts aimed at reducing rates of psychological distress and depression in high-risk populations or subgroups.

Conclusions

Despite the huge volume of research and publications on social support, much remains to be learned about how and why social support matters for health and well-being and about the circumstances and processes that promote and enhance its availability. As outlined in this brief chapter, however, several conclusions are warranted from available evidence. These conclusions may be summarized as follows.

(1) The ever-growing number of studies and reviews on the subject leave little doubt that social support is importantly associated with mental health status generally and with depression in particular.

(2) Combined evidence from laboratory animal studies, experimental human studies, and longitudinal field studies provides clear support for the contention that some part of causality involved in this persistently observed relationship flows from social support to mental health status.

(3) Although social support phenomena clearly involve objective elements (such as network size, structure and density, and actual events and activities), it is one's perception or belief about the availability of support that is most protective against distress and depression. This means that the love or esteem of others – or the availability of emotional, material, or instrumental assistance – is likely to be of little protective utility if kept a secret.

(4) That the perceived levels of social support vary reliably with location in the social system (as defined by SES, marital status, and gender), in combination with an array of other evidence, makes it clear that the experience of being supported by others arises substantially out of the ongoing social context within which the individual is located.

(5) At the same time, the early experience of social support within the family context appears to be a crucial developmental contingency that facilitates the later capacity to develop and maintain supportive relationships and to meaningfully experience the support that others provide.

(6) Social support tends to matter for psychological distress and depression independent of stress level. However, it tends to matter more where stress exposure is relatively high.

11

Outcomes of the Stress Process

Carol S. Aneshensel

Although stress does not "cause" mental illness, exposure to stress does increase the relative risk of experiencing mental health problems. Aneshensel discusses the various research strategies used in the study of the relationship between stress and mental health. There are substantial differences in the types of stressors one is exposed to and in the ways stress is experienced by different groups in society. Furthermore, there are many different mental health outcomes that can be studied when examining the stress process, including emotional distress, substance abuse or dependence, traumatic disorders, and stress outcomes over time. Another question is: How does stress influence mental health outcomes? Researchers have examined a variety of stress mediators (which transmit the effects of stress), including physiological responses to threat, cognitive processes that affect how individuals respond to given situations, and the degree of fit between individuals and their environments. There is a small minority of people whose mental health is seriously damaged by exposure to stress, so current research efforts seek to understand why most people adapt to stress while others do not. Both personal and social characteristics are important in understanding differential responses to stress (stress reactivity), as well as the degree to which an individual is vulnerable to stress (stress vulnerability). The stress experienced by one individual (such as job loss) can also spill over to affect the stress experienced by those (such as family) close to the individual. Think about the way you and your friends respond to highly stressful situations. Are your reactions more similar to or different from each others'?

Stress is a seemingly ever-present feature of contemporary social life, but most people adapt to it and do not develop serious mental illness, emotional distress, or behavioral problems. The majority of those who are exposed to stress, even intense or prolonged stress, continue to function in a normal manner. A sizable minority, however, do become despondent or paralyzed by anxiety, self-medicate their feelings with alcohol or other substances, or engage in maladaptive behavior. A central issue with regard to outcomes of the stress process, then, is explaining why some individuals are adversely affected by stress whereas others are not.

Similarly, most instances of disorder cannot be attributed to the isolated occurrence of a single stressor. Disorders like posttraumatic stress disorder (PTSD) form an exception to this generalization because the diagnostic criteria include exposure to an extreme stressor (e.g., natural disasters): the disorder would not be present if the traumatic event had not occurred. For other conditions, like depression, the occurrence of a specific stressor may seem to trigger the onset of disorder.

In most instances, and even with disorders like PTSD, it is overly simplistic to attribute disorder solely to the occurrence of a single stressor. Instead, a stressor is likely to evoke disorder when it occurs in conjunction with other etiological forces – for example, other stressors, scarce psychosocial resources, poverty, or genetic predisposition. The cumulative burden of multiple risk factors creates a precarious state of heightened susceptibility to stress. In essence, the stressor acts as a catalyst, precipitating a volatile mixture of multiple risk factors.

Exposure to stress, then, does not have a one-to-one correspondence with the development of mental health problems. Those who have been exposed to substantial stress are more likely than those with less exposure to exhibit signs and symptoms of mental, emotional, or behavioral disorders, but most persons who are exposed to stress continue to function within the boundaries of normality. Thus, stress does not "cause" disorder in the deterministic understanding of this term (Little 1991) insofar as stress is neither necessary nor sufficient to produce disorder. Instead, the relationship is probabilistic: exposure to stress elevates the relative risk of experiencing mental health problems, even though this risk remains low in an absolute sense.

The Connection between Stress and Mental Health

The connection between exposure to stress and impaired mental health has been established via several distinct research methodologies, which enhances confidence in its causal interpretation (for reviews, see Aneshensel 1992; Coyne & Downey 1991; Kessler et al. 1985b; Thoits 1983, 1995a). Early research merely demonstrated empirical covariation: individuals who had recently encountered several major disruptions in their lives tended to display more symptoms of emotional distress than those whose recent lives had been in balance. This pattern suggested that exposure to life events generates emotional distress.

However, conclusions from this early work were limited by the correlational nature of the data, which was subject to other interpretations. For example, the association between stress and disorder might be spurious – that is, the result of the influence of a third factor (such as social class) on both stress and emotional distress. Alternately, the correlation could reflect a causal connection flowing in the reverse direction – distressed people tending to cause problems in their own lives.

One approach to these limitations involves the artificial manipulation of exposure to stressful stimuli in controlled laboratory experiments. For example, Choi and Salmon (1995) describe a combined visual-auditory stressor: color names are presented in their own or different colors, and subjects are asked to decide whether the color/name is the same or different while simultaneously listening for and repeating a target word from a recorded list of household objects. In this experiment, stress responses were recorded as changes in heart rate, blood pressure, and mood.

The experimental approach has several advantages. For example, random assignment of subjects to levels of stress exposure resolves some of the limitations of correlational data just mentioned, permitting stronger causal interpretation. This approach has been especially productive in identifying stress reactions at the psychophysiological level.

The experimental approach is limited, however, by the boundaries of the laboratory. The stressors manipulated in this line of research tend to be contrived and trivial compared to misfortune encountered in ordinary life. Also, the only social interactions that can be manipulated are those that occur in the laboratory – not the crucial ties of family, friends, work, and so forth. The subjects participating in this type of research (e.g., college students, patients) are usually quite homogeneous and not representative of the general population. Consequently, this line of research is not especially informative about the natural impact of social stress on mental health in the general population.

Information about the causal impact of stressors occurring during the normal course of everyday life has been derived, instead, from community-based studies following typical populations over time. The longitudinal design of these studies permits stronger causal inferences than the cross-sectional correlational studies mentioned previously. The passage of time clarifies the direction of causal influence. In addition, the analysis of change over time reduces concerns about spuriousness. Finally, the use of community-based samples permits generalization to the population.

Several studies using a longitudinal survey design have demonstrated a link between exposure to stress and changes over time in emotional distress (see e.g. Aneshensel & Frerichs 1982; Billings & Moos 1982; Ensel & Lin 1991). Most of this work has emphasized the impact of major life events on subsequent increases in symptoms of depression. Other studies have documented similar effects for chronic stressors (Aneshensel 1985; Pearlin & Lieberman 1979). In an extremely influential paper, Pearlin, Lieberman, Menaghan, and Mullan (1981) linked life events to emotional distress by demonstrating that some events lead to chronic strains, which, in turn, are depressing. The particular event studied was involuntary job loss, an event known to have substantial and persistent negative effects on emotional well-being (Catalano & Dooley 1977; Kessler, House, & Turner 1987; Liem & Liem 1978). Pearlin and his associates (1981) demonstrated that this relationship is mediated, at least in part, by the intensification of economic strains. They concluded that persistent life strains are both a product of life events and a channel through which life events come to have deleterious effects on psychological well-being.

This tradition of longitudinal survey research has been especially informative about the impact of stress on mental health because it is possible to control for the influence of numerous other factors. For example, the heterogeneity of the samples permits multivariate controls for the impact of sociodemographic and economic factors. This heterogeneity also permits an examination of the extent to which the impact of stress varies across subgroups of the population.

Multivariate analysis of longitudinal data indicates that emotional distress is exacerbated by exposure to stress, irrespective of demographic and socioeconomic characteristics. The addition of controls for age, race, ethnicity, gender, socioeconomic status, and so forth generally does not substantially alter the association between stress and emotional distress. As discussed in what follows, there is some evidence that stress may be especially distressing among certain subgroups of the population. Nevertheless, the positive association between stress and emotional distress has been demonstrated for virtually all subgroups of the population: children through the oldest old; blacks, whites, Latinos, Asian Americans; men and women; those living in poverty and the affluent; and so forth.

That stress processes generalize across subgroups of the population does not imply that the specific dynamics linking stress to mental health are identical in every subgroup. To the contrary, there are substantial differences between groups. For example, the types of events that young adults experience as extremely distressing entail entry into adult social roles: completion of schooling, entry into the labor force, and starting a family. These specific events are not germane to the elderly, who instead often encounter numerous exit events. Therefore, the study of the mental health effects of social stress occurs along two lines: (i) the identification of general processes that span diverse populations and (ii) the specification of the distinctive processes that pertain to select subpopulations.

Mental Health Outcomes of the Stress Process

Social stress acts as a nonspecific risk factor. By this we mean that its impact is not limited to a single disorder, such as depression, but is manifest instead across a broad spectrum of impaired functioning. These outcomes include symptoms of emotional distress, principally symptoms of depression and anxiety; affective disorders, especially depression; and behavioral disorders, particularly substance abuse and dependence. These connections are "robust" in that they have been replicated across different research methodologies.

The increase in risk for any single mental health outcome is relatively small. For example, life event inventories (the most widely used operationalization of stress) typically do not account for more than 10–15% of the outcome variance (Kessler et al. 1985a; Rabkin & Struening 1976; Thoits 1983). Although measures of chronic strains typically perform somewhat better, most of the outcome variance remains unexplained (Kessler et al. 1985b; Pearlin et al. 1981). Thus, stress is reliably related to mental health problems, but exposure to social stress is only one of several influences on mental health.

When mental health outcomes are considered collectively, however, the total mental health burden associated with stress is greater than its etiological impact on any one outcome would suggest (Aneshensel 1996). This point can be made clear by analogy to cigarette smoking: equating the harmful effects of smoking with its contribution to lung cancer alone would substantially underestimate its costs by ignoring other outcomes like heart disease and stroke. Similarly, examining mental disorders one by one, as is the custom in stress research, underestimates the total price exacted by social stress.

Emotional Distress

The most widely studied outcome of the stress process is emotional distress, sometimes referred to as "nonspecific psychological distress." Emotional distress is usually operationalized through a count of symptoms of depression and anxiety experienced over a specific period of time, such as the preceding week. Most measures give heavier weights to symptoms that are experienced as being severe, disruptive, or frequent. Symptom-type outcomes are generally preferred by stress researchers over diagnostic-type outcomes because symptom measures are more sensitive indicators of reactions to changes in the social environment.

As exposure to stress increases, emotional distress tends to increase. This relationship follows a dose–response pattern: Each additional stressor produces, on average, about the same increment in symptomatology. This means that the effects of stress are evident across the full spectrum of levels of exposure.

Not all stressors are of equal consequence, however; some evoke considerably more distress than others. For example, death of one's spouse is substantially more traumatic than having a friend move out of town, and both of these events are more consequential than receiving a traffic ticket. This variation in severity poses measurement problems with regard to assessing the effects of different stressors on mental health, since a simple count of stressors gives equal weight to unequal stressors.

Variation in the severity of stressors tends to be less problematic in practice than one might suppose. One approach is to assess exposure to major life events separately from daily hassles. Within these categories, stressors tend to be more homogeneous, making equal weights acceptable. In other words, the events that figure prominently in stress research tend to be tightly clustered at the high end of a continuum of stress. Their effects tend to be similar to one another and clearly distinct from the effects of daily hassles, which are clustered at the low end of the continuum. Although these types of stressors are distinct, hassles appear to mediate some of the effects of life events on psychological distress (Kanner et al. 1981).

The impact of a major life event tends to be immediate, with the most distress experienced within a few months of its occurrence (Hammen et al. 1986; Paykel 1978). However, the onset of symptomatology may actually precede the event. Obviously, the event cannot cause something that precedes it in time; instead, its anticipation is the source of distress. In other instances, the impact of the event is delayed; the person appears to have adapted but develops symptomatology some time afterward (as in, e.g., PTSD).

Usually, however, the most intense distress accompanies closely in time the occurrence of the event. Thereafter, its effects atrophy over time (Surtees & Ingham 1980). Yet the occurrence of an additional event may reverse this recovery. Distress evoked by the new event is added to the distress remaining from the old event. The combined effect is larger than would be expected if the two events had occurred at completely different times.

The time line for the mental health effects of chronic stressors is difficult to chart. Chronic stressors tend to be insidious, emerging slowly in people's lives without any clear beginning (Pearlin 1983; Wheaton 1996). The individual may not be consciously aware of this type of stressor until it has reached some critical level of severity. For example, marital problems typically accrue for months if not years before either partner recognizes that the marriage is in trouble. The end of chronic stressors is equally difficult to date. When is a troubled marriage back on a firm footing? Is separation or divorce its end or rather its continuation in a new form? Consequently, it is difficult to align the time course of a chronic stressor with the time course of emotional distress.

Aneshensel (1985) compared the impact of both life events and chronic role strains on the course of depressive symptomatology over time. Although events were related to symptoms concurrently and over time, these effects were limited. The occasional occurrence of life events did not have an appreciable impact, but the repeated occurrence of these events over time substantially increased the odds of long-term impairment. Persistent role strains also differentiated those with chronic, recurrent disorder from those with isolated episodes of disorder and from the consistently asymptomatic. Aneshensel (1985) suggests that it is the persistence of risk factors over time that distinguishes the chronic from the transient course of disorder.

Substance Abuse and Dependence

In addition to emotional distress, exposure to stress has been linked to the use of alcohol and psychoactive substances, including patterns of use that are indicative of abuse or dependence. This connection arises, at least in part, because stress generates undesirable internal states – tension, anxiety, nervousness, sadness, or depression – that are, in essence, self-medicated with alcohol and other substances. Using various substances to cope with stress opens the door for the development of substance abuse and dependence (Powers & Kutash 1985).

Lester, Nebel, and Baum (1994) describe a tension-reduction model that links the occurrence of stress to the development of self-sustaining substance abuse and dependence. The first stage in this model is the use of a substance to cope with the emotional impact of exposure to stress. These substances include alcohol; illicit psychoactive substances, like marijuana and cocaine; and prescription medications, especially tranquilizers.

The second stage entails a feedback loop: the reduction of tension achieved via substance use reinforces the use of these substances to cope with the unpleasant effects of stress. Additional reinforcement occurs because many of these substances also elevate mood and generate a subjective sense of emotional well-being. This double reinforcement increases the risk of habitual use.

The third stage entails the psychological reinforcement of drug-taking behavior that goes beyond the actual pharmacological effects of the drugs. This reinforcement entails perceived secondary benefits of drug use, such as generating a sense of belonging to a social group in which substance use is prominent. In this manner, the ritual of drug taking can develop into habitual use, that is, substance use that occurs in the absence of stress. The final stage is addiction: withdrawal creates unpleasant feelings and sensations that help to perpetuate substance use.

In addition, there is some evidence suggesting that stress-induced substance use eventually intensifies some of the negative emotions it initially seemed to reduce (Aneshensel & Huba 1984). In this regard, Freed (1978) notes that alcoholics experience not euphoria but instead increasing dysphoria as a consequence of alcohol consumption, whereas nonalcoholics anticipate and generally attain elevated moods. Lester and colleagues (1994) note that drug taking may emerge as the preferred method of coping, leading the individual to abandon other strategies that were previously used in coping with stressful situations. Pearlin and Radabaugh (1976) similarly note that drinking to control distress tends to leave intact the situations out of which negative emotions have grown.

It should be noted that connections between stress and substance abuse or dependence are probabilistic rather than deterministic: not everyone who self-medicates negative feelings becomes dependent or an abuser. Indeed, the desire to enhance one's mood is one of the most widely cited motivations for drinking (Pearlin & Radabaugh 1976). In other words, many people enter into the first stage of the tension-reduction model. However, most individuals who use alcohol in this manner do so occasionally and only to a limited degree. The progression into problematic drinking just described applies to only a subset of those who ever use alcohol as a coping mechanism. Similarly, the tension-reduction model describes but one of several pathways to substance abuse and dependence.

Traumatic Disorders

In considering the mental health outcomes of the stress process, some disorders are unique because the occurrence of a traumatic event is integral to their diagnosis. These disorders exist exclusively as reactions to trauma. Rabkin (1993) describes two such disorders, brief reactive psychosis and PTSD. Brief reactive psychosis is characterized by sudden onset immediately following exposure to stress. The psychosis lasts at least a few hours (but not more than two weeks) and has a clinical picture including emotional turmoil and at least one gross psychotic symptom.

Posttraumatic stress disorder is an anxiety disorder that may occur months or years after the precipitating traumatic event. Unlike brief reactive psychosis, PTSD may last indefinitely. The clinical picture includes recurrent dreams or daytime flashbacks in which the trauma is reexperienced; emotional numbing; and one or more of several other symptoms such as survival guilt, insomnia, or impaired concentration. In both disorders, the precipitant is conceptualized as being "outside the range of usual human experience" – that is, an extreme stressor or traumatic experience (Rabkin 1993).

These disorders are unique in that their diagnosis is inseparable from the prior occurrence of the traumatic event, a connection that seems to imply the event is the cause of the disorder. However, this perspective is problematic because the occurrence of the event is not, in itself, sufficient to cause the disorder: most people exposed to trauma do not develop PTSD, brief reactive psychoses, or any other disorder. It is therefore necessary to identify the conditions under which exposure to trauma produces disorder. In other words, these disorders are not solely the result of exposure; rather, they result from exposure interacting with other risk factors, including concurrent exposure to other sources of stress.

Stress Outcomes over Time

Although stress research has focused almost exclusively on the present state, current functioning is set within the context of the past and sets the stage for the future. Consider two individuals: one has a history of disorder, the other has maintained a lifetime profile of normality. The first person may be extremely reactive to the emergence of a new source of stress, one to which the second person may appear resistant.

The outcomes, however, are not the same in these two cases: the first concerns relapse whereas the second concerns onset. Hence variation in the impact of stress may not reflect individual differences in stress reactivity so much as more basic differences in the determinants of relapse and onset. Some of the more common psychiatric disorders (e.g., depression) tend to be chronic and recurrent, meaning that studies among adults often concern relapse rather than onset, although chronicity often is not taken into consideration.

There appears to be a self-amplifying relationship between exposure and depression. Hammen and associates (1986) show that negative life events have the largest depressive effect on people who are already symptomatic. Similarly, Coyne and Downey (1991) note that negative life events are more strongly associated with early episodes of depression rather than with later episodes. They describe this as a sensitizing effect that lowers the threshold of exposure necessary to precipitate each successive depressive episode.

Consequently, it is useful to examine the confluence of stress and mental health over time, ideally over the entire life course. The concept of natural history is instructive in this endeavor because it traces a trajectory of experience, arraying critical junctures along a time line. Events of particular interest are *onset,* which marks a turning away from normality; *recovery,* a return to normality; and *relapse,* a further turning away from normality. At issue is the impact of stress on the likelihood that these transitions will occur.

When these transitions are considered collectively, it is immediately apparent that they share an inherent connection with one another. A person is at risk of relapse only after having had a disorder from which he or she has recovered. There is a time connection as well. The period of risk for the onset of disorder varies with age: young people have been at risk for a shorter period of time as compared to persons who are middle-aged or older. The recovery interval begins only with the onset of disorder, and so forth. Furthermore, these intervals may be related to one another; for example, duration varies according to age of onset and remission varies according to duration. These types of contingencies have yet to be systematically taken into consideration in the stress and disorder literature. The life-course literature, however, attests to the importance of incorporating this type of sequential framework (Elder, George, & Shanahan 1996).

Although additional research is needed, there is evidence suggesting that stress influences not only onset but also other transitions into and out of disordered states. Monroe and McQuaid (1994) describe several ways in which stress influences the clinical course of disorder. They note that stress directly influences functioning – for example, decreasing the likelihood of recovery or increasing the likelihood of relapse. Likewise, Aneshensel (1985) links chronic, recurrent emotional distress to the repeated occurrence of life events over time, noting that the impact of isolated events is limited to ephemeral distress. In addition, stress does not appear to be related to the onset of schizophrenia, but it does appear to be related to relapse among those in remission (Rabkin 1993). Stress has also been related to relapse of depression (Surtees & Ingham 1980).

Monroe and McQuaid (1994) also identify indirect effects on the clinical course of disorder. In this instance, stress affects a mediating factor, which then influences mental health. These indirect effects include erosion of social support, decreasing the probability of receiving treatment, and increasing the time between onset of an acute episode and entry into treatment.

Lester and associates (1994) additionally call attention to the *after-effects* of exposure to stress. After-effects are consequences that persist after a stressor has been terminated or resolved, including such behavioral changes as a reduced tolerance for frustration, impaired problem-solving ability, and poorer concentration. These outcomes are especially pertinent to the natural history of disorder because they carry forward in time liabilities that place the person at risk for relapse.

The effects of stress on mental health clearly entail processes that accrue over time. As noted by Wheaton (1990), the impact of life events is best understood in the context of the personal history leading up to the event. A neglected aspect of this context concerns the previous occurrence of disorder. It appears that the stress–disorder relationship follows a developmental trajectory that evolves over the course of time, often in a self-amplifying manner.

Mechanisms Linking Stress to Mental Health

The observation that exposure to stress adversely affects mental health, although critical to understanding the social origins of disorder, raises more questions than it answers. One of the most important pertains to the mechanisms linking stress to mental health: just how does stress exert its inimical effects? This question concerns the internal workings of the stress process, the dynamics that connect stress, on the one hand, to mental health, on the other.

These internal dynamics hinge upon the concept of stress *mediators* – factors that intervene in the stress–disorder relationship. Mediators transmit the effects of stress. This transmission occurs via a series of interlocking pathways: exposure to stress influences the mediator, which then influences mental health. Collectively, these pathways describe the indirect effects of stress on mental health.

Stress mediators have been described at several distinct levels of functioning. One of the earliest and most influential describes physiological responses to threat. This orientation is best encapsulated by the phrase "flight or fight" used to describe arousal of the sympathetic nervous system, including increases in heart rate, blood pressure, respiration, muscle tone, and other systemic changes. Also influential was Selye's (1936, 1993) description of a general adaptation cycle: alarm, resistance, adaptation, and exhaustion.

Recent work in this area emphasizes brain activation, physiological changes, and the functioning of the immune system (Lester et al. 1994; McEwen & Mendelson 1993; Stein & Miller 1993). For example, Frankenhaeuser (1991) describes a psychophysiological model for the stress–health interaction. She notes that the cognitive appraisal of a situation as stressful plays a pivotal role in activating bodily responses. Stressful situations generate signals from the brain's cortex to the hypothalamus that are transmitted to the adrenal medulla via the autonomic nervous system. The adrenal medulla secretes two catecholamines, epinephrine and norepinephrine (often referred to as the stress hormones) that mobilize the "fight or flight" response. It also secretes corticosteroids (e.g., cortisol), an important part of the body's immune defense: this mechanism involves the release of adrenocorticotropic hormone from the pituitary gland. As Frankenhaeuser (1991) notes, these hormones serve important adaptive functions but may be harmful when secreted excessively. In the psychophysiological model, stress mediation occurs at the level of the organism.

A second approach to understanding the connections between stress and mental health can be found in etiological models for specific types of disorders, especially theories concerned with the cognitive antecedents of depression. A prominent example of this approach is "learned helplessness," which refers to the withdrawal of effort and feelings of dejection that accompany exposure to inescapable, uncontrollable negative stimuli (Seligman 1975). As noted by Mirowsky and Ross (1986), this behavioral pattern corresponds to cognitive styles such as externality and fatalism. These cognitive styles, in turn, leave one vulnerable to depression and other forms of emotional distress.

The cognitive approach is similar to the psychophysiological approach insofar as it emphasizes processes occurring within the individual, but it differs in focusing on higher-order processes. In contrast, the psychosocial approach emphasizes exchanges between the individual and his or her environment.

The key element in the psychosocial orientation is the concept of resources, which are used to offset the demands imposed by a stressful event or circumstance. Resources can be material (e.g., financial means), social (e.g., supportive ties to others), or personal (e.g., a sense of self-efficacy). The concept of resources pertains explicitly to the *interaction* between the individual and the environment instead of focusing solely upon individual responses to the environment. This connection is crucial to understanding the social origins of mental health because it places individual experience within a social context.

In addition, the mismatch between person and environment is essential to the concept of social stress. A core element of most definitions of social stress is the idea that the environment imposes demands that either exceed the individual's ordinary adaptive capacity or obstruct his or her ability to attain sought-after ends (Aneshensel 1992; Lazarus 1966; Menaghan 1983; Pearlin 1983). Thus, stress is not an inherent attribute of external conditions but instead emanates from discrepancies with characteristics of the individual, including his or her psychosocial resources.

There is substantial empirical evidence that psychosocial resources are beneficial to mental health. For example, symptoms of depression and anxiety tend to decrease as social support increases (Kessler & McLeod 1985; Ross & Mirowsky 1989; Wethington & Kessler 1986). Similarly, distress and self-efficacy are inversely related to one another (Mirowsky & Ross 1984; Thoits 1987; Wheaton 1980, 1983). The evidence with regard to coping, however, is equivocal because the effectiveness of various coping strategies appears to be situation-specific: what works with regard to one stressful situation may actually exacerbate another (Pearlin 1989; Pearlin & Schooler 1978; Menaghan 1983).

The connection between psychosocial resources and exposure to stress, however, is not well understood at the present time. This gap in the research literature is the result of an overriding concern with mental health outcomes, which has deflected attention away from the stressor–resource relationship.

In theory, resources counteract environmental demands and obstacles. If this is indeed the case then resources should be mobilized by the occurrence of a stressor, a beneficial side effect of exposure referred to as the *stress-suppression* model

(Ensel & Lin 1991; Wheaton 1985). For example, in the face of many difficult life situations, some people turn inward, calling upon their personal abilities and fortitude, or are sustained by others who provide concrete aid, suggestions about coping strategies, and emotional sustenance.

In this model, the direct effects of stress are negative, but they are offset by positive indirect effects achieved through the mobilization of resources. This indirect effect reduces the total impact of stress on mental health. Thus the adverse effects of stress are offset because there is a positive relationship between stress and self-efficacy, social support, or other psychosocial resources.

However, resources may not be mobilized by exposure to stress and instead may remain at a fixed level or, even worse, be depleted, a detrimental side effect of exposure referred to as the *deterioration* model (Ensel & Lin 1991; Wheaton 1985). Those who have been supportive in the past may not want to help with yet another problem and withdraw, for example, or a belief in one's own ability to overcome obstacles may falter in the face of yet another challenge. In situations like these, resources do not offset the adverse mental health effects of stress; instead, the depletion of resources is the means through which stress damages mental health (Wheaton 1985).

Ensel and Lin (1991) provide a comprehensive empirical assessment of competing stress resource models. Their results lend more support to the deterioration model – as stressors increase, resources decrease – than to the stress-suppression model. More work remains to be done in this area, however, before these results can be considered general findings. An important consideration is differentiating the conditions under which resources are mobilized versus depleted.

In general, stress tends to damage mental health when it depletes an individual's connections to other people or their ability to be helpful; erodes a person's sense of mastery, identity, or worthiness; or prompts harmful behavioral adaptations, such as self-medication with alcohol or other mood-altering substances. Conversely, adverse outcomes are contained when one's social networks are mobilized by threatening situations; when overcoming difficulties enhances one's sense of personal efficacy; or when behavioral responses lessen exposure or its impact.

Group Variation in Mental Health Outcomes

As we have noted, successful adaptation to stress appears to be more common than the development of mental, emotional, or behavioral disorder. This modest average effect, however, masks a very large effect among some people that is offset by a very small effect among most people. In other words, two subgroups of the population can be identified: (i) a small minority whose mental health is seriously damaged by their exposure to stress and (ii) the large majority who manifest little if any adverse mental health consequences. A key issue with regard to outcomes of the stress process, then, is accounting for differences in its mental health impact: Why do most people adapt satisfactorily to problematic life circumstances whereas others do not?

Some of this variation in outcomes can be attributed to the unique circumstances inherent in the occurrence of any particular stressful situation. Individual experience is personalized. For example, the very definition of the situation as stressful depends importantly upon the individual's appraisal of both the situation and his or her ability to respond to it – perceptions that are, in turn, shaped by personal history, needs, values, aspirations, self-concept, resources, skills, and so forth. Thus, each person who confronts a potentially stressful situation does so in a singular manner.

This uniqueness notwithstanding, the systematic investigation of social stress and its effects requires that attention focus instead on commonalities in experience that exist across situations and across individuals. These commonalities have been sought along several distinct tracks, often separated by disciplinary lines.

At the individual level, variation in the impact of stress on mental health has been sought in personal attributes that are relatively stable over time. Influential in this regard, although not without substantial criticism, is the concept of "hardiness," which refers to a personality construct that entails orientations toward the self and world that are expressive of commitment, control, and challenge (Kobasa, Maddi, & Kahn 1982; Ouellette 1993). Similar functions have been ascribed to characteristics like optimism, a sense of coherence, and learned resourcefulness (Holahan & Moos 1994).

Physical attributes have been implicated as well. For example, Choi and Salmon (1995) examine physical fitness as a stress modifier. They report that women who exercise differ from sedentary women, exhibiting less heart rate responsivity to stress but more mood fluctuations. The authors also conclude that, contrary to the conventional wisdom, menstrual cycle changes do not alter sensitivity to stress.

Personal characteristics are seen as modifying the impact of stress on the individual. Resources dampen the impact of exposure to stress and thus render the individual stress-resistent or resilient (Holahan & Moos 1994). Conversely, the absence of personal resources leaves one especially vulnerable to the adverse effects of stress. Individual differences in general tendencies to react to external stimuli help to explain variation in responses to specific external stimuli. In other words, those who are generally reactive are more likely to be damaged by their exposure to a particular stressor than those who tend to be generally nonreactive.

Commonalities in reactions to stress have also been sought in the structural arrangements of society, specifically in the attributes that define one's position in status hierarchies. These attributes include many of the socioeconomic and demographic risk factors identified in later chapters, including social class, ethnicity, gender, and age. Here the question has been whether subgroups of the population differ in their general propensity to be harmed by exposure to stress, that is, whether some segments of society are more stress-resistant than others.

Of particular interest is how the organization of the social system shapes individual differences. The biological model is of limited utility in this endeavor because its connection to social processes, essentially unknown, is unlikely to be strong enough to account for the large social variation in risk. This is not to say that genetic predispositions and psychophysiological processes are unimportant to mental health, but rather that the sources of social regularities in mental health outcomes are more productively sought among elements of the social system.

Interest in group variation in stress reactivity, often referred to as "differential vulnerability," arose within the context of attempts to explain the social distribution of emotional distress, especially the inverse relationship between social class and mental illness. Mixed results have been reported for gender, race, social class, and marital status (Kessler 1979; Kessler & Essex 1982; Kessler & McLeod 1984; Kessler & Neighbors 1986; McLeod & Kessler 1990; Myers, Lindenthal, & Pepper 1975; Neff 1985; Newmann 1986; Pearlin & Johnson 1977; Thoits 1987; Turner & Avison 1989; Turner & Noh 1983; Wheaton 1982).

In an influential study, Kessler and McLeod (1984) reported that women are more emotionally distressed than men when bad things happen to friends and family. Turner and Avison (1989) replicate these findings, but note that men and women appear to be similarly affected by stressors to which they themselves are directly exposed. Newmann (1986) similarly reports an absence of gender differences in the depressive impact of chronic stressors. Other studies report a greater depressive impact among men than women for some stressors (Pearlin 1975; Thoits 1987). Gender differences in stress reactivity also are disorder-specific and counterbalance one another across the full spectrum of mental, emotional, and behavioral disorders (Aneshensel et al. 1991). Thus, it appears that both men and women are adversely affected by exposure to stress, yet they differ somewhat with regard to the types of stressors to which they are most reactive and the types of disorder they are most likely to manifest.

The picture with regard to race, ethnicity, and social class is just as complex. Kessler and Neighbors (1986) report an interactive effect such that poverty is more damaging to the mental health of blacks than whites, but they do not examine stress–race interactions directly. In a separate analysis limited to whites, McLeod and Kessler (1990) found class differences in stress reactivity, with vulnerability increasing as social status decreases. In contrast, Neff (1985) found no significant interactions of stress with class, race, or race–class combinations.

Thus, estimates of group variation in stress reactivity are themselves variable. Several conditions contribute to these inconsistencies. First, the type of stressor matters to the assessment of differential vulnerability: groups that are greatly affected by one type of problem may be impervious to other types of problems. Second, vulnerability effects are quite sensitive to the type of outcome examined. Third, an overlooked factor in differential vulnerability is the interaction of various statuses. Gender differences may vary by class, for instance, or be limited to certain age groups. Finally, differential vulnerability is often equated with differential coping resources or abilities, but this explanation has not been empirically demonstrated (Aneshensel 1992).

In summary, stress reactivity is highly specific in nature – unique to certain kinds of stressors and to select outcomes (Aneshensel et al. 1991; Thoits 1987). Any attribution of global group differences in mental health to corresponding group differences in stress reactivity remains speculative at the present time.

The Social Consequences of Stress

Most stress research is concerned solely with the impact of stress on a single person: the individual directly exposed to the stressor. For example, studies investigating the mental health impact of involuntary job loss tend to focus on the person who has become unemployed. However, stress does not occur in a social vacuum; rather, stress tends to impinge upon the lives of others, a contagious effect sometimes referred to as the "high cost of caring" (Kessler & McLeod 1984). For example, involuntary job loss exerts adverse effects not only on terminated workers but also on their spouses and children (Penkower, Bromet, & Dew 1988). This spillover occurs because the lives of family members are interwoven and mutually dependent upon one another.

Pearlin and Turner (1987) provide a conceptual road map for understanding how stress is transmitted among family members. First, the family itself serves as a source of stress, not only as a source of eventful change (e.g., spousal job loss) and the consequent demands for realignment within the family but also as a source of chronic, persistent strains (e.g., interpersonal conflict). Second, the family acts as a conduit for extrafamilial sources of stress. This occurs when emotional disturbances aroused in other social roles are brought into family interactions, for example, when difficulties at work generate tension that then produces arguments between parent and child. In addition, family roles may conflict with the demands of other social roles when the duties, obligations, and investments in outside roles intrude on the expectations and performance of family roles. External conditions may also pose a direct threat to the functioning of family relations, as when a job loss of the family breadwinner alters status relationships within the family.

A related body of work examines mental illness as a family stressor (Avison & Speechley 1987). For example, Coyne and colleagues (1987) report that the spouses of actively symptomatic depressed patients encounter substantial disruption in the ordinary routines of the household, feelings of neglect among others, and problems in other major social roles such as work. These spouses are emotionally upset, worried, nervous, and discouraged. Although these difficulties abate when patients are in remission, spouses of recovered patients fear relapse and are uncertain about the future. The researchers conclude that spousal disorder is a source of stress, even when in remission, and that depressed persons produce distress in others.

This approach inverts the usual stress–disorder model by treating the occurrence of mental illness as a stressor that affects the lives of others. It also adds another link in the causal chain connecting stress exposure to mental health: stress adversely affects the mental health of its primary target; this stress-induced disorder then adversely affects the mental health of family members, who become (in essence) secondary targets of the original stressor. This perspective extends the realm of stress outcomes to include damage to others' mental health.

For example, it has been demonstrated that parental exposure to negative life events ultimately damages the mental health of their sons and daughters (Ge et al. 1994). This study is especially instructive because it describes some of the mechanisms through which the exposure of one person affects the mental health of another person. Specifically: stressful life events generate parental depression; parental depression disrupts parenting practices; harsh, hostile, and inconsistent parenting increases the adolescent's risk of depression. Adolescent emotional distress can thus be seen as an outcome of parental exposure to stress.

A similar scenario arises in the case of paternal unemployment. McLoyd (1989) shows that fathers who encounter job and income loss tend to be depressed, anxious, and hostile – emotions that affect interactions between father and child. In general, fathers who become emotionally distressed also become less nurturant and more punitive and arbitrary. These fathering behaviors increase the child's risk of socioemotional problems, deviant behavior, and reduced aspirations and expectations. McLoyd (1989) itemizes the following adverse child outcomes of paternal job loss: mental health problems, low self-esteem, reduced competence in coping with stress, and serious behavior problems such as delinquency and drug use. In this illustration, parental exposure to stress, which might ordinarily be evaluated through parental mental health outcomes, becomes additionally consequential because parental outcomes influence child outcomes.

These studies illustrate quite clearly that stress-induced emotional and behavioral disorders are consequential to the well-being of other persons, especially family members. Two mechanisms appear particularly salient. First, the initial disorder is distressing in and of itself. Second, this disorder often creates social circumstances that others experience as intensely stressful and, hence, are detrimental to their own mental health. These disorders constitute "secondhand" effects of the stressors generating the initial disorder.

Conclusion

Exposure to stressors tends to create or exacerbate emotional distress, including most prominently symptoms of depression and anxiety. This generalization has been empirically demonstrated for three general types of stressors: major life events, daily hassles, and chronic strains. Although these are distinctive sources of stress, they often coincide in an individual's life. For example, life events are especially distressing when they intensify chronic strains (Pearlin et al. 1981) or generate daily hassles (Kanner et al. 1981). Indeed, whether an event is even experienced as stressful depends upon the context within which it occurs. Thus, Wheaton (1990) shows that seemingly negative life events alleviate emotional distress under some circumstances. This counterintuitive effect occurs when the event brings ongoing problematic life circumstances to an end, a condition Wheaton terms "stress relief." Thus, the harmful mental health effects of exposure to a stressor are not inherent to the stressor; instead, they emerge in interaction with attributes of the individual and his or her life history.

12

Family Structure and Processes

William R. Avison

Avison reviews the major findings concerning family structure and processes and their relationship with mental health. He considers three important issues: the debate over social selection versus social causation in explaining the relationship between marital status and mental health; the link between family structure and socioeconomic disadvantage; and the connection between single parenthood and employment and their combined effects on mental health. Avison discusses family structure, stress, and mental health, and he reviews the literature on such psychosocial resources as mastery, self-esteem, and social support in the stress process. The higher levels of psychological distress experienced by single mothers (compared with married mothers) are more strongly related to their greater exposure to stress and strain than to personal deficits in social competence or resilience. There is also an important connection between single parenthood and poverty. The author concludes by considering the implications of this research for community-based intervention. What types of interventions are advocated by Avison, and how likely do you think it is they can be successfully implemented?

For years, sociologists have been interested in the ways that family structures and processes affect individuals' mental health. There are at least two reasons for the continuing interest in this area in the sociology of mental health. First, a large majority of members of society marry or live together at some point in their lives. This has stimulated ongoing interest in examining differences in mental health among individuals who are married, those who are cohabiting, those who were previously married, and the never married. Second, increments in the rates of marital separation and divorce and in the number of women having babies outside of marriage have resulted in significant increases in the number of single-parent families, most of which are headed by females. Studies that compare the experiences of single mothers with married mothers now constitute a major focus of research on family structure and mental health.

In this chapter, I examine some of the major findings concerning family structures and processes and their relationship to individuals' mental health. I begin with a discussion of the concept of family structure and then turn to a brief review of the research literature. Next, I consider three important theoretical and contextual issues: the debate over social selection and social causation explanations of how marital status relates to mental health; the link between family structure and socioeconomic disadvantage; and the connection between single parenthood and employment and their combined effects on mental health. I then turn to a discussion of family structure, stress, and mental health and follow this with a review of the literature on the roles that such psychosocial resources as mastery, self-esteem, and social support play in the stress process. I conclude with a brief consideration of the implications of this research for community-based interventions.

The Diversity of Family Structure

What do sociologists mean by "family structure"? This term usually refers to the combination of two distinct statuses – marital status and parenthood. The simplest way to examine the intersection of these two statuses is to classify individuals as those who are married (or living as married) or not married and those who are parents or not parents. This cross-classification describes four distinct family structures.

	Parental status	
	---	---
Marital status	Parent	Nonparent
Married	Two-parent family	Childless couple
Not married	Single-parent family	Single person

Of course, this classification is overly simplistic. Among two-parent families, we might wish to distinguish between those where the parents are married and those where the parents are cohabiting in a common-law arrangement. Among single-parent families, we might want to distinguish between female-headed and male-headed families because the circumstances of single-parent mothers are often much different from those of single-parent fathers. As well, we could distinguish between single parents who separated or divorced, those who were never married, and those who were widowed. There might also be situations where researchers wish to distinguish between couples who are childless by choice and those who are involuntarily childless. The important point here is that there are many different family structures that researchers may examine in the sociology of mental health.

To add to this diversity, new family structures emerge over time. For example, in our society we see increasing numbers of same-sex couples. Moreover, not all of these couples are childless. Indeed, there is some indication that the number of same-sex couples with children has also grown in recent years.

Sociologists of mental health have always been aware of this diversity in family structure, yet their research has had a more limited focus. Historically, the central focus of those who studied family structure was to understand the relationship between marital status and mental health. A smaller body of research examined how parenthood was associated with psychological well-being. More recently, as the number of single-parent families has increased in our society, attention has become focused on the impact of single parenthood on mental health.

All three of these areas of research focus on the link between family status characteristics and mental health. For some sociologists, an understanding of the relationships between mental health and *transitions* in family status has been a focus of research. These studies examine how marital transitions – especially separation and divorce – are associated with changes in individuals' psychological distress. Studies on this issue simultaneously consider the effects of marital status and parenthood on mental health. In the next section, I review the sociological research on these three areas of study.

Marriage, Parenthood, and Family Structure

A century ago, Emile Durkheim (1897) explored the relationship between marital status and mental health. In his classic book, *Suicide,* he reported that married people had lower suicide rates than the nonmarried. According to Durkheim, this difference was due to married persons' greater integration into society and their stronger feelings of meaningfulness and security. We now recognize these characteristics as indicators of individuals' psychological well-being.

Since that time, many social scientists have examined the connection between marriage and mental health. The results of this research have been conclusive: the married have fewer mental health problems than the nonmarried. Married persons have lower rates of diagnosed mental disorders such as schizophrenia, major depressive disorder, and substance abuse than people who are not married (Robins & Regier 1991). They also have better mental health than nonmarried persons when this is assessed with scales that measure psychological distress (Kessler et al. 1985b; Mirowsky & Ross 1989b) or alcohol or substance abuse (Horwitz et al. 1996a).

In addition, there is some indication that the mental health advantage of marriage is greater for men than for women (Gove, Hughes, & Style 1984). Studies of gender differences in the effect of marriage on mental health have found that, in terms of their mental health, men benefit more from being married than do women. More recently, in their study of the effects of becoming married on mental health, Horwitz and colleagues (1996a) observe this pattern when depressive symptoms are used as the measure of mental health. However, in examining alcohol abuse, they find that getting married led to similar reductions in drinking problems among men and women. Thus, gender differences in the mental health benefits of marriage may be specific to particular kinds of symptoms. Moreover, recent research has also suggested that this pattern for depression may be declining over time as men's and women's roles become more similar. These differences are not so clear, however, if we distinguish between unmarried persons who have never married and those who are separated or divorced. When we make these distinctions, there is no doubt that the married have a mental health advantage over separated or divorced persons (Gerstel & Reisman 1984; Williams, Takeuchi, & Adair 1992b). In contrast, research provides no conclusive evidence that married people are any more or less likely than the never married to experience psychological distress. While some studies find higher rates of distress among the never married than the married (Horwitz et al. 1996a), others find little or no difference (Fox 1980; Horwitz & White 1991). It thus seems fair to conclude that – although the mental health advantage of marriage over nonmarriage is debatable – there is clear evidence that married people experience fewer mental health problems than do persons whose marriages dissolve.

In the popular media, parenthood is depicted as a role that is largely rewarding and positive in its consequences. In reality, there is surprisingly little empirical evidence to indicate that raising children contributes to the psychological well-being of parents. In fact, much of the research literature reveals no differences in mental health between parents and nonparents (McLanahan & Adams 1987). The arrival of a new baby is usually met with heightened excitement and positive feelings by parents, but research suggests that these feelings often level off when the daily responsibilities of infant care become apparent (Wallace & Gotlib 1990). Moreover, most studies that find no differences in psychological distress between parents and nonparents reveal that the many rewards and benefits of being a parent may be offset by the stresses and strains of raising children.

More recently, research on the family and mental health has focused on family structure in terms of the intersection of marital status and parenthood that we described earlier. Indeed, one of the most significant changes in North American societies over the past several decades has been the increasing number of single-parent families, the majority of which are headed by females. Several statistics attest to this social change. For example, in the United States, the portion of households headed by women increased from 9.3% in 1960 to 15.9% in 1984, and the divorce rate during the same period rose from 0.9% to 5.2% of all married women aged 15 and older (Giele 1988). The proportion of children under age 18 living with one parent increased from 13% in 1970 to more than 25% by 1984. Indeed, Bumpass and Sweet (1989) estimate that 44% of all children in the United States will live in a single-parent family before age 16.

Given these changes in the structure of families, it is no surprise that so much recent research has been directed to the study of single-parent families, especially those that are headed by women. Research on mental health among single mothers has focused largely on symptoms of distress. Results consistently show higher levels of distress among single compared to married mothers (Avison 1995; Furstenberg & Cherlin 1991; Wallerstein & Blakeslee 1989). We know less about the prevalence of diagnosable mental disorders among single parents. Brown and Harris (1978) have clearly documented how many of the social and economic consequences of single parenthood are risk factors for depressive illness. Weissman, Leaf, and Bruce (1987) have compared rates of depressive disorders between single and married mothers using data from the New Haven site of the Epidemiologic

Catchment Area program. For the sample as a whole, they find no significant differences between single and married mothers in six-month prevalence rates of depression. However, among white women, single mothers are almost twice as likely to suffer from depression as other white married mothers (13.1% versus 7.7%); there were no such differences among African-American women. More recent studies suggest that single mothers are two to four times more likely than married mothers to experience major depressive illness (Davies, Avison, & McAlpine 1997; Lipman, Offord, & Boyle 1997). Taken together, these studies of single parenthood clearly reveal that family structure is an important correlate of women's mental health.

We know very little about differences in mental health *among* single-parent mothers. Avison and his colleagues (Avison 1997; Davies et al. 1997) find no differences in rates of depressive illness between separated, divorced, and never-married mothers. This suggests that the social, psychological, and economic experiences of single parenthood itself may be more important determinants of mental health problems than how women become single parents.

Theoretical and Contextual Issues

This wide range of research on the relationship between marriage or family structure and mental health has generated a number of important questions in the sociology of mental health. Most of these questions can be framed within the context of three fundamental considerations. The first concerns the direction of the relationship between marital status or family structure and mental health; this is the well-known debate over social causation versus social selection. The second consideration concerns the frequently noted connection between family structure and poverty or socioeconomic disadvantage. The third issue relates to the connection between single parenthood and employment and their combined effects on mental health.

Social Causation and Social Selection

Almost all researchers agree that marriage is associated with better mental health, but there are at least two possible interpretations of this correlation. The first explanation, the *social causation hypothesis*, asserts that marital status is a determinant of mental health. Researchers who support this theoretical position assert that marriage has various benefits for individuals that being single does not. According to Ross, Mirowsky, and Goldsteen (1990), the two major benefits of marriage are (i) the greater financial and economic resources of married individuals that often result from living in a dual-income family; and (ii) the higher levels of social support (especially emotional support) experienced by married persons. These benefits reduce married individuals' exposure to various stressors and assist them in better coping with whatever stressors they encounter. Thus, the social causation interpretation emphasizes the importance of social relationships and roles as the key elements that account for the positive impact of marriage on mental health.

The second interpretation of the association between marital status and mental health is referred to as the *social selection hypothesis.* According to this argument, individuals' mental health influences whether or not they marry. Moreover, the hypothesis also predicts that, among those who do marry, people with histories of mental health problems will be more likely to separate and divorce. The selection hypothesis emphasizes the influence of individuals' personal characteristics, predispositions, or psychological symptoms on their likelihood of entering into marriage and sustaining a marital relationship.

Over the past 25 years, this causation-versus-selection debate has generated a large body of research. For some time, there has been general agreement that the link between marriage and psychological distress can best be understood in terms of social causation processes whereas the relationship between psychiatric disorder (especially schizophrenia) and marital status is more likely to be the result of selection processes.

It appears that many sociologists now agree that causation and selection processes are *both* likely to influence the relationship between marital status and mental health. This point of view suggests that it is more useful to think instead of chains of events or experiences in people's lives. Some of the links in these chains reflect selection processes while others reflect the effects of social causation. For example, there is evidence that persons with higher levels of psychological distress or earlier experience of mental disorders are less likely to marry (Mastekaasa 1992), and there is also evidence that, among individuals who do marry, divorce results in increased psychological distress and disorder (Menaghan & Lieberman 1986). Forthofer and colleagues (1996) have identified another sequence of individual experiences that links psychiatric disorders with marital patterns: they report that individuals who have experienced a psychiatric disorder marry at younger ages than those who have never had a disorder. They suggest that marriage at an early age is in turn more likely to result in subsequent marital problems (including divorce) than is on-time or late first marriage. Thus, early experience of mental health problems may indirectly contribute to marital conflicts and subsequent divorce. As sociologists continue to follow individuals over the life course, there seems to be a greater appreciation of the interplay of social selection and social causation processes.

Family Structure and Poverty

Sociological investigations of family structure and mental health have frequently observed that there seems to be a strong connection between family structure and socioeconomic disadvantage. A review of the literature on this topic suggests that the relationship is a reciprocal one. On the one hand, disadvantage contributes to marital dissolution and the increase of single-parent families. On the other, single parenthood exposes family members to a wide range of economic adversities.

Some of the most compelling evidence of the effects of economic loss on marital relationships has been presented by Elder and Caspi (1988b) in their studies of families during the Great Depression of the 1930s. This work clearly indicates that economic difficulties increase marital tensions in most families, and especially in those that were most vulnerable prior to the economic hardship. Similar findings have been reported by Conger and associates (1990) in their research on families whose lives were affected by the farm crises of the 1980s.

Other investigations of the effects of job loss and economic stress on family functioning reveal that socioeconomic hardships or disadvantages increase marital conflict, reduce marital satisfaction, and impair family interaction patterns (Voydanoff 1990). Of course, it goes without saying that there is also a strong link between marital or family discord and divorce.

Single parenthood also contributes to family members' economic hardships. Indeed, among the many ongoing stressors to which single-parent families are exposed, poverty may be the most pernicious. In this context, McQuillan (1992) has shown how increases in the rate of labor-force participation of married women has led to substantial increases in total household incomes among two-parent families while demographic changes among single-parent mothers have limited their family incomes. The result has been a consistently widening income gap between two-parent and single-parent families. As a result, poverty is substantially more prevalent among single-parent families than among two-parent families (McLanahan 1983). Recent studies (Avison 1997; Brown & Moran 1997; Lipman et al. 1997) have clearly shown that single-parent mothers experience substantially higher rates of poverty and depression than do married mothers.

Family Structure and Employment

In recent years, sociologists have become aware of the interrelation of family structure and employment status. This has become an especially important consideration in understanding how work and family interact in the lives of working women who have children. Paid work provides obvious financial benefits and opportunities for achievement and advancement, as well as various psychosocial rewards. However, despite the observation that being employed generally has positive psychosocial consequences for individuals, not all employment circumstances are the same. Indeed, there are important variations in the stressors associated with any particular work situation. Work exposes individuals to various kinds of stressful experiences and provides different kinds of rewards for different people – financial rewards, self-esteem, a sense of control over one's life, and so on. It seems, then, that the net effect of paid employment for any individual will depend on the balance of these costs and benefits. To some extent, this balance is conditioned by the individual's location in the social structure of society. In this context, family structure appears to play an important role in affecting the impact of work on mental health.

In their assessment of the research on work and family stress among women, Baruch, Biener, and Barnett (1987) provide an insightful review of the ways in which work and family roles interact in their effects upon psychological distress and depression. Their own research highlights the importance of considering family stressors to which women are exposed as well as work-related stress (Barnett & Marshall 1991).

Relatively few studies have examined how single parenthood and paid employment interact in their impact on mental health problems (Ali & Avison 1997; Avison 1995; Cohen et al. 1990). Those studies that have investigated this issue conclude that differences between single-parent and two-parent families in role obligations and opportunities may have significant effects on the balance between work and family responsibilities. For married mothers, paid employment may be more easily integrated into daily family life. The presence of a spouse provides the opportunity to share some of the child-care responsibilities. Alternatively, dual income families have more funds for outside child care or paid assistance in the home.

Employment for single-parent mothers may represent more of a pressing responsibility than an opportunity for achievement and development. Income from employment may lessen the financial burdens of single-parent mothers; nevertheless, most single-parent families live in poverty or near poverty. Paid employment in such circumstances may alleviate some of the most pressing financial strains, but other strains persist. Moreover, when single-parent mothers obtain employment, they commonly also bear continued sole responsibility for the care and nurturance of their children. Such dual demands may generate a cost to employment – role overload.

Under these circumstances, it seems probable that fewer psychosocial rewards associated with employment (greater self-esteem, self-efficacy, or social support) will accrue to single-parent mothers. This is all the more likely because single parents may be constrained to employment that is not their first choice but which is near their homes and offers hours of work that fit with their children's schedules or with the availability of child care.

These three considerations – social causation versus social selection, family structure and poverty, and family structure and employment – are important issues that have set the context for much of the research on family structure and mental health. As we shall see, each of these contextual issues has influenced the kinds of research questions that sociologists have raised with regard to the relationship between family structure and mental health.

Family Structure, Stress, and Mental Health

As we noted earlier, several studies have documented greater mental health problems among separated and divorced parents than among the married. A central focus of research on single parenthood and mental health has been to explain this pattern and to understand the processes that place single parents at greater risk of psychological distress and disorder.

Exposure and Vulnerability to Stressors

Marital dissolution that results in single parenthood exposes individuals to a wide array of ongoing stressors such as economic hardship, work–home role conflicts, and social isolation. These stressors may continue for long periods of time and may ultimately manifest themselves in elevated levels of distress. For example, McLanahan (1983) finds that separation and divorce trigger chronic stressors such as income reduction and housing relocation. Kitson and Holmes (1992) report that the divorced experience more life events than the married, particularly negative events involving loss. When children are involved, there may be additional strains associated with separation or divorce. The custodial parent, usually the mother, assumes many household, financial, and emotional responsibilities previously shared by two parents (Kitson & Holmes 1992).

Thus, most investigations have employed a social causation perspective to explain the connection between family structure and mental health. From this perspective, single parenthood increases parents' exposure to stressors, which in turn results in increased symptoms of mental health problems. Within this framework, the major source of distress and disorder among single parents is their *greater exposure* to stressors when compared to married parents (Avison 1997; Brown & Moran 1997). By contrast, there is little evidence that single-parent mothers are more distressed because they are any *more vulnerable* to stressors than are married mothers. Indeed, Avison (1997) has shown that stressors have similar effects on married and single mothers, and that the higher levels of distress among single mothers is due almost entirely to their exposure to more stressful experiences. In a comparison of single mothers and married fathers, McLanahan (1985) also reports that higher levels of distress among single mothers are due mainly to greater exposure rather than vulnerability to stressors.

Family Structure and Chains of Adversity

Whereas many sociologists have been interested in the consequences of single parenthood for exposure to stressors and subsequent mental health problems, others have drawn attention to events and experiences that may precede single parenthood. Much less is known about individuals' early psychosocial experiences and structural conditions that may precede arrival into statuses in adulthood. This is certainly true of our knowledge of family structure. The vast majority of studies focus almost exclusively on the consequences of single parenthood. Substantially fewer studies consider earlier experiences and personal histories that are the pathways to single parenthood. This seems to be a curious omission: it is unlikely that becoming a single parent is any more random an event than getting married, getting a job, or becoming a parent. A more complete understanding of the role that family structure plays in the lives of individuals can be attained only by describing the processes that produce different family structures, which in turn result in variations in individuals' well-being. This approach involves conceiving family structure both as a social consequence of prior experience and as a social determinant of subsequent psychosocial outcomes.

Research on adversities in childhood and adolescence and their impact on the timing of depression provide some clues about possible chains of experience that precede single parenthood. First, research indicates that the onset of depressive disorder frequently occurs in childhood, adolescence, or early adulthood (Robins & Regier 1991), prior to marriage and subsequent separation or divorce. Second, the vast majority of current cases of major depression among adults are recurrences rather than first episodes (Kessler & Magee 1993, 1994a). These observations suggest that some of the most important determinants of the onset of depression are experiences that must have occurred in individuals' childhoods or adolescence, prior to their entry into single parenthood. Therefore, to focus solely on the stressful consequences of single parenthood may provide only a partial explanation of the determinants of depression among these individuals. Indeed, such an approach neglects the prior experiences that individuals bring into their adult marital and parenting roles – that is, life histories that may either increase or decrease their risk for depression.

Davies and her associates (1997) have studied these patterns among a large sample of single mothers and a comparison sample of married mothers. They find that single mothers, whether separated or divorced or never married, are almost three times more likely than married mothers to have experienced a major depressive disorder in their lifetimes. At the same time, they are significantly more likely than married women to have experienced several adversities during their childhood and adolescent years. By examining the connections among adversities, depressive episodes, and family structure, Davies and associates show how trajectories that link onset of depression and marital histories are influenced by early exposure to adversities.

These results confirm the importance of considering the role of childhood and adolescent conditions in examining differences in rates of depression among single and married mothers. Higher rates of depression among single women are linked, in part, to greater exposure to stressors in the family of origin, stressors that thereafter increase the likelihood of early onset of depression and subsequent depressive episodes. In contrast, women whose childhoods have been relatively free of adversities are more likely either to report no depressive episodes or to have a later onset of depression associated with their current marital status. These latter trajectories are more common among married as opposed to single mothers.

Thus, it appears that single parenthood may be a product of past adverse experiences as well as a determinant of current stress and distress. In this sense, it seems reasonable to think about family structure as a key element of individuals' life trajectories that reflects previous stressful experiences and also influences subsequent exposure to stressors.

Family Structure and Psychosocial Resources

A central premise of research in the stress process is that psychosocial resources – such as self-esteem, mastery or locus of control, and social support – play important roles in mediating or moderating the effects of stressors on mental health outcomes. The research on the effects of family structure on mental health has also examined how these psychosocial resources influence mental health.

There is general agreement among researchers that married persons have higher levels of self-esteem and a stronger sense of mastery or control over their lives than do the nonmarried (Kessler & Essex 1982). In addition, Avison (1995) reports that married mothers have higher self-esteem and mastery than do single mothers. Substantially more research has focused on marital status and social support. Several studies have reported that separated and divorced women experience lower levels of social support of various types than do married women (Menaghan & Lieberman 1986; Pearlin & Johnson 1977; Weiss 1975).

Research on family structure and social support is less clear. Marks and McLanahan (1993) report that single mothers have more social interaction with their own parents, siblings, and friends and also receive more support from these sources than do married mothers. In contrast, there is evidence that single mothers have lower levels of *perceived* social support than do married mothers (Avison 1997). Other researchers have commented on the experience of social support among unmarried mothers (Furstenberg & Brooks-Gunn 1986; Turner, Grindstaff, & Phillips 1990). It may be that single mothers have more social contact with their social networks but perceive less support from these networks than do married mothers.

Much of the literature indicates that psychosocial resources *mediate* the relationship between family structure and mental health. In other words, these resources constitute "pathways" that connect marital status or family structure to mental health. Studies clearly indicate that single parents encounter a vast array of stressors that appear to erode their self-esteem and challenge their sense of control over their lives. In turn, these challenges or threats to self appear to result in higher levels of psychological distress among single mothers (Avison 1995; Simons et al. 1993). In this way, psychosocial resources mediate the family structure–mental health relationship.

Some researchers have also been interested in the *moderating effect* that these resources have on the stress–distress relationship among mothers. These studies suggest that the moderating effects of psychosocial resources are similar for married and single mothers. Regardless of family structure, mothers with higher levels of self-esteem, mastery, or social support are less affected by stressful experiences than are mothers with lower levels of these resources. That is, these resources moderate or "buffer" the effects of stress on distress for single and married mothers alike.

Implications

These findings are important because they indicate that single and married mothers' responses to stress in their lives are very similar. What distinguishes single mothers from married mothers is the sheer magnitude of stressors in their lives. Indeed, it seems clear that single mothers' higher levels of mental health problems are largely a function of this greater burden of stress. In the research literature, there is little support for the notion that their higher rates of psychological distress or depression are due to some personal vulnerability or to some lack of resilience. This is an important finding because it suggests that social factors such as family structure may have effects on individuals' mental health that are as great or greater than the effects of personal predispositions and characteristics. Stated somewhat differently, it seems clear that single mothers experience mental health problems not because of some personal failing or inadequacy but rather because they face considerably more adversities than do married mothers.

Implications for Intervention

Research on family structure has important implications for programs that are designed to improve the well-being of families. If we review the major findings on family structure and mental health, three critical observations emerge from the literature. First, it seems clear that the higher levels of psychological distress experienced by single mothers (as compared to married mothers) is more strongly related to their greater exposure to stress and strain than to personal deficits in social competence or resilience. Thus, single parenthood should be conceived more accurately as a risk factor for exposure to stress than as an indicator of personal vulnerability. Second, there is an especially important connection between single parenthood and poverty that cannot be ignored. Third, a significant number of single-parent mothers have lives that are characterized by frequent adversities that threaten their mental health. This suggests that interventions that focus solely on factors that occur after entry into single parenthood may fail to address a major source of stressful experience.

These observations clearly demonstrate that family structure has consequences for stress and distress. However, as McLanahan and Sandefur (1994) point out, the problems of single parents are not substantively different from the problems of other families: single parents may simply be exposed to more of these difficulties and to greater levels of challenges. In this context, intervention programs that address the needs of all families in the community are to be preferred to those that target specific types of families, because the former address the entire social and community context in which families live. Such programs attempt to reduce exposure to life stress and improve family members' social and personal well-being indirectly by changing the social systems or the social and economic conditions in which family members live. This approach recognizes that experiences at home, at school, and in their neighborhood have important influences on individuals' social competence, their ability to learn, and their social and emotional well-being.

Ecological or *community-based* programs have considerable promise if they address multiple risk factors, focus on multiple settings (including schools, families, and neighborhoods), and target neighborhoods or communities with high needs (Hawkins & Catalano 1990; Institute of Medicine 1994). These interventions encourage families and neighbors to work together to reduce their exposure to the more stressful aspects of their lives, especially those that occur to children and appear to have long-term effects on their lives. They also assist individuals and families in building stronger social relationships that may enhance their feelings of social support and sense of self. Such interventions challenge value systems that view the family as a private refuge that is immune to outside influences. Rather, they encourage the view that children are the responsibility of the entire community.

Finally, these interventions also recognize the diversity that exists in communities. This resonates with findings of substantial variations in the lives of single and married mothers. Although we have focused on psychological distress and depression, the majority of mothers, whether single or married, have never experienced a depressive episode. Among those who do, considerable variation exists in the timing of onset as well as in the pathways into single parenthood. Moreover, not all mothers with early childhood adversities report episodes of depression. Likewise, not all single mothers experience poverty or a crushing burden of stress. Thus, policies and interventions aimed at improving the conditions of single mothers need to recognize differences in their backgrounds as well as in their current conditions.

The sociology of mental health has made major advances in understanding how family structure is linked to individuals' mental health. Future research in this area is likely to focus on those factors that can reduce single parents' exposure to stress and strain. This, in turn, will emphasize the need for more research on social policies and social programs that reduce inequalities between single and married parents.

13

Social Networks and Mental Health

Nan Lin & M. Kristen Peek

The degree of social integration in our communities and the resources in social environments both affect our mental health. The network approach focuses on the web of social relations in which an individual is located. The logic underlying this approach is that networks offer opportunities through which social support is made available and utilized. Lin and Peek review the empirical data on the relationship of social networks to mental health and also suggest directions for future research. Networks are differentiated by two sets of properties: (1) network versus social composition, and (2) structural versus relational focus. Using these two dimensions, the authors create a typology that contains four types of network properties used to organize their summary of the research on the relationship between networks and mental health. The research has not yielded consistent patterns, in part because social networks have not been examined during the dynamic phases when individuals are utilizing their network for social support. Another reason for the lack of consistent relationships between social network properties and mental health is the degree of variability in each individual's life course and role relationships. Networks are dynamic, and it is difficult to disentangle network characteristics from the sources of stress and from mental health. Community characteristics (i.e., the degree to which one can interact with others in a given community) also need to be included in research on networks and mental health. Students should consider how their intimate ties, network connections, and community interactions differ at various times in their lives and for different locations in which they have lived.

Structural Effects on Mental Health

It has long been observed that people are psychologically affected by the social environment in which they live. This is generally known as "structural effects." Why do structural features affect individuals? In general, two explanations have been offered. One explanation, the *social integration* argument, suggests that a well-integrated community or neighborhood serves two functions. First, it provides a sense of comfort and security to its members. Under the collective umbrella, threat or disruption to one's well-being is minimized. A well-integrated community reduces the likelihood that certain deviant behaviors, such as crimes, will occur. Second, it reinforces one's feeling of identity and worthiness. In a well-connected community, individuals feel the need and the expectation to contribute to the group's well-being; this sense, in turn, affirms their own worth and well-being.

A second explanation – the *support* argument – focuses on the resources individuals can draw from the community and its members. According to this argument, individuals can benefit from resources that the community and its members provide because their own resources are limited and may be insufficient to meet certain needs, especially in time of crisis (e.g., death of a loved one, child care, loss of a job). Another aspect of this explanation is that human beings are social; thus, social contact itself provides psychological support. These explanations offer the theoretical basis for empirical studies on the structural effects of mental health.

Informed by the social integration explanation, community and neighborhood studies document (1) to what extent the community is integrated or disintegrated (e.g., by effects of crime, unemployment, etc.) and (2) how well the members of the community are doing (mortality, illnesses, psychiatric illness, etc.). These studies attempt to demonstrate that, for different communities, varying degrees or extent of integration correspond to varying degrees or extent of rates of mental and physical illnesses.

The idea that social integration affects well-being can be traced back to Durkheim's (1897) study of suicide. His work suggested that social relationships such as marriage, parenthood, religious involvement, and employment promoted health (i.e., reduced suicide), provided a sense of meaning and purpose in life, and at the same time created a set of constraints or controls on individual behavior. Later research focused on the relationship between being embedded in social relationships and the absence of psychiatric disorders. For instance, Faris and Dunham (1939) found, in their study of the ecological correlates of mental disorder in Chicago, that the highest rates of schizophrenia occurred in the most disorganized areas of the city. They attributed the high rates of the mental disorder to a lack of social integration of the respondents. Leighton (1959), in his study on Canadian maritime communities that differed in degrees of social disintegration, determined that one of the main predictors of mental illness was a lack of integration in social relationships, either through the community or through more intimate relationships such as the family. In another study, which focused on residents in midtown Manhattan, Srole and colleagues (1962) showed that social class and lack of social integration were major predictors of mental illness in a large nonpatient population.

More recently, studies have shown that other aspects of the social environment, such as economic change and unemployment, also influence the mental and physical health of individuals (Atkinson, Liem, & Liem 1986; Brenner 1973; Catalano & Dooley 1983; Dooley & Catalano 1988; Dooley, Catalano, & Wilson 1994; Liem & Liem 1978, 1988). The common finding in these studies is that undesirable economic occurrences, such as increases in unemployment and decreases in stock prices, affect illness rates. For instance, economic contraction and unemployment increased undesirable job and financial life events, which in turn increased rates of illness (Dooley & Catalano 1988). Unemployment is of special significance in affecting reactions to economic change (Liem & Liem 1978, 1988). Dooley and colleagues (1994) found that people who lost their jobs had over two times the risk of reporting increased depressive symptoms. Liem and Liem (1988) also reported that unemployment had an indirect effect on the mental health of the partners of the unemployed.

The social support explanation leads to surveys of individuals to determine whether they perceive or draw help from others – especially in time of need or crisis – and whether such perceived or actual help reduces distress. Social support can be defined in many ways but generally refers to help provided by others that promotes emotional mastery, offers guidance, or provides feedback regarding the individual's identity (Brown & Harris 1978; Cassel 1976; Cobb 1976). The simplest and most powerful indicator of social support appears to be the presence of an intimate and confiding relationship. Reviews of the social support literature (Cohen & Wills 1985; House et al. 1988; Thoits 1995a; Vaux 1988) indicate that perceived emotional support is directly associated with better mental and physical health. Furthermore, social support has been found to buffer or mediate the harmful effects of stress or strain on mental health.

The Network Approach

The first approach, where studies are based on the social integration argument, represents a macro-level analysis, using each community as the unit of analysis. It examines the association between community characteristics and outcomes as manifested in community rates of illness (suicide rates, mental illnesses, etc.). The second approach, where studies explore social support's effects on mental health, reflects a micro-level analysis. It examines individuals' support characteristics (e.g., nature of help and whether support is actual or perceived) and assesses their associations with measures of mental health.

A third approach is to understand the social web in which a person is located – the *social network* approach. A social network may be defined as a set of individuals who are either directly or indirectly connected. The theoretical argument for this approach is twofold. First, the network indicates how well a person is connected: how extensively a person is connected to others and how these others are connected among themselves. As such, the social network estimates how well the "community" is integrated and how well a person is integrated into the community, consistent with the integration argument. Second, by further examining what resources (e.g., wealth, social status, caring resources and capacities) these others possess or access, the network approach estimates the capacity of others to provide help if called upon, consistent with the support argument. The contention is that a person in a larger or more integrated network and in a network rich in support resources is more likely to perceive stronger social support and to actually receive social support. Therefore, focusing on the network presumably incorporates both social integration and social support theories and bridges the macro and micro approaches.

Yet, relative to the extensive literatures on community studies and on social support, social network studies are fewer and less consistent in findings. The purpose of this paper is to review research findings regarding how social networks may be related to mental health and to suggest directions in which future research on the effects of social networks on mental health may prove more fruitful.

The study of social networks is an extensive and diverse research tradition. Our decision is to focus on research that directly addresses the relationships between social networks and mental health. However, we exclude: (1) studies that specify types, dimensions, elements, or measurements of social networks and that use social networks as the dependent variables; and (2) studies that do not focus on mental health as the dependent variable.

Typology of Social Network Properties

To review the research literature more systematically, we employ a typology that attempts to capture the relevant elements of social networks. This typology contrasts two important network properties: (1) network versus social composition, and (2) structural versus relational focus. *Network composition* refers to characteristics associated with the distribution of nodes (e.g., individuals in the network) and their connections. One example is density – the extent to which the individuals are actually connected relative to the extent to which they could possibly be connected. Another example is the size of the network – how many individuals are directly and indirectly connected in a defined network. These characteristics are based on the nodes and their connections, without any regard to the social and personal attributes of the nodes. *Social composition,* on the other hand, examines the social and personal attributes of the individuals in the network. The percentage of nodes who are kin to one another is one such measure (a point estimate of a role relationship in the network), and the distribution of income variations among the nodes (i.e., income heterogeneity) is another (a range estimate of the distribution of a social characteristic in the network).

The second set of contrasting properties distinguishes between (a) interrelations among the nodes in the network (the structural focus) and (b) the relationships of the ego (the focal person in the network) to the other nodes (the relational focus). The *structural focus* is on the network rather than on the ego's own connections, and it may reflect either network composition (e.g., density and size) or the social composition of networks (e.g., heterogeneity of education, occupation, or income). The *relational focus* is on the ego's relations with other nodes and is reflected in concepts such as frequency of contact with another individual, strength of tie with another individual, or multiplexity (the number of different roles in which the ego is related to another individual – e.g., the ego may be related to another person as kin and also as co-worker and member of the same church).

Table 13.1. *Typology of social network properties in mental health literature*

	Network composition	Social composition of nodes/ties
Structurally focused	Density Size	Heterogeneity Demographic characteristics (i.e., mean education, mean income)
Borderline	Number of confidants Number of helpers	
Relationally focused (ego–alter)	Frequency of contact Affect with tie Strength of tie (i.e., ties rated as positive or negative, strong or weak)	Heterophily–homophily Multiplexity Role composition (i.e., kin composition, friend composition) Group membership

These two contrasting properties can then be combined into a typology, as shown in Table 13.1. Each cell, or type of network property, represents a combination of one specific aspect from each of the contrasting properties.

First, the upper left cell in Table 13.1 represents the combination of the network composition and the structural focus of the two contrasting properties and its associated concepts or measures, such as density and size. Second, the lower left cell refers to the combination of the network composition with the relational focus of social networks; this cell includes such variables as frequency of contact and content (e.g., strength) of ties. In between the upper and lower cells in the left part of the table is a cell that refers to "borderline" variables. This category represents features of a network that are both structural and relational in nature under network composition; in this cell, the network characteristic that is represented is the number of specific types of relationships in the network (e.g., numbers of friends or family). Third, the upper right cell contains properties that focus on both the structural and social composition aspects of a network. Particularly, this cell refers to heterogeneity (e.g., gender distribution, ethnic distribution) and mean socioeconomic status of network members (e.g., education, income). Finally, the lower right cell deals with the combination of relational and social composition parts of a network such as heterophily–homophily (i.e., similarity or difference of characteristics between ego and alter) and role composition (e.g., percent kin).

This typology and its four specifications will be the guide for a summary of studies relating network features to mental health. The summary will lead to conclusions regarding empirical findings on the effects on mental health of social networks and to some proposed approaches for future studies.

A Summary of Studies and Findings

This summary is based on a brief review of the literature in the last two decades on the associations between social networks and mental health. The format for this review is that studies will be summarized according to the schema of the typology. Thus, in the first section, we discuss network characteristics that fall into the "structural–network composition" cell in Table 13.1. The second section will focus on the network variables that are "relational–network composition" in nature and so forth.

Structurally Focused Network Composition Variables

Two of the main concepts addressed in the structural focus of network composition are size and density. There are no consistent findings on the effects of these two aspects of networks on mental health. In past research, both variables have positive effects in some studies and negative effects in others.

Size. Among the network properties, the most often examined with respect to both physical and mental health is network size (measured in numerous ways but basically refering to the number of individuals in the personal or ego-centered network). Often, size and frequency of contact are discussed together because, especially in earlier research, both size and contact frequency are utilized to create one index of network characteristics. However, we suggest that these two concepts address different aspects of the network; thus, size and frequency of contact are addressed separately.

Studies that have focused on size of network in relation to mental health have found positive effects (Aneshensel & Stone 1982; Barrera 1981; Bowling & Browne 1991; Burt 1987; Cohen, Teresi, & Holmes 1985; Donald & Ware 1982; Dykstra 1990; Lin et al. 1979; Wilcox 1981a; Williams, Ware, & Donald 1981), negative effects (George et al. 1989; Haines & Hurlbert 1992), and no significant effects (Acock & Hurlbert 1993; Andrews et al. 1978; Cohen et al. 1982; Israel & Antonucci 1987; Roberts, Dunkle, & Haug 1994; Schaefer, Coyne, & Lazarus 1981). Clearly there is no consensus on the effects of network size on mental health. For instance, in one study focusing on the effects of networks on psychological adjustment to marital disruption of adults who were recently separated or divorced, Wilcox (1981b) established that those who adjusted successfully to the disruption had larger networks. However, George and colleagues (1989), in their examination of the effects of social support on major depression among middle-aged and older adults, determined that a smaller social network at baseline was related to fewer depressive symptoms at follow-up. This is consistent with the suggestion of other researchers that not all social relationships are beneficial (see e.g. Cohen & Wills 1985; Seeman, Bruce, & McAvay 1996). Furthermore, Haines and

Hurlbert (1992), who focused on network range and health, found that having a large network increased women's exposure to stress, which in turn elevated their distress levels.

On the other hand, several studies have indicated that increased network size is associated with better well-being, greater life satisfaction, lower distress levels, or less loneliness. Though Acock and Hurlbert (1993) found no effect of network size on life satisfaction across different marital statuses, Bowling and Browne (1991) found that, among the very old, greater network size increased life satisfaction. Furthermore, results from two studies – one focusing on the health consequences of social resources (Donald & Ware 1982) and another examining the effects of life events on depression (Williams et al. 1981) – indicated that greater network size was associated with lower distress and better well-being. Other researchers (Bowling & Browne 1991; Dykstra 1990), focusing on determinants of loneliness in the older population, found that larger networks decreased the amount and frequency of loneliness. A study (Siegel, Ravies, & Karus 1994) that examined the well-being of gay men found that increased size of network decreased depressive symptomatology. Finally, Burt's (1987) examination of the connection between friends, strangers, and happiness determined that expressions of happiness increased with the size of a person's discussion network.

Density. Density, or the extent to which members in the network are connected (usually measured by the actual number of ties within the network divided by the possible number of ties), also has mixed results relative to mental health. Like the research conducted on network size, results from studies that examine the effects of density on mental health vary from positive effects (i.e., decreased distress or increased life satisfaction – Acock & Hurlbert 1993; Bowling and Browne 1991; Kadushin 1982, 1983) to negative effects (i.e., poor adjustment to a life event – Wilcox 1981b) to no effects (Haines & Hurlbert 1992; Israel & Antonucci 1987). For example, Kadushin (1982, 1983) elaborated on theories of anomie and alienation to show that the density of the social network, which is a structural aspect of the interpersonal environment, was directly related to lower levels of stress and symptoms of posttraumatic stress disorder (PTSD). Acock and Hurlbert (1993) emphasized the importance of network density with respect to mental health in the context of marital status, finding that dense networks increased life satisfaction for people across all marital statuses. They asserted that social networks increase satisfaction through the provision of social support.

On the other hand, in an earlier study of the effects of networks on adjustment to marital disruption, Wilcox (1981b) established that those who adjusted successfully to divorce and separation had less dense networks. This finding is also consistent with Hirsch (1980), who focused on the influence of social networks on coping among widows and determined that density was negatively related to self-esteem.

Finally, in the Haines and Hurlbert (1992) study on the effects of network range on health, density had very little influence on overall mental health. However, density had a direct positive effect among men on access to companionship and emotional aid, which supports the Acock and Hurlbert assessment that social networks may affect mental health through their connection to social support.

One of the most common explanations for the reason why structurally focused network composition variables should affect mental health is that certain network characteristics represent greater social support, which in turn benefits mental health (Acock & Hurlbert 1993; Wellman & Wortley 1989). An expansion of this argument is that network characteristics represent not only the structure of support (see e.g. House et al. 1988) but also the structure of social resources available to the central person, which may also affect mental health (Haines & Hurlbert 1992; Lin 1982). These explanations apply to size and density in different ways. For example, increased network size may represent a greater number of supporters in the network available for social support. This would presumably benefit mental health, but perhaps only conditionally (i.e., in times of stress). On the other hand, a large network might not have positive effects on mental health if there is considerable tension between network members. Furthermore, a dense network may represent a network that is easily mobilized in times of crisis to aid an individual; however, high density can also be indicative of restricted flexibility and range in accessing different resources (Hirsch 1980).

Borderline Variables

Borderline variables are those that refer to those aspects of a network that are *both* structural and relational in nature. Number of relatives, friends, specific supporters, or confidants are examples of borderline measures. These variables are borderline because they address a structural focus of the network (size) yet also focus on particular relationships between the central person and the rest of the network.

Number of Specific Types of Relationships. The most common finding for borderline variables is that greater numbers of friends and confidants are associated with lower distress or depression of the central person. For instance, in a study that examined the determinants of loneliness in the older population, results suggested that having more friends decreased loneliness (Dykstra 1990). In a study on the effects of social networks on mental and physical health in the Netherlands, Tijhuis (1994) determined that greater numbers of friends decreased psychiatric complaints; on the other hand, results from the same study also indicated that greater numbers of support givers indicated more psychiatric complaints (though this last finding may be largely the result of cross-sectional data – e.g., if people have greater depression then they will likely need more help and call upon more support givers).

Bowling and Browne (1991), in their research on the provision of practical help from informal caregivers and the emotional well-being of the very old, found that both number of relatives and number of confidants had positive effects on emotional well-being. Greater numbers of friends decreased depression, and having more relatives increased life satisfaction for respondents. However, in one study on the effect of number of kin in the network for divorced individuals, Gerstel (1988) found that greater numbers of kin increased depression for men, whereas it decreased depression for women. Furthermore, results from two studies – one addressing the influence of social relationships on depression (Dressler 1985) and the other examining the effects of life events on depression (Warheit 1979) – suggested that number of extended kin and number of relatives living close by had no effect on depression. Finally, Burt's (1987) examination of personal discussion networks found that higher numbers of strangers in the network decreased happiness.

Borderline variables could affect mental health for similar reasons as structurally focused network composition variables in that large numbers of friends, family, and other supporters should theoretically increase social support, which should decrease depression and have beneficial effects on mental health. The findings from borderline variable studies are relatively consistent with this hypothesis. The results generally suggest that higher numbers of these specific relationships benefit mental health.

Relationally Focused Network Composition Variables

This set of measures addresses specific relationships of ego with others in the network but still captures overall network composition. In particular, variables such as frequency of contact between a central person and specific relationships (e.g., friends, family, and confidants) and the "content" of ties (e.g., whether ties are strong or weak, how supportive ties are, etc.) are included as determining both relational characteristics and network composition.

Frequency of Contact. Frequency of contact is typically measured as how often the ego is in contact with specific network members. Research generally indicates that higher frequency of contact is associated either with better mental health or with no significant effects. For instance, in two studies that estimated the effects of frequency of contact on well-being (Donald & Ware 1982; Williams et al. 1981), higher frequency of contact with network members had a positive effect on well-being. Also, several researchers examining frequency of contact as part of an network index found that frequency of contact had a buffering effect (i.e., frequency of contact acted to reduce the effects of stress on the outcome variable) with respect to mental health. Having a high frequency of contact with other network members buffered the effects of stress on depression for those with high numbers of undesirable life events (Kessler & Essex 1982; Linn & McGranahan 1980; Monroe et al. 1983; Thoits 1982b).

However, other researchers examining similar measures found no buffering relationship (Andrews et al. 1978; Husaini et al. 1982; Lin et al. 1979; Roberts et al. 1994; Warheit 1979). Furthermore, George and colleagues (1989) determined that lower frequency of contact was related to lower depression. Still other researchers found no effects at all associated with frequency of contact (Cohen et al. 1982; Eaton 1978).

Affect and Strength of Ties. The content of ties refers to numerous aspects of network ties. Social support is one important content of a tie, for example. However, the research covered in this chapter will not focus on support, since there is a large literature elsewhere that focuses on social support (see Chapter 10). Therefore, content in this chapter refers to satisfaction with particular ties or network structure, how the ties are rated (e.g., positive or negative), how adequate the ties are, and whether the ties are strong or weak (Granovetter 1973).

One study emphasized that social networks have both positive and negative elements (which a number of other researchers corroborate; see e.g. Seeman et al. 1996) and that positive and negative aspects of networks should therefore have independent contributions in predicting depression (Pagel, Erdly, & Becker 1987). These authors assessed how helpful and upsetting each tie in the network was, as well as overall network satisfaction, and found that higher network satisfaction reduced depression but that neither helpful nor upsetting dimensions of network ties had any significant effects once satisfaction with the network was controlled for in the model. Also, Rook's (1984) examination of the effects of supportive and problematic ties on the well-being of older women determined that increased numbers of negative ties both decreased life satisfaction and increased loneliness. Furthermore, results from another study, which focused on whether positive and negative network ties moderated the impact of negative life events on distress for older people, suggested that positive ties had no main effects on distress but buffered the effects of negative events on distress (Okun, Melichar, & Hill 1990). These researchers also emphasized that negative ties increased psychological distress (which is corroborated in other research; see e.g. Siegel et al. 1994).

Two other studies that focused on content examined adequacy of ties and strength of ties (Dykstra 1990; Lin, Woelfel, & Light 1986c). Lin and colleagues, in their study on the buffering effects of strong ties, determined that strong ties decreased the effects of undesirable life events on depression. In two other of their studies (Ensel & Lin 1991; Lin, Dumin, & Woelfel 1986b), they found that strong ties with confidants both decreased distress and increased perceived social support, which then decreased depression. Finally, in her study on how primary relationships influenced the well-being of older people, Dykstra (1990) found that feelings of ties being adequate decreased neurotic symptoms under conditions of high adversity (essentially a buffering effect).

Relationally focused network composition variables can affect mental health by representing social support and integration or by directly affecting social support.

For instance, frequency of contact could reflect availability of social support but could also represent an individual's amount of social integration. Again, both social support and social integration influence mental health (see House et al. 1988 for reviews). As far as strength of ties is concerned, the hypothesis is that stronger ties provide better social support (e.g., Dykstra 1990; Lin et al. 1986b), which in turn should benefit mental health.

Structurally Focused Social Composition Variables

This section focuses on those variables that address either the structural features of the network (e.g., not specific ties but the network as a whole) or the sociodemographic characteristics of nodes and ties in the network (e.g., overall education or average age of all people within a specific network). As with the other variables that have been reviewed thus far, there are no consistent findings with respect to mental health.

Heterogeneity. Heterogeneity generally refers to the diversity of the network with respect to such characteristics as sex, age, and geographic composition. Heterogeneity is a potentially important network variable because it represents the diversity of resources within the network. However, it is one of the least studied characteristics in network research with regard to mental health. One study (Haines & Hurlbert 1992) examined the effect of network range on health and found that men whose networks had an increased geographic range experienced less distress. Results from another study that concentrated on the relationship between presence of resources and mental health in the context of marital status suggested that networks of wide range (one indicator was age heterogeneity) enhanced well-being by providing instrumentally useful resources (Acock & Hurlbert 1993). It was found that the never married suffered from networks with high age heterogeneity whereas the divorced benefited from age-diverse networks.

Finally, one study found no significant effects of heterogeneity on mental health. Tijhuis (1994) examined personal networks of the Dutch and found that heterogeneity of gender, proportion of colleagues in the network, and heterogeneity of labor-force participation had significant effects on physical health but not on mental health.

Demographic Characteristics of Nodes and Ties. Like heterogeneity, the demographic characteristics of nodes and ties represent, to a certain extent, the different types of resources available through the network (e.g., mean age and education of network members). And as with heterogeneity, demographic characteristics of nodes and ties have not been examined frequently with respect to mental health. The one study that has examined these characteristics is that of Acock and Hurlbert (1993), who addressed whether social networks affected two aspects of well-being (life satisfaction and anomie) and whether effects differed across marital statuses. They determined that mean age of network members had no significant effects on either variable. However, higher mean education increased life satisfaction across all marital statuses.

A resources argument is the most common explanation for the effects on mental health of structural–social composition variables such as heterogeneity and demographic characterization of network members (Acock & Hurlbert 1993). The argument is basically that access to a wide range of social resources (including support, money, and information) is beneficial to mental health (see also Haines & Hurlbert 1992). For example, greater heterogeneity signifies many different types of relationships within the network that are potentially important resources for an individual. Also, average education and income of network members could indicate how many resources possessed by these individuals could help others.

Relationally Focused Social Composition Variables

Finally, in this section we cover measures that address both specific relationships within the network and the social composition of the people involved in those relationships. These variables include measures that consider how similar and different "ego" and "alter" are, how many different types of roles are present in a relationship between ego and alter, and the proportion of different types of relationships within a network.

Heterophily–Homophily. Heterophily and homophily refer to the difference or similarity over a particular set of characteristics between a central person and an alter. In other words, these variables address how similar or different are the central person and the other node with respect to various characteristics (e.g., age, education, gender, and income). This is another type of measure that has not been addressed much in network research. The main study that has focused on homophily addressed the question of whether the access to and use of strong and homophilous ties buffered potentially harmful effects of undesirable life events and if these effects varied across marital status (Lin et al. 1986c). These researchers found that homophilous ties reduced depression for both married and unmarried individuals. Age and education homophily reduced depression for married respondents, whereas occupational status homophily reduced depression for unmarried respondents. Another study (Lin et al. 1986b) found, in the confidant network, that gender homophily with confidant actually increased psychological distress and that education homophily reduced distress.

Multiplexity. Multiplexity refers to the number of social roles between ego and an alter in the network. As in the case of heterogeneity, there is very little research dealing with the relationship between multiplexity and health. Hirsch (1980) found that multidimensional or multiplex relationships are positively related to self-esteem for young and mature widows. However, Haines and Hurlbert

(1992) determined that, for men, an increased number of multiplex ties (each involving more than one role) *increased* exposure to stress, which elevated the distress levels of men. Another study (Lin et al. 1986b) found that, whereas having a multiplex relationship with spouse or partner significantly reduced psychological distress, having multiplex relationships with other family members or friends increased depression.

Role Composition. Role composition refers to the *proportion* of certain types of role relationships in the network. Examples include kin, friends, non-kin, helping professionals, and so forth. The proportion of kin to non-kin in the network is one of the most frequently examined types of role composition with respect to mental health. For example, Acock and Hurlbert (1993) concentrated on network composition with regard to well-being in the context of marital status. They determined that the mental health of the never married benefitted from a network with a high proportion of kin, whereas the divorced with a high proportion of kin in their network suffered. In a study on the effects of kin composition on distress, Peek (1996) determined that high kin composition directly decreased psychological distress for younger people and indirectly decreased distress for older people (for older people, higher kin composition was associated with greater social support, which then reduced distress). However, two other studies (Dykstra 1990; Haines & Hurlbert 1992) found that higher proportions of kin increased distress and loneliness. Furthermore, in her study of the effects of kin ties on depression for divorced individuals, Gerstel (1988) found that higher proportions of kin decreased distress for women and that higher kin proportions increased depression for men.

Other studies have determined that the composition of the network (particularly presence of a spouse and number of good friends) has a buffering effect on depression (Monroe et al. 1983; Thoits 1982b). In other words, the presence of spouses and good friends in the network was shown to buffer against depression for those with high numbers of stressors in their lives (Eaton 1978; Kessler & Essex 1982; Linn & McGranahan 1980; Monroe et al. 1983; Thoits 1982b).

Still another researcher (Tijhuis 1994) found that kin composition had no effect on mental health but that other types of composition affected depression. In this study, respondents with higher proportions of people who are close to them living nearby, and those with high proportions with whom they had frequent contact, reported less depression or psychiatric complaints. Finally, Kadushin (1983) found that a higher proportion of veterans in urban respondents' networks was associated with decreased incidence of PTSD.

Group Membership. Group membership refers to what types or how many different social organizations the focal person or ego is involved in (these typically include churches, clubs, and voluntary associations). Group membership has, to a certain extent, become more a measure of social integration than of social networks. Therefore, the studies that are reviewed here are from earlier studies, since later studies that examine group membership tend to focus on multiple roles with less reference to social networks (e.g., see reviews by Adelmann 1994; Moen, Dempster-McClain, & Williams 1989; Thoits 1987).

Researchers focusing on group membership as part of a network index typically find either positive effects or insignificant effects of group membership on mental health. For instance, results from two studies (Donald & Ware 1982; Williams et al. 1981) indicated that group membership increased well-being. Kessler and Essex (1982) determined that group membership (again as part of a network index) buffered the effects of stress on depression. Also, in their study on distress among Chinese Americans, Lin and associates (1979) found that group membership decreased distress. However, a number of other studies found no significant effects of group membership on mental health (Andrews et al. 1978; Cohen et al. 1982; Eaton 1978; Husaini et al. 1982; Thoits 1982b). Other researchers examine the "supportiveness" of social networks with a high proportion of kin (Wellman 1990; Wellman & Wortley 1989). Their studies are relevant to this discussion because, according to social support research (e.g., George 1996; Lin & Ensel 1989), greater support generally is associated with lower depression and better mental health. Wellman and Wortley (1989) find that most of the networks with a high proportion of kin are supportive in several ways. First, almost all parents and adult children in their study provide emotional support, instrumental services (siblings provide this as well), and financial aid (though less so than the other categories). Therefore, a high proportion of kin is thought to have beneficial effects on mental health by increasing social support.

One of the predominant explanations is that relational social composition variables influence mental health through their effects on social support. The best example is kin composition. Higher kin composition indicates the network's ability to provide support (see e.g. Seeman & Berkman 1988; Wellman & Wortley 1989). Another example is multiplexity, where the greater the number of roles that ego has with an alter may indicate stronger ties; this in turn should offer more social support and thus benefit mental health (Lin et al. 1986b).

Reconceptualizing Network Effects in the Process of Support

This review of the literature shows that the effects of social networks on mental health are moderate at best. For each of the social network's properties, there were findings of insignificant as well as significant effects on mental health. For example, under the category of structurally focused network composition variables, density and size had generally positive effects, but there were some findings of negative effects on mental health as well as findings of nonsignificance. From the literature reviewed here, there were approximately four findings in support of density having positive effects on mental health, two insignificant findings, and one negative finding. For size, there were about twelve findings that suggested size had beneficial effects on mental health, but there were also at least two negative findings as well as six insignificant findings.

Under the classification of borderline variables, the results were again relatively positive (abount six results suggest that higher numbers of certain types of relationships in the network promote mental health). However, as with the other network characteristics, there were also findings of nonsignificance and results that suggested negative effects on mental health. In the category of relationally focused network composition variables, the effects of frequency of contact and of affect and strength of ties are generally positive for mental health. There were approximately six beneficial effects of frequency of contact on mental health; on the other hand, there were also six insignificant findings and one negative effect. Positive affect and strong ties are two of the only network properties that have consistently positive effects on mental health.

The results were even less consistent under the general category of social composition of the network. For example, among the structurally focused social composition measures, two positive effects of heterogeneity on mental health were established, but one negative effect and one insignificant effect were also found. For demographic characteristics of nodes and ties, one positive effect and one insignificant effect were found. Under the category of relationally focused social composition variables, all the effects of homophily on mental health were positive or beneficial to mental health. However, the results were mixed for the remaining properties of multiplexity, role composition, and group membership. For instance, there were four positive results for the effects of multiplexity on mental health, but there were also three negative results. Furthermore, for role composition, approximately eleven beneficial effects on mental health were determined, but also there were four negative findings and two insignificant effects. Finally, there were about four positive effects of group membership on mental health, but there were also four insignificant findings.

These inconsistencies can in part be attributed to the variation in ways that social network variables are measured. For example, heterogeneity can refer to several different types of diversity, and studies that have focused on heterogeneity do not all focus on the same types; for example, Acock and Hurlbert (1993) focused on age heterogeneity, whereas Tijhuis (1994) focused on gender and labor-force heterogeneity. Multiplexity is perhaps a better example of how one concept can be measured very differently. The Haines and Hurlbert study (1992) measured multiplexity as the number of contents per tie across a relatively large network, whereas Lin and colleagues (1986b) defined multiplexity as a relationship where ego discussed three or more problems with an alter in the context of a specific support network. These are just two examples of how one concept can be addressed in several different ways, which of course can influence the measured effects of the concept on mental health.

Inconsistencies in the findings may also be attributable to variations in the study populations and samples. For example, several studies focused only on the older population (e.g., Bowling & Browne 1991 and Roberts et al. 1994 examined people aged 85 and older; Dykstra 1990 examined respondents aged 65–75), whereas others examined all ages or those aged 18 and older (e.g., Acock & Hurlbert 1993; Lin 1986; Tijhuis 1994). The focus of other studies varied from hospitalized patients (George et al. 1989) to working-class women with children at home (Brown et al. 1986a) to black communities in the South (Dressler 1985) to Vietnam veterans (Kadushin 1983). These vastly different samples make it difficult to compare the effects of network properties across studies.

Still another factor in accounting for conflicting results is the variation in outcome measures. Outcome variables include psychological distress (e.g., Lin et al. 1986b), well-being (Bowling & Browne 1991), loneliness (Dykstra 1990), life satisfaction and anomie (Acock & Hurlbert 1993), depression (Dressler 1985), and adjustment (Wilcox 1981b). These are diverse outcomes, and factors of significance for life satisfaction levels need not be so predictive for (say) depression.

Nevertheless, if social network variables had an intrinsic direct effect on mental health, such effects should be consistently evident even under differing conditions of measurement, populations, and outcomes. Take, for example, life events and social support. These factors – even when measured differently, applied to different populations and samples, and linked to different types of mental health outcomes – tend to show consistent effects. Thus, it is inappropriate to argue simply that – given the "proper" measures, samples and populations, or outcomes – social networks "should" have significant direct effects.

The appropriate question, then, is why social network properties have not shown consistent patterns of relationships with mental health. We propose two reasons why the relationships have not been consistently found: (1) social networks should be examined in the dynamic process of support, and (2) conditions of life course and role relationships must be taken into account.

Networks must be viewed as one dynamic element in the process of support. That is, the effects of the social context on a person's psychological well-being must be mediated by a process in which these contexts offer opportunities for ego to find and form relations with the few people who could provide support in time of need or crisis. As proposed elsewhere (Lin 1986: 341), mental health may be directly affected by ego's access to and use of intimate ties, ties with whom ego can confide and share important and "inner" thoughts. The extent to which ego may be able to identify and access such intimate ties is contingent on the network in which ego is involved and on the properties of the network. That is, networks may exert effects on a person's mental health indirectly because the social network, in part, determines whether a person may draw upon a particular tie (node) for intimate and confidential interactions.

This conceptualization is consistent with the assumptions many researchers use to study network effects on mental health. The general assumption is that networks are effective because they offer opportunities through which social support becomes not only available but also more likely to occur. Because it is generally known that stronger or more intimate ties tend to provide better support, it may be inferred that networks offer opportunities to establish such stronger or more intimate ties. It can be hypothesized that increased network size, density, and heterogeneity offer more opportunities for ego to identify and access an intimate tie.

A more complete picture of the mediated effects of the social context can also include community characteristics. Network size, density, and heterogeneity may be affected by the extent to which individuals participate in the community and, in addition, by the amount of possible interactions in the community. Community, network, and intimate ties thus form three layers of the social context, with the community as the outer layer, the network as the intermediary layer, and the intimate ties as the inner or core layer for the ego. While the inner-layer relations directly affect ego's mental health, the outer layers dictate both opportunities and constraints for ego to find the alters who will be able and willing to provide support in time of need.

A second dimension of the effects of social networks on mental health may be appreciated by focusing on the fact that the utility of network characteristics in providing support (through intimate ties) varies depending on the individual's social position, stage of life course, and composition of role relationships in his or her network. The significance of a spouse is expected to vary depending upon the absence or presence of children, whether both spouses participate in the labor force, or the extent to which the spouses maintain their own networks. Relations with a supervisor or co-workers may be more or less supportive or stressful depending on possibilities for moving to other jobs, offices, or organizations. Likewise, a "significant other" at one time in a person's life may become less significant at a later phase, when someone who is less significant will assume more significance. Siblings may be important for teenagers, but not as important for the individuals when they form their own marriages, families, and careers. Yet, as people age, as their children grow up and depart, and as they lose their spouses, siblings may again assume significance as confiding partners. In other words, advantages of certain social compositions in one's network differ over the life course, and the variations may be curvilinear rather than linear over the life-span.

These considerations help clarify the lack of findings for direct effects of network properties on mental health; they also focus research attention to placing networks in the process of support where "structural effects" reflect the opportunities and constraints for individuals to develop meaningful and intimate relations with a few others who can provide expressive and instrumental support in time of need or crisis. This "process" view links the three aspects or layers of the social context to mental health, and it postulates that the contributions of the community and the network should not be expected to be direct. Instead, the significance of social networks lies in the opportunity structure they provide for ego to find intimate ties. Likewise, we should not expect the same network or social composition of the network to exert constant effects across the life course, because changing configurations of role relationships call for different alters to fill the support needs. In sum, then, it would be impossible to understand the process of support without a firm understanding of the structure from which support is derived – namely, the social network.

14

Socioeconomic Stratification and Mental Disorder

William W. Eaton & Carles Muntaner

This chapter reviews sociological theories and measurements of stratification and social class in the process of relating inequality to mental disorder. Eaton and Muntaner argue that processes of stratification and periods of high vulnerability to mental disorder are related to different stages in the life course. Consequently, stratification and one's place in the socioeconomic system have a complex relationship to the occurrence of mental disorder. Both individual and environmental factors must be taken into account. Eaton and Muntaner review the major research studies, noting differences in indicators of social class and methodological variations. In general, researchers have found that socioeconomic status (SES) is inversely related to mental disorder; that is, those in the lower classes experience higher rates of disorder. Two contrasting frameworks for understanding the relation of SES to mental disorder are selection and drift on the one hand and social causation on the other hand. *Selection* refers to the idea that individuals who are predisposed to mental disorder have lower than expected educational and occupational attainment.*Drift* refers to the idea that those with mental disorders are likely to drift down the SES ladder, as they will have more trouble with employment and other means of attaining higher-SES positions. In contrast, *social causation* explanations emphasize how the social experiences of members of different social classes influence their likelihood of becoming mentally ill or distressed. The authors conclude by reviewing two studies that illustrate the complexity of the relationship between social class and mental disorder. We need more research on the specific ways in which social class affects mental disorder and on how mental disorder affects the attainment of social status. Students should compare the selection and drift frameworks. Is it likely that an individual born of a wealthy family will drift down the socioeconomic ladder if they experience a mental health problem? Consider the role of social support and stress in understanding the relationship between SES and mental health.

Introduction

Inequality is the simplest concept that applies to the group but not the individual. As such, the study of inequality has always been central to sociology. Inequality in social resources seems to be present in every current society (Flanagan 1989) and brings with it a wide range of associated differences that might be related to mental disorder. Although the study of mental disorders formed part of the earliest empirical work in sociology, as in Durkheim's (1897) *Suicide,* the initial work on the relationship of social inequality to mental disorder was done by individuals in other fields (e.g., Commission on Lunacy 1855; Nolan 1917). A review of the literature on social status and specific mental disorders in 1969 included 25 studies of social class and mental disorder, of which 20 revealed the inverse relationship between social class and prevalence of disorder: that is, the highest rate of disorder in the lowest social class (Dohrenwend & Dohrenwend 1969). A review in 1990 referred to 60 studies published between 1972 and 1989 (Ortega & Corzine 1990). Of these, 46 revealed an inverse relationship between social class and mental disorder. The strength and consistency of the relationship is impressive, as is its enduring interest for sociologists. The literature reflects slow progress in specifying useful details and implications of the overall research. Gradually, however, a picture is emerging that reflects the complexity of mental disorders as well as the complexity of social class and socioeconomic status.

Definition of Mental Disorder

Mental disorders are defined here as disturbances in the mental life of the individual that have deleterious consequences for the individual's relationship to others. The concept of "mental disturbance" focuses (a) on time-limited perturbations from the individual's usual pattern of thinking and feeling, such as a sudden panic attack or a months-long episode of depression, and (b) long-term deviations – in this case, from the statistical norm of mental functioning of most individuals – that have no apparent cause, like schizophrenia and antisocial personality disorder. This definition places less emphasis on behavioral deviations that have little cognitive or emotional component, such as those that can occur with addictions or homicides. Use of alcohol or other psychoactive substances does not, in itself, meet the criteria for mental disorder unless there is other evidence of mental disturbance.

Most mental disorders involve deviations in cognition or emotion that are part and parcel of everyday human existence, necessitating an arbitrary threshold of measurement. The requirement that mental disturbances lead to interference with social relationships excludes trivial disturbances such as daydreaming, brief confusion, temporary irritation, or trivial anxiety. Thus, the individual's relationships to others operationally defines the threshold for presence of disorder. Deterioration in social functioning can have a variety of causes, such as physical illnesses or injuries, and is not in itself a mental disturbance. Mental disturbances – even nontrivial ones such as the trance of a shaman (Ellenberger 1970) – do not qualify as mental disorders unless they bring about a disruption of the individual's social relationships. Thus, the social network is a defining concept in the operational definition of mental disorder.

This definition focuses on the nature of the disturbance (mental) and its implication for functioning (social); it thus requires psychological *and* sociological conceptualization and measurement. However, this definition does not specify the nature of the cause. Mental disorders can have infectious, toxicologic, genetic, neurodevelopmental, psychological, and social causes.

Definition of Socioeconomic Stratification and Social Class

Socioeconomic stratification is defined as the process by which individuals are accorded unequal access to rewards and resources in society. Individuals in social structures with socioeconomic stratification are hierarchically ordered as to wealth, power, and prestige – that is, economic, political, and cultural rewards and resources.

An important form of socioeconomic stratification is the social class structure. *Social classes* are defined here as groups of individuals who are similar in their wealth, power, and prestige and who either (1) interact with one another more often than randomly or (2) are aware of some common interest. According to the Marxian tradition, social classes are groups of individuals defined by their relationship to the ownership and control of the means of production, or by the process of appropriation, production, and distribution of surplus value in the economy. This definition leads to at least two basic classes: those who own and control the means of production and receive the benefits of others' labor (i.e., the capitalist class) and those whose labor is exploited in that the surplus value produced is taken from them (i.e., the working class). Although Marx emphasized the process of exploitation as the major determinant of class, later evolutions of this concept have emphasized the importance of power and the capacity of the individual to influence decisions about the structure of the economy. Individuals in similar socioeconomic strata form into social classes, in part, in order to retain control over the economic and political process (Mills 1956). Some recent theorists have emphasized the importance of the relational concept of exploitation based on control of productive assets beyond the material means of production to organizational power and the influence of credentials such as educational degrees, as opposed to simple measures of domination or power (Western & Wright 1994; Wright 1985). For the purposes of our discussion, the glue holding these notions of social class together is the concept of the social group: social classes, according to this view of the Marxian tradition and its heirs, are social groups with differential control over productive assets. In itself, socioeconomic stratification indicates only an ordering of individuals who may or may not be formed into groups.

The study of social class and socioeconomic stratification includes many diverse traditions (Collins 1994; Farley 1994; Matras 1984). These various perspectives on socioeconomic stratification and social class have formed a central part of the discipline of sociology, and it is reasonable to consider different mental health outcomes associated with various definitions.

Education, measured either as years of education or as credentials such as certifications and degrees, is the most common index of social class in psychiatric epidemiology and public health research (Liberatos, Link, & Kelsey 1988). Its stability over adult life – as well as it reliability, efficiency of measurement, and good validity – are presumably the main reasons for its popularity (Kaplan & McNeil

1993). Education represents knowledge, which might have an influence over health behaviors (Sorlie, Backlund, & Keller 1995). According to neoclassical economists, education might also increase the value of an individual's contribution to the productive process, which translates into greater social rewards. On the other hand, some neo-Marxists maintain that the social rewards associated with greater education stem from the association with skills that are in short supply (Wright 1985). Another view is that the credential provided by educational attainment may be more a sign of life-style, class of origin, or "attitude" than of actual ability; these latent features may be what actually generates the higher salary.

Occupation, measured according to the Bureau of Census Classification of Occupations or as occupational prestige, is a major social class indicator in psychiatric epidemiology (Muntaner & Eaton 1996). Occupation strata identify technical aspects of work (Muntaner et al. 1991) and are also associated with prestige, wealth, skills, and specific working conditions (Sorlie et al. 1995). Some authors in the functionalist tradition of medical sociology emphasize that occupational prestige and socioeconomic status are consequences of educational achievement (Ross & Wu 1995). Other models of occupational stratification emphasize that the rewards associated with positions in society derive from their location in the hierarchical structure of the workplace and not from the workers' education (Krieger et al. 1993). For example, managerial and professional occupations obtain higher wages partly as compensation for self-monitoring.

A third way of measuring social stratification has been the assessment of a person's *economic resources,* using mostly measures of personal and household income (Kessler et al. 1994) but occasionally measures of poverty (Bruce, Takeuchi, & Leaf 1991) or wealth (Muchtler & Burr 1991). In a money economy, income and wealth are the most straightforward measures of ability to acquire resources and influence a wide range of outcomes. But these measures present their own set of limitations. Questions about income typically show a higher nonresponse rate than those about education and occupation, presumably because respondents are unwilling to disclose their financial situation (Kaplan & McNeil 1993; Liberatos et al. 1988). Furthermore, although income can be conceptualized as a measure of social class, several research programs consider income as a dependent variable to be explained by social class theories (Halaby & Weakliem 1993; Robinson & Kelley 1990; Smith 1990; Wright 1979). Positions in the social structure are associated with various kinds of income (e.g., rents derived from renting land versus wages derived from being an employee) and differentials in wealth (e.g., value of assets owned) (Callinicos & Harman 1989; Wright 1993). Finally, because wealth is more unequally distributed than income (Matras 1984; Wolff 1995), it is likely that reliance on income as the preferred indicator of economic resources may overlook larger differentials in mental health.

Marxian *class analysis* represents an alternative approach to measurement (Wright 1993). Class analysis maintains that several societal relations (e.g., owner versus worker, manager versus nonmanager) generate inequalities in social resources such as income. For example, in traditional Marxian analysis, owners of the means of production generate excess wealth for themselves from the surplus value they appropriate from laborers. In some modern versions of Marxian class analysis, managers are thought to receive higher income to reward their additional loyalty in supervising others in line with the desires of owners (Wright 1985).

The Causes of Inequality

There are two main contending paradigms for explaining the existence of social classes and socioeconomic differences (e.g., as in Matras 1984). One explanation arises from the sociological theory of *functionalism,* a major sociological paradigm (Davis & Moore 1974; Merton 1956). With respect to socioeconomic stratification, functionalists argue that in a complex modern society there are differences in the individual qualities required for different occupations. Some occupations require extremely persistent, skillful, and intelligent individuals, whereas other jobs can be performed by almost anybody. In addition, some jobs are more important than others for the welfare of the society as a whole. Rewards are distributed unequally in society in order to attract individuals with specific and rare skills and abilities into important jobs. Thus, the social class system serves the function of sifting and sorting people into appropriate occupations for the greatest good of society.

The second main explanation for the existence of socioeconomic stratification and social classes comes out of the *conflict* paradigm, which finds its most developed expression in the Marxian tradition. According to this tradition, classes are thought to exist because individuals higher up in the hierarchy are more powerful, preserving the class structure in order to hold on to privileged and advantageous positions for themselves and their heirs (Mills 1956). Such control is exercised in a variety of ways. For instance, the upper classes may attempt to manipulate the political process to favor those already in power (Ferguson 1995; Navarro 1994). High-status individuals will attempt to ensure that their sons and daughters are provided with educational credentials for entering high-status positions in the occupational structure. The upper classes, consciously or unconsciously, may manipulate the mass culture so that explanations for the class system are expressed in terms of individual differences in ability instead of differences in power or inequalities of institutions (Chomsky 1989). The functional explanation of the class system just described may here be thought of as an ideology that elites maintain to draw attention away from their privileges and power (Laurin-Frenette 1976).

Socioeconomic stratification is a process generating a structure that tends to persist through time, even though the individuals holding positions within the structure are constantly being replaced over the generations (Erikson & Goldthorpe 1993).

Each generation of individuals joins the current structure of socioeconomic stratification via both *inter*generational mobility (i.e., from one generation to the next) and *intra*generational mobility (i.e., within one generation, over the lifetime of an individual).

If individuals – regardless of their personal characteristics – inherit class position from parents, then the class system is said to be "rigid" or "closed," and the data is thought to support the conflict interpretation for the existence of classes. If individuals can enter the upper class no matter what their background then the system is thought of as "open" and the functional theory is supported.

In the last few decades, there have been considerable advances in the quantitative study of the dynamics of this replacement process (sometimes referred to as "status attainment" – a phrase and an approach with a slightly functionalist orientation). The quantification of the process of stratification has the potential to illuminate the relative adequacy of the functionalist versus conflict explanations for the existence of socioeconomic inequality. For example, useful empirical studies of the stratification process have taken the form of path models of intergenerational mobility – that is, the relationship of the acquisition of socioeconomic position of the child to the position of the parents (Blau & Duncan 1967). In Western societies during the first three quarters of the twentieth century, there was considerable intergenerational movement from the lower class into the middle and upper-middle classes. The movement was due partly to the expansion of the middle class. But along with the movement out of the lower class, there was a strong tendency for those born into the upper class to remain there throughout their lifetimes. In other words, some evidence is consistent with the functionalist approach and some with the conflict approach.

The Life Course

At any given point in time, the individual brings to the social environment a biological organism with a history of learning and experience. These all affect the numerous capabilities and inclinations that make the individual unique and contribute to his or her sense of identity and life plan. The organism begins at conception with genetic material, and the history of learning and experience start at that moment. The organism is sometimes obdurate in the face of environmental experience (e.g., sustaining personal identity in an oppressive prison or concentration camp) and sometimes exquisitely sensitive (e.g., exhibiting neurological changes as a result of experience; Eisenberg 1995). It is still hard to predict the realms, and the times, of obduracy and sensitivity. As the life course progresses, the capabilities and inclinations that make the individual unique are constantly evolving as experience is acquired. Age-related periods of relatively rapid or relatively stable evolution are called "developmental periods"; these are demarcated by more or less regular age-related patterns – in the way the environment changes and in the way the organism matures – called "life transitions" (Baltes, Reese, & Lipsitt 1980).

The process of stratification, and the periods of highest vulnerability to mental disorder, are developmentally staged. During some stages of life, the effects of the environment, the choices individuals make, and the successes and failures in tasks (related to the social environment in particular) are more important for the future evolution of the life course than they are at other stages. Adolescence and young adulthood appear to be important developmental periods, both for the process of socioeconomic stratification and for the onset of mental disorders. For example, elaborations of status attainment models show that the period of high school and young adulthood are very important in determining ultimate socioeconomic position. In high school, educational and occupational aspirations (as well as other factors such as the socioeconomic position of the family) are influential in determining whether the individual attends college; college attendance, in turn, is important in determining the first job (Sewell, Haller, & Ohlendorf 1970). Still other models of the process show that the first job has a strong influence on the entire later career (Blau & Duncan 1967). Likewise, the age of risk of first onset for many mental disorders is in adolescence and young adulthood. For males, schizophrenia arises just after adolescence; for females it arises about a decade later, during young adulthood (Eaton 1985). Depression arises in adolescence (Giaconia et al. 1994; Lewinsohn et al. 1993). Simple phobic disorder, extreme shyness, and general nervousness usually start as early as when the infant learns to talk (Eaton, Dryman, & Weissman 1991; Giaconia et al. 1994), but social phobia arises in puberty (Giaconia et al. 1994) and panic attacks start in adolescence (Hayward, Killen, & Taylor 1989). Conduct disorder arises in males in the middle of their childhood, followed by mental disturbances connected to use of alcohol and drugs after puberty and to antisocial personality disorder in the late teenage years (Mrazek & Haggerty 1994).

The general focus of this developmental approach is the ongoing reciprocal relationship between the age-graded expectations of the social system, the adequacy of the individual's performance in the context of those expectations, and the consequent mental life of the individual. The rating of performance by others affects aspirations for future performance; the school system and the occupational system both regularly provide such ratings (Kellam et al. 1983). How does the attainment of a given letter grade in elementary school affect risk for conduct disorder in the following year, and vice versa? How does the onset of depression or other disorder affect educational, occupational, and income aspirations (Crespo 1977; Kessler et al. 1995b; Link 1982), and vice versa? How does significant others' influence regarding occupational aspirations affect risk for schizophrenia, and vice versa (Parker & Kleiner 1966)? How does the first job affect risk for schizophrenia (Link, Dohrenwend, & Skodol 1986), and vice versa? How does the occupational career affect panic disorder, and vice versa (Keyl & Eaton

1990)? How does an episode of schizophrenia affect occupational mobility after the first job, and vice versa (Goldberg & Morrison 1963)? The point of listing these questions, and repeating the obverse, is to show the reader that the process of socioeconomic stratification is related to the occurrence of mental disorder in a subtle and complex manner. The effects of many variables that mediate the relationship ebb and flow over the life course, interacting in a constantly evolving co-dependent manner.

Class as Cause of Mental Disorder: Environmental and Individual Factors

The New Haven Study

The monograph *Social Class and Mental Illness* (Hollingshead & Redlich 1958) is the strongest early study of the relationship of class to mental disorder that assumes the direction of causation from class to mental disorder. It represents one of the strongest collaborations between sociology and psychiatry. Hollingshead, the sociologist, had done earlier work on the structure of social class in America. This work included creation of the Hollingshead Index of Social Position, which produced five categories of social class by combining information about education, occupation, and area of residence for each respondent. This index presumes that social class can be represented and measured via a single dimension. Although the Index of Social Position was ordinal in nature and is named with reference to the individual, the presentation in *Social Class and Mental Illness* indicates that the concept is consistent with the foregoing definition of social classes: that is, groups of individuals that are not only similar (in terms of wealth, power, and prestige) but that also exhibit structured patterns of interaction and discontinuous culture and life-styles. This conception of social class is no longer dominant in sociological research, even if the Index of Social Position still appears in psychiatric journals, four decades later. The monograph – often referred to as the New Haven study – presents no theory as to how social class might cause mental illness. Instead, the focus was on presenting the details of the relationship, by type of disorder and by treatment facility. The impact of this study on the popular culture was dramatic, powerfully linking social class with mental illness in the public mind.

Social Class and Mental Illness had the advantage of presenting data on specific categories of disorder, but it also had the disadvantage of using data only from facilities that treat mental illness. Table 14.1 presents the central findings. Psychosis is strongly associated with class, showing more than eight times the prevalence in the lower class as in the upper two classes (1,505 versus 188 per 100,000). Some of this association must be due to higher chronicity among the lower classes, since the relationship of class to incidence is weaker (73 versus 28 per 100,000). Chronicity

Table 14.1. *Social class and mental disorder in the New Haven Study (rates per 100,000)*[a]

	Level of social class			
Disorder	I–II	III	IV	V
Neurosis				
Prevalence	349	250	114	97
Incidence	69	78	52	66
Psychosis				
Prevalence	188	291	518	1,505
Incidence	28	36	37	73

[a]Prevalence rate is point prevalence; incidence rate is annual.
Source: Hollingshead and Redlich (1958, Table 16).

of neurosis, on the other hand, is associated with higher class status, even though the relationship of neurosis to incidence is flat. Treatment for psychosis was available in 1950 through publicly financed mental hospitals, but long-term treatment for neurosis had to be paid for by the patient. The higher prevalence rate of neurosis for the upper classes thus presumably reflects data gathered solely from treatment facilities and not the general population.

Selective Review of Incidence Studies

The New Haven study was the first among many later examples of studies of socioeconomic stratification and mental disorder. Most of the studies are cross-sectional in nature, yielding only *prevalence* rates; thus, the observed association between class position and mental disorder could have resulted either because lower class position causes mental disorder ("causation") or because those with mental disorder end up in lower class positions ("selection"). Prospective studies of *incidence* – new cases – of mental disorder show that the class position actually precedes the disorder and thereby establish class as a more credible potential cause. The incidence results from the New Haven study regarding schizophrenia (Table 14.1) have been replicated in dozens of studies, with all but a handful showing the inverse relationship of incidence with social class (Eaton 1985) and thus providing consistent support for the causation explanation. Because schizophrenia is so rare, data on its incidence are uniformly from treatment agencies. Yet because schizophrenia is a severely impairing disorder, most schizophrenics are treated by psychiatrists, and data from the treatment sector are more credible than for other disorders (Eaton 1985).

There are much more limited incidence data for other disorders. Data from the Epidemiologic Catchment Area (ECA) program show that indicators of poverty (Bruce et al. 1991) and of occupational status and education (Anthony & Petronis 1991) are risk factors for depression, supporting the causation model for that disorder. Likewise, ECA analyses on panic disorder (Keyl & Eaton 1990), agoraphobia (Eaton & Keyl 1990), and social phobia (Wells et al. 1994) all show statistically significant relationships between indicators of low social class and incidence, supporting the causation explanation for anxiety disorders generally.

Lower-Class Status and Mental Disorder: Individual and Situational Factors of Causation

Some explanations for the effects of lower class status on mental disorder concentrate on the social environment of the individual, especially its stressful qualities. Other studies focus on individual differences in coping with the social environment. Still other possibilities exist in the way in which socioeconomic position brings individuals into contact with the physical environment.

Increased stress is the most widely accepted causal explanation for higher rates of mental disorder among the lowest class. Stress evolves from the "discrepancy between the demands of the environment and the potential responses of the individual" (Mechanic 1978). This is closely allied with "distress," which may be defined as the individual's *perception* of the discrepancy between the environment and the individual's potential to respond (i.e., a subjective assessment of stress). The idea that lower-class life produces mental disorder through increased stress fits naturally within the conflict theory of formation and maintenance of the social classes. Conflict theorists would contend that lower-class life is certainly less pleasant than life in the upper class, in part because of additional stresses. Many of these stresses are described in vivid detail in Marx's depiction of lower-class life in nineteenth-century England (Engels 1958; Marx 1967, chap. 10).

A variety of stresses that are relatively normal can contribute to one's mental disorder if they cluster together in a short period of time. These "life event" stresses are more frequent in the developmental periods of adolescence and young adulthood (Goldberg & Comstock 1980). Many of these relatively normal stresses involve the economic system, where the lower-class person is at a distinct disadvantage compared with the upper-class person. Individuals in the lower class are more likely to have financial difficulties, for instance (Wright 1979), or to lose their jobs (Granovetter 1995). Stresses resulting from illness in oneself or one's friends and from death of friends or relatives are important causes of mental disturbance, and these illness-related stresses have repeatedly been shown to be more common in lower classes than in the upper classes (Marmot & Koveginas 1987; Susser, Watson, & Harper 1985). Contemporary reviews of a variety of causes of morbidity and mortality confirm the finding (Krieger et al. 1993). Another major

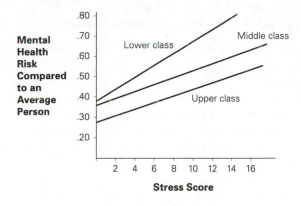

Figure 14.1. Social class and stress in Manhattan. *Source:* T. S. Langner, "The Stress Score, Impairment Risk, and Socioeconomic Status" (Figure 14-2, p. 382). In *Life Stress and Mental Health* by Thomas S. Langner and Stanley T. Michael. Copyright © 1963 by The Free Press, a Division of Simon & Schuster. Adapted with permission of the publisher.

type of stress is related to divorce and separation, and these events may occur more frequently in the lower classes as well (Cherlin 1992). Stress indices, which collect these types of stressful life events into a score, are related to lower social class position (Turner et al. 1995).

Class and Stress in Manhattan

This class research was conceived by sociologists and psychiatrists working together, but the major psychiatrist (Thomas Rennie) died before the collection of data began (Langner & Michael 1963). The methodology shifted considerably: data were collected via household surveys, and the emphasis was on a global concept of mental illness rather than specific diagnostic categories. The substantive focus shifted from social class to social stress, but the issue of social class remained important. The concept of social stress provided an etiological explanation for the association of social class and mental disorder, as shown in Figure 14.1. This example is one of many ways in which lower social class position could raise the risk for mental disorder. The figure shows that higher levels of stress are related to higher risk for mental illness, all along a continuum of stress from very low to very high. It also shows that individuals in the lower class have a higher risk of mental illness for any given level of stress. Finally, the figure suggests that stress is a more potent activator of mental illness in the lower class than in the middle and upper classes: the slope of the line for the lower class is steeper. This difference in slope picks up the issue of the linearity of the relationship of social class to mental illness, which is a continuing theme in the literature (Kessler 1979; Kohn 1968).

Class, Family Life Stage, and Depression in London

The most convincing demonstration of social factors in the etiology of any mental disorder is *Social Origins of Depression,* by George Brown and Tirril Harris (1978). That work demonstrates the importance of life event stresses and chronic difficulties in depression for females. The methodology involved in-depth diagnostic and etiologic interviews with a sample of 114 patients, as well as a sample of 220 community residents of a lower middle-class area of London. Of particular interest was the relationship of social class to onset of depression (Brown et al. 1975). Social class was defined by combining measures of occupation, educational attainment, and assets. Women living alone who were professionals, managers, or small business owners – or whose husbands (or fathers, if not living with their husbands) were professionals, managers, or small business owners – were defined as belonging to the middle class. Those in skilled manual or routine nonmanual occupations were included in the middle class if they or their husbands had completed school through age 16 *or* if they had both a car and a telephone. The lower class included semiskilled or unskilled workers or, for those with intermediate occupations, those who did not own both a car and a phone.

There was strong evidence of a relationship between life event stressors and depression. For example, 86% of the recent cases from the community, and 75% of patients, had a severe event or major difficulty, but only 31% of the women without depression had such events or difficulties (Brown et al. 1975). There also was strong evidence of a relationship between social class and depression. For example, 25% of the lower class in the community residents – versus 5% of the middle-class community residents – were recent or chronic cases (Brown et al. 1975). Likewise, there was strong evidence that stresses were related to social class (e.g., 54% of the lower class, versus 30% of the middle class, had a severe event or major life difficulty). Of interest here is the elaboration of this relationship when the data are analyzed in terms of (a) life stage and (b) the availability of an individual with whom the respondent could talk about personal problems or intimate relationships. Figure 14.2 shows the complexity of the relationships by combining two separate analyses from Brown and colleagues (1975). The bottom two lines in the figure show that social class interacts with life stage in affecting depression: there are no statistically significant differences between the classes, except for women who have one or more children less than 6 years old living with them. But for women at this life stage, more than 40% are recent or chronic cases of depression in the lower class, versus only 5% in the middle class. That three-way relationship stretches the data about as thinly as is possible, but there is evidence of a separate interaction of class with the availability of a confidant in the top two lines in Figure 14.2. Here again, the classes differ most in the life stage of women who have children younger than 6 living with them. Less than 40% of lower-class women report having someone they can talk to about personal problems, whereas more than 75% of middle-class women have this kind of

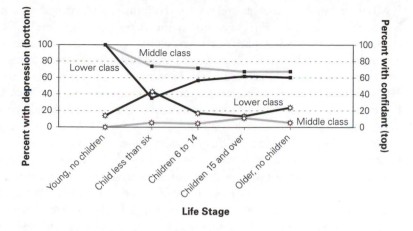

Figure 14.2. Class and depression in London (life stage and intimacy as mediators). *Source:* Adapted from G. W. Brown, M. N. Bhrolchain, and T. Harris, "Social class and psychiatric disturbance among women in an urban population," *Sociology* 2: 225–54. Copyright 1975 American Association for the Advancement of Science.

relationship available to them. Since most of these women are married, this suggests that lower-class marital life does not support or include a psychologically intimate component during this life stage. Other data in the London study, as well as data reviewed elsewhere in this volume, strongly suggest that social supports of this type are an important buffer of social stress, protecting the individual from onset of depression and other types of psychopathology. It could be that social supports are more important for women than for men in influencing risk for mental disorders (Kessler & McCleod 1984). Regardless of this possibility, the London study reinforces the importance of life stage in understanding the relationship of class and mental disorder; it also reveals (again) the importance of young adulthood as a critical developmental period.

Socioeconomic Position and Individual Coping

Variation in the population regarding many individual characteristics tends to expand over the life course, as the combination of genetic endowment and environmental experiences produces individuals with more and more unique qualities (Baltes et al. 1980). A natural research focus for the functional perspective is the study of individual differences in ability – whether they are presumed to be inherited or the result of socialization processes. The question for the functionalist is: How does an individual with a given set of characteristics end up in a given social position? In the field of socioeconomic stratification, any abilities that are broadly advantageous in a range of occupational positions are important.

Many cognitive abilities are relevant to performance of occupational duties. Some scholars feel that intelligence – the ability to perform in modern school systems and to survive and advance in a given culture – is a broad, stable, and general dimension along which individuals differ (Anastasi 1988). There is considerable controversy over how broad and general the trait of intelligence is (Sternberg 1995). This concept of general intelligence, if correct, has consequences for the functionalist theories of class because more intelligent individuals will be suited to a wider range of jobs than less intelligent individuals. There is evidence (reviewed by Jensen 1969) that intelligence as measured by standard psychometric tests is correlated with socioeconomic position. The continual calibration and recalibration of intelligence tests, with validation by a range of indicators, naturally tends to produce a measure that predicts broadly for the majority of the population and is longitudinally stable. But the degree to which intelligence tests actually are predictive, whether it is fair to use them in judging individuals' abilities, and the degree of changeability over the life-span are issues of intense debate.

Ambition is also important to consider. In a true functionalist "meritocracy," the only determinants of reward should be an individual's ambition and intelligence (Young 1994). At any given level of ability, ambitious people who set high aspirations for themselves are likely to have higher educational and occupational attainments.

Some status attainment models have incorporated measures of mental ability and ambition (Sewell et al. 1970). The occupational status of the parents, as well as the mental ability of the offspring, have strong influences on ultimate attainment. Mental ability has a strong influence on grades, which in turn affect educational ambition and educational attainment. Thus, early variables like mental ability and parental occupational status also pass effects on status attainment through sociopsychological variables (e.g., ambition and peer effects) measured in high school. But social class background also affects aspirations because individuals may become aware that upward mobility is closed to them, or because they are taught that it is inappropriate for them to aspire to upper-class status. Stress is a situation requiring intensive problem solving, to which the general trait of intelligence is relevant. The power of early measures of intelligence in predicting later performance in the occupational system – as shown, for example, in the Wisconsin model of status attainment (Sewell et al. 1970) – is strong enough to consider in any comprehensive model of social stratification and mental disorders.

Other types of coping abilities are important to consider. Kohn (1977) feels that lower-class children are brought up in an atmosphere that encourages a "conformist orientation," without the flexibility necessary to deal with a stressful situation. Lower-class adults, perhaps because of the type of occupations in which they find themselves (Kohn & Schooler 1983), value conformity to authority more than upper-class people and socialize their children to their own value systems. Upper-class individuals and their children value self-direction more than conformity to authority. Conformity to authority contributes to inflexibility in coping

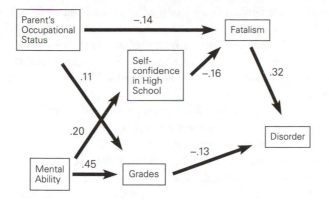

Figure 14.3. Fatalism model of SES and psychological disorder. *Note:* Residual and unanalyzed correlations are omitted. *Source:* Adapted from Wheaton (1980, Table 5 and Figure 5).

with stress; this inflexibility, interacting with genetic factors, could explain some or all of the social class differences in rates of mental disorder. Kohn (1977) provides abundant data, from several industrialized nations, showing that social classes do differ in their conformity orientations in this way; as yet, however, there is no evidence that the differences are connected to mental disorder.

The relationships of social class, stress, coping, and psychological disorder have been examined in detail by Wheaton (1980) in what he terms an "attributional" theory. As a result of reinforcement contingencies associated with social class position, individuals develop biases in their attribution of the causes of changes in their situations. The general notion from attribution theory is that success is more likely to be attributed to the individual's efforts, whereas failure is more likely to be attributed to the external environment. Because of their disadvantaged position in the social structure, lower-class individuals are less successful in the everyday challenges of life and so acquire the habit of attributing causes to the external environment. Upper-class individuals are more successful, in general, and attribute causes to their own efforts. The external attribution, termed "fatalism," increases vulnerability to psychological disorder because active attempts at coping are viewed by the individual as unlikely to be successful. In this case, the individual's characteristics interact with the stressful environment to precipitate disorder. Individuals may not emerge successfully from stressful situations when they do not attempt to deal with them actively but instead let events overtake them (Seligman 1975). Upper-class individuals are more optimistic because their backgrounds have led them to think of themselves as successful, and this optimism leads to greater persistence in the face of stress.

Wheaton (1980) provides analyses from three separate longitudinal data sets that are consistent with the fatalism theory. Figure 14.3 shows the simplified model of one of them. The data derive from a study of all 17-year-old male high school students in the Lenawee County (Michigan) school system in 1957. In 1972, 291 of these were reinterviewed. The father's occupational status is weakly related to the school ability of the respondent (correlation of 0.16). School ability affects self-confidence in high school, and school ability and father's occupational status are both related to the grades received in school. The fatalistic orientation is affected both by the father's status (−0.14) and the level of self-confidence (−0.16). Poor grades affect vulnerability to disorder (−0.13). There is a relatively strong effect of fatalism on disorder (coefficient of 0.32).

The advantage of this analysis is that it provides an empirical test of an explicit model of the effects of low social class on mental disorder. The model has the advantage of its foundation in social psychological theory and of linkage to laboratory studies of attribution for success and failure. It builds elegantly on advances in stratification theory and research.

Socioeconomic Position and the Physical Environment

Many mediators of the effects of low social class have been overlooked or undervalued, perhaps because they require multidisciplinary work. The physical and biological environment can affect the individual's risk for mental disorder at any time from the moment of conception to death. Because there are enormous differences in life-styles between the various social classes, and because the causes of mental disorders are not yet well understood, there are numerous other specific possibilities (e.g., fetal damage or toxic environments) for explaining why lower-class life may cause an increased risk for mental disorder.

A variety of disturbances during pregnancy and birth can increase the risk of disease, injury, or death of a newborn child (Bracken 1984). These pregnancy and obstetric complications can also lead to relatively subtle disturbances in mental functioning in later life (Pasamanick & Knobloch 1961). The link to social class exists because many aspects of fetal damage are more common among the lower classes (e.g., mortality – Bakketeig, Hoffman, & Titmuss-Oakley 1984; low birth weight – Strobino et al. 1995; prematurity – Alberman 1984). This suggests the possibility that lower-class infants are more likely to be born with some slight fetal damage, which may contribute later to a mental disorder. The pregnancy and obstetric complications also may interact with social class in that fetal damage may be potentiated only among lower classes (Drillien 1964).

Mental disorders can be produced by toxins and physical deprivation. Many aspects of lower-class residential environments are potentially toxic. Lead and other heavy metals, which can cause mental deficiencies (Needleman & Bellinger 1991), are more common in lower-class urban neighborhoods. Toxic waste sites are more likely to be situated in lower-class than in upper-class residential neighborhoods (Bullard 1993). Dangerous occupational environments contribute to risk for mental disorder and are found more frequently in jobs held by lower-class individuals. The dangers include toxins (such as heavy metals) found in battery plants as well as organophosphate herbicides and pesticides used by migrant workers (Needleman 1995). Other dangers include the psychological characteristics of the occupational environment. For example, Link and others have suggested that jobs with certain noisome characteristics (steam, heat or cold, odors, confined spaces) contribute to risk for schizophrenia (Link et al. 1986; replicated by Muntaner et al. 1991), and that jobs where individuals have little influence over the pace of work may contribute to risk for depression (Link et al. 1993).

Selection and Drift: Individual Impairments and the Social Environment

Mental disorder could be inversely related to socioeconomic stratification because mental disorder affects the educational and occupational career. The notion that mental disorder leads to a lowering of socioeconomic status is here termed "drift," which refers to *intra*generational mobility. The notion that the predisposition to mental disorder could affect attainment of socioeconomic position over the entire life course is here termed "selection." Selection can be observed in longitudinal research on *inter*generational mobility.

Mental disorders with significant chronic impairment are likely to affect attainment of occupational roles. Consider the contrast in the manner of hiring that might occur in lower- versus upper-class occupations. Application for a job as construction worker or fruit picker is sometimes as simple as showing up at the construction trailer or street corner when workers are needed. Verbal or social skills, judgment, independence, persistence, and other traits may not be assessed prior to being hired. Application for an executive or professional position is more likely to require the possession of professional certifications, assessment by professional placement firms, and interviews – sometimes over several days – with prospective supervisors and co-workers. Paper-and-pencil tests, including intelligence tests, may be included in the requirements for obtaining positions, or for the educational background of degrees and certifications required even to apply. Social impairment is one of the defining criteria for mental disorders, and the more severe disorders like schizophrenia involve lower cognitive ability in some persons (Bilder et al. 1992). Individuals with chronic social and cognitive impairments, as is likely to be the case for schizophrenia and antisocial personality disorders, are likely to suffer in the more rigorous selection procedure and so gravitate down the social scale to positions with less demanding entrance requirements.

Lunacy and Poverty in Nineteenth-Century America

A classic early study of social class and mental disorder concluded that selection and drift, rather than social causation, were the dominant explanation. In 1854,

Edward Jarvis led a legislative commission "to ascertain the number and condition of the insane in the State, distinguishing as accurately as may be between the insane, properly so considered, and the idiotic or *non compos*; between the furious and the harmless, curable and incurable, and between the native and the foreigner, and the number of each who are State paupers" (Commission on Lunacy 1855: 9). Letters of inquiry were sent to hospitals, to physicians in each town, and to clergy and other responsible persons in towns without physicians. It was apparently assumed that the physicians could make a reliable diagnosis, as they were presumed to "understand the nature of defective or diseased minds, and [were] competent to testify" (Commission on Lunacy 1855: 17). The study gives the appearance of extreme effort to be comprehensive and of exacting efforts in the presentation of data. At the tenth meeting of the Association of Medical Superintendents of American Institutions for the Insane (the forerunner organization of the American Psychiatric Association), a motion was unanimously adopted praising the Jarvis commission work "as the first successful attempt, in America, to secure entirely reliable statistics on this subject" (Grob 1971: 65).

A principal finding of the Jarvis report was that poverty was associated with lunacy. There were 2,622 lunatics in a population of more than one million, for a prevalence proportion of 2.33 per thousand. This proportion is slightly lower than (but on the same order of magnitude as) the prevalence of psychosis today, which might be estimated as about one half of one percent, or 5 per thousand. The prevalence of lunacy among paupers, who formed about 2% of the population, was 65 per thousand (over 6%) but only 1 per thousand among persons of independent means. The resulting odds ratio, estimated and presented by Jarvis in the report (pp. 52–3) is nearly 70 – a size any modern-day epidemiologist would pay attention to.

What did Jarvis conclude from these data? One conclusion was that insanity caused individuals to become paupers – this is the "drift" interpretation: "It needs no philosophy to show that some, perhaps many, lunatics, by their disease lose their power of self-sustenance, and are thereby removed from the independent to the pauper class" (Commission on Lunacy 1855: 53). But he also concluded (p. 55) that "much of poverty has a common origin with insanity" – this is the "selection" interpretation:

> it is worth while to look somewhat at the nature of poverty, its origin, and its relation to man and to society. It is usually considered as a single outward circumstance – the absence of worldly goods; but this want is . . . only one of its manifestations. Poverty is . . . enrooted deeply within the man . . .; it reaches his body, his health, his intellect, and his moral powers, as well as his estate. In one or other of these elements it may predominate, and in that alone he may seem to be poor; but it usually involves more than one of the elements, ... Hence we find that, among those whom the world calls poor, there is less vital force, a lower tone of life, more ill health, more weakness, more early death, . . . less self-respect, ambition and hope, more idiocy and insanity, and more crime, than among the independent.(Commission on Lunacy 1855: 52)

The Jarvis report raises several issues that form themes for much of the later work on the subject. The comprehensive definition of the target population and the comprehensive quality of case finding is important, and it would appear that the Jarvis commission was more inclusive in this respect than other work until the ECA study, more than 120 years later. The use of specific categories of mental disturbance ("lunatic" and "idiot"), and the presentation of data that allows distinctive relationships to social variables between the categories, contrasts favorably with some later work. However, the categories studied – both the focus variables of lunacy and idiocy and the social definition of "pauperism" – are on the rare end of the continuum.

The idea that mental illness produces a downward shift in the individual's financial status (drift), or that some trait or group of traits of the personality structures of affected individuals predisposes them simultaneously to pauperism and insanity (selection), is not proven in the cross-sectional work of Jarvis but is consistent with the functionalist view of the formation and maintenance of the social classes. This point of view suggests that individuals in poverty acquire that status because of their own lack of ability or ambition.

Curiously, results for the fatalism model of Wheaton (1980) are consistent with Jarvis's contention that "among those whom the world calls poor, there is less vital force, a lower tone of life, more ill health, more weakness, . . . less self-respect, ambition and hope"; for "less self-respect, ambition, and hope" substitute "fatalism." Data from the Jarvis commission, and from the Lenawee County study one century later, provide strong evidence that mental disorder is related to social class position. Jarvis's notion that a wide range of personal dispositions is associated with mental disorder and with social class position receives empirical support from the work of Wheaton and others. The direction of causation is presumed by each author, but differently: from disorder to class for Jarvis; from class to disorder for Wheaton. The presumption of direction may have been affected by Jarvis's focus on relatively severe disorders as opposed to the relatively milder distress studied by Wheaton.

Follow-up Studies

Because they sort out temporal order, longitudinal data are preferred for assessing the selection/drift theory. This assessment requires a longitudinal follow-up of the social class attainment of a population of individuals *after* the occurrence of mental disorder in some proportion of them. About a dozen studies address the issue of mobility of individuals with severe mental disorders; most indicate some support for either the selection or drift hypothesis (e.g., Eaton & Lasry 1978). A methodologically rigorous study of intragenerational mobility in England gave strong evidence of downward mobility following an episode of schizophrenia (Goldberg & Morrison 1963). Two convincing studies compared intergenerational mobility of schizophrenics and control individuals born in the same cohort and showed that the trajectory for individuals who would later be diagnosed as schizophrenic was not as high as that in the general population (U.K. cohort – Goldberg & Morrison 1963; U.S. cohort – Turner & Wagenfeld 1967). These studies of intergenerational mobility suggest that the incidence findings are artifactual, because many schizophrenics have insidious onset of disorder and this type of onset is presumed to hinder upward mobility. There are very few follow-up studies of the effects on attainment of socioeconomic position of such milder mental disorders as depression, anxiety, and alcohol dependence.

Two Later Studies of Social Class and Mental Disorder

Comparing the Forces of Stress and Selection: The Israel Study

In reviewing the evidence on social class and mental disorder, Dohrenwend and Dohrenwend (1969) helped to inaugurate the so-called third generation of research, in part because they showed that results for social class differed for specific disorders, thus challenging the point of view that mental disorder was a global concept. They decided upon a strategy of research that would support either the stress or selection interpretation of the social class–mental disorder relationship. They argued that individuals in certain ethnic groups, such as African Americans in the United States, have less opportunity for upward mobility in societies that discriminate against them. These persons in disadvantaged ethnic groups also suffer a greater amount of stress than those in advantaged ethnic groups. The finding that social class is related to mental disorder is hard to interpret because social class status is constantly changing over the lifetime of the individual. But ethnic status does not change over the lifetime. This situation is an experiment of nature, or quasi-experiment, that provides the leverage to decide between stress and selection as an explanation for the social class–mental disorder relationship (Dohrenwend & Dohrenwend 1974b).

In analyzing data on social class, ethnic group, and mental disorder, it is important to compare rates in ethnic groups at the same level of social class. At any given level of social class, if *stress* is the explanation then the more highly stressed individuals (i.e., those in the disadvantaged ethnic groups) will have *higher* rates of disorder. If selection is the explanation, then: (a) upwardly mobile individuals (in the advantaged groups) will leave behind a residue of impaired individuals in lower levels of the class structure; whereas (b) healthy individuals in disadvantaged ethnic groups, who would otherwise be upwardly mobile, will be held to lower class positions. Hence the quasi-experimental design predicts that, if *selection* obtains, disadvantaged ethnic groups will have a *lower* rate of mental disorder.

The quasi-experimental design was executed in Israel, which was in many ways an ideal setting. Israel possessed excellent record-keeping systems that facilitated

Table 14.2. *Education and ethnic status in Israel*
(one-year prevalence in percent)

Educational attainment	European ($n = 1,197$)		North African ($n = 1,544$)	
	Male ($n = 602$)	Female ($n = 595$)	Male ($n = 852$)	Female ($n = 692$)
Schizophrenia				
Less than high school	4.18	0.84	1.91	0.00
High school graduate	0.29	0.39	0.17	0.00
College graduate	0.00	0.39	0.00	0.00
Major depression				
Less than high school	3.01	4.81	3.47	6.60
High school graduate	2.06	2.93	4.61	12.11
College graduate	0.66	1.68	2.94	10.70
Antisocial personality				
Less than high school	0.73	0.82	6.97	0.73
High school graduate	0.15	0.00	0.79	0.30
College graduate	0.00	0.00	0.00	0.00

Source: Reprinted with permission from Dohrenwend et al., "Socioeconomic status and psychiatric disorders: The causation–selection issue," *Science* 255: 946–52, Table 2. Copyright 1992 American Association for the Advancement of Science.

drawing samples, and is sufficiently small so that high completion rates could be achieved. Israeli society fit the design requirements of an open society with substantial upward mobility yet with large differences in social advantage between certain ethnic groups. The Dohrenwends focused on the comparison between Jews born in Israel from European heritage versus those born in Israel of North African (mostly Moroccan) heritage, using educational attainment as the indicator of social class. Table 14.2 shows the results for three disorders: schizophrenia, major depression, and antisocial personality disorder. The selection interpretation is supported for schizophrenia, because the Jews of European heritage have higher rates at each level of education, for both sexes (e.g., 4.18 per thousand for European heritage males with low education versus 1.91 for North African heritage males; 0.84 versus 0.0 for females with low education). The results for antisocial personality disorder, on the other hand, support the stress interpretation for males, because the North African heritage group has higher rates than the European heritage group at all levels of educational attainment (e.g., 6.97 per thousand versus 0.73 at the lower level of education; 0.79 versus 0.15 at the middle level of education). For depression the results are equivocal: even though the North African group has the higher rate at all levels of education and for both sexes, the table does not display the expected inverse relationship between social class and disorder.

The quasi-experimental strategy is bold in conception, and its execution in Israel was methodologically rigorous. However, it requires assumptions that vitiate its power. It must be assumed that the stresses (and psychological consequences of stresses) associated with low social class status are similar or identical to those associated with membership in a disadvantaged ethnic group. The perceived cause of the stress will render different psychological consequences: lower-class individuals in the dominant ethnic group may be more willing to blame themselves for the stresses they suffer, in part because of the functionalist ideology (Hochschild 1995; Matza 1967), whereas individuals in disadvantaged ethnic groups may be more likely to blame the structure of society for the stresses they suffer. The quasi-experiment requires the assumption that ethnic groups do not differ in their genetic propensity for mental disorders. Although there is wide variation within any given ethnic group (often greater than variation across ethnic groups, as shown by Cavalli-Sforza, Menozi, & Piazza 1994), it is nevertheless true that a large number of diseases differ greatly in their prevalence between groups (McKusick 1967); often the differences are larger than differences shown in Table 14.2. The quasi-experiment requires the assumption that mental disorders are equivalent across cultures and can be measured equivalently. The quasi-experimental data cannot determine whether or not both the causation and selection processes are operating simultaneously – the results reflect only the relative preponderance of one or the other process. Finally, the quasi-experiment fails to provide evidence as to how lower social class position affects risk for mental disorder.

Comparing Different Indicators of Socioeconomic Position: The Baltimore ECA Follow-up

In spite of the central importance of social class to sociology – and despite the importance of the issue of mental disorders and social class – there has been only limited comparison of the effects of different measures of social class on the rate of mental disorder (Eaton 1974; Eaton & Kessler 1981; Kessler & Cleary 1980). Therefore, the Baltimore ECA follow-up included several measures whose effects could be compared. The goal of including the different measures is to gain insight into the nature of the relationship between social class position and mental disorder.

The ECA program (Eaton et al. 1981; Eaton & Kessler 1985; Regier et al. 1984) was designed to estimate prevalence and incidence of specific mental disorders, to study risk factors, and to study patterns of use of facilities. It consisted of panel surveys of populations of community mental health catchment areas in five metropolitan areas of the United States, with one year between panels. About 20,000 individuals were interviewed with a structured survey questionnaire called the Diagnostic Interview Schedule (DIS). During 1993–96, the Baltimore ECA site followed up its cohort of 3,481 individuals, again using the DIS. Of the 2,635 individuals known to be alive and with an address, 73% participated in reinterviews (Eaton et al. 1997).

Results from the Baltimore ECA follow-up regarding social class are shown in Table 14.3. The DIS produces specific diagnoses according to criteria used by psychiatrists. Table 14.3 includes the diagnosis of major depression and a group of anxiety disorders (including panic disorder, phobic disorders, and obsessive-compulsive disorder). The table explores differences between the two types of mental disorders, as well as differences that may exist between measures of social class. The numbers shown are odds ratios from a multivariate logistic regression, with all variables included together in the same model. Each variable includes a category that is designated as the "reference," with odds ratio of 1.0. Odds ratios for other categories in that variable are estimated relative to the reference category. When odds ratios are close to 1.0 there is no association, when they are greater than 1.0 there is positive association, and when they are less than 1.0 there is inverse association. The association is statistically significant when the confidence interval for the odds ratio does not include the value of 1.0, in which case the odds ratio (OR) is followed by an asterisk.

Education is not significantly related to major depression or to anxiety disorder, but low household income is related to both disorders. Respondents whose household income is less than $17,500 are 16 times as likely to meet the criteria for major depressive disorder as those whose household income is over $35,000; those with household incomes in the middle range are 11 times as likely to meet the criteria for major depressive disorder. For anxiety disorders, the relationship is significant but smaller (nearly three times the rate of anxiety disorder in the low-income group as in the reference group).

Measures of assets – such as owning one's home, having a car, owning stock, or having a savings account – are not related to rate of depression or anxiety disorder, with income and education controlled. But receiving income from property, royalties, estates, or trusts is strongly associated with low rate of anxiety disorder (OR = 0.1). This type of income protects individuals from year-to-year fluctuations in salary and possibly inoculates them, to some degree, from day-to-day difficulties in achieving success at work.

The occupational setting is related to depression and anxiety disorder, but not in the predicted direction. After adjusting for education, income, and assets, the respondent's occupation does not have a strong effect. But the organizational assets of the individual do have effects in that supervisors have higher rates of depressive disorder (OR = 2.9, not significant) and anxiety disorder (OR = 2.6, significant) than both management and workers. The concept of organizational assets derives from a reconceptualization of Marxian class theory in the modern context (Wright 1985). Supervisors are in the lower tier of management, with authority over other workers. But they have little influence over the decisions made by top management, and are accountable to them for the performance of workers. This

Table 14.3. *Prevalence (in percent) of major depression and anxiety disorder by social class, Baltimore ECA follow-up, 1993–94 (n = 1,865)*

Measures of social class	Major depression		Anxiety disorder	
	%	OR	%	OR
Education of respondent				
Less than high school	1.2	1.0	16.0	1.0
High school graduate	2.5	1.9	14.8	1.3
Some college	2.7	3.5	7.6	0.3
College graduate	2.7	6.5	13.3	0.8
Graduate school	0.7	1.9	13.9	0.8
Household income				
<$17,500	1.2	16.2*	19.1	2.9*
$17,500–$34,499	3.8	11.5*	16.3	1.6
$35,000+	2.0	1.0	10.8	1.0
Household physical assets				
Does not own car	1.8	0.6	19.3	1.6
Owns car	2.1	1.0	13.0	1.0
Does not own home	2.2	1.3	19.3	1.1
Owns home	1.8	1.0	12.1	1.0
Household financial assets				
No dividend income	2.0	1.0	16.3	1.0
Dividend income	2.1	2.9	11.6	1.2
No savings income	2.9	1.5	18.3	1.2
Savings income	1.5	1.0	13.3	1.0
No property income	2.0	1.0	15.7	1.0
Property income	1.9	1.8	4.7	0.1*
Respondent occupation[a]				
Labor	2.9	—[b]	14.8	0.5
Craft	1.9	1.1	8.5	0.3
Service	0.9	0.6	14.1	0.6
Technical	2.7	0.6	19.0	0.8
Professional	2.6	1.0	14.7	1.0
Respondent organizational assets[a]				
Nonmanagement	1.4	0.5	15.7	2.1
Supervisor	3.6	2.9	15.7	2.6*
Manager	1.0	1.0	8.1	1.0

Note: OR = odds ratio – adjusted for age, gender, and race/ethnicity, as well as for other variables in the table.
*Statistically significant (95% confidence interval).
[a] The sample for measures of occupation and organizational assets is limited to 877 respondents who were in the labor force at the time of the interview.
[b] There were no sample respondents with major depressive disorder in this occupation category.

class location is often filled by former workers, who may experience role conflict and divided loyalties. They have the trappings of authority but may experience little freedom in controlling their own day-to-day work. This finding is consistent with studies of the role of direction, control, and planning in the workplace as it relates to depression.

Conclusion

As long as inequality exists, it is likely to be associated to some degree with the extent of mental disorder in society. Changes in socioeconomic structure will lead to consequent changes in the mental structure of society, including rates of mental disorders. Thus, research describing the relationship will always be central to sociology's interest in the causes and consequences of inequality. As society evolves, there is a continuing role for descriptive studies of social class and mental disorder because the possibilities for both causation and selection to operate will continue to exist. In the half-century since the New Haven study there have been many descriptive studies of prevalence of mental disorders that document the evolving relationship. There has been slow but measurable progress in understanding the mediators: how social class affects mental disorder; and how mental disorder, or the predisposition to it, affects attainment of social status. Research on the mediating variables may eventually prove more helpful in improving the lives of individual human beings. Eliminating social inequality may be impossible, but identification of causal mechanisms may lead to (less global) societal programs for preventing the onset of mental disorder. Identification of factors mediating the process of selection may lead also to programs that lessen the impact of mental disorder once it has occurred.

15

Work and Unemployment as Stressors

Mary Clare Lennon

Lennon examines the mental health consequences of work and unemployment. Changes in the nature of work and the entry of women into the work force have had important consequences for psychological well-being. Jobs that are stressful or that provide few opportunities for control have negative consequences for mental health. Lennon discusses various theoretical models for understanding the relationship between control and psychological well-being. She also considers the effect of unpaid work (specifically, housework) on mental health and well-being. Like paid work, housework involves varying levels of control and stressful demands. Unemployment has a negative effect on well-being because it produces anxiety and depression and reduces self-esteem and economic security. Yet it is also important to examine the economic context within which individuals experience unemployment. Several recent approaches that integrate community variables and individual characteristics are described. Lennon concludes by arguing for policies that improve work opportunities. Who would benefit most from such policies?

This chapter considers some of the mental health consequences of work and unemployment. In examining the effects of work, it focuses on specific work conditions that both theory and empirical studies indicate are important for psychological well-being. Rather than restrict attention to paid work, this chapter will also examine research on unpaid work. In examining unemployment, it gives attention to effects of individual job loss as well as of community-level unemployment.

Background

Americans spend large portions of their adult life working. The average wage-earner's work week is about 35 hours (U.S. Department of Labor 1995). Because about 90% of men and three quarters of women aged 25–54 are employed (U.S. Department of Labor 1995), jobs hold a central place in the daily lives of most of the adult population.

Recently, various social and economic changes have affected the availability and quality of jobs for a substantial number of workers. The latter half of the twentieth century has seen dramatic changes in the labor-market experiences of a large share of the population. Two major changes involve the nature of work and the participation of women in the labor force. Each of these changes will be described briefly as context for considering the relation of work and unemployment to mental health.

First, there have been a number of changes in the types of work available in the United States. Looking at changes by industrial sector (e.g., mining, manufacturing, retail trade, services), the percentage of workers holding jobs in the manufacturing sector has declined from 32% (of nonfarm, private workers) in 1972 to 19% in 1994, while the proportion of employees in the services sector has increased from 20% to 33% during the same period (U.S. Department of Labor 1995; see also Bell 1973; Gittleman & Howell 1995; Wetzel 1995).

This shift in the economy has transformed the job experiences of many workers. Analyses of changes in the occupational structure indicate that job quality has declined within the low-skilled occupational sector (Gittleman & Howell 1995) while rates of joblessness have increased (Swinnerton & Wial 1995). These declines have disproportionately affected young inner-city minority men (Kasarda 1995; Wilson 1985), but the effects are also felt by a broader range of the population (Levy 1995; Newman 1993; Swinnerton & Wial 1995). Moreover, research (reviewed in what follows) suggests that the experience of poor-quality jobs and unstable employment undermines the individual's sense of competency, psychological well-being, and health.

Second, women have entered the labor force in increasing numbers, partly in response to changes in the occupational structure. The most dramatic increase is seen for married women with young children. In 1960, one in five married women with children under age 6 was in the labor force; by 1990, this rate had tripled (McLanahan & Casper 1995). Participation of mothers of older children is even greater: about three quarters are in the labor force (McLanahan & Casper 1995). A large body of literature has considered the consequences of maternal employment for women, their spouses, and their children. Even with the decline in quality of men's jobs (Gittleman & Howell 1995), the average woman's job continues to be of lower quality, more insecure, and less well-paid than the average man's job (Gittleman & Howell 1995; Kilbourne et al. 1994). Moreover, when married women are employed, they remain responsible for the bulk of household chores (Lennon & Rosenfield 1994). This situation means that the work women do in the home is likely be an important factor in their psychological well-being.

These broad social changes – in the nature of work and in women's participation in the labor force – have wide-ranging effects on individuals, not the least of which involve their sense of psychological well-being. Both the type of work available and the unavailability of work affect mental health in many ways, some of which will be outlined here. Starting with paid work, I will review studies linking job conditions to psychological well-being. I then examine extensions of this framework to the study of the unpaid work done at home. Finally, the consequences of job loss are considered.

Paid Work and Psychological Well-Being

Paid work can have a range of mental health consequences, both positive and negative. Jobs provide economic rewards and may be a source of identity, competence, and self-esteem (Jahoda 1982; Morse & Weiss 1955). Jobs may also entail excessive pressures and demands or exposure to dangerous or toxic conditions, and they may be unchallenging and routine – all of which can undermine physical and mental health (Frankenhaeuser, Lundberg, & Chesney 1991; Kahn 1981; Karasek & Theorell 1990). The focus of this section is on the stressful aspects of work; the benefits of work will be examined indirectly, when the effects of unemployment are considered.

Studies of the relation of work to health and mental health have generally posited a central role for control over work (e.g., Ganster 1989; Spector 1986; Link et al. 1993). Control over one's life has generally been shown to contribute to satisfaction and well-being (Costello 1982; Pearlin et al. 1981; Rosenfield 1989; Ross & Mirowsky 1992; Rotter 1966). In the workplace, control may be experienced by the worker who can set the pace of the work, as well as by the worker who can determine whom to hire or fire. Because various dimensions of "control" have been examined in the literature (for reviews see Frese & Zapf 1989; Kasl 1989), central domains of work control are only briefly discussed here.

In evaluating the distinctive contribution of different dimensions of control, it is especially important to distinguish between autonomy and other aspects of control. Although the terms "autonomy" and "control" have often been used interchangeably in the literature (see Halaby & Weakleim 1989), "control" tends to have a broader usage, ranging from freedom from close supervision, to control over others, to control over general organizational policies and procedures. Autonomy is a major component of control. It involves the exercise of discretion in one's own work activities. This concept is similar to what Karasek and colleagues (1988) call "decision authority" and what Blauner (1964) calls "control." Autonomy may entail a number of components: freedom of physical movement, freedom to establish plans for one's own task accomplishment, or freedom from close supervisory attention (Schwalbe 1985).

Another form of control is what Kohn, Schooler, and colleagues (Kohn & Schooler 1982) call "occupational self-direction," defined as the use of initiative and personal judgment on the part of the worker. Occupations that permit self-direction involve substantively complex work with data, people, or things; work that is not closely supervised; and work that is not routine. This configuration, which occurs more frequently in highly skilled occupations, promotes intellectual flexibility in job incumbents and enhances the perception of self as competent and in control of one's own fate (Kohn & Schooler 1983).

Yet another important dimension of control is control over others' work activities. This differs from self-direction in that it involves not only control over one's own work but also over the work of others. Existing literature on the psychological consequences of control typically does not distinguish control over others' work from control over one's own work. Still, a number of studies do implicate self-direction or control over one's own work as consequential for well-being (Kohn & Schooler 1982; Kohn et al. 1990), and other investigations have demonstrated psychological consequences of the direction, control, and planning of others' activities (Lennon & Rosenfield 1994; Link et al. 1993; Semmer 1982). At this time it is unclear whether these latter findings are due to the high levels of self-direction that accompanies controlling others' work or to the control over others' work per se.

Another dimension of control is organizational control: the ability to direct and plan organizational procedures and policies. This has not been investigated adequately relative to other dimensions of control in terms of its impact on psychological functioning. However, it is an important aspect of control and thus is expected to contribute to feelings of mastery and well-being.

Two theoretical frameworks are prominent in the sociological literature that assesses the relation of control at work and psychological well-being. The first, by Kohn, Schooler, and colleagues (Kohn & Schooler 1982, Kohn et al. 1990), attempts to explain social class differences in psychological functioning by positing the importance of occupational self-direction. They argue that certain structural imperatives of work permit the exercise of self-direction: work that entails complex tasks related to data, people, and things; work that is not routine; and work that is not closely supervised. In terms of its mental health consequences, substantively complex work is expected to reduce anxiety and improve self-esteem. Kohn, Schooler, and colleagues have conducted a number of studies that support their arguments empirically. These studies include cross-sectional and longitudinal designs, samples of men and women, and a range of cultural settings (Kohn & Schooler 1982, 1983; Kohn et al. 1990; Miller et al. 1979; Schooler et al. 1983). Their results generalize to nonoccupational activities, including housework (Schooler et al. 1983).

The second framework frequently used in sociological studies of work stress was proposed by Karasek and colleagues (1988; Karasek & Theorell 1990). Their theoretical model posits that control over work is related to health outcomes primarily among individuals who experience high levels of psychological demands on the job. In their early work, Karasek and colleagues (1988) defined control as consisting of two dimensions: (1) skill discretion, which involves nonrepetitive work, high skill requirements, and new learning on the job; and (2) decision authority (or freedom to decide) about aspects of tasks at work or about nonwork elements, such as breaks and telephone calls. It is important to note that there is considerable overlap between these elements and the components of self-directed work. High skill requirements and new learning are involved in substantively complex work; nonrepetitive work and nonroutine work overlap considerably; and decision authority includes freedom from close supervision.

However, Karasek's model differs from that of Kohn, Schooler, and colleagues on a number of dimensions. One important difference is that, for Karasek and colleagues, low control is problematic for health primarily when demands are high. They define "high-strain" jobs as those in which the worker experiences excessive demands but little control. Although job strain has been shown to predict cardiovascular disease (Karasek 1979; Theorell & Karasek 1996), empirical evidence for an interaction of job control and demands in predicting psychological distress is mixed. Even so, many studies demonstrate direct effects of control and demands on mental health problems (Bromet et al. 1988; Lennon 1994; but see Roxburgh 1996). Karasek's framework has been expanded to incorporate the role of social support in the workplace (Johnson & Hall 1988; Johnson, Stewart, & Hall 1996). Jobs with low support and low control are associated with greater mortality from cardiovascular disease (Johnson & Hall 1988). Whether this model holds for mental health outcomes remains to be demonstrated.

As Kohn and Schooler (1983) recognized, one mechanism by which lack of job control can increase psychological distress is by contributing to a more general sense of not being in control of one's life. Link and colleagues (1993) investigated this in relation to depression and depressive symptomatology. They defined job control somewhat differently than either Kohn and Schooler or Karasek, arguing that jobs that permit direction, control, and planning (DCP) of others' work activities may protect against the development of depression and psychological distress by contributing to a sense of mastery over the environment. They argued further that mastery protects against depression. To investigate this issue empirically, these authors use data from a case control study and a community cross-sectional design. They show that (1) individuals of lower socioeconomic status (SES) are less likely to be involved in DCP occupations than individuals of higher SES; (2) exposure to occupations involving DCP accounts for the associations of SES with depressive disorder and psychological distress; and (3) the association between DCP and depressive disorders is mediated by mastery. Moreover, these relationships cannot fully be accounted for by social selection processes, which could cause depressed persons to gravitate toward the type of work that does not require exerting control over the work of others. In conclusion, Link and colleagues suggest that DCP operates as a protective factor that reduces the risk for development of depression and psychological distress.

Moreover, lack of self-direction or control in one's current work situation may be compensated for by the anticipation of future control. Thus, jobs that offer opportunities for advancement may mitigate the negative consequences of low levels of job control. In this regard, advantage will accrue to individuals employed in the core industrial sector, characterized by well-defined internal labor markets that present opportunities for advancement (Edwards 1979; Ward & Mueller 1985). Low-level jobs in the core sector may not be as stressful as low-level jobs in the peripheral industrial sector, where chances for advancement and job security are limited.

Taking a broad view of occupational control as encompassing self-direction, decision latitude, control over the work of others, and autonomy, it is clear that control over work is central to psychological well-being. The role of demands, such as time pressure and excessive hours, is less clear. According to Karasek and colleagues, the effect of demands occurs in interaction with control: only at low levels of control are demands hypothesized to be salient. However, evidence to support this view is mixed, as many studies find independent rather than interactive effects of demands and control (Bromet et al. 1988; Lennon 1994).

An alternative way of conceptualizing the role of workplace demands is suggested by Rosenfield (1989) in her studies of power and demands in family life. Rosenfield hypothesized that excessive household demands (such as having a number of young children at home or having sole responsibility for housework) undermine an individual's sense of control, leading to higher levels of depressive symptoms. Thus, she argues that excessive demands have a similar psychological effect as low levels of control: to undermine personal sense of control or mastery. Rosenfield (1989) finds support for this perspective with respect to conditions of family life. If her reasoning generalizes to other spheres of life, then it is plausible that excessive work demands may also limit the exercise of control. Jobs that entail heavy work loads and frequent deadlines can make it difficult for the worker to control the pacing or scheduling of tasks. Thus, job demands may reduce the possibilities for exerting control. Following Rosenfield, then, we would expect to find that demands of the job, like demands at home, operate through the same mechanism as lack of control or power: to diminish both opportunities for control and feelings of mastery. This would be a fruitful area for future researchers to examine.

Unpaid Work and Psychological Distress

The study of work stress has generally focused on paid work. However, many women, at some point in their lives, devote substantial effort to unpaid work in the home. The study of housework as work attempts to extend the study of work conditions from the job into the home. Many researchers seeking to understand gender differences in mental health have often compared homemakers to employed wives, generally assuming that full-time housework will increase levels of distress. More symptoms among housewives, found in several studies (e.g., Gove & Geerkin 1977; Rosenfield 1980), are assumed to derive from the burdensome and tedious nature of housework or from the positive features of employment. In these investigations, the characteristics of housework and paid work are not examined directly. However, research makes clear that conditions of housework, like job conditions, vary among women and may include positive as well as negative dimensions (Berk & Berk 1979; Bird & Ross 1993; Oakley 1974; Schooler et al. 1983). In addition, like paid work, housework involves varying levels of control and demands. For example, in households with low levels of income and many young children, housework may be quite demanding. In dual-career households, housework may be highly routinized and scheduled; once a routine becomes established, opportunities for control become restricted (see Oakley 1974).

Several investigators have systematically examined housework as work (Berk 1985; Berk & Berk 1979; Oakley 1974). A number of more recent studies have used comparable measures of dimensions of paid work and housework (Bird & Ross 1993; Kibria et al. 1990; Lennon 1994; Schooler et al. 1983). A few of these have compared the conditions of work for full-time homemakers and employed women (Bird & Ross 1993; Lennon 1994). Bird and Ross (1993) report that housework is more routine, is less intrinsically gratifying, and provides fewer extrinsic rewards than paid work. These authors also find that routine, ungratifying, and unrewarding work accounts for homemakers' lower sense of personal control relative to employed women. I found similar results in a study comparing conditions of housework for homemakers with conditions of jobs for employed wives. Homemakers experienced more advantageous work conditions in terms of greater autonomy, fewer time pressures, and less responsibility for matters outside their control, whereas they experience less advantageous conditions in terms of more routine, more physical demands, and more interruptions (Lennon 1994).

In contrast to the differences in the job conditions of employed wives and housework conditions of homemakers, the housework conditions of employed wives are surprisingly similar to those of full-time homemakers (Lennon 1998). Employed wives and full-time homemakers alike consider housework as permitting a high degree of autonomy, being highly routine, involving extensive physical effort, subject to frequent interruptions, and entailing a moderate degree of responsibility for things outside their control. There are, however, two interesting differences between these groups: homemakers see housework as more complex and less time-pressured. Employed wives and homemakers differ as well on the number of hours that they spend on housework each week, with employed wives averaging fewer hours than full-time homemakers. However, when hours on the job are added to the time spent on housework, employed wives exceed homemakers in total hours per week (Lennon 1998).

Differences in specific work conditions and hours have implications for levels of depressive symptoms among employed wives and homemakers. Before these are taken into account, employed wives and homemakers do not differ in levels of depressive symptoms. However, when the impact of housework conditions is statistically controlled, employed wives average significantly fewer depressive symptoms than nonemployed wives. In other words, the relationship between work status and symptoms appears to have been suppressed by the characteristics of housework that distinguish employed wives from homemakers.

Employed women experience more time pressure in their housework than do full-time homemakers, but they appear to be no more disadvantaged than homemakers with respect to depressive symptoms. This suggests that they experience rewards from paid work that offset the difficulties encountered with housework.

Benefits of employment, such as earnings and access to networks of social support, may compensate for disadvantages of housework. Hence, future research on these issues should consider aspects of jobs as well as aspects of housework in understanding symptoms among employed wives.

Unemployment and Psychological Well-Being

A large number of investigators have documented the detrimental effects of unemployment on psychological well-being (for reviews see Dew, Penkower, & Bromet 1991; Horwitz 1984; Perrucci & Perrucci 1990; Warr, Jackson, & Banks 1988; see also Brenner 1973 and Catalano et al. 1981 for ecological studies). Research on this topic ranges from Durkheim's (1897) classic study of suicide to studies of the impact of the economic depression of the 1930s (Eisenberg & Lazarsfeld 1938; Elder 1974; Jahoda 1982) to recent investigations of the effects of the economic changes of the 1970s and 1980s (Conger & Elder 1994; Dooley, Catalano, & Rook 1988; Kessler et al. 1989). Cross-sectional, longitudinal, and prospective studies of individuals and time-series aggregate studies of communities have shown that unemployment increases symptoms of anxiety and depression and reduces self-esteem and security (for an exception, see Kasl & Cobb 1979). Evidence suggests that this effect is not entirely due to selection processes through which individuals in poor mental health are more apt to become unemployed. In fact, when unemployed persons obtain new jobs, their distress levels decline (Warr & Jackson 1985), suggesting that the episode of unemployment had contributed to their initial poor mental health.

Although most research on the consequences of unemployment is descriptive, some investigators provide conceptual frameworks for understanding the mechanisms through which unemployment comes to have negative psychological effects. Jahoda (1982) asserts that unemployment is stressful because it involves the loss of connection to important social institutions and associations. Pearlin and colleagues (1981), based on their stress process model, consider unemployment as a primary stressor that may set into motion disruptive secondary stressors, such as economic deprivation (see also Conger & Elder 1994). Thus, unemployment may bring in its wake a range of losses, including social ties and economic stability, and these losses may be stressful in themselves.

Many studies find that the effect of unemployment is more negative among persons of low socioeconomic status (Dooley & Catalano 1979; Pearlin & Lieberman 1979). Because the pre-unemployment economic circumstances of women (especially single mothers) are likely to be more precarious than that of men (Bianchi 1995; Dew et al. 1991), it is likely that the economic effects of unemployment will be more problematic for women, especially those who are single parents. The poverty rate for single-parent families headed by women is 25% if just one member of the household has a job. Unemployment for the breadwinner in these circumstances can exacerbate an already precarious financial situation.

In addition to examining mediators and moderators of unemployment on an individual level, research on unemployment has been extended into two promising areas: specifying further the effect of the broader economic context in which unemployment occurs, and assessing the effects of unemployment on family members. I shall next describe briefly the research efforts in these two areas.

A number of investigators have shown the importance of examining the economic context in which individuals experience unemployment. The meaning and consequences of job loss will vary depending upon the state of the economy at a given point in time and at a given place. There are a number of ecological studies that examine changes in broad economic indicators, such as the presence of manufacturing jobs, in relation to indicators of mental health problems, such as rates of psychiatric hospitalizations (Brenner 1973, 1987). Problems with ecological-level studies have been well documented (Catalano 1981; Kasl 1982; Perrucci & Perrucci 1990). Although much of this criticism is justified, such studies have the advantage of emphasizing the broader economic forces that may lie behind individual episodes of unemployment.

One promising line of research examines the effects of macroeconomic conditions, including community-level unemployment rates, in addition to individual unemployment. Several investigators have reported results from such cross-level analyses. Prominent among these is the research program of Dooley, Catalano, and colleagues (Catalano & Dooley 1977, 1983; Catalano et al. 1981; Dooley et al. 1988), which found independent effects of community-level unemployment rates as well as of individual unemployment. Aggregate unemployment is associated with subsequent increases in depressive mood and stressful life events in metropolitan areas (Catalano & Dooley 1977). However, these investigators did not find evidence for an interaction between these broad economic changes and unemployment on an individual level.

Another cross-level study conducted by Turner (1995) did find such an interaction effect. In areas where unemployment was high, the currently unemployed had higher rates of depressive symptoms. Moreover, this association was stronger among those with lower levels of education. The author notes that low education is a risk factor for unemployment. Thus, those with low education are more likely to become unemployed, and when unemployed would have less chance of being reemployed. Adding to this the greater mental health cost to this group (due to being unemployed in an adverse economy), individuals with low educational attainment appear to be highly vulnerable to macroeconomic downturns.

Most studies that examine community-level factors do so using regression models that do not take into account the clustering of individuals within economic structures. Thus, they do not adjust for the nonindependence of observations that occurs when persons are examined within clusters (such as those in high unemployment areas). Future research in this area will be enhanced by utilizing random effects models, which permit the modeling of community and individual effects simultaneously. The increasing availability of computer programs to conduct random effects models (e.g., Bryk & Raudenbush 1992) makes it possible to simultaneously examine effects of context and individual-level characteristics.

Conclusion

Research on the relation of work and unemployment to mental health has demonstrated both the rewards and stressors associated with working and the difficulties that are likely to ensue when jobs are lost. For the most part, however, studies of job conditions and unemployment have not been integrated. One promising area for research involves examining the effects of macroeconomic changes, such as high levels of unemployment, on the conditions of work for those who retain their jobs. One such study, conducted by Fenwick and Tausig (1994), examined the relationship between community-level unemployment and levels of job stress. The authors hypothesized that widespread unemployment would be detrimental not only to those directly affected (i.e., the unemployed) but also to those workers who remain employed. If these workers are easily replaced, then employers may reduce beneficial aspects of the job – for example, by increasing work loads. The authors also observe that, in times of economic downturns, firms that survive hard times are likely to do so at the expense of the quality of jobs they offer workers. Fenwick and Tausig find support for their hypotheses in that higher occupational unemployment rates were associated with decreased life satisfaction and increased stress. This effect was mediated by lower decision latitude and increased job demands associated with higher occupational unemployment. Thus, broad economic downturns have implications for mental health not only by increasing unemployment risk for individuals but also by reducing job quality.

In addition to investigating the interaction between community economic changes and individual work experiences, more remains to be learned about the effects of unemployment on families. Investigations of families in the economic depression of the 1930s noted the consequences of husbands' unemployment for their spouses and children (Elder 1974). Research conducted in the 1980s by Conger and Elder (1994) have extended the scope of study to examine the consequences of unemployment in either spouse. They find that when mothers experience economic deprivation, their distress influences their children's well-being. In a similar vein, McLoyd and colleagues (1994) find that current unemployment is associated with adolescent depression primarily through the effect of unemployment and maternal depression on the quality of interactions between mothers and their children.

An area where the study of work and unemployment has immediate policy relevance involves the changes underway in welfare reform. It is likely that counterproductive consequences may arise from reducing expenditures on welfare benefits alone without improving the employability and job conditions of (former) recipients. If, as expected, more single mothers enter low-skill, low-paying jobs, then both they and their children may be negatively affected and may require additional expenditures in the health-care sector. However, research indicates that mothers and their children are each likely to benefit from efforts directed at improving employment and providing higher-quality jobs, because such good jobs can compensate for other difficulties that single families generally face (Menaghan, Kowalski-Jones, & Mott 1997). The costs of not improving work opportunities are likely to be high, not only for poor women but for their children as well.

16

Race and Mental Health: Emerging Patterns and Promising Approaches

David R. Williams & Michelle Harris-Reid

Williams and Harris-Reid provide an overview of the mental health status for several minority populations, and they evaluate the available evidence of racial variations in mental health. Because of different research methodologies and varying criteria for identifying both mental disorder and minority status, it is difficult to generalize about these mental health differences. Studies that assess the mental health of African Americans find few differences between blacks and whites. The mental health picture for Hispanics is more complicated, though their rates of disorder tend to be higher than that of whites. Given the small size and diversity of the Asian-American population, there is little conclusive data on their mental health. Finally, little is known about the mental health status of American Indians. Hence, despite decades of research, we lack a clear picture of the mental health status of major minority populations. Research must overcome problems of inadequate coverage of the minority population and find ways to capture the considerable heterogeneity of minority groups. A second group of problems concerns limitations on the measurement of mental health status among minorities. Finally, culture affects the manifestation of mental health problems, because cultures emphasize different emotions and standards for acceptable expression and emotion. Culture also affects the interpretation of symptoms of disorder. Research must identify the ways in which social, economic, political, and cultural factors have impacts on the health status of minority groups. Racism and migration experiences are also critical to mental health and need further investigation. Students should discuss why there is so little available data about minority mental health. Does this provide further evidence of racism?

The United States Government requires federal agencies to report statistics for four racial groups (white, black, Asian or Pacific Islander, and American Indian or Alaskan Native) and for the ethnic category Hispanic (U.S. Department of Commerce 1978). However, because these categories are socially constructed and since almost 70% of Hispanics would prefer to have Hispanic included as a racial category (Tucker et al. 1996), this chapter treats all five groups as "races" and examines the extent to which these categories predict variations in mental health status. These racial groups are more alike than different in terms of biological characteristics and genetics. Human beings are identical for 75% of known genetic factors, with 95% of human genetic variation existing within racial groups (Lewontin 1972; Lewontin et al. 1984). Historical events and political factors have played an important role in determining which racial categories are officially recognized at a given time. The current categories capture the majority white and the principal minority populations in the United States. "Minority" does not refer to numeric size but rather reflects the convergence of geographic origins, exposure to prejudice and discrimination, and socioeconomic disadvantage (Williams 1997). Consensus does not exist within the official racial groups on a preferred racial label. Accordingly, in an effort to respect individual dignity, this chapter uses the most preferred terms for each group (Tucker et al. 1996) interchangeably (i.e., black or African American, Hispanic or Latino, white or Caucasian, and American Indian or Native American).

This chapter provides an overview of the mental health status for each minority population and evaluates the available scientific evidence of racial variations in mental health. In considering directions for future research to enhance our understanding of race and mental health, we emphasize the need for identifying the ways in which the mental health problems of each group emerge from the larger social context in which the group is embedded.

African-American Mental Health

Blacks have historically constituted the largest and most visible minority racial group in the United States, and early studies of racial differences in mental health focused largely on this population. These studies reflected the prevailing social ideology of their time. Historically, racial categories have been used not only to classify human variation but also to provide an apparent scientific rationale for the exploitation of groups that were regarded as inferior (Montagu 1965). Initially, the very first Article of the United States Constitution provided for the enumeration of three races: whites, black slaves (who were legally regarded as three fifths of a person), and Indians who paid taxes (Anderson & Feinberg 1995). The discounting of blacks and the exclusion of "noncivilized" Indians reflected this nation's relative ranking of these groups. Early studies of racial comparisons in mental health status also reflected this racist ideology. Krieger (1987) provides several examples of how these studies, irrespective of their findings, were used to demonstrate black inferiority and provide a scientific rationale for policies of inequality. A report based on rates of mental illness from the 1840 U.S. Census deliberately falsified black insanity rates to show that the further north blacks lived, the higher their rates of mental illness. This was interpreted as evidence that freedom drove blacks crazy. In fact, blacks were regarded as so constitutionally suited for slavery that the very desire to escape slavery was defined as a mental illness, "drapetomania." Another disease, "dysesthesia Ethiopia," readily identifiable by slave masters, was the attempt to avoid work. Sleeping during the day was one of its symptoms.

Consistently, reports of the mental health status of blacks interpreted any available evidence within the context of racial ideology and their social position. For example, Babcock (1895) argued that the newly emancipated black would be less prone to mental illness than whites because of the excellent care and supervision received during slavery. On the other hand, Lind (1914) indicated that rates of mental illness would be high for blacks because of their inherent biological inferiority. In the early twentieth century, the best available data (rates of insanity from the U.S. Census based on counts of the institutionalized and noninstitutionalized mentally ill) indicated that the rates of mental illness were lower for blacks than for Caucasians (Malzberg 1944). In 1930, the Census restricted its prevalence rates of mental illness to counting persons in state mental health facilities. After this change, census data indicated that blacks had higher rates of mental illness than whites (Malzberg 1944). Other early studies focusing on first-admission rates of patients in mental hospitals, both nationally and in selected states, also found elevated rates of psychiatric illness for the African-American population (Fischer 1969).

Methodologically, all studies based on treatment rates are seriously flawed. Because these rates do not reflect the psychiatric problems of persons who have not entered treatment, they are importantly affected by health care access and financing options, distance, available transportation, racial discrimination, the client's economic status, and other structural and cultural barriers that affect the likelihood of seeking and receiving medical care, as well as by accuracy of diagnosis. For example, recent national data of population-based rates of treated and untreated cases of mental illness indicate that only 40% of persons who have had a psychiatric illness have ever received treatment (Kessler et al. 1994). Moreover, almost half of all persons in treatment do not meet the criteria for psychiatric illness. State hospitals continue to be an important source of mental health care for African Americans, and studies indicate that rates of mental illness for persons in these health facilities are higher for blacks than for whites (Snowden & Cheung 1990).

As studies expanded their population to include outpatients, private patients, and community residents, the biases inherent in some of the earlier treatment studies were reduced and findings of racial differences became more inconsistent (Jaco 1960). One Baltimore study found, for example, that blacks had higher rates of mental illness than whites only when the analyses were restricted to patients in state hospitals. Rates for whites exceeded those for blacks when the state hospital data were combined with data from private mental hospitals, Veterans Administration hospitals, and a community survey of Baltimore residents (Pasamanick 1963).

After World War II, community surveys emerged as a new source of information on the distribution of mental health problems. These surveys used statistical methods to select a sample of residents representative of a total community and thus avoided the selection biases associated with treatment samples. However, psychiatry had not reached consensus on the criteria for the formal diagnosis of discrete psychiatric disorders, and the technology to obtain standardized information based on structured or semistructured interviews did not yet exist. Accordingly, these studies did not collect information on discrete psychiatric disorders. Instead, measures of psychological distress that assessed nonspecific emotional symptoms were utilized. These scales of psychological distress were easy to administer, were not time-consuming, and provided a continuous distribution of mental health status. These symptom checklist scales typically include items that assess depressed mood, psychological distress, and indicators of dysfunction (Link & Dohrenwend 1980a; Vega & Rumbaut 1991).

Many of the early classic community studies in psychiatric epidemiology (Weissman, Myers, & Ross 1986) did not make special efforts to include African Americans in sufficient numbers to make reliable racial comparisons. The landmark New Haven study of social class and mental illness included only 96 blacks; the Sterling County Study, an important ongoing prospective study of mental illness, had 47 blacks; and the Midtown Manhattan Mental Health Study, an important early study of mental health status in an urban population, was drawn from a population that was 99% white.

In an early review of community-based studies, Dohrenwend and Dohrenwend (1969) indicated that half of the eight studies they reviewed showed higher rates of mental health problems for blacks; the other half showed higher rates for Caucasians. Subsequent studies have frequently found higher rates of psychological distress for blacks than for whites, but with the racial difference reduced to nonsignificance when adjusted for socioeconomic status (Neighbors 1984; Williams 1986). However, the pattern is not uniform. A recent review of the literature on minority mental health status showed that some recent studies find higher levels of distress for blacks whereas others find lower levels, as compared to whites (Vega & Rumbaut 1991). For example, although one recent study utilizing a national probability sample found that blacks had lower levels of psychological distress than whites (Williams in press), another recent study utilizing a probability sample of the Detroit metropolitan area found no racial differences in distress (Williams et al. 1997). The reasons for these inconsistencies are not well understood.

An important methodological innovation in the 1970s was the development of semistructured and structured interviews to obtain standardized information that could be used to generate the diagnosis of psychiatric illness. One of the first studies of this kind was a community survey in New Haven, Connecticut, that found no significant racial difference for anxiety disorders but higher rates of major depression, minor depression, and depressive personality for nonwhites (mainly blacks), compared to whites (Weissman & Meyers 1978). One of the limitations of this study was that nonwhites were only 12% of the 511 respondents.

The Epidemiologic Catchment Area (ECA) project is the largest mental health study ever conducted in the United States (Robins & Regier 1991). Between 1980 and 1983, almost 20,000 adults in five communities were interviewed in order to estimate the prevalence and incidence of specific psychiatric disorders in samples of institutionalized and noninstitutionalized persons. The ECA study utilized the Diagnostic Interview Schedule (DIS), a research instrument that utilizes operational criteria and algorithms based on the APA's *Diagnostic and Statistical*

Table 16.1. *Rates of psychiatric disorders for blacks, whites, and Hispanics – ECA study (percentages)*

Disorder	Current			Lifetime		
	Black	White	Hispanic	Black	White	Hispanic
Affective	3.5	3.7	4.1	6.3	8.0	7.8
Alcohol abuse	6.6	6.7	9.1	13.8	13.6	16.7
Drug history	—	—	—	29.9	30.7	25.1
Drug abuse	2.7	2.7	1.9	5.4	6.4	4.3
Schizophrenia	1.6	0.9	0.4	2.1	1.4	0.8
Generalized anxiety	6.1	3.5	3.7	—	—	—
Phobic	16.2	9.1	8.1	23.4	9.7	12.2
Any disorder	26.0	19.0	20.0	38.0	32.0	33.0

Source: Robins and Regier (1991).

Manual to assign persons to specific diagnostic categories (Robins et al. 1981). The DIS is a fully structured, lay-administered interview that generates diagnoses based on the presence, severity, and duration of symptoms. Its structured nature allows for the reliable assessment of psychiatric illness without clinical judgment.

Table 16.1 presents current and lifetime rates of disorder by race. These data come from a summary of ECA findings that uses a somewhat questionable strategy of weighting the five-site data toward the national demographic distribution in order to produce prevalence rates for the United States (Robins & Regier 1991). Overall, the first two columns under the current and lifetime categories of Table 16.1 show very few differences between blacks and whites in the rates of psychiatric disorders. Especially striking is the absence of a racial difference in history of drug use and the overall prevalence of alcohol and drug abuse or dependence. More detailed analyses reveal that the age trajectory of lifetime rates of alcoholism varies by race. Whites have a rate of alcohol abuse about twice that of blacks in the youngest age group (18–29), but the black lifetime rate exceeds that of whites in all remaining age groups, with the gap being largest in the 45–64 age category. African-American and white rates of depression are generally similar. Blacks have rates of schizophrenia that are higher than those for Caucasians, but this difference disappears when adjusted for age, gender, marital status, and socioeconomic status (SES).

Anxiety disorders stand out as the one area where blacks had considerably higher rates than whites, and this disparity is responsible for the elevated rates for blacks in the category of "any disorder." African Americans have higher lifetime rates of simple phobia, social phobia, and agoraphobia than whites (Brown, Eaton, & Sussman 1990). The findings are less consistent for other anxiety disorders.

Table 16.2. *Overall prevalence and ethnic ratios of psychiatric disorders –*
National Comorbidity Survey

Disorders	Prevalence in general population (%)	Ethnic ratios	
		Black/white	Hispanic/white
Any affective disorder	11.3	0.78	1.38
Any anxiety disorder	17.1	0.90	1.17
Any substance abuse or dependence	11.3	0.47	1.04
Any disorder	29.5	0.70	1.11

Source: Kessler et al. (1994).

Whites tend to have lower rates of generalized anxiety disorder than blacks, but there are no consistent racial differences for panic disorder. However, comparisons of current and lifetime rates suggest that, compared to whites, blacks have longer durations of panic disorder but briefer durations of phobic disorders (Brown et al. 1990).

Findings from the National Comorbidity Survey (NCS) are even more striking (Kessler et al. 1994). The NCS interviewed over 8,000 adults and was the first study to use a national probability survey to assess psychiatric disorders in the United States. Table 16.2 presents findings from this study. The first column shows the overall rate for each major class of disorders, and the second column shows the black/white ratio. (A ratio greater than 1 means that blacks have a higher rate of disorder than whites.) The pattern in Table 16.2 is impressive. Blacks do not have higher rates of disorder than whites for any of the major classes of disorders. Instead, lower rates of disorders for blacks than whites are particularly pronounced for the affective disorders (depression) and the substance abuse disorders (alcohol and drug abuse). Instructively, the NCS reports no racial differences in panic disorder, simple phobia, or agoraphobia (Kessler et al. 1994). However, detailed analyses suggest that the associations between phobia and race may be importantly patterned by gender. Using data from the NCS, Magee (1993) found that white males tend to have higher current and lifetime rates of agoraphobia, simple phobia, and social phobia than their black counterparts, whereas black women have higher rates of agoraphobia and simple phobia than white women.

Hispanic Mental Health

Hispanics comprise a large and rapidly growing minority group in the United States. Between the 1980 and 1990 Censuses, the Hispanic population increased by 53% to well over 22 million persons (U.S. Bureau of the Census 1991a). Although most Hispanics have language, religion, and various traditions in common, the timing of immigration and incorporation experiences in the United States have varied for the more than 25 national origin groups that make up this category, so each group is distinctive. The largest Hispanic groups are Mexican Americans (63%), Puerto Ricans (11%), and Cubans (5%). The remainder come from several countries in Central and South America and the Caribbean. It is projected that Hispanics will become the largest minority group in the United States early in the next century.

Research on the mental health of Hispanics does not provide a clear picture of the distribution of mental health problems for the Hispanic population, compared to other major racial groups or for subgroup variations within the Latino category (Rogler 1989; Vega & Rumbaut 1991). For example, utilizing two Alameda County samples, Roberts (1980) found that Mexican Americans did not differ from whites and blacks on measures of psychological distress. At the same time, two other California studies found that Mexican Americans have higher rates of distress than either blacks or non-Hispanic whites (Frerichs, Aneshensel, & Clark 1981; Vernon & Roberts 1982). Inpatient and outpatient treatment data from the Los Angeles County Mental Health System reveals that Hispanics tend to have lower levels of psychotic disorders than whites (Flaskerud & Hu 1992). Some studies suggest that Puerto Ricans may be especially vulnerable to mental health problems. In a study of 1,000 New York City residents, Dohrenwend and Dohrenwend (1969) found that Puerto Ricans reported more psychiatric symptoms than whites or blacks, even after SES was controlled. Immigrants from Cuba and Mexico seem to enjoy better mental health than non-Hispanic whites, but the opposite seems to be true about immigrants from Puerto Rico (Vega & Rumbaut 1991).

One of the best sources of comparative data on Hispanic populations is the Hispanic Health and Nutrition Examination Survey (HHANES). The HHANES, conducted between 1982 and 1984, was a major federal effort to obtain comparable data on the Mexican, Cuban, and Puerto Rican origin populations in the continental United States. It utilized a stratified cluster sample drawn from specific geographic areas where large proportions of Latinos live. The sample size was over 8,000. Mental health status was assessed by a scale of depression symptoms and by DIS results for major depressive disorder. The HHANES data revealed that Puerto Ricans had the highest levels of psychological distress and the highest rates of depression (Narrow et al. 1991). In addition, Cuban Americans had lower levels of psychological distress and lower rates of major depression than either the Mexican-American or Puerto Rican population. At the same time, scores for Mexican Americans on the depressive symptoms scale were lower than those found in previous studies of non-Hispanic whites and in previous community samples of Hispanics (Moscicki et al. 1989).

The ECA study is another important source of information on the distribution of psychiatric disorders for Latinos. However, it is limited in that the Hispanic sample comes from one geographic area (the Los Angeles ECA site). Table 16.1

shows that, compared with blacks and whites, Hispanics have the lowest current and lifetime rates for schizophrenia and drug abuse. They also have the lowest rates of histories of drug use. Nonetheless, their *current* rates of alcohol abuse and affective disorder are *higher* than those of both blacks and whites. Current rates of anxiety disorder are intermediate between those of blacks and whites. The NCS also provides data on the prevalence of psychiatric disorders for the Hispanic population. These data, shown in Table 16.2, should be interpreted with caution because of the relatively small size ($N = 737$) of the Hispanic population (Kessler et al. 1994). In contrast to the pattern for African Americans, Hispanics have rates of the major psychiatric disorders that tend to be higher than those of whites.

Thus, given the quantity and quality of the available evidence, it is difficult to arrive at firm conclusions about the distribution of mental health problems for the Hispanic population and for major subgroups within that population.

Asian-American Mental Health

Asians and Pacific Islanders comprise 3% of the American population, and they include an ethnically and nationally diverse group of peoples who originate from China, Japan, Korea, the Philippines, the Pacific Islands, the subcontinent of India, and the countries of Southeast Asia. Japanese Americans represented the majority of Asian Americans up to the 1960s, but the 1990 Census revealed that Filipinos and Chinese now occupy that position. Asian countries have been major contributors to the U.S. immigration stream over the last few decades. This has significantly changed the population composition of the Asian-American community. In contrast to the 1960s, when most Asian Americans had been born in this country, the current population consists of a large number of foreign-born persons.

Because Asian Americans constitute only a small portion of the U.S. population, traditional surveys do not include adequate numbers of this diverse racial group to yield reliable estimates of the distribution of health problems. Accordingly, early research on Asian-American health attempted to estimate the level of mental health problems based on the utilization of mental health services. These early studies found that Asian Americans were consistently underrepresented in clinical populations, and it was assumed that they experienced lower levels of mental health problems (Sue et al. 1995). However, several small community studies suggest that at least some Asian population groups in the United States are experiencing more mental health problems than previously thought. A small community sample of Chinese Americans found between 20% and 40% reporting that they experienced high levels of psychological distress (Loo, Tong, & True 1989). Similarly, a study of Asian Americans in Seattle found that Chinese, Japanese, Filipino, and Korean Americans reported higher levels of depressive symptoms than did white Americans (Kuo 1984). The sampling strategies utilized in this study reflect some of the challenges in attempting to sample a relatively rare population. The Seattle

Table 16.3. *Lifetime prevalence rates of psychiatric disorders – three studies (percentages)*

Disorders	CAPES	ECA	NCS
Generalized anxiety disorder	1.7	—	5.1
Major depression	6.9	4.9	17.1
Simple phobia	1.1	11.3	11.3
Panic disorder	0.4	1.6	3.5

Note: CAPES = Chinese American Psychiatric Epidemiological Study; ECA = Epidemiologic Catchment Area study; NCS = National Comorbidity Survey.
Source: Adapted from Sue et al. (1995).

sample was compiled from lists provided by ethnic organizations, pooling Asian last names from the telephone directory, as well as lists generated from "snowball" techniques. Other evidence suggests that the Chinese and Japanese American elderly have higher rates of suicide than their non-Asian peers (Lui & Yu 1985). Refugees, especially those from Southeast Asia, have been a part of recent waves of immigration. Several studies have found high rates of mental health problems for this group (Buchwald et al. 1993; Kinzie et al. 1990; Lum 1995).

Large epidemiologic surveys like the ECA and NCS provide no comparative data on the mental health problems for Asian Americans. A recent Los Angeles study, the Chinese American Psychiatric Epidemiological Study (CAPES), represents the largest mental health study of any Asian group to date (Sue et al. 1995). This study collected data from a probability sample of 1,700 native-born and immigrant Chinese living in the Los Angeles area. Table 16.3 presents rates of psychiatric disorder from the CAPES study, compared with the overall rates reported in the ECA and NCS. Overall, the rates of mental health problems for Chinese Americans are low when compared with the other reported rates. Rates of generalized anxiety disorder, simple phobia, and panic disorder are considerably lower than those reported in the other studies. However, the rates of major depression are higher than reported in the ECA study yet considerably lower than reported in the NCS.

Much remains to be learned about the extent of psychopathology for the diverse populations that make up the Asian American and Pacific Islander category.

American Indians

According to the 1990 Census, American Indians and Alaskan Natives make up only 1% (just over two million persons) of the American population. Even though they comprise the smallest racial group, the diversity within their ranks is impressive, with over 500 federally recognized tribes and entities. Some original languages have been lost over time, but many tribes have their own language and distinct customs. Almost one third of this population lives below the poverty level, with an average per-capita income of $8,328 (U.S. Bureau of the Census 1991b). The median age for Native Americans is 26.9 years, the lowest of any major racial group in America (U.S. Bureau of the Census 1991b).

There is a dearth of information from epidemiological studies regarding the mental health of American Indians (Manson, Walker, & Kivlahan 1987). Two issues that have received some research attention are substance abuse and depression. The available evidence suggests that Indian adolescents abuse alcohol at two to three times the rate of their non-Indian peers (Mail 1989; Mail & Johnson 1993). Many researchers believe that drug and alcohol abuse may exacerbate some of the health and social problems that American Indians experience; consequently, there have been many studies examining the high rates of alcohol problems within some American-Indian communities (Heath 1989; Johnson 1994; Silk-Walker, Walker, & Kivlahan 1988). Closely related to the problem of alcohol abuse is the high rate of suicide among American Indians. It is estimated that Native Americans commit suicide at two times the national average (Debruyn, Hymbaugh, & Valdez 1988). Alcohol plays a role in a majority of Indian suicides (Johnson 1994; Kettle & Bixler 1993).

Studies of clinic populations or convenience samples suggest that there might be high rates of depression among American Indians (Kinzie et al. 1992; Napholz 1994). For example, a study of 102 clinic patients (Wilson, Civic, & Glass 1994) found that 21% met DSM-III-R criteria for depressive disorder. Other data suggests that, as in the general population, comorbid psychopathology may also be prevalent for Native Americans (Walker & Kivlahan 1993). For example, in a study of 104 adult Indians from three reservation-based mental health clinics, Shore (1987) found that 83% of the adults had more than one psychiatric disorder. Of the 86 individuals diagnosed as depressed, half had a secondary diagnosis of alcohol abuse.

Cross-Cutting Issues in Minority Mental Health

Our review of the available evidence clearly indicates that, despite decades of research, we lack a clear picture of the mental health status of the principal minority populations in the United States. There are several issues that must be resolved before we can obtain an accurate picture of the distribution of mental health problems for minority populations, and there are some important issues that must be addressed to enhance our understanding of the determinants of variations in mental health status. These issues will be considered in this section. They include quality of data as well as the need to pay more attention to the specific social conditions faced by minority populations.

Data quality issues that are crucial to the assessment and interpretation of minority mental health status include coverage of the population, limitations of the measurement of mental health status, and the role of culture.

Coverage of the Population. Despite large epidemiologic studies like the NCS and ECA, we still lack a complete picture of the mental health of the black population (Williams & Fenton 1994). Noncoverage of African-American males is a serious problem in most epidemiologic surveys. Black males tend to have low response rates in survey research studies, and they are overrepresented in marginal and institutional populations that are likely to have higher rates of morbidity. High rates of nonresponse in a particular group may bias estimates of the distribution of disease for that group. This problem is typically addressed in epidemiologic studies by using poststratification weights to make sample distributions correspond to U.S. Census estimates of the population. This strategy does not solve the problem because it is likely that nonrespondents differ systematically from respondents and because the degree of Census undercount has an important effect on Census estimates of the population (the Census estimates that more than 10% of all black males between the ages of 25 and 64 are not counted; Williams 1996a). These national estimates are likely to vary by specific geographic areas and can seriously distort estimates of the population in particular areas. Although the Census has historically devoted more attention to the undercount problem for the black and white population, evaluation of the 1990 Census suggests that the undercount problem may also be acute for Hispanics and American Indians (Williams 1996a). Low response rates for racial minorities can be eliminated by a commitment of adequate financial resources and the use of appropriate field methods (McGraw et al. 1992).

Another issue related to data coverage is the considerable heterogeneity of minority populations. There is considerable ethnic heterogeneity within each of the five racial categories, and an understanding of mental status requires that health status variations within these categories be disaggregated whenever possible. Subgroups of the Asian, American-Indian, Hispanic, and even the black and white populations vary across a broad range of sociodemographic characteristics. There is also considerable heterogeneity within even a subgroup of a global racial category. For example, the Chinese-American population, one of the largest subgroups of the Asian and Pacific Islander category, is in itself diverse (Sue et al. 1995). It consists of individuals born in the United States as well as immigrants born in different regions of China who speak a variety of dialects and languages. Some of these individuals are highly educated; others may be barely literate.

The problem of noncoverage in psychiatric epidemiology studies is also evident in the absence of small groups that are relatively rare and widely dispersed in the population. The small sample size available for the Asian, Hispanic, and American-Indian populations in most mental health studies is a particularly serious problem. The lack of adequate data yields unreliable estimates of the distribution of disease and precludes the assessment of heterogeneity within a given racial group. The small sizes and geographic concentrations of these populations suggest the importance of geographically focused surveys (as opposed to national ones) as the optimal cost-effective strategy to obtain data for these groups. However, if racial identifiers exist for these populations that capture the heterogeneity of these populations in national data bases, combining multiple years of data can be a useful strategy for obtaining mental health data for rare populations.

Measuring Mental Health. Historically, mental disorder and normal functioning have been conceived as polar ends of a scale, with self-reported symptoms of psychological distress or depression placed on a continuum with defined psychiatric disorders. Thus, some researchers viewed scales of psychological distress as a substitute for studies of psychiatric disorders. However, there is growing recognition that scales of psychological distress capture qualitatively different phenomena than measures of psychiatric disorder. Research has shown that although most clinically depressed persons have scores in the depressed range on self-report questionnaires, relatively few persons from community samples who have high scores on self-report scales of depression meet diagnostic criteria for clinical depression (Downey & Coyne 1991). In addition, the social correlates of self-reported symptoms differ from those of interview-generated diagnoses of clinical depression (Downey & Coyne 1991).

It is important to note that conclusions about the distribution of mental health problems for at least some minority populations appear to be linked to the measurement of mental health status. We noted earlier that, compared with whites, African Americans tend to have higher levels of symptoms but equivalent or lower rates of disorder. Some limited evidence suggests that Puerto Ricans (Canino et al. 1987a) and Chinese Americans (Sue et al. 1995) may also have high levels of symptoms but low rates of disorder. This pattern is consistent with the notion that psychological distress scales capture not clinical diagnosis but aspects of demoralization that are likely to be more common at the low end of the SES spectrum (Link & Dohrenwend 1980a). Future racial comparisons of mental health status must pay more careful attention to distinctions between distress and disorder.

Another problem affecting the quality of measures of psychiatric status is language proficiency. Language barriers often exacerbate the challenges associated with mental health assessment among racial and ethnic minorities. This problem is especially acute for subgroups of the Asian-American and Hispanic populations that have a high percentage of foreign-born persons. A lack of language proficiency in the client or clinician can create bias in the diagnostic process. Fluency is particularly important in the determination of psychotic thought processes. If a clinician has difficulty comprehending the speech pattern of an individual with limited mastery of the English language, he or she could erroneously diagnose a patient as having a thought disorder (Cervantes & Arroyo 1994).

Williams and Fenton (1994) note that many of the racial differences in disorder in the ECA study were evident only for measures of lifetime prevalence. There are validity problems with the lifetime measures of psychiatric illness that may be especially acute for members of minority populations. The available evidence indicates that respondents have difficulty in accurately recalling and dating psychiatric episodes that occurred over their lifetime (Rogler et al. 1992). These recall problems are likely to differ by racial group status because both education level and level of language proficiency are probably associated with accuracy of recall.

Culture. Inattention to the role of culture in shaping the manifestation of mental health problems could also contribute to systematic patterns of misdiagnosis across racial groups. If races have different cultures, they may also have distinct belief systems and standards for acceptable behavior. It is thus possible that the specific symptoms related to a psychiatric disorder would vary across different cultural groups. Depression, for example, may have a stronger somatic component for individuals raised in cultures that repress overt expression of emotion. Manson (1995) emphasizes that the cultural context is important in the presentation of symptoms among Native Americans. He indicates that cultures may differentially emphasize particular emotions, intensity of emotional expression, and the ways in which emotion is expressed. For example, some evidence suggests that Eskimos seldom display anger (Briggs 1970). Rogler, Cortes, and Malgady (1991) call attention to another methodological issue that can affect diagnosis of mental health. Researchers, in deciding what measures to use to determine mental health, tend to use "etic" classifications: broad taxonomies of mental health that tend to ignore unique domains of the patient's culture. These cultural factors can influence how symptoms are interpreted and treated. On the other hand, "emic" classifications would reflect forms of psychological distress specific to a cultural group – for example, expressions of anger among the Eskimo. When researchers privilege the etic over the emic, they may tend to categorically apply to one culture a malady classification that was developed for another culture.

Williams and Fenton (1994) review several studies that indicate differences between blacks and whites in the type and quantity of symptoms displayed for both depression and schizophrenia. We do not currently know how generalizable this problem is, but it is likely that the standard measures of mental health may not appropriately fit all of the racial and ethnic subgroups that make up America's multiracial diversity (Rogler et al. 1991). The literature also describes several examples of how culture affects the assessment of mental health status for Hispanics. Studies have revealed that the assessment of mental health status of Puerto Ricans often confounds beliefs in spiritualism with psychotic symptoms (Guarnaccia 1992). As a result, cultural adaptations were made to the DIS for the assessment of several disorders (obsessive-compulsive disorder, psychosexual dysfunction, dysthymia, and cognitive impairment) in Puerto Rico (Canino et al. 1987b).

An emerging strategy in the health field is the use of in-depth cognitive interviewing to assess the extent to which there might be subgroup differences in the understanding and interpretation of questions. Cognitive interviewing techniques are designed to identify the extent of variation in comprehension and other cognitive processes (e.g., the response editing of sensitive questions) that survey respondents use in answering standardized questions (Forsyth & Lessler 1991). If racial groups belong to different subcultures, then a single approach to eliciting symptoms could be insensitive to cultural nuances and lead to significant response errors. Cognitive interviewing has not yet been systematically applied to the examination of potential racial differences in answering questions in standardized psychiatric diagnostic interviews.

The problem of misdiagnosis may be exacerbated when sociocultural distance between clinician and client is combined with racial bias. A number of researchers have addressed the misdiagnosis of major psychotic illnesses and psychological distress in racial and ethnic minorities (Lum 1995; Neighbors et al. 1989). In a review of the literature pertaining to the diagnosis and treatment of African-American patients in the mental health system, Worthington (1992) reported that the misdiagnosis of black patients is common. Loring and Powell (1988) investigated the objectivity of psychiatric diagnosis using the formal diagnostic criteria of the DSM-III. They presented two case studies of undifferentiated schizophrenia to a random sample of psychiatrists. This study found that, even in the face of unambiguous diagnostic criteria, diagnosis was related to the race and sex of the client and to the race and sex of the clinician. For example, black male and female psychiatrists both tended to give the least severe diagnosis to white male patients. The most severe labels of psychopathology tended to be diagnosed in black patients, where ascriptions of violence, suspiciousness, and dangerousness were often made even though the case studies of the black males were identical to those for the white males.

Mukherjee and associates (1983) had similar results in a study that reviewed the records of 76 outpatients of an inner-city hospital for a history of previous misdiagnosis of schizophrenia. These patients had been diagnosed with bipolar disorder but had experienced full remission of symptoms. Compared with white patients who were displaying similar symptoms, black and Hispanic patients were more likely to be diagnosed as schizophrenic and delusional. Instructively, both the Loring and Powell (1988) and the Mukherjee et al. (1983) studies revealed that black and Hispanic psychiatrists also misdiagnosed or failed to correct the misdiagnosis of minority patients. Thus, skin color match between the client and the clinician may not overcome deeply entrenched stereotypes and norms of medical practice.

The Social Context of Minority Mental Health

Greater attention to understanding what racial categories measure can lead to the development of research agendas that shed light on the distribution of diseases across social groups. Williams and Fenton (1994) emphasize that research that will enhance our understanding of racial differences in mental health must seek to identify the ways in which social, economic, political, and cultural factors – as well as racism and the migration experience – shape the experiences of minority populations in ways that can adversely affect their mental health.

Socioeconomic Status. This is one of the strongest known determinants of variations in health status, both in developed countries and in the developing world (Williams & Collins 1995). There is also a well-established pattern of variations in mental health status by SES in both early (Hollingshead & Redlich 1958) and more recent (Holzer et al. 1986) studies. For example, in the ECA data, low-SES persons exhibited rates of psychiatric illness that were twice as high as those of high-SES individuals (Holzer et al. 1986). Race is strongly associated with SES. American Indians, Hispanics, blacks, and certain subgroups of the Asian and Pacific Islander population have lower levels (than the white population) of education, income, and employment (Williams 1996a). Accordingly, adjusting racial differences in mental health status for SES substantially reduces and sometimes eliminates these differences. This pattern has been consistently found for black–white differences in psychological distress (Neighbors 1984) and for the higher rates of schizophrenia for blacks (as compared with whites) in the ECA data (Robins & Regier 1991). Lower levels of socioeconomic status can lead to greater exposure to stress (Kessler 1979) as well as to higher levels of alienation and powerlessness (Mirowsky & Ross 1989b). Moreover, socioeconomic status also predicts variations in mental health status within racial groups (Williams et al. 1992a).

There is growing recognition that the relationship between race and SES is neither simple nor straightforward. Kessler and Neighbors (1986) reanalyzed data from eight epidemiologic surveys and showed that there was a robust interaction between race and SES. That is, although adjustment for SES tends to reduce elevated black levels of psychological distress to nonsignificance, low-SES blacks have higher rates of psychological distress than low-SES whites. A similar pattern was found by Ulbrich, Warheit, and Zimmerman (1989). Cockerham (1990) found no racial differences in psychological distress at low levels of SES, although higher-income blacks had lower levels of distress than high-income whites. Analyses of the ECA data suggest that the association between race and SES also varies importantly by gender (Williams et al. 1992a). Among women, low-SES black females had higher rates of alcohol and drug abuse disorders than their white counterparts. Surprisingly, however, low-SES white males had *higher* rates of psychiatric disorder than their low-SES black counterparts.

The health literature has also been giving increasing attention to the nonequivalence of SES measures across racial groups. There are racial differences in the quality of education, income returns for a given level of education, wealth or assets associated with a given level of income, purchasing power of income, stability of employment, and health risks associated with occupational status (Williams & Collins 1995). The literature has also recently emphasized that SES is not just a confounder of the relationship between race and mental health but part of the causal pathway by which race affects health status (Cooper & David 1986). That is, race is antecedent to SES, and SES differences between the races reflect (in part) the impact of economic discrimination produced by large-scale societal structures. Socioeconomic status is measured with considerable error, so there is need for continuing efforts to identify all of the relevant aspects of position in social structure that might be linked to health status (Krieger, Williams, & Moss 1997).

Racism. Understanding the social contexts of minority populations will require increased attention to the ways in which racism affects health (Krieger et al. 1993; Williams 1996b; Williams, Lavizzo-Mourey, & Warren 1994). The term "racism" as used here includes ideologies of superiority to and negative attitudes and beliefs about outgroups, as well as differential treatment of members of those groups by individuals and societal institutions. There is growing attention to the pervasiveness and persistence of racial discrimination in the United States (Essed 1990; Feagin 1991; Kim & Lewis 1994; Telles & Murgia 1990). Descriptions of these experiences suggest that they incorporate important elements of stressful situations that are known to adversely affect mental health status (Essed 1991; Feagin 1991). The literature on the health of the black population has long indicated that prejudice and discrimination can adversely affect black health (McCarthy & Yancey 1971). It has been argued that racial discrimination is a significant part of the stressful life experiences of minority group members that is *not* captured by traditional scales used for assessing stress (Williams et al. 1997).

Several studies have indicated that racial discrimination adversely affects mental health status. Two studies have indicated that Mexican-American women experience high levels of racial discrimination and that these experiences of stress predict higher levels of psychological distress (Amaro, Russo, & Johnson 1987; Salgado de Snyder 1987). Similarly, studies of African Americans also indicate that racial discrimination adversely affects psychological distress and psychological well-being (Jackson et al. 1996; Williams & Chung in press). One recent study of a large metropolitan area attempted to measure major episodic experiences of discrimination (such as being fired and failing to get a promotion) as well as more routine, everyday experiences of unfair treatment, such as poor service in restaurants and stores or being treated with lack of courtesy and respect (Williams et al. 1997). This study found that African Americans report higher levels of both types of discrimination than whites, and that the chronic everyday experiences of discrimination are more adversely related to both physical and mental health status than the major episodic experiences (Williams et al. 1997). Discrimination may also be a potent influence in affecting the mental health status of Asian Americans (Kuo 1995; Young & Takeuchi 1998). Future research in minority mental health status must give more serious and sustained research attention to categorizing exposure to discrimination and patterns of response and to systematically assessing their implications for mental health.

The literature also suggests that the internalization of racist beliefs within the larger culture can lead to negative self-evaluations that can adversely affect psychological well-being. Research by Taylor and colleagues (Taylor & Jackson 1990, 1991) indicate that African Americans' internalized racism (belief in the innate inferiority of blacks and feeling uncomfortable around other blacks) was positively related to alcohol consumption and psychological distress. Similarly, analyses of the National Study of Black Americans found that blacks who believed that societal stereotypes of blacks were accurate had higher levels of psychological distress and lower levels of psychological well-being (Williams & Chung in press). Williams-Morris (1996) outlines a number of ways in which racism in the larger culture can adversely affect the psychological development of minority children. She indicates that a potential role of racism is implicit in most of the major theoretical models in developmental psychology, and she proposes a research agenda in that area.

Coping Processes and Resources. Minority racial status can capture not only differential exposure to stress but also variations in coping processes and in resources available to cope with stress. There are a range of social and psychological factors that have emerged as risk factors for health status or that can reduce levels of stress or the adverse consequences of stress on mental health. These psychosocial variables include self-esteem, social support, perceptions of mastery or control, anger or hostility, feelings of helplessness or hopelessness, and the repression or denial of emotions (Kessler et al. 1995c). The literature clearly documents that the distribution of most of these risk factors varies by SES and race (Mirowsky & Ross 1989b; Williams 1990), but few attempts have been made to explore systematically how psychosocial risks and resources relate to race and combine with environmental constraints to affect mental health. The literature also indicates that there is need to pay greater attention to the health-enhancing cultural resources of minority group members that may shield them from some of the adverse consequences of stress (Rogler, Malgady, & Rodriguez 1989; Williams & Fenton 1994). It has been suggested that a broad range of cultural resources, including family support and religious involvement, may play an important role in buffering minority populations from the negative effects of stress. However, the processes and mechanisms through which these resources operate to affect mental health status are not well understood.

Recent analyses of the Detroit Area Study data highlight the importance of understanding coping processes and of testing for interactions among the predictors of mental health status. In this study, for both measures of mental health status (psychological distress and psychological well-being), the mental health of blacks was better than that of whites once adjustment was made for race-related stress (Williams et al. 1997). This pattern is consistent with the notion that these stressful experiences may more adversely affect the health of whites than of blacks. A recent review noted that, for a number of child and infant health outcomes, although blacks are more exposed to adverse risk factors, these factors have a larger impact on the health status of whites than of blacks (Williams & Collins 1995). Kessler (1979) documented a similar pattern for the relationship between stressful life events and psychological distress for nonwhites (mainly blacks) and low-SES persons. Both of these economically disadvantaged groups were more exposed to stress. However, compared to nonwhites and low-SES individuals, comparable stressful events more adversely affected the mental health of whites and high-SES persons, respectively. Kessler (1979) suggested some possible reasons for this relative advantage. First, owing to earlier or more frequent exposure to adversity, African Americans could become sufficiently accustomed to dealing with stress that a new stressful experience has less of an impact. Second, compared with whites, African Americans may respond to stress with greater emotional flexibility (i.e., emotional expression), which may facilitate recovery. In addition, African Americans may have greater access than Caucasians to other coping resources, such as religious involvement, that some have argued may importantly reduce the negative effects of stress (Williams & Fenton 1994).

Migration and Acculturation. The migration experience is a salient characteristic of the lives of many minority populations, and it may be an important influence on the level of mental health problems within these groups. However, despite numerous studies on this topic, our understanding of the ways in which acculturation and migration affect mental health status is still modest (Rogler et al. 1991). Several studies of Asian-American students have found an inverse relationship between length of time in the United States and levels of psychological distress (Sue et al. 1995). Similar findings also come from probability samples of Asian populations (Sue et al. 1995). Other studies of nonrefugee immigrants show that the stressors associated with migration constitute the most significant risk factor for mental health (Furnham & Shiekh 1993; Lum 1995). These stresses include feelings of isolation from peers, the challenges of economic survival in an unfamiliar socioeconomic system, and the difficulties involved in acquiring a new language. The new immigrant must also learn the behavioral norms and values of the host country.

In the Los Angeles site of the ECA project, rates of depression were lower for immigrant Mexicans than for U.S.-born Mexican Americans (Burnam et al. 1987).

In contrast, Puerto Ricans in New York seem to have higher levels of depressive symptoms than island Puerto Ricans (Haberman 1976; Vega & Rumbaut 1991). In an analysis of the literature on acculturation and mental health among Hispanics, Rogler and associates (1991) reviewed the results of 30 studies (published since 1960) on the subject. The authors found that twelve studies showed a negative relationship – that is, individuals who are high in acculturation (more fully integrated into the host society) are more prone to suffer from low self-esteem and psychological distress. Presumably, integration into the host society leads to self-depreciation or self-hatred and isolation from traditional support systems. However, thirteen studies reported a positive relationship between acculturation and mental health. Individuals who became more and more integrated into the new society experienced greater psychological well-being. In three other studies, a curvilinear relationship was found. Good mental health was a product of the ability to obtain a balance between traditional cultural norms and the host country's norms and values. As one moves away from this equilibrium toward either of the acculturation extremes, psychological distress increases (Rogler et al. 1991).

When migration is coupled with refugee status, there are further implications for mental health. A prospective study of 467 adult refugees who sought health care in ten public health clinics in four states found a 20% prevalence rate for depression based on the Vietnamese Depression Scale (Buchwald et al. 1993). A study of 322 refugees at a psychiatric clinic reported that 70% of the Southeast Asian refugee patient sample met the criteria for current posttraumatic stress disorder (PTSD) and that 82% of these individuals experienced the most common symptom of PTSD – depression (Kinzie et al. 1990). What is striking about this study is that most of the individuals who were assessed had experienced the trauma more than a decade prior to the assessment. High rates of refugee trauma were also found in Southeast Asian refugee populations outside the United States. The Harvard program in refugee trauma assessed the mental status of displaced Cambodians living on the Thailand–Cambodia border. Using a household survey of 993 randomly selected adults, researchers found a prevalence rate of 55% for depression and 15% for PTSD (Mollica et al. 1993).

Conclusion

One of the most critical issues in the study of the mental health of U.S. minority populations is the identification of the extent to which minority status itself is a predictor of increased risk for mental health problems (Vega & Rumbaut 1991; Williams & Fenton 1994). Such research is contingent on delineating the specific factors linked to race that influence health status. Challenges due to socioeconomic disadvantage and adaptation to mainstream American culture can lead minority group members to experience high levels of stressful experiences that could adversely affect health. Recent research reveals that comprehensive measures of stress account for substantially more variability in mental health status than did previous studies of life events and chronic stressors (Turner et al. 1995). Future research must characterize this full range of stress variables for minority populations and identify how they combine with stressors (such as residence in deprived geographic areas and discrimination) that may be unique to, or more prevalent among, racial minority populations. An enhanced understanding of the role of the larger social environment in mental health requires integrative models that examine how stress in the larger environment develops over the life course and combines with appraisal processes, emotional states, and behavioral, psychological, and physiological responses and vulnerabilities – in additive and interactive ways – to affect mental health.

Acknowledgment. Preparation of this chapter was supported in part by grants 5 T32 MH16806 and 1 RO1 MH57425 from the National Institute of Mental Health and by the John D. and Catherine T. MacArthur Foundation Research Network on Socioeconomic Status and Health.

17

Social Stressors in Childhood and Adolescence

Elizabeth G. Menaghan

Menaghan argues that the major mental health concerns in children and adolescents are linked to behavioral problems and various high-risk behaviors. She defines and examines two dimensions of such problems: externalizing and internalizing behaviors. Social stressors linked to family composition, occupation, and various economic factors are related to the development of behavior problems. Large family size, unstable family composition, difficult working conditions, and inadequate incomes have negative impacts on parenting abilities and also exacerbate developmental problems in children. Individual characteristics of parents and children also shape the development and course of behavior problems, the socialization experience of children, and the quality of the interaction between parents and children. Further research is needed to determine the causal linkages between social stressors, parent and child characteristics, and the quality of parent–child interactions as well as to develop effective interventions for reducing the number of children with behavioral problems. What types of stressors seem most critical to the development of childhood mental health problems? What types of interventions (see Chapter 5) would have the most impact on children's mental health?

An enduring interest for social scientists and everyday observers alike is the question of continuity and change in individual personality and well-being. Some accounts emphasize the genetic and biological determinants that underlie emotional responsiveness, discuss "set points" for happiness to which people tend to return, and in general take a "biology is destiny" view that looks for enduring patterns of responsiveness and well-being over time. Most sociologists, on the other hand, counter such claims with emphasis on the importance of social experiences and social contexts in shaping individual and group behavior. As well, changes in social contexts should be linked to changes – for better and worse – in well-being. In this chapter we focus on only one subset of the social stressors that impinge on children and adolescents: stressors that are linked to their social memberships in particular families. We focus on the effects of family composition, family economic well-being, and parental occupational characteristics on patterns of parent–child interaction as well as on the development and persistence of behavior problems. We attempt to summarize what is known about the linkages between social stressors and child and adolescent well-being, and we also identify some of the complexities and insufficiently studied possibilities in this area that make it ripe for additional research.

A better understanding of how social stressors affect the next generation is a critical need. National data suggest that increasing numbers of children and adolescents in the United States are exhibiting severe manifestations of aggressive and depressed behavior. Successive birth cohorts have shown increased rates and earlier onset of depression and suicide. Intentional injury, assault, and homicide rates have also been increasing, especially among nonwhite youth (National Research Council 1993). The major current health concerns for children and adolescents are linked to behavior problems and high-risk behaviors that threaten long-range life chances.

These trends raise questions about how changes in children's and adolescents' well-being may be linked to changes in their everyday life conditions. A better understanding of these processes promises both social and scientific benefits. It can contribute to social scientific theories regarding the development of social competence and mental health over the life course. It also can help identify children who are otherwise likely to reach adulthood without the behavioral skills needed to attain economic self-sufficiency, to be effective parents to their own children, and to enjoy a satisfying level of emotional well-being. Finally, it may suggest strategies for social interventions that can improve the life chances of those children.

Behavior Problems: Explanations for Persistence over Time

What do we know about behavior problems in childhood and adolescence? Two dimensions of behavior problems repeatedly emerge in the literature (see e.g. Achenbach 1984; Rutter 1970). *Externalizing* behavior, also referred to as undercontrolled or troublesome behavior, refers to behavior that is troubling to others – especially aggressive and antisocial behavior. *Internalizing* behavior, sometimes labeled overcontrolled or troubled behavior, is marked by withdrawal from interaction, anxiety, and depressed mood. In community samples, we observe a fairly high correlation between the two sets of problems, produced in part by the tendency of most children to be low on both. Both sets of difficulties may also have shared consequences in that they disrupt interaction with others and thus make it more difficult for children to learn other, more socially accepted ways of perceiving the social world and responding to others (Elder & Caspi 1988a).

Researchers are concerned with the origins of these problems early in the life course precisely because they believe that, once established, they tend to persist. However, the actual research evidence for this is somewhat mixed. Some studies of children's behavior problems have suggested that (a) except for extreme outliers, problems observed in early childhood are not necessarily enduring, yet (b) the period of middle childhood is marked by increasing stabilization of behavior problems (Achenbach 1984). Other studies, however, emphasize that high levels of antisocial behavior at early ages do tend to persist unless active intervention occurs. As children approach adolescence, empirical data suggest that behavior patterns are increasingly stable. Studies suggest that both aggressive, externalizing behaviors and excessively inhibited and fearful styles of interaction tend to persist into and beyond the adolescent years (Caspi, Elder, & Bem 1988; Elder & Caspi 1988a; Patterson, DeBaryshe, & Ramsey 1989; Robins 1966, 1979).

Parker and Asher (1987) have reviewed many of these studies of continuity and change in behavior problems and have pointed out common limitations. Very few are prospective studies, following a group of children forward over time and observing variations in outcomes. They tend instead to be retrospective and selective, identifying a sample with current problems and tracing these back to earlier difficulties. Because all of the children studied have the same outcome – that is, they all have current problems – we are in a weak position to make claims about cause and effect. Suppose we find that everyone with serious behavior problems at age 12 was rated by their kindergarten teachers as having trouble with self-control and following rules. We may be tempted to conclude that early problems predict later problems. But if we had studied all of the kindergarteners so rated, we might find that only a small subset, perhaps 10%, also had serious problems at age 12. In fact, if we had studied all the children in kindergarten, we might find that the same proportion of children who didn't have problems at age 5 nevertheless had difficulties later on. If 10% of each group – those with and without early problems – had problems later on, then we would conclude that there is not much linkage over time.

In addition, many of these samples include few nonwhite children, focus only on middle-class samples, or consist only of children in treatment for serious difficulties. These restrictions in the children studied make it impossible to generalize to other children. Finally, most of the longitudinal studies in this area focus on describing the magnitude of behavioral change or continuity over time; they rarely focus on specifying how problem levels tend to stabilize over time or on specifying the conditions under which changes will occur. It is clear that some change is possible, but we are still trying to understand the conditions under which children either will persist in the patterns of behavior established in childhood or will alter their trajectory.

At any particular point in time, such behavior problems may be painful but self-limiting expressions of temporary emotional distress, or they may become an established pattern of learned behavior that tends to be self-reinforcing. What seems to make the difference? Elder and Caspi (1988a) discuss two major processes that sustain maladaptive behavior over time: interactional and cumulative continuity. The idea of *interactional* continuity refers to the repeated give and take between individuals who interact with one another over long time periods. They tend to fall into recurrent patterns, each playing the same role or repeating the same behavior and in turn evoking the same response from the other. These established patterns of interaction, particularly family interaction, may repeatedly provide short-term reinforcements or rewards for problematic behavior, making its recurrence more likely (see also Patterson 1988). The idea of *cumulative* continuity emphasizes more long-range consequences. Over time, the consequences of such behavior cumulate, systematically selecting children into environments that reinforce and sustain established behaviors. Elder and Caspi's accounts predict fairly high continuity in behavior over time, not because it is biologically or genetically inevitable, but because of social patterns that stabilize and maintain it. Unless something alters these interaction patterns, behavior patterns will tend to persist.

Children's internal explanations and beliefs about themselves and others also play a role in maintaining established patterns. Dodge (1993) discusses how children develop attributions about the motivations and intents of others that shape their own behavior. For example, when children perceive hostile intent, they are more apt to exhibit "preemptive aggression" or harsh retaliatory behaviors. This type of behavior is self-fulfilling: the child who strikes out first, anticipating the worst, is likely to elicit an angry or punitive response – just what they expected. Hence, their own actions tend to elicit behavior that confirms their initial reading of the situation. This is similar to Caspi and Bem's (1990) concept of "evocative interaction," in which individuals elicit responses from others that tend to reinforce their own initial behaviors and attitudes. They note as an example Clausen's (1991) finding that personal competence tends to "pull" affirmative responses from others, whereas personal irritability and explosiveness tend to evoke reciprocal hostility from others, reinforcing an individual's initial tendency to respond explosively to evidence of personal threat. These arguments suggest that, once problematic styles of interaction have become established, they are likely to persist – although changes in interaction patterns and environments may produce change in behavior.

Social Stressors and Behavior Problems

The story thus far emphasizes forces for continuity once behavior difficulties are established. But what establishes them in the first place, and under what conditions may they change? Social stress research emphasizes the roles of compositional, occupational, and economic factors. An extensive literature links family composition and adult economic activity, particularly maternal employment, to children's outcomes, although much of this work concentrates on the early childhood years. For children of all ages, family composition and adult economic activity have powerful effects on the economic resources available in the child's household. These economic resources shape relations among adults in the household as well as relations between parents and children, including the strategies of child socialization, support, and control that are used, the overall affective climate of the family, and the consistency and contingency of parental action. These factors are also likely to be implicated in our explanations of both continuity and change. Available research suggests that behavior becomes increasingly stable over the middle childhood period, but this may largely reflect the greater stability and chronicity of economic and family conditions that characterize families with school-aged and adolescent children as compared to those with preschoolers. Improvements in family life, interruptions in parental employment, economic losses, or parent departure may each alter children's behavioral patterns.

Family Circumstances

Relatively difficult family circumstances, including fewer adults and larger numbers of children, constrain parental nurturance and stimulation, and they have negative effects on the quality of children's home environments and on child intellectual and behavior outcomes (Blake 1989; Bradley 1985; Bradley & Caldwell 1984; Bradley et al. 1988; Haveman, Wolfe, & Spaulding 1991; Menaghan & Parcel 1991; Mercy & Steelman 1982; Parcel & Menaghan 1990; Rogers, Parcel, & Menaghan 1991b; Steelman & Powell 1991; Zajonc 1976; Zuravin 1988). Some of these effects stem from economic causes. As discussions of the feminization of poverty make clear (see e.g. McLanahan & Booth 1989; U.S. Bureau of the Census 1989; U.S. Congress 1990), family composition is a major predictor of family economic well-being. Family households that do not include a wage-earning man are significantly more likely to experience poverty or near-poverty incomes. When women's earnings are the primary source of family income, they are often insufficient to avoid poverty.

Some researchers have argued that "absent father" effects may actually indicate other characteristics of the mother, or may largely reflect associated economic deficits (Mott 1991, 1992, 1993). Other theorists argue that the absence of nurturance from fathers does shape children's beliefs and behavior. Scott Coltrane (1988) reviews a variety of socialization arguments advanced by Margaret Mead, Philip Slater, and Nancy Chodorow that converge in predicting that men who are reared primarily by women and with little nurturance from fathers will be "hypermasculine," define themselves in opposition to women, and exaggerate the differences between men and women. Using data on 90 nonindustrial societies, he concludes that societies with greater father involvement in patterns of child socialization produce men who are less hostile and aggressive toward women. If differences among societies can also be applied to intrasocietal differences, they suggest that, at least for boys, little contact with fathers will predict increased aggressive and acting-out behaviors. Implications for girls are less clear. Other studies also suggest possible gender differences in effects of family composition, favoring boys or girls depending on particular circumstances. The varying results of this large and growing body of literature partly reflect the heterogeneity of the samples, methodological orientations, and availability of appropriate controls.

Other theorists focus on the quality of parent–child interaction as a key factor linking family experiences to child outcomes. Dodge (1993) reviews literature that suggests that both aggressive and depressed children display processing biases and deficits in social cognition. Aggressive children selectively attend to hostile acts directed toward the self and evaluate aggression more positively than other children do. On the other hand, Dodge finds that depressed children attend to failure, loss, and negative self-reference and tend to blame problems they may encounter on their own shortcomings (1993: 564). Given the specific deficits shown, Dodge derives a set of hypotheses regarding what sorts of social and family experiences are likely to promote one rather than the other set of difficulties. He argues that early experiences of physical abuse, exposure to aggressive models, and insecure attachment relationships lead the child to see the world as a hostile place, to be hypervigilant and hyperreactive to possible hostility, and to be prone to aggressive behavior. In contrast, either interpersonal loss and instability or pressure to achieve at an unrealistic level (especially when combined with a parent who models depressive affect) leads the child to develop a negative self-schema, to attend to negative aspects of events, to attribute negative events to internal, stable, and global factors, and to be prone to depressive behavior.

Independent of family composition, the number and spacing of children have clear influences on children's socialization experiences. Family size is an established predictor of children's cognitive and educational outcomes (Blake 1989) and is also linked to greater behavior problems (Cooksey, Menaghan, & Jekielek 1997). However, the effects of a larger number of siblings vary somewhat depending on birth order and spacing, with at least one study finding that a closely spaced younger sibling is particularly problematic (Desai, Chase-Lansdale, & Michael 1989).

Changes in Family Composition

Neither adult family membership nor number of children are stable properties of families, and changes in family composition are expected to alter the quality of home environments. Such alterations have implications for changes in child behavioral outcomes as well. Additions to the household because of cohabitation, marriage or remarriage, or combining households across generations – as well as reductions in the number of available adults that occurs when young single mothers move out of their parents' households – alter the supportive economic, emotional, and cognitive resources available to children. Breakup of marital or quasi-marital relationships may be particularly negative, as the surrounding emotional and economic difficulties tend to compromise parents' abilities to provide appropriate stimulation and support, at least in the short run (Hetherington, Cox, & Cox 1978; Patterson & Bank 1989; Patterson et al. 1989; Rickel & Langner 1985; Wallerstein 1984).

Conversely, the addition of a male partner or spouse should increase family economic resources and improve the overall quality of home environments and so provide for added support for child development. Some evidence suggests, however, that stepfathers are less involved in interaction with children than are fathers, and that mother–stepfather families remain similar to single-mother families in patterns of interaction and in child outcomes (Bray 1988). Rogers and colleagues (1991b) find that both recent marital disruption and recent remarriage are associated with elevated behavior problems for young children. In longitudinal studies, the introduction of a "new man" is associated with increased difficulties (Mott, Kowaleski-Jones, & Menaghan 1997). Additional work suggests that advantages or disadvantages accruing to children in these new family forms may vary for boys and girls (Mott 1991, 1992, 1993) and that the benefits of living with both biological parents may be greater for boys than for girls, at least in white households (Mott 1994). Finally, some studies suggest that informal unions are particularly problematic for children (Menaghan et al. 1997).

Parental Employment and Occupational Conditions

As employment of American mothers of young children has risen, much research has considered possible effects of parental work experiences on their children's lives. Fathers' unemployment or underemployment has long been recognized as a risk factor for children (see Elder 1974 and McLoyd 1989). In contrast, mothers' foregoing employment, especially when their children were young, has been viewed as beneficial. However, maternal employment has become economically essential for many families even when a second adult is present, and maternal employment is a key to lifting single-mother families from poverty. It appears that the economic advantages of mothers' more continuous long-term labor-force attachment may outweigh the attendant disadvantages in terms of reduced home time and increased demands. It seems plausible that these effects may vary depending on the other economic resources available to the family. For example, maternal employment may have more positive effects in single-mother families and in families with lower levels of income from other sources.

Occupational Stressors

Occupational Quality. Studies of whether or not parents are employed may be somewhat misleading if they do not also consider the kinds of employment held. It is likely that the effects of both parents' employment depend in part on the quality and quantity of their work. Sociopsychological theory and empirical research both suggest that the conditions adults experience at work, particularly their opportunities to exercise self-direction in substantively complex work, affect their own cognitive functioning and emotional well-being and shape their attitudes and values, including the values they hold for their children (Kohn & Schooler 1983; Kohn et al. 1990; Miller et al. 1979; Schooler 1987; Siegal 1984; Voydanoff 1987). In terms of values, these studies suggest that when parents' work is more substantively complex and offers greater opportunities for self-direction, parents place greater value on their children's developing self-direction and are less concerned with behavioral conformity per se (Kohn & Schooler 1983; Spade 1991).

Such parents display more warmth and involvement; they also restrict their children's actions less frequently and report fewer spankings (Luster, Rhoades, & Haas 1989). In particular, studies of employed mothers show that the complexity of current maternal occupation exerts a significant effect on a child's family environment (Menaghan & Parcel 1991). For mothers who move into employment, effects are better the higher the complexity of work she obtains (Menaghan & Parcel 1995).

The effects of work quality are not limited to shaping parental attitudes. Work stress research has shown that the conditions of work that are more common in less desirable jobs – routinization, low autonomy, heavy supervision, and little opportunity for substantively complex work – exacerbate psychological distress and reduce self-esteem and personal control. When work experiences leave parents feeling uncertain of their own worth and emotionally distressed, they are less able to be emotionally available to their children or to provide them with responsive, stimulating environments (Belsky & Eggebeen 1991; Menaghan 1991). Such effects may be exacerbated by other difficult family conditions, such as absence of a spouse or large family size.

Work Hours. Controlling for the quality of employment, higher total hours in employment may negatively affect home environments and children's behavioral outcomes (Piotrkowski, Rapoport, & Rapoport 1987; Voydanoff 1987). Coleman (1988) and others argue that time spent in employment competes with time needed to provide suitable home environments for children and to support cognitive and social development. These arguments suggest that when labor-force participation of mothers leaves less time to transmit values, norms, and skills from parents to children, the families' higher economic well-being may not translate into better environments for children. On the other hand, longer work hours are apt to prompt mothers to demand greater independence of their children and to expect greater participation in domestic household work. If not excessive, such demands foster children's maturity and responsibility, contributing to positive outcomes. These arguments suggest a curvilinear effect of work hours on children's outcomes. It is also possible that the quality and extensiveness of employment will interact, with the combination of long work hours at a low-quality job particularly adverse for child rearing. Effects are also likely to be more negative when available parenting time must be distributed across more children. In short, work and family social circumstances may interact in complex ways to shape parent–child interaction and children's outcomes.

Economic Stressors

A large literature supports the negative effects of economic pressures on child outcomes; McLoyd (1989) provides a particularly thoughtful review of the theoretical and empirical underpinnings for this link. Persistence of low overall economic levels and the experience of economic losses can each lead to parental demoralization or depression and hence disrupt skillful parenting (Conger et al. 1992; Elder, Van Nguyen, & Caspi 1985). Some studies suggest that such effects appear reversible if economic pressures are lifted, whereas others (e.g. McLeod & Shanahan 1993) argue that early poverty has significant adverse effects even when conditions later improve.

Many studies have demonstrated associations between economic stressors and parent–child interaction and family environments, but it is unlikely that all of the effects of economic location work through parent–child interaction. Family economic resources are also reflected in the quality of the school, community, neighborhood, and mass media that children experience. As Maccoby (1984: 212–13) points out, it is likely that, by the preadolescent years, children have begun to understand their family's position in a stratified social system and to develop attitudes about what this position implies about their own opportunities and probabilities of success. These dawning understandings and conclusions about their own life chances may make family income levels increasingly important as children grow older.

The Role of Parent and Child Characteristics

Particularly for initial levels of behavior problems, the characteristics that parents and children bring to their interaction also have important effects on child behavior outcomes (see also Elder & Caspi 1988a). Earlier studies have shown strong effects of maternal educational attainment and maternal cognitive skills on such outcomes (Bradley 1985), in part because they are associated with preferable parenting actions. Social psychological theory suggests that mothers' *psychological* resources, such as self-esteem and sense of mastery over life events, will also have positive direct and indirect effects (Clausen 1991); empirical studies confirm this (Gecas 1989; Menaghan & Parcel 1991; Mirowsky & Ross 1986; see also Moore & Snyder 1991). Mothers' commitment to mothering and involvement in their children's lives are also critical: although general "mothering" traits are difficult to assess, they are partially captured by observed characteristics of a mother (such as use of prenatal care, early postbirth well-care, not smoking or drinking during pregnancy), which may be viewed as overt manifestations of more subtle parenting concerns. Finally, many of the mother's prior psychological or intellectual traits may directly affect the nature of her employment as well as the characteristics of her spouse or partner. Children's own attributes may also be correlated both with home environments and with other explanatory variables. For example, serious child health problems may simultaneously strain family economic resources, constrain maternal employment, and prompt parents to try to compensate for children's limitations by providing an especially stimulating and supportive environment. Health problems may hinder children's social development by limiting normal educational and social opportunities. Children's physical size and progress toward puberty also have implications for children's interactions with others and for behavioral outcomes.

It is clear that research linking social stressors and child outcomes need to take such parent and child factors into account. In much nonexperimental research, observed associations between contemporaneously assessed family circumstances, on the one hand, and children's outcomes, on the other, may largely reflect effects of such parental characteristics (see Zaslow, Rabinovich, & Suwalsky 1991 for a thoughtful discussion of this issue). Similarly, without appropriate controls for child characteristics, one can easily obtain "perverse" research results – for example, that better family environments produce poorer child outcomes (see Mott 1991 for discussion of how these selective biases can affect interpretations of early childhood research).

What Aspects of Parent–Child Interaction Matter – And for Whom?

Much of this account emphasizes the role that family environments play in mediating the effects of family composition and patterns of parental employment on children. Several dimensions of family environments have significant implications for children's development (Bradley 1985; Bradley & Caldwell 1984). Providing appropriate cognitive stimulation and more complex and interesting materials and activities should encourage active cognitive efforts. Parents' efforts to organize the child's immediate physical environment in order to provide both stimulation and safety should also make a positive difference. Maternal warmth is related to more positive outcomes for children, including more cooperative and task-oriented classroom behavior (Bradley et al. 1988; see also Crouter, Belsky, & Spanier 1984; Estrada et al. 1987; Howes 1988).

These studies have focused particularly on the early childhood period. Studies of children in the early school years reinforce these findings. They also suggest other important aspects of childhood socialization: particularly, the form and consistency of discipline and the extent of parental monitoring and supervision (Crouter et al. 1990; Maccoby 1984), explicit parental socialization and control efforts, and appropriate autonomy opportunities. Both theory and research suggest that parental control must gradually yield to co-regulation of behavior and eventual self-regulation. However, too-early relinquishment of parental authority and granting of autonomy, which may be more common among hard-pressed single mothers, is likely to backfire (Steinberg et al. 1992). Baumrind (1971, 1991) emphasizes that warmth must be combined with firm control to ensure optimal child outcomes. Baumrind terms this combination authoritative parenting, and contrasts it with authoritarian (high control–low warmth) approaches and with indulgent (low control–high warmth) or neglectful (low control–low warmth) parenting. Steinberg and colleagues emphasize the importance of older children's participating in rule making (Lamborn, Mounts, & Steinberg 1991; Steinberg et al. 1992), rather than feeling powerless to affect such rules. Finally, Ann Crouter notes that, as children spend more and more time away from direct supervision of parents, parents must increasingly turn to more long-range monitoring and more distal supervision strategies. Crouter and associates (1990) find that parents vary widely in their knowledge of their children's daily schoolwork demands and after-school activities; not surprisingly, more active parental efforts to monitor activities and obtain information have been found to increase parental knowledge and improve child outcomes.

Other Complexities in Studying Continuity and Change

We have emphasized the possibility that social stressors interact and that the effects of social stressors may differ depending on parent and child resources (see also Achenbach 1984). For example, stress-buffering models suggest that strong maternal resources may significantly moderate the adverse impacts of stressful circumstance, while stress-amplifying arguments posit that the combination of difficult circumstance and weak personal or familial resources will be particularly adverse. Such considerations challenge any simple summations of how families influence the mental health of children.

Elder and Caspi (1988a) also argue that the effects of stressful changes are generally contingent on what the individual brings to the situation. For example, the effects of economic deprivation on paternal behavior varied depending on the quality of his behavior *prior* to the stressor. If the same argument applies to children's behavior problems over time, the effects of stressful change in family work and family circumstances may be greater for children who are already having difficulties prior to the change.

More generally, it is important to take explicitly into account the level of prior behavior problems when assessing the effects of subsequent economic events or family changes. The need for such controls for prior status has become increasingly clear. For example, some analyses of longitudinal data archives suggest that much of the "effects" of family disruption on children actually predate the family disruption itself, suggesting that prior research may have misspecified causal linkages (Cherlin et al. 1991).

These considerations suggest several critical contrasts for research on social stressor effects on children and adolescents. First, among children who begin middle childhood at deviant levels, what distinguishes children who persist in their outlier status versus outliers who return to the normative range? Second, among children who were "okay" at the beginning of this period, how do we account for the emergence of problem or outlier children versus those who remain within the normal range of behavior problems? The interactive arguments just reviewed suggest, at a minimum, that factors sufficient to maintain an already established level of problems may *not* be sufficient to induce meaningful changes from that level over time. If such patterns are found, they also suggest that initial levels of problems can help to identify children who are likely to need special support and assistance under stress.

Beyond the Family

Although we have emphasized stressors that are measured at the individual family level, an important emerging focus of research considers social stressors beyond the family. For example, Brooks-Gunn and her colleagues (1993), using data from samples of low-birthweight children and of adolescent girls, have demonstrated significant neighborhood effects on childhood and adolescent development even after adjusting for differences in individual families' socioeconomic characteristics, suggesting that such contextual features can provide additional insight. The National Research Council's (1993) report on high-risk youth, *Losing Generations,* also suggests that the state of the economy – and its reflection in unemployment and poverty rates – creates a powerful but insufficiently studied climate of hope or pessimism that affects both parents and children.

One's membership in dominant versus subordinate ethnic minorities may also condition the effects of both parent and child resources and social stressors. Prior research has found ethnic differences in home environments, even when variations in individual resources are controlled (Baker & Mott 1989; Bradley & Caldwell 1984; Elardo & Bradley 1981; Menaghan & Parcel 1991). American black and Chicano families tend to score lower than other families. Laosa (1981) argues that maternal ethnicity influences maternal values and assumptions regarding appropriate mother–child interaction. Peters and Massey (1983) suggest that African-American parents are both more restrictive and more overprotective with their children (see also Mott 1994). To the extent that children share these assumptions, the same qualities of parental action may have somewhat differing effects depending on the larger context within which children and parents operate.

More generally, what parents do and how effective their socialization efforts are may both vary depending on the supportiveness or constraints present in the family's community. This in turn may explain observed ethnic differences. Ethnic minorities face greater economic hardships and, at any given level of economic resources, tend to live in poorer areas with greater crime and fewer community resources. Parents who fear for their children's safety are likely to be more restrictive toward their children and possibly more punitive when children violate family rules. In addition, although parental restrictiveness may in general be associated with more adverse child outcomes, this may be less so when both parents and children view this behavior as an expression of parental care and protection. Future research should examine whether parental behavior patterns are different in better and worse social contexts, independent of the individual parent's characteristics. It should also examine whether parental–child interaction patterns have different effects on a child's behavior in differing contexts, independent of the other individual level controls. On the one hand, we may expect that levels of parental stimulation, support, and supervision are particularly important when family economic well-being is low and community contexts are more negative and have fewer resources. In these circumstances, the home environment may function as a critical factor, amplifying or blunting the impacts of family and community economic factors (see Ross & Mirowsky 1989 for a parallel argument). More pessimistically, the effectiveness of home environments in shaping more positive child outcomes may be overwhelmed at very low levels of economic and community support. Adjudicating between these alternatives is an important task for future research.

Conclusion

In summary, we argue that parental resources, social stressors, and family patterns combine to shape the development of children's behavior problems during childhood and adolescence. Stable maternal characteristics – including such resources as intellectual skills, educational attainment, and self-esteem – shape children's socialization experiences and thus influence their trajectory of behavior problems. Where fathers are present, their resources also influence children's socialization environments. Because these parental characteristics are relatively stable over time, such influences are likely to have their strongest effects on initial levels of children's behavior problems and on their stability over time.

Social stressors – particularly large family size and unstable family composition, difficult parental working conditions, and inadequate incomes – undermine the quality of parental child rearing and so make the development of behavior problems more likely. When such stressors increase, children will exhibit more behavior problems. Conversely, decreases in social stressors should diminish children's behavior problems over time.

It also appears that the quality of children's socialization, which is affected by parental resources and social stressors, has significant independent effects on children's behavior problems. It is likely that the critical components of socialization vary by children's age. Overall warmth and stimulation are important at all ages, but indirect monitoring and negotiation of behavioral rules and expectations become increasingly important in the middle childhood years as children spend increased time away from home, beyond the reach of direct parental intervention.

All three sets of these interdependent explanatory variables – parent and child characteristics, social stressors, and the quality of parent–child interaction – contribute to a social explanation of children's behavior problems. By investigating the causal linkages among these three sets of variables and estimating both direct and indirect effects, social scientific research may suggest the most promising pathways for social intervention to reduce the proportions of children who emerge with behavioral styles that have poor outcomes when they become adults.

18

Well-Being across the Life Course

John Mirowsky & Catherine E. Ross

Middle age is the best time of life in terms of depression; older and younger adults report higher levels of depression. In explaining this pattern, Mirowsky and Ross provide an overview of the five aspects of age – age as maturity, age as decline, age as life-cycle stage, age as generation, and age as survival – and describe how these aspects help account for age differences in depression. Also important are the conditions, beliefs, and emotions that define and shape one's well-being and that differ across age groups. The authors utilize data from the 1995 U.S. survey of *Aging, Status and the Sense of Control* to illustrate the impact of age on mental health. Age is related to many of the conditions critical to well-being, including economic prosperity, employment, marriage, children, education, one's childhood family, and physical health. The most critical process is a sense of mastery (controlling one's own life). Those who are middle-aged are at the peak of their earnings and their children have grown; their marriages are stable and jobs secure; the tensions and conflicts of young adulthood have lessened, and the problems of old age have not yet set in. According to Mirowsky and Ross, this is why the best years are in the middle.

The best years of adult life? Some claim the heady springtime must be the best. Looking back on early adulthood, it sparkles with romance, aspirations, adventure, and the elemental energies of life. But what of the golden years – that time of life when the work is done and the harvest is in? Looking forward to late adulthood, it glows with a relaxed and genial aura. It beckons as a time of mellow reflection retired from obligation. What time of life is best? The answer may surprise you: middle age. Forget the midlife crisis. Forget the empty nest. People in their forties and fifties have it made. If you are young, do not pity the middle-aged man with a soft waist and thinning hair or the middle-aged woman with bifocal lenses and crow's-feet wrinkles. Some day, with care and perseverance, your life may become as good as theirs.

How do we know that middle age is the best time of life? The term "best" implies a common standard of value by which we can measure and compare. The frequency of depression serves as that standard. Depression is a feeling of sadness and dejection marked by trouble sleeping, concentrating, and acting. Depression feels unpleasant; it exhausts and debilitates, sapping vitality and well-being. Depression arises from a variety of stresses and strains, from the assaults of microorganisms to the insults of dashed hopes or diminished status. Depression arouses the attention of psychiatrists when it is extreme, prolonged, or inexplicable. More commonly, depression comes and goes with the challenges and adaptations of life.

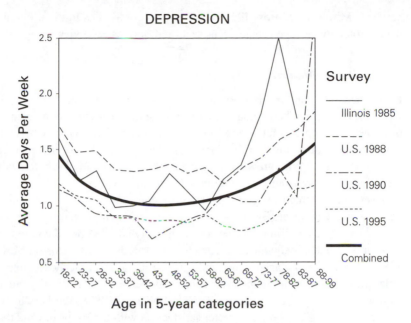

Figure 18.1. Prevalence of depression by age in four surveys with a total of 18,450 respondents, with nonlinear regression line fit in the combined samples (see the Appendix for a description of the samples).

Measured in terms of depression, middle age is the best time of life. Figure 18.1 shows the results of four surveys taken over the past ten years. The four surveys combine the reports of 18,450 American adults selected at random. (A description of the samples at the end of this chapter gives details.) Each jagged line traces the average level of depression across five-year age groups in one of the surveys. The smooth line summarizes the overall pattern (it shows the curve fit by statistical regression.) The figure shows that middle-aged Americans report a lower average frequency of depression than younger and older adults do. It looks as if depression starts relatively high in early adulthood, drops to a lifetime low somewhere in the range of 40 to 60 years old, and then rises in old age.

What makes the pattern? What accounts for the differences in depression between age groups? Explaining the pattern requires that we understand the five aspects of age, the conditions, beliefs, and emotions that affect depression, and the circumstances that characterize each part of life.

The Five Views of Age

The time elapsed since birth defines a person's age. This simple physical measure marks five distinct aspects of age: maturity, decline, life cycle, generation, and survival (Mirowsky & Ross 1992). Each aspect contributes to the differences in depression between age groups. This section describes each view of age.

Age as Maturity

People become more experienced, accomplished, and seasoned as they age. In a word, they mature. Each human sums a lifetime of experience, composing a self of elements arranged to function efficiently and successfully. Personal growth and development require time. Aging increases practice with living and the extent of self-composition. With growing insight and skill, social and psychological traits merge into an increasingly harmonious and effective whole.

Several developments suggest that maturity comes with age: lower crime rates, safer habits, a more orderly life-style, greater satisfaction, and a more positive self-image. Rates of crime decline steeply in early adulthood and continue to decline throughout subsequent ages (Hirschi & Gottfredson 1983; Ross & Mirowsky 1987). People in older age groups lead a more routine and orderly life, take fewer risks, avoid fights and arguments, drink more moderately and carefully, and refrain from the recreational use of illegal drugs (Umberson 1987). Workers in successively older age groups report greater satisfaction with their jobs beyond that due to their higher rank and pay (Kalleberg & Loscocco 1983). People in successively older age groups rate themselves more helpful, supportive, disciplined, able, and satisfied with life, as well as less emotional, nervous, and frustrated; they report greater self-esteem and, until age 75, less of a sense that life is empty and meaningless (Campbell, Converse, and Rodgers 1976; Gove, Ortega, & Style 1989).

Age as Decline

Just as humans sum and integrate experience, they also sum and integrate failures, faults, injuries, and errors. Often the slow and steady deterioration produces little apparent effect at first. Many defects accrue too slowly to notice the changes from year to year. Eventually, though, the accumulation becomes apparent, like the wrinkling of skin or the graying of hair. Many physical problems that accumulate also compound. For example, weight gained in body fat reduces physical activity and then lower physical activity increases the rate of weight gain. Accumulating and compounding decline may affect behavior and emotions, too, as a consequence of physiological decline or as an independent process (Aneshensel, Frerichs, & Huba 1984).

Several facts point to accelerating decline with advancing age. Many physical and mental abilities hold roughly stable throughout most of the adult years but erode at a slowly accelerating rate to produce substantial declines beyond age 70 (Schaie 1983). The incidence and prevalence of chronic disease increase at an accelerating rate with age (Collins 1988; Hartunian, Smart, & Thompson 1981). So does the average level of dysfunctions, such as trouble seeing, hearing, walking, lifting, climbing stairs, grasping, and manipulating (Waldron 1983; Waldron & Jacobs 1988). Those dysfunctions interfere with the performance of daily activities such as shopping, cooking, cleaning, gardening, bathing, grooming, dressing, and eating (Berkman & Breslow 1983; Guralnik & Kaplan 1989). Both the peak performance of athletes and the typical levels of physical activity among nonathletes decline (Shephard 1987). So does carbohydrate metabolism (the process that fuels the muscles), lung capacity, and bone density (Rowe & Kahn 1987). Mental functions also decline, including orientation to time and space, recall, attention, simple calculation, language comprehension, and the speed of perceptual, motor, and cognitive processes (Holzer et al. 1986; House & Robbins 1983; Rowe & Kahn 1987; Schaie 1983).

Age as Life-Cycle Stage

Age marks a person's stage in the life cycle. Human life progresses through common sequences of roles: from school to job to retirement, from single to married to widowed (Hogan 1978). Over the lifetime, adult status and prospects rise and fall. The phased roles interlock with a flow and ebb of freedoms, prerogatives, privileges, options, opportunities, scope, and resources. The achievements and acquisitions of early adulthood build the rank and prosperity of middle age that eventually erodes in the retrenchment and loss of old age.

Changes in marital, job, and economic status index the social life cycle. Most Americans begin their 18th year single, in school or recently graduated, and with little wealth or personal earnings. The progression to middle age increases the prevalence of marriage, parenthood, and employment. It generally increases the earnings of the employed and the total household income (Mirowsky & Ross 1989b). Beginning around age 60, the progression into old age sharply increases the prevalence of retirement and widowhood, thus decreasing personal earnings and total household income.

Age as Generation

Age marks a person's place in the major trends of recent history. At any given stage in their lives, the members of younger generations benefit from material, economic, and cultural progress. In the United States, twentieth-century trends increased average education, income, female employment, and life expectancy, but decreased family size and rural residence (Bianchi & Spain 1986; Sagan 1987). In the past 50 years alone, median family income (adjusted for inflation) more than doubled, life expectancy at birth increased 20%, age-adjusted annual mortality rates dropped 60%, the proportion living in rural areas dropped from 45% to 25%, total fertility rates dropped 20%, and the proportion of women in the labor force more than doubled, from 25% to over 50% (Bianchi & Spain 1986; Hoffman 1991; Sagan 1987). Fifty years ago, 6% of Americans aged 25–29 had less than five years of formal education, and only 6% had completed four years of college (Hoffman 1991). Today, under 1% has less than five years of education and 25% have at least four years of college. In 1900, one American in 10 could not read; in 1940, it was one in 25. Today, it is less than one in 100. Aggregate increases in education may have generated the favorable trends in income, life expectancy, family size, and female employment (Sagan 1987).

Age as Survival

Age indirectly indexes traits associated with differences in survival. Other things being equal, traits that confer a selective advantage become more common with age while those that confer a selective disadvantage become scarce. Being older increases the likelihood of having the traits associated with survival, particularly after age 70. Those traits may create a false impression of aging's effect, perhaps making it appear beneficial or benign when it is actually destructive. Lower survival among the most depressed groups can make aging seem less depressing than it is.

Depression and the things that cause it tend to reduce survival. Severely depressed people die at two to four times the rate of others who are similar in terms of age, sex, socioeconomic status, preexisting chronic health problems (e.g., hypertension, heart disease, stroke, and cancer), and signs of fitness (e.g., blood pressure, blood cholesterol, lung capacity, weight for height, and smoking habits) (Bruce & Leaf 1989; Somervell et al. 1989). Many of the same statuses and conditions that produce depression also reduce survival. Life expectancy at birth is 4.4 years lower for minorities than for others (and 6.4 years lower for blacks than for others) (Kessler & Neighbors 1986; Mirowsky & Ross 1990; National Center for Health Statistics 1990). Unemployment, low education, and poverty all increase the age-specific rates of mortality (Antonovsky 1967; Berkman & Breslow 1983; Comstock & Tonascia 1977; Kitagawa & Hauser 1973; Kotler & Wingard 1989; Leigh 1983; Sagan 1987). So does being divorced, separated, or widowed (Berkman & Breslow 1983; Bowling 1987; Kaprio, Koskenuo, & Rita 1987; Kotler & Wingard 1989; Litwack & Messeri 1989).

Although most traits that increase depression also reduce survival, there is one major exception: being female. Women are more depressed than men but they live an average of 6.8 years longer (Gove 1984; Radloff 1975; National Center for Health Statistics 1990; Waldron 1983).

Concentric Spheres of Experience

Depression emerges from a matrix of conditions, beliefs, and emotions that shape and define well-being. We may say that conditions, beliefs, and emotions form "concentric spheres" of experience. *Conditions* make up the most external sphere. They define the hard realities of status and circumstance that enable or restrain action (Aneshensel 1992). *Beliefs* crystallize around the hard realities, forming interpretations and mental maps that blend observation, judgment, and prediction. Beliefs form the mental bridge between external conditions and emotional response. *Emotions* arise from those beliefs. For example: poverty is a condition, hopelessness a belief, and despair an emotion. Maturity, decline, life cycle, generation, and survival define the conditions that shape beliefs and emotions.

This section describes the conditions, beliefs, and emotions that differ across age groups and affect well-being. The facts and figures come from the 1995 U.S. survey of *Aging, Status and the Sense of Control* (ASOC). References mention reports from other surveys with similar or related findings. We (the authors) designed the ASOC survey and analyzed the data. (An appendix to this chapter gives details about the ASOC.) The National Institute on Aging (NIA) funded the survey to find out why older Americans often feel helpless and depressed and how lifetime conditions and experiences shape those feelings. We hope that information from the ASOC survey will help Americans of all ages plan gratifying and productive futures for themselves and others.

Conditions

People of different ages live under very different conditions. Age is itself one of the most powerful ascribed social statuses. Society assigns many rights, obligations, and opportunities based on age. These include the right to drive, drink alcohol, get married or vote; the obligation to serve in the military, hold a job, and raise a family; and the opportunity to go to college, run for congress, or head a corporation. Law prescribes the ages for some rights, obligations, and opportunities, but tradition prescribes the ages for most. In sociological terms, society is stratified by age. Different age groups form the graduated layers in a system of responsibility and privilege.

Economic Prosperity. Our list of conditions that affect emotional well-being begins with economic prosperity. A proverb says that money cannot buy happiness. Technically this may be so. No material or symbolic reward can guarantee happiness; even the rich suffer disappointment and loss. But money goes a long way toward reducing the frequency, intensity, and duration of misery. People in need of money carry more than an equal share of society's total burden of depression (Pearlin & Schooler 1978, Pearlin et al. 1981; Ross & Huber 1985).

The competitive logic of our society guarantees that young adults need money more than others. American society is designed for achievement. For the most part, people must earn what they get. Even when society gives an advantage of birth to some over others, that advantage comes chiefly in the form of more and

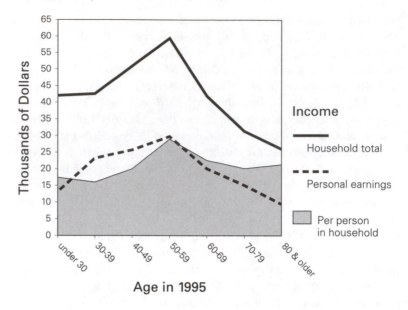

Figure 18.2. Income and earnings by age (1995 ASOC data).

better education. Rather than give money itself, Americans try to give their children a superior ability to achieve. Whatever one's advantages or disadvantages, making money takes time. Our system of competition and achievement produces a marked relationship between age and economic prosperity, illustrated in Figure 18.2. That, in turn, accounts for part of the relationship between age and depression.

Average personal earnings and household income peak in the 50–59-year-old bracket, about the same time of life when depression reaches its lowest levels. Many studies conducted since the 1950s find that higher earnings and income reduce an individual's probable level of depression (Kessler 1979, 1982; Kessler & Cleary 1980; Mirowsky & Ross 1989b; Wheaton 1978, 1980). Why? Two possibilities stand out. One is that earnings and income mark one's worth and status in the eyes of others. People judge themselves partly by seeing how others judge them. Thus, low earnings or income can feel shameful whereas higher earnings and income can feel honorable. Americans do harbor these feelings to some extent, but the main connection between economic and emotional well-being lies elsewhere. Higher earnings and income reduce depression mostly by reducing economic hardship (Ross & Huber 1985). People find it distressing to have difficulty paying the bills or buying household necessities such as food, clothing, or medicine. Economic hardship threatens one's personal security. Worse than that, it threatens the security of children, partners, and others whom one loves and sustains.

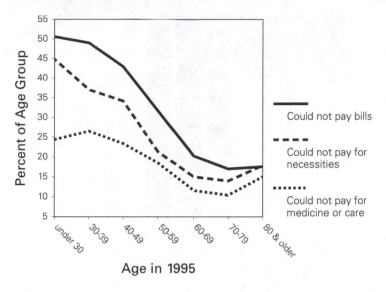

Figure 18.3. Economic hardship in past year, by age (1995 ASOC data).

Economic hardship generally decreases with older age, as shown in Figure 18.3. Young adults have by far the highest levels of economic hardship. Half say they had difficulty paying bills in the past year. About 40% report at least one period when they did not have the money to buy food, clothes, or other household necessities; 25% report a time when they did not have the money for needed medicine or medical care. The levels of economic hardship drop sharply between the ages of 40 and 60. Hardship remains relatively low among those aged 60 and older. (Even then, one person in five reports a period of economic hardship during the previous year.) Clearly, earnings and income are not the only things that determine the risk of economic hardship. The elderly have relatively low rates of hardship despite low earnings and household income for two reasons. First, older adults have fewer dependents. As shown in Figure 18.2, the amount of income per person in the household stays level above the age of 60 even though earnings and total income drop. Second, accumulated wealth and government programs such as Social Security, Medicare, and Medicaid meet many needs.

Employment. The life cycle of employment generates the rise and fall of earnings and household income. Figure 18.4 illustrates the cycle. Employment also improves emotional well-being apart from its impact on household economics. Adults employed full-time enjoy the lowest average frequency of depression (Gove & Geerken 1977; Kessler & McRae 1982; Kessler et al. 1989; Pearlin et al. 1981; Ross, Mirowsky, & Huber 1983). (Full-time employment

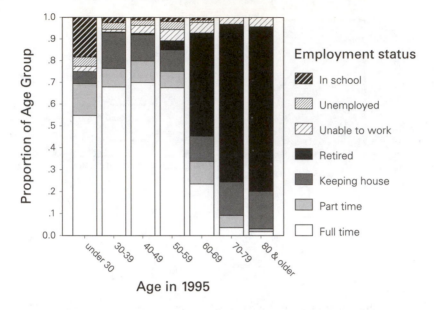

Figure 18.4. Employment status by age (1995 ASOC data).

improves physical health, too; Ross & Mirowsky 1995b). With the exception of full-time students, adults who are not employed full-time suffer from depression more frequently than those with full-time jobs. Adults who are unemployed, laid off, or unable to work because of disability carry the highest burden of depression. They experience symptoms two to four times more often than people with full-time jobs. Luckily, they comprise less than 10% of the typical random sample. Retirees and part-time employees make up much larger fractions: about 16% and 9%, respectively. Both of these groups have slightly more depression than the full-time employees but not a lot more (about 10–20%). Women keeping house make up the second largest group not employed full-time (after the retirees): about 12% of adults. Women keeping house feel depressed about 37% more often than the women and 75% more often than the men who hold full-time paying jobs. The fact that women often keep house rather than hold a full-time paying job accounts for part of the difference between men and women in frequency of depression.

The quality of a job can also affect well-being. Many aspects of paid jobs improve with age for those who remain employed. In addition to earnings, these aspects include deciding what to do or how to do it, influence over work group goals, a higher management level, greater prestige and recognition, freedom to disagree with one's supervisor, and performing tasks that are less routine or unpleasant and more interesting and enjoyable.

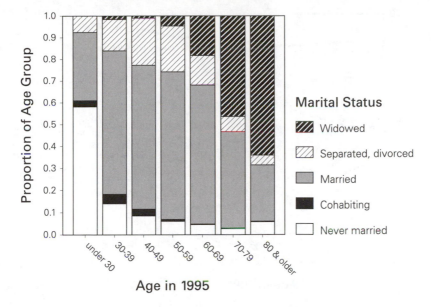

Figure 18.5. Marital status by age (1995 ASOC data).

Marriage. Marriage and family form another major aspect of the adult life cycle that affects well-being (Hughes & Gove 1981). Middle-aged adults are the ones most likely to be married, as shown in Figure 18.5. Married people feel depressed about one third less often than others. People who are recently separated or widowed feel depressed the most often, with two or three times the frequency of symptoms as married persons. The level of depression drops with time for the divorced or widowed, but it remains about 40–50% higher than among married persons. Adults who never have been married also experience about 40–50% more symptoms than those who are married. People living together with someone as if married are between the married persons and others in their frequency of symptoms.

Marriage reduces depression for two main reasons: social support and household income. Marriage improves well-being by improving emotional and economic security. Adults benefit from a partnership that provides mutual intimacy and reliance (Gove et al. 1984; Mirowsky 1985; Pearlin & Johnson 1977; Ross et al. 1990). Of course, some marriages meet these needs better than others. The quality of one's marriage affects well-being; a bad marriage can be worse than none. The quality of marriages improves with age for the ones that stay intact. Older married persons feel happier with their partners, divide housework more fairly, and think of separating less often, as shown in Figure 18.6. The quality of marriage improves with age for two reasons. First, people become more adept at

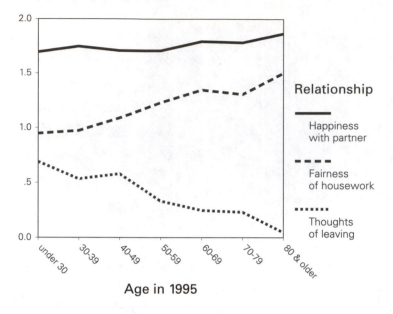

Figure 18.6. Subjective quality of marriage by age (1995 ASOC data).

managing their relationships as they mature. Second, the worst marriages break up. Learning by trial and error leads to improvement over time.

Children. Child care introduces the major strain associated with marriage (Ross & Huber 1985; Ross & Mirowsky 1988). Children improve the well-being of parents in conducive circumstances: adequate household income and a stable, supportive partnership with fair sharing of chores and sacrifices. Ready availability of affordable child care helps a lot, too. Unfortunately, a large minority of parents find themselves in circumstances far from this ideal. Some lack the money. Some lack a partner or a helpful partner. Some mothers find themselves in extremely depressing circumstances: a failed or unsupportive marriage, a low-paying job that does not accommodate family responsibilities, and no ready source of affordable child care. Adults in their 20s, 30s and 40s bear most of the child care responsibilities, as indicated by Figure 18.7. Few adults over the age of 50 have children in the household. Younger parents bear the greatest child-care strains because they have lower income and younger children who need closer attention.

Most of the conditions discussed so far define the economic and family life cycles that account for much of the relationship between age and depression. However, the changes between generations also account for some of the pattern. Increasing education leads as the most important of those changes for well-being.

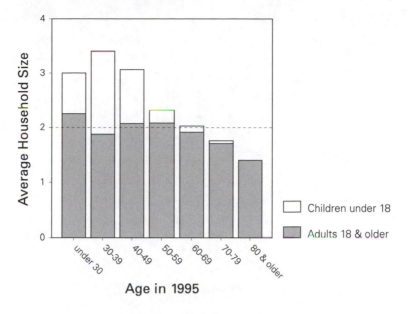

Figure 18.7. Number of children and adults in the household by age (1995 ASOC data).

Education. Younger generations benefit from higher levels of education. The frequency of depression drops with each additional year of education (Mirowsky & Ross 1990, 1992; Ross & Huber 1985). It takes an especially big step down with the high school degree. For the most part, though, it is the years of education rather than the formal degrees that make the difference. The effect of education on depression does not fade with time as people grow old. Likewise, the effect does not fade in successive generations with rising educational standards. Each additional year of education reduces the average level of depression by the same amount as does an additional $40,000 in household income. Remarkably, the education of one's parents has a similar (though smaller) lifelong effect. Each additional year of one's parents' education reduces the average depression by the same amount as an additional $10,000 in household income. Figure 18.8 shows the average education of the respondents and their parents in ten-year age categories. The middle-aged and older respondents finished about three or four years of education more than their parents did. If Americans under the age of 30 eventually do the same, they will complete an average of 16 years of education. That will do two things. It will help bring their depression down from current levels, and it will help keep their depression below the levels of previous generations at each stage in life.

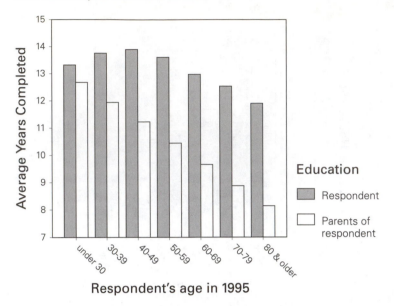

Figure 18.8. Education of the respondent and parents by age of the respondent (1995 ASOC data).

Childhood Family. The main trends of recent history generally improve the well-being of Americans with each new generation. Unfortunately, one harmful trend works against the helpful ones: the increasing breakup of childhood families. Figure 18.9 illustrates the trend. Less than 10% of the adults now in their 70s, 80s, and 90s experienced the breakup of their childhood families, yet almost 33% of the adults now in their 20s did. The death of a parent became less common in succeeding generations, but the divorce of parents increased dramatically. As with the education of one's parents, the breakup of their marriage has a lifelong effect on the frequency of depression. Adults from divorced childhood families feel depressed about 22% more often than adults from families that remained intact. The effect does not vanish as people grow older, and it does not abate as parental divorce becomes more common. The effect remains the same among young adults with a high prevalence of parental divorce as among old adults with a low prevalence. A single parent or the death of a parent have even worse effects, raising the frequency of depression by 98% and 57% respectively. (See also Brown & Harris 1978 on the lifelong effects of parental death.) Fortunately, these latter conditions remain relatively uncommon. The broken childhood family increases later depression in two ways. First, it reduces the average level of education attained compared with others of the same generation from similar backgrounds

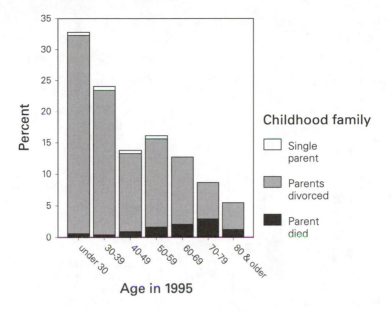

Figure 18.9. Disruption of respondent's childhood family by age at interview (1995 ASOC data).

(McLanahan & Bumpass 1988). Second, it reduces the quality and stability of the respondent's own marital relationships (Webster, Orbuch, & House 1995). Adults from divorced or never-married childhood families have more marriages of their own that they find less pleasing, fair, or promising. In fact, they feel greater mistrust and suspicion of others in general. (The death of a parent does not have these negative interpersonal effects.) Thus, the breakup of childhood families creates an intergenerational cycle that increases the prevalence of breakups, despite the harm done and in part *because* of the harm done.

Health and Physical Function. Like it or not, life comes to an end. Most people think of old age as a time of rising disease and disability leading ultimately to death. As people grow old, they feel less healthy, have more impairments and medical conditions, and expect to live fewer additional years (Mirowsky & Hu 1996; Ross & Bird 1994). A large majority of Americans over the age of 60 have a serious chronic disease such as hypertension, heart disease, diabetes, cancer, osteoporosis, or arthritis. About 70% report some difficulty with common activities such as carrying a bag of groceries, and almost a fourth report a severe impairment of some type. Most physical problems increase in prevalence and severity with age. (There are a few welcome exceptions: older people report fewer headaches

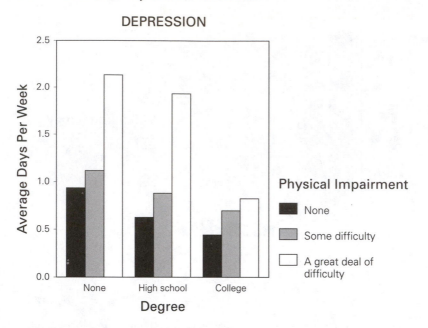

Figure 18.10. Depression by level of education and physical impairment (1995 ASOC data).

and allergies.) The problems take many forms: discomforting aches and pains, threatening diagnoses, disabling impairments, and a shortening future. People find all of these depressing, but impairments are the worst by far. Serious impairment can triple the frequency of depression, as shown in Figure 18.10. Even moderate difficulty climbing stairs, kneeling, carrying, walking, hearing, seeing, or the like increases depression as much as not having finished high school. A major disability produces as great an effect as that of not finishing high school, marital breakup, and economic hardship combined. Impairment depresses employment-aged adults the most, but the majority of them are unimpaired and few have serious difficulties. The burden of impairment lies heaviest on the oldest adults.

There is some good news about physical impairment. Rising levels of education may reduce both the amount of impairment and its impact on well-being (Ross & Wu 1995). Figures 18.10 and 18.11 compare people with a high school degree to those with more and with less education. Those with college degrees appear to cope with impairment much better than others, as Figure 18.10 suggests. Furthermore, education seems to slow the rise of impairment with age, as shown in Figure 18.11. People with college degrees have about the same level of impairment in their 70s as high school graduates in their 60s and as high school dropouts in

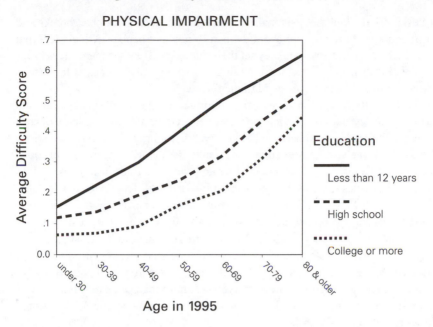

Figure 18.11. Physical impairment by education and age (1995 ASOC data).

their 40s. Rising levels of education may help today's younger generations delay impairment longer and manage it better.

Beliefs and Emotions

The members of different age groups live under different conditions that influence their beliefs and emotions. The various conditions just described combine to produce the fall and rise of depression across age groups. Together those external conditions shape beliefs and stimulate emotions that produce the age-group differences in depression. Mostly they work through two channels: the sense of controlling one's own life and the feelings of anger and anxiety. As detailed next, old adults suffer from a lack of control; young adults suffer from an excess of anger and anxiety.

Sense of Control. The perception of directing and regulating one's own life varies by degree, ranging from fatalism and a deep sense of powerlessness and helplessness to instrumentalism and a firm sense of mastery and self-efficacy (Mirowsky & Ross 1989b, 1990, 1991; Rodin 1990). Some people feel that any good things that happen are mostly luck – fortunate outcomes they desire but do not design. They feel that personal problems mostly result from bad breaks and feel little ability to regulate or avoid the bad things that happen. Others feel that they can do just about anything they set their minds to. They see themselves as responsible for their own successes and failures, viewing misfortunes as the results of personal mistakes they can avoid in the future.

This sense of control links the socioeconomic, interpersonal, behavioral, and physiological systems. It is the human awareness at their hub. A firm sense of control averts the tendency to become helpless in frustrating and aversive situations (Hiroto 1974). It also decreases autonomic reactivity. A low sense of control correlates with higher circulating catecholamines and corticosteroids in humans, as does learned helplessness in both humans and animals (Gold, Goodwin, & Chrousos 1988a,b; Rodin 1986a,b). The catecholamine norepinephrine (noradrenaline) is implicated in depression and anxiety. The anti-inflammatory corticosteroid cortisol (hydrocortisone) may produce sleep disorders related to depression, particularly those involving agitation and early-morning rising (Greden et al. 1983). Cortisol regulates the metabolism of cholesterol (its parent compound), mobilizing energy to resist stress (Steward 1986). Improving the sense of control of nursing-home patients lowers their odds of dying by a factor of 2.5 (18-month follow-up) (Rodin 1986a,b).

Certain objective conditions create a sense of detachment from one's own actions and outcomes that people find demoralizing and distressing (Erikson 1986; Mirowsky & Ross 1989b; Seeman 1959, 1983). Many of those conditions represent classic interests of sociology such as alienated labor, powerlessness, structural inconsistency, dependency, and so on. Structural social psychology looks for alienating situations that undermine the individual's sense of control (Kohn et al. 1990; Kohn & Slomczynski 1990; Mirowsky & Ross 1983, 1984, 1990; Pearlin et al. 1981; Rosenfield 1989; Ross & Mirowsky 1992; Wheaton 1980). Old age is one such situation.

The average sense of control declines sharply among Americans over 50, as shown in Figure 18.12 (Mirowsky 1995; Mirowsky & Ross 1990, 1991). Adults younger than 50 typically report a firm sense of directing and regulating their own lives. They see themselves as responsible for their own successes and failures and usually view their misfortunes as the results of personal mistakes that can be avoided in the future. In older age groups, the balance of perceived control shifts from a sense of mastery toward one of helplessness, from instrumentalism toward fatalism.

A number of factors come together to produce the low sense of control observed among old Americans. They represent many aspects of age, including physical decline, the life cycle of employment, earnings, and marriage, and the generational trends in education and in women's employment. Health problems account for much of it. Subjective life expectancy has the single biggest effect on the sense of control. The less time people expect to live, the less they feel in control of their own

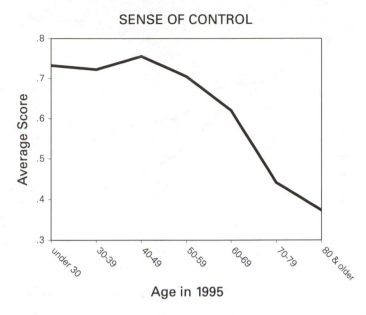

Figure 18.12. Sense of control over personal events and outcomes by age (1995 ASOC data).

lives and outcomes. People find it hard to plan for a future that looks short; hard to manage a life that might end soon. Physical impairments have the next biggest effect. Difficulty performing common daily tasks puts real limits on personal control. A general feeling of health and fitness bolsters the sense of control, but sickness and disease undermine that feeling. Specific diagnoses such as heart disease, cancer, or arthritis reduce the sense of control by making people feel sick, impaired, or near the end of life. Social and economic losses undermine the sense of control, too. Widows feel less in control of their own lives than do married people of the same age. A full-time job, substantial personal earnings, and employee medical insurance all increase the sense of control, but they become scarce as people grow old.

A large fraction of the fatalism and powerlessness that characterizes the elderly comes from having lived in harder times (Mirowsky 1995). Members of older generations had lower education than is common today, and they were raised by parents who had even less. Both forms of human capital affect the sense of control. Together, personal and parental education account for about a third of the association between old age and low sense of control. For women, the history of employment contributes, too. Retirees who held full-time paying jobs most of their lives feel more in control than those who did not. Women who are over the age of 70 lived in a period when few women held full-time jobs during most of the years before retirement.

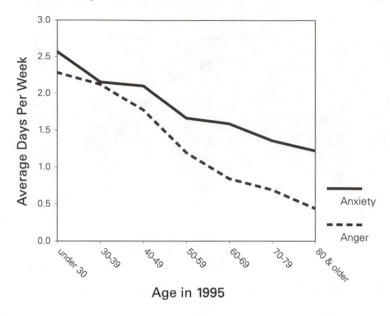

Figure 18.13. Prevalence of anxiety and anger by age (1995 ASOC data).

Anxiety and Anger. Just as fatalism and helplessness tarnish old age, anxiety and anger tarnish early adulthood. Restlessness and worry find close companions in hostility and ire (Conger et al. 1993; Gove 1978; Mirowsky & Ross 1995). Young adults report double the old-age frequency of anxiety and triple the frequency of anger, as shown in Figure 18.13. Much of the tension revolves around marriage, children, and money. People start having children at a time in life when money is scarce, jobs are uncertain, and relationships are unseasoned. Children often increase the need for money while decreasing the household income. That income is greatest when both parents remain employed full-time with no prolonged absence from employment. Many women suspend full-time employment when they have children, which reduces the income available for supporting the children. In addition to creating economic strains, children engage parents in conflict over behavior and instigate conflict between parents over housework and child care. These tensions sorely test even the strongest parental relationships and break many others.

Well-Being across the Life Course

Adulthood begins as a time of hopes and tensions as people acquire full adult status. Young adults must complete an education, establish an occupation and household, acquire recognition and prosperity, and develop marriage and family relations that profit all involved. The overwhelming majority of young Americans feel in control of their lives, responsible for their outcomes, and able to meet the challenges of life. For most, the trials and errors lead to improvements that create a steady decline in tensions.

Late in life, in old age, people walk a narrowing path. Those who proceed with health, function, wealth, and marriage intact find old age an enjoyable time of relaxation and companionship. Even those who lose a spouse or suffer a medical crisis often rebuild a gratifying life within a year or two. But physical impairment can impose demoralizing limitations; the shorter and less certain life appears, the less it seems possible to recover and rebuild. Well-being in old age rests on economic, interpersonal, and physical fitness built throughout adult life. For those of us not yet old, now is the time to build.

Late middle age marks the time of life when everything comes together. Earnings and household income reach a peak. The children are grown and probably out of the house. Marriages are more congenial and less discordant; jobs are more secure and enjoyable. The tensions and conflicts of young adulthood have abated, and the problems of old age have not arisen. That is why the best years of adult life are the years in the middle.

Appendix: Description of the Samples

The 1995 U.S. survey of *Aging, Status and the Sense of Control* (ASOC) used randomly dialed households to select a national sample of 1,405 persons aged 18–59 and 1,098 persons aged 60–95. The ASOC survey is supported by a grant from the National Institute on Aging (AG 12393; Principal Investigators John Mirowsky and Catherine E. Ross). All of the findings reported in the section on "Concentric Spheres of Emotions" and its figures (18.2–18.13) come from analyses of the ASOC data.

The 1990 U.S. survey of *Work, Family, and Well-Being* (WFW) also randomly dialed households to select 2,031 respondents ranging in age from 18 to 90. The WFW survey was supported by a grant from the National Science Foundation (SES-8916154; Principal Investigator Catherine E. Ross).

The 1988–89 *National Survey of Families and Households* (NSFH) randomly chose census blocks and then households within those blocks for 13,017 face-to-face interviews (Sweet, Bumpass, & Call 1988). Of these, 12,752 provided sufficient information on age and depression for analysis. The NSFH is conducted under a grant from the Center for Population Research of the National Institute of Child Health and Human Development (HD 21009; Principal Investigators James A. Sweet and Larry L. Bumpass).

The 1985 *Illinois Survey of Well-Being* (ISW) used randomly dialed households in Chicago and its suburbs, as well as randomly selected numbers from current telephone directories in all other areas of Illinois, for a total of 809 respondents ranging in age from 18 to 85. The ISW was supported by the University of Illinois Research Board (Principal Investigators Catherine E. Ross and John Mirowsky).

19

Gender and Mental Health: Do Women Have More Psychopathology, Men More, or Both the Same (and Why)?

Sarah Rosenfield

Are there differences between men and women in mental health? Rosenfield shows how classical psychoanalytical theory and more recent developmental approaches answer this question. In contrast, social theorists focus on how the different positions men and women hold as adults affect mental health. While there are no differences in their overall *rates* of psychopathology, men and women do differ in terms of the *type* of psychopathology experienced. Women have higher rates of depression and anxiety (referred to as "internalizing" disorders), and men have higher rates of substance abuse and antisocial disorders (also called "externalizing" disorders). Rosenfield considers various explanations for these gender differences. Divisions in power and responsibilities are critical; women earn less relative to men, tend to have jobs with less power and autonomy, and are more responsive to problems of people in their social networks – all of which can contribute to psychological distress. An unresolved question is whether men and women have different reactions to similar situations, or whether they face different circumstances and stressors. Rosenfield concludes by suggesting that socializing practices that encourage high self-regard and mastery, along with a strong regard for others' interests and well-being, would most benefit the mental health of both men and women. Students may want to discuss their own socialization into "appropriate" feminine and masculine behaviors.

Among the most profound social divisions in our culture is the one we make by gender. Whether we are male or female shapes our access to resources and our life choices and options. It colors the ways we relate to others, what people expect of us, and what we expect of ourselves. Clearly, then, this division should affect our internal states and compasses: the way we feel about ourselves, how we experience the world, and our emotional reactions. Because our social practices are fundamentally gendered, mental health and emotional troubles should also differ for men and women.

For some time, however, there have been heated debates over the differences between mental health of men and women. Some argue that women have more psychopathology than men, and some claim men have more. Others think that both sexes suffer equally but from different maladies. In debates about cause, some claim that biology creates sex differences in personal problems, and some look to psychological reasons. Others hold that social experiences spawn any diversity. Finally, in debates over social causes, some argue that men and women's troubles result from encountering very different life circumstances and stresses. Others claim that the sexes face similar trials but react to them differently. Evidence on these debates ultimately points us toward the situations that are best for the mental health and well-being of men and women. With that in mind, this chapter focuses on these questions and that evidence.

Do Women Have More Psychopathology Than Men, or Men More, or Both the Same but Different Types?

There are intense disagreements about which sex is psychologically superior or inferior to the other. Freud was probably the first to design a systematic theory comparing men and women's mental health. Classical Freudian theory holds that men are superior to women psychically – a view that persists among many today. For those reasons, I start this debate with Freud's approach.

Generally, Freud posits that humans acquire a separate sense of self – including an ego and a superego – in the course of several stages of development. In the phallic stage of development (around ages 3–5), an event occurs that marks the beginning of a radical distinction between the sexes in the nature of the self. This event involves children's recognition of the genital differences between males and females. At this point, boys are indifferent to or deny the sight of the female genitals (Freud 1959a). For girls, however, this discovery is a major crisis in their development. In Freud's words, girls "notice the penis of a brother or playmate, strikingly visible and of large proportions, at once recognize it as a superior counterpart to their own small and inconspicuous organ, and from that time forward fall victim to envy for the penis" (Freud 1959a: 190). The "normal" outcome of this crisis for girls is hostility and resentment toward their mother for bringing them into the world "so ill-equipped." As a result, the girl turns from her mother to her father as her primary love object, which forms the female Oedipus complex (Freud 1949, 1959a,b, 1966a).

For boys, the dynamics of development are less complicated. A boy's crisis in the phallic stage comes when his attachment to the mother intensifies and becomes more sexual in tone (Freud 1949). This desire for the mother and the resulting rivalry with the father constitutes the Oedipal situation for boys. In trying to deflect this situation, the parents threaten the boy with castration, which is taken seriously only when he recalls the earlier sight of female genitals (Freud 1949, 1959a). This results in the castration complex, in which the boy perceives that the girl has been castrated and therefore believes that the threat to himself is real. The boy renounces his desire for possession of the mother and represses the Oedipus complex (Freud 1949). As the replacement for this loss, the child identifies with the authority of the father and with the position that he will some day inherit. This identification with the morals and standards of the father forms the basis for the superego or conscience (Freud 1959a,c).

There are several ways that girls or boys can veer off these normal paths of development. But only for females is the normal path itself flawed. According to Freud, women are stunted in both ego and superego development. In turning toward the father, girls repress active sexual impulses, which results in passivity as a personality characteristic (Freud 1959b). Similarly, the shift from mother to father attachment involves turning aggression toward the self, resulting in masochistic tendencies (Freud 1966b). The wound to girls' self-image in discovering they have no penis predisposes them to more vanity and jealousy than boys (Freud 1959a). Finally, there is no force comparable to the castration complex in boys to motivate girls to give up the Oedipal complex: they may remain in this situation indefinitely (Freud 1959a). Since the superego depends on resolving the Oedipal situation, girls have an underdeveloped superego and less of a sense of justice than males.

Although some of Freud's own followers criticized his positions on women (see e.g. Horney 1926 and Thompson 1942), more recent systematic approaches turn his general views upside down. Daniel Stern (1985) questions the basic assumptions of Freudian theory as well as most current theories of development (see e.g. Erikson 1950 and Kohlberg 1969). All of these theories assume that humans start out totally connected to the world around them, especially their mothers, unable to make a distinction between themselves and the external world. Mature, successful development involves becoming an independent, self-sufficient, autonomous adult. This version of development links what we think of as masculine (autonomous, separate) with mature, developed selves and links what we think of as feminine (connected, attached to others) with immature, undeveloped selves. Therefore, these basic assumptions about how people develop favor males and produce the view that male psychology is superior. Stern (1985) proposes instead that humans start out as separate, unconnected creatures and become more and more attached to those around them over time. A recent theory from the Stone Center at Wellesley takes this a step further. The self-in-relation theory posits that females' sense of self is based strongly in connections to others. Using this as a standard, the hallmark of maturity is the development of greater and greater complexity in relationships over time (Jordan et al. 1991). Thus, the model of development is reversed in these approaches. Connections with others is the mark of maturity; the model of male as superior is replaced with a model of female as superior.

Some argue that models of female superiority are just as problematic and insidious as models of male superiority. Either way, they piece apart the world and set up destructive hierarchies (Tavris 1992). A few theories, in contrast, attempt to disadvantage neither sex by emphasizing the problems and strengths in both male and female development. Nancy Chodorow's object relations theory (1978) is probably the best known of these. Chodorow claims that certain positive and negative characteristics of females and males come from the fact that women are mostly responsible for parenting. Out of their presumed similarity, mothers tend to identify more strongly with their daughters than with their sons. Because of this overidentification, mothers often hold daughters back from experiences of independence. Sons, in contrast, are pushed away into a position of independence too early. These different ways of treating daughters and sons underlie the development of the self, which is reinforced later by more obvious forms of socialization. Girls experience a greater preoccupation with their relationships with others. This gives them a lifetime capacity for rich social connections, more flexible boundaries between themselves and others, and a large capacity for empathy. Boys' greater separateness and distance set them up to adapt effectively to the work world. However, each sex also suffers from tendencies toward problematic extremes. The overembeddedness and lack of separation for girls leads to dependency on others for a sense of self. Low self-esteem also results from identification with a mother whose own self-regard is often low and whose social position is undervalued (Chodorow 1974). Boys, on the other hand, experience problems with and fears of emotional connection. In sum, Chodorow writes that the result of present family structures for girls and boys, respectively, are "either ego-boundary confusion, low self-esteem, and overwhelming relatedness to others, or compulsive denial of any connection to others or dependence upon them" (Chodorow 1974: 66).

These theories represent the three general views on gender and mental health. Although there are disputes within each of these approaches, they illustrate the positions that women exceed men in psychopathology, that men exceed women, and that both men and women experience problems but of different types. These theories focus on childhood development specifically. Other ideas about gender and mental health concentrate on adult social positions and experiences.

What Situations in Adulthood Could Shape Psychopathology in Men and Women?

In order to understand how adult experiences shape male and female emotional make-up, we first examine the broader social forces that affect them. To start, I give a brief historical perspective on some of the definitions of gender we now take for granted.

The rise of industrial capitalism in the 1800s heralded a shift of major consequence in the social situations of males and females. Before this, both men and women produced goods within the home. In addition to raising children, women had central productive responsibilities along with men. With industrialization, the workplace became divided from the home. Men began to leave home to work and women stayed to care for the children and the household. This seemingly simple split in the realms of men and women had ramifications throughout all levels of social and personal life. The productive work of the public sphere became primarily associated with males and masculinity. The socioemotional work and domestic labor of the private sphere became primarily linked with females and femininity. A so-called cult of domesticity arose to validate the assignment of women to the private sphere. This primarily middle-class ideology dictated that women were fragile and emotional beings and that children required their mothers' (not fathers') special care for moral and psychic development. Thus it was that public and private realms became divided and gendered: men belonged in the realm of economic productivity and women belonged in the realm of emotions, social relations, and caretaking.

This division of public and private has had strong implications for power differences between the sexes. The economic resources of the public sphere are more transferable than the socioemotional resources of the private sphere (Lennon & Rosenfield 1994). Money is a resource that can be used or transferred within any context, exchanged for the same rewards, and accumulated without limit. In contrast, caretaking skills and emotional sensitivity are resources that are tailored to particular individuals – one's specific husband, children, or friends – and are not easily transferable to other individuals or extended indefinitely. In this sense, the economic resources of the public sphere bring greater power, and are hence more socially valued, than the socioemotional resources of the private sphere. Since males and females are split along public–private lines, they hold different amounts of power and esteem in the social eye (Blood & Wolfe 1966; Rosenfield 1995).

These differences in power and responsibilities have ramifications for myriad life circumstances – both chronic difficulties and events – that could shape divergent psychological troubles. For example, women's income is less than men's overall, whether we look at labor-force earnings or at how money is distributed within the family to husbands versus wives and children. In the labor force, women earn less than men even in jobs requiring comparable training and experience, a wage gap due in part to the devaluation of women's skills (Kilbourne et al. 1994). Often, income is also divided unequally within the family, with husbands receiving more than wives, who spend larger proportions of their share on their children (Becker 1976). Scores of studies attest to the negative effects of low income on mental health (see Chapter 14 in this volume).

The division of public and private spheres also results in women's greater responsibility for domestic labor, regardless of their employment status. Most women are employed currently, including those with small children. Women do the bulk – an average of 66% – of child care and housework, even if they work hours comparable to their husbands outside the home (Lennon & Rosenfield 1994; Pleck 1985). Employed women sleep half an hour less per night and do an extra month of 24-hour days' work each year (Hochschild & Machung 1989).

The separation of spheres by gender also has consequences for the social relationships of males and females. Consistent with their identification with the private sphere, women maintain more social ties that are emotionally intimate (Belle 1987;

Turner 1981). Although such ties bring women support that benefits well-being, they also bring sources of negative interactions, such as conflicts, demands, and guilt (Cohen & Wills 1985; Turner 1981; Turner 1994).

Differences in power and connections connote different experiences for men and women even within the same social institutions. For example, given the general distribution of economic and social resources between the sexes, marriage has different implications for men and women. On the whole, women more than men depend on marriage for financial security. Men more than women depend on marriage for socioemotional sustenance. Research on divorce clearly reveals these differences. Both husband and wife suffer high distress when their marriage dissolves. But it is the greater loss of income with the dissolution of marriage that causes women to be depressed and anxiety-ridden. The greater loss of social support from the marriage causes men to suffer distress. Negative reactions occur, but for the very different reasons based in the circumstances of marriage for males and females (Gerstel, Riessman, & Rosenfield 1985).

Given These Ideas about Sex Differences in Childhood and Adulthood, What Is the Evidence on Sex Differences in Mental Health?

Several recent large-scale epidemiological studies have assessed the rates of mental disorders in the United States (Kessler 1993; Kessler et al. 1993; Kessler et al. 1994). Taking all psychological disorders together, these studies show that there are no differences overall in men and women's rates of psychopathology. This also holds for some of the most severe disorders such as schizophrenia. It is therefore clear from the evidence that neither sex is worse off than the other overall.

However, there are sex differences in particular types of psychiatric disorders. Women have higher rates of depression and anxiety than men. This includes both milder and more severe forms of depression, as well as most types of anxiety, including generalized anxiety disorder and phobias. On the other hand, men have higher rates than women of substance abuse and antisocial disorders. This includes both alcohol and other drug abuse as well as antisocial personality disorder, the recent term for people formerly called psychopaths or sociopaths. What do these differences mean? Greater depression means that more women than men live with feelings of profound sadness and loss. It means women have serious problems with negative self-concept and suffer feelings of guilt, self-reproach, and self-blame much more often than men. Women experience a great loss of energy, motivation, and interest in life more often than men. They feel more often that life is hopeless, coupled with a deep sense of helplessness to improve their circumstances. They more often have trouble concentrating. They have problems with sleeping and with their appetites, both of which can be too much or too little. They suffer more often from feelings of great anxiety, ranging from fears of specific objects or situations (phobias) to panic attacks and free-floating anxiety states that attach themselves to seemingly random thoughts and situations (APA 1994).

In contrast, men more frequently consume excessive amounts of alcohol and other drugs – in both quantity and frequency – than women. They more often experience extreme physical consequences from substances, such as blackouts or hallucinations. Drugs or alcohol interfere with their lives more often, causing problems at work or school or in the family. They are more likely to be dependent on a substance, needing to use more and more to get the same effect, and to have serious psychological or physical consequences from attempts to stop it. Furthermore, men are more likely to have enduring personality traits that are antisocial in character. They are more often aggressive or antisocial in a wide range of areas, beginning at an early age, with accompanying problems in forming close, enduring relationships (APA 1994).

Some researchers group the disorders in which men and women vary into more general categories. The cluster of disorders in which women exceed men are called *internalizing* disorders, because the problematic feelings focus more on the self. Disorders in which males predominate are called *externalizing* disorders, as problematic emotions are expressed in outward behavior rather than turned against the self. Given these findings on sex differences in psychopathology, we move to research on the explanations for these differences.

What Evidence Is There Concerning Reasons for Sex Differences in Psychological Disorder?

Sex differences in externalizing and internalizing disorders are remarkably wide-ranging and consistent. They are found not only in the United States but also in other cultures. They cut across both urban and rural areas. They appear in recent studies as well as studies done in the past. Because these differences have been so tenacious across so many populations, many argue for a biological root. For this reason, we first consider physical explanations. Evidence that sex differences begin in adolescence suggests the role of hormonal differences (Kessler et al. 1993). Biological studies have tried to link women's hormones to their higher rates of depression. Even though some women experience depressive symptoms during premenstrual periods and the postpartum period, this increase is not enough to account for women's overall excess in depression. Thus, women's greater rates cannot completely be explained by physical differences between males and females (Brooks-Gunn & Warren 1989; Nolen-Hoeksema 1987; Paikoff, Brooks-Gunn, & Warren 1991).

Although there is little evidence for a biological cause of sex differences in depressive disorders, we lack direct information about the role of biology in men's predominance in substance abuse and antisocial behavior. However, there is another way to test whether sex differences are biologically versus socially caused. If sex differences are socially caused, these differences should change under certain social conditions. Since many speculate that conventional gender roles underlie women's higher rates of depression, one test is to examine sex differences when men and women are in more and less conventional roles. One such study compared married couples in which wives are employed to couples in which wives are homemakers. The study used data collected in the 1960s, when women's employment was a nonconventional role (Rosenfield 1980). Overall, in this research, husbands had significantly lower scores than wives on depressive symptomatology. In addition, when wives were homemakers, their scores were much higher than their husbands'. However, when wives were employed, the sex differences reversed: wives who were employed had lower scores on depression and anxiety than their husbands. Similar reversals between husbands and wives occurred in relation to anger. When wives were homemakers, husbands had higher rates of anger, whereas employed wives reported more anger than their husbands.

Other research demonstrates that sex differences change depending on marital status as well as employment status. A recent study finds that married men and married women are significantly different in distress – which is a combination of depressive and anxious symptoms – with men having lower rates. However, single women and single men experience similar levels of distress symptoms. Furthermore, although married women score relatively high in depression, they drink less. Thus, different social statuses are associated with very different rates of psychological problems both between and within the sexes (Horwitz, White, & Howell-White 1996b).

The evidence from these studies shows that men and women do not always have higher rates of typically sex-linked disorders, and that under certain social conditions they have the same or reversed rates. This kind of evidence counteracts a biological argument for sex differences and points to social causes. It further leads us to the evidence about what exact social causes account for these differences.

What Does Research Show about the Social Situations of Males and Females That Leads Them to Different Psychiatric Disorders? Do Men and Women Face Fundamentally Different Kinds of Life Circumstances, or Do They React Differently to the Same Circumstances?

Differences in Life Circumstances

There is evidence that the divisions in power and responsibilities just discussed have implications for the different psychiatric problems among males and females. When women *or* men earn less in general and less relative to their spouses, they experience more symptoms of depression and anxiety (Rosenfield 1989, 1992a). That women more often earn less than their husbands contributes to their greater rates of distress (Rosenfield 1989). Consistent with their differential earnings, women also tend to have jobs with less autonomy and less complexity than men. Both low complexity and low autonomy on the job decrease psychological well-being (Lennon 1987; Lennon & Rosenfield 1992; Pugliesi 1995). In this sense, women have problematic job conditions and low income, both of which disadvantage mental health.

Furthermore, women's greater responsibility for the private sphere, regardless of employment status, results in an overload of demands. The result of such role overload is greater levels of depressive and anxious symptoms in women (Rosenfield 1992a). The stress of managing often unpredictable child care arrangements also takes a psychological toll, and women who have trouble with such arrangements suffer high levels of distress (Mirowsky & Ross 1988, 1989b). In contrast, when child care is secure and when husbands share the work at home, women's symptoms of distress resemble men's. Thus, a part of women's excess in depression and anxiety appears to be the typically greater overload of work and family demands.

Finally, the negative aspects of women's closer social ties and connectedness contributes to their higher rates of psychological distress. In general, the negative aspects of social ties have a stronger destructive effect on well-being than the positive effect of supportive aspects (Rook 1984). Because the bad parts can offset the good, women do not profit overall from their greater social ties (Turner 1994). In addition, women experience more distress about the problems of those they care about than do men (Kessler, McLeod, & Wethington 1985a). For this reason also, women do not necessarily benefit in well-being and may actually suffer greater anxiety and depression – what some call the "costs of caring" – from their closer social connections (Kessler et al. 1985a; Turner 1994).

Why are these circumstances differentiating the sexes so problematic for mental health? One reason is that each of them – income and job autonomy, role overload, and the nature of social relations – affects personal resources that are crucial for well-being (Pearlin et al. 1981). These personal resources include basic dimensions of the self such as our sense of self-esteem and mastery over the world. Pearlin and colleagues (1981) describe self-conceptions of self-esteem and mastery as fundamental goals to enhance and protect the self, measuring the destructiveness of life circumstances by how much they damage these self-concepts (Pearlin et al. 1981). Recall that, in theories (such as Chodorow's) of childhood development, these dimensions are also central for shaping sex differences. Experiencing few opportunities for independence in childhood, or being overwhelmed by demands and trapped by low power in adulthood, compromises feelings of having control over one's life. This low sense of control, in turn, generates the sense of hopelessness and helplessness that characterizes depression (Rosenfield 1989). Also, in childhood or adolescence, difficulties with significant others – who are a primary source of our opinions about ourselves – can produce the low self-esteem that typifies depressive reactions (Mead 1934; Rosenfield & Wenzel 1996).

Summarizing so far, it is easy to notice that we have concentrated on the disadvantages for females of the gendered division of spheres. This is in part because, although both sexes suffer from the limitations inherent in dividing the world by gender, women's lower power has particularly damaging effects. For example, women suffer more than men from marital dissolution even when both male-linked symptoms such as drinking and female-linked symptoms such as depression are considered (Horwitz et al. 1996b). However, there is also a dearth of research on sex differences in disorders that characterize men. The study I just mentioned demonstrates the importance of considering both. Although women suffer more overall from marital dissolution, their rates are highest when only depressive symptoms are considered and are somewhat less when both depression and drinking are examined (Horwitz et al. 1996b). The most balanced account of the consequences of social experiences, therefore, must evaluate both male-dominated and female-dominated disorders (Aneshensel et al. 1991). Another study demonstrates that, though men are considered to be privileged overall by this division, there are serious costs of gender divisions for men as well as women. Like women, men experience great stress when they are faced with requirements associated with the opposite sex. In a study of medical students, male students increased their drinking when they had to begin caring for patients (Richman & Rospenda 1991). The few other studies that consider both men's and women's types of disorders focus on differences in reactions.

Differences in Reactions

Sex differences in power and responsibilities also shape men's and women's responses to the same circumstances, which could account for their divergent troubles. First, the meaning of circumstances can color the reactions of men and women, especially if they threaten cherished goals and ideals (Brown & Harris 1978). Thus, for example, women's greater responsibility for caretaking and for domestic life can make problems with their children particularly stressful. Thoits (1992) suggests that situations that challenge valued aspects of the self – what she calls identity-relevant stressors – are especially destructive. Applying this to gender, there are different meanings for males and females in combining work and parent roles (Simon 1995). Men's conceptions of themselves as a paid worker are consistent with their conceptions of being a good parent. They see breadwinning as part of their parental role. For women, paid work and being a parent overlap less – income is not as central to their notion of parenting. Because of these different social conceptions, women with children more often experience intense internal conflicts and challenges to identity when they are employed. These reactions in turn contribute to their higher levels of distress in combining these roles compared with their husbands (Simon 1995).

As I have suggested, certain personal resources – which can be mobilized in the face of difficulties – vary by sex. Low self-regard and personal control increase the risk of depression in particular: threatening events loom even larger when we doubt ourselves and our ability to handle situations (Rosenfield 1992a; Rotter 1966; Thoits 1995a). Women on the whole are lower in their self-esteem and perceptions of personal control than men. Such differences in reacting to stress clearly account for some of the sex differentials in the rates of depressive disorders.

Consistent with this, men and women differ also in very specific strategies for coping with stress. Men are more stoic and less expressive in their responses to stressors than women. They more often try to control the problem, accept the problem, not think about the situation, and to engage in problem-solving efforts. Women more often pray, solicit social support, express their feelings, and try to distract themselves (Thoits 1995a). Overall, coping strategies that reflect a high sense of mastery, such as problem-solving efforts and attempts to control the problem, are associated with lower depression and may help explain men's lower rates (Folkman & Lazarus 1980; Kessler et al. 1985a). However, certain strategies are more effective for certain kinds of problems (Mattlin et al. 1990; Pearlin & Schooler 1978). Generally, strategies that keep partners engaged are most effective for interpersonal problems. For impersonal problems like those on the job, coping mechanisms that allow distancing or devaluation of the problem are most helpful. In this sense, women's typical coping techniques stand them in good stead for dealing with problems in relationships; men's techniques benefit them for dealing with problems at work. We see the division of spheres again reflected in this distribution. We also see that flexibility in coping may be the most effective strategy of all, allowing one to use the best technique for the specific problem at hand.

Finally, in relation to responses to stress, some question whether the different disorders of males and females really reflect different circumstances or instead different normative reactions to the same circumstances. Norms for the expression of emotion, or what are called "feeling rules," vary dramatically for men and women and may prompt different responses even to similar situations. Males are expected to suppress emotions in general, and especially those defined as feminine and weak. Thus, men are discouraged from showing feelings like helplessness, worry, and insecurity – all of which are associated with anxiety and depression. Anger is somewhat more tolerated even though not welcomed. In contrast, emotions such as fear and helplessness – consistent with anxiety and depression – are more normative for women. Cross-sex emotions such as anger and antisocial behavior are discouraged. We can witness the operation of these norms clearly when men and women display the "wrong" emotional problems for their sex. For example, men who come into psychiatric emergency rooms with depressive symptoms are hospitalized at much higher rates than women with the same symptomatology. Likewise, women who come in with antisocial disorders or substance abuse are more likely to be hospitalized than men with the same problems. These cases of double deviance are treated much more severely, showing us there are norms even in deviating (Rosenfield 1984).

Some argue that these feeling rules leave men and women little choice in expressing their troubles. For example, since open displays of anxiety and depression are relatively forbidden, men may attempt to hide, remove, shorten, or deflect any such feelings. Drinking accomplishes this goal, under the cover of relative acceptability. For these reasons, some see substance abuse as a male version of depression, that is, a gender-equivalent expression of depression (Horwitz et al. 1996b). Both come from the same underlying feelings, one allowing direct expression and the other indirect. As some evidence of this, low-level jobs increase psychological distress for women and increase drinking for men. Thus, the same problematic circumstances can produce divergent disorders in men and women (Lennon 1987).

In summary, the evidence supports claims that males and females have different disorders because they encounter different social experiences *and* because they have different kinds of reactions to circumstances. This brings us to our last issue: identifying situations that are most beneficial for the mental health of men and women.

What Are the Best Situations for Men's and Women's Mental Health?

Based on the evidence presented here, we can point out some conditions that are positive for women and for men. The same principles hold for both sexes: greater power and reasonable levels of demands are beneficial for mental health. Thus, for women or men, one positive situation is full-time employment when there are no children in the home. Women who are employed part-time with kids at home also seem to be in good shape (Rosenfield 1989). Those women who work full-time with kids at home benefit only if they have secure child-care arrangements or if their husbands share in the domestic labor. There is, however, some evidence of negative effects for men when household labor is shared (Rosenfield 1992a). Thus, since men and women gain and lose (respectively) from the same conditions, a danger is trading off benefits for one sex at the expense of the other.

Within the workplace, high job autonomy and complexity – as well as low time pressure – are the most positive conditions for mental health for both men and women. Other research shows that positive job conditions can even offset negative family arrangements. Specifically, autonomy as well as low time pressure on the job reduce the stress women experience in combining jobs and families and the negative effect of child care demands (Lennon & Rosenfield 1992, 1994).

It is also clear that certain kinds of social relations and dimensions of the self are quite beneficial for males and females. Thus, in addition to high power and low demands, high self-esteem, mastery, and reciprocally supportive relationships are necessary for optimal mental health. More generally, a balance between the interests of others and the interests of oneself also reduces the chances of veering toward externalizing or internalizing disorders. Given that such orientations come from social experiences beginning from childhood, socializing practices encouraging high self-regard and mastery tempered by strong regard for others' interests would have the most benefit for mental health.

In concluding, I have reviewed some of the evidence for differences between the sexes in mental health and the social underpinnings of those differences. Looking at numerous levels, from broad sociohistorical forces to current social practices in the workplace and the family to aspects of the self, we see how social differentiation by gender shapes the psychological problems of men and women. This differentiation falls along the lines of a public–private split. On the private side is a constellation of low power, caretaking responsibilities, nonreciprocal social relationships emphasizing giving, feeling rules dictating expressivity of less potent and active emotions, and low personal resources. These social or internal stances disadvantage the self relative to others, and in this sense are highly consistent with internalizing disorders. Because women have been more identified with the private sphere, women have higher rates of such internalizing disorders.

On the public side, we see a constellation of greater power, productive responsibilities, nonreciprocal relationships in which the ratio of giving to receiving is tipped toward receiving, feeling rules of emotional stoicism with the exception of more potent and active emotions, and personal resources of high mastery and self-esteem. Such social and internal stances advantage the self relative to others, which in turn is consonant with externalizing disorders. Given the association of men with the public realm, such externalizing behaviors are more typical of men.

This is not to belittle the variation that exists among men and among women. As many observe, there is great diversity among particular men and women. But we are talking about general tendencies and about the differences in those tendencies. In general, men earn more than women. In general, women do more of the child care. And, in general, women have more depression whereas men are more aggressive.

We also do not want to go to the other extreme and imply that there is something necessary about these differences. Ultimately, sex differences are largely due to things other than gender. They are rather due to certain social practices, such as economic inequality, that have become associated with gender but whose associations can be altered. Going full circle back to Freud, we can trace the advances in understanding the differences between the sexes, showing us that anatomy is not necessarily destiny. Instead, research shows a complexity of social forces that converge to push men and women toward different psychological troubles. The more we understand these forces and their sources and consequences, the more reasons and power we gather to change them.

20

The Labeling Theory of Mental Disorder (II): The Consequences of Labeling

Bruce G. Link & Jo C. Phelan

Although labeling can have positive effects by bringing individuals into treatment, it can also have negative effects of increasing stress and decreasing the individual's ability to cope with stress. Link and Phelan review the issues associated with the impact of labeling and then review the research literature on both the positive and negative effects of labeling. It shows that many treatments (especially medication) have proven to benefit individuals suffering from various forms of mental illness. However, labeling also produces stigma – when individuals labeled with mental illness are seen as possessing undesirable characteristics. Debate centers on whether labels, or behaviors associated with labels, produce stigma and negative social reactions. Link and Phelan discuss the research difficulties in assessing the impact of stigma and also review various means for reducing the level of stigma associated with mental illness. Students should discuss the common stereotypes associated with mental illness, analyzing the degree to which these stereotypes contribute to stigma.

Many people with symptoms of mental illness never receive treatment for those symptoms (see Chapter 21). For those who do, there are potentially important consequences, both positive and negative. The treatment they receive may ameliorate their symptoms and improve their well-being and ability to function. Along with this treatment, however, comes an official label. A specific diagnostic label such as "schizophrenia" or "depression" may become attached to the person. More generally, he or she becomes identified as someone who has received mental health treatment – a "mental patient," a "psychiatric patient," a "mentally ill" person. For this reason, another way that entering treatment may importantly change people's lives is in terms of other people's reactions to them based on these labels. It is easy to imagine that people may have negative stereotypes of the mentally ill – such as unpredictability or dangerousness – that would be applied to the labeled individual, and that people may reject or attempt to maintain distance between themselves and the labeled person as a result of those stereotypes. It is equally easy to imagine that these reactions on the part of others might have a variety of negative consequences for the labeled person. Such reactions may, for example, introduce a new source of stress into ill people's lives, directly limit their life chances through discrimination, damage their self-concepts, and impair the way they cope with and confront the world.

Theoretically, then, it is possible for mental health treatment, and the labeling it necessarily entails, to have positive effects, negative effects, or simultaneous positive and negative effects on the person who receives it. There is no consensus among sociologists of mental health, however, about what the actual consequences of labeling are. The benefits of treatment, the presence and strength of stigmatizing reactions on the part of others, and the impact of those reactions on the lives of people with mental illness have all been subjects of debate. These debates have been framed by labeling theory. In this chapter, we briefly review the labeling theory of mental illness and the alternative positions proposed by the theory's critics; we then review and evaluate the evidence concerning both positive and negative consequences of labeling.

The Labeling Debate

Scheff's (1966a) labeling theory of mental illness posits that the labeling of an individual as mentally ill is an important event with strong social antecedents and consequences. Concerning the social processes leading to a label, Scheff argues that behaviors associated with mental illness – such as apparent inappropriate affect or saying things that do not make sense to other people – are quite common and occur in many people for a variety of reasons, but such behaviors usually are not considered noteworthy by others, do not become labeled as symptoms of mental illness, and consequently are only transitory. The circumstances that determine whether such behaviors will become labeled as mental illness are social in nature and involve, for example, the race or social status of the person committing the deviant act. Evidence regarding factors that lead to social labeling is reviewed in Chapter 7, where theory regarding this first component of the labeling approach is also discussed more thoroughly. Regarding the consequences of labeling, Scheff says that, once a person does become labeled as mentally ill, a set of expectations and pressures are set in place that eventually lead to a stable pattern of deviant behavior that conforms with the cultural stereotypes associated with mental illness. Mental health professionals and lay persons expect the labeled people to behave as if they are "insane," and labeled individuals are rewarded for conforming to the mentally ill role and punished for not conforming. For example, Scheff would argue, psychiatric patients are praised and encouraged when they acknowledge that they are ill and accept and value the professional help that is offered to them. Conversely, they are punished if they attempt to break out of the mentally ill role by insisting they are not insane or by attempting to live and work in the community as if they were "normal." Scheff argues that, in the stressful circumstances that surround having one's sanity called into question, those who have been labeled may be especially confused and vulnerable and may adopt the role expected of them: "In a crisis, when the deviance of an individual becomes a public issue, the traditional stereotype of insanity becomes the guiding imagery for action, both for those reacting to the deviant and at times the deviant himself" (Scheff 1966a: 82). The endpoint of this process, according to Scheff, is that the labeled person comes to adopt a stable pattern of behavior that conforms with cultural expectations of a person with mental illness: "his amorphous and unstructured rule breaking tends to crystallize in conformity to . . . expectations, thus becoming similar to the behavior of other deviants classified as mentally ill, and stable over time" (Scheff 1966a: 82).

Clearly, then, Scheff's theory emphasizes the negative effects of labeling. Scheff's critics, most notably Gove (1970, 1975, 1980, 1982), have challenged each major component of the theory, instead emphasizing labeling's positive consequences and downplaying the negative ones. First, Gove argues that symptomatic behavior, not social contingency, is the prime determinant of labeling. (Evidence regarding this question is reviewed in Chapter 7.) Second, he argues that the consequences of labeling are overwhelmingly positive rather than negative. He argues that, rather than leading to a stabilized pattern of mentally ill behavior, treatment diminishes the symptoms of mental illness. Finally, Gove argues that the extent to which a label of mental illness evokes negative reactions in others is quite minimal. He concludes that there is little evidence that people with mental illness are rejected or devalued by others and that, to the extent that such reactions do occur, they are due to the disturbed behavior of people with mental illness and not to the mental illness label per se.

In the remainder of this chapter, we review the evidence on both positive and negative effects of labeling. Specifically, we consider the benefits of mental health treatment, the extent to which a label of mental illness elicits stigmatizing perceptions or reactions from others, and the consequences of stigma for people with mental illnesses.

The Positive Effects of Labeling through Mental Health Treatment

According to the original theory (Scheff 1966a), labeling exposes people to "agents of social control" (mental health professionals) who assign them to coercive and often inhumane mental health treatment settings that strip them of their identities, trap them in a deviant role, and end up producing much more harm than good. In this formulation, the potential benefits of treatment are not considered. However, evidence concerning the effectiveness of mental health treatment interventions gathered in the last three decades suggests that treatment can have positive effects.

Consider first the extensive literature that consistently indicates that psychotherapy has positive effects. The evidence comes from large-scale meta-analyses of many forms of psychotherapy applied to many conditions (Smith, Glass, & Miller 1980), including more traditional literature reviews (Meltzoff & Kornreich 1970), reviews that consider only well-defined interventions on specific forms of disorder such as major depression (Robinson, Berman, & Neimeyer 1990; Weissman,

Jarret, & Rush 1987), and exacting studies that randomly assign patients with one well-defined disorder (major depression) to different forms of well-specified treatment (interpersonal psychotherapy, cognitive behavioral therapy) (Elkin et al. 1989). Whether one considers all studies (Smith et al. 1980) or only the most methodologically sophisticated ones (Weissman et al. 1987a), the answer is the same: psychotherapy, on average, has positive effects.

The evidence for the effectiveness of drug treatments is extensive as well. Many studies document that phenothiazines reduce relapse rates in schizophrenia (Davis 1975), that lithium reduces relapse rates in manic depressive or bipolar disorder (Prien et al. 1984), and that the symptoms of such conditions as obsessive-compulsive disorder can also be controlled with drugs (Clomipramine Collaborative Study Group 1991). With respect to schizophrenia, newer drugs have been developed that are effective even for people who were unable to benefit from earlier-developed drugs, and the evidence suggests that the benefit may extend not only to the positive symptoms of schizophrenia (e.g., delusions and hallucinations) but to the negative symptoms (e.g., blunted affect and psychomotor retardation) as well (Kane et al. 1988).

It is quite clear from these studies that both psychotherapy and drugs can have important benefits. This is not to say that they are panaceas – neither form of intervention has shown compelling evidence for long-lasting effects. Few studies assess the long-term effects of mental health interventions, and those that do so indicate that the positive effects of treatment erode rapidly (see e.g. Smith et al. 1980). In recognition of this fact, research studies have identified the need for "booster" sessions and "maintenance" doses to extend the benefits of psychotherapeutic and pharmacological interventions, respectively (Frank, Kupfer, & Perel 1989; Kupfer, Frank, & Perel 1989). Moreover, mental health interventions have undesirable effects of their own. Drugs such as the phenothiazines can have very serious side effects in the form of conditions like tardive dyskinesia. Psychotherapy is expensive and time-consuming, and it can be culturally biased in favor of advantaged segments of society (Link 1983; Link & Milcarek 1980; Schofield 1964). Moreover, though the evidence of effectiveness is undeniable, treatments have usually been evaluated under relatively ideal conditions, not the conditions existing in typical treatment settings where providers might be poorly trained, hurried, or too culturally dissimilar from their patients to provide effective care. Thus we know relatively little about the real-world as-delivered effects of psychotherapy and pharmacotherapy on the mental health of the population. Despite these qualifications, however, the evidence is persuasive that psychotherapy and drugs can effect significant improvement in patients.

The Negative Effects of Labeling through Stigma

When we turn from evidence concerning the effectiveness of treatment to the literature on the negative consequences of stigma, we turn from an area that is the domain of psychiatrists, psychologists, and social workers to an area that is inherently sociological. Although major theoretical statements about stigma have been made from a sociological vantage point (Goffman 1961), the importance of stigma in mental illness has been an area of controversy among sociologists. Much of the controversy stems from the debate over labeling and whether the stigma of mental illness was a sufficiently important factor in the lives of people with mental illness to produce serious untoward consequences. We begin our evaluation of this evidence by providing a definition of stigma.

Stigma Defined

Our conceptualization of stigma starts with Jones et al.'s (1984) two-part definition of the concept as a "mark" (i.e., label) that (1) sets a person apart from others and (2) links the marked person to undesirable characteristics. When a person is linked to undesirable characteristics, a third aspect of stigma comes into play – people reject and avoid the stigmatized person. Thus, with respect to mental illness, a clear example of stigma would exist if a person were hospitalized for mental illness (a mark or label) and then assumed to be so dangerous, incompetent, and untrustworthy that avoidance and social isolation ensued. Stigma is a matter of degree; the mark or label can vary in the extent to which it sets a person apart, the marked person can be strongly or weakly linked to a variety of undesirable characteristics, and the rejecting response can be more or less strenuous.

The Position of Labeling Critics on Stigma

The critics of labeling theory not only attacked the position that labeling was the prime determinant of stable mental illness (a criticism that may be valid, according to evidence reviewed here and in Chapter 7), they also denied that labeling-induced stigma might have detrimental effects on jobs, social networks, self-esteem, or the course of disorder. For example, Gove (1982: 280) claims that for the "vast majority of mental patients stigma appears to be transitory and does not appear to pose a severe problem"; Crocetti, Spiro, and Siassi (1974: 88) claim that former psychiatric patients "enjoy nearly total acceptance in all but the most intimate relationships."

Three general types of evidence have been used to support the conclusion that stigma is unimportant in the lives of people with mental illnesses. First, when members of the public are asked so-called social distance questions about whether they would, for example, be willing to work on the same job or fall in love with a former psychiatric patient, most say that they would be willing to do so. Such findings led Crocetti and associates (1974: 89) to conclude that "neither our study or other recent studies document the presence of clear prejudice toward those who have been mentally ill." Second, experimental studies that vary labeling (e.g. "former mental patient" versus no mention of mental illness) and behavior (normal behavior versus behavior indicative of mental illness) have generally shown behavior to be a stronger determinant of rejection than labeling (for a review see Link et al. 1987; for a more recent example see Aubry, Tefft, & Currie 1995). Third, surveys of people who have been psychiatric patients report few concrete instances of rejection (Clausen 1981; Gove & Fain 1973) and indicate that many former patients view their hospitalization experience favorably (Pugh et al. 1994; Weinstein 1979, 1983).

Based on this evidence, the view that the stigma of mental illness was relatively inconsequential was dominant during the late 1970s and early 1980s. For example, the editors of the proceedings of a 1980 conference sponsored by the National Institute of Mental Health decided not to use the term "stigma" in the title of its proceedings – even though the purpose of the meeting was to review evidence on that topic (Rabkin 1984). Apparently, the argument that behaviors and not labels were the prime determinants of rejection was so forcefully articulated that the editors of the proceedings decided that stigma was not an appropriate designation when "one is referring to negative attitudes induced by manifestations of psychiatric illness" (p. 327). And, though it may no longer be dominant, this view is still articulated. For example, Aubrey and colleagues (1995) claim that people with mental illness are not burdened by stigma and can receive equitable treatment "if their presentation shows only minor deviations from the norm" (p. 48).

Evidence Bearing on the Validity of the Claim That Stigma Is Inconsequential

Despite their widespread acceptance at one time, the aforementioned three sources of evidence are too methodologically weak and too limited in scope to allow the broad conclusion that labeling and stigma are unimportant. The social distance questions upon which Crocetti and associates based their conclusion are completely undisguised as to their purpose. Consequently, they allow – almost invite – the kind of nonrejecting responses that research has shown to be socially desirable. A study by Link and Cullen (1983) underscores the influence of social desirability. Respondents were assigned randomly to one of three conditions with respect to how social distance questions were asked about a hypothetical person whose description included symptoms of mental illness. In one condition, respondents were asked how an "ideal person" would react; in another, how they themselves would respond; and in a third, how "most people" would respond. The authors found that, when the description included a reference to a history of psychiatric hospitalization (i.e., a label), the "ideal person" way of asking questions elicited the most accepting responses and the "most people" version produced the most rejecting responses, with the "self" version falling in between. In contrast, when the vignette subject was *not* labeled as a former patient, the "self" responses were the most rejecting. These findings suggest that people respond in a socially desirable way when reporting their own attitudes toward a group they have learned they should accept, such as mental patients. In this way they challenge conclusions about the widespread acceptance of people with mental illness that have been based on responses to undisguised social distance items.

In addition, studies that compare mental illness to other potentially stigmatizing conditions reveal a rather distinct hierarchy, with mental illness falling at or near the most-stigmatized end of a list of conditions including epilepsy, prostitution, alcoholism, drug addiction, and ex-convict status (Albrecht, Walker, & Levy 1982; Brand & Claiborn 1976; Drehmer & Bordieri 1985; Hartlage & Roland 1971; Lamy 1966; Skinner et al. 1995; Tringo 1970). These studies are instructive in that, while they ask questions in a straightforward way, they also demand that respondents compare stigmatizing conditions. Thus we must conclude either that people accept everyone – drug addicts, ex-convicts, and prostitutes – or that mental illness is indeed a stigmatized condition in our society. Because the latter view seems far more plausible, the comparative approach leads us to conclude that public attitudes are not nearly as favorable as Crocetti and associates have claimed.

Finally, a few studies have investigated how people respond not to hypothetical scenarios but in situations where they are personally involved – circumstances that are much less likely to induce socially desirable responses. For example, Page (1977) obtained a sample of advertisements for apartments to rent and randomly assigned landlords to receive calls from collaborators feigning different conditions. In some conditions, a caller working with Page's research team indicated that he was a patient in a mental hospital who would be released in a day or two, whereas in a control condition no mention of mental hospitalization was made. When the "mental patient" label was applied, landlords were much less likely to indicate that the apartment was available (27%) than in the control condition (83%). Similar effects of labeling have been found on willingness to hire a job applicant (Brand & Claiborn 1976; Farina & Felner 1973).

The claim that it is only the deviant behavior associated with mental illness that leads to rejection – not labeling per se – has been refuted by numerous experimental and nonexperimental studies. Social psychological experiments have shown that labeling can affect responses even when no deviant behavior is involved. In fact, these studies show that a self-fulfilling prophecy is invoked such that labeling actually causes behavior that leads to rejection. Sibicky and Dovidio (1986) randomly assigned 68 male and 68 female introductory psychology students as mixed-sex pairs to one of two conditions. In one condition, a "perceiver" (random assignment here as well) was led to believe that a "target" was recruited from the psychological therapy clinic at the college. In the other condition, the perceiver was led to believe that the individual was a fellow student in introductory psychology. In fact, the target was always recruited from the class, and targets and perceivers both were led to believe that the study was focusing on "the acquaintance process in social interaction." Each member of a pair completed a brief inventory of their courses, hobbies, and activities. Then the experimenter

exchanged the inventories and provided the perceiver with the labeling information (student or therapy client). Subsequently, the two engaged in a tape-recorded
interaction that was later reliably evaluated by two raters blind to the experimental conditions. Even before meeting them, perceivers rated the therapy targets less
favorably. Moreover, the judges' ratings revealed that, in their interactions with
therapy targets, perceivers were less open, secure, sensitive, and sincere. Finally,
the results showed that the behavior of the labeled targets was adversely affected
as well, even though they had no knowledge of the experimental manipulation.
Thus, expectations associated with psychological therapy color subsequent interactions, actually calling out behavior that confirms those expectations.

In Sibicky and Dovidio's study, targets were labeled without their knowledge.
Similar processes have been observed when targets believe they have been labeled but actually have not been. In an experimental procedure similar to Sibicky
and Dovidio's, Farina and colleagues (1971) asked former psychiatric patients to
interact with a person they believed might be a prospective employer. Former
patients in the experimental condition were led to believe that their interviewer
knew of their hospitalization; in the control condition, no such information was
conveyed. Those who believed they had been labeled behaved in less socially
attractive ways and were judged less favorably by their interviewers. Thus, the behavioral sequences leading to self-fulfilling prophecies can be initiated by either
the stigmatized or the nonstigmatized member of a dyad (see also Farina, Allen,
& Saul 1968; Harris et al. 1990).

In another study, Link and associates (1987) responded to the fact that previous research on labeling versus behavior was incomplete because it failed to take
into account what the label "former mental patient" actually meant to respondents.
They conducted a vignette experiment similar to those that led previous researchers
to conclude that behaviors, not labels, were important in determining societal reactions. However, their study also incorporated a measure of the extent to which
people believed that mental patients in general were "dangerous." They found
that, when the vignette described a subject without a mental illness label, beliefs
about the dangerousness of people with mental illness played no part in determining social distancing responses to the person described in the vignette. When the
vignette described a labeled subject, however, these beliefs became a potent determinant of responses: respondents who believed mental patients to be dangerous
reacted negatively to the person described in the vignette as having experienced
mental hospitalization. This pattern of results held regardless of the degree of
deviant behavior. In fact, Link and associates were able to show that labeling-
activated beliefs about dangerousness predicted social distance responses just as
strongly as did variations in behavior. Apparently, a mental illness label activates
beliefs about the dangerousness of mental patients, making such beliefs important
for determining how much social distance is desired from labeled people regardless of their behavior. Finally, it should be noted that if Link and associates had

proceeded without bringing the measure of perceived dangerousness into the analysis – thus achieving a more complete specification of labeling processes – then
they, too, would have found large effects of behavior and no effects of labeling.

Studies like those described here make it clear that labeling exerts an independent effect on the rejecting responses of the public. But several studies also
suggest that the "labeling versus behavior" conceptualization is overly simplistic for two important reasons. First, several studies, including the one by Farina
and colleagues (1971) described previously, have shown that labeling can produce
behavior in the labeled person that then leads to rejection. Under such circumstances, it would be short-sighted to attribute the subsequent rejection solely to
behavior, since that behavior was induced by labeling. Second, labeling can provide an interpretive context that changes the meaning of "behaviors." In a pair
of experiments, Riskind and Wahl (1992) demonstrate how labeling could change
the interpretation of a behavior as straightforward as the amount of hand and leg
movement a person exhibits. Activity level (active versus inactive) and labeling –
patient on leave from a mental hospital versus "clown" (study 1) and "ordinary person" (study 2) – were both significantly related to perceived dangerousness, but the
study also showed that activity level increased the perceived dangerousness more
in the mental hospital patient condition than in the other two conditions. Given
that labeling can induce behaviors that lead to rejection and can also change the
interpretative framework in which behaviors are evaluated, it seems vastly over-
simplistic to continue to cast the debate as an issue of "labeling" versus "behavior."

A Model for Understanding the Effects of Labeling and Stigma on People with Mental Illness: Theory and Concepts

Our evaluation of the evidence in the previous section led us to reject the claim
that labels per se are inconsequential. But does labeling-induced stigma affect the
lives of people with mental illness and so produce serious negative consequences?
And if it does, how does it do so?

Link and colleagues have offered an explanation that identifies a mechanism
through which patient attitudes about stigma may strongly affect their life circumstances (Link 1987; Link et al. 1989). Their "modified labeling theory" posits that
a mental illness label gives personal relevance to an individual's beliefs about how
most people respond to psychiatric patients. According to this view, people develop conceptions of what others think of mental patients long before they ever
become patients. These conceptions are often quite negative among the general
public and also among psychiatric patients. Moreover, researchers note that such
beliefs take on new relevance when an individual becomes a psychiatric patient for
the first time. What once seemed to be an innocuous array of beliefs about others'
attitudes toward mental patients is now applicable personally and no longer innocuous. Being marked as a mental patient transforms a person's beliefs about

the devaluation and discrimination of mental patients into personal expectations of rejection. Once such people expect rejection, the theory goes, interactions with others may be strained, and strategies aimed at minimizing the rejection they fear – such as withdrawing from social contacts – may impair their ability to function. In this approach, people can be harmed by labels even when there are no direct negative reactions from others. This research emphasizes that people's internalization of negative stereotypes produces negative labeling effects.

To test this explanation, Link (1987) constructed a twelve-item scale measuring the extent to which a person believes that mental patients will be devalued and discriminated against. This scale was administered to mental patients and nonpatients in an epidemiological "case control" study of major depression and schizophrenia. Link (1987) shows that the degree to which a person expects to be rejected is associated with demoralization, income loss, and unemployment in individuals labeled mentally ill but *not* in unlabeled individuals, thereby supporting the notion that labeling activates beliefs that lead to negative consequences.

In a subsequent paper, Link and associates (1989) extend the foregoing reasoning in two ways. First, they bring into the analysis empirical measures of coping strategies of secrecy (concealing a history of treatment), withdrawal (avoiding potentially threatening situations), and education (attempting to teach others in order to forestall the negative effects of stereotypes). Consistent with the notion that the stigma of mental illness labeling activates expectations of rejection, they show that patients tend to endorse these strategies as a means of protecting themselves. Second, the researchers extend the analysis to a consideration of the effects of stigmatization on social network ties. Patients who fear rejection most and who endorse the strategy of withdrawal have insular support networks consisting mainly of household members.

In more recent work, Link and colleagues (1997) have extended their conceptualization and measurement of stigma to include reported experiences of rejection. In earlier research, these investigators had not included this aspect because both Clausen (1981) and Gove and Fain (1973) had indicated that reported experiences of rejection in areas such as jobs and housing were very rare. As a result, it did not seem as though such experiences could produce pervasive negative effects, so Link and colleagues instead focused their attention on the social psychological mechanism of expectations of rejection. However, when attention is turned from severe exclusions in jobs and housing to more minor insults and slights, rejection experiences turn out to be much more prevalent (Link et al. 1997). It might seem that relatively minor events such as these would also be relatively inconsequential, but in the context of cultural stereotypes that people with mental illness frequently internalize, these seemingly minor rejections can elicit powerful reactions. A comment about "crazy" people can remind those who hear it that they are part of a group that is feared, devalued, and discriminated against. The power of day-to-day, taken-for-granted experiences in activating stereotypes has been demonstrated in the work of Steele and Aronson (1995) regarding stereotypes about the academic ability of African Americans. The authors show that African-American college students perform much worse on SAT-like tests when they have been led to believe that the test measures their intellectual ability than when they are not led to have such a belief. The performance of white students, in contrast, is not significantly affected by statements about the meaning of the test. This "stereotype vulnerability" may also operate for people with mental illness, with stereotypes being activated by what seem to be mild or inadvertent slights and insults.

Taken together, the evidence indicates that there are pervasive negative consequences that follow from labeling. The studies that lead us to this conclusion have varied in design, have been conducted in a variety of samples, have used many different types of outcome measures, and are individually robust to the kinds of counterexplanations that the critics of labeling theory have championed. Just as advocates of labeling theory would be hard put to deny the benefits of treatment, labeling theory's critics are almost certainly incorrect to claim that labeling has no meaningful negative consequences. Existing data simply do not justify a continued debate concerning whether the effects of labeling are positive *or* negative – clearly, they are both. The data, however, strongly motivate further study of both the positive and negative consequences and the way in which they come together in the lives of labeled individuals (Herman & Miall 1990). In this vein, two recent studies have explicitly taken up the issue of the co-occurring and opposite effects of stigma and treatment.

In the first, Rosenfield (1997) examined the effects of both treatment services and stigma in the context of a model program for people with severe mental disorder. She shows that both the receipt of services (specific interventions that some people in the program receive and others do not) and stigma (Link's 1987 measure of perceived devaluation or discrimination) are related – in opposite directions – to multiple dimensions of a "quality of life" measure (Lehman 1983). Services had positive effects on dimensions of quality of life such as living arrangements, family relations, financial situation, safety, and health, whereas stigma had equally strong negative effects on such dimensions.

In the second study, Link and associates (1997) conducted a longitudinal study of men who were dually diagnosed with mental disorder and substance abuse. The men were followed from entry into treatment (when they were highly symptomatic and addicted to substances) to a follow-up point one year later (when they were far less symptomatic and largely drug- and alcohol-free). Despite these dramatic benefits, the results also showed that perceptions and reported experiences of stigma continued to affect the men's levels of depressive symptoms. The effects of stigma endure and are apparently unaffected by treatment benefits.

These two studies are important to the labeling debate in that they acknowledge both positive and negative consequences of labeling and thus achieve a partial accommodation of the so-called labeling and psychiatric perspectives (see also Herman & Miall 1990; Link & Cullen 1990). However, they also pose an important new challenge for future research. To the extent that treatment benefits erode with time, as research suggests they do, the tradeoff between treatment benefits and the effects of stigma may also change with a longer-term perspective. What happens when people like those studied by Rosenfield and Link leave treatment? If the benefits of treatment dissipate with time, it becomes critical to know whether the effects of stigma also evaporate. If the effects of stigma endure then the ultimate tradeoff between the positive and negative effects of labeling needs to be reassessed in longer-term studies. Thus the accommodation between the labeling and psychiatric perspectives achieved in these two studies is only partial, since we need to know much more about the interplay between stigma and treatment over the long run. Moreover, it is important to note that the negative consequences documented in the studies reviewed here are not full-blown, stabilized mental illness. Thus, these studies do not directly support Scheff's most provocative hypothesis – that labeling causes stabilized mental illness. Future work needs to address the nature of the "package deal" that people with mental illness receive when they are officially labeled.

Future studies of stigma must recognize that the content of this package deal can change. For example, it is clear that the benefits of labeling through treatment have improved dramatically over recent years. The enormous expenditures of human and financial resources that have been invested in the development of treatment interventions have had a distinct payoff. In contrast to this enormous investment in enhancing the positive benefits of labeling, the investment in understanding and combating the negative effects of stigma have been appallingly small. This means, of course, that the information available concerning how to combat stigma is necessarily sparse. Nevertheless, in light of research documenting the negative effects of stigma, it is important to offer an evidence-based consideration of ways to reduce the negative consequences of labels.

What Can Be Done? Efforts to Overcome Stigma

The theory and evidence reviewed here suggest that cultural conceptions of mental illness shape the behavior of both labeled and unlabeled individuals in ways that are damaging to people with mental illnesses. Such conceptions lead the public to devalue, reject, and avoid people with mental illnesses. At the same time, they lead persons labeled as mentally ill to expect such rejection and to make efforts to protect themselves from it. Expectations of devaluation and discrimination, as well as the coping efforts activated by these expectations, may have negative consequences for the labeled person's social, psychological, and occupational functioning. This framework suggests several points of intervention in efforts to overcome the effects of stigma.

Because cultural beliefs and stereotypes are the origin of stigma in this model and lead to negative outcomes through their impact on the public and on people with mental illness themselves, those cultural beliefs must be considered a prime target of intervention. However, the kind of intervention that may be successful in changing beliefs and attitudes is not obvious. In the past few decades, there have been many public education efforts aimed at disseminating scientifically based information about mental illness (Wahl 1995). Although the effectiveness of these efforts has not been formally evaluated, the evidence we have reviewed points to continuing stigma despite those interventions. In fact, recent evidence shows that, when asked to describe how they view mental illness, a significantly greater proportion of people mentioned characteristics like unpredictability and dangerousness in 1996 than they did in 1950 (Phelan et al. 1996). Moreover, one effort (evaluated in a quasi-experiment) to change public attitudes toward mental illness was found to be unsuccessful in its goal of reducing feelings of social distance and increasing feelings of social responsibility (Cumming & Cumming 1957). This was an intensive intervention in a single community – described by the investigators as an "all out attempt to improve attitudes towards mental illness" (p. 88) – that included numerous meetings with local groups and clubs, newspaper editorials, radio programs, and films. Not only did attitudes remain unchanged, but over the course of the education campaign, the community became clearly suspicious of and hostile toward the research team that had initially been warmly welcomed.

Such facts are not very encouraging with respect to the ease with which cultural stereotypes can be changed, yet two studies by Penn and colleagues (1994, 1998) suggest that careful attention to the type of information conveyed in public education efforts may lead to greater success. For example, Penn and associates (1998) asked college students to read a vignette describing a person who was labeled as having schizophrenia; they then assessed the extent to which the students thought people with mental illness might be dangerous. The researchers' experimental manipulation involved the nature of the information that accompanied the vignette. If the vignette was accompanied by a general description of the symptoms and course of schizophrenia or by a statement describing the limited types of symptoms that elevate the risk of violence among persons with schizophrenia, perceptions of dangerousness were not altered. However, if the vignette was accompanied by a statement indicating that people with schizophrenia were less dangerous than people with other mental disorders such as substance abuse, then perceptions of dangerousness were reduced when compared with the vignette-only condition. In their 1994 study, which also used a vignette experiment with a student sample, Penn and colleagues showed that revealing information about a person's past symptoms had markedly negative effects on responses. Although limited to the experimenters' sampled student populations, these findings nevertheless suggest the possibility that standard approaches to public education about mental illness – the provision of general, descriptive, scientifically based information about mental disorders – may be less effective in changing attitudes than other, more specific and strategically chosen, types of information.

Other ideas about the particular types of information or conceptualizations that may help reduce the stigma of mental illness have been proposed. For example, some have hypothesized that viewing mental illness in biological terms (e.g., as a brain disorder or brain disease) should lead the public to view and react to mental disorders in the same way they do to other diseases and consequently should have a destigmatizing effect (Bar-Levav 1976; Crocetti, Spiro, & Siassi 1971; Schwartz & Schwartz 1977). However, available evidence suggests that describing psychiatric problems in terms of disease rather than psychosocially may result in less favorable evaluations of and behavior toward the labeled person (Mehta & Farina in press; Norman & Malla 1983; Ommundsen & Ekeland 1978; Rothaus et al. 1963; Wheeler 1989).

A final consideration of public conceptions of mental illness involves media portrayals of people with mental illnesses. People with mental illness are commonly portrayed (on television, in films, and in the news) as being distinctly different from normal people, as being ineffectual, and especially as being dangerous. For example, in a content analysis of prime-time television dramas over a period of 17 years, Signorelli (1989) found that 72.1% of mentally ill characters were portrayed as being violent and 21.6% were portrayed as murderers. It is not clear to what extent such images may actually shape public attitudes and beliefs about mental illness. However, certain aspects of theory and research on persuasion and attitude change suggest that they should. Accordingly, Wahl (1995) suggests that, because they arouse emotions yet are not viewed as deliberate attempts to change attitudes, such dramatic images may be particularly potent at shaping attitudes and beliefs; they may be very difficult to counteract with didactic messages that are not highly emotion-arousing and that may be seen as deliberate attempts at persuasion. If this is correct then it suggests the possibility that reducing stigma may require reducing the frequency, intensity, and inaccuracy of such negatively stereotyped fictional images rather than counteracting those influences with competing destigmatizing messages.

Another approach to combating stigma involves "inoculating" those with mental illnesses against cultural stereotypes about them. Link, Mirotznik, and Cullen (1991) argue that three individually based stigma-coping efforts (secrecy, withdrawal, and education) are either ineffective or actually harmful, but it is nevertheless possible that group-reinforced coping efforts might be effective. In particular, it may be possible for people with mental illness to use group-based social support to reject cultural stereotypes – to effectively see the problem as originating in the ignorant, overgeneralizing attitudes of the stigmatizers. Although some interventions along these lines have been developed, perhaps the most active efforts are consumer-based self-help and empowerment approaches (e.g. Fisher 1994;

Rosenfield 1992b). On the positive side, these approaches not only offer a means of effectively coping with stigma but also hold out the possibility of achieving broader social change. To the extent that people with mental illness are empowered to "come out" and challenge stereotypes, the broader public may come to view mental illness differently than they now do. Among the possible difficulties of such approaches is the personal risk that challenging stereotypes might entail if identification leads to devaluation and discrimination. In addition, it may be (as the recent work of Phelan et al. 1996 shows) that trends in public stereotyping are moving in the wrong direction. If they are then it suggests that the empowerment movement, and all who seek to diminish stigma, are confronting powerful social forces that run counter to their goals. If so, it will be extremely difficult to overcome such forces without directly confronting them. Of course, the empowerment and self-help movements can play a role in such a confrontation and can also offer some protection against the effects of stereotypes, whatever direction they are moving in. A general conclusion suggested by the data reviewed here is that, although modifying cultural stereotypes must be considered an important means of reducing the stigma of mental illness, more research is needed to understand what needs to be changed and how it might be changed. We suggest that large-scale public education efforts should be guided by smaller-scale experimental studies focused on different potential sources of cultural stereotypes. Moreover, such studies should assess the effects of various types of messages and focus on different means for conveying those messages.

Conclusion

The original labeling theory of mental illness strongly emphasized the negative consequences of labeling, whereas critics emphasized the benefits of treatment and have denied negative consequences. The evidence we have reviewed indicates that labeling can have both positive and negative consequences. For the most part, the positive consequences have been demonstrated for outcome variables that focus on clinical conditions (e.g., symptoms of depression or the florid symptoms of schizophrenia). Extensive research suggests that psychotherapy and drug treatments have positive effects. There are problems with the equitable and effective distribution of these treatments, but the evidence suggests that they can be viewed as beneficial effects of labeling. At the same time, labeling has pervasive negative consequences for psychological and social functioning. It appears that, when people are labeled as mentally ill, powerful cultural forces are brought to bear that determine what the labeling process means to individuals and to those around them. For many, the labeling experience evokes a potent expectation of rejection that, along with the actual responses of others, can disrupt social interaction, diminish self-esteem, and negatively influence performance in social and work roles.

These negative consequences have not been definitively linked to the stabilization of severe mental disorders, but there are plausible theoretical reasons to suggest that they might have such effects by increasing stress and by affecting the individual's means of coping with stress (Link et al. 1989).

Part III
Mental Health Systems and Policy

Teresa L. Scheid & Allan V. Horwitz

Mental health care must be understood in terms of its wider social context: the care and treatment provided to individuals with mental health problems reflects wider social values and priorities. Hence, the mental health system (the network of organizations, services, and health-care professionals) will change as social factors change. Specifically, widely held values and beliefs about mental health, attitudes toward the mentally ill, and professional ideologies and treatment preferences will all shape the political climate, economic priorities, and the types of services available. Beliefs about illness also influence the willingness of people to seek help. In Chapter 21, Pescosolido and Boyer provide an overview of the available systems of care and describe the different theories of help-seeking behavior.

The needs of those with severe, persistent illness are central to understanding the mental health system. Hence, the chapters in this part of the book will focus more on those with chronic, as opposed to acute, illnesses. The unique needs of those with severe and persistent illness have not been adequately recognized; these individuals require long-term care, and there is a notable lack of efficacious treatment technology (Rochefort 1989). We do not know how to "cure" such illness, and there is wide disagreement over what services can provide those with severe mental illnesses the best quality of life.

Care to people with severe mental illness can be differentiated by inpatient versus outpatient and public versus private services. Chart III summarizes 1990 data from the Center for Mental Health Services (CMHS 1994c: 5). In terms of inpatient care, the majority of individuals receive treatment from general hospitals that offer both general medical care and psychiatric care. Future years will see further integration of medical and mental health care, an issue relevant to health-care reform and the development of managed care systems; see Chapter 22 (by Manderscheid, Henderson, Witkin, and Atay). Close to 20% of inpatient care is provided by private psychiatric hospitals, while 16.4% is provided by public, state, and county mental hospitals. Yet in 1990, inpatient care episodes were a small fraction of outpatient care episodes; most clients now receive care on an outpatient basis, with some

Chart III. *Mental health organizations and patient care*

Type of organization	Patient care episode (percentages)			
	Inpatient	Outpatient	Partial care	Total
State and county hospitals	16.4	2.1	3.7	6.0
Private psychiatric hospitals	9.3	3.4	9.2	7.9
VA psychiatric organizations	9.5	7.8	6.1	8.2
Nonfederal psychiatric hospitals with psychiatric units	44.1	16.8	12.7	23.7
Residential treatment centers for emotionally disturbed children	3.0	3.4	5.0	3.4
Freestanding psychiatric clinics	—	15.4	—	10.4
Freestanding psychiatric partial care organizations	—	—	4.4	0.3
Multiservice mental health organizations	7.7	51.1	58.9	40.1
Number of patient care episodes per 100,000 population				
1955	795	233	—	1,028
1990	917	2,354	220	3,491

Source: CMHS (1994c: 5).

receiving partial care (partial hospitalization). The majority of outpatient care, as well as partial care, is received in multiservice mental health organizations.

Who provides this care? Most people tend to think of a psychiatrist in a white coat as the typical mental health–care provider, but in fact most clients of mental health services will see a psychiatric nurse (if they are in an inpatient setting) or a social worker (if they are in an outpatient setting). Scott and Lammers (1985) reported that psychiatry, psychology, social work, and nursing are the most prevalent fields in the mental health–care sector. Psychiatric nursing and clinical social work are fast-growing disciplines, with specific certification rules for mental health care. Psychiatrists make decisions about medication while other mental health professionals provide therapy or supportive case management. Mental health–care providers can also be distinguished as either paraprofessionals (who provide direct care but lack formal qualifications or direct authority over clients) or professionals (who possess a qualifying degree). Increasingly, care is provided by multidisciplinary treatment teams.

Care of those with mental illness has exhibited four phases that reflect changing societal values, professional ideologies, and economic priorities:

(1) *institutionalization* (late 1800s to mid-1900s) – mental hospital as the primary locus of care;

(2) *deinstitutionalization* (1950s to 1970s) – mental hospitals de-emphasized in favor of community-based care;

(3) *consolidation of community-based care* (1980s to early 1990s) – emphasis placed upon coordinating and integrating community mental health services, developing centralized authorities, and extending services to those most in need;

(4) *managed care* (early 1990s to present) – cost cutting and rationing of mental health services and contracting out services to private providers (i.e., privatization).

This summary briefly describes each of these trends. The chapters in Part III provide in-depth analyses of mental health care services and policy.

Institutionalization

One of the most well-known books in the sociology of mental illness is Erving Goffman's *Asylums,* published in 1961. Goffman (1961: 4) describes the state mental hospital as a "total" institution (in the same category as prisons) designed to care for those who are "felt to be incapable of looking after themselves and a threat to the community." These two criteria (ability to look after oneself and potential danger to the community) provide the basis for continued debate over appropriate services to those with mental illnesses. A total institution represents a closed world, where all of the individual's needs are met and life is highly regimented and controlled.

The state mental hospital became widespread in the 1800s and was the primary locus of care for those with mental illness until the mid-1900s. During that period, afflicted persons either stayed with family or friends or were sent to the state hospital. On the one hand, state hospitals provided all their services – housing, food, treatment, medical care, social interaction – at a single location, so problems of service integration did not arise. On the other hand, the variety of mental health services that exist today simply was not present in that era. Furthermore, although reliance on state hospitals has declined since the 1960s, these institutions continue to dominate mental health policy debates, and many individuals with severe, persistent mental illness still face the likelihood that they will spend some time in a state mental hospital.

Dowdall (1996) provides a sociological analysis of the state mental hospital, drawing on organizational theory to explain its growth, decline, and future prospects. He argues that state mental hospitals are "maximalist" organizations (1996: 23) – that is, they live very long lives and are unusually resistant to change. This is certainly the case today; most of the several hundred state mental hospitals created since 1773 are still in existence (in 1990 the NIMH listed 286). The average state spends 57% of its state mental health dollars on hospitals (Dowdall 1996). However, patient populations have fallen sharply since 1950. If fewer patients are served, why do states still fund state hospitals at such a high level? Vested interests are part of the explanation; communities fight to maintain their state mental hospitals because they provide local jobs. Also, the state hospital provides custodial care to the minority of patients who cannot survive in the community, who cannot afford private residential treatment, or who are unable to utilize community services. State hospitals have also diversified; many now provide a range of outpatient and rehabilitation services to assorted groups of clients. Many now provide more comprehensive treatment to persons with serious mental illnesses – including outpatient and day treatment as well as inpatient treatment – in addition to such services as case management, family care, sheltered workshops, and vocational rehabilitation (Gudeman 1988). But the future of the state mental hospital is uncertain owing to contracting state budgets, the emergence of managed care, and consumer preference for community treatment.

Deinstitutionalization

Deinstitutionalization, the process of closing state hospitals and the transfer of inpatients to community-based mental health services, began in the 1950s (see Morrissey 1982). It received much of its impetus from the view that public asylums were little more than warehouses for the "custodial care of the poor and immigrant insane" (Williams, Bells, & Wellington 1980: 57). Goffman's analysis of these total institutions, among others, led to the recognition that inpatient care could stigmatize individuals and prevent their return to society. Furthermore, state hospitals provided little therapy or treatment; instead, they served custodial functions and ensured that the most basic needs (food and shelter) of patients were met.

Harsher critics charged that asylums served primarily to control those with mental illnesses and to violate their constitutional rights. Thomas Szasz (1963) argued that civil commitment procedures violated the rights of the individual to be secure in person and possession against unreasonable searches (4th Amendment); against self-incrimination (5th Amendment); to a speedy trial (6th Amendment); to a trial by jury (7th Amendment); against cruel and unusual punishment (8th Amendment); and, most importantly, due process and protection against deprivation of life, liberty, and property (14th Amendment). Goffman's (1961: 361) observation – that, in the state hospital, the "patient's life is regulated and ordered according to a disciplinary system developed for the management by a small staff of a large number of involuntary inmates" who are rewarded for "quiet, obedient behavior" – was portrayed to mass audiences in the popular film adaptation of Ken Kesey's *One Flew over the Cuckoo's Nest*.

In addition to changing social values of society toward greater concern with the rights of the mentally ill, the 1950s and 1960s saw the advent and expansion of psychotropic drugs (Gronfein 1985b). At the same time that the more liberal attitudes of the 1960s resulted in a series of court cases that mandated care in the least restrictive environment, psychotropic drugs provided community mental health workers with the technology to actually maintain patients in the community. With the shift from hospital- to community-based care, individuals with mental illness become clients rather than patients. We will first discuss the legal impetus behind deinstitutionalization and then turn to a brief discussion of psychiatric medication.

The legal rationale for asserting State control over those with mental illnesses (i.e., the ability to commit an individual involuntarily to the hospital) originates in the State's police power and *parens patriae* functions. Under its police power, the State has the obligation to protect the community from potential harm; under *parens patriae,* the State has the obligation to serve the best interests of individuals, which means it must protect those with mental illness from potential harm (Wexler 1981). Courts have interpreted this to mean that the state can exercise this power only when individuals are found to be dangerous to themselves or others. The "least restrictive" interpretation represents a second major restriction on the State's power to commit individuals to mental institutions. As articulated in a case heard in the District of Columbia Circuit Court (see Reisner 1985): "Deprivation of liberty solely because of dangers of the ill persons themselves should not go beyond what is necessary for their protection" (*Lake* v *Cameron,* 364 F.2d 657, U.S. Court of Appeals, District of Columbia, 1966). The State's power to commit is limited by the constitutional imperative that government should use methods that curtail individual freedom to no greater extent than what is essential to secure valid community interests. As delineated by subsequent court rulings, the doctrine of the least restrictive alternative mandates that health officials and courts find or create settings that allow patients to move from large custodial state institutions to facilities that (i) are smaller, less structured, and integrated into the community, and (ii) allow for independent living (Levine 1981).

While legal rulings provided formal guidelines that facilitated deinstitutionalization, new advances in drug therapy allowed community-based care to become a reality. A great deal of controversy exists over the use of psychiatric drugs. Psychiatric drugs control the overt symptoms of mental illness so that medicated individuals are able to live in their communities. For many, drug therapy has been of tremendous help in the control of their symptoms of mental illness. For example, Prozac (an antidepressant) has helped millions of people to deal with their depression (Wurtzel 1994; Kramer 1993). Clozaril and other new psychotropics such as risperidone have helped even those with the most debilitating forms of schizophrenia to live more stable lives in their own communities.

The primary problem with psychiatric medication, however, is the resulting side effects. All of the major psychiatric drugs, including fluphenazine deconoate (prolixin), lithium carbonate (lithium), thioridazine (mellaril), haloperidol (haldol), and methylphenidate (ritaline), are capable of causing drowsiness, nausea, blurred vision, and sinus problems. Many of these drugs – most notably prolixin, which is commonly used in the treatment of schizophrenia – may also affect the motor movements of patients, resulting in Parkinson-like symptoms. These include akinesia (weakening and general muscular fatigue), akathisia (the jitters), and dyskinesia (neck spasms, stiffness, grimacing, and speech impairment). The most serious side effect of psychotropic medication is *tardive dyskinesia* – a neurological disorder whose symptoms (rhythmical involuntary movements of the tongue, face, mouth, or jaw) may persist after the individual is taken off the medication. Although many of these side effects can be treated with anti-Parkinsonian drugs such as cogentin or artane, these drugs also produce side effects. Fortunately, the new neuropletics (such as clozapine and risperidone) produce fewer side effects and may reduce the signs of tardive dyskinesia (Borison et al. 1992; Carpenter et al. 1995; Meltzer 1995).

The concerns over psychiatric medication and side effects are central in the treatment of those diagnosed with schizophrenia. First, the medications used to treat bipolar disorder and severe depression (e.g., lithium, prolixin) are less likely to produce side effects and more likely to be effective in reducing the symptoms of the illness. Second, schizophrenia is chronic, severe, and debilitating. Third, the medications used to control the symptoms of schizophrenia are most likely to produce lasting side effects. Drug dependency and side effects are themselves stigmatizing and serve to further separate those with schizophrenia from the community. Scheid and Anderson (1995) found that although compliance with medication allowed schizophrenics to work, their medication slowed them down so much that their work performance was impaired.

In addition to changes in the social environment (greater liberalization and preference for community-based care), liberalized legal statutes, and the growth in new drug therapies, there were important economic reforms during the first two decades of deinstitutionalization. Changes in the financing of mental health care provided the impetus for wide-scale institutional reform. New sources of public funding at the federal level for community mental health centers together with extension of welfare benefits to those with mental illnesses allowed community-based care to become a reality. Andrew Scull (1977: 131) has argued that the segregative social control of the state hospital simply became too costly to maintain, so those with severe mental illnesses were returned to the community, where costs are lower. However, Schull's argument ignores the fact that governmental expenses – especially through funding the federal programs of Medicaid, Medicare, SSI, and SSDI – increased dramatically during the period of deinstitutionalization.

The political mechanism for deinstitutionalization was President Kennedy's stated commitment to community mental health, which resulted in the Community Mental Health Centers Act of 1963. The CMHC Act directed each state to develop a statewide plan designating catchment areas that would serve 75,000 to 200,000 people. A community mental health center (CMHC, which now comprise the majority of those multiservice mental health organizations identified in Chart III) would serve each catchment area. The legislation was designed in such a way that a federal agency, the National Institute of Mental Health (NIMH), would deal directly with localities and CMHCs, bypassing state governments (Levine

1981). This bypassing of state authorities resulted in conflict between state and local authorities because states continued to fund state hospitals while communities assumed fiscal responsibility for CMHCs.

In theory, the CMHC had many roles (Adler 1982), including: (1) to provide focused individual competency-building programs; (2) to coordinate agencies that serve the mentally ill (i.e., transportation, housing, income maintenance, vocational rehabilitation, crisis intervention, and emergency hospitalization); and (3) to promote social support networks for those with mental illnesses. These functions of the CMHC reflect a social rather than a medical model of mental illness; the CMHC is expected to develop the adaptive capacities of the client in the community as well as to foster community attitudes of tolerance, respect, and helpfulness toward the patient (Bockoven 1972).

Yet CMHCs were quickly criticized for having little direct impact on the mental health field (Gronfein 1985a; Kaplan & Bohr 1976; Kirk & Therrien 1975; Stern & Minkoff 1979). The CMHCs neither directly reduced hospital populations nor served the needs of those with severe mental illness. Instead, they served new patient populations: those with less acute disorders and segments of the middle class, sometimes referred to as the "worried well." Policies promoting deinstitutionalization assumed that community mental health centers would accept responsibility for patients' release from the state mental hospital and would work to prevent their reinstitutionalization into hospitals (or jails). It was also assumed that communities would accept the mentally ill. Both assumptions were false (Morrissey, Goldman, & Klerman 1980). For former hospital patients, the CMHC became part of the "shuffle to despair" (Wilson 1982: xviii) as they revolved in and out of state hospitals. These failures were compounded by the programmatic chaos that resulted because deinstitutionalization occurred before a coherent policy was developed and before public consensus was built.

Consequently, deinstitutionalization encountered administrative and system difficulties involving the delineation of agency and staff roles, breakdowns in the referral of patients from one agency to another, opposition from the medical profession and from the community, oversaturation of certain neighborhoods with released patients, and a lack of residential alternatives (Halpern et al. 1980). These problems resulted in the revolving door of frequent hospital admissions (and shortened stays) when patients could not be maintained in the community, and also in transinstitutionalization, where former patients wound up in nursing homes, board and care homes, and other such facilities. A recurrent issue is the relationship of the criminal justice system to the mental health system, which Dr. Hiday discusses in Chapter 28. Because of the greater difficulties in entering state mental institutions, many seriously mentally ill people were jailed or imprisoned for violations that could be attributed to their mental illnesses. Other critics pointed to the rise in homelessness brought about by the wholesale dumping of the mentally ill into the community. Many of the problems associated with deinstitutionalization were attributed to the failure of the CMHC to provide or coordinate the necessary support services (Ahmed & Plog 1976; Mechanic & Rochefort 1990; Morrissey, Tausig, & Lindsey 1984; Rochefort 1989; Shadish, Lurigio, & Lewis 1989).

Gronfein (1985a) maintains that CMHCs had neither the incentive nor the means to deal with people having serious and persistent mental illnesses. The CHMCs were inadequately funded, and work with chronic patients involves greater expenditures of time with very little professional return. There is also a notable dearth of solutions and proven technologies (beyond psychiatric medication) to aid mental health professionals in their work (Mechanic 1986; Stern & Minkoff 1979). Consequently, those with severe or persistent mental illness are often viewed as the least desirable clients (Atwood 1982; Lang 1981; Stern & Minkoff 1979). Much of the necessary care is not therapy but rather the provision of supportive services and case management (Mechanic 1986). Case management involves coordination of those services and supports (income, housing, medical care, skills training, medication, therapy) necessary to maintain the client in the community. It has become the primary form of treatment for individuals with severe and persistent mental illnesses (Harris & Bergman 1987), but this sort of work is generally not viewed as professionally challenging or rewarding, nor is it well paid. Most mental health professionals are trained for psychotherapy and have neither the skills, training, nor desire to engage in case management.

In a review of studies and evaluations of CMHCs in the 1980s, Dowell and Ciarlo (1989: 223) conclude that CMHCs need to rethink their role and develop a "community based thrust for chronic patient care." The central problem remains coordinating the various services needed (Aviram 1990; Dill and Rochefort 1989); behind coordination problems lie economic and funding constraints.

Consolidation of Community-Based Care

Because those with serious mental illnesses need long-term, continuous care, mental health services must be coordinated. Yet, economic considerations rather than treatment ideas and philosophies shape systems of long-term care (Frisman & McGuire 1989). Funding of long-term care is not market-driven but results instead from governmental policies that affect the funding of CMHCs. The federal government provides direct support to states and local communities via the Alcohol, Drug Abuse, and Mental Health Block Grant as well as the Social Service Block Grant, which helps fund the many supportive services needed by those with severe mental illnesses. Federal policies affecting housing and welfare are also critical. Federal policy is currently in a state of flux, with serious ramifications for mental health service delivery. Descriptions of the effects of various policy reforms on mental health care are provided in Chapter 23 (by Schlesinger and Gray) and in Chapter 25 (by Rochefort).

With the decline in funding, which began with President Reagan's Omnibus Reconciliation Act of 1980, mental health researchers, administrators, and advocates turned to a variety of strategies to improve existing service delivery. The NIMH provided funding for training programs and services research, and it also contributed to the development of the Community Support Program (CSP). The CSPs provide coordinated case management; assessment, identification, and diagnosis of those in need of crisis intervention (to prevent hospitalization); psychiatric treatment; support for activities of daily living; psychosocial rehabilitation; client advocacy; and residential, vocational, and recreational services (Tessler & Goldman 1982).

Another attempt to improve service delivery to those with severe, persistent illnesses was the Robert Wood Johnson (RWJ) Program on Chronic Mental Illness (Shore & Cohen 1990; see also the 1994 *Milbank Quarterly,* vol. 72, no. 1). The Program on Chronic Mental Illness sought to improve service delivery by establishing centralized authorities that would provide coordinated care. Hence both the CSP and other innovations of the 1980s emphasized integration and coordination of existing services.

Coordination of care operates at several distinct levels: the client, the organization, and the system (Dill & Rochefort 1989). Case management and multidisciplinary treatment teams operate at the individual level because mental health professionals direct attention to individual clients. Operating at the organizational level are Community Support Systems and other organizational structures, such as Assertive Community Treatment, that seek to coordinate and integrate the services offered by different community agencies. Finally, mental health authorities (such as those promoted by the RWJ initiative) operate at the system level, overseeing services to a defined population group. In Chapter 24, Morrissey provides a more detailed discussion of some of the most recent approaches to coordinated care at the systems level.

At present, a number of federal programs reimburse individual care for chronic patients; these programs include Supplemental Security Income (SSI), Social Security Disability Insurance (SSDI), and Medicare. With health-care and welfare reform, the exact contributions of federal, state, and local communities to these forms of individual support is currently in a state of flux, and cutbacks at all levels are being anticipated. Few would disagree that funding is inadequate or that wide gaps exist in the provision of services. Current funding mechanisms simply do not allow for either long-term care or the continuity of care needed by those with severe, persistent mental illness. In addition, this population is aging, and many in it face problems with HIV infection (the mental health needs of those with HIV/AIDS are addressed by Crystal in Chapter 29). Hence, the need for coordinated mental health as well as medical services for long-term, chronic-care populations will continue to put pressures on the service system.

One consequence of the community mental health–care movement has been a growth in rehabilitation as a treatment modality, as opposed to the primary reliance on reducing psychiatric symptoms that is characteristic of the biomedical view of illness. With rehabilitation, the treatment goal is the improvement of social functioning and not merely the relief of symptoms. Pickett, Cook, and Razzano provide a discussion of the outcomes of psychiatric rehabilitation in Chapter 26.

Psychiatric rehabilitation emphasizes "normalization," whereby the client is able to live a normal life in the community, and is based on conformity to the Western ideals of independence and self-reliance. Treatment provides a socialization function – clients learn appropriate social norms and skills needed to "fit in." Bayley (1991: 88) suggests that such conformity to American ideals of individualist achievement and independence may be "profoundly unhelpful" to those with mental illnesses and disabilities. Lefley (1984) charges that such emphasis on Western ideals represent a type of professional ethnocentrism that may be inappropriate for clients in different cultural contexts and for many minorities. That which is defined as "normal" is culturally specific and valued. Issues regarding cultural diversity and mental health treatment are taken up in Chapter 30 (by Takeuchi, Uehara, and Maramba); in Chapter 31, Lefley examines mental health systems in a cross-cultural context. Of course, many of the goals of the normalization movement (such as vocational training, provision of social skills, and destigmatization) are widely shared social values.

In contrast to normalization are various models for consciousness raising, mutual self-help, and empowerment. Rose and Black (1985) first presented the empowerment paradigm as an alternative to traditional, psychiatric-based mental health care. Those with mental illnesses should be treated not as subjects but as active agents, with control and autonomy over their own lives and decisions. An extension of the consumer rights movement, which was part of the seminal ideology of the community care movement, empowerment calls on consumers (here, those with mental illness who receive services) to take an active role in the creation and delivery of mental health services; it calls on mental health professionals to act as advocates for their clients. Rather than seeking to rehabilitate or resocialize those with mental illness, this movement believes that mental health providers should work with consumers to help them articulate their concerns and to develop action strategies. Kaufmann provides an analysis of the mental health consumer movement in Chapter 27. The issues of normalization and empowerment are also central to questions of culturally appropriate treatment and service delivery, as well as to alternative forms of mental health care that are discussed in Lefley's chapter.

Managed Care

Mental health care has been subject to the same attempts to "rationalize" services as has physical health care (Brown & Cooksey 1989). Cost containment is a driving force behind this rationalization (Pollack et al. 1994). The goal is to limit unnecessary services, yet there is also pressure to ensure access to care as well as to provide quality care. State and local mental health authorities are modifying the funding and organization of services, with movement to managed care a common strategy (Essock & Goldman 1995).

In 1989, the Institute of Medicine defined managed care as "a set of techniques used by or on behalf of purchasers of health care benefits to manage health care costs by influencing patient care decision making through case-by-case assessments of the appropriateness of care prior to its provision" (quoted in Wells et al. 1995: 57). That is, managed care is any system that seeks to control access to care or that seeks to regulate the type and amount of care received. With specific reference to mental health, the following types of managed care have been widely utilized.

(1) *Precertification* – services must be preapproved before a patient may receive them. Typically, physicians must make a recommendation and have this approved before insurance plans or HMOs will pay for mental health services.

(2) *Concurrent review* (also referred to as *case management*) – occurs when there is ongoing review of treatment at regular intervals. The purpose here is to allocate services, select less costly treatments, and ensure that those most in need receive appropriate care.

(3) *Gatekeepers* – primary care providers who are responsible also for allocating mental health care.

Whatever the form of managed care, and wherever such management occurs (in a health maintenance organization, a preferred provider network, an independent practice association, or in the public system of services), it always involves some form of cost containment and rationing of services. Providers of mental health care are seeking to minimize the costs of treatment and promote fiscal efficiency. Managed care needs to be differentiated from managed competition, which attempts to encourage competition among providers under the assumption that competition leads to lower prices for services rendered.

The primary ways in which managed care controls costs are by limiting access to services and by limiting the utilization of more costly services while encouraging the use of less costly services. Managed care also emphasizes measurable success, or outcomes – a problematic feature for mental health care, where treatment success is more difficult to define (see Part I of this volume) or measure. Managed mental health care pursues the following goals:

(1) functional improvements (i.e., some gain in the client's ability to function in society – be it work, community integration, or some other measure that enables social roles to be fulfilled);

(2) measurable outcomes within a reasonable time frame;

(3) utilization of less costly services when possible (e.g., group therapy and/or medication as opposed to inpatient hospital stays or residential placements).

Most managed care plans do not cover chronic mental illness in their standard benefit packages, and the amount of money generally allocated for mental health services is not considered sufficient for adequate treatment (Iglehart 1996). As described by Iglehart (1996), a typical benefit may allow a maximum of 20 outpatient visits and 30 days of inpatient hospitalization a year. This is barely sufficient to deal with a spell of acute depression (such as following a divorce) and a fortiori with serious and persistent mental illnesses. "Parity" legislation may redress this imbalance by prohibiting differential coverage of physical and mental health problems. The Domenici–Wellstone amendment (enacted September 1996, effective January 1, 1998) prohibits different annual reimbursement levels and lifetime caps for mental health. However, the legislation is limited in that it affects only those plans that already cover mental health, and those plans may elect to drop it (Frank, Koyanagi, & McGuire 1997). In other words, there is no mandate that plans provide mental health benefits, yet if they do, they must not have different annual and lifetime limits for reimbursement.

However, mental health–care providers may actually face pressure from their managed care organization to provide even less treatment than what is covered by a patient's benefit plan. This is most likely to occur where fees are "capitated" (i.e., a set fee is paid for each enrollee). If treatment costs are below the capitation fee then the managed care company will retain a profit; if treatment costs are higher than the capitation fee then the company loses money. Many managed care firms offer bonuses to providers when patient care costs are kept low. In behavioral health (mental health and substance abuse), providers join panels or a network, and the managed care company refers their enrollee (the client) to a given provider (this is authorization). Providers must apply to be on a panel or network and are paid fees that are lower than what they would charge on their own (generally $75–$80 an hour for a M.S.W. or psychologist as opposed to $100–$125, in 1997 dollars). Provider networks are increasingly selective, and providers who are seen by the managed care company as "costly" will be dropped from the network. Hence the patient's interests may well be at odds with those of the managed care company, and the provider is placed in the difficult position of having to negotiate between the two. This is most apparent when providers seek additional treatment for their clients or are reluctant to provide information about the client's mental health problems to the managed care company (e.g., homosexuality or other problems that may result in some risk to the client if made public).

In addition to challenging the professional authority and autonomy of the provider, managed care may represent a threat to the mental health professions. Shore and Biegel (1996) note that managed care companies have a financial incentive to have more providers at lower levels of professional training because the fees will be lower. Consequently, outpatient networks consist primarily of social workers and psychologists (rather than psychiatrists or those with Ph.D.s).

> The challenges to the definition of illness, professional ethics, the allocation of professional resources, and professional accountability brought by the emergence of managed behavior health care will not disappear and must be resolved by professionals and managed behavioral health care companies working together to craft new forms of professional practice. (Shore & Biegel 1996: 118)

Managed mental health care already exists in many different forms, which is the major reason why there is no conclusive data about the effect of managed care systems on access to care or the quality of care. There are simply too many different kinds of managed care programs to allow for effective evaluation. For example, Medicare's prospective payment system (PPS) is a form of managed care that relies on a preset reimbursement for a given diagnosis related group (DRG). Many insurance companies also use prospective payment systems. Other types of insurance coverage may utilize "carve-out" arrangements – where a managed care firm may contract out its mental health services to a specialty mental health provider (perhaps a group practice or a mental health HMO).

Managed behavioral care is a quickly changing sector. In a study of 106 behavioral health care organizations from 1990 to 1994, Kihlstrom (1997) found the field to be highly turbulent, with an increasing number of mergers and consolidations. The majority were for-profit and had parent companies that were insurance or managed care corporations. This scenario is similar to that experienced by hospitals, and it represents increased consolidation and concentration of ownership.

Beyond the wide variety of private insurance arrangements, state mental health authorities (SMHAs) have also embraced managed care (Essock & Goldman 1995). The SMHAs have utilized managed mental health–care vendors – that is, managed care firms that offer their services to help state and local mental health authorities manage care. These companies (private in nature) assist states and public mental health agencies with cost containment, coordinating care, and contracting for services. In general, public agencies hire a managed care manager, or a consulting firm, for a limited period of time to assist them with reform. Another device widely used by public mental health agencies to manage care is contracting services out to private organizations.

One important obstacle to evaluating managed mental health care is the great difficulty in assessing treatment effectiveness. Not only is it difficult to define the nature of the problem, but different types of treatment work with different clients; moreover, client confidentiality limits collection of and access to data. Mental health treatment does not result in the same kind of measurable outcomes as does the treatment for physical diseases. Even determining whether managed care has resulted in fiscal savings is often impossible owing to the complexity of funding mechanisms for care and the diversity of mental health systems providing treatments (Wells et al. 1995). Often, mental health and substance abuse services are managed separately, under a wide variety of "carve-out" arrangements; at other times, services and recipient populations are integrated in order to better coordinate care.

There has been widespread concern regarding people with severe mental illnesses that "an already vulnerable population" will be placed at "even greater risk for being managed toward the bottom line rather than toward improved client outcomes" (Durham 1995: 117). Of critical importance is the motive behind a given managed care system; is it to manage care (seeking to improve outcomes as well as care) or to manage reimbursements so as to reduce costs? A concern with cost containment may result in the reduction of services deemed costly, intensive, and long-term. Yet those with serious mental illnesses generally require long-term care and integrated services (Mechanic 1994). Furthermore, many of those with severe mental illnesses lack insurance and are served largely by the public sector. The private sector, however, has little experience in dealing with severe and persistent mental illnesses such as schizophrenia. Mechanic, Schlesinger, and McAlpine (1995: 20) articulate the alternative outcomes of managed mental health care: "Managed care is a strategy that may increase availability of treatment, contain costs, and increase quality, but it could result as well in denial of needed treatment, reduction in quality of service, and cost shifting to patients, families, professionals, and the community."

The motto of managed care seems to be "less is more," as the primary emphasis has been upon cost-cutting and rationing of care. However, there are countervailing forces that seek to ensure that the goal of quality care is not abandoned. In 1996, the Institute of Medicine formed the Committee on Quality Assurance and Accreditation Guidelines for Managed Behavioral Health Care. The committee's mission was to "develop a framework to guide the development, use, and evaluation of performance indicators, accreditation standards, and quality improvement mechanism" (Institute of Medicine 1997: v). This is a very useful volume for both the practitioner and researcher, as it presents a good overview of the many complex issues facing managed behavioral health care.

The National Association for Healthcare Quality (NAHQ) is another organization that seeks, by establishing standards, to improve the quality of care provided to enrollees of managed care organizations. Another group active in care to those with severe mental illnesses is the National Alliance for the Mentally Ill. In a 1997 study of nine managed behavioral health care companies, NAMI found that managed care is failing to bring the best clinical practices to those with severe mental illness. As with physical health care, managed behavioral health care saves money by restricting inpatient hospital care, which can have detrimental effects for someone who is suicidal or overtly psychotic. The NAMI also found that managed care firms neglect critical community support services (such as housing and rehabilitation) that can help keep those with severe mental illnesses out of the hospital.

There is much apprehension over the future of mental health–care services. Both public and private mental health services are undergoing rapid change as a variety of managed care systems reshape mental health care. Federal and local governments are also considering different forms of mental health parity whereby employer-sponsored benefit plans provide a minimal level of mental health services as well as more traditional forms of health care. Such measures may work toward a more integrated health care system. Mental health advocates and professionals are working to ensure that these types of coverage are adequate and provide also for those with severe and persistent mental illnesses. Another law relevant to mental health is the Americans with Disabilities Act (ADA, passed in 1990), which mandates that employers must hire those with mental handicaps who are qualified to perform the essential functions of the job and to provide reasonable accommodations for these employees. Both measures (parity and the ADA) point toward greater recognition, and perhaps acceptance, of mental health problems, and they may lead the way to an improved mental health service system. Yet the history of mental health reforms indicates that persons with the most serious mental illnesses often do not benefit from reforms that are initially aimed to help them. It remains to be seen whether the most recent round of changes in mental health services will follow this pattern.

21

How Do People Come to Use Mental Health Services? Current Knowledge and Changing Perspectives

Bernice A. Pescosolido & Carol A. Boyer

This chapter focuses on how people come to seek help from mental health services. Services can include: (1) the formal system, consisting of specialty mental health care and general medical care; (2) the lay system, including friends and family as well as self-help groups; (3) the folk system of religious advisors and alternative healers; and (4) the human–social service system of clergy, police, and teachers. The authors provide a review of the research on mental health–care use and describe and contrast the dominant theories of help-seeking behavior (the sociobehavioral model, the health belief model, and the theory of reasoned action). These models provide a profile of users of services; more recent dynamic approaches also focus on when care is received and develop models of illness careers. For example, the help-seeking decision-making model assumes that individuals pass through each stage laid out in the model. The authors propose an alternative, the network–episode model, which views help seeking as a social process managed by the social networks people have in the community, the treatment system, and social service agencies. The network–episode model incorporates four components: the illness career, the social support system, the treatment system, and the social context. Students may want to investigate their own communities to discover what types of services are available for people who need help for their mental health problems.

I had felt this way before, but this started just before Thanksgiving. I went into a depression . . . . The feeling that I have is that I've been feeling this way for years and years but to tell somebody about it was, it was silly or it was being childish and . . . . And a couple of times I called help lines or stress centers and talked to somebody on the phone and they would always either pray with me or just give me enough strength to keep going on. . . . Well the first person I talked to was Rita. I work with her. And it was just the same day that I came in here. I hadn't done anything prior to that. . . . I remember going to work so angry inside . . . . And in my job I have to talk to people all day long on the phone, you know, and I couldn't do it that day . . . so Rita asked what was the matter. She goes, "I know something's wrong with you. You don't even have make-up on." So we talked and I just told her, you know. And that's when she told me she'd try to find me some help. "You need help. You don't need to go through this alone."

(Pam, diagnosed with major depression, 1991)

When people experience mental health problems – whether stresses associated with the normal ups and downs of life or serious problems diagnosed as a mental illness – two basic questions arise: "How are these problems seen by people? What kinds of help exist, and when do people use different sources of care?" In this chapter, we go beyond how clinicians define mental illness and examine how people give meaning to psychiatric symptoms and act on them. We pay particular attention to the social processes involved in responding to mental health problems and if, when, and how individuals receive care from a wide range of people in the community – their friends and family, physicians, and mental health specialists. We consider how the new fiscal and organizational contours of the medical system brought on by health-care reform affect how society allocates the quantity and quality of mental health services and what this means for how people and professionals respond to illness.

Generally, research in mental health utilization or "help seeking" involves the study of how individuals make contact with the *formal* system of care. Much of what we know about the use of services has focused on the two separate but overlapping sectors that characterize this formal medical system:

(1) specialized mental health care – professionals including psychiatrists, psychologists, psychiatric nurses, and social workers, as well as specialized hospitals, inpatient psychiatric units of general hospitals, and outpatient mental health programs; and

(2) general medical care – including primary care practitioners, community hospitals without specialized psychiatric services, and nursing homes.

Even within these sectors, there is considerable variety in the scope and nature of the clinical resources available to ill individuals and the providers who care for them.

As Pam's story makes clear, whether individuals eventually receive formal care often depends on three other "systems": the *lay* system of care, including friends, family, co-workers, and an increasingly visible set of support or self-help groups (Regier et al. 1993); the *folk* system of religious advisors and alternative healers (Kleinman 1980); and the *human–social service* system that includes police, clergy, teachers, and social security clerks (Larson et al. 1988). Together, these systems of care form a complex web of community resources for dealing with mental health problems. There is remarkably little evaluation of how these various services affect outcomes for the people who use them.

Challenges in Understanding the Utilization of Mental Health Care

To understand the behavior of individuals suffering from mental health problems and their entry into treatment, three basic ideas are important. First, only a small percentage of people with mental health problems ever receive formal treatment. Even fewer people are treated by specialized mental health professionals. With the increasing recognition of the high prevalence of mental disorders, their disabling nature, and the distress they cause for individuals and families (Mechanic 1996), it may seem surprising that the majority of people with psychiatric disorders remain untreated or, if they make contact, do not stay in care. Yet many large studies show this gap between need and care (e.g., Shapiro et al. 1985; Ware et al. 1984). In the United States, the most common estimate is that only 20% of individuals (one in five) with mental health problems receive treatment. The National Comorbidity Survey, which administered structured psychiatric interviews to a national probability sample, found the prevalence of psychiatric disorders to be higher – but the percentage of people who received professional treatment to be even lower (by at least 25%) – than that commonly held estimate (Kessler et al. 1994). This higher prevalence of psychiatric disorders, when coupled with lower treatment rates, suggests considerably more unmet need for mental health services than previously thought.

Second, the treatment of mental health problems, as well as the public's view of mental illness, has changed dramatically over the last century. The turn of the last century saw the coming of the "asylum" that was intended to be a place of respite for those suffering from mental illness. Following World War II, a transfer of care occurred for persons with severe and persistent mental disorders from long-term treatment in these mental institutions to treatment anchored in the community (Bachrach 1976; Bell 1989a; Brown 1985; Morrissey & Goldman 1986). Today, these large, old state mental hospitals continue to close or decline in size. Outpatient mental health programs are struggling to meet the increased need for community care for those in greatest need. However, these kinds of services are also available to and used more by individuals suffering from less severe psychological problems, signaling a greater public acceptance of mental health care (Kulka, Veroff, & Douvan 1979). This increase in use by the "worried well" and a longstanding reluctance (at times, an unwillingness) to provide ongoing care for those with severe mental illness produces a system under great strain.

Third, a major change is now occurring in how mental health services are organized and financed in the United States. Although the Clinton Health Security Act (based on managed competition, a global or capped national budget, and universal access to care) failed, it was followed by a "silent revolution" that continues to shift fee-for-service arrangements to various managed care strategies. Different forms, financing arrangements, and regulations may be labeled "managed care," but every version is designed to control costs, access to care, and the types and amount of care delivered (Wells et al. 1995; see Chapters 22 and 23 in this volume). As Mechanic and colleagues (1995) explain, managed care organizations make treatment decisions that previously were made by individual patients or their medical care providers. Managed care introduces an additional party into models of utilization – an organization that allocates care and may even provide that care. At the same time, managed care plans also place greater responsibility for providing care on those outside the formal system, shifting more of the burden of care to families and neighborhoods (Pescosolido & Kronenfeld 1995). We are only beginning to understand the extent of the impact of such plans on individuals' access to care, use of services, quality, and outcomes.

Contributions of Sociology to the Study of Utilization

A substantial body of good theory and relevant findings illustrate how social science theory and methods provide insight into who uses medical or psychiatric care. This research offers an important part of the story of what happens to ill individuals, a part that cannot be known from clinical research. In a perfect world, the mere presence of symptoms would be sufficient for people to desire and obtain treatment. Since this is not the case, knowing who receives care or who has a propensity to seek care informs us about what happens to people with mental health problems.

Sociologists contribute to understanding the use of mental health services in three ways. First, sociologists have documented that "users" and "nonusers" of mental health services have different sociodemographic characteristics and hold different views of medical and mental health treatment. This systematic difference between people who tend to get treatment and those who do not illustrates a major sociological concept, that of social selection (Greenley & Mechanic 1976; Mechanic 1975). The extent to which individuals and social groups with similar psychiatric symptoms ("need") suffer different fates with regard to the use of medical care poses questions about their personal and social lives quite apart from their symptoms. Many of the earliest (and now classic) studies surprised clinical researchers and medical providers by showing that socioeconomic status is predictive not only of who came to treatment but also of how they were treated by the medical system. For example, Dunham (1959) found that individuals from poorer neighborhoods in Chicago had higher rates of first psychiatric admissions to hospitals than those from wealthier areas. Hollingshead and Redlich (1958) found that individuals from lower social classes were more likely to be brought to Yale–New Haven hospital by the police than others. Once hospitalized, these patients were more likely to be given serious diagnoses than individuals from other social classes. It may be tempting to conclude that these actions reflected real differences in mental health problems, but a long tradition of research shows that mental health professionals see problems of the lower social classes differently (i.e., more seriously) and respond to them with more invasive treatments (see e.g. Loring & Powell 1988).

Second, sociologists, as well as anthropologists, focus on understanding individuals in their social contexts. Whereas early clinical researchers looked at the social and clinical profiles of individuals in care, sociologists were the first to follow individuals from the community into the treatment system. This distinctly social science approach provided new and important information. For example, a classic study by Clausen and Yarrow (1955) examined how and when men, later diagnosed with schizophrenia, came to be cared for at St. Elizabeth's Hospital in Washington, D.C. To the surprise of many treatment staff, the authors documented that even individuals with serious mental illness entered care only after years, sometimes decades, of displaying severe and disabling symptoms of schizophrenia. Clausen and Yarrow provided a stunning picture of how these men and their wives struggled, often for years, to understand and normalize strange behaviors before talking to family or friends. Rather than documenting a social process of quick and efficient entry into care for men with serious mental health problems, Clausen and Yarrow described how puzzling mental health symptoms were to families and how the quality of the marriage shaped the responses of wives. These researchers also showed that, beyond extensive and painful delays in getting into treatment, other people in the community – from family and friends to the police and the clergy – played crucial roles in getting these men into care.

Third, sociologists, along with psychologists, have organized psychological, cultural, and medical characteristics into comprehensive theoretical frameworks of who enters care and why they seek care. These theories laid the groundwork for empirical studies and interventions that have been conducted since the late 1960s. Subsequent revisions of these theories improved their sensitivity to measuring new challenges in access, quality, and equity. The current shift in how mental health services are organized and financed will require sociologists to reconsider once again how we conceptualize and study individuals' use of services. As the organizations providing mental health care (e.g., hospitals, outpatient programs, health maintenance organizations, and office-based professionals) undergo radical transformations, pressures for more cost-effective care alter the types and amount of services available as well as referral patterns. For example, many managed care plans prohibit individuals from going directly to psychiatrists. Their primary care physicians serve as "gatekeepers" to the mental health system. Insurance companies now routinely require prior authorization for emergency care or psychiatric hospitalization. Less expensive forms of outpatient treatment, such as group therapy, are being substituted for more expensive individual therapy, and mental health professionals are being encouraged to use drug therapy exclusively or to avoid more lengthy care plans that include "talk" therapy of any sort. Private insurance plans that specialize in managing services for individuals with severe and persistent problems are enhancing outpatient programs and case management to reduce hospital stays and re-admissions. Many states are restructuring their Medicaid programs in order to control the usual 20% of their budget that goes to the care of individuals with serious mental illnesses. At the same time, advocates for persons with mental illness have raised expectations for treatment and alternative services based on self-help and empowerment philosophies (Cook & Wright 1995). All of this restructuring of health care changes how people come into the treatment system, whether and for how long they stay there, and what services they receive.

An Overview of Prior Research on Mental Health–Care Use

Not surprisingly, the single best predictor of the use of mental health services is the need for care. Whether "need" is defined by the level of psychological distress, one or more psychiatric symptoms, limitations in mental health functioning, self-reports of mental health, risk factors associated with mental illness, or a psychiatric diagnosis, individuals with greater need are more likely to enter treatment (Greenley & Mechanic 1976; Gurin et al. 1960; Leaf et al. 1985; Portes, Kyle, & Eaton 1992; Scheff 1966b; Ware et al. 1984).

This research finding illustrates how the larger social context influences entry into treatment. "Need" is a relative concept shaped both by the people who use the term and by their social and cultural circumstances (Cleary 1989). For individuals, need may mean the extent to which psychiatric symptoms cause distress and disrupt work, family, and other social activities. Symptoms causing embarrassment, fear, inconvenience, and uncertainty are more likely to lead to help than other psychiatric symptoms (Mechanic 1978). For families, need reflects the degree of bizarre and dangerous behavior, aggressiveness, or suicidality (Clausen & Yarrow 1955; Lefton 1966). Under strained conditions, families are more likely to report higher need and pressure their family members into treatment. For health professionals, need frequently translates into whether symptoms or disorders can be treated with available knowledge and technology (Cleary 1989). For researchers, need is variously defined as a minimum score on symptom scales or through measures of distress, life events, risk factors, self-reports, diagnostic instruments, or proxies (e.g., expenditures).

Because fewer than one fourth of all individuals with mental health problems receive care, the relationship between need and use of services is far from perfect. If the magnitude and seriousness of psychiatric symptoms alone do not lead to treatment, what other factors are important? Drawing on much of the social science literature that examines social selection into treatment, we discuss four main factors – gender, race and ethnicity, age, and social class – that have been shown to be the strongest and most consistent predictors of outpatient mental health–care utilization.

Gender

Most studies show that women are more likely to receive treatment than men for distress or mental illness (Gove 1984; Greenley & Mechanic 1976; Kessler,

Brown, & Broman 1981; Veroff 1981). Although this gender difference may reflect the higher prevalence of psychiatric symptoms and disorders in women (Kessler et al. 1994), gender differences may also be due to (i) the greater propensity of women to recognize, acknowledge, or report psychiatric symptoms or (ii) gender biases in the measures used or in the judgments of clinicians (Horwitz 1977a,b; Kessler et al. 1981). Recent evidence suggests that gender differences in the use of services may also be related to sources of care. Women make more mental health-related visits than men to physicians in the general medical sector, but women and men do not differ significantly in their rates of use of outpatient specialty mental health care. The higher level of outpatient mental health service visits reported by women may stem from their greater use of medical practitioners overall (Horgan 1984; Leaf & Bruce 1987).

Race and Ethnicity

The gap between need and the actual use of outpatient mental health services is greatest among blacks and Hispanics (Hough et al. 1978; Padgett et al. 1994; Sussman, Robins, & Earls 1987; Wells et al. 1988). When the level of symptoms or distress is controlled, significantly fewer blacks, Mexican Americans, and Asian Americans receive outpatient mental health treatment than do whites (Cole & Pilisuk 1976; Leaf et al. 1985; Mechanic, Angel, & Davies 1991; Neighbors et al. 1992; Scheffler & Miller 1989; Sue 1977; Wells et al. 1988). For example, in a study of federal employees, blacks and Hispanics reported both significantly lower probabilities of one mental health visit and lower total visits overall than whites (Padgett et al. 1994). But some studies show that, once treatment begins, no significant differences exist across ethnic and racial groups in the number of times services were received (Hu et al. 1991; Wells et al. 1988).

Among minority groups, there are greater economic barriers to getting into care as well as greater suspicion about how they will be treated once in the system and whether treatment will help them (Rogler & Cortes 1993; Rogler et al. 1989). For example, when asked about the primary reason for not seeking treatment for a major depressive episode, blacks were significantly more likely than whites to fear being hospitalized (Sussman et al. 1987). The racial and ethnic background of clinicians also may be important, especially for retaining people in long-term care. For example, Asian Americans whose care providers matched their ethnic background were significantly less likely to drop out of treatment than individuals treated by professionals with different racial or ethnic backgrounds (Sue et al. 1991).

Age

For the most part, age shows a curvilinear relationship with entering outpatient mental health treatment. Younger and older age groups have the lowest rates of use, while the middle-aged (25–64 years old) use the most outpatient mental health services (Horgan 1984; Shapiro et al. 1984). Precisely the opposite occurs for physical ailments, where the very young and the elderly are the highest consumers of services (Anderson & Andersen 1972). It is possible that, when these groups visit physicians for physical ailments, emotional and psychological problems are treated as related distress. However, it may also signal poor detection of mental problems by physicians, parents or schools, and caretakers (Morlock 1989; Wells et al. 1986). Some studies report that general practitioners diagnose psychiatric disorders less often but are twice as likely to report a mental health reason for visits, whether or not they provided psychotherapy, therapeutic listening, or prescriptions for psychotropic drugs (Allen, Burns, & Cook 1983; Morlock 1989; Regier et al. 1979).

Social Class

Social class is perhaps the most intriguing of social selection factors and the most problematic to study. Early researchers constructed summary measures of social class (using occupation, income, and residence) and documented important differences in the utilization of mental health services by social class. In Hollingshead and Redlich's (1958) study, individuals in upper social classes were more likely to use outpatient mental health services than those in lower social classes. Similarly, Kadushin (1966) showed that upper-class individuals were more likely to support the use of psychotherapy.

Since these early studies, research has focused on components of social class – education and income. The effects of education on use of services are rather consistent. People with better education have a higher probability of using outpatient mental health services (Greenley, Mechanic, & Cleary 1987; Veroff, Kulka, & Douvan 1981). The effects of income on the use of mental health services are far from clear. Several studies have reported that income is not significantly related to the use of mental health services (Leaf et al. 1985; Veroff et al. 1981). When high use rates are shown among the more affluent, this may reflect their ability to pay for more services, their better insurance coverage, or their self-selection of better insurance coverage (Wells et al. 1986). Medicare, Medicaid, and expanded private insurance coverage for mental health services have made psychiatric services more financially accessible to greater numbers of people. Almost all private insurance plans include some coverage for outpatient mental health services, although higher co-payments, special deductibles, and lower limits of reimbursable services than for general medical care are likely. The most recent research from the RAND Health Insurance Experiment, where effects of insurance and income were separated, show that higher-income groups are more likely to use specialty mental health providers than general medical practitioners or services for mental health problems (Wells et al. 1986).

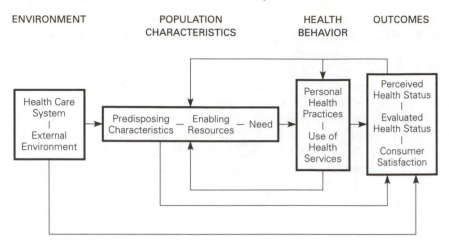

Figure 21.1. Andersen's (1995) revised sociobehavioral model. *Source:* Reprinted with permission from the *Journal of Health and Social Behavior* 36: 1–10.

Combining Social Correlates: Dominant Theories of Help Seeking

Although listing social correlates is informative, a more comprehensive picture of service use emerges through theories of utilization that posit how and why these factors work together. Three dominant theories of utilization guide research in the use of health services: the sociobehavioral model, the health belief model, and the theory of reasoned action.

In the late 1960s, Ronald Andersen (1968; Andersen & Newman 1973) developed the *sociobehavioral* model (SBM). The original model (and still its core) detailed three basic categories: need, predisposing, and enabling factors (see Figure 21.1). Some *need* for care must be defined or individuals are not likely to consider whether or not to use services, what services to use, and when to go. The nature of the illness and its severity (e.g., the "hurt," "worry," "bother," or "pain" that it causes) reflect not merely a biological imperative but also how people perceive this need and how they experience symptoms.

Mental health researchers have developed an extensive array of symptom scales and structured clinical interviews to measure psychiatric need for care. For psychiatrists, the "gold standard" is based on criteria from the American Psychiatric Association's *Diagnostic and Statistical Manual* (DSM-IV; APA 1994). In order to establish a reliable and valid diagnosis according to DSM, standardized information is collected about the person's past history, current social functioning, and symptoms, using one of several structured interviews – for example, the Diagnostic Interview Schedule (DIS; Robins et al. 1981), the Composite International Diagnostic Interview (CIDI; WHO 1990), or the revised CIDI (Kessler et al. 1994).

Some researchers argue that this diagnostic approach alone misses a great deal of social phenomena surrounding symptoms, especially how individuals and professionals socially construct mental health problems (Leaf et al. 1985; Mirowsky & Ross 1989a). In an interesting study, Mechanic and his colleagues (1991) combined interview and claims data from the RAND Health Insurance Experiment to create a measure of "risk" defined as the threat of danger or disruption. This risk measure was more important than psychiatric symptoms in explaining referrals from general medical practitioners to specialty mental health professionals.

In the SBM, gender, race, age, education, and beliefs (to name but a few) are defined as *predisposing* characteristics – those social and cultural factors that are associated with an individual's tendency to seek care. However, even in the presence of need and a profile of predisposing social characteristics, individuals must be able to act on a desire to receive care: *enabling* characteristics are the means and knowledge to get into treatment. Geographical availability, having a regular source of care, travel time, and financial ability (via income, insurance, or the existence of public clinics and programs) limit or facilitate the use of services.

Because Andersen and his colleagues (see Aday, Andersen, & Fleming 1980) were fundamentally concerned with issues of access, organizational characteristics of the health system and types of health insurance benefits figured prominently among enabling characteristics. Managed care arrangements, for example, tap into an important part of enabling characteristics because they are designed to control access to care, types and amounts of care available, and the costs of care. The bulk of research on managed care shows that individuals in both prepaid or managed care plans and fee-for-service arrangements have a similar likelihood of making a single outpatient mental health visit, but those in prepaid plans are less likely to have long-term, continuous care (Diehr, Williams, & Martin 1984; Norquist & Wells 1991; Wells et al. 1986). In the Medical Outcomes Study conducted in Boston, Chicago, and Los Angeles, depressed persons covered by prepaid plans had five fewer outpatient visits in a six-month period (Sturm et al. 1995). In the public sector, where more disadvantaged individuals with severe mental illnesses are treated, the results are more mixed. In Hennepin County (Minnesota) and in the Utah Prepaid Mental Health Plan, individuals with serious mental illnesses who participated in the prepaid versus fee-for-service plans had no significant decreases in inpatient or outpatient use of services (Manning et al. 1993; Moscovice et al. 1993). However, in a capitated program in Monroe County (New York), inpatient psychiatric admissions and days hospitalized decreased while the use of outpatient services increased (Babigian et al. 1992). Finally, in Massachusetts, inpatient admissions from emergency rooms and length of stay declined in both managed care and comparison groups (Stroup & Dorwart 1995).

Over time, Andersen has revised the sociobehavioral model by incorporating more variables measuring the organizational structure, goals, and policies of health-care systems, the insurance industry, and state regulation (Andersen 1995).

Furthermore, the revised SBM considers the effects of service use and, in particular, how previous experience alters need, predisposing, and enabling characteristics. These revisions mirror growing policy concerns about "effective" (i.e., having actual health benefits) and "efficient" (i.e., having the least cost) care. Figure 21.1 shows Andersen's more complicated and complete contextual model of how individuals evaluate their problems (need), their own tendency to seek care as shaped by social and cultural circumstances (predisposing characteristics), and the kinds of access they have or perceive they have to the formal system (enabling characteristics). The environment shapes these population characteristics as well as health behaviors and outcomes.

A second influential theory of help seeking, the *health belief* model (HBM; Rosenstock 1966) came originally from social psychology. It has been revised several times by a multidisciplinary team including sociologist Marshall Becker. In a recent version, this model includes the same kinds of factors as the sociobehavioral model, but its emphasis and intent are quite different. Where the SBM focuses on the influence of the system and issues of access in attempting to understand the use of curative services, the HBM examines the meaning of "predisposing" characteristics. As depicted in Figure 21.2 (from Eraker, Kirscht, & Becker 1984), rather than looking generally at social and cultural factors, the HBM analyzes how individuals' general and specific health beliefs (e.g., beliefs about the severity of symptoms) and preferences (e.g., perceived benefits of treatment), as well as their experiences (with health problems and providers) and knowledge, all affect decisions to seek care, health behavior, and outcomes.

The most recent model in this tradition is Ajzen and Fishbein's (1980) theory of *reasoned action* (TRA). "Expectancy" becomes key as individuals rate how current and alternative actions can reduce health problems. Like the HBM, this model focuses primarily on motivations, assessment of risk, and avoidance of negative outcomes. Individuals evaluate whether or not to engage in healthy (e.g. exercise) or risky (e.g. smoking) behaviors and whether to seek preventive (e.g. mammography) as well as curative medical services. Like the SBM, it takes into account access to the system.

In sum, these utilization models provide a comprehensive listing of contingencies that affect an individual's decision to use services. The contingencies range from the psychological (e.g., patient preferences in the HBM) to the system level (e.g., external environment in the SBM). Over time, each model has broadened its focus to include factors considered central in other approaches. For example, the HBM originally focused heavily on social psychological factors (e.g., general and specific beliefs) to the near exclusion of measures of access to system resources. Developed within the disciplines of sociology and health services administration, the SBM included structural factors and consolidated the sociopsychological detail of the HBM into the residual category of predisposing factors. Revised versions of all the models have been more inclusive and, in keeping with policy concerns, now incorporate a focus on outcomes (Weinstein 1993).

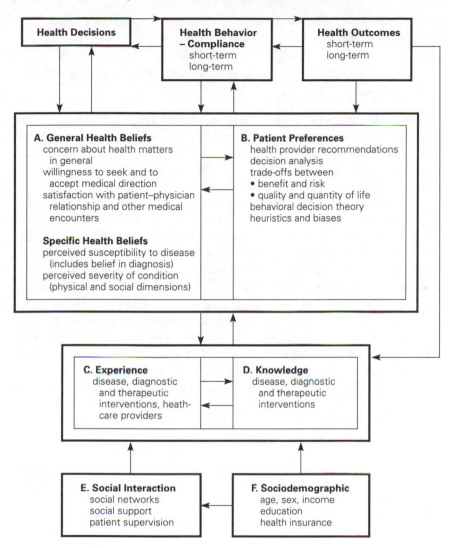

Figure 21.2. Eraker and associates' (1984) revised health belief model. *Source:* Reprinted with permission from the *Annals of Internal Medicine* 100: 258–68.

These theories depend on certain assumptions about service use: *individuals decide whether or not to use medical services by weighing costs and benefits of treatment, given their own assessment of their health profile and the options open to them* (Pescosolido 1992). The first assumption is that the underlying mechanism is rational choice. Individuals are seen as weighing in their minds whether their need can be met by the resources available (in the SBM) or whether their risk of illness is offset by the health-care system treating them (HBM and TRA). The second assumption is that service use is "help seeking," a voluntary choice made by individuals. These are issues to which we will return.

Dynamic Approaches to Studying Utilization in a Changing Health-Care System

The models just described have provided some strong and consistent findings about who uses services and some interesting explanations of why they do so. In essence, these models have provided a profile of service users. A more process-oriented approach to studying the use of services complements these traditional models and is uniquely sensitive to the challenges raised by recent reforms in the health-care system. In general, dynamic approaches focus not only on *who* receives care but also on *when* care is received and *how* the whole episode of illness proceeds. Such approaches treat the use of services more as a socially embedded process, tied not only to the decision making of individuals with psychiatric problems but also to the communities in which they live and the people who surround them in their daily lives and in the treatment system.

Dynamic models challenge the underlying image of traditional models in examining mental health utilization. The very nature of mental illness (and the stress of many other major illnesses) calls into question individuals' ability to engage in the complicated cognitive processes on which some theories rely. Psychiatric symptoms of confused thinking, cognitive disorganization, delusions, and surges or deficits in affect make a "rational choice" approach a poor candidate for understanding the mechanisms underlying use of health services. What happens to these individuals rarely happens as part of a subjective process in people's heads. Individuals who use services may have chosen to do so, may have been forced into treatment, or may have struggled haphazardly (like Pam) in trying to cope with psychiatric problems. But they rarely do this in isolation. Family, police, or other institutional agents (e.g., judges, teachers) suggest that they go for care; such agents bring them in at their own request or use "emergency detentions" and "involuntary commitments" to initiate treatment (Bennett et al. 1993; Grisso & Appelbaum 1995; Hiday 1992a; Matthews 1970; Miller 1988; Perelberg 1983; Suchman 1964). People can be hospitalized involuntarily and treated over their objections, including an outpatient treatment plan of regular, court-ordered injections of such antipsychotic medications as Prolixin or Haldol. For some people, then, the term "help seeking" and the image of individual choice assumed in some utilization models does not fit with their experiences. In fact, fewer than half of the stories people told us about how they came into the mental health system revealed an individual cost–benefit assessment where the individual made the decision to seek care, even when it was suggested by supportive friends and relatives (Pescosolido, Gardner, & Lubell 1995). This issue may be more pronounced in the area of mental illness, but it is not limited to this health problem. Prior research suggests that, in general, traditional utilization models are better adapted to acute than to chronic problems, and they offer better answers to questions about whether individuals *ever* use services than about when they go, how they get there, whether recommendations are followed, and whether they stay in care (Apsler & Rothman 1984; Haug & Lavin 1983; Pescosolido 1991, 1992; Wolinsky & Amold 1986).

These concerns raise some important additional questions: How do we move from a static to a dynamic model of utilization? How do we track the pathways from the community through the medical system and the social service system? What is the underlying mechanism at work? Fortunately, we have a start in some early work that developed the idea of an "illness career."

Attempts to Model Illness Careers and the Use of Services

Research looking at the use of services as a social process dates back to the studies by John Clausen and his colleagues at the Socio-Environmental Laboratory at the National Institute of Mental Health. They developed the concept of "pathways" into care, framed the use of health services as part of an "illness career," and described the sequence of lay people, professionals, and agencies seen during the course of an illness (see also Horwitz 1977a; Janzen 1978; Young 1981). Clausen and his research team talked about different patterns of the recognition of a mental health problem by family and friends. In each case, the wives of the men that they studied tried to understand and adapt to their husbands' changing pattern of behavior until some "trigger" event forced them to recognize that something was wrong. Of course, for many of these men, there were periods in which everything seemed to go smoothly, to be normal. Only a few of the wives thought that the problem might be mental illness; many tried to explain away strange behaviors with different theories (e.g., stress at work, after-effects of service in the military, character flaws, or physical illness).

Other studies in anthropology and sociology described and conceptualized these careers in different ways. Romanucci-Ross (1977) defined "hierarchies of resort" – how individuals set priorities to move from one type of medical system to another. For example, those who followed "acculturative" patterns went first to the formal medical care system, then used folk healers as a back-up, and eventually depended only on their family, friends, or others in the community. Some health researchers defined "stages" that defined points or phases that individuals pass through as they cope with illness (Parsons 1951; Roth 1963). Figure 21.3 shows an update of a stage model, the *help-seeking decision-making model* (HDM; Goldsmith, Jackson, & Hough 1988). Symptoms appear, the problem is recognized, services are used, and particular types of providers are accessed. More recently, Alegría and her colleagues (1991) added a stage that extends the social process to what happens after people make initial contact with help or treatment. Individuals may continue in treatment, change practitioners or services, or discontinue care. The

Figure 21.3. Goldsmith and associates' (1988) revised help-seeking decision-making model. *Source:* M. Alegría, "Mental health care utilization among Puerto Ricans," NIMH grant no. R01 MH 42655.

HDM blended this idea of the stages of a career with the sociobehavioral model, suggesting that at each stage we need to consider how enabling, predisposing, and need contingencies affect the movement from one stage to the next.

The problem with many stage models is that they are rigid – individuals logically passed through every stage laid out in the model. The case of mental illness showed how often this did not fit with what actually happens to people. For many of the men in Clausen's study, the first indication of a serious mental illness was *not* recognizing it but rather wondering why and how they ended up in a psychiatric hospital, sometimes after the police brought them there. More recent models, such as the one shown in Figure 21.3, adopt a broader and more flexible view. Individuals might skip over stages or repeat them; "advisors" include friends, family, and folk healers as well as general and specialty providers in the formal medical sector (see also Twaddle & Hessler 1977).

Another proposed model is the *network–episode* model (NEM; Pescosolido 1991, 1992), which draws from the strengths of the dynamic and contingency models described earlier. The NEM starts with a basic idea: dealing with health problems is a social process that is managed through the contacts (or social networks) that individuals have in the community, the treatment system, and the social service agencies (including support groups, churches, and jails – where we know many individuals end up for the disruptive behavior associated with their illnesses; see Teplin 1994 and Teplin, Abram, & McClelland 1996). How people respond to illness is as much a process of social influence as it is a result of individual action. In the NEM, individuals are seen as pragmatic users of common-sense knowledge and cultural routines as well as seeking out and responding to others when psychiatric symptoms or unusual behaviors occur. The NEM does not suggest that people are not rational, but it questions whether every action in coping with illness is a result of a complicated, cost–benefit calculus. There may be times when people have to weigh the costs and benefits of a whole list of factors (e.g., when faced with the decision to "pull the plug" on a relative on a respirator). In general, however, people are social. That is, they face illness in the course of their day-to-day lives by interacting with other people who may recognize (or deny) a problem, send them to (or provide) treatment, and support, cajole, or nag them

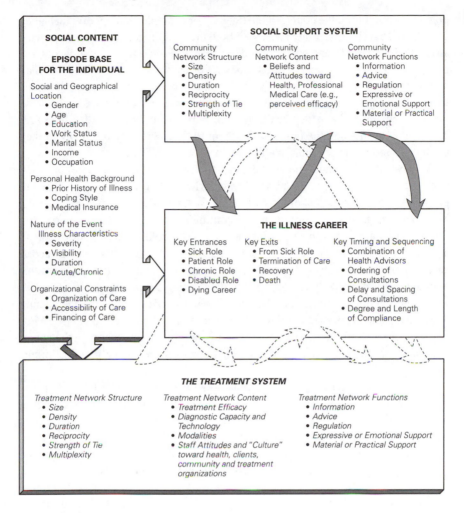

Figure 21.4. Revised network–episode model.

about appointments, medications, or life-style. Figure 21.4 shows a revised version of the NEM and its four basic components: the illness career, social support system, treatment system, and social context.

From career and stage models, the NEM conceptualizes service use not as a single, yes–no, one-time decision but rather as the patterns and pathways of practices and people consulted during an episode of illness. Pictured as the "middle stream" (right side of Figure 21.4), the illness career marks all the individuals' attempts to cope with the onset of an episode of mental health problems, charting what they do and when they do it. Patterns of care describe the combination of advisors and practices used during the course of an illness. For example, some individuals may go only to a psychiatrist; others may visit both their family physician and a psychiatrist. Pathways add the element of order – that is, the sequences of advisors and practices used over the course of an illness. For example, some individuals may pray for help, then go to their pastor, and then to a counselor. Others might have their family try to help them through a bad time and eventually see a physician but never end up in the mental health system. For some individuals, the illness career might begin when the police bring them to an emergency room where they are transferred to the psychiatric unit and nurses contact their family.

We have little information about either patterns or pathways to care, but such knowledge could inform us about whether and when individuals with mental health problems agree to treatment or are willing to take the advice of nurses and doctors. For example, there is an important and continuing debate about the merits and limits of involuntary treatment. Some mental health professionals, policy makers, and advocates argue that these legal measures ensure that patients receive needed care, that the length of hospitalization is reduced, the quality of life improves, rehabilitation is more likely to happen, and debilitating symptoms lessen (Gardner et al. 1993). Others believe that the use of coercion undermines the therapeutic relationship and is not successful in ensuring compliance with treatment (see Mulvey, Gelber, & Roth 1987). Only by following individuals and mapping the nature of their contacts, experiences, and resulting outcomes can we address this important issue.

Whatever the patterns or pathways, the NEM does not assume that illness careers occur in a vacuum. Rather, they are embedded in personal lives and changing communities. The NEM conceptualizes the idea of "community" through the idea of a dynamic social support system (top stream of Figure 21.4). It does this by breaking down the community into individuals' social ties or social networks. The structure (e.g. size), content (e.g., beliefs about and experiences with the medical system), and functions (e.g., support or coercion) of social networks capture that all communities hold vast reserves of people who might be consulted during the course of an illness. At any time in the illness career, network advisors may or may not be consulted, may or may not change over time, and may or may not be consistent in their advice.

In any case, the nature of the encounters people have in their day-to-day lives help to provide meaning to the symptoms of illness. If individuals see mental health problems as crises of faith, as bad marriages, or as any of a number of other things besides illness, they may consult faith healers, spiritualists, the clergy, or other people (Lubchansky, Egri, & Stokes 1970; Rogler & Hollingshead 1961). If they, or others around them, see the problem as "bad behavior" rather than illness, then they might seek out police and lawyers (Cumming & Harrington 1963; Hiday 1992a). If they conceptualize their problem as physical illness (e.g., "fatigue" associated with depression), then they may visit physicians, try an exercise regime, or start taking vitamins. As we would expect, studies find that when the social network ties around ill people – especially friends and relatives – hold positive attitudes toward psychiatry or have been in treatment themselves, ill people are more likely to use medical services (Fisher 1988; Greenley & Mechanic 1976; Greenley et al. 1987; Weinstein 1993). However, social networks also may deter the use of services or have no effect (Geertsen et al. 1975; McKinlay 1972; Salloway & Dillon 1973; Suchman 1964). Following Freidson (1970a,b), the NEM evaluates the power of social networks in terms of how their structure (e.g., their size and amount of support) and the kinds of advice they offer (e.g., supportive or resistant to mental health treatment) work together. Among studies of the middle and upper classes in New York City (e.g., Kadushin 1966), networks facilitated use. Among the poor in Puerto Rico, however, large and supportive networks substituted for informal care and harbored negative beliefs about the efficacy of the mental health system, thus lowering the probability of using formal providers (Pescosolido et al. 1996a). The NEM suggests that both of these characteristics of social networks must be taken into account in order to provide a sense of how much influence is being exerted on the ill person and to determine the trajectory of that "push" – for example, into or away from formal medical or mental health treatment.

Although every society has some kind of treatment system, what that system looks like, who has access to it, what it offers, and how difficult it is for people to get care can vary substantially even within a given society (Andersen 1995). As we have described, our medical system is currently undergoing very dramatic changes. The NEM conceptualizes the medical system as a changing set of providers and organizations with which individuals may have contact when they are ill (bottom stream, right-hand side, Figure 21.4). Like the community and the episode of illness, the elements of this set change over time in response to the health problems people have, to the technology and medical knowledge that exists, to the resources that society makes available, and to community preferences and demands. In the same way that social networks can help us break down the community into the set of contacts people have, the network perspective allows us to unpack what happens to people when they go for treatment and to think about how their experiences affect whether they stay in treatment, take their medications, and get better. The treatment system shapes a set of network contacts for ill people, their families, and other people who become involved in the illness career (e.g., police or social service workers). Like the community, the treatment system can provide a rich set of helpful, supportive people for individuals or can allow for contacts that are only brief, impersonal, and antagonistic. The kinds of social networks that exist in the treatment setting create a climate of care, affect the work of medical providers, and shape reactions of individuals who come for treatment (Pescosolido 1996, 1997; Pescosolido, Wright, & Sullivan 1996b).

The left side of Figure 21.4 represents the foundation: the larger social context for the dynamic streams of the illness career, the social support system, and the treatment system. All are anchored in the social locations, histories, and problems that people have. For example, in studies showing the effects of predisposing characteristics, women tend to have more social network ties, to be more involved in caretaker networks, and to use more formal services than men (Cook 1988; Mechanic 1978; Thoits 1995a). In research that looked at the differences in service use between the Mariel Cubans and Haitian refugees arriving in southern Florida during the early 1980s (Portes et al. 1992), it became clear that *where* the immigrants came from mattered a great deal. The Mariel Cubans had greater mental health problems, but these needs were also more likely to be met. Their past experience with the Cuban health system (a socialized set of services) combined with the strong and supportive ties in the vibrant Cuban community in southern Florida to provide them with mental health treatment. The Haitian refugees, who did not have a history of using mental health facilities before immigration and who found only a small and limited ethnic community upon their arrival, had a lower use of services after arrival. The severity and nature of mental health problems also shape the illness career and the extent to which individuals in the social support and treatment systems experience burnout (Tausig 1992; Wright 1994).

The NEM and other process models provide a more complex picture of what happens when people experience mental health problems. They raise questions concerning how we think about, study, and collect data on the complicated and often messy realities of dealing with illness, particularly as society and treatment systems change.

Conclusion

In this chapter we have provided an overview of the issues, theories, ongoing changes, and challenges that surround efforts to understand how, when, and why individuals enter or fail to come for treatment of mental health problems. A great deal is known about the use of mental health services by different social groups, but we are far from understanding the nature of the process and timing by which people reach treatment in the mental health system. We have suggested that one way to proceed is to tie together the community, the illness career, and the treatment system. This link between the day-to-day lives of individuals and their interactions in the community or the treatment system cannot be ignored. Such interactions shape how individuals who may need care – as well as those who provide care – view mental health problems, how they embrace or scorn what the treatment system offers, and whether they are encouraged or dissuaded to receive or provide care.

One issue that we did not explore in detail was the impact of different kinds of "need" – social, financial, or medical – that mental health problems raise for individuals and their families. We have focused on medical or mental health needs and, for the most part, on how individuals get into care. However, the onset of a serious mental illness, such as schizophrenia, interferes with schooling, employment, and intimate relationships. Further, even for individuals who are hospitalized in acute psychiatric units, where stabilization or resolution of the acute symptoms may occur, ongoing psychiatric treatment and rehabilitation is critical. We know relatively little about what happens after people get into the system. We have addressed the issue of pathways to care, but there should be a parallel focus on pathways *from* care. We do know that the likelihood of following through with aftercare in the community is quite low (Boyer & Mechanic 1994). We need to ask how different sectors (e.g., psychiatric and medical care, housing, employment, substance abuse) work smoothly or erratically, and in coordination or in opposition, to address individuals' mental health and related social problems (see Bachrach 1980; Morrissey et al. 1994; Pescosolido 1996; Rosenfield 1991).

After decades of concentrating on who used what types of mental health services, social scientists have now turned toward addressing other challenging sociological questions about the patterns and pathways into care and about how incentives (financial or otherwise) affect use of services and their allocation in a radically changed health-care environment. As reforms are implemented and as communities react to these and other changes, the experiences individuals confront, their perceptions of mental health problems, and their response to them and use of services may be different than in the past. With managed care rapidly becoming a mainstay of health-care delivery in the United States, a process approach may better capture how service use changes over time, how managed care allows or limits the use of specialty mental health services, and how families and other social service agencies assume the added burden of care resulting from decreased hospital stays and limits on outpatient services.

22

Contemporary Mental Health Systems and Managed Care

Ronald W. Manderscheid, Marilyn J. Henderson,
Michael J. Witkin, & Joanne E. Atay

Mental health care has become a commodity under managed care systems, where cost is a principal determinant of care. Managed care places greater reliance upon prior review (internal or external) to control who receives what type and what intensity of care. To understand how managed care affects service delivery, a profile of the current mental health system must be available. This chapter provides that framework. Information on the mental health service system is available from the perspective of consumers (the ECA study), from providers (survey data collected by the Center for Mental Health Services and the National Center for Health Statistics), and from a system framework. The authors use the system framework to provide a statistical profile of the current mental health system, presenting data from national surveys of specialty mental health services for 1990 and 1992. The statistical profile includes the numbers of individuals (adults, children, and adolescents) who received care; the number of service organizations, services, and service episodes; and an assessment of financial and human resources. The authors conclude by identifying the major trends that will affect mental health services: the growth of managed care, evolution of a multitiered system, growth of the consumer movement, and growth of population-based planning. Do students think that these trends will increase or rather decrease the services available to consumers?

Introduction and Purpose

Managed care has already had a profound effect on mental health care (Freeman & Trabin 1994; Manderscheid & Henderson 1996). Inpatient mental health care has become less frequent, and ambulatory care has become more common. At present, the effects of these changes on quality and outcome of care are virtually unknown. It is clear, however, that mental health care has become a commodity under managed care, and that cost is the principal mechanism for assigning quality at present.

What is managed care? It is primarily a reform in the financing of care through which great reliance is placed on prior review to control who receives what type and intensity of care. This review may be external or internal (Manderscheid & Henderson 1996). An example of the former would be when a health insurance company hires a utilization review firm to serve as a control point from which providers must receive approval before giving care to a prospective client. An example of the latter would be a health maintenance organization (HMO) that both delivers care and monitors level of utilization by clients.

The movement toward managed care is as profound as the deinstitutionalization process of a generation ago (Bachrach 1976). Hence, it is exceedingly important to develop a statistical profile of the mental health care system prior to implementation of managed care. The purpose of this chapter is to offer such a baseline, which can be used by students, faculty, researchers, and policy makers as a framework for examining the effects of managed care. In a sense, this statistical profile can provide a window to the future.

Recent Descriptions of the Mental Health System

Relatively few synoptic descriptions of the mental health service system have been provided in the past. To develop those descriptions that are available, researchers examined service delivery through the eyes of those who use care or through the eyes of those who deliver care. Major examples of each approach are provided below.

The Client's Perspective

The Epidemiological Catchment Area (ECA) project provided a classical analysis of the mental health service system. Based upon interviews of adults in the community and in institutional settings conducted during the early 1980s, Regier et al. (1993) compiled an overview of the de facto mental and addictive disorders service system for adults in the United States. Currently, similar information is not available for children and adolescents.

Figure 22.1 summarizes the major findings from the ECA work. For 1990, the results showed that about 28.1% of the adult population of the United States – about 52 million persons – had a mental or addictive disorder during that year. However, only about 14.7% of the adult population – almost 27 million adults – received any care. More than half of all adults served had diagnoses in the year in which services were provided.

Mental health care was provided in several types of settings: by mental health and substance abuse providers (5.9% of all adults were served); by primary care physicians (5.0% of all adults); and by social service providers or self-help groups (3.8% of all adults). These findings were shown to be valid through independent data sources (Manderscheid et al. 1993).

The Provider's Perspective

Information from providers was used to develop a more detailed picture of the mental health care delivered by mental health practitioners and primary care physicians.

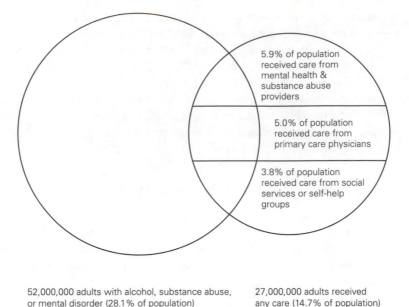

52,000,000 adults with alcohol, substance abuse,   27,000,000 adults received
or mental disorder (28.1% of population)   any care (14.7% of population)

Figure 22.1. Perspective on population problems and services delivered from the ECA project. *Source:* Adapted from Regier et al. (1993).

Schulberg and Manderscheid (1989) used survey data collected by the National Institute of Mental Health and the National Center for Health Statistics to construct this picture. Findings regarding service use generally confirmed those just noted for the ECA project.

The results showed that major shifts have occurred since the 1950s in terms of the sites in which mental health care is delivered in the United States. However, in the 1980s, the new patterns stabilized. Generally, with the advent of deinstitutionalization in the 1950s, the use of inpatient care stopped growing, the use of ambulatory care expanded dramatically, and service sites became considerably more heterogeneous. For example, the use of general hospital psychiatric services grew, partial care was introduced as an alternative to inpatient care, and a broad array of different organizations and practice arrangements were used to deliver ambulatory care. Of note, this work offers a similar perspective on patterns of care as that of the ECA study.

A System Framework

To help organize client and provider information on mental health services, work has been undertaken to apply systems analysis to national data on mental health

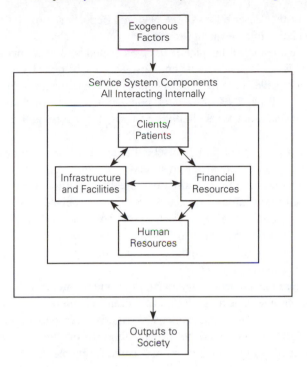

Figure 22.2. System framework to organize information on the mental health service delivery system. *Source:* Adapted from Katzper and Manderscheid (1984).

service delivery (Katzper & Manderscheid 1984). As shown in Figure 22.2, this work has resulted in a system framework that organizes such data. It shows that Exogenous Factors, such as population and socioeconomic and political factors influence how the service system operates. The service system itself is comprised of four components, all of which interact internally. These are Infrastructure and Facilities, Financial Resources, Human Resources, and Clients. In turn, these components and their interactions lead to Outputs to Society. This system framework will be used to guide the present analyses.

The Current Mental Health System

In this section we present findings from national surveys of specialty mental health services for 1990 and 1992. Although important, descriptions of mental health care provided by primary care physicians, social service agencies, and self-help groups are beyond the scope of this paper. For the specialty mental health services covered in this report, detailed descriptions of the surveys that served as sources are available (Manderscheid et al. 1986; Redick et al. 1983). The reader is referred to those sources for further descriptions of the National Reporting Program and the Mental Health Statistics Improvement Program.

In order to set the context for the picture to be presented here, it is important to specify what is and is not included in the findings. This can be done by looking at the population that received care from the mental health organizations described. Recall from Figure 22.1 that 5.9% of the adult population received specialty mental health and/or substance abuse care in 1990. Overall, this represented about 10.9 million adults in that year.

From information presented by Manderscheid et al. (1993), one can estimate that of the 10.9 million adults who received specialty care in 1990, about 5 million were cared for by private practitioners, slightly more than 1 million were cared for by substance abuse organizations, and about 5.8 million received care from the mental health organizations described in the next section. (The total of these numbers is greater than 10.9 million, since slightly more than half of all persons who received inpatient care also received ambulatory care from a provider organization or private practitioner in the same year.)

Thus, in 1990, these mental health organizations provided care to about 5.8 million adults. To this number, one must also add children and adolescents under age 18 who received care from these organizations. Currently, exact person counts are not available for these children and adolescents, although our findings (derived from data in Table 22.7) suggest that the number cared for by mental health organizations each year is approximately 1 million.

Service Organizations and Services

Although the overall number of mental health organizations grew from 5,284 to 5,498 between 1990 and 1992, the distribution of organizations changed only slightly (Table 22.1). Organizations that specialized in the provision of inpatient and residential treatment comprised a smaller proportion in 1992 as compared with 1990. These include state and county mental hospitals, private psychiatric hospitals, general hospitals with separate psychiatric services, and residential treatment centers for emotionally disturbed children. On the other hand, organizations that provide services predominantly in ambulatory settings, such as outpatient or partial care settings, comprised a larger proportion of total organizations. These include freestanding psychiatric outpatient clinics, freestanding psychiatric partial care organizations, and multiservice mental health organizations.

In addition to the distribution of organizations, Table 22.1 also gives the distribution of services that are provided in specific settings. For multiservice mental health organizations, the large increase in the proportion providing inpatient and/or residential services was due to a change in definition rather than a change in service delivery.

Table 22.1. *Distribution of U.S. mental health organizations and associated services, 1990 and 1992*

Organization type	1990				1992			
	Total organizations	Number with specific service			Total organizations	Number with specific service		
		Inpatient and/or residential treatment	Outpatient treatment	Partial care		Inpatient and/or residential treatment	Outpatient treatment	Partial care
TOTAL	5,284	3,430	3,189	2,430	5,498	3,934	3,390	2,548
	Percent of column total							
State and county mental hospitals	5.2	8.0	2.6	2.3	5.0	6.9	2.2	1.8
Private psychiatric hospitals	8.7	13.5	5.5	12.9	8.6	12.1	5.8	15.0
Nonfederal general hospitals with separate psychiatric services	31.7	45.7	19.8	17.2	29.5	38.6	18.2	16.6
VA medical centers	2.7	3.8	4.4	2.9	2.9	3.4	4.7	2.7
Residential treatment centers for emotionally disturbed children	9.5	14.6	5.1	8.2	9.0	12.6	4.9	7.7
Freestanding psychiatric outpatient clinics	14.1	-	23.3	-	15.7	-	25.5	-
Freestanding psychiatric partial care organizations	1.8	-	-	3.8	2.9	-	-	6.2
Multiservice mental health organizations	26.3	14.4	39.3	52.7	26.4	26.4	38.7	50.0

Table 22.2. *Distribution and rates of U.S. patient care episodes by organization type, 1990 and 1992*

Organization type	Total patient care episodes in thousands			Total episode rates per 100,000 civilian population		
	1990	1992	Change in percent 1990-92	1990	1992	Change in percent 1990-92
TOTAL	8,617	8,809		3,487.8	3,474.3	-0.4
	Percent of column total					
State and county mental hospitals	6.0	5.6	-0.4	207.7	196.2	-5.5
Private psychiatric hospitals	7.9	9.3	1.4	276.8	322.7	16.6
Nonfederal general hospitals with separate psychiatric services	23.7	21.3	-2.4	827.7	741.1	-10.5
VA medical centers	8.2	7.7	-0.5	285.0	268.9	-5.6
Residential treatment centers for emotionally disturbed children	3.4	3.3	-0.1	118.1	114.3	-3.2
Freestanding psychiatric outpatient clinics	10.4	11.0	0.6	361.0	380.9	5.5
Freestanding partial care organizations	0.3	0.3	0.0	9.8	11.4	16.3
Multiservice mental health organizations	40.1	41.5	1.4	1,401.7	1,438.8	2.6

Service Episodes

Table 22.2 gives the percent distribution and rates per 100,000 civilian population for total patient care episodes by organization type; Table 22.3 gives the percent distribution of patient care episodes provided in inpatient, outpatient, and partial care settings. *Patient care episodes* are defined as the number of persons receiving services at the beginning of the year plus the number added to the rolls during the year. Although the overall number of patient care episodes increased from 8.6 to 8.8 million between 1990 and 1992, the total episode rate per 100,000 civilian population decreased slightly from 3,488 to 3,474 (−0.4%) (Table 22.2).

The largest changes in rates were for private psychiatric hospitals and freestanding partial care organizations, which increased 17% and 16%, respectively; the largest percent decreases in rates occurred in nonfederal general hospitals with

Table 22.3. *Number and distribution of U.S. patient care episodes by service type and organization type, 1990 and 1992*

Organization type	Inpatient care episodes in thousands			Outpatient care episodes in thousands			Partial care episodes in thousands		
	1990	1992	Change in percent 1990-92	1990	1992	Change in percent 1990-92	1990	1992	Change in percent 1990-92
TOTAL	2,263	2,307		5,810	5,959		544	544	
	Percent of column total			Percent of column total			Percent of column total		
State and county mental hospitals	16.4	15.7	-0.7	2.1	2.0	-0.1	3.7	2.8	-0.9
Private psychiatric hospitals	19.3	21.4	+2.1	3.4	4.2	0.8	9.2	14.0	4.8
Nonfederal general hospitals with separate psychiatric services	44.1	42.8	-1.3	16.8	13.8	-3.0	12.7	12.1	-0.6
VA medical centers	9.5	8.6	-0.9	7.8	7.8	0.0	6.1	4.0	-2.1
Residential treatment centers for emotionally disturbed children	3.1	2.7	-0.4	3.4	3.5	0.1	5.0	3.9	-1.1
Freestanding psychiatric outpatient clinics	-	-	-	15.4	16.2	0.8	-	-	-
Freestanding partial care organizations	-	-	-	-	-	-	4.4	5.3	0.9
Multiservice mental health organizations	7.6	8.8	1.2	51.1	52.5	1.4	58.9	57.9	-1.0

separate psychiatric services, which decreased 11%, and state and county mental hospitals and VA medical centers, which decreased 6% each (Table 22.2). Each of the latter organizations were downsizing or remaining the same with respect to numbers of episodes in the 1990–92 time period for all three settings (Table 22.3). Private psychiatric hospitals gained, particularly in the number of partial care and hospitalization episodes (Table 22.3), as partial hospitalization became a covered service under Medicare, and also (but to a lesser extent) in the number of inpatient and outpatient care episodes.

Financial Resources

Although the total expenditures by mental health organizations increased in actual dollars from $28.4 billion in 1990 to $29.8 billion in 1992, the expenditures per capita of the United States civilian population decreased from $116.39 to $111.27 (Table 22.4). However, if the expenditures are expressed in constant dollars – that is, adjusted by the medical care component of the consumer price index (1970 = 100) – then the expenditures overall decreased from $5.6 billion to $5.0 billion,

Table 22.4. *Expenditures of U.S. mental health organizations, 1990 and 1992*

Organization type	Expenditures in thousands of dollars		Change in percent 1990-92	Expenditures per capita	
	1990	1992		1990	1992
TOTAL	$28,410,261	$29,765,202		$116.39	$111.27
	Percent of column total				
State and county mental hospitals	27.4	26.8	-0.6	31.85	31.25
Private psychiatric hospitals	21.5	17.8	-3.7	24.99	15.36
Nonfederal general hospitals with separate psychiatric services	16.4	17.4	1.0	19.10	20.36
VA medical centers	5.2	5.1	-0.1	6.06	6.00
Residential treatment centers for emotionally disturbed children	6.9	7.3	0.4	8.07	8.50
Freestanding psychiatric outpatient clinics	2.4	2.8	0.4	2.75	3.22
Freestanding partial care organizations	0.2	0.4	0.2	0.33	0.47
Multiservice mental health organizations	20.0	22.4	2.4	23.24	26.11

a decrease of 10.3% (Manderscheid & Sonnenschein 1994, 1996). Organizations comprising a larger proportion of total expenditures in 1992, as compared with 1990, included all organizational types *except* state and county mental hospitals, private psychiatric hospitals, and VA medical centers (Table 22.4), three organizations with decreasing numbers of patient days and shorter lengths of stay in 1992 as compared with 1990.

To provide context for these numbers, additional information is required on total mental health spending. Frank and associates (1994) estimated the total funding for mental health services in 1990 at $42.4 billion. With this figure as the denominator and with our $28.4 billion figure as the numerator, one can estimate that about two thirds of spending on mental health care was organization based, with the remainder going principally to individual and group practitioners.

Human Resources

As shown in Table 22.5, the number of full-time equivalent (FTE) staff (based on a 40-hour workweek) increased from 563,619 in 1990 to 584,977 in 1992 (3.8%).

Table 22.5. *FTE staffing, by discipline, in U.S. mental health organizations, 1990 and 1992*

Staff discipline	Full-time equivalent staff		
	Number of FTEs		Change in percent 1990-92
	1990	1992	
All staff	563,619	584,977	
	Percent of column total		
Patient care staff	73.8	73.9	0.1
Psychiatrists	3.3	3.9	0.6
Other physicians	0.7	0.7	0.0
Psychologists	4.0	4.3	0.3
Social workers	9.5	9.7	0.2
Registered nurses	13.8	13.4	-0.4
Other mental health professionals (B.A. and above)	14.9	17.4	2.5
Physical health professionals and assistants	2.3	2.8	0.5
Other mental health workers (less than B.A.)	25.3	21.7	-3.6
Administrative, clerical, and maintenance workers	26.2	26.1	-0.1

The relative distribution of patient care staff to administrative, clerical, and maintenance staff was approximately 3 to 1 in each year (Table 22.5).

However, within specific staff disciplines of the patient care staff, notable changes occurred between 1990 and 1992. With the exception of registered nurses, all professional staff disciplines comprised a larger proportion of total staff in 1992 as compared with 1990. Other mental health professionals (B.A. and above) – including occupational therapists, recreation therapists, and vocational rehabilitation counselors in particular – comprised over 2.5% more of the total FTE staff in 1992 as compared with 1990, an indication of the increased intent of organizations to expand their treatment and rehabilitation services rather than just provide custodial services. At the other extreme, registered nurses and, in particular, other mental health workers (less than B.A., including aides and orderlies) decreased as inpatient units downsized, particularly those in state and county mental hospitals.

Table 22.6. *Distribution of U.S. residents under care and admitted, by treatment modality, 1986*

Organization type	Persons under care			Persons admitted		
	Inpatient	Outpatient	Partial care	Inpatient	Outpatient	Partial care
TOTAL	170,486	1,405,076	133,194	1,687,464	2,180,507	156,912
Percent of column total						
State and county mental hospitals	59.1	3.9	2.9	20.3	2.7	4.3
Private psychiatric hospitals	10.1	3.3	5.9	13.1	4.0	3.7
VA medical centers	7.7	5.2	7.6	10.6	2.7	3.0
Nonfederal general hospitals	20.2	13.5	8.1	50.4	14.5	16.0
Multiservice mental health organizations	2.8	56.0	69.0	5.5	56.1	67.7
RTCs for emotionally disturbed children		0.7	1.9		1.0	2.4
Freestanding partial care organizations			4.7			3.0
Freestanding outpatient clinics		17.3			19.1	

Service Recipients

The most recent national information about characteristics of service recipients dates from 1986. Information is presented for two groups of recipients, those continuing care at a point in time (beginning of the survey), as well as those admitted during a one-year period. Adding these two groups together provides an estimate of the total number of recipients within the year. Approximately 5.7 million people were seen in the inpatient, partial care, and outpatient programs of specialty mental health organizations in 1986. Outpatient programs provided care to the largest number, approximately 3.6 million persons. Slightly less than 2 million persons were seen within inpatient programs, and a much smaller group, under 300,000 persons, was seen within partial care programs.

Striking differences existed among inpatient, outpatient, and partial care programs with respect to the number and locus of care for persons admitted during the year versus those in active treatment at the beginning of the year (Table 22.6). In outpatient and partial care programs, the numbers of persons under care at a given time and those admitted during the year were approximately equal and were concentrated primarily in multiservice mental health organizations. In inpatient programs, this was not the case: the number of admissions overall was much higher than the number of residents. Over half of residents under care were in state and county mental hospitals, and another one fifth of residents were in nonfederal general hospital psychiatric services. Among persons admitted, these percentages were reversed, consistent with the shorter stays and greater turnover found in the general hospital psychiatric settings. With the increased emphasis

Table 22.7. *Client characteristics of U.S. residents under care and admitted,*
by treatment modality, 1986

Client characteristic	Persons under care			Persons admitted		
	Inpatient	Outpatient	Partial care	Inpatient	Outpatient	Partial care
TOTAL	170,486	1,405,076	133,194	1,687,464	2,180,507	156,912
Percent of column total						
Gender						
Male	59.1	48.7	55.6	56.7	52.4	56.7
Female	40.9	51.3	44.4	43.3	47.6	43.3
Race						
White	71.8	84.6	75.9	75.7	85.0	80.5
Races other than white	28.2	15.4	24.1	24.3	15.0	19.5
Age						
Under 18	9.8	16.3	13.0	7.0	26.2	11.7
18-24	11.8	9.3	9.7	13.5	14.0	17.0
25-44	47.7	45.9	44.1	52.1	44.7	48.7
45-64	19.3	22.1	25.4	18.7	12.0	17.8
65 and Over	11.4	6.4	7.9	8.7	3.1	4.8

on short inpatient stays within psychiatric hospitals, it is not surprising to find a smaller number of persons under care at any one time and a larger number of persons moving in and out of care. It can be expected that this pattern will become more pronounced over time.

Table 22.7 summarizes the basic patient characteristics of gender, race, and age. With the exception of persons under care in outpatient programs, males comprised slightly larger percentages of recipients than females, even though they made up slightly less than half (48%) of the civilian population in 1986. Persons who were white made up the preponderance of persons under care and admitted to each program type, but were particularly highly represented in outpatient programs. Inpatient programs tended to have higher proportions of persons who were from races other than white, particularly among those under care, where minority races made up 28% of residents as compared with only 15% of the U.S. civilian population in 1986.

In all settings, persons between the ages of 15 and 44 made up the largest percentage of the recipients (Table 22.7). Both the elderly and youngest populations tended to be underrepresented within specialty inpatient, outpatient, and partial care programs when compared with their numbers in the general population.

Table 22.8. *Selected diagnoses for U.S. residents under care and admitted, by treatment modality, 1986*

Diagnostic grouping	Persons under care			Persons admitted		
	Inpatient	Outpatient	Partial care	Inpatient	Outpatient	Partial care
TOTAL	170,486	1,405,076	133,194	1,687,464	2,180,507	156,912
Percent of column total						
Alcohol-related disorders	6.2	4. 9	1.8	14.4	9.4	9.3
Drug-related disorders	3.0	1.9	1.1	6.4	3.1	2.1
Affective disorders	21.7	22.1	17.0	31.7	14.3	22.5
Schizophrenia and related disorders	43.6	21.3	47.4	23.0	7.7	32.0
Personality disorders	2.4	6.0	4.9	1.8	6.7	3.8
Adjustment disorders	3.8	16.7	5.2	7.4	23.0	11.1

Children and youth under 18 represented a higher percentage of persons in ambulatory care settings than in inpatient settings, a finding consistent with the emphasis on providing services in the least restrictive settings, particularly for children and youth.

Differences also exist in the diagnostic distributions for persons seen within the three service settings. To illustrate differences among the settings, Table 22.8 presents several major groupings of principal diagnoses: alcohol-related disorders, drug-related disorders, major affective disorders, schizophrenia and related disorders, personality disorders, and adjustment disorders. Approximately two thirds of the persons under care in inpatient and partial care programs received principal diagnoses within the groupings of either affective disorder or schizophrenia, and about half of persons admitted to inpatient and partial care programs received these diagnoses. Persons diagnosed with schizophrenia and related disorders tended to have longer hospital stays and hence were concentrated within the "under care" caseload counts when compared with admission counts.

As could be expected, in outpatient settings more focus was given to less severe disorders, such as adjustment disorders and social conditions. This points to very different groups of people being seen in each setting. The question of which programs will serve more severely ill persons as the system continues to decrease the use of inpatient care (and the length of stay for such care) remains to be resolved.

Major Current Trends

The information presented here tells an important story. It also provides an essential baseline for current developments. Several of the most significant of these current trends are described next.

Dramatic Growth of Managed Care

Currently, about 150 million persons are covered by private managed behavioral health-care plans, and 45 states have received waivers from the U.S. Health Care Financing Administration to convert their Medicaid mental health programs to managed care. The rate of conversion to managed care has been unprecedented, especially since the demise of President Clinton's national health-care reform initiative.

Managed care will lead to dramatic changes in the statistical profile that we have presented. For example, the number of mental health organizations will likely decrease; the use of inpatient care will diminish further; the number of providers will become smaller; provider composition will change; financial resources will shrink; and client characteristics will change. The entire mental health delivery system will change as control of care moves from individual providers to the entities that pay for care and their representatives. The effects that these profound changes will have upon quality and outcome of care are yet to be determined.

Further Evolution of a Multitiered System

Historically, a strong distinction has existed between private mental health care and that provided by public sector organizations (Nakao et al. 1986). When private insurance benefits were exhausted, the consumer of care moved from the private to the public sector. Such "dumping" had the effect of keeping private sector insurance costs artificially low while encouraging the development of a large public safety net of mental health services.

Modern managed care replicates this historic pattern. Because of the failure of national health-care reform, the United States does not have universal health insurance coverage. Currently, more than 43 million Americans are without any health insurance (U.S. Bureau of Census 1996, Table 173). At the same time, private and public managed care plans are being developed independently. This multitiered system encourages dumping from one level to another – dumping from private to public settings and dumping from public settings to the streets or jails. Clearly, we have yet to develop a comprehensive solution to this problem.

Consumers as Providers

Another hallmark of the present era is the dramatic growth of a mental health consumer movement in the United States. Over the past 20 years, consumers have organized affinity groups that have articulated common consumer values (Consumer Managed Care Network 1996). Among these values are concepts related to care (personhood, recovery, and independence) as well as concepts related to participation (organization, operation, and evaluation of care systems). The rapid expansion of self-help approaches attests to the expression of these values.

Of particular note in the present context is the rapid expansion of consumer affairs offices in state mental health agencies and the emergence of consumers in the role of peer counselors. The consumer affairs offices provide policy guidance on the organization and operation of state systems; peer counselors provide direct care in local communities. These trends are altering both our concepts of care delivery and the statistical profile presented earlier.

Growth of Population-Based Planning

To be most efficient and effective, modern managed care needs to engage in population-based planning. Information of the type presented in the ECA study is required to define the mental health status of populations, their needs for mental health interventions, and potential directions for prevention activities. Only through a comprehensive, population-based approach will level of service needs be controlled and the effects of prevention optimized.

State mental health agencies have begun to engage in population-based planning for adults and children with serious mental disorders. This effort has been facilitated through the planning requirements of the Community Mental Health Services Block Grant (authorized by Part B of Title XIX of the Public Health Service Act – 42 U.S.C. 300x et seq.). Similar planning has been initiated in the private sector with respect to particular mental health benefit plans. Thus, current efforts could be said to reflect planning for particular population segments but without comprehensive planning for all persons in a geographical area. More comprehensive, geographically based planning approaches can be expected in the future.

Conclusions and Next Steps

It is critical to reiterate the importance of system descriptions as benchmarks against which future developments can be assessed. The statistical information presented in this chapter can serve as an important benchmark for examining the effects of the trends described here. Hence, a critical application of the information presented in *Mental Health, United States* (Manderscheid & Sonnenschein 1994, 1996), a biennial statistical publication of the U.S. Center for Mental Health Services, is to benchmark the developments that are occurring. Sociologists are well trained to study and explain these trends, and to help plan new and improved systems for the future. The critical challenges currently faced in mental health will require the very best that can be offered.

23

Institutional Change and Its Consequences for the Delivery of Mental Health Services

Mark Schlesinger & Bradford Gray

Schlesinger and Gray examine the mental health delivery system from the wider perspective of institutional change and transmission. Wider institutional changes transmitted from outside the mental health–care system are not adapted to the unique characteristics of mental health care, and they may produce a downward spiral in the effectiveness of services. This argument is illustrated with two examples: the growth of proprietary ownership among psychiatric hospitals and the spread of various forms of managed care in third-party arrangements paying for mental health services. These institutional changes diffused from the general health-care system into the mental health–care system and represent a fundamental shift toward technical considerations of efficiency. Yet mental health is a less technically driven system; consequently, the long-term effects may be quite different from those found in other parts of the health-care system. The long-term dynamics of each of these types of institutional change will have diverse effects, which the authors examine and describe. Furthermore, they examine the transmission of these institutional changes from three different perspectives arising from organizational sociology – transmission as a form of diffusion of innovations, as a form of institutional isomorphism, and as a form of intersectoral bridging. The institutionalist interpretation broadens our understanding of the ongoing changes in mental health care. Students should (a) discuss the ways in which the mental health system is different from the medical system and (b) assess whether they think the "downward spiral in the effectiveness of mental health services" will increase with the advent of managed care.

The past half-century has seen significant change in mental health services in the United States. Policies shifting treatment from inpatient settings to the community – the "deinstitutionalization" movement – are perhaps the best known of these changes. But there have also been dramatic shifts in the ways in which mental illness is treated in civil or criminal legal proceedings, in the availability of government financial subsidies to people disabled by mental disorders, in the role of public and private health insurance programs in paying for treatment of mental illness, in the types of hospitals where inpatient care is provided, as well as in the roles of various health care professionals in providing those services (Applebaum 1994; Levin & Petrila 1996).

These changes can be traced to a variety of influences. Some reflect the introduction of new technologies, such as psychoactive pharmaceuticals or information processing systems (Grob 1994a). Others can be traced to changing popular conceptions of mental illness or the perceived rights of people with mental disorders (Rochefort 1993). However, perhaps the most consistent source of institutional change in the mental health care arena has little to do with the characteristics of mental illness, individuals with mental disorders, or the nature of mental health services. Change most often comes to mental health care as a sort of spillover of ongoing changes in the broader systems that deliver health and social services, a process that we will refer to here as "institutional transmission."

Past research on the diffusion of innovations emphasizes the importance of social networks as conduits of change (Anderson & Jay 1985; Fennell & Warnecke 1988). The field of mental health services is composed of two distinct (albeit somewhat overlapping) networks of purchasers, providers, and the government regulators who oversee their practices. The first network involves those aspects of mental illness that have come to be viewed as the responsibility of the *private* sector – in this case, largely through employer-based insurance and worksite-based treatment programs known as employee assistance programs (EAPs) (Frank, McGuire, & Newhouse 1995; Gerstein & Harwood 1990; Roman & Blum 1992). This responsibility has generally been limited to acute illness or acute episodes of chronic conditions that are sufficiently mild that the affected individual continues to be largely or at least periodically functional. State governments oversee this sector primarily through regulation of private insurance coverages and practices.

Individuals who are more severely disabled typically are seen as the responsibility of the *public* sector. State departments of mental health, or their functional equivalents, are the primary actors in this sector, either directly providing services or contracting for their provision from the private sector (Rochefort 1993). When mental illness leaves people disabled or indigent, federal agencies become involved – most commonly the Health Care Financing Administration (which is responsible for overseeing the operation of the Medicare health insurance program for the disabled and elderly and the Medicaid program for the indigent) or the Veterans Administration (which provides a substantial amount of mental health care for veterans with service-connected disabilities).

Change can be transmitted through several different social networks. In the private sector, innovation in the treatment of mental health care may be shaped by contemporary practices in employee benefits more generally. In the public sector, change may be induced as a part of broader efforts to reform the policies of state or federal governments. As we will demonstrate in this chapter, innovations that begin in the private sector may spill over to the public sector, particularly in periods that favor "reinventing" government in the image of private institutions.

Our central contention in this chapter is that institutional transmission has important implications for the quality and appropriateness of mental health services. Because mental health care is in some important ways different from other health and social services, reforms that are sensible in these broader contexts may have unexpected and unfortunate short-term consequences in the mental health–care arena. But we further suggest a troubling corollary: under certain circumstances, the institutional changes that have been transmitted from outside of mental health care are not adapted to its unique characteristics, even in the longer term. Consequently, institutional transmission can produce a downward spiral in the effectiveness of arrangements to address mental health needs, with the initial inadequacies of borrowed institutional arrangments exacerbated over time. Under these circumstances, institutional change may have even more dramatic and problematic consequences over time than are discernible with contemporary evidence.

We illustrate these claims with two examples: the growth of proprietary ownership among psychiatric hospitals and the spread of various forms of managed care in third-party arrangements paying for mental health services. Each of these developments represents a significant change in the institutional context within which mental health care is provided. We describe how these two institutional changes have migrated from the rest of the health-care system into the mental health sector, assessing their transmission in light of three different theoretical perspectives suggested by organizational sociology. Synthesizing the findings of published research with previously unpublished data, we identify some problematic implications that each form of institutional change has had for the delivery of mental health services. We then explore some preliminary evidence suggesting that the two examples of institutional transmission will have quite different long-term dynamics: the growth of proprietary hospitals stimulating a strong countervailing process that limits its negative effects; the growth of managed care inducing a sort of self-reinforcing process that exacerbates the short-term problems it creates. We conclude with some speculations about the future of the mental health system and mental health policy in the United States in light of these institutional dynamics.

The Origins of Institutional Transmission to Mental Health Care

There have been a number of institutional innovations that were initially adopted for some health and social services and subsequently applied to mental health care. Over the past 15 years, two examples of institutional transmission have had significant consequences for the delivery of mental health services: the growth of for-profit hospitals as a substantial source of inpatient treatment and the application of various forms of managed care to mental health services. In this section we briefly discuss the origins of each change and then examine the processes through which they were brought into mental health care.

The Growth of Proprietary Psychiatric Hospitals

The Origins of Proprietary Hospitals. At the beginning of the twentieth century, the majority of American hospitals were run on a proprietary basis

(Bays 1983). Most for-profit facilities were relatively small, owned and run by a single physician or a small partnership of practitioners as an adjunct to their clinical practice. As hospitals became the locus of more sophisticated technologies, small proprietary hospitals were replaced by or evolved into larger nonprofit facilities (Steinwald & Neuhauser 1970). By the mid-1960s, just over 5% of the beds in community general hospitals operated under proprietary auspices (Bays 1983).

The role of for-profit hospitals providing inpatient psychiatric services was even smaller. The earliest national statistics, collected in 1949, reported that only about 1.5% of all psychiatric inpatient beds were in proprietary settings. This share declined over the subsequent two decades, so that by 1965 less than 1% of all beds devoted to psychiatric care in long-term and short-term hospitals were in proprietary institutions (American Hospital Association 1950, 1965).

The rebirth and reconfiguration of the for-profit hospital sector can be traced to the expanded role of government financing in the 1960s. Medicare and Medicaid not only provided insurance coverage for previously indigent patients, they also had generous capital financing arrangements that allowed hospitals to receive substantial revenues by depreciating the purchase price of newly acquired facilities. These incentives encouraged the immediate growth of multifacility corporations both among general hospitals (Gray 1991) and nursing homes (Vladeck 1980).

In their early years, hospital corporations grew primarily by acquiring freestanding for-profit hospitals, with the construction of new facilities accounting for no more than 20% of their expansion (Gray 1991). By the mid-1980s, these opportunities became increasingly limited. The federal government revised its rules on depreciation of assets, so that the acquisition of new hospitals was no longer a source of substantial revenues. Also, in 1983 both Medicare and Medicaid began to change the ways in which they paid hospitals, foreshadowing subsequent declines in the profitability of treating government-financed patients (Russell 1989; Bentkover et al. 1988).

Expansion into Mental Health Care. Seeking more profitable conditions, the hospital corporations began to invest in other markets – including home health care, renal dialysis, ambulatory care centers, and psychiatric hospitals. The latter appeared a particularly promising new venue for several reasons (Dorwart & Schlesinger 1988). First, they were exempted from Medicare's new payment arrangements and so appeared to have greater potential for long-term profitability. Second, during the late 1970s and early 1980s, a number of states had required private insurers to add inpatient treatment of mental illness to covered benefits. This had expanded the market for privately insured patients at a time when public sector facilities were being closed and established nonprofit psychiatric facilities were unwilling or unable to increase their capacity. Third, at this time psychiatry and substance abuse were largely overlooked in growing efforts by purchasers to introduce practice standards to the health-care system.

The response was dramatic. Between 1984 and 1989, the proportion of the for-profit hospital industry that specialized in the treatment of mental illness doubled, from 27% to 55% of total capacity (Gray 1991). The expansion was most pronounced in the states in which private insurers had been required to cover inpatient care. For example, by the mid-1980s, 22 states had required that private insurers cover inpatient mental health care. For-profit hospitals represented 43% of the facilities offering inpatient psychiatric care in those states but only 13% of the facilities in states without mandated inpatient coverage (Marmor, Schlesinger, & Smithey 1986). In some of the potentially most profitable local markets, as many as eight new psychiatric facilities were constructed simultaneously (Dorwart & Schlesinger 1988).

The profitability of treating mental health care on an inpatient basis was significantly undermined by the subsequent expansion of managed care to oversee the treatment of mental illness (Mechanic et al. 1995). As a result, investment by for-profit corporations in psychiatric hospitals began to flag by the early 1990s. Nonetheless, the involvement of proprietary hospital corporations had significant short-term consequences for the treatment of mental illness, which we explore in more detail later in this chapter.

The Spread of Managed Care to the Treatment of Mental Illness

The Origins of Managed Care. "Managed care" is a catch phrase applied to a variety of interventions through which purchasers of health services attempt to shape clinical practices. Managed care approaches can be most simply grouped into two broad categories. The first involves arrangements in which the purchaser contracts with a group (or "panel") of health-care providers. Enrollees covered by that health insurance plan must receive their treatment from affiliated providers. This category includes prepaid health plans (often referred to as health maintenance organizations, or HMOs) and preferred provider organizations (PPOs).

Closed-panel health plans make use of a variety of interventions to shape the ways in which enrollees are treated. These include: (1) administrative requirements, such as primary care gatekeeper programs, under which enrollees must obtain a referral from their primary care provider before seeing a specialist; (2) financial incentives, either for the plan as a whole or for subsets of providers within the plan; and (3) educational or informational interventions, including the "profiling" of provider practice patterns in comparison with others affiliated with the plan (Luft 1981).

The second form of managed care involves third-party review of clinical practices, typically by an organization that contracts to provide such services. These are sometimes referred to as utilization review organizations (UROs). As of 1993, UROs reviewed treatment for roughly 122 million Americans (Schlesinger et al.

1996b). They may provide only episodic review of treatment, triggered by a clinician's decision to hospitalize a patient, or they may utilize more extensive ongoing supervision in the form of intensive case management (Gray & Field 1989). Utilization management techniques are also commonly used with HMOs and PPOs, in addition to the other interventions described previously (Gold et al. 1995).

Prepaid health plans had their origins in employer-sponsored health arrangements and mutual aid societies in the late nineteenth century, but it was not until a half-century later that the federal government began to actively encourage their expansion (Brown 1983). The most dramatic expansions occurred later in the 1980s, when private and government purchasers of health care grew more concerned about increasing costs and saw HMOs as a means of containing costs. Enrollment in prepaid plans increased from 9 million in 1980 to 36 million in 1989. The dramatic expansion of HMO enrollment continued into the 1990s, spurred on by the embrace of managed care as a reform strategy favored by both the Clinton Administration and its opponents in the Republican Party.

The role of UROs also expanded rapidly during this period. Early experiments with utilization review by Blue Cross plans during the 1960s had limited application and little evident impact on medical practice (Gray & Field 1989). Spurred by purchasers' concern with the cost of private insurance, as well as by supportive federal and state government policies, the scope of utilization management grew exponentially during the 1980s. Between 1982 and 1986, the prevalence of prior authorization among Blue Cross plans grew from 28% to 95% (Scheffler et al. 1991). By 1990, 95% of private fee-for-service insurance incorporated some form of utilization control; the vast majority required prior authorization for some hospitalization, and most reviewed the length of stay of hospital admissions (Hoy, Curtis, & Rice 1991).

Expansion into the Treatment of Mental Illness. In its early forms, managed care paid little attention to the treatment of mental illness. Most early prepaid plans excluded psychiatric care from their covered benefits. In order to obtain certification as a "federally qualified" HMO during the 1970s, plans were required to add some minimal coverage, but they were allowed to routinely exclude coverage for any mental illness that was diagnosed as chronic in nature (Schlesinger 1986). Early forms of utilization review focused on preventing unnecessary hospitalization for surgery, which made them of little relevance to people with mental illness (Ermann 1988).

During the 1980s, managed care began to have a larger impact on the treatment of mental illness. Private insurers and employers grew increasingly concerned about the costs of mental health benefits (Frank et al. 1991; Schlesinger & Dorwart 1992). Managed care plans covering mental health care of the privately insured initially relied almost exclusively on utilization review, though by the 1990s many had developed networks of affiliated providers and the capacity to more actively manage services (Englund 1994). As they evolved, these "carve-out" plans came to resemble a sort of specialized HMO, with purview limited to problems of mental illness and substance abuse (a.k.a. "behavioral health"). By 1994, companies specializing in managed behavioral health care oversaw the treatment of more than 100 million Americans, with UROs still the most common form (37 million covered individuals) and carve-out plans the fastest growing (over 20 million covered) (Frank et al. 1995).

States were similarly concerned about the rising costs of care for the mentally ill. But they also saw managed care as a mechanism for improving the quality of services by better coordinating a fragmented treatment system and facilitating the shift of resources from hospital to community-based services (Elias & Navon 1995; Essock & Goldman 1995). Early experiments during the 1980s incorporated the models of prepaid care used by private sector HMOs (Mechanic & Aiken 1989a), which were further adapted and refined during the 1990s (Christianson et al. 1995; McFarlane et al. 1995).

A second avenue through which managed care spread to the care of the seriously mentally ill involved its incorporation into state Medicaid programs (Iglehart 1995). Although initially restricted to families covered under Aid to Families with Dependent Children, during the 1990s managed Medicaid was extended to other eligibility categories, which included a substantial number of individuals with serious mental illness (Callahan et al. 1995; Durham 1994).

Theoretical Perspectives on Institutional Transmission

How might we understand the spread of managed care and for-profit hospital corporations to mental health care? Organizational sociology offers several alternative conceptual frameworks. The first treats the spread of for-profit corporations and managed care into the mental health field as cases of more general processes of diffusion of innovations (Fennel & Warnecke 1988; Meyer & Goes 1988; Rogers 1995a). From a Weberian perspective, the innovations spread because of their demonstrated benefits and market pressures that motivate capitalist organizations to become more efficient. They entered the mental health–care arena later either because the need for innovation was less salient there (e.g. market pressures were weaker) or because the existing institutions in the mental health field had less capacity to innovate.

A second perspective views institutional transmission as an example of more general processes of institutional isomorphism (Dimaggio & Powell 1983). From this perspective, mental health–care organizations adopted similar institutional arrangements to those existing in acute medical care because there are broad forces that constantly push for congruence among organizations operating in the same "field" – in this case, health care. These include: (a) "mimetic isomorphism," that is, efforts by less-established organizations to mimic traits of their better-known counterparts as a means of gaining greater legitimacy; (b) common norms, including the professionalized training and socialization of the professionals who deliver the services in health and mental health care organizations; and (c) "coercive isomorphism," or pressures from central authorities striving for greater congruence in organizational behavior in an effort to produce more accountability or equity in health care.

A third possible explanation links institutional transmission to the differences in the networks of organizations that respond to mental and physical illnesses, termed either "societal sectors" or "institutional fields" by organizational sociologists (Scott & Meyer 1991). From this perspective, general and mental health care are parts of two quite different sectors, and the transmission of innovations is shaped in fundamental ways by their differences (Powell 1991).

Transmission as a Form of Institutional Diffusion. This is essentially a story of learning. From this perspective, effective institutional alterations are adopted most rapidly in those sectors that have the greatest resources or capacity for innovation. Their merit is established in these pioneering settings, which are then emulated by other organizations.

This perspective does not provide an adequate explanation for the spread of proprietary hospital corporations into mental health care. Proprietary corporate affiliation was expected by its proponents to carry two advantages over freestanding nonprofit hospitals: (1) the corporation was supposedly able to capture cost advantages through economies of scale in purchasing and other administrative functions, and (2) for-profit hospitals were purportedly better able to motivate affiliated health-care professionals to practice in a cost-efficient manner. But the early experience with for-profit general hospitals provided little evidence in support of either proposition. Empirical research suggested that system-affiliated hospitals had patient care costs that were no lower than their unaffiliated counterparts and were actually more likely to have high administrative costs (Dranove, Drake, & Shanley 1996). Nor did for-profit hospitals appear any more efficient than otherwise comparable nonprofit facilities (Gray 1991).

Consequently, there is little reason to believe that investor-owned hospitals spread to the mental health field because they had proven to be a successful innovation in acute care settings. But while not necessarily efficient from a societal perspective, this innovation may have been quite rational from a narrower perspective. Investors looked for continued growth of hospital corporations as a marker of future profitability. At the first sign of limits to growth, the market value of corporate stock fell precipitously. This produced its own self-reinforcing cycle: falling stock prices made it harder to raise money to pay for future acquisitions, which further inhibited future growth. To avoid this fate, proprietary corporations were forced to place a premium on continual expansion.

This pattern was first observed in the collapse of stock prices in the nursing home industry in the late 1960s, a time in which "the bubble had burst" for the industry (Vladeck 1980). It was replicated in the early 1980s in the hospital industry. In one particularly striking episode, a report from a single hospital company that predicted limited future growth led to what the New York Times described as "panic selling" in the entire industry: the collective stock value of proprietary hospital corporations declined by $1.5 billion in a single day (Gray 1991).

The transmission of managed care to mental health initially appears to fit more readily into a conventional model of innovation and diffusion. Both HMOs and UROs had demonstrated their ability to limit spending on health care, without substantially worsening health, long before they were incorporated into the treatment of mental illness (Gray & Field 1989; Luft 1981). But here again, the diffusion story is too simple, because there were reasons for doubting that the lessons for acute medical care applied to the treatment of behavioral health problems. Mental illness and substance abuse problems have certain characteristics that make it difficult to apply conventional managed care techniques without producing problematic side effects (Mechanic et al. 1995; Scheffler et al. 1993; Schlesinger 1986). Moreover, until recently there was very little experience with managed care for populations insured by government programs (Medicare, Medicaid, and state departments of mental health). The track record that did exist was not especially promising (Freund & Hurley 1995; Iglehart 1995).

If the purported efficacy of managed care had not been demonstrated for the most seriously mentally ill, what accounts for the widespread willingness of state governments to adopt this innovation? To some extent, the spread of managed care into the public sector was driven by the same investor expectations that drove the expansion of hospital corporations, leading managed care companies to market themselves to state officials. Because the private sector carve-out of mental health benefits is now the rule rather than the exception, there is little new business for managed mental health care vendors in that market. Furthermore, the initial savings associated with reductions in utilization and in fees have already been realized for clients in that market. Therefore, these managed care firms are now looking to public sector mental health services as their next sales frontier (Essock & Goldman 1995: 37).

Transmission as a Form of Institutional Isomorphism. Dimaggio and Powell (1983) argue that three sets of influences encouraged organizations in a common field (in this case, health care) to become like one another over time. Consequently, once for-profit hospital corporations and managed care had established their legitimacy for the health system as a whole, a combination of mimetic, normative, and coercive pressures would encourage their diffusion into mental health care.

For investor-owned hospitals, the evidence suggests that if any of these three isomorphic pressures were at work, only the third had a substantial effect – and even in that case, the documentation of isomorphic pressures is not fully convincing. We consider each of the three forms of isomorphic pressures in turn.

Although the behavioral health field has considerably less legitimacy than do other forms of health care – and is often referred to as the "neglected stepchild of health services" (Boyle & Callahan 1995: 9) – there is no evidence that providers of mental health services mimicked the pattern of for-profit ownership as a means of enhancing their legitimacy. Because of public controversies over the appropriateness of profit making in health care, profit-oriented hospitals offered little opportunity to enhance the legitimacy of mental health care (Schlesinger & Dorwart 1984). Nor did professional norms encourage the spread of proprietary ownership. Most health-care professionals have resisted, and in some cases have actively opposed, an increased role for investor-owned health care facilities (Gray 1991). Nor did coercive isomorphism play much of a role. Although large multistate employers may prefer to deal with hospital corporations that can provide services in a broad array of locales (Dranove & Shanley 1995), for-profit psychiatric hospitals were largely limited to particular parts of the country; hence they offered few advantages to purchasers with a nationwide workforce (Dorwart & Schlesinger 1988).

If institutional isomorphism seems to be a poor explanation for the spread of proprietary psychiatric hospitals, it offers a more persuasive rationale for the incorporation of managed care into mental health care. Mimetic and coercive pressures appear to have played the largest role. Professional norms are less of a factor, because the health-care professions are deeply divided in their assessment of managed care in general (Clancy & Brody 1995; Emanuel & Dubler 1995) and of its implications for the treatment of mental illness (Boyle & Callahan 1995; Iglehart 1996; Schreter, Sharfstein, & Schreter 1994a).

Mimetic processes appear to be more important, particularly in the acceptance of managed care by state policy makers. In this case, however, those seeking legitimacy are not the mental health–care providers but rather the purchasers of services. State officials responsible for mental health care suffer from the same lack of legitimacy, relative to their peers in state governments, as do mental health–care providers relative to their professional counterparts. As noted by one former commissioner of a state department of mental health, "in many states, the mental health authority is deeply buried in the bureaucracy, with little identity or influence" (Bevilacqua 1995: 45). In an era of seemingly constrained public sector budgets, the only way for state officials concerned about mental health care to demonstrate their legitimacy is to show that they can assure the availability of "cost-effective services for persons disabled by psychiatric illness" (Essock & Goldman 1995: 37). With little evidence about what services are effective (let alone cost-effective), officials have a strong incentive to emulate the practices that have a reputation for encouraging more efficient treatment – namely, managed care. Under these circumstances, state mental health officials "have little choice but to get on board with managed care contracting" (Bevilacqua 1995: 45).

Coercive pressures are also at work. Large employers and public officials have grown increasingly concerned with regional inconsistencies and inequities in the treatment of mental illness and substance abuse (Englund 1994). Managed care practices have the potential to standardize clinical practices in a manner that can limit, if not fully eliminate, these inconsistencies (Iglehart 1996). This potential is enhanced as managed care firms increasingly operate nationwide (Essock & Goldman 1995; Schlesinger et al. 1996b). Again, the processes producing isomorphism arc associated with the perceptions and decisions of those purchasing services, not of mental health–care providers.

Transmission as a Form of Intersectoral Bridging. Although some organizational sociologists include mental health within the broader organizational field of health care, others have argued that the two belong to entirely different sectors of American society. Scott and Meyer (1991), for example, suggest that acute medical care organizational practices are influenced by both social norms (labeled the "institutional environment") and what they term the "technical environment" (primarily market processes linked to considerations of efficiency and other outcome measures). They argue that mental health, in contrast, belongs (along with schools, legal agencies, and churches) to the sector in which only social norms shape organizational behavior.

These differences might explain why both managed care and for-profit ownership emerged first in the general health care arena, because organizational success in this sector depends on technical efficiency and because proprietary corporations and managed care were both perceived as having the potential for achieving greater efficiencies (Gray 1991; Gray & Field 1989). But these intersectoral differences ought to have inhibited institutional transmission between health and mental health fields.

Organizations in sectors that emphasize technical efficiency are thought to have their performance judged in terms of measures of process and outcome (Scott & Meyer 1991). Organizations functioning in sectors that are highly developed institutionally but not technically will be subjected primarily to controls that emphasize structural measures. Previous studies have concluded that, in sectors like education and mental health, primary emphasis was placed on such structural controls as accreditation, certification, and licensure (Scott & Meyer 1991: 136).

Yet even as these words are written, they are seemingly invalidated by the spread to mental health care of both proprietary corporations and managed care, each of which injects greater control over the process of care and a stronger orientation to measurable outcomes, particularly cost containment. This convergence can be traced to two developments that serve to bridge what had previously been two distinct sectors within health care.

The first bridge grew out of state requirements, first enacted in the mid-1970s, that private health insurance policies cover the treatment of mental illness and substance abuse. When states began to mandate that private insurers pay for these services, insurers naturally sought to apply the coverages and service arrangements that were familiar to them from the treatment of medical conditions. For example, privately insured patients with substance abuse problems were (in the early years of the mandates) treated largely in hospital settings, although specialists in substance abuse had previously concluded that inpatient treatment was unduly expensive and no more effective than outpatient treatment (McAuliffe 1990; Schlesinger & Dorwart 1992).

Insurers provided a bridge for institutional transmission in several different ways. Most directly, by simultaneously operating in both acute care and mental health fields, they had both opportunity and incentive to borrow techniques that worked well in one field and apply them to the other. This provided an important initial impetus for the spread of managed care into behavioral health. In addition, the insurers' role inadvertently created the conditions that encouraged institutional transmission. By paying for inpatient treatment for psychiatric disorders and substance abuse at a time when public officials were emphasizing outpatient treatment, insurers provided an impetus for the hospital corporations to view behavioral health care as a lucrative new market in which they could deal with organizations that were familiar to them from their experience with acute medical care.

A second bridging factor is of more recent vintage. There remains a widespread perception among the general public and government officials that much that is diagnosed (or paid for by third parties) as mental illness is little more than malingering or neurosis, which distinguishes it from other health care (Boyle & Callahan 1995). Over the past ten years, however, emerging scientific evidence has identified biological markers for certain mental disorders. If mental illness is in fact biological in origin, then a strong case can be made that it should be treated in a manner comparable to other health needs; this perspective is captured by the doctrine of "parity" (Lefley 1996a). Although providing a strong intellectual rationale for common institutions in health and mental health care, the parity argument has emerged sufficiently recently that it probably cannot account for institutional transmission that occurred during the 1980s.

The spread of proprietary hospitals and managed care can thus be explained in part by all three perspectives: as diffusion of an innovation, as a process leading to institutional isomorphism, and as the result of institutional change that bridged previously distinct sectors in society. The first and third perspectives offer the most convincing explanations for the transmission of proprietary hospital ownership, whereas institutional isomorphism appears to have played a larger role in the spread of managed care.

Some Implications of Institutional Transmission

Institutional transmission of this sort may have a variety of practical consequences for the delivery of mental health services (Dorwart & Schlesinger 1988; Mechanic et al. 1995). From a sociological perspective, however, perhaps the most interesting results involve the changing bases of institutional legitimacy in the field. The incorporation of proprietary ownership and managed care into mental health care reflects a fundamental shift toward what Scott and Meyer term "technical" considerations of efficiency. These considerations conflict with preexisting patterns of authority that are based on professional norms (Dimaggio & Anheier 1990; Hafferty & Wolinksy 1991; Marmor et al. 1986; Scott & Meyer 1991). One important implication of both institutional changes involves growing constraints on professional autonomy.

This is not simply a process of convergence between mental and general health care. The characteristics of behavioral health problems that have traditionally made them a less technically driven field still exist. Most notably: (1) much of the cost of inappropriately treated problems is felt by the family of the patient or by society as a whole (Flynn 1994; Steinberg 1992); (2) the professional norms of appropriate treatment are relatively weak and vague (Boyle & Callahan 1995); and (3) because these conditions are chronic, they are not readily cured and instead require continued care (Grob 1994a). The superimposition of efficiency considerations onto these other characteristics leads to outcomes that may be importantly different than those that occur in other parts of the health-care system.

Short-Term Effects: Growing Constraints on the Delivery of Mental Health Care

For-Profit Psychiatric Hospitals. The expansion of for-profit psychiatric hospitals attracted considerable interest in the mental health care literature (Dorwart et al. 1991; McCue & Clement 1992; McCue, Clement, & Heorger 1993; Schlesinger 1995; Schlesinger & Dorwart 1984; Schlesinger et al. 1997a,b; Wolff 1989). All of these studies draw data from one of several different national surveys of psychiatric hospitals. They generally conclude that, compared with otherwise similar private nonprofit hospitals, for-profit hospitals: (1) treat fewer patients with severe diagnoses, (2) provide less treatment for uninsured patients, and (3) are more likely to transfer unprofitable patients to other mental health–care facilities in the community.

Some of this variation in outcomes may be produced by the different ways in which for-profit hospitals compensate their affiliated health professionals (Gray 1991) or by differences in the array of services that the hospital offers to patients (Schlesinger et al. 1987). For-profit hospitals may also try to shape the behavior of health-care professionals more directly by regulating their practice patterns.

Evidence on these forms of private regulation is available from a national survey of psychiatrists conducted in 1988 by the American Psychiatric Association (Dorwart et al. 1992). Respondents were asked about ways in which the hospital constrained clinical autonomy, including pressures to avoid admitting patients who were uninsured, covered by Medicaid, or who had particularly severe mental illness – as well as limits on the length of admission or requirements that the provider order particular tests (Schlesinger et al. 1996a). To assess the role of

Table 23.1. *Hospital characteristics and the prevalence of constraints on physician autonomy*

	Difference[a] in constraints on treatment practices	
Hospital type	Hospital limits length of stay	Hospital requires tests
For-profit specialty	+23.2**	+14.4
Private nonprofit specialty	+20.7**	+14.0
For-profit general	+31.0**	+1.8
Private nonprofit general	+10.7	−1.9

	Difference[a] in constraints on admission of patients		
Hospital type	Uninsured	Medicaid	Severely mentally ill
For-profit specialty	+96.6**	+150.1**	+53.0
Private nonprofit specialty	+88.6**	+86.8**	+51.5
For-profit general	+77.6**	+110.0**	+122.1**
Private nonprofit general	+35.8	+2.2	+84.3*

Notes: Numerical values (percentages) reflect predicted change in prevalence of constraints relative to the average prevalence for that constraint. $N = 1,339$ observations.
* Statistically significant (10% confidence level).
** Statistically significant (5% confidence level).
[a] Compared with government-run general hospitals.

hospital ownership in the prevalence of practice constraints, psychiatrists' reports were used as dependent variables in a set of regression models while controlling for: other characteristics of the hospital (e.g., specialization in psychiatric care, competitive conditions in local markets, region of the country); the prevalence of state regulations (e.g., insurance mandates); and characteristics of the responding psychiatrist (e.g., age, specialty area, preference for inpatient treatment) that might affect the reported prevalence of these external constraints. Table 23.1 presents the estimated effects of hospital ownership, controlling for these other factors.

Practice constraints are generally more common at private hospitals than government-run facilities and are also more common at for-profit than nonprofit hospitals, though not all of the latter differences were statistically significant. One might expect that the relatively weak norms of professional practice in mental health care would make psychiatrists more at risk for hospital-based constraints than would be true for other physicians. Unfortunately, we have no directly comparable data for other medical specialties. A previous study (Schlesinger et al. 1987) did examine the relationship between hospital ownership and the extent of admission constraints for uninsured and Medicaid patients, controlling for a similar set of independent variables. The differences between public and private (as well as between for-profit and nonprofit) hospitals were less pronounced than those reported here, suggesting that hospital-related pressures may in fact be more prevalent in the mental health–care arena. However, this other study drew data from 1984 as opposed to 1988, so other changing features of the health care system may have accounted for these differences.

Managed Care and Constraints on Clinical Autonomy. By design, managed care is intended to alter clinical practices. Whatever the impact of managed care on clinical autonomy generally, there are reasons to expect that it will have a particularly substantial influence on the treatment of mental health and substance abuse (Mechanic et al. 1995). Because professional norms of appropriate practice tend to be weaker for mental health care than for many other medical interventions, external reviewers are likely to reject a larger portion of proposed treatments as insufficiently justified (Schlesinger 1989). Because many of the costs of inadequately treated mental health and substance abuse are borne by family members or society as a whole rather than the medical care system, health plans that are prepaid to provide services have inadequate financial incentives to address those problems (Schlesinger 1986).

The published literature on managed mental health care has been reviewed in several articles (see e.g. Mechanic et al. 1995; Wells et al. 1995). It demonstrates the large impact that managed care has on treatment practices, associated with significant declines in aggregate levels of inpatient care (Wickizer, Lessler, & Travis 1996). The impact on professional autonomy has received less attention.

Some insights can be gained by examining the comparative impact of utilization review on mental and general health care. The 1988 survey of psychiatrists just described found that 20–25% of hospital-affiliated psychiatrists reported that they "often" or "always" had to deal with insurance company review when deciding on inpatient care (Schlesinger et al. 1996a). A survey conducted in 1990 by the American Medical Association found that psychiatrists were the specialty reporting the largest constraints on clinical autonomy as a consequence of external review (Emmons & Chawla 1991).

We can obtain a more refined comparison by drawing on some unpublished data from a recent national study of the utilization review industry in 1993 (Schlesinger et al. 1996a). The survey included a variety of measures of the extent to which external review limited clinical autonomy, including the frequency with which utilization review organizations deny requests for hospitalization. As we have suggested, the weaker professional norms for the treatment of mental illness appear to make practitioners in this field more vulnerable to external review. Those UROs specializing in behavioral health care denied 11.9% of their requested hospitalizations, compared with 6.5% for the review organizations covering medical and surgical admissions. (This difference was statistically significant at a 1-percent confidence level.)

Table 23.2. *Practices of utilization review organizations specializing in psychiatric treatment versus those reviewing all conditions*

	Type of review	
Measures of impact on clinical autonomy	All conditions	Behavioral health problems only
Review criteria adjusted to regional practice patterns		
Variation in hospital admission rates[a]	2.99	2.73
Variation in length of stay in the hospital[a]	2.38	2.27
Allowances for practices that violate review criteria		
Successful appeal rate	19.6%	7.2%*
Exceptions based on adamancy of clinicians[b]	2.60	2.60
Adjustments made to review criteria over time in response to:		
Changes in average clinical practice[c]	3.90	3.20*
Request made by individual clinicians[c]	2.73	2.87

*Difference statistically significant at a 5% confidence level (*t*-test with unequal variances).
[a]Measured on a five-point scale, from "never" (= 1) to "always" (= 5).
[b]Measured on a five-point scale, from "not important" (= 1) to "critically important" (= 5).
[c]Measured on a five-point scale, from "not important" (= 1) to "extremely important" (= 5).

A more detailed portrait emerges by comparing the review process among UROs that specialize in mental health care with those that review hospitalization requests for all conditions. The extent to which the review process limits clinical autonomy can be measured by: (a) the extent to which UROs attempt to eliminate existing patterns of regional variation in treatment practices; (b) the ability of clinicians to affect reviews, either by advocating with reviewers or by formally appealing denials; and (c) the impact of clinicians' concerns and practices on changes over time in the review process. The evidence summarized in Table 23.2 suggests that UROs specializing in mental health care allow substantially less clinical discretion than do their counterparts reviewing general medical care.

Utilization reviews are used also by HMOs, PPOs, and other forms of managed care that rely on closed panels of providers. But managed care has other means of affecting clinical practices, either by socializing providers to follow the practice norms of the health plan or by threatening to drop them from the provider panel if they do not conform (Mechanic et al. 1995). Little is known about the consequences of these pressures on clinical autonomy, though we can glean some insights from the findings of a small 1995 survey of providers (with primary responsibility for treatment of patients with severe mental illness) who have had experience with managed mental health care (Wolff, Schlesinger, & Vajhe 1997). The majority of providers reported that they felt some obligation to practice in a manner that protected the interests of their colleagues in the plan and also felt threatened by the potential for the managed care plans to drop providers from their

Table 23.3. *Pressures on clinical autonomy among mental health–care providers in managed care plans*

	Distribution of responses (percentages)				
Forms of inducement	Strongly disagree	Somewhat disagree	Neutral	Somewhat agree	Strongly agree
Socialization					
In making decisions about treatment, a provider owes it to his or her colleagues in the plan to avoid treatment that is excessively costly.	14.2	26.1	6.0	45.5	8.2
When mental health professionals affiliate with a managed care plan, they should follow the rules of the plan.	5.9	25.2	14.8	46.7	7.4
Fear of disaffiliation					
Providers who complain about inappropriate utilization review practices are likely to be dropped by managed care plans.	2.3	12.1	26.5	49.2	9.8

panels (Table 23.3). Preliminary analyses suggest that providers who are more rule-abiding or more concerned with being disaffiliated are less likely to actively advocate for their patients in the utilization review process (Wolff et al. 1997).

Longer-Term Implications: Countervailing Pressures and Self-Reinforcing Cycles

The spread of for-profit hospitals and managed care into mental health services has constrained the practices of mental health care professionals and hence the treatment of people with mental illness. But the full consequences of these forms of institutional transmission depend on longer-term institutional dynamics. It is at this stage that the two stories of institutional transmission begin to diverge more sharply.

Proprietary Ownership and Countervailing Pressures. As we have documented, the growth of for-profit psychiatric hospital care affected the autonomy of mental health–care professionals. In addition to more aggressively "weeding out" unprofitable patients, for-profit hospitals also made an effort to attract profitable clients. This took the form of advertising directly to the public to attract clients who would refer themselves or family members to the hospital for treatment (Busbin 1993; Dorwart & Epstein 1991). Among the most popular and effective marketing efforts were addressed to parents who had troubled relationships with their adolescent children (Weithorn 1988).

With their aggressive marketing campaigns, proprietary hospitals were simply replicating practices that they had pioneered for community general hospitals (Naidu & Naryana 1991; Tucker et al. 1992). But here, too, the circumstances associated with mental health care differed from those associated with physical illness. People rarely admit themselves to the hospital for a physical illness without first being examined by a physician, yet self-referral to psychiatric facilities is quite common. With relatively weak norms for determining when hospitalization was appropriate, the potential for unnecessary and in some cases harmful excessive treatment was viewed as a major concern. Suspicion grew when evidence suggested that the average length of a hospital stay for many behavioral health problems almost exactly equalled the average coverage that states required private insurers to provide for these conditions (Gerstein & Harwood 1990).

Although health-care professionals had worried about the influence of for-profit psychiatric hospitals on clinical autonomy (Dorwart & Schlesinger 1988; Schlesinger & Dorwart 1984), it was not until concerns about excessive hospitalization emerged that policy makers responded. The reaction included Congressional hearings, a spate of reports in the national news media, federal criminal investigations, and lawsuits by major insurers attempting to recover costs for hospitalizations that they judged inappropriate (Lutz 1994; Meyerson 1994; Modern Healthcare 1995). These culminated in 1992 with a series of raids by U.S. marshals of the offices of several of the largest proprietary hospital corporations, seizing evidence to be used in legal actions initiated on behalf of Medicare and Medicaid programs to recover costs for inappropriate treatment or fraudulent claims. Given the sensitivity of investors to uncertain future growth, these controversies played a major role in deflating the expansion of for-profit psychiatric hospitals. Growth of for-profit facilities came to a virtual halt.

Managed Care and Self-Reinforcing Cycles. Like for-profit ownership of hospitals, managed care techniques were first transmitted to the mental health field in the 1980s. In this case, however, the immediate consequences of institutional transmission actually reinforced the factors that encouraged the initial entry of managed care, building pressures for additional expansion.

The initial rationale for the spread of managed care involved the relatively weak professional norms for appropriate treatment of mental illness and substance abuse. When independent clinicians are seen to practice in a haphazard and possibly self-serving manner, concerns about inappropriate care seemed quite reasonable and fears about the loss of clinical autonomy associated with managed care less compelling. When state governments had difficulty successfully transferring treatment from hospital settings to the community, the evidence that managed care could reduce the use of inpatient settings looked particularly attractive.

After roughly a decade of experience, the performance of managed behavioral health care has left a rather mixed track record. It clearly reduced the costs of treatment for mental illness and substance abuse, although there is some disagreement over the magnitude of these savings (Callahan et al. 1995; Frank & McGuire 1995). On the other hand, there is also a body of evidence suggesting that:

(1) the treatment of privately insured patients with depression is decidedly worse under managed care than for patients covered by fee-for-service insurance (Wells & Sturm 1995);

(2) outcomes for patients with more severe mental illness affiliated with state-run programs are mixed, with some evidence of worsened outcomes (Mechanic et al. 1995); and

(3) some nonclinical outcomes, such as return to employment, may also be undermined by managed care (Mechanic et al. 1995).

Coupled with the evidence just presented that managed care exerts particularly strong constraints on the clinical autonomy of mental health professionals, the balance sheet for managed behavioral health care is hardly impressive.

Indeed, one could readily make the case that the drawbacks associated with managed care are at least as problematic as those observed for proprietary hospitals. Nonetheless, enthusiasm among purchasers for managed care remains strong, and various forms of managed care continue to spread through private and public insurance programs (Iglehart 1996). What can explain the continued expansion of managed care when comparable concerns appear to have undercut the growth of the for-profit psychiatric hospital industry?

There are a variety of plausible explanations. The simplest, albeit most cynical, interpretation suggests that costs may simply count for more than care in contemporary American medicine. Despite concerns about the ethical implications of proprietary hospitals, they continued to expand as long as they were perceived as paragons of efficiency. However, once evidence emerged that they actually *increased* costs by encouraging unnecessary treatment, collective approval vanished. Conversely, managed care continues to have legitimacy when applied to mental health care because it has demonstrated its ability to reduce spending, even though it raises a number of red flags in terms of other outcomes.

Three other explanations can be drawn from the three theories of institutional transmission we developed earlier. From the diffusion perspective, for-profit ownership and managed care spread because they were effective responses to institutional failures in health care in general and mental health care in particular. To the extent that the diffusion of both managed care and for-profit ownership reflects pressures for greater efficiency, the evidence favoring the cost-saving potential of the former was simply stronger than that for the latter. And the countervailing pressures were weaker. Opposition to both forms of institutional transmission reflected concerns about the need to preserve clinical autonomy. However, as indicated earlier, the spread of managed care – by creating a divided set of loyalties for mental health professionals – can undermine patients' confidence that their providers will act reliably in their behalf (Mechanic & Schlesinger 1996).

Isomorphic processes offer a third explanation for the differing outcomes in the spread of for-profit ownership and managed care. Isomorphic pressures expanding for-profit ownership were based in the private sector, whereas the spread of managed care to mental health care reflected at least as much a desire by state mental health officials to acquire greater legitimacy. Consequently, the long-term dynamic may differ because expectations adjust differently in public and private sectors. More specifically, private sector expectations may adapt more quickly to newly emerging evidence. Consequently, even though the "balance sheets" of for-profit hospitals and managed care might be viewed as roughly equivalent, the continued spread of managed care may result simply because public officials are slower to adjust their expectations following recently emerging negative aspects of both types of reform.

The third institutional explanation is linked to the process of intersectoral bridging. Recall that we hypothesized that the values of "technical" performance and efficiency were transmitted to the mental health sector primarily as a result of the spread of private insurance coverage in response to state mandates. If this is correct, then the specific forms of efficiency that are relevant to institutional change in mental health care will be the forms of efficiency that are most salient to these private insurers and not to some broader notion of societal efficiency. Even if for-profit hospital corporations had been able to deliver services more efficiently, their higher charges and inflated levels of utilization undermined insurers' efforts to constrain rapidly growing premiums. Even if managed care creates some social costs by less effectively ensuring that people with mental illness remain employed, such costs are not borne by the insurance companies and are thus not relevant to their assessment of the merits of managed care. In other words, private notions of rationality are those that are deemed relevant, not calculations from a broader societal perspective.

Some Concluding Thoughts

Throughout its history, the mental health service system has borrowed institutional innovations that originated in other sectors. In some cases, these have transformed in important and positive ways our understanding of mental illness, mental health care, and the role of people with mental illness in society. In other cases, however, the adoption process has been more problematic and the adaptation process less complete, as illustrated with the two examples described in this chapter.

There is every reason to expect that this process of institutional transmission will continue. Compared with acute medical care, mental health services remain relatively low in professional status, lacking in public legitimacy, and limited in the availability of resources. Future institutional innovations, therefore, are likely to emerge first for general health care and then migrate to behavioral health care. It therefore behooves us to better understand the process of institutional transmission and the role of public policy in shaping outcomes.

The three conceptual perspectives explored here offer some insights into both the origins of institutional innovation and their longer-term consequences. Interpreted through these three perspectives, historical evidence suggests that innovations in mental health care are more fully explained by isomorphic pressures and intersectoral bridging than by conventional models of diffusion. All three theoretical perspectives suggest that the primary dynamic involves the factors that legitimize particular institutions to the purchasers of mental health services, rather than to the providers of those services. Of course, the two examples considered here – for-profit hospitals and managed care – do not necessarily explain all the processes of institutional change in mental health care. Nor have we been able to fully explore all aspects of these changes; it would also be useful to better understand the forces that affect the timing of institutional transmission and that lengthen or shorten the delays between innovation outside mental health care and the appearance of that innovation in the behavioral health context.

These issues are important for better understanding the evolution of mental health services. But one can also see the mental health field as an illustration, a useful case study, of broader processes of institutional transmission. The "new institutionalism" as applied to organizational sociology has provided some important insights into organizational behavior and social structure (Powell & Dimaggio 1991), yet it remains in the early stages of development, with some plausible conceptual models but all too little grounding in the study of actual processes of institutional diffusion and adaptation. With just the two examples introduced in this chapter, we have seen the limits of extant theories for explaining institutional change. More specifically, our discussion suggests that factors rarely explored in the new institutional theories – distinctions between public and private sectors, the importance of resource-rich versus resource-poor sectors, and the relative social legitimacy of the activities conducted in the sectors – may play critical roles as mediating factors.

Better understanding the process of institutional transmission also promises some insights into other topics of concern to sociology in general and medical sociology in particular. For example, sociologists recognize that the spread of managed care has had important implications for the changing role of professionals in American medicine (Hafferty & Wolinsky 1991; Ritzer & Walczak 1988). The interactions between professionals and managed care organizations are typically characterized as a struggle for authority and legitimacy between the healthcare professionals and the purchasers of medical services (Light & Levine 1988). When the spread of managed care is seen instead as a process of institutional transmission, it suggests a very different set of factors that are likely to be relevant to the interaction of managed care plans and health-care professionals. Clinical autonomy becomes juxtaposed with standardization, technical criteria against professional norms. From this perspective, the spread of utilization review reflects changes in the interaction among medical specialties as well as a countervailing force constraining the previously broad authority of the profession as a whole.

Viewed from a variety of perspectives, an institutionalist interpretation of the ongoing changes in mental health care can enrich our understanding of ongoing changes affecting the mentally ill and the professionals who treat them. It calls for understanding the role of the treatment of mental illness and substance abuse in a broader institutional field or sector and for focusing on the changing place of mental health services in the general health and social service system of contemporary postindustrial societies.

24

Integrating Service Delivery Systems for Persons with a Severe Mental Illness

Joseph P. Morrissey

Obtaining care for severe mental illness is challenging because each service area has its own special purpose and funding mechanisms, whereas people with severe mental illnesses need a broad array of services. Hence there has been much effort to produce service integration. Morrissey reviews the experiences of service integration and considers four major innovations: Community Mental Health Centers; the Community Support Program and its spin-off, the Child and Adolescent Service System Program; the Program on Chronic Mental Illness; and efforts to introduce managed mental health care. Recent demonstration programs to integrate services have been subjected to comprehensive outcome evaluations. The research from two of these demonstrations produced similar findings; there was strong evidence for service system change and improvement but little consistent evidence for improved client-level outcomes. The chapter concludes by describing opportunities for further research. Without a national policy for health and welfare programs, it is difficult to meet the various needs of those with severe mental illness. Students may want to list the number of agencies in their own communities who provide services for those with severe mental illnesses and to question providers about gaps in such services as well as about issues of coordination.

Over the past fifty years, the U.S. mental health system has shifted from a centralized, institutional model based largely on state mental hospitals to a decentralized, community-based system involving several thousand public and private providers (Grob 1991). In this process of deinstitutionalization (Mechanic & Rochefort 1992; Morrissey 1982), many thousands of long-stay patients who had a severe mental illness (SMI) were transferred to nursing homes or released directly to community settings. In addition, the growth of psychiatric services in community mental health centers attracted many more thousands of formerly unserved patients. As a result, the mental health services system expanded enormously and moved from a predominantly inpatient to a predominantly outpatient array of services (Goldman & Taube 1989). These changes have benefitted persons with acute care needs and those with milder conditions but, in a number of respects, they have disadvantaged persons with SMI. Members of the latter group often present a multiplicity of needs, not only for medical psychiatric treatment but also for social rehabilitation, income maintenance, housing, health care, employment, social supports, and substance abuse counseling (Rosenblatt & Attkisson 1993). Obtaining appropriate care to meet these needs in community settings has been a challenge because the human service system in the United States is organized largely on a categorical or single-problem basis. Each categorical program area or service sector has its own special purpose, its specific sources of financing, its particular eligibility requirements, its own geographical service area, and its individual mode of operation. Moreover, persons with a SMI often have cognitive and functional impairments that reduce their motivation to seek out care or to comply with treatment plans once contact is established.

The disjuncture between the needs of persons with SMI and the contours of the community care system have led to a variety of efforts to decategorize the various service sectors and to integrate or bundle the services in a more accessible and effective way. The quest for improved service arrangements has been advanced under the banner of "services integration" (SI), a broad-based movement that has sought to develop linkages between sectors at the service delivery and administrative levels that enhance the effectiveness, efficiency, and economy of human service programs for such persons at risk as the poor, the disabled, the mentally ill, dependent children, and delinquents (Kusserow 1991).

This chapter reviews the experiences with SI in the broader U.S. health and welfare arena as a context for considering its applications in the mental health field over the past few decades. Four major innovations will then be considered as examples of SI in the mental health field: Community Mental Health Centers (CMHCs); the Community Support Program (CSP) and its spin-off, the Child and Adolescent Service System Program (CASSP); the Program on Chronic Mental Illness (PCMI), co-sponsored by the Robert Wood Johnson Foundation (RWJF) and the U.S. Department of Housing and Urban Development; and the now rapidly proliferating efforts to introduce managed mental health care. The effectiveness of SI will then be considered with a focus upon evaluation findings from the RWJF–PCMI (Goldman, Morrissey, & Ridgely 1994) and the Ft. Bragg children's mental health demonstration (Bickman et al. 1995). These reviews will lead to a discussion of research opportunities for a more definitive test of the relationship between SI and improved client outcomes. Here, the ACCESS demonstration for persons who are homeless and severely mentally ill (Randolph 1995) will be highlighted as the most recent and the most comprehensive effort yet undertaken to demonstrate the client-level effects of service system integration in the mental health field. In this discussion several directions for further research are identified.

Services Integration: Setting the Context

Although the roots of SI as a health and welfare policy can be traced back to the charity organization societies at the turn of the nineteenth century and early decades of the twentieth century (Kagan 1993), the real impetus came from the New

Frontier and Great Society programs spawned by the Kennedy and Johnson administrations during the 1960s. Initiatives were undertaken on juvenile delinquency, neighborhood service centers, community action, Community Mental Health Centers, Model Cities, Head Start, Older Americans Act, and the War on Poverty, to name just a few of the major projects. Between 1962 and 1966, the number of federal categorical grant programs increased from 160 to 349, and by 1971 there were 500 (Banfield 1971). These projects focused on substance (target-group needs) over structure (coordination within and between programs). Their funding was appropriated on a categorical basis that was restricted and restrictive with tight eligibility, accountability, and personnel requirements (Kagan 1993).

By the early 1970s, services coordination had become a watchword within the Department of Health, Education, and Welfare (DHEW). In speeches, DHEW Secretary Richardson often lamented that these programs were suffering from a "hardening of the categories" (Kusserow 1991). He initiated a number of reforms to foster the integration of services across categorical program areas, including research and demonstration projects, proposed legislation, technical assistance efforts, and internal departmental reforms. These efforts were continued throughout the 1970s and 1980s by his successors. Most of these projects promoted linkages, coordination, and comprehensiveness in the context of federal categorical legislation. The 1970s saw a shift in strategy from redesigning the system through the aid of the federal government to "capacity building" at the level of local government (Morris & Hirsch-Lescohier 1978). At the state level, strategies included the development of comprehensive human resource departments, "umbrella agencies" or interdepartmental planning councils, information and referral systems, community-based care, case management, and other forms of service coordination mechanisms. Service Integration Targets of Opportunity (SITO) projects focused on interagency program linkages, core services, and case coordination. Partnership Projects targeted the management of service systems at the state and local levels as well as program planning and design.

Despite the DHEW's demonstration projects and capacity-building efforts, progress in services integration was slow throughout the 1970s and 1980s; this was due in part to the lack of documentation on examples of successful service integration or on the efficacy of state-level administrative reorganizations. For instance, Baumheier (1982) describes how, in much of the public administration literature of this decade, no established causal links were made between interorganizational and intraorganizational coordination, even with well-controlled structures of authority. So the question of whether changes in formal structures would enhance coordination among organizational units remained largely unanswered. Overall, services integration projects of the 1970s and 1980s showed little impact (Kusserow 1991). Attention began to shift dramatically from broad national initiatives to narrower initiatives focused at the level of the provider and the client, a trend that was sustained into the 1990s. Service needs emphasized case management strategies and networking among agencies and providers within a community (Kagan 1993; Kahn & Kammerman 1992).

Past services integration efforts have been criticized for lacking accountability, evaluation, and measurable outcomes. Evaluations that did take place merely identified implementation problems and failures to be avoided in future efforts. Baumheier (1982) offers four reasons for the failure of integration efforts: (1) target grant programs are inadequately funded; (2) coordination is aimed at existing service techniques and approaches that have been proven to be inadequate; (3) the root barriers to coordination are not susceptible to managerial solutions – revised national policy is needed rather than administrative coordination; and (4) the true source of the coordination problem is the fragmentation and pluralism of American policies, opinions, and interests.

This leads to the question of why interest in services integration has persisted. Warren (1973) answers this question by identifying the latent functions of services coordination that sustain interest in integration despite its limited success. He uses the example of the Model Cities project to describe the ways in which it succeeded not in improving the conditions of the inner city but rather in reinforcing the reliance on policies of comprehensive planning and coordination. The various projects he studied met with varying levels of success and were burdened by local political shifts, economic conditions, and unemployment. However, the critics of these projects were largely ignored, while proponents offered statements about unrealistic expectations and suggestions for subsequent integration projects. Consequently, Warren identifies a number of latent functions as the factors that sustain interest in coordination. In his view, the coordination strategy serves to strengthen existing local agencies, reduce competition, provide money for agency expansion, define poverty in terms of needed services, secure roles for agencies in channeling efforts, produce an aura of change without threatening the status quo, and provide a stimulus for additional funds and employment. Finally, he notes that the habit of simply writing about how to improve subsequent SI efforts avoids the question of how outcomes can be measured.

In a similar vein, Morris and Hirsh-Lescohier (1978: 22) state that

> integration and coordination are often turned to because the real problems of social organization and social distress are too difficult to deal with frontally or directly. Inequity, inequality, serious deprivation, and disability are impossible to overcome without serious expenditure of resources. . . . [Integration is a] less painful way to make the existing welfare system function more efficiently by presumably stretching its resources further.

These authors opt for identifying specific defects in the service system that integration or coordination might likely improve, rather than working to reconstruct the entire human services system.

Table 24.1. *Profile of service integration strategies for persons with a severe mental illness*

Level of integration	Mechanisms	Problem to be solved
Client	Case management	Fragmented and uncoordinated office-based services
	Assertive community treatment	Inaccessible services
Organization	Community Mental Health Centers	Lack of comprehensive services and of continuity of care
System	Local mental health authorities	Lack of organization and accountability at system level
	Managed care	Lack of incentives for cost-efficient performance

Mental Health Services Integration Strategies

The experience with services integration in the welfare field underscores that it is a multilevel process that can be focused at system, organization, or client interventions (Agranoff 1991; Kagan 1993; Kahn & Kammerman 1992). Table 24.1 presents a profile of the major service integration mechanisms that have been pursued in the public mental health system for persons with a SMI. This configuration is based on discussions by Mechanic (1991) and by Hoge and colleagues (1994). Each strategy emerged as a response to a specific set of problems; in many respects, each strategy in isolation is only a partial solution for the services integration problems facing SMI persons.

At the *system* level, two main interventions have been attempted: creating mental health authorities and (more recently) implementing managed care. Both strategies focus on the organization and financing of services. The idea of a mental health authority was the central focus in the Robert Wood Johnson Foundation Program on Chronic Mental Illness (see the following section). The assumption was that lack of accountability and organization within the mental health system made it difficult to meet the needs of SMI persons, so that a single entity had to be created that would assume systemwide responsibility for the clinical, fiscal, and administrative aspects of care.

Managed mental health care is still more of a concept than an everyday reality within the public mental health sector, but things are changing rapidly. Managed care is a new way of financing services that shifts risk from the payer to the provider of services, limits choice of provider, and manages utilization through a variety of gatekeepers, periodic reviews, and authorizations. The main problems to which it is addressed are the lack of incentives for cost-efficient performance in the traditional fee-for-service or indemnity insurance reimbursements (Frank & Morlock 1997).

At the *organizational* level, the principal mental health innovation of the past 25 years was the Community Mental Health Centers program (Schulberg & Killilea 1982b). Its goal was to create a new community-based treatment program that would supplant the state mental hospitals. The underlying problems to which it was addressed were the lack of comprehensive and coordinated services and the discontinuity of care.

At the *client* level, two interventions have been carried out within a services integration framework: case management and assertive community treatment. Both of these focus on the needs of individual clients and avoid efforts at reorganizing the structure or financing of services. Case management is an effort to increase the accessibility of services and entitlements from a complex and diverse network of provider agencies. Assertive community treatment is an effort to integrate major responsibilities for patient care within a single, multidisciplinary, and largely self-contained team. It represents a response to the fragmented and uncoordinated care and largely office-based practices of most community mental health programs.

Mechanic (1991) argues that systems which employ mutually reinforcing combinations of these strategies provide a more viable framework for achieving true services integration and overcome some of the barriers that have undermined or constrained individual strategies when used in isolation. He believes that such a framework would provide incentives and foster favorable professional behavior for integrated service delivery. In the following section, the evolution of these strategies will be highlighted as a basis for considering current research evidence on their effectiveness.

The Evolution of Mental Health Services Integration

The issue of service integration, especially the linkage between state mental hospitals and community programs, was an active concern throughout the 1950s. This concern intensified between 1960 and 1995, a period of rapid and tumultuous change in mental health care. Here, the applications of services integration to mental health will be highlighted in terms of four programmatic efforts: Community Mental Health Centers, the Community Support Program, mental health authorities, and managed mental health care.

Community Mental Health Centers

The most ambitious effort to deliberately integrate the delivery of mental health services on a national scale was the CMHC program initiated by the National Institute of Mental Health (NIMH) in the mid-1960s (Schulberg & Killilea 1982b).

The goal was to develop closer-to-home or community-based services (vs. the often distant state mental hospitals) that were comprehensive (e.g., providing emergency, inpatient, outpatient, and partial hospitalization services), had catchmented responsibilities (serving population areas of 125,000–250,000 persons), and were organized under one administrative umbrella (either as a freestanding center or a consortium of providers with affiliation agreements). The program was founded to promote early treatment, continuity of care, and a preventive orientation. Citizen boards and consultation and education services to schools and other community agencies were also key features.

Such centers would seem to be ideally suited to meet the multiple needs of persons with SMI. Ironically, at the outset, the CMHC system was never fully intended nor utilized for such persons. For much of their early history, CMHCs concentrated largely on heretofore unserved populations and those persons with acute, episodic, or less severe conditions (Chu & Trotter 1974; Windle & Scully 1974). Indeed, despite the clustering of services and their delivery in "single stop" locations, most CMHC patients were one-service (predominantly outpatient) users (Morrissey & Lindsey 1987). Gradually, with the growing concerns about deinstitutionalization beginning in the 1970s, the CMHCs began to serve SMI persons. This trend was accelerated in 1981 when the Omnibus Budget Reconciliation Act (P.L. 97-35) repealed the major provisions of the Mental Health Systems Act, thereby eliminating authorization for using federal funds specifically earmarked for community-based services for persons with SMI. Federal funding for substance abuse and mental health programs was consolidated into a block grant and allocated to the individual states at levels below previous apportionment (Tessler & Goldman 1982). At roughly the same time, Medicaid funds were capped, which also reduced the availability of federal funds for providing mental health services to the poor (Morrissey & Goldman 1984; Sharfstein 1982). With the transfer of operational responsibility for the CMHCs from NIMH to state governments, the centers became much more dependent on state funding (Tessler & Goldman 1982). As states began to give priority to SMI persons, CMHCs were induced to increase their services to this population in order to secure state contractual funding. Today, CMHCs are among the primary (outpatient) service providers for SMI individuals.

However, with the growing ranks of the homeless mentally ill across the country and with widespread concern about the adequacy of funding for public mental health services, CMHCs in many large cities were often seen as impediments to – rather than vehicles for – alleviating these problems (Shore & Cohen 1990). It was thought that catchmenting (assigning specific geographic districts to each center) and the decline in federal funding of CMHCs led to a fragmentation of services for those SMI persons with stable housing (i.e., there was not enough of a critical mass of chronic patients in any one catchment area to warrant the development of multiple, specialized services) while encouraging denial of responsibility for problems seen as "out-of-area" or citywide in scope, such as those presented by persons who are mentally ill, homeless, and on the streets. Homeless mentally ill persons often congregate in central city areas, where the assigned CMHC may be overburdened, whereas other contiguous CMHCs might have fewer homeless persons to serve.

Community Support Program

Beginning in the early 1970s and intensifying throughout the decade, the concept of deinstitutionalization was severely criticized because of the emergence of new patterns of exclusion, neglect, and abuse among persons with SMI. The General Accounting Office issued a report in November 1977 that called for immediate efforts to address the needs of the thousands of state mental hospital patients who had been "deinstitutionalized" into local communities without adequate provision for their overall care (Morrissey et al. 1980). In 1978, the President's Commission on Mental Health issued a similar call for action.

In response to this criticism, the NIMH created the Community Support Program (CSP), which was designed "to improve services for one particularly vulnerable population – adult psychiatric patients whose disabilities are severe and persistent but for whom long-term skilled or semi-skilled nursing care is inappropriate" (Turner & TenHoor 1978: 319). Initially, $3.5 million was allocated annually for contracts with 19 states for three-year pilot demonstration programs designed to provide psychosocial rehabilitation services, medical and mental health care, case management for the chronically mentally ill, supportive living and working arrangements, and crisis care services (Tessler & Goldman 1982). In addition, CSP supported state-level planning and policy development activities in an effort to induce legislative changes and new sources of funding for local programs.

In a sense, CSP may be viewed as a fourth cycle of reform in that it advocated a whole system of care and treatment approach for the mentally ill (Goldman & Morrissey 1985; Morrissey & Goldman 1984). Unlike earlier reform efforts (asylums, psychopathic hospitals, and CMHCs), CSP offered direct care and rehabilitation for the chronically mentally ill, rather than a focus on preventing chronicity via the early treatment of acute cases. An additional difference was the importance of developing a system of support services for SMI persons among the currently existing community agencies. Advocates of CSP recognized that SMI is, first and foremost, a social welfare problem. Thus, they did not recommend mental health solutions to social problems; rather, they proposed social welfare solutions to mental health problems (Goldman & Morrissey 1985). These included a community support system with health and mental health services in addition to incorporating critical entitlement programs that assist with income supports, transportation, and housing.

Despite the repeal of the Mental Health Systems Act in 1980, the NIMH community support program continued to receive an annual appropriation (approximately

$6 million in the early 1980s), and block grants, though limited, also contained provisions for continued financial support of community-based mental health services. In the early 1980s, the program was expanded to younger age groups with the Child and Adolescent Service System Program (CASSP). This initiative followed a similar strategy of advocacy, planning, and local service development. The central concept was a system or "continuum of care" to provide individualized mental health services in the least restrictive setting in the community, involving families and close collaboration among child-service agencies – particularly schools, social services, youth services, the courts, and health care providers (Behar 1988; Knitzer 1982; Looney 1988; Stroul & Friedman 1986). In 1989, CASSP was a key stimulant for the Robert Wood Johnson Foundation Mental Health Services Program for Youth, a five-year, $20.4-million initiative designed to demonstrate that mental health and community support services for young people with serious mental illness can be organized, financed, and delivered more effectively (Beachler 1990).

Local Mental Health Authorities

The next (and, in many respects, the most well-conceived) effort to create a truly comprehensive system of care for persons with SMI was launched by the Robert Wood Johnson Foundation on a pilot demonstration basis (Aiken, Somers, & Shore 1986; Shore & Cohen 1990). The Program on Chronic Mental Illness (PCMI) was a unique public–private partnership between the Foundation and the U.S. Department of Housing and Urban Development (HUD). Nine cities from among the nation's largest were selected on a competitive basis in 1986 to receive support in the form of grants, low-interest loans, and federal rent subsidies (Section 8s) to develop more effective systems of care and housing for the chronically mentally ill. The demonstration was funded for a five-year period from January 1987 through December 1992.

The mandate to the demonstration sites was severalfold: create local mental health authorities to take clinical, fiscal, and administrative responsibility for services to SMI persons; develop mechanisms to promote continuity of care; create independent and supported housing for the target population; develop flexible and expanded funding arrangements; and promote psychosocial supports for persons with SMI. The form and function of these authorities varied widely among the nine cities (Goldman, Morrissey, & Ridgely 1990b).

Local mental health authorities (LMHAs), owing in large part to the publicity surrounding the PCMI, were touted as the systems development model for the 1990s. As a result, the MHA concept has come under a great deal of scrutiny, and not all of the commentary to date has been favorable. Rosenberger (1990) criticizes LMHAs as politically flawed because, like CMHCs, they are an organizational solution imposed upon communities from above, rather than a negotiated agreement between agencies and government units whereby some authority and power is voluntarily ceded in order to accomplish systemwide goals. Dill and Rochefort (1989) make a related point in arguing that the most serious obstacle for services integration and consolidation of funding streams under a LMHA is "geopolitical" – the operation of federal, state, county, and municipal public and private providers under many separate jurisdictions. Rarely have the prerequisites for integration been present. These include not only a special will and energy for system transformation on the part of service workers, recipients, and citizens, but also mechanisms to organize and channel these feelings. As a result, Dill and Rochefort believe that the promise of local or substate mental health authorities still exceeds their performance.

Greenley (1992) has questioned the viability of LMHAs because their design neglects a number of organization and management issues. Reflecting on the experience with local mental health authorities in Wisconsin (Stein & Ganser 1983), he points out that services are highly variable across the state even though county-level LMHAs have control and responsibility for service delivery. In his view, LMHAs will not succeed unless managers and others in these systems go beyond administrative structures and "pay attention to issues of setting goals, monitoring care, giving feedback, and promoting desirable interorganizational cultures" (Greenley 1992: 382).

Managed Care

The concept of health care reform was in no way a new idea introduced by the Clinton administration. Grappling with our nation's health care costs has been part of virtually every political platform since the Great Depression in the 1930s. However, if Clinton's tenure is remembered for no other reason, he and Hillary Rodham Clinton should be credited with bringing the issue of health-care reform to the forefront of public consciousness in America during 1992–94. Armed with the knowledge that escalating health costs had a stranglehold on the national economy, Clinton's health-care reform plan aimed both to provide universal coverage and to reduce cost through capitation. There now seems to be no political relief in sight for the 40 million uninsured and underinsured Americans, but strides had previously been and continue to be made regarding cost containment.

"Managed care" equates to cost containment and is a catchall phrase coined to encompass a broad range of financing arrangements, organizational forms, and regulatory mechanisms that affect patient care (Mechanic et al. 1995). The Institute of Medicine (1989) defines managed care as "a set of techniques used by or on behalf of purchasers of health care benefits to manage health care costs by influencing patient care decision making through case-by-case assessment of the appropriateness of care prior to its provision" (see also Frank & Morlock 1997; Wells et al. 1995). More generally, the term is now used to define programs that control access to care, the types of care delivered, and the amount or costs of care.

Managed care has developed within the private health-care sector over the past 20 years through Health Maintenance Organizations (Paley 1993) and other pre-paid arrangements, but to date its applications in public sector settings for persons with SMI are limited (McFarland 1969; Mechanic et al. 1995; Wells et al. 1995). Mental health and substance abuse benefits are increasingly being specified and managed separately from general health benefits in employer-sponsored insurance (Hoy et al. 1991). In these "carve-out" situations, a managed care organization may be used to provide care and manage costs. These arrangements are now becoming increasingly common in public sector mental health programs that carve mental health services out of capitated health plans and set them up under separate auspices.

At the time this chapter was written (early 1997), it is uncertain whether the Medicaid program – the principal source of funding for SMI services – will be transferred to the states under a federal block grant to be administered under varying types of managed care arrangements. These changes are occurring so rapidly that systematic research on the structures, processes, and impacts of these arrangements is lagging far behind (Mechanic et al. 1995). Hence, as yet there is no clear analysis of the roles and responsibilities of managed care in the delivery of public mental health services (Cuffel et al. 1994). But there is much concern that "managed care" really means "managed money," so that clients with multiple and long-term needs (i.e., expensive cases) such as persons with SMI might be disadvantaged under these arrangements.

Effectiveness of Mental Health Services Integration

Unlike earlier efforts in human services integration, recent demonstration programs seeking to integrate services for persons with SMI have been subjected to comprehensive outcome evaluations sponsored by both government agencies and private foundations. Media reports throughout the late 1970s and 1980s about the failures of deinstitutionalization contributed to this concern, as did the increasing visibility of homeless mentally ill persons living on the streets of urban America (Goldman & Morrissey 1985). The rise of mental health advocacy and consumerism also contributed to the critique of mental health policies and to public demands for reform. Responding to criticisms of its role in encouraging deinstitutionalization, the National Institute of Mental Health began in the early 1980s to shift its goals and research programs toward persons with SMI. Increased NIMH grant funding in these areas spawned the growth of a mental health services research community that attracted many young social and behavioral scientists and clinicians who studied ways in which services can be improved for SMI persons. Findings from two of these demonstrations – the PCMI sponsored by the Robert Wood Johnson Foundation for adults, and the Ft. Bragg demonstration for children and youth, sponsored by the U.S. Department of the Army – will serve to highlight current evidence about the effectiveness of services integration strategies.

Program on Chronic Mental Illness

The PCMI systems evaluation focused on the extent of change in the performance of the local mental health authorities and on the development of community support systems for the nine cities involved (Goldman et al. 1990a). Parallel measures of local mental health authority and community support system performance were obtained from two data sources (key informant and interorganizational network surveys) conducted at each site at two times during the demonstration (1989 & 1991). Findings indicate that the local authorities were successfully implemented at most demonstration sites, but that changes in the community support systems lagged behind authority performance levels (Morrissey et al. 1994).

The outcome study was fielded at two points in time in four of the nine demonstration cities (Lehman et al. 1994). Two cohorts of clients were followed for a twelve-month period: cohort 1 beginning in late 1988 and extending through late 1989; cohort 2 beginning in late 1990 and extending through late 1991. Clients entered the study cohorts just prior to discharge from local inpatient or crisis residence units, on the assumption that such clients were at maximum likelihood of exposure to the demonstration (e.g., case management, housing, entitlements, rehabilitation). Data collection focused on the client's personal and treatment history, current level of psychosocial functioning, housing, continuity of care, and quality of life. The core hypothesis tested was that cohort 2 would outperform cohort 1 on all outcome measures because the system of care would be better developed later in the demonstration. The improvement in services at the system–provider level was expected to translate into improvements in services at the client level, leading in turn to better client outcomes.

Contrary to expectations, the results showed that there was no detectable improvement in outcomes between the two cohorts in any of the cities across multiple domains (Lehman et al. 1994). Positive results were found for case management in three of the four cities where a significantly higher proportion of clients in cohort 2 received this service during the two-month period after hospitalization. In addition, a greater proportion of cohort 1 than of cohort 2 changed case managers (a measure of *dis*continuity of care) during the one-year period in two of the cities (there was a clear trend in this direction for all four sites). Both of these findings support the hypothesis that improvements at the system level are associated with improvements in the services available to clients. However, for all five client outcome measures, the only significant difference between cohorts was on symptomatology at twelve months, and the effect was in the *opposite* direction than that predicted (i.e., cohort 2 had more symptoms than cohort 1). Similar findings of no outcome effects were also reported for a companion study of the PCMI demonstration in Denver (Shern et al. 1994).

Ft. Bragg Demonstration

Would a "continuum of services" for children and youth lead to improved treatment outcomes and lower costs per client in comparison to usual care? This was the central question addressed in the Ft. Bragg Child and Adolescent Mental Health Demonstration, which was sponsored by the U.S. Department of the Army from 1989 to 1995 (Bickman et al. 1995). The $80-million demonstration was operated under contract by a private mental health agency for an eligible pool of 42,000 military dependents residing in south-central North Carolina. Families seeking services for their children were required to use the demonstration's clinical services, which were free, or seek and pay for services on their own. The contract agency either provided services directly (outpatient) or contracted with local providers (for both outpatient and acute hospitalization) to form a continuum of community-based nonresidential and residential services. The continuum offered intake and assessment, outpatient therapy, day treatment, acute inpatient hospitalization, in-home therapy, after-school group treatment, therapeutic homes, case management and interdisciplinary treatment teams (for cases requiring more intensive care), and 24-hour crisis services.

The evaluation consisted of a three-year assessment of program implementation, quality, mental health outcomes, and cost–utilization components (Bickman et al. 1995). The "usual care" comparison group consisted of children receiving traditional CHAMPUS (health insurance for military dependents) services at two other comparable army posts. Families were interviewed at intake and then six and twelve months later. Findings indicated that the demonstration successfully implemented a coordinated, individualized, community-based and family-focused system of care. Quality-of-care results showed that the demonstration had greater continuity of care and fewer dropouts, used less restrictive settings, provided more individualized care, and delivered services more quickly than the comparison sites. Furthermore, most of the children at each site improved on a battery of clinical outcomes over the twelve-month follow-up period, although few were free of mental health problems at year's end (e.g., 80% of the children had at least one diagnosis at the twelve-month interview). However – and this is the key finding vis-à-vis the central question addressed – no consistent clinical outcome differences were found to favor the demonstration site (Ft. Bragg) over the comparison sites, and the costs per treated child were greater at the demonstration site ($7,777) than at the comparison sites ($4,904). Finally, and not surprisingly given the free and virtually unlimited needs-based care, parents and adolescents at the demonstration site did show a higher level of satisfaction with services.

Interpretations

Both of these demonstrations produced similar findings in that there was strong evidence for service system change and improvement yet no consistent evidence for client-level improvements. The PCMI investigators interpreted their findings as evidence that service system change was a necessary but not a sufficient condition for positive outcome effects for clients (Goldman et al. 1994; Lehman et al. 1994). They suspected that this set of results may reflect the lack of attention to improving clinical services in the design and conduct of the demonstration. From the outset, the focus of the PCMI was on structural change and continuity of care, not on developing specific clinical services other than case management. As a result, attention was deflected from the treatment needs of persons with SMI, and no consistency was achieved in delivering services according to models with demonstrated efficacy such as assertive community treatment (Santos et al. 1995) and other high-quality clinical, rehabilitative, and supportive services (Lehman et al. 1994).

The Ft. Bragg evaluators suggest that, in any situation where there are no outcome effects, alternative explanations must be considered; that is, the results must be due either to theory failure or implementation failure or both (Bickman 1996a,b). In this case, they rule out implementation failure because their data clearly indicate that the continuum of care at the demonstration site was implemented successfully and with fidelity. Instead, they suggest that the most parsimonious interpretation of their findings is that the program theory underlying the continuum of care idea is wrong – that is, exposure to a continuum does *not* improve child and family outcomes as assumed. The underlying issue in their view is the general ineffectiveness of clinical services in community (noncontrolled) settings. The meta-analyses conducted by Weisz and Weiss (1993) – documenting the ineffectiveness of psychotherapy for children and youth in community mental health settings – are consistent with this view. These authors found that children were as likely to improve while on the waiting lists as they were after receiving treatment services.

Investigators associated with the PCMI and the Ft. Bragg evaluations therefore point to failures associated with clinical interventions as the most plausible explanation for the negative results. Whereas the PCMI investigators point to the inadequate use of effective mental health treatments for adults, the Ft. Bragg investigators point to the absence of effective treatments in community settings for mentally disturbed children and youth. In the latter case, it would appear that the methods for improving service system performance (e.g., mental health authorities or financing strategies) are far more developed than are the clinical interventions (e.g., parent–child counseling) employed in everyday community settings. In both cases, the interpretations are speculative, since neither study conducted controlled evaluations of specific treatments. As such, these explanations offer a number of leads for further research on integrated mental health service systems.

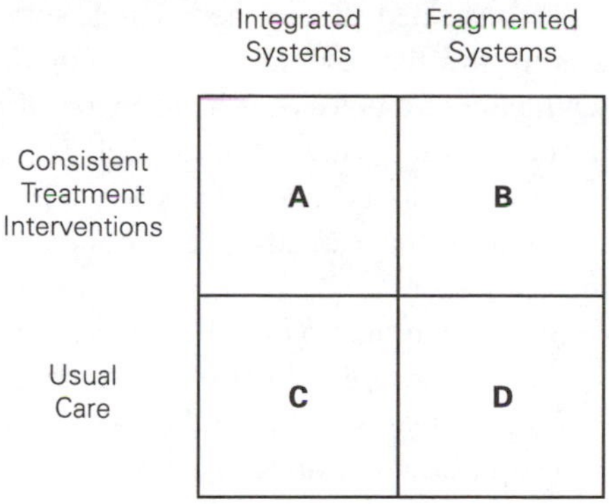

	Integrated Systems	Fragmented Systems
Consistent Treatment Interventions	A	B
Usual Care	C	D

Figure 24.1. Research design for strong tests of integrated mental health service systems.

Opportunities for Further Research

The idea that system change is a necessary but not a sufficient condition for improving client outcomes is suggestive of the kinds of field research opportunities that must be found or created to conduct more definitive tests of these relationships. A schematic representation is given in Figure 24.1. On one axis, studies must involve comparisons between consistent treatment interventions and usual care on a communitywide basis. On the other axis, studies must simultaneously contrast integrated systems versus communities functioning under the more usual situation of fragmented or minimally coordinated and unmanaged service delivery. Comparisons among the four cells on a set of clinical outcome measures would provide the information needed to assess the validity of the "necessary and sufficient" hypothesis. The A+B versus C+D comparison would test the main effects of consistent treatment, and the A + C versus B + D comparison would test for the main effects of system integration (e.g., continuum of care). A comparison of A versus B + C + D would be the most direct test of the necessary and sufficient hypothesis that the combination (interaction) of consistent treatment and system integration will deliver outcomes that are superior to any other combination.

How feasible would such a study be? It is difficult to imagine another opportunity similar to the level of funding associated with the Ft. Bragg project but with a larger number of sites. Nonetheless, ongoing changes in the financing of mental health services – and the possibility that the Medicaid program will be transferred to the states under a federal block grant – suggest that opportunities for multi-site field-based research will occur in the next few years. Both the PCMI and Ft. Bragg demonstrations indicate that technologies for improving and integrating service systems are reasonably well developed. Moreover, there are current treatments for both adults and children (e.g., assertive community treatment and multisystemic therapy) that have demonstrated effectiveness in field settings (Santos et al. 1995). The challenge is to find the resources and the commitment to introduce and maintain these treatments in a consistent manner for all providers in settings of integrated care or a continuum of care. Short of such grand designs, we next describe the research opportunities associated with a current federal mental health services demonstration program that can advance our understanding of the effectiveness of integrated service systems.

In May 1990, the Federal Interagency Council on the Homeless convened the Federal Task Force on Homelessness and Severe Mental Illness to develop a plan of action to end homelessness among people who are severely mentally ill (CMHS 1995). The task force consisted of representatives from all major federal departments whose policies and programs directly affect the homeless population with severe mental illness, including the Department of Health and Human Services as well as the Departments of Housing and Urban Development, Labor, Education, Veterans Affairs, and Agriculture. The task force also sought advice from experts in mental health research and housing administration, citizen advocates, mental health consumers, and state and local officials. Recognizing that there is no single, simple solution to the problems of homelessness among this population across the nation, the task force recommended the development of new incentives to promote integrated systems of care that offer access to essential services and to affordable and safe housing. To advance this agenda, a new ACCESS (Access to Community Care and Effective Services and Supports) initiative was proposed (Randolph et al. 1997).

Applications were solicited from the states, and ultimately nine were selected for participation in a five-year demonstration sponsored by the Center for Mental Health Services (CMHS) involving grants totaling about $45 million (Randolph 1995). Two communities in each state were identified as demonstration sites to participate in a quasi-experimental program design. Both sites received funding to recruit and enroll 100 homeless mentally ill persons each year and to engage them into comprehensive services. One site selected at random (integration site) would receive additional funding to develop systems integration strategies while the other (enhancement site) would not receive such funds. In this way, the ACCESS program is designed to assess what gains in quality of life and psychosocial functioning are obtained by systems integration over and above what can be accomplished by an array of comprehensive services alone. Many of the sites are implementing assertive community treatment teams as part of the services plan. The ACCESS evaluation is carried out by a consortium of private and public organizations under contract with CMHS (Randolph et al. 1997). The component parts involve an implementation study, a systems integration study (Morrissey et al. 1997), and a client outcome study (Rosenheck & Lam 1997). As a formative evaluation, there is feedback of results to demonstration sites on a regular basis and technical assistance to ensure that full implementation is provided to each site through the CMHS. The implementation study involves periodic site visits and semiannual reporting on progress from the sites. The client outcome study involves baseline, two-month, and twelve-month follow-up interviews with enrolled clients covering a wide array of clinical, social, housing, and service utilization topics. The systems study component, in turn, obtains data at three points in time (1994, 1996, 1998) about interagency relationships in the local systems of care (density, fragmentation, and centralization of interorganizational networks) in addition to ratings of the performance of the overall system (services accessibility and coordination).

This is not the definitive test depicted in Figure 24.1, as the ACCESS comparisons only approximate the A versus B contrast and the other cells are not represented (at least by design). Nevertheless, a number of important policy-relevant questions can be answered from the ACCESS evaluation. Data from each study component will be used to answer the central questions of the demonstration: (1) Does providing a comprehensive service package for persons who are homeless and mentally ill yield improvements in clinical outcome, housing, and quality of life for the participants? (2) Are these improvements greater in systems integration sites than in enhancement sites?

With the changing political climate at both the federal and state levels, the ACCESS demonstration may also have the distinction of being the last broad national services research effort the federal government will sponsor in the foreseeable future. Opportunities for services integration and related efforts now shift to the states and localities, where tremendous changes will be occurring on a state-by-state basis in the ways that mental health services are financed and delivered.

Conclusions

The public asylums created in the early part of the nineteenth century were the first mental health service "carve outs." The mentally ill were placed in separate facilities under the superintendency of psychiatrists for short-term care and restoration to functioning. Policies over the succeeding century led to the segregation of the mentally ill in a separate system of care that was governed by considerations of public welfare, charity, and the care of dependent populations yet was cut off from developments in the broader health care field (Grob 1973, 1983). The progressive dismantling of the asylum system during the past 50 years under policies of deinstitutionalization have returned responsibility for the care of mentally ill persons to local communities (Mechanic & Rochefort 1992; Morrissey 1982; Morrissey et al. 1980). The underdeveloped system of care in most communities, and the inadequate health and welfare coverage for persons with SMI, place such individuals in an extremely vulnerable position. Current changes in the financing and organization of care and the growth of various managed care arrangements raise further uncertainties about the integration of these persons in the community.

There are also renewed debates about the relative advantages and cost implications of Medicaid carve-in versus carve-out arrangements for persons with SMI (Frank & Morlock 1997; Mechanic et al. 1995; Wells et al. 1995).

At this time, it is difficult to predict future developments. A few things seem certain, however. For one, there is little chance of a wholesale return of SMI persons to the public asylum system, yet "asylum" (the function, *not* the facility) is needed in community settings for a relatively small group of SMI persons. For another, services may become more fragmented and less integrated in the absence of national policy and the growth of 50 different state mental health systems. Third, the mismatch between the needs of persons with SMI (e.g., for social rehabilitative care) and public spending (e.g., acute care hospitals) may continue indefinitely. The United States is moving into a period of retreat from a national health and welfare program. However, until these issues are addressed as national policy for all citizens, it is difficult to see how the needs of SMI persons can be adequately met at the community level.

In this political and economic climate, many of the key decisions about financing and organization will not be made on the basis of research findings. The knowledge base about the costs and benefits of alternative service delivery arrangements is still exceedingly primitive. In such situations, interest-group politics often prevail. The mental health services research community – including social scientists, clinicians, economists, and health policy analysts, among others – that crystallized within the past decade is now addressing issues of the organization and financing of mental health care in a rigorous way. Whether and how this research capacity is sustained during this period of transition and innovation in the delivery of mental health services will have much to do with how soon SMI persons will receive effective services and community supports.

25

Mental Health Policy Making in the Intergovernmental System

David A. Rochefort

This chapter examines the politics of mental health–care reform. Central to understanding mental health policy development is federalism – the interactions among national, state, and local governments. Also critical is the ultimate form Medicaid will take, whether as a continued federal entitlement or as a block grant giving the states enhanced authority. Rochefort reviews basic organizational aspects of American government and ties together the operation of federalism with mental health policy making via ten overarching principles that bear on mental health services. Included in this discussion is a review of past policy-making efforts and consideration of future reforms. What emerges is a picture of recurrent internal tensions and ambiguities. Problems of mental illness pose a number of fundamental questions of social justice: Is the receipt of health care a right? Do mentally ill persons have a guarantee to adequate community care? Is a two-tiered system of public and private mental health care acceptable public policy? Is it appropriate for mentally ill persons to receive care of widely disparate quality simply as a function of where they live?

By all signs, the United States is in the midst of a wrenching reexamination of the relationship between federal and state governments. On issues ranging from welfare to health care to education, major reforms have been proposed (or already enacted) that redirect power from Washington, D.C., to state and local officials. Philosophies of federalism have also been at center stage in recent elections, as presidential candidates and other office seekers attempt to clarify their views of the proper role for government in this society. Listening to the rhetoric, the changes under review sound deeply transformative – which they may well prove to be in some policy areas. Yet this is the kind of fundamental debate that Americans engage in not once a generation, or even once a decade, but almost continually in this era of the advanced welfare state.

In such a political environment, understanding federalism – the interactions among national, state, and local governments – becomes crucial to making sense of mental health policy development. From the earliest days of the republic, mental health care was a sector operating at the intersection of state and local levels of government. The advent of Medicaid and Medicare in the 1960s, coupled with the national community mental health center (CMHC) program, eventually created a major federal presence in financing mental health services. Yet the role of states and local communities within the mental health system continued alongside such initiatives and in some ways was elaborated by the partnership required by some of these programs. At present, one of the most critical issues in the evolution of U.S. mental health care is the ultimate form to be taken by Medicaid – whether as a continued federal entitlement or as one of a variety of species of block grants giving enhanced authority to the states.

The purpose of this chapter is to analyze the structure and process of mental health policy making from an intergovernmental perspective. As general background, I will first review basic organizational aspects of American government. Then I will link the operation of federalism and mental health policy making with the aid of ten overarching principles that bear on the formulation, implementation, financing, and management of mental health programs. This will demonstrate how the politics of our diffuse intergovernmental apparatus play a pivotal part (a) in both creating and limiting opportunities for mental health system change and (b) in shaping the performance of mental health programs. Thus, in the U.S. context, intergovernmental relations have significant "macro" and "micro" effects on mental health care, making them relevant to a broad variety of topics discussed elsewhere in this volume.

Fundamentals of U.S. Governmental Structure

"The most distinctive, and consequential, feature of governance in the United States is its elaborate machinery for dispersing authority"; so observes the political scientist Everett Carll Ladd (1993: 97). Born out of a rebellion against centralized political control, the American polity was designed to restrain the concentration of power in the new nation. On the contemporary scene, distrust of governmental authority persists as a basic American trait, showing itself in tax revolts, the drive to privatize public services, and suspicion of government regulation, to mention just a few tell-tale signs. According to public opinion polls, the citizenry is willing to countenance the idea of big government attacking specific social problems where it might prove more effective than the private sector or states and localities (Ladd 1993: 276–81). Yet, with rare exception, our political culture gives little support for developing the kinds of public programs through which this kind of centralized problem solving could be attempted.

The first, and most widely noted, structural mechanism for fragmenting public authority in the United States is the formal separation of powers, which warrants only short treatment here. Under the Constitution, three independent branches of the national government – Congress, the presidency, and the Supreme Court – are given a specific basis of existence and set of legislative, executive, and judicial functions, respectively (Ladd 1993). At the same time, distinct as they are, the three branches have overlapping powers that often bring them into conflict and circumscribe their individual autonomy.

The limited capability of the president to control the policy process was well demonstrated by the recent collapse of President Clinton's health-care reform proposal (Johnson & Broder 1996). After many months of internal deliberations and with a full media blitz, the Health Security Act was introduced to the Congress in September 1993 as a top administration priority. The bill remained a focus of legislative action but briefly, however. Remarkably soon, a phalanx of senators and representatives were vigorously advancing their own versions of health reform before a variety of committees (and interested news media), with neither the president nor the Democratic leadership of Congress able to hammer out a majority position. Then, as control of the Congress shifted from Democratic to Republican in the 1994 elections, the president's chances of dominating the health-care issue dropped from extremely slim to nil. The contrast between this governmental structure and a parliamentary system is sharp. In the latter, the prime minister generally has much greater influence over the legislative branch owing to the executive's control of party organization as well as to the principle of party discipline within Parliament (Landes 1987).

The second structural device for dividing governmental authority in the United States is federalism, or the distribution of political power between the national and subnational levels. Although the details of intergovernmental relations are less often an object of journalistic (and hence popular) attention than struggles among the three branches of national government, some scholars maintain that "federalism clearly is the preeminent institution of American domestic policymaking" (Anton 1989: v; see also Walker 1995). As a British expert on American government has put it, "The unique advantage of federalism is that it makes the United States possible" (Nicholas 1986: 16).

One great irony of the American penchant for limited government is that it has spawned so much of government. In fact, in a certain sense, we are the most "governed" nation in the world (Anton 1989). According to the U.S. Bureau of the Census, there are more than 82,000 units of government in the United States; these units are defined as bodies with specific jurisdiction over a public activity – including, for most, the authority to make policy and raise resources. This list includes one national government, fifty state governments, and also, as legal creations of the states, 40,000 municipal governments, 26,000 special districts, 15,000 school districts, and more (Anton 1989). This proliferation of government alone guarantees the significance, and complexity, of dealings across levels.

Consulting the Constitution, we are not surprised to find ambiguity regarding the relative powers of the federal versus state governments. The most important single constitutional provision speaking to the issue of overlap is the Tenth Amendment. It states that "The powers not delegated to the United States by the Constitution, nor prohibited by it to the States, are reserved to the States respectively, or to the people." But what, exactly, do these "reserved" powers include? Supreme Court interpretations of this Constitutional statement have varied over time, with some recent cases on state sovereignty in the area of commerce turning on very close decisions (Bowman & Kearney 1990; Ladd 1993).

Significantly, the calendar for the Supreme Court continues to strain with issues of states' rights in the form of cases in such areas as free speech, gun control, and sexual assault (Greenhouse 1996). Decisions on these and future cases will continue to demarcate federal–state prerogatives without any final settlement of the problem, simply because the changing political complexion of the nation shapes perceptions of a proper balance. All that can be said for sure is that both the national and subnational levels of government are intended to be strong under our system of government and will remain so.

It is important to note that the subject of federalism encompasses both structural and behavioral dimensions (Agranoff & Robins 1984). Federalism is equally about the formal powers attached to each level of government and the variable ways that actors at these levels choose to exercise such powers. It is about how national and state and local officials compete to control policy in specific domains and how they attempt to cooperate to accomplish shared objectives. Not least, federalism is also about the financial transfers that serve simultaneously to supply governments with resources and as the expression of symbolic values that the intergovernmental system is meant to embody.

We turn now to the ways in which this intergovernmental system, a defining characteristic of the American polity, has helped to determine the content and process of mental health policy activity.

Ten Principles of Intergovernmental Relations and U.S. Mental Health Policy

A set of ten principles serves to organize this discussion of the intergovernmental aspects of mental health policy making. The purpose of the first principle is to sketch the intertwining of federalism issues with the lengthy history of mental health services in our society. The subsequent principles are more generic observations about intergovernmental mechanisms with specific application to the mental health sector.

1. The History of U.S. Mental Health Care Can Largely Be Told in Terms of Changing Federal, State, and Local Responsibilities

There are several possible perspectives from which to trace the history of the mental health sector in the United States. One approach might be to focus on changing ideas about the causes and treatment of mental illness. Another would be to emphasize evolving concepts of rights for the mentally disabled. Far from discounting such vantage points, an intergovernmental perspective shows how changes in federal, state, and local responsibilities have often provided the vehicle for directing the mental health sphere in line with clinical and humanitarian concerns. Occasionally, shifts in federalism have themselves provided the impetus for implementing new values in a status quo organized around particular intergovernmental arrangements. Or, as Grob has written, "[governmental] structure can transform priorities, which in turn reshapes the content of policy in distinct ways" (1994b: 471–2).

During the colonial era, care of the mentally ill was a local responsibility. The primary public policies that community officials relied on for dealing with the mentally ill were poor relief measures and use of local jails. This period, however, marks the last time in American history that the mentally ill fell under the undivided jursidiction of a single level of government, a reflection both of the absence of a formal mental health system and the polity's undeveloped state.

By the early 1800s, a distinct mental health policy – centered around specialized hospital facilities – was coming into being in the new nation. Parallel to developments in the private sector, state legislatures around the country began to finance the establishment of dozens of public mental hospitals to implement the new regimen of "moral treatment." Under this therapeutic system, controlled institutional environments were essential for delivering humane and individualized care focused on restoring patients' psychological balance. Yet state authorities did not seek to eliminate local involvement in care of the mentally ill; instead, state laws continued to stress local autonomy and to refer to different categories of mentally disordered persons who would be handled differently by state and local officials. As Grob (1994b: 473–4) has described, the state hospital was envisioned first and foremost as a facility for commitment of the dangerously ill. Admission of other types of patients depended more on local discretion (and available space). Complicating this arrangement were provisions in most states that required local communities to pay for their residents in state hospitals. These provisions set in motion an intergovernmental financial dynamic for mental health care with implications for decision making on patient placement and discharge as well as for institutional fiscal management. They also ensured ongoing negotiations between state and local officials on matters small and large, from the treatment of individual patients to the state's cost-sharing formulas (Grob 1994b). To avoid these costs of asylum care, many local governments continued to rely extensively on local welfare institutions, resulting in tremendous variation in policies and practices both within and across states. This situation was not resolved until the late 1800s, when most states passed acts designating insane individuals as the responsibility of state government alone (Goldman, Frank, & Gaynor 1995).

Advocates who sought the federal government's support for mental health care during the 1800s never did achieve their objective. Not until after World War II did mental health care become accepted as a priority on the national level in the United States, an intergovernmental shift that was again associated with an important change in treatment philosophy and practices. Highly critical of the role being played by large custodial state institutions, federal policy makers tipped the balance toward community care as national mental health policy by financing a host of alternative services in commmunity clinics, private hospitals, and doctors' offices. It is important to note that, of the three major pieces of federal legislation providing this funding (the Community Mental Health Centers Act, Medicaid, and Medicare), only Medicare did not require states to share in the costs. Moreover,

Medicaid gave the states considerable discretion over eligibility and the services to be made available under the program.

The federalism initiatives of the Reagan administration during the early 1980s inaugurated another noteworthy change in intergovernmental responsibilities for mental health care. After nearly two decades, the CMHC program was converted from a categorical grant to one element of the block grant for Alcohol, Drug Abuse and Mental Health. Key to the block-grant mechanism is a lessening of federal requirements and controls coupled with greater state discretion over types of activities funded, the recipients of funding, and general program priorities (Conlan 1988). State officials generally seized on this opportunity to better integrate the community mental health system with state planning and service structures. Also, original federal concepts of what the community service system should look like (e.g., the use of local "catchment areas" as the geographic basis of service delivery) were sometimes abandoned. Finally, the move to a block-grant approach was accompanied by a substantial cut – 21% in the first year – in the overall level of federal funding for community mental health care, making it a time of severe retrenchment as well as reconfiguration (Rochefort 1993).

In the 1990s, mental health reform has been linked with the drive for expanded insurance for general medical care. As the health insurance issue progressed from the state to federal levels in the late Bush and early Clinton years, so too did the effort to improve the availability of mental health benefits (Scallet & Havel 1994). For some advocates, national health-care reform was not only a means of giving more people access to mental health care but also a chance to eliminate the traditional two-class system of private and public services.

President Clinton's health care proposal, which included substantial mental health benefits plus the promise of complete parity of health and mental health coverage by 2001, took a significant step in the direction desired by mental health reformers (Arons et al. 1994). The demise of that proposal was a setback for the mental health issue, but not a fatal blow; two years later, the federal mental health reform strategy won an important victory with a new law guaranteeing partial parity of health and mental health insurance benefits for large employee groups (Pear 1996b).

As such determinative episodes illustrate, the course of U.S. mental health policy history has been inseparable from changing decisions about the involvement of government at different levels as provider, payer, and regulator of mental health services.

2. Federalism Presents an Inescapable Tension between the Values of Diversity and National Policy Standards

Our federal system prizes the states for the diversity they present. In the realm of public policy, this diversity is justified with two chief tenets. First is the belief that government should be as close to the people as possible, reflecting the values that differ from region to region. Second is the concept of the states as "laboratories" for experimenting with innovative public policies, a phrase first introduced in the 1930s by Justice Louis Brandeis, in a dissenting opinion for the Supreme Court, and still used widely today (Ladd 1993: 128).

In fact, many important social policies in the United States have followed this path of diffusion from state to state before being adopted on the national level. For example, basic elements of the Social Security Act of 1935, the framework of the American welfare state, were put in place initially on the state level (Patterson 1986). Welfare reform is another example. During the 1980s, dozens of states had implemented employment and training programs for welfare recipients before Congress used the same basic model in the Family Support Act of 1988 (Gueron & Pauly 1991). Once again, in the 1990s the prevalent concepts of national welfare policy making – including time limits and other benefit restrictions – have first been employed on the state level (Pear 1996a).

However, there are also instances where national standards are viewed as essential, signifying that states and localities cannot simply choose to go their own ways. In this context, it is the value of "national purpose" that takes priority over the value of "states' rights" (Anton 1989: 11). The classic example where this conflict has been waged in the United States, with a settlement in favor of one national policy, lies in the area of civil rights.

For mental health policy, this tension between national uniformity and state variation has also been consequential, although with a clear tipping of the balance toward the latter. On the one hand, it is true that federal legislation like the recent parity bill will institute new national protections for mental health care, to be applied equally to covered workers and their families throughout the country. The mental health–care benefits provided under Medicare are another example of uniform national policy encompassing users of mental health services (Lave & Goldman 1990). Yet such programs are much more the exception than the rule in mental health.

We do not have one mental health system in the United States; we have 50 state systems. Perhaps no fact is more central to understanding the nature of mental health care in this country. The states vary enormously with respect to a broad array of mental health resource, utilization, and manpower indicators, and this makes it misleading to present national averages as descriptive of general trends (Reamer 1989). So, too, with the financial aspect of mental health care. For example, in 1990 New York spent $118 per capita on mental health and substance abuse care; Iowa spent $17, a sevenfold difference (Arons et al. 1994). Although the correspondence is not exact, analysts have pointed out that such patterns of financial inequality are matched by important variations in the performance of state mental health systems (see e.g. Torrey, Wolfe, & Flynn 1988).

By far the most important federal program for mental health care in this country is Medicaid, judged both by levels of expenditure and the variety of services supported (Lave & Goldman 1990; Taube, Goldman, & Salkever 1990). What we find with Medicaid is not a uniform national program but rather a federal–state endeavor. It is a partnership that sets in place a basic foundation of mandatory services to be funded in all states, but with a wide range of optional add-ons and choices about eligibility. This discretionary element has proved perhaps the most important aspect of the program for mental health care, and the program continues to grow more diverse still. By 1996, a majority of states had either received or applied for waivers from the federal government to develop a variety of managed care arrangements for their Medicaid populations (Bazelon Center 1996). Such waivers are a mechanism by which states may gain exemption from certain standard national requirements under Medicaid in order to expand eligibility or develop innovative service system solutions (Holahan et al. 1995). Should the program next be transformed into a block grant, the trend toward devolution will be amplified, along with increasing interstate variability.

3. Devolving Federal Responsibilities to State Governments Is Inherently Neither a Conservative Nor a Liberal Act

The move to decentralize federal programs is generally taken to be a right-wing political strategy. It is, first of all, compatible with the states'-rights theme, a traditional mainstay of American conservatism (Conlan 1988). Moreover, the devolution policy currently tends to receive its most enthusiastic and consistent support from politicians inside the Republican party. (In the final 1996 presidential debate, Bob Dole even claimed he carried a card in his pocket with the Tenth Amendment printed on it.)

Historically, however, block grants and other steps to devolve federal programs have enjoyed broad bipartisan support as a way to clean up a federal grants process that had grown extremely cumbersome (Advisory Commision 1977; Agranoff & Robins 1984). Thus, the first block grants ever created were fashioned during the Johnson era in the mid-1960s and with the backing of that Democratic administration. This reaction against the rigidity of the federal grants system still can be seen today in the widespread sentiment among governors of both parties for federalism changes. Without doubt, President Clinton's own openness to augmenting state powers and responsibilities partly reflects his background as governor of Arkansas.

The programmatic repercussions of devolution also are neither inherently conservative nor liberal in character. Much depends on who is in power nationally and in the states when changes are effected. When Reagan created his block grants, encompassing dozens of federal categorical grants of different types, the programs were leaving the control of a very conservative national administration for disposition by a group of state officials including, at that time, many Democratic governors and legislatures, not to mention centrist Republican administrations. As a result, many states infused their own resources into mental health care and other areas to help offset federal cuts. It seems clear, in these locales at least, that the programs fared better than they would have if the dominant federal role had continued (Nathan et al. 1987).

Of course, it could work the other way too, should a liberal administration decide to turn over programs to conservative state policy makers having little interest in the maintenance of a particular policy area. Thus, the consequences of possible future devolution for mental health care are very hard to predict without knowledge of the political balance of power on the national and state levels over coming years.

Mental health services are a long-established responsibility of state governments around the country, which to some extent insulates them from major sudden budget cuts. At the same time, the political power of the mental health–care constituency is not as strong in most state capitals as on the federal level, exposing this service area to possible reductions with increased state control, no matter whether under Democratic or Republican auspices. A host of forces – political, bureaucratic, economic, and cultural – influences mental health policy making on the state level. In general, reducing national control over mental health care cannot be seen as expressing a singular policy theme, conservative or liberal, because its main effect is to expose these programs to all such forces that produce innovation and stagnation across the individual states.

4. Programmatic Shifts between Levels of Government Impact Differently on Different Groups, Depending on Patterns of Advantage and Disadvantage under the Prior Intergovernmental Arrangement

The distribution of intergovernmental responsibilities is a policy choice about power and the setting of priorities. Redistribution, therefore, inevitably works to strengthen or weaken the position of different interests involved with a program area.

Some of the implications of change are overt and readily recognizable. For example, as already noted, federal intervention in the mental health system after World War II was intended to weaken state control over mental health policy, which was identified with an antiquated public mental hospital system. Accordingly, federal policy makers deliberately structured the grant-in-aid process so as to bypass state authority and the state mental health–care agenda (Grob 1987). When the community mental health centers program was converted into a block grant in the 1980s and turned over to the states, this marked a diminution of the federal role – in particular, that of the National Institute of Mental Health, which had supervised CMHC grant giving – and an enhancement of the influence of state mental health departments.

Other, more subtle differentials also occurred under this block-grant shift. Those CMHCs in midstream of a promised federal funding cycle suddenly lost their guarantee of a certain level and period of support. By contrast, other community mental health providers – including, but not limited to, CMHCs that had become ineligible for continued federal grant support – now had a chance to compete for new state monies (Rochefort 1993).

And what about service constituencies? They, too, felt different impacts from this block grant funding. Research has shown that state officials around the country tended to direct new resources to the severely and chronically mentally ill, a population of traditional concern within state care systems (Rochefort 1993). Mental health consumers with mild and short-term disorders received service cuts. Special target populations, such as children and the elderly, were treated inconsistently from state to state.

The passage of national health insurance including mental health benefits would also have distributional impacts, although not all analysts agree on their form (Hudson & DeVito 1994). Some have argued that, since there is a middle- and upper-class bias in who chooses to enter psychotherapy, expanded coverage for mental health care could end up having the poor subsidize care for the rich. More commonly, it is expected that universal health insurance would lower financial barriers to mental health treatment for lower-income groups, thereby reducing social class disparities in the receipt of mental health care. But specific conclusions must depend on the structure of any new national program, including service exclusions, required cost sharing, and the overall basis of funding.

5. The Intergovernmental System Serves as a Context for Public Organizations to Engage in Political and Fiscal Games against Each Other as a Means of Avoiding Unwanted Burdens and Striving for Control over the Use of Their Own Resources

Almost by definition, federalism means a social service system featuring overlap and gaps in public programs due to the difficulties of coordinating policy making across a disorganized polity. Often, this leads to ambiguity about where primary responsibility lies for groups making use of services provided by different levels, or for groups having service needs not well met by any available program. Government departments and agencies are no exception to the general tendency of organizations to defend themselves against commitments that strain resources, especially if there is doubt about assignment of responsibility (Bardach 1977, Perrow & Guillén 1990). As a result, the intergovernmental environment can become host to its own version of such familiar games as hot potato, tug-of-war, and hide-and-seek, wherein public officials dispute who the clients of different service systems are and how they should be assisted.

The homeless mentally ill are an example of a population group with extensive needs in health care, mental health, housing, and income support (Federal Task Force 1992). In response, federal, state, and local governments have all created programs rendering them a variety of forms of assistance, and there is clear recognition of the need to coordinate these diverse public (and private) activities. Nonetheless, the plight of the homeless mentally ill has sometimes given rise to disruptive bureaucratic conflict and avoidance.

For a poignant illustration, consider a hospitalization plan attempted in New York City a few years ago (Rochefort 1993). Beginning in late 1987 and continuing into the winter of 1988, the administration of Mayor Edward Koch undertook a well-publicized roundup of the city's homeless mentally ill. Under Koch's plan, the homeless individuals first were to be taken for evaluation and basic medical and psychiatric care at Bellevue Hospital, a municipal facility. They would then be transferred to other service centers as appropriate, with most expected to move on to the state-run mental hospital and state-funded community housing.

State officials, however, objected to the large influx of new patients produced by the program. These administrators supported a policy of deinstitutionalization, not reinstitutionalization, and they lacked sufficient capacity in their housing programs to handle a sudden upsurge in demand. Accusing Mayor Koch of launching a poorly conceived initiative to shift an unwanted burden to the state, they called on New York City to develop more housing programs of its own. For his part, Koch was quite open about having mounted his hospitalization effort as a way of forcing an expansion of state resources for the homeless mentally ill.

In the end, Koch's program collapsed under the weight of conflict between these two levels of government. Reflecting the inadequacy of community services, city and state inpatient facilities quickly became overcrowded. Ultimately, the city began discharging homeless hospital patients to city-run homeless shelters after brief hospital stays, from which the homeless individuals soon exited back onto the streets.

Albeit in unusually public and exaggerated form, this scenario depicts the kind of governmental tensions that typify long-term, community-based mental health care in the United States (Goldman et al. 1995). In California, legislation was passed to realign responsibilities between state and county levels, clarifying the latter's fiscal responsibility for mental health care and limiting their ability to transfer patients into state programs (Austin, Blum, & Murtaza 1995). These modern-day situations echo the contested responsibility between states and localities dating back to the earliest development of public mental hospitals. Then, as now, the services available to patients, transfers between programs, and the strategies of administrators are inexplicable without reference to intergovernmental constraints and opportunities.

This problem of dispersed local responsibility for the mentally ill is widely acknowledged, so much so that the Robert Wood Johnson Foundation (one of the nation's premier sponsors of health-care research and demonstration programs) recently funded a major pilot initiative to create new municipal mental health authorities to focus capacity and responsibility for persons with chronic mental illness. This effort, a collaborative venture between the foundation and the U.S. Department of Housing and Urban Development, sought simultaneously to expand the continuum of community-based services and to consolidate the structure of financing and administration in mental health–care systems. However, despite some local mental health authorities' success in gaining new funds from state sources, formidable organizational and political barriers impeded full implementation of this model program, and state–local control issues persisted throughout the project (Goldman et al. 1990b, 1994).

6. Intergovernmental Changes by One Part of Government Need Not Be Consistent with the Actions and Decisions of Other Parts

Federalism is usually cast by public officials as an overarching philosophy about government in our society. In this sense, it is presented as a doctrine for ordering roles and responsibilities among federal, state, and local levels according to a consistent ideology. Within certain program areas, however, the polity may seem Janus-faced as to the intended locus of control and the preference given to such values as geographic uniformity and variation. This is especially true for a domain such as mental health, in which key policies emanate from divergent sources within government and are sometimes offshoots of other social programs

During the 1980s, for example, there were actually many inconsistencies in federal mental health policy when viewed from the perspective of augmenting state control over mental health services. As I have described, the Alcohol, Drug Abuse, and Mental Health block grant was created, and imbued with a very strong rhetoric of change via political decentralization, as a core part of Reagan's New Federalism. In contrast, at about this time and somewhat more quietly, the Health Care Financing Administration and the National Institute of Mental Health began collaborating on bringing hospitals around the country under a standardized federal prospective payment system for psychiatric patients (Lave et al. 1988).

The 1980s also saw a substantial expansion in Medicaid waivers and options by the federal government, giving greater programmatic flexibility and discretion to the states (Koyanagi & Goldman 1991). Yet this same federal government instituted a sweeping crackdown on the recipients of disability programs, including the mentally ill, that mandated tougher eligibility standards and procedures throughout the nation (Goldman & Gattozzi 1988).

Today, the tides of change for mental health care have their own cross-currents – for example, the devolution of Medicaid versus federal parity insurance legislation, and the encouragement of managed mental health plans versus increasing state and federal interest in the regulation of managed care. The pattern is a puzzle, to the extent one assumes a single government is in charge. But actually it reflects decisions by a host of different centers of power and policy making, with varying agendas, constituencies, and program histories. As federalism specialist

Thomas Anton (1997) maintains, the division of governmental responsibilities in the United States is not so much theoretical as it is political and pragmatic in its inspiration.

7. State Competition for Federal Resources Can Be Expressed in the Most Technical Forms

Any federal program that distributes resources to the states must operate under an allocation formula. But what should this formula have as its quantitative basis? The nuts-and-bolts of intergovernmental policy often come down to vigorous legislative and bureaucratic struggles in which the states compete to influence such technical questions.

For example, numerous adjustments have been made in the distribution formula of the mental health block grants over time, and they have been the product of contending forces of rational planning and power politics (Rochefort 1993). At first, a state's share of the block grant was tied proportionally to its preexisting CMHC funding. Then the formula was altered to factor in a state's population size and per-capita income. Acknowledging a high-risk population group, the size of a state's urban population subsequently was added into the formula. When small states and rural states complained that this emphasis disadvantaged them, still more changes were incorporated into the equation. Note that this process of formula development refers only to funding that the federal government gives to the states. Moving down the intergovernmental continuum, the states in turn have had to fashion their own internal methods for distributing federal monies, entailing an additional round of negotiations with public and private interests.

Medicaid policy making has its technical side as well, which takes on heightened importance as prospective intergovernmental reforms are entertained. The authors of a recent analysis by the National Health Policy Forum write:

> The most contentious battle in the Medicaid reform debate has centered on how a capped amount of federal money would be distributed among the states. Here, party politics breaks down and broadly pits southern and western states – which have high population growth and comparatively low per capita expenditures – against those in the Northeast and the Rust Belt – which have lower expected growth and higher current Medicaid spending. Certainly, a 4% growth cap imposed evenly across the states would punish states, such as Florida and Texas, that have higher growth rates of elderly and low-income people. Those with slower growth or expected declining populations, such as Michigan, would stand to gain. Also on the losing end would be those states that have reduced Medicaid costs through certain program efficiencies; they would presumably have less fat to cut. (1995: 7)

As these funding issues make clear, the acquisition of increased control by states over federal programs always creates uncertainties and risks, simply because the transition brings with it new funding conflicts – technical in part – that pit states and regions against each other. And because not all states have the same power (either structurally or operationally) in the legislative branch, the federal government is likely to function less as an impartial arbiter of these disputes than as a mirror of inequalities in state influence and access within the national government.

8. The Intergovernmental System Can Serve to Energize the Public Policy Process by Providing Additional Access Points for New Issues and Unheard Interests

Although federal, state, and local divisions in the United States are often criticized for contributing to inefficiency and inequity, there is another, more positive aspect to this method of governmental organization. The sheer number of units and levels of policy making create innumerable policy windows where new issues can be introduced or existing issues redefined.

In other words, if the balance of political forces, or institutional procedures, at one level of government is excluding a certain set of interests, then those interests have the opportunity to regroup and seek influence at another access point. When congressional committees prove inhospitable, there are always state legislatures to turn to. When bureaucracies at any level resist change, there is always the court system – on federal, state, and local levels. According to Baumgartner and Jones, this permeability of the intergovernmental system is a crucial part of its role in public policy change:

> Federalism in America creates a great number of distinct and partially autonomous venues for policy action. . . . Most research on the federal system has emphasized its role in limiting comprehensive policy change. Ironically, however, the federal system can promote change because no group can control all parts of the system, closing out consideration of policies that it does not favor. Federalism does not so much limit change as it makes such changes less controllable by anyone. The numerous venues provided by federalism make change far more unpredictable than in a unitary system. (1993: 216–17)

Change of this nature is easiest to recognize in an area such as mental health policy precisely because of its lengthy history. Benefiting from a panoramic perspective, we can see how critical policy innovations related to the use of institutions, community care, and insurance practices have all been associated with shifts in the level of governmental involvement.

Courts have played their own distinctive role in the modern era of community mental health care (Marmor & Gill 1989). Their support for such principles as the right to treament in the least restrictive setting, the right to refuse treatment, and the right to minimum-quality hospital standards has imposed legal requirements on other parts and levels of government or limited their range of action. When the Reagan administration carried out its administrative purge of the disability rolls in the early 1980s, it was the courts that reinstated the benefits of thousands of mentally ill recipients, leading ultimately to the passage of a new law by Congress to curb the president's policy (Goldman & Gattozzi 1988). And when Mayor Koch ordered his roundup of homeless mentally ill, a variety of state courts having original and appellate jurisdiction were drawn into the fray by civil liberties advocates who charged the program with violating New York's involuntary commitment statute (Ludwig 1991).

In this fashion, the dual system of American checks and balances – federalism and separation of powers – interlace. The most effective organized interests become well acquainted with the policy-making possibilities created by such an expansive framework and learn to "shop" for venues offering them the best advantage (Baumgartner & Jones 1993) – a test court case here, a regulatory decision there, a model program somewhere else. One adaptation on the part of the nation's leading mental health advocacy groups, including the Mental Health Association and the Alliance for the Mentally Ill, has been to develop networks of affiliated national, state, and local organizations that are capable of multilevel monitoring and mobilization.

9. Federalism Initiatives, Like Most Other Public Policies, Are Uncontrolled Experiments Whose Precise Effects Remain Unknown (and Unknowable)

The requirements for rigorous public policy evaluation are widely recognized: randomization of program participants, control groups, identification of key outcome variables, before–after quantitative measurements, and testing for statistical significance. Very few public policies, however, have ever been implemented on a large-scale basis according to this format. Time and resource demands are a discouraging factor. Moreover, the experimental framework is at odds with basic dynamics of a policy process in which constituency building, affirmation of social values, and demonstration of decisive leadership all take precedence over a research orientation.

The problems with introducing federalism changes as social experiments are multiplied because of the systemic character of the intervention. For obvious political reasons, it is simply implausible to think of including some states, but not others, in a devolution of power or in the creation of a new federal grant program. In practice, states do collaborate with the federal government to different degrees and in different ways – for example, by choosing whether to take advantage of waiver options, or by applying for different federal support programs. (Arizona did not even enter Medicaid until the early 1980s.) Yet there is an element of self-selection for these "natural experiments" that confuses any attempted comparative analysis.

A substantial amount of true experimental research has been carried out in the mental health policy field, for example, in regard to the impacts of hospitalization versus community care (for a summary, see Kiesler & Sibulkin 1987). However, these have all been closely managed, local-level studies. No precedent exists for a macro research effort that would provide definitive findings regarding mental health policy change on an intergovernmental scale. Thus, although various commentators may talk broadly about the "success" or "failure" of a realigning policy like deinstitutionalization, the data do not exist for linking the program's multiple interventions to results in a rigorously empirical way (Mechanic & Rochefort 1992).

In the case of the 1980s block grants, all states were phased into participation at the same time, a problematic approach from the research standpoint. Further, the block grant's effect was muddled by its coincidence with large federal funding cutbacks. What we know about the repercussions of the block grant, then, is pretty much confined to description of managerial performance and program priorities in the states, plus changing service, staffing, and revenue patterns among community mental health centers (Rochefort 1993). Client outcomes have been much more difficult to trace, and it is not possible to distinguish with any precision the influence of block grants versus contemporaneous changes in Medicaid and other programs affecting the mentally ill.

Shifting public philosophies and political power, administrative concerns, and the emergence of new policy priorities will continue to be the mainspring of federalism changes (Anton 1989; Conlan 1988; Walker 1995). Meanwhile, firm knowledge about programmatic consequences will remain elusive and of secondary importance in the hierarchy of policy-making values.

10. Intergovernmental Conflicts Can Mask the More Fundamental Questions of Social Philosophy and Resource Commitment That Are at Stake for a Policy Domain

Having highlighted the many ways that federalism in the United States serves to channel resources and express policy priorities, it is necessary, finally, to note its role in issue obfuscation. Nicholas puts it well: "the history of American politics is also, at almost every point, a constitutional history and, as often as not, the constitutional conflicts are not the real ones, but the smokescreen behind which the real political differences are being thrashed out" (1986: 22). Even more importantly, these conflicts can be the mask for leaving basic differences unresolved; intergovernmental strife can be a self-revealing symptom of a polity shirking its social responsibilities.

Problems of mental illness pose a number of fundamental questions of social justice in response to which the American political system has always hedged. Is the receipt of health care, including mental health services, a right? Do mentally ill persons have a guarantee to adequate community care, including needed housing arrangements and social support? Is a two-tiered system of public and private mental health services acceptable public policy? Is it appropriate for mentally ill persons to receive care of widely disparate quality simply as a function of where they happen to live?

Disputes over how mental health grant monies should be transferred from one level of government to another, or which public department should be providing services to the homeless mentally ill, pertain directly to these profound issues of social obligation. Aside from the larger currents of federalism in which mental health policy partakes, these ever-unsettled intergovernmental questions reflect the special politics of a marginal and unempowered social group.

Conclusion

Mental health policy making in the United States bears the indelible stamp of our intergovernmental political structure. It is a system in which all major objectives and values seem to function in tandem with their limiting opposites: variation and uniformity, autonomy and dependence, fragmentation and coordination, localism and centralization, permissiveness and authority, conflict and cooperation, change and stability (Anton 1989: 208–12; Walker 1995: 306–12). The result is part paradox, part self-regulation. A close examination of virtually any major mental health policy – taking into account its legal authority, funding basis, administrative organization, and delivery mechanism – will disclose these recurrent internal tensions and ambiguities.

Whether the needs of persons with mental illness could be better met under different governmental arrangements is an interesting question, but beside the point of this chapter. From a more pragmatic point of view, the challenge is to understand how the *existing* policy-making framework has shaped past mental health policy activities, what we may expect of it in the future, and how it can be used to advance needed change.

26

Psychiatric Rehabilitation Services and Outcomes: An Overview

Susan A. Pickett, Judith A. Cook, & Lisa Razzano

Whereas previous chapters have focused on the help-seeking behavior of individuals with mental health problems in general, this chapter focuses on services for those with severe mental illness. Given the debilitating effects of illnesses such as schizophrenia, individuals need rehabilitation services that enhance better overall functioning and include management of psychotropic medications, skills training, and services that promote better community integration. Psychosocial rehabilitation refers to the array of services that are provided. The difficulty is to understand how such rehabilitation services produce disparate versus uniform outcomes. The authors provide a review of the literature on psychosocial rehabilitation, the major aspects of rehabilitation programs, different kinds of outcomes, and the factors that predict these outcomes. Finally, they indicate promising directions for future research about psychosocial rehabilitation. What other mental health outcomes should researchers examine?

Rehabilitation services for individuals with severe mental illness are designed to promote functioning at optimal levels with the least amount of intervention from professionals (Dion & Anthony 1987). Psychiatric (or psychosocial) rehabilitation programs typically involve services for the management of psychotropic medications, skills training, and creation of a supportive network to assist community living (Attkisson et al. 1992). This chapter describes rehabilitation principles, program models, the services typically provided by such programs, as well as client outcomes. It also considers issues regarding outcome research and implications for future directions of outcome research in this area.

Review of the Literature

Psychiatric Rehabilitation Programming and Principles

In the 1950s and 1960s, the development of new, effective psychotropic medications for mental illness, coupled with policy changes within the social service system, resulted in the move away from institutional to community care. These changes meant that persons with severe mental illness were no longer committed for long periods in state hospitals. Instead, these individuals now reside and receive treatment within their communities and experience, when necessary, short hospital stays (Cook & Wright 1995).

Psychiatric rehabilitation (PSR) programs seek to help persons with mental illness live successfully within the community (Cook & Hoffschmidt 1993). A central goal of psychiatric rehabilitation is enhancement of quality of life through prevention of unnecessary rehospitalization. Accordingly, an emphasis is placed on developing strategies to manage symptomatology and to develop skills that will enable persons with mental illness to lead productive lives in the community. Another basic element of PSR programs is that they are organized as programs to which persons "belong" and in which clients are considered "members." As such, programming is designed to foster client empowerment, consumer involvement, and peer support (Cook, Graham, & Razzano 1993), giving more of an emphasis to these processes than to achievement of behavioral outcomes. Tanaka suggests the following general definition for a psychiatric rehabilitation program:

> A goal-oriented program for the mentally ill which provides coping experiences toward improved living in the community. The program emphasizes common sense and practical needs and usually includes services of vocational, residential, socialization, education, personal adjustment, and the prevention of unnecessary hospitalization. The psychosocial rehabilitation setting is purposefully informal to reduce the psychological distance between staff and member and consciously engages the member as an active participant in program planning, development, policy making, implementation, and evaluation. (1983: 7)

Cook and Hoffschmidt (1993) describe several fundamental principles that underlie psychiatric rehabilitation. A *biopsychosocial* approach suggests that the rehabilitation process should take a holistic stance, acknowledging that mental illness affects such diverse areas of clients' lives as intrapsychic functioning, vocational and educational achievement, social interactions, and physical health and well-being (Dincin 1990). *Client choice* means that clients are actively involved in decisions surrounding the treatment process. They participate in the development of their rehabilitation treatment plans and play an active role in the ongoing implementation and future refinement of those plans (Cook & Pickett 1995).

Comprehensive *rehabilitation* plans are necessary to address the goal areas that clients choose to work on. These plans detail the changes that occur in clients' lives and environments and are continually updated to reflect those changes (Anthony & Liberman 1986). Given the recurring nature of psychiatric symptomatology, the rehabilitation process may be lengthy, and clients often require ongoing support to help them attain and maintain certain goals. Thus, PSR services are delivered on an ongoing basis for as long as clients are interested and able to participate (Anthony, Cohen, & Farkas 1990).

Psychiatric rehabilitation places an emphasis on strengths and wellness as well as the remediation of deficits, focusing on the enrichment of talents and skills instead of solely addressing symptoms and deviances (Cook et al. 1996). Situational *assessments* – observations of persons demonstrating skills in naturalistic settings – are used in place of traditional diagnostic or standardized psychological assessments and so redirect the focus from clients' deficits to clients' strengths (Anthony & Jansen 1984).

One rudimentary principle of PSR services is the use of in vivo (real-world) environments and community settings as well as the inclusion of nondisabled partners in the treatment process. Recognizing that mental illness impairs clients' ability to transfer training from one environmental situation to another – and also that many of the benefits of "normalization" cannot occur in segregated settings – the rehabilitation process emphasizes social and community *integration* (Cook & Hoffschmidt 1993). Thus, PSR services are delivered to clients in the community, at their homes, and at the workplace. Finally, instead of maintaining rigid boundaries between clients and service providers, relationships that emphasize *advocacy and partnership* are developed. Psychiatric rehabilitation staff work together with clients and on the behalf of clients, rather than taking a neutral position. In addition, clients' families, friends, employers, and other service providers are encouraged to take part in the rehabilitation process.

In short, PSR programs provide the services that persons with mental illness need in order to avoid unnecessary psychiatric hospitalizations and to live successfully in their communities. Clients are actively involved in the decisions related to the PSR services they receive and are viewed as equal partners in the treatment process. Services are delivered to clients in a variety of community settings, and families, employers, and other service providers are viewed as partners in the rehabilitation process in order to strengthen and help maintain clients' social and community integration (Razzano, Pickett, & Astrachan in press).

PSR Program Models

Several models of psychiatric rehabilitation programs exist. Typically, these programs provide a variety of services based upon the needs of their clients. Although no model can meet every client need, most endeavor to provide a comprehensive array of services focusing on stabilizing psychiatric symptomatology, training in life skills, and developing supportive community networks (Cook & Hoffschmidt 1993).

Fairweather Lodges and Clubhouses. Fairweather Lodges were one of the earliest established PSR models. At Fairweather Lodges, clients reside together, work at a small community business, and co-facilitate the program with staff (Fairweather 1980). The clubhouse model was developed at Fountain House in New York City (Beard, Propst, & Malamud 1982) and offers vocational training, social activities, housing assistance, and adult education courses. Clubhouse models are structured so that clients are able to explore opportunities for managing the program and participate in service delivery, evaluation, and administrative responsibilities.

Assertive Community Treatment. Assertive community treatment programs consist of teams of interdisciplinary staff – social workers, nurses, and psychiatrists – who provide case management and skills training services directly to clients in the community, rather than requiring clients to visit a specific service site (Stein & Test 1980). These programs emphasize direct assistance with an individual's problems of living in the community by providing ongoing support and treatment targeted at the client's unique needs and utilizing available natural supports. The individualized interventions may include teaching clients how to take medication, social skills training, independent living skills training, and strengthening clients' support systems by working with friends and family. The assertive community treatment (ACT) models focus on providing continuity of care; clients are the responsibility of the entire team, not of just one case manager.

Skills Training Programs. Skills training programs seek to overcome the cognitive deficits present in severe mental illness by teaching clients the social, intellectual, and physical skills needed to live in the community (Liberman et al. 1993). The goal of skills training programs is to teach clients new behaviors that they will adopt through training and practice. Clients typically work in small groups of ten or fewer individuals who are led by a trainer. Sessions are held two to three times a week for approximately one hour and last from six to twelve months. Clients may work step-by-step through a training curriculum focusing on a particular goal, such as symptom management or social living skills.

Supported Education. Supported education programs focus on improving clients' academic skills through remedial reading and math courses, assessment and treatment of learning disabilities, and college preparatory classes. In supported education models, clients attend college classes with other nondisabled students but receive additional academic supports (e.g., teaching clients how to take notes when they are having trouble concentrating), mental health services, and (in some programs) job training from PSR staff (Cook & Solomon 1993; Unger 1994). In addition to increasing academic opportunities, the on-campus setting allows in vivo social skills training by providing clients with opportunities to interact with nondisabled student peers.

The Nature of PSR Outcomes

With the increasing development of this field and with expansion of mental health services research (Taube, Mechanic, & Hohmann 1989), questions were raised about the efficacy of psychiatric rehabilitation programs. In addition, the advent of managed mental health care turned attention to the relative effectiveness of psychiatric rehabilitation versus other community-based alternatives such as partial hospitalization or outpatient day programs (Anthony 1993). This, in turn, led to an increasing focus of assessing outcomes of PSR services.

Despite differences in the type of services clients may receive, common psychiatric rehabilitation outcomes exist. As described by Cook and Jonikas (1996), there are seven typical outcomes of PSR services. *Unnecessary psychiatric hospitalizations are reduced,* which may be assessed by changes in the clients' number of admissions during the course of a year of program tenure and by duration of the admissions. *Vocational outcomes* are measured by employment status (i.e., employed vs. unemployed), number of hours worked per week, hourly wage, and job type and tenure. *Residential outcome* indicators involve level of skills needed to live independently, degree of supervised support, housing permanence, whether the housing is restricted to mental health consumers, and client housing preference. *Educational outcomes* are assessed by clients' attainment of academic skills, marked by achievements both at remedial and postsecondary levels. *Social skills outcomes* are reflected by changes in leisure activities and communication skills. *Client satisfaction outcomes* are determined by the extent to which clients state that services meet their needs and help them to achieve their goals and whether they would recommend the program to others or would themselves return for additional services. *Quality-of-life outcomes* encompass several domains, such as satisfaction with social relationships, job opportunities, housing, and overall life satisfaction ratings.

Reduction of Unnecessary Psychiatric Hospitalization. Psychiatric rehabilitation services such as crisis intervention, symptom awareness training, and medication management are geared toward helping clients avoid unnecessary psychiatric inpatient stays. Research has documented that PSR services are effective in reducing both the number and length of inpatient admissions (Arana, Hastings, & Herron 1991; Bond et al. 1984; Test & Stein 1980). In a study conducted by Dincin and Witheridge (1982), clients who participated in a clubhouse model spent significantly fewer days in the hospital compared with clients who participated in a peer support group. Bond and his colleagues (1990) found that ACT clients experienced a significant reduction in the number of inpatient admissions from the year prior to receipt of services to one year after receipt of services.

Vocational Outcomes. Helping clients obtain and maintain meaningful, productive work is a common goal of PSR programs. Vocational services provide clients the opportunity to develop general and specific work skills, improve interactions with supervisors and co-workers, and explore potential career interests. Evaluations of PSR models have demonstrated that these vocational services effectively increase clients' ability to find and keep paid jobs in the community (Cook & Pickett 1995; Cook & Solomon 1993; Fountain House 1985; Rogers et al. 1991a). In addition, recent research in this area has found that PSR clients who are immediately placed in jobs had higher employment rates, earned higher salaries, and reported higher levels of job satisfaction when compared with those who undergo lengthy preemployment training (Bell, Milstein & Lysaker 1993; Bond et al. 1995).

Residential Outcomes. Independent living – assisting clients to live successfully in the community in the least restrictive setting – is another important aim of psychiatric rehabilitation programs. Some programs may offer housing services, such as supervised group homes or apartments, but most programs work with residential facilities already established in the community. Placement of clients in a particular residential setting is related to availability of housing, level of functioning, compliance with treatment, and client preference (Cook et al. 1996). Most PSR clients prefer to live in settings that maximize their autonomy and privacy, opt for living with nondisabled persons rather than other clients, and prefer staff assistance on an as-needed rather than an on-site basis (Carling 1993; Tanzman 1993). Psychiatric rehabilitation residential services may range from teaching clients basic skills (e.g., preparing meals, housekeeping, and budgeting) to helping clients establish and maintain relationships with neighbors and landlords. Research on residential outcomes has found that clients who had longer PSR program tenures were more likely to be living independently in the community (Cook et al. 1996; Stein & Test 1980).

Educational Outcomes. First episodes of mental illness frequently occur in late adolescence or young adulthood, interrupting completion of secondary and postsecondary education. Since education is related to increased vocational opportunity and success, many PSR models view education as an important part of their program (Cook & Solomon 1993). As previously noted, these educational services may include remedial, secondary, and postsecondary courses as well as on-campus supports. Studies have found that clients who receive PSR educational services are more likely to return to college on a full-time basis (Hoffman & Mastrianni 1993; Unger et al. 1991).

Social Skills. Psychiatric rehabilitation programs seek to help clients learn the skills needed to better manage their symptoms and daily life stressors, make friends, and increase their participation in social activities. Skills training involves helping clients develop new knowledge or skills, providing opportunities to practice these skills, giving feedback about performance of these skills, and encouraging clients to incorporate these skills in everyday situations. Research has found that skills training is an effective tool in helping clients reduce symptoms and improve personal interaction (Liberman et al. 1993; Wallace 1995). In addition to skills training itself, PSR programs may help clients practice and improve their skills through evening and weekend recreational activities and holiday parties, which provide clients with opportunities for interaction as well as peer support. These gatherings facilitate clients' reintegration into social and community settings (Cook, Pickett, & Jonikas 1989).

Client Satisfaction. Given that psychiatric rehabilitation programs view clients as equal partners in the treatment process, it follows that a key PSR outcome would be clients' satisfaction with the services they receive. Unfortunately, many programs perceive clients as being unable to provide such information and so do not measure clients' positive and negative feelings about rehabilitation services (Leete 1988). This perception, however has begun to change in recent years. Increasingly, PSR programs are actively asking clients to provide feedback about which elements of the program are helpful to them, which elements are not useful, and what actions are needed to improve the program. Results of this research indicate that, overall, clients are satisfied with the PSR services they receive (Massey & Wu 1993; Mowbray & Tan 1992). Kaufmann, Ward-Colasante, and Farmer (1993) found that clients requested increased program hours, staff, and transportation. In a study conducted by Beall (1992), clients reported that increased collaboration between clients and staff was needed.

Quality of Life. Psychiatric rehabilitation programs seek to improve clients' quality of life by helping them achieve reduced psychiatric hospitalizations, increased employment and educational opportunities, independent living in the community, and satisfying interpersonal relationships. Results from two studies suggest that PSR programs do help clients improve their quality of life. Rosenfield and Neese-Todd (1993) found that clients who felt empowered (e.g., felt that they were involved in the decisions regarding their treatment or were heard and supported) also noted significant improvements in social relationships, health, and residential situations. Similarly, Rosenfield (1992b) found that vocational services were positively related to clients' reported quality of life.

Issues in Studying PSR Outcomes

Attempts to study psychiatric rehabilitation services have been hindered by the fact that many treatment models consist of an integrated set of services aimed at enhancing client strengths and addressing deficits caused by the illness (Attkisson et al. 1992). This creates a need to develop multidimensional outcome models that take into account the possibility of multiple changes in a series of goal areas (Anthony & Farkas 1982). For example, clients involved in supported education programs may, in addition to achieving academic success, learn skills that help them obtain and maintain paid employment, which in turn may enable them to afford stable community housing. The likelihood that treatments will influence different outcomes in various ways coexists alongside the possibility of unintended negative outcomes (Vitalo 1971). For example, ongoing vocational services may enhance job retention while increasing social coping difficulties because of the challenges of full social integration into the lives of co-workers (Cook & Razzano 1992). Similarly, the achievement of residential independence demands more autonomous functioning and may distance the client from sources of social support previously available from group home or familial environments (Cook 1994).

Further evidence for variability in client outcomes comes from research suggesting that changes in one outcome area may not be accompanied by changes in another. This idea was articulated in Anthony and Jansen's influential review article on predictors of vocational outcomes, which cited literature indicating that "a person's ability to function in one environment (e.g., a community setting) is not predictive of a person's ability to function in a different setting (e.g., a work setting)" (1984: 539). For example, improvement in client vocational functioning has been found to be unrelated to changes in psychosocial functioning among rehabilitation clients with a variety of disabilities (Bolton 1974; Growick 1979). A study of clients in an aftercare program following psychiatric hospitalization (Summers 1981) indicated that improvement in social functioning over a one-year period was not accompanied by similar improvement in vocational functioning. Tessler and Manderscheid's (1982) research involving over 1,400 individuals with severe mental illness found weak correlations between being employed and level of social participation or basic living skills. In a randomized study of outcomes following psychiatric rehabilitation (Dincin & Witheridge 1982), clients in the experimental group experienced significantly less inpatient treatment than those in the control group, yet there were no significant differences between the two groups in employment rates. The results of these studies raise the question of how achievement in one area of functioning is related to success in another for persons with severe mental illness.

Another feature of this research was that it typically did not conceptualize PSR service delivery as individually designed programming. Current rehabilitation technology emphasizes rehabilitation plans that are tailored to clients' particular situations and that address their own goals for their unique environments (Cook, Jonikas, & Solomon 1992). This makes it difficult to define standard treatment protocols or duration, because clients are able to design and access programming at will. The variability in such real-world experiences stems from clients' ability to move in and out of widely varying job and residential settings (Cook 1994). Consequently, the effects of receiving services in real-world environments also must be assessed. These issues suggest that research on PSR outcomes must include variables that accurately operationalize the ways in which clients use available programming, how long clients receive services, which services they receive, and the nature of service continuity (Cook 1995).

Directions for Future Research

The issues described here with regard to studying psychiatric rehabilitation services suggest that a multidimensional outcome model is needed that simultaneously measures multiple outcomes and determines whether clients improve at different rates on different outcomes (Cook & Jonikas 1996). Along with this, a longitudinal approach is needed in order to understand how clients' attainment of PSR goals change over time and whether additional services are needed to help clients maintain desired outcomes (Cook 1995). For example, skills training may help provide clients with basic social skills needed to establish friendships, but these initial skills may fade over time, and clients may need "refresher courses" or additional training in negotiating such difficult situations as how to refuse drugs and alcohol in work-related situations (Cook & Jonikas 1996).

Another area of future research involves greater client definition in determining and assessing their own rehabilitation outcomes. Some programs operate under a "one plan fits all" approach; however, in recent years several programs have begun to recognize that no one approach works best for all clients and that rehabilitation plans must be continually changed according to changes in clients' lives (Cook 1995). In addition, research needs to examine the relevance of certain outcomes for certain groups of clients. For example, independent living may be an irrelevant goal for some clients from racial and ethnic cultures that emphasize family co-residence (Cook & Mock 1990). Similarly, the rehabilitation goals of female clients may differ from those of male clients. Women may be more likely to need services to help them care for their children or to express greater concern about personal safety (Jonikas & Cook 1993; Mowbray et al. 1995).

Finally, as Cook and Jonikas (1996) note, PSR outcome research is too often geared toward the perspectives of service providers, researchers, and policy makers. Results are defined according to markers of success established by those who seek to have their programs re-funded, their grants renewed, and tax dollars allocated to their community. Clients' perspectives are often ignored even though they – not the service providers, researchers, or policy makers – are the actual users of PSR services. Therefore, clients should be fully included in the research process and be actively involved in each step, from hypothesis development to questionnaire design, assessment of administration, data analysis, and outcome interpretation.

Incorporating these issues in future psychiatric outcome research will provide information necessary for understanding the complexity of multiservice models designed to promote successful community adjustment for persons with severe mental illness. These future findings will sharpen current definitions of psychiatric rehabilitation goal achievement and will help to both shape and improve future services.

27

An Introduction to the Mental Health Consumer Movement

Caroline L. Kaufmann

Consumers of mental health services are an important group influencing mental health policies. Kaufmann provides an overview of the consumer movement and of self advocacy in mental health, describing the origins and purposes of the consumer movement. Sociologists have long studied the power of groups to affect broad social changes, and Kaufmann utilizes social movement theory to assess the likely impact of consumers on the delivery of mental health services. A critical problem for any social movement is the mobilization of resources, and the consumer movement is currently highly dependent upon the public mental health system. A key objective of the consumer movement is an expanded consumer role (for example self-help groups or consumer-run services); this is part of a broader movement toward consumer empowerment. Consumer groups also share the goal of combatting the stigma of mental illness. However, Kaufmann describes areas of tension among different consumer advocacy groups – especially over the etiology of mental illnesses. The chapter ends by considering the challenge of managed care to service delivery and advocacy groups. An important issue is whether cost-conscious managed care organizations (both public and private) can also respond to the needs of people who have severe mental illnesses.

I saw the second best minds of my generation destroyed by sanity . . . .
Aaron David (1973, cited in Zinman et al. 1987)

Introduction

People with mental illness deal with both disabilities and stigma. The disabilities affect a wide range of human activities involving emotional integration, perception, and reason. Stigma produces social degradation and limits social interaction for individuals with mental illness. Of the two human predicaments, stigma is the most detrimental.

Sociologists document and analyze the process of social degradation attendant upon the experience of being a mental patient; Goffman's (1961) work is a classic example. Relatively little effort has been focused on the collective efforts of people with mental illness to combat that degradation process. The mental health consumer movement is an effort by people with mental illness to establish control over psychiatric treatment and the severe social stigma that attends a psychiatric diagnosis. Participants in this movement also try to acknowledge diversity among people with psychiatric diseases and to develop systems of care that reflect the diverse

493

needs and wishes of mental health consumers. The purpose of this chapter is to examine efforts in mental health consumer self-advocacy as a social movement.

What's in a Name – From Mental Patient to Mental Health Consumer

The recent history of the contemporary mental health consumer movement begins roughly in 1970. By this time, the nationwide policy of deinstitutionalization had already produced a rapid decrease in the number of individuals held in state psychiatric hospitals and a corresponding increase in people needing community-based services.

Deinstitutionalization brought thousands of people with serious mental illnesses out of state psychiatric hospitals, where their social roles as mental patients were originally defined and learned. They were now "ex-patients." Outside the hospital, psychiatrists no longer had primary responsibility for, or control over, former patients. Community mental health centers (CMHCs) were established to meet the needs of former state hospital patients in local settings. Once discharged, former mental patients received care from CMHCs (for a review, see Schulberg & Killilea 1982a). Patients' rights groups in a number of states – notably Oregon, California, Massachusetts, New York, and Pennsylvania – were formed by relatively small numbers of people who had undergone psychiatric hospitalization. These groups worked to improve conditions in hospitals and community treatment centers (Zinman, Harp, & Budd 1987).

Within the burgeoning consumer movement, a number of personal accounts of hospitalization, treatment, and discharge were published that highlighted the passivity and degradation imposed upon psychiatric patients (Chamberlin 1977; Chesler 1972; Gotkin & Gotkin 1975). These accounts emphasized the lack of privacy and dignity accorded patients in psychiatric hospitals.

To support their opposition to forced treatments, early consumer activists drew upon writings by R. D. Laing and Thomas Szasz (Hirsch et al. 1974). Laing and Szasz criticized then current practices in psychiatry, claiming that the system of care was itself a major cause of psychiatric distress. Reformers from within the ranks of psychiatry gave legitimacy to patients' complaints about dehumanizing and ineffective treatments (Breggin 1991).

Some early consumer groups took an antipsychiatry position, rejecting the label of mental patient and the interpretations of mental illness offered by psychiatrists (Hirsch et al. 1974). They declared themselves to be "psychiatric survivors" because they had endured what they saw as harsh and unwarranted treatment in psychiatric institutions. However, former patients who were dependent on community services after their release rejected this antipsychiatry position. In large measure, the mental health consumer movement embraced the expanded role for clients described in the psychosocial rehabilitation literature (see Chapter 26).

People discharged from psychiatric hospitals had difficulty establishing meaningful lives outside the hospital (Susko 1991). They frequently lacked money, job skills, and social supports essential in the transition to community life. The shift from the hospital to the community produced a change in roles for those receiving care from the mental health system. The old institution of the hospital had taught most former patients to be dependent and behave in ways that were meaningful in the context of a psychiatric hospital. Most of those who left psychiatric hospitals took on new social roles as "clients" in the community mental health system.

The client role was somewhat less restrictive than the patient role. It implied a degree of freedom that was not available to hospitalized patients. At the same time, the newly emerging clients were learning to depend on a fragmented system of community treatments and welfare services. Clients needed experience and ingenuity to navigate the maze of local agencies that controlled the systems of health care, rehabilitation, and welfare upon which they came to depend. Many people had difficulty negotiating a fragmented system of services while struggling with conditions of severe mental illness, social isolation, and limited finances.

Emergence of the Mental Health Consumer

The term "consumer" has been in use within the movement generally since the early 1980s. Already preferred among activists in the disability rights movements, the consumer rubric trades on issues of choice and freedom in an ideal market for mental health services. The mental health consumer as a social role is based on experiential knowledge developed through interactions with the mental health treatment and welfare systems. In dealing with these systems, those seeking services face a largely voluntary system that does not impose service but assumes that the consumer can and should be actively involved in the design and implementation of treatments. Consumer nomenclature has been readily adopted by more moderate factions in the movement who are uncomfortable with terms such as "ex-inmate" or "psychiatric survivor." As mental health consumers, activists acknowledge the existence of mental illness but also claim the right to choose the types of services they want to use. At the same time, there exists a weak consensus among movement participants over the appropriate name to use in referring to people with psychiatric disabilities (Chamberlin 1984). To avoid conflict, a number of writers use three terms combined – consumer/survivor/ex-patient, abbreviated as "c/s/x" – as a way of acknowledging the diverse identities among movement participants (Van Tosh & Del Vecchio 1998).

Resources for Consumer-Run Organizations

Organizing former mental patients and recruiting them to the consumer movement requires financial support. One theory of social movement organization –

resource mobilization theory – has interpreted the relationship between resources and social movement growth in ways that are particularly relevant to the consumer movement. According to resource mobilization theory, as resources in the social environment increase, assets available to the social movement also increase. An increase in resources leads to an increase in the number of social movement organizations and overall growth in what McCarthy and Zald (1977) termed the "social movement industry." New organizations representing ideological factions within the movement emerge. These factions become financially dependent upon what McCarthy and Zald call "conscience constituencies." Conscience constituencies are individuals or groups sympathetic to the specific interests and ideologies of the faction. This dependence influences the agenda for change among the organizations and determines the modes of action organizational activists take (McCarthy & Zald 1977: 1224ff).

Resources to organize come from a variety of channels, most notably federal, state, and local authorities. The Center for Mental Health Services (CMHS), housed within the Substance Abuse and Mental Health Services Administration, continues to provide financial support for innovative services that emphasize consumer involvement (CMHS 1994a; Knowledge Exchange Network 1997). Antipsychiatry groups have little in the way of support from the professional mental health system and function as isolated social movement organizations, heavily dependent on contributions from their constituencies. More radical factions in consumer advocacy find themselves "shut out" of key roles in planning and funding. Attempts to include representatives from other factions of the movement meet with serious and strident opposition from representatives of the more moderate organizations.

Social movement organizations have varying degrees of participation among members, including full-time (or nearly full-time) professional activists, paid or volunteer staff, and occasional workers. Membership also affects the types of activities likely to be taken up within the organization. The community mental health system, combined with various subsidies from Social Security and state welfare programs, supports many individuals regarded as seriously mentally ill. Because these systems provide some degree of financial support without a significant requirement to work, many consumers have a great deal of free time. According to resource mobilization theory, the more the organization consists of workers with discretionary time, the more likely it is that the organization can develop "transitory teams." Transitory teams are composed of workers assembled for a specific task of relatively short duration. People become directly linked to the organization through these specific tasks. Among consumer organizations, the ready availability of workers for relatively short projects facilitates activities such as conferences, afternoon workshops, and letter-writing campaigns.

Consumer-run services reflect the social support functions of more traditional community mental health programs. For example, self-help groups formed by relatively small numbers of consumers in local neighborhoods have established consumer-run "drop-in centers" that offer clients a place for leisure, social interaction, and tangible assistance from their fellow consumers (Emerick 1989; Kaufmann et al. 1993; Segal, Silverman, & Temkin 1995a). Examples of consumer-run alternative services currently exist in every state, sponsored partly through funds from the local and state mental health authorities and private foundations (National Mental Health Consumer Self-Help Clearinghouse 1998). Most of these services operate under the auspices of a community mental health center or a local mental health association. The movement has borrowed resources from the community mental health systems to operate its own service programs.

The 1990s have seen the growth of formal consumer organizations developed partly with funding from state and federal government agencies. The number of consumer organizations has increased as a direct function of the allocation of public funds at the state and national levels to the generation of "consumer associations." The National Mental Health Consumer Association, formed in 1987, works to "fight the stigma of mental illness, improve the quality of life of people with psychiatric histories, and empower these people to speak for themselves" (Rogers 1987). The founding members of the association include many of the early activists who advocated for more humane and caring services for people with mental illness. The National Mental Health Consumer Self-Help Clearinghouse, located in Philadelphia, has been in operation since the 1980s and continues to expand its activities. The Clearinghouse is one of two technical assistance centers funded by grants from the Community Support Program of the CMHS (CMHS 1994a; Rogers 1995b). Another technical assistance center, the National Empowerment Center in Lawrence, Massachusetts, is headed by a psychiatrist who is also a mental health consumer. The Empowerment Center offers consumer-run training and services to providers and consumers (Fisher 1996).

State consumer organizations have been established with funds provided by the Center for Mental Health Services under a service system improvement program. From 1991 through 1993, CMHS provided grants to "empower consumers and family members and expand their roles in planning and providing services" (CMHS 1994a). The federal program offered funds to state offices of mental health to support organizational development among consumers and family members. These state grants helped establish and enhance local chapters of the National Alliance for the Mentally Ill (NAMI) and state Mental Health Consumer Associations (MHCAs). Though not successful in all cases, CMHS promoted collaboration among consumer groups and state mental health authorities. In some instances, consumer associations were successful in obtaining ongoing funding for consumer-run services initially established through the federal CMHS grant.

The CMHS provided start-up funds and ongoing support for a limited period of time, usually three to five years. After that time, MHCAs were expected to obtain continued support from state and local mental health authorities as well as from private foundations.

Community mental health agencies are another source of funding for consumer organizations. Since the late 1980s, consumer self-help has received attention as a possible therapeutic modality (Chamberlin & Rogers 1990; Kaufmann, Freund, & Wilson 1989). Local mental health agencies have allocated funding for consumer-run services and self-help groups, using both state and local tax revenues. These organizations exist under the direct administrative authority of the community mental health agency and tend to focus on activities consistent with community support programs (Mulkern 1995). Consumers work in paid or unpaid positions to provide informal social supports, leisure activities, and recreation to individuals served by the mental health agency.

Among advocates for change in the mental health system, one of the largest and most influential organizations is the National Alliance for the Mentally Ill. A social movement organization founded by family members of people with mental illness, NAMI has a unique and ambivalent role with respect to the mental health consumer movement. It was originally formed to counteract a dominant perspective among some psychiatrists that parents, particularly mothers, were the main cause of severe mental illness. Earlier research on families of patients with severe psychotic disorders suggested that disturbed communications between parents and children could explain the occurrence of severe psychosis in the child (Lidz, Fleck, & Cornelison 1965). This area of research popularized the concept of the "schizophrenigenic mother." Many family members felt that psychiatrists blamed them for causing their children's mental illnesses (Bernheim 1987).

In reaction to strong feelings of blame and degradation among family members, NAMI launched a political campaign to enhance the role of the family in managing severe mental illness. More recently, NAMI has directed efforts toward maintaining and enhancing services to people with chronic mental illness. The term "seriously and persistently mentally ill" was coined by NAMI in order to focus attention on the needs of individuals with long-term psychiatric disabilities. The group of "seriously and persistently mentally ill" were contrasted to the "worried well," who were regarded as healthier and hence less in need of publicly funded mental health services. Much of NAMI's efforts in system reform have been devoted to allocating scarce mental health resources to support, treat, and eventually cure family members with serious psychiatric disability. The organization endorses the psychiatric definition of mental illness as a type of neurological disease (McLean 1990) and lobbies at the local and national levels for increased funding for research into causes of and cures for all forms of psychiatric disease.

Ideological differences between family members and consumers tend to build up around issues of personal autonomy and social control. The National Alliance for the Mentally Ill *opposes* the views of some factions of the consumer movement on issues of involuntary commitment and treatment of psychiatric diseases. Some state and local chapters of NAMI have supported legislation making it easier for families to obtain court orders for involuntary commitment of mentally ill family members. Many NAMI members endorse the use of psychiatric treatments, including medication, with or without a patient's consent.

The Social Psychology of Movement Participation

The problem for movement advocates lies in shaping a common social identity among the diverse population of people with psychiatric disabilities. The majority of people who recover from psychiatric diseases may be reluctant to acknowledge their status as people with mental illness. The reluctance to disclose one's experience as a mental health consumer poses special problems in recruiting members to the movement.

How does a social movement assist members in forming a positive social identity – a new sense of themselves (Blanche & Penney, 1995)? People with psychiatric disabilities may resist participation in the consumer movement because of internalized beliefs that they and others like them are unworthy. Mental illness is different from most other forms of human distress because it calls into question the social worthiness of the mentally ill person.

One team of researchers has noted that "accounting for mental illness unavoidably entails giving account of oneself, so closely implicated are the person and the illness" (Estroff et al. 1991: 333). In contrast, movement activists place responsibility for the problem of mental illness in factors that are external to the individual. According to this view, accounting for mental illness requires consideration of social, economic, and political factors that influence the illness experience.

A social psychological perspective explains how a contextualized definition of the problem of mental illness works to build a positive social identity among movement participants. Some theorists have suggested that "individuals derive their interests through their memberships in groups, particularly those in which active social interaction occurs" (Ferree & Miller 1985: 41). Social movements provide a person with a way of seeing his or her social circumstances as the product of controllable forces that are not directly attributable to individual abilities, talents, or skills. Individuals who suffer hardships do not necessarily experience them as grievances if they adopt an explanation that attributes their present circumstances to their own individual qualities. Social movements allow individuals the opportunity to reinterpret selected life experiences in terms of external causes rather than personal attributes.

Because they attribute a significant portion of suffering to external forces in the larger society, movement participants focus on changing society. Consumer activists acknowledge that participation in movement activities may improve an individual's well-being. However, their salient goals are to combat stigma and to reform the mental health system, rather than to change the behaviors of their fellow consumers. The search for "empowerment" in the experience of mental illness and its treatment reflects the consumers' desire for control over their illnesses and their treatments (Segal, Silverman, & Temkin 1995b).

Williams (1995) observes that social movements operate between the social psychological level of recruiting people to join particular social movement organizations and the broader level of political activity. Social movements link personal identity, sense of self, and interpretation of one's circumstances to a larger sphere of social and political activity. Social movements furnish new arenas for action. Members of the consumer movement assume roles as advocates, service providers, and peer counselors. Their experiences as ex-patients and psychiatric survivors become a source of quasi-professional expertise, as opposed to a basis for social stigmatization.

So long as the dominant paradigm for dealing with mental illness remains a disease-based model, the major legitimate activity for someone who is mentally ill consists of being treated for an illness. People with mental illness are confined to a relatively narrow social role defined in terms of their relationships within the treatment system. The consumer movement reinterprets psychiatric diseases in terms of legitimate social and political activity. The mental health consumer movement is a strong mechanism for reconnecting individuals with social interactions outside the domain of clinical psychiatry and mental health treatment.

Reframing the Problem of Mental Illness

Frames and frame alignments provide a link between the experience of mental illness and participation in the social movement of mental health consumers. The concept of "frames" is based on Erving Goffman's (1974) *Frame Analysis*. Frames are defined as schemata of interpretation that allow an individual to identify and label life experiences (Goffman 1974: 21). In order for people to ally themselves with a social movement, they must see that their way of interpreting their life experiences is consistent with the image promoted by those in the movement.

The notion of framing is particularly salient with respect to mental health consumers. For people who are frequent or long-term clients of professional mental health services, individual interpretations often follow from attitudes learned while in the role of client or patient. The professional literature in psychiatry and psychology provides a well-developed frame for interpreting the behaviors of those in the client role. Long-term users of mental health services come to interpret their experiences in therapeutic terms. The psychomedical system provides a frame for clients to interpret their experiences of emotional distress as treatable psychiatric disease, and it encourages consumers to rely on their therapists or other community mental health professionals for assistance in managing their disability.

Self-esteem and sense of efficacy are often lost through ongoing clinical encounters that focus on symptoms of psychopathology and mental health disabilities (Sherman & Kaufmann 1995).

In the United States, few people now assume social roles as long-term inmates of psychiatric hospitals. However, many recipients of community mental health services see their involvement with the mental health system as a life-long career. The client role discussed earlier includes a readily available interpretive schema for severe emotional distress, along with a course of action leading to its relief. The person in the client role is expected to regard his or her condition as a disease and to interpret personal experiences with reference to psychiatric symptoms. Within this interpretive frame, the primary objective is relief of symptoms. In contrast, the consumer movement offers an expanded frame for defining mental illness in which symptom relief is but one of several factors important to well-being (Campbell & Schraiber 1989). The mental health consumer movement has promoted the ability to develop social roles apart from psychiatric interpretations and controls.

Tensions within the consumer movement develop around competing and contradictory ways for framing mental illness. Proponents of an antipsychiatry point of view explain mental illness as a product of the social stigmatization of people whose behavior does not conform to social expectations. Antipsychiatry advocates describe mental illness as the inability of so-called sane members of society to tolerate the emotions and perceptions of others. Antipsychiatry advocates claim that society rejects people who do not – or cannot – conform to social norms. According to this view, psychiatry is primarily a form of social control, and mental illness is a problem of intolerance in human societies. Those who espouse this point of view challenge society to increase acceptance of human diversity (Breggin 1991).

The Support Coalition International, an advocacy group based in Oregon, espouses positions consistent with an antipsychiatry point of view. Coalition members publish *Dendron,* a periodical highlighting cases of psychiatric abuse (Dendron 1996). They also sponsor an annual "counter-conference and protest" held at the same place and time as the annual meeting of the American Psychiatric Association. This counter-conference provides a forum for those claiming status as psychiatric survivors to protest "forced electroshock and psychiatric drugging" (Oats 1992). The antipsychiatry views of the Coalition have not been embraced by mainstream factions in the movement. However, the Coalition's protest activities have included transitory participants from more moderate consumer groups.

In contrast, the NAMI Consumer Counsels tend to support the dominant interpretation of psychiatric disability within a disease-related interpretive frame. The Consumer Counsels also endorse therapeutic interventions such as psychotropic medications. Within the movement, organizations such as the NAMI Consumer Counsels and the National Mental Health Consumers Association enjoy national prominence.

Providers as Advocates for the Consumer Movement

In the mental health consumer movement, community-based providers sympathetic to the ideals of self-help and individual autonomy promote many of the movement's activities. Their relationship to the mental health consumer movement is complicated by their ambiguous relationship with consumers. On the one hand, community providers exist to deliver services to their clients. On the other hand, they are responsible for maintaining control over potentially disruptive clients. Although providers may support the idea of "consumer liberation" from an oppressive bureaucratic system of care, they maintain positions of power over consumers that derives from that system. (See Pinderhughes 1983 for a discussion of reciprocal empowerment of clients and professionals in social work practice.)

In the psychiatric hospital, medically trained psychiatrists hold ultimate authority over patients. The "definition of the situation" on an inpatient ward is heavily, if not exclusively, determined by a medical or psychiatric interpretation of mental illness and its treatment (Goffman 1961). Psychiatric diagnosis is a significant determinant of how inpatients will be treated. In some hospitals, diagnosis determines ward placement at admission. Those diagnosed with schizophrenia may be admitted to a "schizophrenia ward." Change in diagnosis can mean a transfer to another service and application of a different treatment regimen. Because psychiatric treatments combine both behavioral and pharmaceutical therapies, patients in a psychiatric hospital face a network of relationships and social environments that are heavily determined by their diagnoses.

Many professionals who practice outside psychiatric hospitals have negative views of the diagnostically driven approach typically found in psychiatric hospitals. There are at least three reasons for this. First, the physical separation between staff and patients commonly found in psychiatric hospitals is largely unattainable in most community mental health settings. In situations of close physical and social proximity, community-based providers find it difficult to establish social and emotional distance from the recipients of their services. Although there are designated "staff only" areas in most treatment settings, clients spend long periods of time in unstructured social interactions and group sessions with staff and fellow clients. In these circumstances, it is difficult for staff to use hospital-based perspectives in interacting with clients.

Second, the majority of community-based staff are not psychiatrists but rather are paraprofessionals or hold bachelor's or master's degrees. Psychiatrists are infrequent visitors in many community mental health programs, confining their interactions largely to assessment of patients, management of medications, and authorization of services that require the authority of a licensed physician. Although psychiatrists may see a host of patients during clinical appointments, they usually do not have extended daily contact with a particular group of patients and rarely visit the "drop-in centers" and residential facilities where clients socialize and live. Under these circumstances, staff have limited contact with psychiatrists.

Third, in most community mental health programs, specific diagnoses are less important in determining the type of behavioral and rehabilitative services clients receive. Staff who run residential and social support services may not have access to a client's psychiatric medical record on a daily basis, and exact clinical diagnosis may be unknown to them. Staff providing social support and psychosocial rehabilitation are more concerned with the client's ability to function in the community than in the diagnosis associated with the disability. Many professionals in community mental health settings prefer to describe clients in terms that suit adult-oriented rehabilitation and social service. They may be uncomfortable with the social control functions that hospital staff often assume. Furthermore, they lack sufficient resources in the community to provide complete custodial care for people with serious and long-term psychiatric disabilities.

The community mental health system is largely voluntary. Court-ordered psychiatric treatment – though available through the community mental health centers – is difficult to enforce in a community treatment setting. Community-based providers lack the means to physically restrain or confine clients. Most involuntary treatment takes place in psychiatric hospitals. This allows community-based treatment settings to develop alternative ways of providing for people with long-standing psychiatric disabilities based on consumer choice and self-determination (Mulkern 1995).

Community mental health workers find common ground with the mental health consumer movement in designing treatment alternatives. New methods in psychosocial rehabilitation promote client involvement in the design and implementation of community services. Those at the forefront of psychosocial rehabilitation see client responsibility, personal control, and independence as primary goals (for a review, see Anthony & Liberman 1986).

Consumer Demands for System Change

Mental health consumer organizations tend to make "reactive" demands of the evolving service system. Reactive demands are proposals for change drafted in the language and perspective of social and politically powerful groups (Ferree & Miller 1985). Dominant institutions teach subordinate people what to expect from those institutions. The ascendancy of more moderate advocacy groups, along with the ostracism of antipsychiatric factions in the consumer movement, has produced an agenda for reform consisting largely of reactive demands.

For example, most of the state-sponsored consumer associations have voiced strong support for the ideology of community support. This includes insistence on social support and psychosocial rehabilitation as a cornerstone of community-based treatment. Further, moderate advocates have supported recent moves toward vocational rehabilitation for people with severe mental illnesses. The demand is couched in terms borrowed directly from the public rhetoric promoting work rather than welfare (Sherman & Kaufmann 1995).

What do consumers want from mental health services? In reviewing the various positions of organizations representing mental health consumers, it is difficult to uncover a specific set of demands for reform. Some common principles do emerge, however. Virtually all consumer groups agree on the need to reduce public stigmatization of people with mental illness. The National Alliance for the Mentally Ill has mounted several successful antistigma campaigns and has endorsed celebrities who have "gone public" with personal accounts of mental illness. Calls for increased funding for consumer-run services have also received support within the movement. There is strong opposition among a small but vocal group of consumers concerning the need to protect confidentiality of patient records. Confidentiality is a special concern when consumers sign "blanket" consent forms that authorize release of confidential mental health records to insurance companies and other third-party payers. Problems of confidentiality in computerized clinical records have also been raised (Mental Health Report 1997).

The problem for the movement lies in the difficulties that individuals and organizations have in drafting specific programs for change. Although most consumers support ideals of personal choice and improved quality of life, they disagree on what choices should be offered to them and how best to improve the quality of life for people with mental illness. They lack a consensus on the role of professional psychiatry and psychiatric research in improving the lot of people with mental illness. Most movement advocates call for increased funding for consumer-run self-help groups and other types of mutual aid. However, consumer groups compete with one another for scarce funding. They experience ideological differences that make consensual action difficult on a national level.

How can organized consumer advocacy organizations present proactive demands? In order to develop proactive demands, individuals with a potentially common grievance need the opportunity to interact in homogeneous groups. This close, face-to-face social interaction, central to the experience of consumers in an inpatient treatment setting, is being replaced partly by an evolving network of telecommunications.

Telecommunications and computer networks have enhanced communication among elite professionals in the consumer movement. State mental health consumer advocates, the Consumer/Survivor Research and Policy Work Group, and the ThisIsCrazy news group communicate using distance-based teleconferences and computer news groups (see e.g. Caras 1994). The use of the Internet to form support groups of current and former mental health consumers opens membership in the consumer movement to individuals from a wide range of social and economic backgrounds.

Many Internet users have the sense that their privacy is maintained on a network where communications are on a first-name basis and where no face-to-face contact occurs. This leads to frank discussions among individuals who may not be members of the community mental health system, allowing them to develop relationships outside formal psychiatric treatment centers. Users share experiences of individual hardship and personal coping strategies. The free flow of communication across geographic boundaries adds to the storehouse of shared experiential knowledge among mental health consumers. On the other hand, access to computer technology is limited to consumers who have the resources and expertise to use Internet technology. The National Mental Health Consumer Self-Help Clearinghouse has made an effort to train consumer groups in the use of telecommunications.

The Impact of Changes in the Mental Health Service System

As the mental health consumer movement has grown and changed in the last ten years, the system that provides many of the services that people with psychiatric disabilities rely on has undergone even greater changes brought on by managed care. Managed behavioral health care is both an organizational form and a mechanism for financing mental health services based on contractual agreements between providers and payers (CMHS 1994b). Consumer efforts to change current practices in the care of people with mental illness have been overwhelmed by the rapid incursion of private managed behavioral health care into traditionally public mental health services.

Throughout this century, people with serious mental illnesses – those experiencing lengthy periods of hospitalization and long-term functional disabilities – have received care through the public mental health system. Historically, public agencies have provided the bulk of services to people with mental illness in state-run psychiatric hospitals. As a result, public interests have shaped the advocacy agenda in mental health. In the second half of this century, state hospitals have dissolved into a system of publicly funded community mental health agencies and short-stay inpatient psychiatric units in general hospitals (P. Brown 1985). However, advocates for the rights of people with mental illness continue to target public institutions. Managed care has refocused attention on issues more common to a private, market-based system of service delivery. The consumer movement has seen the arena for reform shift from public agencies to private corporations.

With the advent of managed care, some aspects of the dominant ideology represented in community mental health services has been lost or severely modified. For example, community mental health organizations have developed coordinated programs of care that provide a range of services not easily recognizable as medical or psychiatric in nature (Ray & Oss 1993). In contrast, managed care firms are based on a medical/surgical model for treatment and delivery. This means that such psychiatric treatments as electroconvulsive shock, which look more like medical procedures, are readily accommodated in a managed care environment. Medication, brief psychotherapy, short-term inpatient care, and electroshock "therapy" are relatively easy to define in terms that are synonymous with traditional medicine.

Long-term social supports, supported housing, supported employment, and other forms of social services are harder to describe in the language of medical treatments. In addition, social support services are labor-intensive (Olfson 1990). The cost of delivering the services cannot be readily contained without decreasing the amount of contact with the patient.

Prior to community mental health reforms, people with psychiatric disabilities had ample opportunities to interact in homogeneous groups on wards in state and community psychiatric hospitals. With the development of community mental health centers, the "catchment area" system (based on geographic residency) also allowed patients to have ongoing social contact with people they originally met on the inpatient psychiatric wards. Sustained, face-to-face interaction in the hospitals and communities among people sharing the common predicament of psychiatric disability promoted feelings of collective grievance and needs for system reform. State psychiatric hospitals and community mental health centers were a good place to recruit new members to the movement.

The shift to short-term treatments and the de-emphasis of inpatient modalities weakens the communal experience among consumers. At a time when the consumer movement is beginning to develop proactive demands (Trochim, Dumont, & Campbell 1993), the conditions that facilitate their formation may be evaporating. Unlike the community mental health system, managed care organizations emphasize the individual as the unit of care. Programs designed for geographic communities are less common. Programs that aggregate individuals into treatment groups are peripheral to the core practice of managed care. Managed behavioral care organizations show a preference for funding services to individual patients, rather than programs that support a broadly defined set of consumers.

Conclusions: The Future of Mental Health Consumer Advocacy

In an organizational society, the shape of social movements is closely tied to the technologies, social institutions, and opportunities created within that society (Zald & McCarthy 1987: 319). Historically, changes in social movement organizations parallel changes in other large-scale organizations. In both the public and private sectors, there is scarcity of resources, abundance of bureaucratic controls, and circumspection over individual rights. These broad social forces have influenced the mental health consumer movement in dramatic ways.

The current shift toward fiscal restraint and cost savings throughout the service economy has produced a scarcity of resources in the behavioral health care sector. As a result, I anticipate increasing intensity of competition among consumer organizations as they struggle to secure a niche in the social movement industry. I also expect to see increasing tension among moderate groups as competition for funding increases. Similar tendencies have been documented in other social movement sectors (Benford 1993). As public dollars become harder to obtain, the consumer movement may look to the private sector of managed behavioral health care to subsidize some of its activities. Although it is clear that the managed care industry is sensitive to consumer satisfaction and other factors affecting the market for behavioral health care services, more radical alternatives are unlikely to receive much substantive support. Smaller consumer groups may be poorly prepared to negotiate with managed care organizations. Accrediting bodies such as the National Committee on Quality Assurance (NCQA) are adopting "practice guidelines" for psychiatric services that recommend only those services that carry scientific proof of efficacy. Consumer-run services have not yet been submitted to the rigorous empirical tests that would be necessary to prove their effectiveness.

Rapid change in the mechanisms for funding and coordinating services should foster increased activity within the consumer movement. However, consumer organizations have had to move quickly to readjust the focus of their protests from public agencies to private industry. Tactics such as "sit-ins," pickets, and letter-writing campaigns may be less effective on a system that is organizationally complex and, so far, free from public regulation. On the other hand, corporate service organizations are intensely sensitive to any type of public pressure. Once the behavioral managed care sector learns of real or suspected criticisms from consumer groups, it responds with attempts to change procedures and address individual complaints. Managed care organizations incorporate consumer representatives and organizations into planning and quality assurance. Highly skilled members of the consumer movement can be co-opted by the corporate sector.

What tactics are likely to work best to change corporate for-profit structures? Consumer monitoring of managed care contracts is one clear avenue. Here the consumer movement may find itself limited in its ability to launch legal challenges to contracts negotiated between providers and payers. Consumer-controlled mechanisms for quality assurance, with requirements for external monitoring of treatment processes and outcomes, may be an essential pivot for turning managed behavioral health care in the direction of the mental health consumer movement.

28

Mental Illness and the Criminal Justice System

Virginia Aldigé Hiday

Hiday examines two prevailing beliefs about mental illness and the criminal justice system: that deinstitutionalization has led to criminalization of the mentally ill, and that mentally ill persons are dangerous and likely to commit crimes. The chapter reviews the available empirical evidence for these beliefs. Although arrest rates and incarceration rates are indeed higher for mentally ill persons than for the general population, criminalization may be too extreme a characterization. Furthermore, most people with mental illnesses are not violent, and only a small proportion become violent. The chapter goes on to examine how mentally ill persons are handled by the criminal justice system. Hiday hypothesizes that there are three subgroups of persons with severe mental illness who come into contact with the criminal justice system: (1) those committing only misdemeanor offenses that often involve survival behaviors; (2) those with accompanying character disorders who also abuse alcohol and drugs, both of which contribute to their high rates of criminal offenses, arrests, and incarceration; and (3) a much smaller subgroup who fit the stereotypical image of a severely disordered person driven to criminally violent actions by delusions. All three groups live in impoverished communities where it is difficult to survive with a major mental illness. She concludes that the criminal justice system is left to pick up the pieces after the failure of other social institutions. What types of social stressors contribute to the criminalization of the mentally ill? What failures of social institutions have led to incarceration of those with mental illnesses?

Two prevailing beliefs of the public (and of many professionals) connect mental illness to the criminal justice system: first, a belief that deinstitutionalization has led to criminalization of the mentally ill; and second, a belief that mentally ill persons are dangerous and likely to commit crimes, especially violent crimes. If these beliefs were accurate, they would lead to the criminal justice system processing and holding significant numbers of sick persons. The first two sections of this chapter examine the evidence to ascertain whether and to what extent empirical evidence supports these beliefs. The third section describes how mentally ill persons are handled and fare in the criminal justice system and after release, whether or not these beliefs hold true. The concluding section hypothesizes that there are three types of persons with major mental illness who are arrested and incarcerated.

Criminalization of the Mentally Ill

Following procedural and substantive legal changes that restricted civil commitment (Bloom et al. 1986; Hiday 1988; LaFond & Durham 1992), reports of criminalization of the mentally ill appeared – reports of large numbers of sick persons arrested and incarcerated in jails and prisons who were previously treated in state mental institutions (Abramson 1972; Bonovitz & Guy 1979; Dickey 1980; Geller & Lister 1978; Lamb & Grant 1982; Rachlin, Pam, & Milton 1975). Initial reports faulted the legal changes for denying treatment, but soon many mental health and criminal justice professionals attributed responsibility to the larger process of deinstitutionalization (including restrictive civil commitment laws) for criminalization of mentally disordered persons (Goldsmith 1983; Hiday 1991, 1992b; Lamb et al. 1995; Miller 1987; Roesch & Golding 1985; Stelovich 1979; Teplin 1983; Torrey 1995). These professionals saw deinstitutionalization as limiting the ability of society to care for mentally ill persons in large public hospitals and placing substantial numbers of mentally ill persons in the community, thus putting them at risk for arrest. Believing society to be intolerant and fearful of the bizarre, unpredictable, and dangerous nature of some symptoms of mental disorder (Gerbner et al. 1981; Link et al. 1987; Monahan 1992; Nunnally 1961; Rabkin 1972; Steadman & Cocozza 1978; Weiss 1986), these observers argued that the criminal justice system was controlling mentally ill persons by getting them off the streets through arrests for both nuisance offenses and more serious allegations, with resulting criminal sentences to jail or prison or commitments to mental hospitals. This thesis suggests that the criminal justice system processes mentally ill persons differently, being quicker to arrest and incarcerate them than persons not mentally disordered.

The possibility that society would turn to the criminal justice system after deinstitutionalization should have been anticipated, because the police are entrusted with ensuring social order. Undoubtedly, citizens would call law enforcement when they could not control observable disordered behaviors of the mentally ill, especially when they felt these behaviors were dangerous. The released mentally ill would be likely to commit minor infractions such as vagrancy, disorderly conduct, trespassing, and shoplifting, especially since they would often return to poor neighborhoods with few material and social resources. Additionally, because of their vulnerabilities, the severely mentally ill who did violate the law would be less likely to escape detection and more likely to be caught. But would police involvement lead to criminalization, that is, would it lead to arrest and incarceration? To answer this question, researchers have investigated police encounters with mentally ill persons, arrest rates, prevalence of mental illness among jail and prison inmates, and mentally ill offenders sent to forensic units.

Police Practices

Even before deinstitutionalization was underway, law enforcement officers frequently dealt with mentally disordered persons (Bittner 1967; Cumming, Edell, & Cumming 1965). Since deinstitutionalization, police have increasingly been called to control the mentally ill who are disruptive (Bonovitz & Bonovitz 1981; Teplin et al. 1980). Sometimes they intervene directly in observed disturbances; but often family, friends, or others in instrumental roles such as landlords or physicians call police to quell disorders or to provide transportation to psychiatric emergency facilities. These calls come especially from poor, undereducated urban families (Teplin et al. 1980).

When police are called, they settle encounters (not only those with the mentally ill) most frequently by informal means – mediating disputes, offering solutions, placating complainants, and in general "cooling out" situations (Bittner 1967; Bonovitz & Bonovitz 1981; Teplin 1984b). Police resort to formal dispositions (including both arrest and hospitalization) infrequently, only in those situations that are likely to escalate and require police to return (Bonovitz & Bonovitz, 1981, Teplin 1984b). When police do take formal action, they are likely to opt for hospitalization over arrest when they perceive that the individual lacks criminal intent or needs treatment, or when they know the individual to be a former mental patient (McNiel et al. 1991; Monahan, Caldeira, & Friedlander 1979; Teplin et al. 1980). Officers opt for hospitalization and treatment more frequently when their police department has a cooperative program with a mental health facility (Kneebone, Rogers, & Hafner 1995; Lamb et al. 1995; McNiel et al. 1991; Steadman, Morris, & Dennis 1995; Teplin et al. 1980). Thus, we find police playing a major and expanding role in bringing patients to psychiatric emergency facilities (Cohen & Marcos 1990; Durham, Carr, & Pierce 1984; Finn & Sullivan 1988; Lamb et al. 1995; Steadman et al. 1986).

Police may resort to arrest even when treatment is clearly needed. Teplin (1984a,b) found that Chicago police arrested mentally ill persons when treatment was preferable in cases of deviant behavior that were so public and visible as to exceed the limits of tolerance, and when deviant behavior was likely to continue, proliferate, and require later police intervention if the person were not removed from the site. Police also resorted to arrest when treatment facilities refused to accept a mentally disordered individual. Psychiatric staff, in attempting to control their work environment, commonly refuse persons with criminal charges or criminal records and persons with substance abuse comorbidity. Substance abuse facility staff likewise refuse substance abusers with comorbid mental illness, leaving police with little choice but arrest (Teplin 1984b, 1985). Ironically, police sometimes resort to arrest when psychiatric emergency staff turn down mentally disordered persons who are neither sick enough nor dangerous enough to meet civil commitment criteria for involuntary hospitalization (Steadman et al. 1986).

Mentally Ill Persons Arrested

Prior to deinstitutionalization, mental patients released from public hospitals had lower arrest rates than the general population; following deinstitutionalization, arrest rates of former mental patients rose both absolutely and in relation to the general population (Melick, Steadman, & Cocozza 1979; Monahan & Steadman 1982; Rabkin 1979). This trend would seem to support a criminalization hypothesis; however, increased arrest rates may be accounted for by a new type of patient who was sent to mental hospitals, persons whose former criminal behavior was viewed as sick rather than bad. Support for this alternative explanation comes from studies showing that, when arrests are decomposed by arrest record prior to hospitalization, patients with no prior arrests are no more likely than the general population to be arrested after hospitalization, whereas patients with arrest records are much more likely to be arrested (Cirincione et al. 1994; Melick et al. 1979; Steadman, Cocozza, & Melick 1978). Rather than criminalization of the mentally ill, higher arrest rates of former mental patients may result from another trend, the medicalization of deviance, in particular the trend to hospitalize substance abusers and persons with antisocial personality (ASP) (Kittrie 1971; Steadman et al. 1978; Stone 1975).

Most studies of arrest of former mental patients do not control for diagnosis, even though research shows that patients with character disorders and substance abuse have much higher arrest rates than other patients (Bloom, Shore, & Arvidson 1981; Harry & Steadman 1988; Holcomb & Ahr 1988; Schuerman & Kobrin 1984; Robins 1993; Rice & Harris 1992). Another problem with these studies of arrest rates is that most patients sampled were hospitalized in state mental institutions, where patients are disproportionately young, male, unmarried, and of lower socioeconomic status. Since these traits are associated with crime and are underrepresented in the general population, comparing former mental patient and population arrest rates without adequate sociodemographic controls yields a distorted picture (Hiday 1992b; Monahan & Steadman 1982).

Only a few arrest studies not using state mental hospital patients have been conducted, and they reported mixed outcomes. One study, of a Community Mental Health Center (CMHC) catchment area centered on a small city in Missouri, reported that first-admission outpatients had lower arrest rates than the general population whereas inpatients had higher rates (Harry & Steadman 1988). Younger age, ASP, and prior arrests significantly contributed to explaining arrests among both groups of patients, but gender, education, and employment did not affect arrests. Clients of the Los Angeles County Department of Mental Health, some of whom had never been hospitalized, had higher arrest rates than the Los Angeles adult population, and substance abusers had the highest rates; however, the never hospitalized were not analyzed separately to discern whether their rates were lower (Schuerman & Kobrin 1984).

Arrest rates can be misleading because they do not indicate the percentage of patients who have been arrested. High arrest rates may be due to arrests that are concentrated in a small group of patients who revolve in and out of both the mental health and criminal justice systems; such rates would thus *not* reflect criminalization (Hiday 1991, 1992b). On the other hand, a sample of psychiatric patients' families – who were more likely to be sociodemographically similar to the general population because of their Alliance for the Mentally Ill membership – reported that 52% of their mentally ill relatives had been arrested at least once, averaging 3.3 arrests each (McFarland et al. 1989). When age and gender were adjusted to the general population distributions, the standardized percentage fell to 28%, a rate still significantly higher than the region's population arrest rate (McFarland et al. 1989). Families reported that most arrests were associated with acute psychotic crises in which substance abuse and medication noncompliance were involved, suggesting that appropriate treatment might have prevented the incidents and the arrests (McFarland et al. 1989).

One group of mentally ill persons that appears to have a high rate of arrests is the homeless mentally ill (Belcher 1988; Crystal, Ladner, & Towber 1986; Fischer 1988; Martell, Rosner, & Harmon 1995; Morse & Calsyn 1986). Although the public has been greatly concerned with the criminal behavior of homeless mentally ill persons, little empirical research has been directed to the criminalization of the mentally ill via homelessness. Two studies of temporary housing and shelter residents in New York and St. Louis reported that almost half of mentally disordered persons (broadly defined) had been arrested (Morse & Calsyn 1986) or jailed (Crystal et al. 1986); however, because a broad definition of mental illness can encompass substance abuse and situational depression and anxiety, one must be careful in generalizing these results to persons with severe mental illness. One in-depth study of persons with major mental disorders who became homeless shortly after hospital discharge to a Midwestern city found that 64% were arrested (Belcher 1988). Those arrested who self-medicated with alcohol and street drugs (rather than taking their prescribed medication) became increasingly impaired in cognitive and social functioning, wandered aimlessly, appeared psychotic much of the time, and manifested bizarre and often threatening behaviors in public places (Belcher 1988).

Mentally Ill Persons Incarcerated

Some researchers have turned to studies of incarcerated populations to investigate whether mentally ill persons have been criminalized since deinstitutionalization. They have analyzed two types of data: archival records on psychiatric hospitalization of prison populations and survey data of the mental status of incarcerated persons.

Initially, criminalization adherents pointed to growth in the numbers of persons incarcerated in state prisons after deinstitutionalization as evidence of criminalization of the mentally ill. Clearly, there has been a long-term trend of substantial increases in prison populations and rates of prison incarceration across the nation following deinstitutionalization (Steadman et al. 1987; Steadman & Morrissey 1987). To discern whether these trends were either a result of or coincidental with deinstitutionalization requires knowing whether the increases were accounted for by persons previously hospitalized in mental institutions. The evidence here is mixed. The trend of increased prison populations was accompanied in some states by increases in the proportion of incarcerated prisoners with prior mental hospitalization; however, in just as many states, the proportion of prisoners who had prior mental hospitalization decreased (Steadman et al. 1984; Steadman & Morrissey 1987). Records of prior hospitalization would capture most mentally ill persons incarcerated prior to deinstitutionalization, but in the postdeinstitutionalization period this measure is a particularly inadequate indicator of criminalization because mentally disordered young adults became less likely ever to have been hospitalized.

Surveys of correctional institutions using clinical evaluations and standardized instruments avoid the problem of changes in hospital experience affecting the amount of measured mental disorder. Prison surveys consistently have found higher levels of mental illness than found in the general population (Collins & Schlenger 1983; James, Gregory, & Jones 1980; Jordan et al. 1996). However, the higher overall rates are due mainly to inordinately high rates of ASP and substance abuse or dependence that often can be psychiatric labels for criminal behavior. For instance, male felons in North Carolina had a lifetime ASP rate of 28.9%, 14 times higher than in the North Carolina ECA sample (2.1%); an alcohol abuse/dependence rate of 49.5%, three times higher than the ECA sample (17.0%); and a drug abuse/dependence rate of 18.8%, 23 times higher than the sample (0.8%) (Collins & Schlenger 1983). Female prisoners a decade later also had higher rates than the North Carolina ECA sample but lower rates than the males on ASP and alcohol abuse (11.9% and 38.6%, respectively; Jordan et al. 1996). The female rate of drug abuse was higher than that of the males, reflecting the spread of drugs, especially crack, over the intervening decade.

Rates of severe mental illness (bipolar, severe depression, schizophrenia or schizophreniform) among prisoners are significantly higher than those of the general population: the rate of schizophrenia and schizophreniform for male felons is 1.2%, versus 0.6% for the general population; the comparative rates for major depressive episode are 5.3% to 2.1% (Collins & Schlenger 1983). A later survey – one that focused on amount of current dysfunction and disruptive behavior rather than diagnosis – also reported relatively high rates: 8% of New York state prison inmates had severe mental disabilities and an additional 16% had significant mental disabilities (Steadman et al. 1987; Dvoskin & Steadman 1989).

The population in county and local jails has burgeoned since the 1970s (Steadman, McCarty, & Morrissey 1989; Steadman et al. 1995). As with prisons, jail surveys have found high rates of all mental disorders after deinstitutionalization. (City and county jails hold persons serving short sentences or awaiting trial; state and federal prisons hold persons found guilty of more serious crimes and serving longer sentences.) Several researchers reported extremely high prevalence rates of the more severe psychoses (17–75% – see Lamb & Grant 1982, 1983; Swank & Winer 1976; Valdiserri, Carroll, & Hart 1986), but these rates were biased in that they were based on jail inmates referred for mental health evaluations rather than the general jail population. Rates of severe mental disorder based on random inmate samples are much lower (5–8% – Swank & Winer 1976; Teplin 1990a; Washington & Diamond 1985), although one study found a higher lifetime prevalence rate (18.5%) among women jail detainees due in large part to their high rate (16.9%) of major depressive episode (Teplin et al. 1996). Even though higher than the general population, current rates of major mental illness in jails may be no higher than they were prior to deinstitutionalization. Because comparable studies of the earlier era are not available, we cannot know from this type of data whether there has been a criminalization of the mentally ill since deinstitutionalization. One would expect to find greater numbers of mentally ill persons incarcerated in jails, even if the proportion incarcerated remained the same, simply because of the huge overall increases in number of persons jailed.

Mentally Ill Persons in Forensic Units

The fourth type of evidence used to support the criminalization thesis is data on the number of offenders who are evaluated and treated for mental illness while incarcerated. One study reported an increase in referrals to a prison's psychiatric unit following enactment of restrictive civil commitment criteria and a corresponding increase in the proportion of unit inmates who were less serious offenders (Bonovitz & Guy 1979). Other studies have supported the criminalization argument with data showing increases in commitment to psychiatric treatment following judgments of both incompetency to stand trial (IST) and not guilty by reason of insanity (NGRI), verdicts that send mentally ill persons to forensic psychiatric units in jails or hospitals, or to general units in state hospitals for treatment, instead of punishment (Abramson 1972; Arvanites 1988; Dickey 1980; Morrissey & Goldman 1986). However, there are alternative interpretations for these data. Commitments of offenders could have increased in response to reform limitations in length of confinement for IST and NGRI (LaFond & Durham 1992; Wexler 1981). With shorter stays, offenders who are committed may now revolve in and out of the criminal justice system and forensic treatment units, just as the non-offending mentally ill revolve through mental hospitals (McMain, Webster, & Menzies 1989; Menzies 1987; Menzies et al. 1994). Medicalization also could explain increases in these commitments, as when prisoners previously thought to be "normal" are redefined as disordered. Such redefinition is expected owing to medicalization in the larger society and also to relatively new mental health training programs for criminal justice officers (Bonovitz & Bonovitz 1981; Finn & Sullivan 1988) and a more general increased sensitivity throughout society to problems of mental illness (Veroff et al. 1981). And, as stated before, increases in jail populations would lead to increases of mentally ill persons in forensic units even if the proportion of mentally ill remained stable from pre- to postdeinstitutionalization.

Arrest rates and incarceration rates are higher for mentally ill persons than for the general population, and the police may handle, arrest, and incarcerate more mentally ill now than they did before deinstitutionalization. Even so, criminalization of the mentally ill may be too extreme a characterization of these trends, because arrest is rare among the mentally ill persons that police encounter (Teplin 1984a, 1985). As well as overstating conditions, the term "criminalization" connotes little appreciation for the role police play as "street-corner psychiatrists" who not only quell disorder but also assist in maintaining many mentally ill persons in the community (Teplin & Pruett 1992). Regardless of how one chooses to view the term, there can be no doubt that the criminal justice system is responsible for the care and control of many severely mentally disordered persons.

Criminality of the Mentally Ill

The second belief linking mental illness and the criminal justice system is that mentally ill persons are dangerous and likely to commit crimes, especially violent crimes. Going back at least to the Greco-Roman period, the public has believed that a disproportionate number of the mentally ill were unpredictable and dangerous (Monahan 1992; Rosen 1968). This belief is reinforced today in fiction and human interest news stories (Gerbner et al. 1981; Steadman & Cocozza 1978). The frenzied madman, the "psycho" who is driven to harm others, and the delusional paranoid who unexpectedly and randomly kills are regular grist for television and motion picture studios as well as features for the news media (Wahl 1995).

Unlike criminalization (which holds society responsible for processing the mentally ill through the criminal justice system instead of treating them more humanely with mental health and social services), the criminality thesis blames mental illness for behavior that the criminal justice system must control. Indeed, the legal verdict of NGRI is premised on the understanding that mental illness can make an individual insane – that is, it can override an individual's ability to control criminal behavior. To evaluate the criminality of the mentally ill, researchers have looked to arrest rates and incarceration surveys and have examined data on dangerous behavior that is not punished or treated by the criminal justice system.

Arrest Data

Some observers have cited the previously discussed higher arrest and incarceration rates of mentally disordered persons as evidence supporting the criminality (instead of criminalization) of the mentally ill (Hodgins 1995; Rabkin 1979; Sosowsky 1980). If the criminality concept is correct – that is, if mentally ill persons are more dangerous – then they should be arrested predominantly for violent behavior that threatens or brings physical harm to others. However, most studies find the distribution of offenses for mental patients to be similar to that of the general population: most arrests are for misdemeanors (83% for mental patients, 75% for the general population) rather than felonies (Schuerman & Kobrin 1984); most are for less serious offenses (75% for mental patients, 84% for general population) rather than for the more serious FBI "index" crimes (Hiday 1992b). A minority of offenses of mentally ill persons are violent; few (either absolutely or proportionately) are arrested for the violent crimes the public most fears: murder, rape, aggravated assault, and arson (Bloom, Williams, & Bigelow 1992; Feder 1991; Harry & Steadman 1988; Hiday 1991, 1992b; Holcomb & Ahr 1988; Teplin 1994). A Milwaukee study of persons arrested for deadly and dangerous crimes against others found no support for the stereotypical madman violently out of control (Steury & Choinski 1995). Even homeless, severely mentally ill persons, whose homelessness puts them most at risk of arrest, are arrested predominantly for nonviolent crimes (Belcher 1988; Fischer 1988). Remember, with the same distribution of offenses as the general population, mentally ill persons will have higher arrest rates for violent crime because of their higher overall arrest rates. Thus, several studies report that mental patients are more likely to be arrested for violent offenses than nonpatients in the same community (Hodgins 1992, 1993; Link, Andrews, & Cullen 1992).

In order to address the question of the criminality of the mentally ill, we must be able to ascertain whether mental illness causes the violent crime or whether coincidental factors are causal. Robins (1993) reported that the association between crime and major mental illness in the ECA data completely disappeared when controls were placed for age, gender, ASP adult symptoms, childhood conduct disorder symptoms (generally considered integral to ASP diagnosis), and substance abuse. She concluded that the association of major mental illness with crime is not direct but occurs when severe mental illness is secondary to ASP and substance abuse. Recidivism studies that compare disordered to nondisordered offenders' arrests after imprisonment also fail to find severe mental illness to be the causal factor in crime and violence. Among Teplin's (1990a) jail detainees, severe mental illness did not predict the probability of arrest or the number of arrests for violent crime over a three-year or a six-year postrelease period (Teplin, Abram, & McClelland 1994; Teplin, McClelland, & Abram 1993). Among a sample of offenders admitted to a maximum security forensic institution for competency assessment, four fifths of whom had at least one violent offense, schizophrenia was negatively associated with violent recidivism over an eight-year mean risk period (Rice & Harris 1995). Psychopathy and alcohol abuse were the factors that placed this sample of offenders at high risk for violent recidivism. In a study examining only schizophrenic defendants who were evaluated in a forensic psychiatric hospital, Rice and Harris (1992) found the predictors of both general and violent recidivism to be the same as those that predict recidivism for nondisordered offenders: prior offenses and aggressive behavior, age, alcohol abuse, and psychopathy (Harris, Rice, & Cormier 1991).

Incarceration Data

As we have seen, recent studies of random samples of jail and prison inmates reported higher prevalence rates of mental disorder and of major mental disorders than in the general population (Collins & Schlenger 1983; Coté and Hodgins 1990, 1992; Jordan et al. 1996; Teplin 1990a; Teplin et al. 1996). Further analyses of samples from two of these studies have revealed that severely mentally disordered inmates tend to be substance abusers and/or have ASP disorder (Abram 1989, 1990; Abram & Teplin 1991; Coté & Hodgins 1990). For instance, only 6% of jail detainees with severe psychotic illness in Teplin's (1990a) sample had neither substance abuse/dependence nor ASP: 84.8% suffered from alcohol abuse/dependence and 57.9% from drug abuse/dependence, while 68.7% met criteria for a diagnosis of ASP (Abram & Teplin 1991). Furthermore, these detainees were likely to have been using drugs or alcohol at the time of their arrests (Abram & Teplin 1991) – as was also reported for Danish male homicide offenders with a major psychosis, 89% of whom were intoxicated at the time of the homicide (Gottlieb, Gabrielsen, & Kramp 1987). Furthermore, Abram (1990) found that, among those with major depression, ASP was the primary syndrome in that it appeared in their lives before both substance abuse/dependence and the depression. Likewise, Hafner and Boker (1982) found that, among violent mentally ill offenders, a history of antisocial traits preceded the onset of their psychosis. They also found antisocial history to be what distinguished offending from non-offending mentally disordered persons.

Unofficial Dangerous Behavior

The behaviors of both mentally disordered and nondisordered persons that violate criminal statutes do not always result in arrest. More violence actually occurs than is revealed in offense charges of arrest records. Many physical assaults and threats by both the mentally ill and others are not reported to police and thus cannot result in arrest (Hiday & Markell 1981; Hiday & Smith 1987; Lagos, Perlmutter, & Huefinger 1977); moreover, as we have seen, much of such behavior that is reported does not result in arrest (Monahan & Steadman 1982; Teplin 1984b, 1985). Frequently, law-breaking behavior by the mentally ill, including violent behavior toward others, leads instead to mental hospitalization.

Studies of legal records for involuntary hospitalization and of medical records of both voluntary and involuntary hospital admissions indicate that mental patients often are hospitalized because of dangerous behavior. Depending on the definition used, rates of violence toward others vary. Definitions restricted to threats of physical harm and physical assaults yield lower rates than definitions including loss of impulse control, hostile verbalizations, and thoughts of harming others physically (Hiday 1988). By the more restrictive definition of physical assault, studies report between 10% and 40% of persons admitted to mental hospitals are violent in the community in the weeks immediately prior to hospitalization (Monahan 1992). However, one must use caution in measuring violence mentioned in admission records, because physicians and families may use allegations of dangerousness to obtain admission for a person they think is in need of hospital treatment, given that mental hospitalization is now often limited to those who are dangerous (Hiday 1988; Miller 1987). As a result, court hearings often find that allegations of violence in commitment petitions and medical records cannot be substantiated (Hiday & Markell 1981; Warren 1977, 1982).

Inside the hospital, most violence occurs during the first week after admission, especially on the first day (McNiel & Binder 1987; Yesavage et al. 1982). Patients who do behave violently in the hospital tend to do so only once (Werner et al. 1983). Reports of hospital violence range from 10% to 40% of patient samples (McNiel & Binder 1994; Monahan 1992). Hospital rates of violence are likely to be higher than community rates because of selection processes, close observation, and hospital rules requiring violence to be reported in patient charts and violence indexes (Hiday 1988; Menzies et al. 1994). Still, much violence goes unrecorded in these settings (Lion, Snyder, & Merrill 1981). On the other hand, medication, therapy, ward structure, removal from hostile environments in the community, and staff intervention before tense situations erupt are all likely to reduce the amount of violent behavior that would otherwise be expected.

After patients leave the hospital, official legal and medical records indicate that approximately 20% threaten or assault others (Hiday 1990; Steadman & Morrissey 1982); however, as we have seen, these records have many weaknesses. Recent studies using self- and collateral interviews report more violence. A six-month follow-up study with detailed measures of violence found that 44.3% of voluntary and involuntary patients who visited an urban psychiatric emergency service engaged in a violent incident as defined by laying hands on another or threatening another with a weapon (Lidz, Mulvey, & Gardner 1993; Newhill, Mulvey, & Lidz 1995). Most incidents involved hitting and fighting; about one fifth were minor incidents (involving shoving, slapping, etc.); but 28% were serious, including murder, attempted murder, assault with injury needing medical treatment, sexual assault, robbery, and use of (or threatening to use) a weapon (Newhill et al. 1995). Alcohol consumption, along with age, was significantly related to violence in this sample; surprisingly, gender was not (Lidz et al. 1996; Newhill et al. 1995). Preliminary results from the MacArthur study, using similar measures with emergency service patients, show that 27% report at least one violent act within an average of four months after release into the community (Monahan 1992). Substance abuse or dependence comorbidity greatly increased the likelihood of violence (*Psychiatric News* 1995). Because these studies sampled only patients who were recently hospitalized owing to mental deterioration accompanied by crisis situations, their violence rates cannot be generalized to all mentally ill persons. Furthermore, most of these samples include patients with substance abuse, personality, and other disorders yet who do *not* have severe mental illness.

Recent epidemiological studies, which avoid the aforementioned problems, have shown that most mentally ill are not violent, that only a small minority with severe mental illness commit any violent act in a year's time, but that their low rate is higher than what is found among those with no mental illness (Link et al. 1992; Link & Stueve 1994; Swanson 1994; Swanson et al. 1990). These findings held with controls for age, gender, and socioeconomic status. Further analysis in one sample showed that substance abuse or dependence comorbidity greatly raised the violence rate above that for severe mental illness alone (Swanson 1994; Swanson et al. 1990). In the other sample, psychotic symptoms – especially those that produce feelings of personal threat or involve intrusion of thoughts that can override self-control – accounted for all violence differences with the nondisordered (Link et al. 1992; Link & Stueve 1994). Three other studies also support the finding that active symptoms of psychosis are predictive of violent behavior (McNiel & Binder 1994; Mulvey et al. 1996; Swanson et al. 1996). But it must be emphasized that, although these findings are significant, only a small proportion of persons with severe mental illness and active psychotic symptoms become violent. Traits that are far more predictive of violence than mental illness include being single, a young adult, male, of low socioeconomic status, and a substance abuser (Hiday 1995; Link et al. 1992; Monahan 1992).

The Mentally Ill in the Criminal Justice System

We have seen that the mentally ill are more likely to be detected when they commit an offense and more likely to be arrested during encounters with police than are persons without mental disorders. Are they also differentially handled once they enter the criminal justice system?

Based on our society's moral values, legal advocacy system, and presumptions about voluntary behavior, the law provides for different processing when a defendant's mental status impairs his or her capacity to meet the assumptions underlying legal procedures. The law holds that, to be found guilty of a crime and punished for it, a person must be blameworthy – that is, able to choose rationally to commit the offense. In addition, to defend oneself against criminal charges, a person needs to understand the nature and purpose of the criminal proceedings and be able to assist counsel in his defense (American Bar Association 1989). If the accused cannot understand and assist, then that person is "incompetent to stand trial" (IST, also called "unfit" and "incompetent to proceed"). When the accused is competent but mental illness interfered with his ability to make rational choices concerning the offense, then that person is not responsible or blameworthy and thus is legally insane or "not guilty by reason of insanity" (NGRI). Note that neither legal incompetence nor legal insanity is equivalent to mental illness. A person can be mentally ill, even with a severe psychosis, yet still meet the legal definitions of competence and sanity.

Consistently, 80% of defendants who are referred for IST evaluations are found to be fit, though they may be mentally ill (Roesch & Golding 1980; Roesch, Ogloff, & Eaves 1995). The competent are returned for continued criminal processing; those whom the court finds IST are committed for "fitness treatment" – that is, treatment to bring back competence. Discharge from IST commitment thus resumes the adjudication process on the original charge(s). Many go on to plead NGRI successfully. In fact, 40–60% of insanity acquittees are hospitalized and treated as IST prior to NGRI adjudication (Golding, Eaves, & Kowaz 1989).

Unlike competency, the insanity defense generates a degree of controversy that is greatly out of line with the frequency of its use and success. The public tends to dislike the insanity defense because of the perception that NGRI is a common loophole in the law whereby guilty persons who commit murders avoid punishment for their heinous crimes (Callahan, Mayer, & Steadman 1987; Hans 1986; Morse 1985; Pasewark & Pantle 1979; Pasewark & Seidenzahl 1979; Steadman & Cocozza 1978; Steadman et al. 1993). Even attorneys and judges tend to share these opinions (Burton & Steadman 1978). However, studies of various states from the 1970s and 1980s report that the insanity defense is seldom used (pled in less than 1% of all felony cases, on average, across states) and seldom successful (receiving an NGRI verdict in only a fraction of the 1%) (Pasewark & Pantle 1979; Sales & Hafemeister 1984; Silver, Cirincione, & Steadman 1994). Many more defendants are held in forensic psychiatric facilities to be evaluated for competency and to be restored to competency after being found IST (Marques, Haynes, & Nelson 1993; Wack 1993). Furthermore, the criminal charges that NGRI defendants face cover the full range from nuisance to serious, with a significant proportion facing only minor offense charges (from 20% to 30% of all cases). Although there is variation across jurisdictions, a minority (10–40%) involve murder, while the majority of cases judged NGRI do involve violent offenses (Draine, Solomon, and Meyerson 1994; Golding et al. 1989; Silver et al. 1994; Steadman et al. 1993).

Some states have enacted a "guilty but mentally ill" (GBMI) verdict in response to public concern over NGRI leniency, especially after John Hinckley's successful insanity plea for the attempted assassination of President Reagan. Intended to protect society by reducing NGRI verdicts and providing lengthy prison terms instead of brief hospitalization (Callahan et al. 1992; Ogloff 1991; Steadman et al. 1993), GBMI holds mentally disordered persons responsible when their mental illness was not directly causal in their offense. Empirical studies have found GBMI legislation to have little impact on NGRI acquittals because the GBMI verdict has been given primarily to those who previously would have been found guilty (Callahan et al. 1992; Keilitz 1987). A study in one state, however, did find that GBMI decreased the rate of both guilty and NGRI verdicts out of all insanity pleas (Callahan et al. 1992). The intended effect of more societal protection has been found consistently: GBMI verdicts lead to more incarceration, longer sentences, and longer imprisonment than guilty or NGRI verdicts for the same offenses (Callahan et al. 1992; Keilitz 1987; Steadman et al. 1993).

By law, defendants found GBMI are guilty and must be punished despite their mental disorders. Although some state statutes call for evaluation and treatment of their mental illness, in practice no special treatment is given beyond that provided to all inmates under the constitutional right to necessary medical care, which includes psychiatric and psychological services (Callahan et al. 1992; Dvoskin & Steadman 1989). But because of our moral values and legal philosophy, statutory law provides that those found IST and NGRI are to be treated without punishment. Where IST defendants are treated for the purpose of being returned to fitness to stand trial, NGRI acquittees are treated as long as they are mentally ill and dangerous. In both cases, treatment may be for periods that extend beyond what defendants found guilty of the same offenses would serve in prison (Golding et al. 1989).

The public's concern about "coddling" and subsequent release of NGRI offenders into the community seems to be unwarranted. Research indicates that the overwhelming majority of NGRI acquittees suffer severe mental disorders (Sales & Hafemeister 1984) and are ordered to treatment in mental hospitals (84.7%) for substantial time periods, with only a small proportion being released outright (1.1%) or ordered to treatment in the community (14.2%) (Silver et al. 1994). A multistate study found that courts are more likely to release convicted felons after a verdict than they are to release NGRI acquittees (Silver 1995). Although results are mixed across jurisdictions and time as to whether NGRI acquittees serve longer confinements than comparable offenders (Sales & Hafemeister 1984; Silver 1995), unsuccessful NGRI defendants have been found to have longer detention times than convicted felons who did not raise the insanity defense (Braff, Arvinites, & Steadman 1983). Among NGRI acquittees, those charged with more serious crimes serve longer periods of confinement in the hospital (Golding et al. 1989; Silver 1995; Silver et al. 1994). In fact, offense seriousness has been found to be the most important predictor of length of confinement – more important than mental disorder or response to treatment (Golding et al. 1989; Pasewark, Pantle, & Steadman 1982; Silver 1995).

Although the public and the law give much attention to incompetent and insanity defendants, only a small proportion of offenders with major mental illness are evaluated for IST and an even smaller proportion raise the insanity defense. Most mentally ill offenders go undetected during pretrial and adjudication stages and proceed through conviction to imprisonment (Freeman & Roesch 1989; Marques et al. 1993; Teplin 1990b; Wack 1993). These legally "fit and sane" mentally ill detainees and prison inmates constitute a minority who serve longer incarceration times than nonmentally ill offenders, require significant management attention by correctional authorities (Kropp et al. 1989), and need mental health services (Dvoskin & Steadman 1989). They are more likely to be held in custody awaiting trial because of denial of bail, and this "dead time" commonly exceeds the length of sentence ordered for the substantive offense (Freeman & Roesch 1989). Once imprisoned, they are more likely to be denied parole and to serve a greater proportion of their maximum sentences, in large part because parole boards find few community programs willing to service and supervise offenders with mental illness (Feder 1994; Porporino & Motiuk 1995). Community agencies frequently refuse to take mental patients with criminal records into their programs, causing mentally ill offenders to be detained longer (once imprisoned) than nondisordered offenders (Feder 1994; Porporino & Motiuk 1995).

Diversion

Some mentally ill offenders are never incarcerated or are held only a short time before diversion out of the legal system. Pretrial diversion programs began during the 1960s when minor cases increasingly clogged courts, and popular rehabilitative and therapeutic philosophies encouraged their use (Kittrie 1971; LaFond & Durham 1992; Roesch & Corrado 1983; Roesch et al. 1995). Initially, courts relied on informal arrangements with other community agencies, but they soon established many formal diversion programs to turn minor offenders into law-abiding citizens (Roesch et al. 1995).

Diversion programs are also used for mentally ill offenders to prevent disruption in the antitherapeutic, crowded, noisy cell blocks of jails (Kropp et al. 1989; Steadman et al. 1989, 1995). Often, the diversion is ad hoc and passive rather than programmatic; that is, court officers merely drop charges and dismiss a case when they learn that the mental health system is treating the defendant's mental illness (Hiday 1991; McFarland et al. 1989; Steadman et al. 1989). Formal diversion programs, run mostly by the larger jails, consist of: initial screening of all detainees; evaluation of possible cases by mental health professionals; negotiation with court officers and community mental health providers to agree on a treatment or service instead of prosecution, or as a condition of reduction in charges; and, finally, referral to the treatment or service itself for residential placement, outpatient treatment, and case management (Steadman et al. 1995). Unfortunately, few of the formal programs have specific follow-up procedures once initial placements are made.

Community Tenure and Management

When mentally ill inmates are released from imprisonment or from forensic commitment to a psychiatric facility, mental health treatment is often a condition of probation or parole. But mental health services seldom exist for severely disordered persons with antisocial and substance abusing behaviors, and too often mental health practitioners do not want to engage such persons with criminal records

(Draine & Solomon 1992; Freeman & Roesch 1989; McFarland et al. 1989; Mc-Main et al. 1989). The lack of services for mentally ill offenders in the community and their depressing and unstable living situations – along with their comorbidities – lead to a strong likelihood of re-arrest, ranging from 24% to 56% (Bieber et al. 1988; Corrado, Doherty, & Glackman 1989; Draine et al. 1994). However, they are neither more criminal nor more violent than released nondisordered offenders (Feder 1991; Teplin et al. 1993, 1994). Mentally ill persons are also likely to be rehospitalized in psychiatric institutions following criminal justice release. The extensive follow-up study of the Metropolitan Toronto Forensic Service reported that the overwhelming majority of patients have repetitive cycles of institutionalization in both hospitals and prisons (McMain et al. 1989; Menzies et al. 1994).

To break the cycles of institutionalization and to protect society from both feared and actual violent behavior, some observers have called for an assertive case management model for this population (Draine & Soloman 1994; Dvoskin & Steadman 1994). Assertive case management, which has successfully aided community adjustment of chronically mentally ill patients discharged from mental hospitals, uses case management teams to work intensively with individual clients in obtaining services, resources, and social support such as medication, therapy, housing, and financial assistance (Stein & Test 1985). For mentally ill offenders, establishment of a therapeutic relationship along with assessment and planning begin with the inmate in the prison or forensic unit during the month before discharge. Thereafter, most case management occurs out of the office on the streets and is available after normal work hours, when these clients are likely to get in trouble. Careful monitoring is employed; probation and parole officers become treatment allies, and case management continues into the criminal justice system when a client is jailed (Dvoskin & Steadman 1994; Steadman et al. 1989, 1995). Only two studies have evaluated assertive case management programs with mentally disordered offenders. Both offer preliminary support for its usefulness. The Vancouver program reported that clients had more community time before reconviction (271 vs. 120 days) and fewer days in correctional facilities (80 vs. 214 days) than a comparison group of released mentally disordered offenders (Wilson, Tien, & Eaves 1995). Dvoskin and Steadman (1994) reported that 75% of mentally ill offenders in a Texas program had no arrests after one year of program entry, 92% did not return to state prison, and 80% of those on parole had no parole violations.

A few states have created programs of mandated community forensic treatment of insanity acquittees that emphasize both management of aggressive behavior and treatment of psychopathology (Heilbrun & Griffin 1993; Lamb, Weinberger, & Gross 1988). In Oregon's well-established and -evaluated program, the state Psychiatric Security Review Board (PSRB) holds jurisdiction and supervision over all insanity acquittees for as long as the maximum sentence that could have been imposed with a conviction. The PSRB can place an acquittee in a maximum security hospital and can grant conditional release or outright release. It sets the conditions for release, monitors patients closely, and responds immediately if hospitalization is necessary (Bloom & Bloom 1981). Before granting conditional release, the PSRB carefully screens NGRI acquittees, keeping higher-risk individuals hospitalized and out of the community. Results indicate a relatively low re-arrest rate (13%) during conditional release but a high rehospitalization rate for deterioration of mental condition or nonadherence to the conditions of release (Bloom et al. 1986, 1992; Rogers, Bloom, & Manson 1984). Rather than failure, PSRB sees rehospitalization as an integral part of ongoing treatment and as a preventive measure against possible criminal recidivism (Heilbrun & Griffin 1993; Rogers et al. 1984).

Summary

There is no doubt that the criminal justice system deals with a significant number of mentally ill persons on the street, and that it processes and holds a significant number in its correctional and forensic facilities. But whether there has been a criminalization of the mentally ill since deinstitutionalization became public policy cannot be answered definitively because necessary longitudinal data do not exist. Whether mentally ill persons are dangerous and likely to commit crimes – that is, whether mental illness causes criminality – remains uncertain.

My reading of the literature leads me to hypothesize that there are three subgroups of persons with severe mental illness who come into contact with the criminal justice system for violating laws. One group commits only misdemeanor offenses, some of which (e.g., disturbing the peace or loitering) would not lead to arrests of nondisordered offenders. Others in this group commit survival behaviors such as shoplifting and failure to pay for restaurant meals (Steadman et al. 1995; Teplin 1984b; Torrey 1995). This group violates the law and becomes criminal not because their mental illness forces them to do so but rather because their social background and their mental illness leave them poor and marginal, and because they do not get the necessary care and services they need in order to survive in the community without getting into trouble. For this group, the American Bar Association (1989) recommends diversion to mental health, not arrest. Prior to deinstitutionalization, this group would have been hospitalized for much of their adult lives and not at risk for criminal offending and arrest.

The second group with severe mental illness who come into contact with the criminal justice system have accompanying character disorders and abuse alcohol and drugs. They are aggressive, often threatening or intimidating, and are likely to have a history of violent acts (Belcher 1988; Corrado et al. 1989; Draine et al. 1994; Lamb et al. 1995). As with the first group, they have few resources and are extremely needy of food, clothing, shelter, direction, and protection. Many of them become homeless. Some fall between the cracks of mental health and substance abuse systems, but others are frequent and demanding users of multiple community agencies such as hospitals, "detox" facilities, emergency shelters, welfare, and community mental health centers. Often their abusive and uncooperative behavior (plus lack of agency coordination and concerted action) deprive them of service benefits. They have high rates of criminal offenses, arrests, and incarceration, which are often for violent behavior (Corrado et al. 1989; Martell et al. 1995). This group is most visible and disturbing to the public. However, their criminal and violent behavior seems to be driven by their character disorders, substance abuse, and desperate situations, and not by mental illness.

Finally, there seems to be a much smaller subgroup consisting of severely mentally ill persons who fit the stereotypical image of the madman out of control. Delusions and hallucinations drive them to criminally violent behaviors. This very small group is the one that receives the most media and fictional attention. These three groups are different – both from each other and from the larger population of mentally ill persons who are not arrested and incarcerated. It is thus incorrect to generalize from their behavior to all persons with major mental illness, because they are not representative of that population.

All three of these groups tend to live in impoverished communities and within social environments that have substantially deteriorated in the late twentieth century, making it more difficult for persons with major mental illness to survive outside of institutions. Many individuals in these groups come from broken families and disorganized communities that are unable to give desperately needed support and care. In addition, the high prevalence of drugs, alcohol, and violence entrap these very vulnerable persons in greater pathology. Mental health and social welfare systems try to ameliorate the effects of such deleterious social conditions, but the criminal justice system is often left to pick up the pieces when these other systems fail.

29

The HIV–Mental Health Challenge

Stephen Crystal & Lori R. Schlosser

The mental health problems associated with HIV infection begin when people learn they are HIV-positive; individuals face severe anxiety and depression. A second set of mental health problems emerges with the resulting strain to community relations experienced with HIV infection. The third set of mental health problems comes when people experience the symptoms of HIV-related illnesses. Finally, those with preexisting mental health problems and substance abuse problems are disproportionately represented among those with HIV infection. Consequently, the HIV–AIDS pandemic represents a serious challenge to mental health service delivery. Crystal and Schlosser review the available research in each of the four areas of mental health problems just identified, noting the additional difficulties that result from the stigma associated with HIV infection. More training and support for mental health professionals is needed; increased levels of burnout are likely as mental health professionals are called upon to work with an increasing number of HIV-seropositive individuals. A number of current program models are described, many of which are based upon "continuity of care" concepts developed initially by programs that provide care to those with severe mental illnesses. These HIV-related issues illustrate sharply that physical and mental health problems cannot be separated. Students should consider the ways in which these two service systems can be better integrated.

The human immunodeficiency virus (HIV) has posed a variety of new challenges to mental health professionals since its emergence in the 1980s. It has challenged policy makers and program designers to find ways to meet new care needs despite scarce resources; it has created new ethical and policy challenges in balancing individual rights with public health and social responsibility concerns; and it has challenged society to reexamine the health risks and social circumstances faced by the often stigmatized groups among whom the epidemic has had its greatest impact: gay men, drug users, and the inner-city poor. Indeed, social marginalization and stigma have been central aspects of America's experience with HIV, and these themes are intertwined with all aspects of the effort to respond to the mental health needs of those who are HIV-affected.

Essentially, HIV (and its sequel, acquired immunodeficiency syndrome or AIDS) is a highly stressful condition that has disproportionately affected individuals who are already experiencing stresses related to social marginality – that is, being "different" from the social norm in one or more socially important ways. Particularly in the early years of the HIV epidemic, when public understanding of the details of HIV transmission was limited, the HIV-infected were often the object of fears of pollution almost like those associated in the past with leprosy or bubonic plague (Hall 1992). Even today, living with HIV – and disclosure of one's HIV status – places individuals at risk of strained relationships with family, friends, co-workers, and others in one's social world, adding to the emotional stress imposed by anxiety about one's medical future and, as the disease progresses, the discomforts and disabilities created by the disease process itself.

The mental health problems associated with HIV infection begin at the asymptomatic stage of the disease – in fact, at the point at which one learns that one is HIV-positive. Episodes of depression or severe anxiety states may need to be addressed. A second set of issues emerges in dealing with strains in social relationships that are commonly experienced in the wake of HIV infection. A third set of mental health issues involves the stresses of life that occur as asymptomatic HIV infection progresses to symptomatic illness. As the disease progresses, it imposes a broad range of physical sequelae that can include fatigue, interference with the ability to work, impairment in the ability to perform tasks of daily living, periodic episodes of acute illness related to opportunistic infections, and numerous other impacts. These impacts again create an elevated risk of depression, anxiety, and other mental health difficulties. Additional strain increasingly revolves around the need to adhere to complex and difficult treatment regimens with often toxic antiviral and other drugs. Finally, a fourth set of mental health issues concerns preexisting mental health and substance abuse problems that are disproportionately represented in the HIV-positive population.

The HIV–mental health challenge occurs at personal, clinical, and systems levels. At the personal level, the HIV-infected individual is faced with psychosocial issues that change during the various stages of the disease. At the clinical level, there are an insufficient number of appropriately trained mental health professionals to provide needed assessments and interventions to the affected populations. Further investigation is also needed to identify methods of reducing stress and preventing burnout in mental health professionals who serve individuals with HIV (Sheridan et al. 1989). At the systems level, existing mental health policies and programs are inadequate to meet the present and anticipated needs of HIV-infected patients. Better evaluation research is needed to assess the effectiveness of the interventions currently being utilized.

This chapter examines current issues and prior research on HIV and mental health, with a specific focus on adults diagnosed as HIV-seropositive. The psychosocial issues that individuals report during the clinical course of the disease are reviewed. The chapter begins with a discussion of psychological reactions to notification of HIV seropositivity and continues with an examination of the literature on coping with the diagnosis and the role of social support in this process. A review follows of the persisting psychological distress, psychiatric symptoms, and neuropsychiatric complications that are frequently reported as the disease progresses. The focus then shifts to a review of the unique needs and problems of various high-risk groups. These include the gay male community, injection drug users, and two newly emerging risk groups: heterosexual females and the seriously mentally ill. The conclusion of the chapter examines a variety of mental health programs and interventions currently provided for individuals with HIV. The educational needs and support of mental health professionals who serve HIV-seropositive clients are also discussed.

Psychological Reactions to Notification of HIV Seropositivity

On learning that they are HIV-positive, individuals must struggle with processing the information that they are infected with the virus, cope with the anxiety and fear that such information can engender, and deal with the reformulating of self-concepts and perspectives on one's future that are called into question in this process. Choosing to be tested – a choice that has remained largely a voluntary one in the United States, outside of the military and a few other situations – involves a tradeoff between reduction of uncertainty and the fear of having to deal with bad news (McCusick 1986). Negative (i.e., HIV-negative) results are likely to reduce anxiety. Even for those who previously suspected they might be infected but were living with uncertainty, there may be beneficial effects (alongside the distressing impacts) of positive test results because the uncertainty has been eliminated – but these uncertainties are replaced with a new set of uncertainties that are part and parcel of the ambiguous experience of living with HIV (Crystal & Jackson 1989; Weitz 1991). That many individuals who receive the HIV antibody test never return to obtain their results is evidence that this cost–benefit calculation is not an easy one.

Perry et al. (1990) studied emotional distress at time of testing, two weeks before notification, immediately prior to and after notification, and then at two and ten weeks after notification. Relationships with previous psychiatric disorders were also examined. Subjects were 218 volunteers recruited through advertising and contacts with medical clinics, all physically well and unaware of their antibody status. High rates of distress were reported just prior to notification. Distress was reported to fall quickly regardless of test result. Relief was sustained for those who received a negative test result. Not surprisingly, seropositive subjects who had incorrectly predicted a negative result reported higher levels of distress than those who suspected they might be HIV-positive. The distress scores of this former group decreased significantly, however, ten weeks after notification. These findings may suggest that fear and uncertainty of HIV seropositivity may create more distress than a definitive positive result (King 1993).

The finding that most individuals experience a high distress level at time of antibody testing prompted Perry and colleagues (1991) to explore effective elements of pretest counseling. The authors compared the effects of three interventions: (1) counseling only; (2) counseling plus a three-session, interactive, educational video about HIV; and (3) counseling plus six individual sessions of stress prevention training. The third group received training in cognitive behavioral methods to enhance self-control and challenge dysfunctional thoughts as well as in problem solving and assertiveness. For those subjects whose test results were negative, no significant difference was noted in the effectiveness of the three interventions. For those with a positive test result, however, the counseling plus stress prevention training had a significant distress-reducing effect compared with the other two interventions.

Similarities and Differences in the Psychosocial Impact of HIV and Other Terminal Illnesses

Many authors have examined the similarities between the psychosocial impact of AIDS and that of other terminal illnesses, particularly cancer. Both AIDS and cancer are life-threatening and often strike young adults. Both diseases often create stress on the patient's social network (Wolcott, Fawzy, and Pasnau 1985). Crystal and Jackson (1989) note that psychosocial adaptation to these and other catastrophic, terminal illnesses follows a multistage reaction process from initial shock through anger, denial, and finally acceptance and preparation for death. Coates, Temoshok, and Mandel (1984) compared reactions of gay men to a diagnosis of HIV with those of a matched group of men to a diagnosis of malignant melanoma. Highly similar reactions were found in a period two months after diagnosis. Woods (1985) conducted a similar study comparing the following four groups of men in the areas of depression, anxiety, distress, and locus of control: those with AIDS-associated Kaposi's sarcoma (KS) soon after diagnosis; those with acute leukemia soon after diagnosis; a healthy homosexual-identified control group; and a healthy heterosexual-identified control group. The groups with KS and acute leukemia were similar to one another and to the healthy gay-identified control group on measures of depression, anxiety, distress, and locus of control. The finding that the healthy gay-identified men shared high levels of psychological distress with their counterparts diagnosed with KS or leukemia suggests that the impact of being at risk for the disease may be as powerful psychologically as the actual diagnosis (McCusick 1986).

Societal responses to HIV – and hence stresses that persons with HIV must cope with – are inextricably bound with moral judgments (Auerbach et al. 1994). Issues of stigmatization, past sexual behavior, and drug use are unique psychosocial characteristics of HIV infection. Hall (1992) indicates that diseases are often understood through metaphors, with "plague" being the principal metaphor for HIV. Thus, the disease may be considered by some to be appropriate punishment for devalued and stigmatized groups (Auerbach et al. 1994).

Kelly and associates (1987) surveyed 157 physicians in three cities using descriptive vignettes. They found that physicians expressed less willingness to interact with AIDS patients than with leukemia patients, regardless of patients' sexual orientation. Blendon and Donnelan (1988) examined data from 53 national and international opinion surveys and found that many Americans feel that AIDS is a deserved punishment for offensive or immoral behavior (Hall 1992).

Baker and Seager (1991) compared the psychosocial support required by, and given to, HIV-positive and HIV-negative hospice patients of the same average age. The study involved interviewing staff about the time spent and stress associated with caring for AIDS patients compared with non-AIDS patients. An analysis of the amount of support received from family, congregation, and neighbors was also conducted through a review of clinical records. The record review indicated that AIDS patients required contact over two and a half times as often by telephone and over two times as often in person. Staff reports corroborated these findings. Ninety-two percent of staff reported that AIDS patients usually required more time than non-AIDS patients of similar ages. They stated that AIDS patients needed more time because they had more physical and emotional needs, were generally unsupported by the community, and were emotionally devastated. They also stated that AIDS patients frequently had less support and more unresolved issues than non-AIDS patients (Baker & Seager 1991).

Coping and Social Support

A substantial literature has emerged on the psychological and social variables that predict psychological distress in persons with HIV. Frequently studied variables include coping style, social support, symptom burden, and life stress. The literature also includes a number of studies on the relationship between sociodemographic characteristics and psychological distress.

A number of studies have identified coping style as a significant predictor of psychosocial functioning. Most studies compare the effects of *active-behavioral* coping, which mobilizes energy to deal directly with the illness while turning to others for emotional, informational, and instrumental support (Wolf et al. 1991), with those of *avoidance* coping, which avoids thinking about or behaving in direct response to illness. The effects of *active-cognitive* coping – using thoughts and attitudes to defend against concerns or to create meaning in light of a dismal prognosis – have also been examined. Namir and colleagues (1987) found that active-behavioral coping decreased the likelihood of psychological distress whereas avoidance coping increased it. Similar findings were noted by Wolf and associates (1991) in a study of 29 homosexual and bisexual men. Active-cognitive coping has been generally found to be unrelated to distress.

In addition to the effect of coping style, researchers have examined the effect of social support on psychological distress. Dew, Ragni, and Nimorwicz (1990) examined the effects of psychiatric history, demographic characteristics, social support, coping skills, and life stress on psychiatric symptoms in 75 hemophiliacs. Results indicated that individuals with a personal or family history of psychiatric illness, a high-school education or less, low levels of support from spouse, family, or friends, a poor sense of mastery, and recent exposure to life events involving loss are more likely to report depression and anxiety. In this study, coping style was not found to be a significant predictor of psychological distress. Blaney and colleagues (1991) reported that social support decreased the likelihood of distress in a sample of HIV-seropositive men. Similar results were noted by Wolcott et al. (1986), Zich and Temoshok (1987), and Ostrow et al. (1989) using a variety of instruments to measure a number of dimensions of both psychological distress and social support.

Hays, Turner, and Coates (1992) used data from the San Francisco Men's Health Study to examine the effects of emotional, informational, and practical support (counting on others for such favors as borrowing money or helping in a crisis) on depression. The effects of HIV antibody status, knowledge of HIV antibody status, and number of HIV symptoms were also examined. These authors found that number of HIV symptoms experienced was a strong predictor of depression and that satisfaction with each type of social support was associated with decreased depression. Neither HIV status nor knowledge of one's HIV status was found to be significant predictors of depression. When changes in depression after one year were assessed, early depression scores were found to be highly correlated with depression one year later. Social support scores continued to predict lower depression at follow-up even after controlling for previous depression level. When the impact of each type of social support and the number of symptoms were examined, the combination of symptoms and information support was found to have a significant impact on depression.

These findings demonstrate the beneficial effects of social support. They also suggest that the support needs of HIV-positive individuals may change as their disease progresses. As symptoms become more apparent, the need for informational support may take precedence over other forms of support. The authors suggest that gathering information about AIDS may serve to reduce stress by creating a sense of control and predictability (Hays et al. 1992).

A major limitation of the research studies noted here is that participants are predominantly white, middle-class, and well-educated gay men (Auerbach 1994; Hays 1992). Further research is needed to investigate whether these findings can be generalized to females, minorities, and those with other risk factors.

Crystal and associates (1993) extended the knowledge base regarding the relationship between coping style, social support, and psychological well-being in a study involving the responses of 267 adults participating in a New Jersey Medicaid waiver program. The authors investigated whether coping factors had an impact on the effects of life stress and social support on psychological distress. The authors found that coping style changed the impacts of stressful events, physical symptoms, and social support on both anxiety and depression.

Fleishman and Fogel (1994) conducted a variety of statistical analyses using data from 1,031 individuals participating in a Robert Wood Johnson (RWJ) Foundation demonstration of community-based care for people with AIDS. The authors found that minorities, injection drug users, females, and those with lower incomes had higher scores for avoidance coping than their respective counterparts. The greater the number of months since notification of HIV infection, the less likely it was that an individual would engage in positive coping. The greater the number of close friends, however, the more likely one was to engage in positive coping. The number of close relatives did not increase the likelihood of positive coping. Avoidance coping was significantly related to symptom intensity and number of months since HIV infection. Women had higher levels of depressive symptoms than men. Blacks had lower levels of distress than whites, but Hispanics had higher levels. Injection drug users were more distressed than gay and bisexual respondents. Individuals in the lowest income category had significantly higher levels of depressive symptoms than those in the highest income category. Symptom severity, functional impairments, and months since HIV notification were related to higher levels of distress. These clinical variables reduced the effect of the sociodemographic characteristics noted previously.

The authors also analyzed the combined effect of symptoms and perceived tangible support as well as the combined effect of functional impairment and perceived tangible support. The latter had a significant effect on depression. This suggests that the relationship between depressive symptoms and the physical progression of HIV is reduced as the level of perceived tangible social support increases.

Fleishman and Fogel's findings are consistent with the foregoing studies in suggesting: (a) a strong relationship between HIV-related symptoms and psychological distress; (b) that social support may reduce psychological distress; and (c) that avoidance coping may increase psychological distress. Their findings extend prior research by identifying sociodemographic differences in coping and levels of depressive symptoms. They also lend additional support to the concern that estimates of HIV-related psychological distress that are based on studies of white, gay men may be limited in generalizability. These authors suggest that mental health services for people with HIV should be sensitive to sociodemographic differences in reactions to stress, and that measuring coping style may be a clinically promising method to identify individuals who are particularly at risk for adverse psychological consequences (Fleishman & Fogel 1994). Further research is needed to examine whether factors that detract from or protect one's mental health change over time.

Psychological/Psychiatric Disorders in HIV

Information about the types of psychological and psychiatric problems to which HIV-seropositive individuals are most vulnerable is critical in effective diagnosis and treatment. Although significant work has been done in this area, most studies have been based on small, nonrepresentative samples, particularly of those who have advanced HIV disease or who have been referred for psychiatric services

(Whitaker & Ostrow 1991). The majority of studies have been conducted on samples of gay white men.

Psychological reactions to HIV are best understood in relation to disease progression. They vary with the diagnostic or illness events that occur during the trajectory of the disease: learning that one is seropositive, experiencing a dramatic drop in one's CD4 cell count, developing physical symptoms, beginning antiretroviral therapy, and developing neurologic symptoms or opportunistic infections. Availability of adequate support systems and the presence or absence of preexisting psychological strengths or vulnerabilities may also cause variations in each individual's reaction to the disease.

Initial reactions to knowledge of HIV seropositivity have been reported to include a mixture of denial and disbelief. In early studies, some individuals demonstrated heightened activity – addressing financial matters, executing wills, finishing work or educational projects, and deciding who should be told. Others, particularly injection drug users, acknowledged their seropositivity but denied that their behaviors were involved. Shock was also commonly reported. Shock can be immediate or delayed, occurring at various points during the course of the illness. Some patients reacted to a diagnosis of HIV seropositivity with guilt and self-blame about life-style and sexual orientation (Dilley et al. 1985). Recently diagnosed individuals may report an obsessive preoccupation with physical health. Frequent body checks for moles, marks, and blemishes are common (Miller 1990).

As disease symptoms appear, HIV-positive individuals' reactions may shift to depressed mood. The clinical manifestations of the disease, feelings of helplessness, and intensified feelings of loss of physical strength and attractiveness create psychological distress (Chesney & Folkman 1994; Sheridan & Sheridan 1988). Symptoms of depression include sadness, hopelessness, and helplessness. Miller (1990) reports that many patients who appeared to have successfully adjusted to their diagnoses over many months appear to relive the original trauma of their status when infections or illnesses emerge. Depressive reactions often result in a decrease in functioning, and depressed patients frequently withdraw from social interactions. Withdrawal may restrict a patient's exposure to positive interventions and social support (Miller 1990). A complicating factor in diagnosis of depression is the frequent overlap in the symptoms of depression itself and those created by medication side effects (Whitaker & Ostrow 1991). Many of the medications used to treat infections or cancers are known to cause side effects of depression as well as neurologic complications.

Miller (1990) reports that anxiety is a ubiquitous feature in the life of an HIV-seropositive person. Common anxiety symptoms include panic attacks, agitation, insomnia, tension, anorexia, and tachycardia (Holland & Tross 1985). In addition, symptoms of diarrhea, nausea, sweating, tremors, visual disturbances, dizziness, skin rashes, and lethargy – all manifestations of anxiety – can be misinterpreted as clinical manifestations of HIV, thus further increasing anxiety. Some

HIV-positive individuals may self-medicate their anxiety through abuse of alcohol or recreational drugs (Miller 1990).

Sheridan and Sheridan (1988) report that persons with no history of suicidal ideation frequently begin to discuss thoughts of suicide as a result of overwhelming anxiety and an inability to cope. Depressive symptomatology and reported physical symptoms have been found to be associated with suicidal thoughts (Belkin et al. 1992). A literature has emerged that suggests that suicides and suicide attempts by HIV-seropositive individuals are more common than was originally believed. Marzuk and colleagues (1988) reviewed all suicides certified by the Office of Chief Medical Examiner in New York in 1985. They used review of medical records, interviews with family members, autopsy evidence, police reports, and suicide notes. In addition, the New York City AIDS surveillance unit cross-matched registry information with the 1985 suicide list. They determined that the rate of suicide for HIV positive individuals was 66 times higher than the rate for the general population, and that HIV-positive men aged 22–55 were 36 times more likely to commit suicide than their counterparts of the same age without an HIV diagnosis (King 1993; Marzuk et al. 1988). Of the AIDS-related suicides reviewed by Marzuk and his colleagues, most victims were white; the mean age at suicide was 37.5; 75% were homosexual or bisexual; and all committed suicide within nine months of receiving the diagnosis. Two of these individuals had psychiatric hospitalizations within one month before the suicide. In four cases, families reported that their deceased family member had been previously depressed. King (1993) points out that statistics based on death certificates may actually underestimate the true rate of suicides.

Studies investigating the timing of suicide attempts have shown mixed results. O'Dowd and McKegney (1990) reported that suicide was more likely in earlier stages of HIV infection than in patients with full-blown AIDS, whereas Gala and associates (1992) reported that vulnerable periods were within six months of testing and with the development of AIDS (King 1993).

A large-scale study by Belkin and colleagues (1992) examined the effects of demographic variables, social support, physical disability, and cognitive impairment on depressive symptoms and the presence of suicidal thoughts. One thousand thirty-one clients in nine communities were interviewed. Significant associations between depression and functional limitations, gender, number of days in bed, social support, and number of mental health services since HIV notification were also identified. Women and those with less social support were more likely to be depressed. Results regarding suicidal thoughts were similar. Physical symptoms, days bed-bound, and less social support all had a significant relationship with suicidal thoughts. Women, however, were less likely to have suicidal thoughts than men. Further study revealed that the magnitude of the relationship between depression and suicidal thoughts increased as symptom intensity increased. The burden of physical symptoms appears to be a strong predictor of depressed mood.

Neuropsychiatric Complications

Early in the epidemic, clinicians attributed most of the psychiatric symptoms experienced by persons with HIV to the emotional repercussions of contracting the disease. Researchers later identified the important role of organic mental syndromes in individuals with HIV disease, particularly at its advanced stages. Neuropsychiatric complications result from the effects of malignancies and opportunistic infections as well as from the direct effects of the virus on brain tissue. Studies have found evidence of central nervous system (CNS) involvement in 80% of postmortem examinations (Zeifert, Leary, & Boccellari 1995). The presence of organic disorders creates a diagnostic dilemma, as it is often extremely difficult (if not impossible) to differentiate the organic from the functional (McCusick 1986; Perry & Jacobsen 1986).

Signs of depression, withdrawal, somatic preoccupation, anxiety, forgetfulness or disturbances in memory or concentration, panic attacks, paranoia, bipolar episodes, and schizophreniform psychosis (McCusick 1986; Perry & Jacobsen 1986) all may result from the presence of organic mental disorder. Early in the epidemic it was suggested that, owing to the prevalence of neuropsychiatric complications in patients with HIV, the presumption should be of organic deficit unless proven otherwise (Ostrow, Atkinson, & Grant 1990; Perry & Jacobsen 1986; Tross & Hirsch 1988). The situation is further complicated because CNS disease may be present despite normal results on neurodiagnostic tests. The presence of CNS involvement thus presents another aspect of the HIV mental health challenge. Mental health professionals involved in diagnosis and treatment of individuals with HIV must be aware of the possibility of neurological disease. They should develop skill in screening for cognitive impairment and an awareness of the potential need for referring to neurological specialists. Although newer, more effective antiviral treatments are maintaining patients in better health and cognitive functioning for longer periods, late-stage HIV disease may still bring cognitive impairment in its wake.

A general understanding of the physiology of the brain is helpful in understanding theoies regarding the mechanisms by which HIV disease enters and affects the brain (Zeifert et al. 1995). A tight network of cells, called the blood–brain barrier, protects the brain by allowing entry only of blood cells it recognizes as "self" into the brain. It has been theorized that HIV uses a "Trojan horse" technique to gain entry to the brain: HIV hides in cells called *macrophages* (Auerbach et al. 1994), and the blood–brain barrier allows these HIV-infected macrophages into the brain. Upon entry into the brain, HIV can replicate in the macrophages and other cells (Zeifert et al. 1995). Some studies have suggested that HIV does not directly kill or infect nerve cells (Auerbach et al. 1994). Rather, it disrupts brain functioning by causing a reduction in myelin tissue, or "white matter." White matter insulates the branches of the neurons that allow for the electrochemical flow of brain impulses, speeding transmission of neural impulses and thus permitting a person to think and initiate motor activity quickly. When the myelin tissue is reduced, cognitive and motor impairment result (Zeifert et al. 1995). Early studies suggested that up to two thirds of AIDS patients became demented. More recent reports indicate a drop in the prevalence of HIV-associated dementia since the advent of increasingly effective antiviral treatments (Atkinson & Grant 1994).

Still, HIV-associated dementia (HAD) is the most common CNS dysfunction identified in individuals with HIV. Also known as nonfocal encephalopathy or subacute encephalitis, this disorder was first identified by Snider and associates (1983), who noted that the early symptoms are so similar to those of depression that they cannot usually be distinguished without neuropsychological testing. These symptoms occasionally are the presenting condition for persons with HIV disease (Holland & Tross 1985). Initial symptoms of forgetfulness and poor concentration are followed by psychomotor retardation, decreased alertness, apathy, withdrawal, diminished interest in work, and loss of libido. Late-stage symptoms include severe confusion, disorientation, seizures, mutism, loss of bowel and bladder control, gait disturbances and/or inability to walk, profound dementia, and death. Nielsen and colleagues (1984) found evidence of HAD in 19 of 40 subjects with AIDS. The researchers described similar symptoms in these patients to those reported by Snider, including depression, lethargy, and withdrawal and progressing to psychomotor retardation and ultimately dementia (Faulstich 1987). Despite this general pattern, the clinical course of dementia in each individual is highly variable, progressing gradually in some or appearing with dramatic onset and rapid progression in others. Sometimes, psychosis and delirium complicate HAD (Atkinson & Grant 1994). In the late 1990s, the incidence of HAD decreased as newer, more effective antiviral treatments became available.

Another group of organic nervous system disorders are the result of opportunistic infections or systematic organ dysfunction from immunosuppression. The most commonly reported are toxoplasmosis, cryptococcal meningitis, progressive multifocal leukoencephalopathy (PML), and lymphoma (Zeifert et al. 1995). Toxoplasmosis (*toxoplasma gondii*) is a parasitic infection. It is difficult to diagnose because it may affect a variety of parts of the brain, thus causing a variety of symptoms. Symptoms range from fever and constant headache to motor weakness and seizures (Zeifert et al. 1995). Cryptococcal meningitis is a fungal infection. Patients with this infection often present with seizures and altered mental status (Wolcott et al. 1985). The latter can range from mild changes in personality to severe confusion and memory loss. Antifungal drugs have been reported to be effective (Zeifert et al. 1995).

Progressive multifocal leukoencephalopathy is a viral infection in the white matter of the brain. Most patients diagnosed with PML become bed-bound and severely incapacitated. They require major assistance with activities of daily living and often experience loss of vision and impairment in walking. It is reported that death usually occurs within several months of onset, although some cases were responsive to antiviral treatment (Zeifert et al. 1995).

As treatment of HIV disease with antiviral medications – including protease inhibitors as well as prophylactic (preventive) use of antibiotics and antifungals – improved, by the late 1990s the incidence of opportunistic infections such as pneumocystis carinii pneumonia and toxoplasmosis declined and the duration of survival with HIV disease increased. However, after years of living with the virus, persons with HIV increasingly experienced cancers such as lymphoma, which has been identified in approximately 7% of AIDS patients. This cancer, which begins in the lymphatic system, invades the brain and causes cognitive impairment and behavioral changes. Although these neoplasms respond to radiation therapy, life expectancy in the early 1990s was only about six months after diagnosis (Zeifert et al. 1995).

Risk Groups – Special Populations

The epidemiology of HIV infection is changing, and the list of groups at risk has expanded. The newly emerging high-risk groups involve groups within the population who have been disadvantaged and discriminated against in the United States (Bell 1989b). In this country, HIV first became apparent largely among men who had sex with men. Although there is some evidence that HIV seroprevalence rates among gay men have plateaued (Auerbach et al. 1994), high seroprevalence rates remain. Gay men who are outside of AIDS epicenters, and those who are young, minorities, hidden and hard to reach, and/or do not self-identify as gay, remain at elevated risk (Kelly & Murphy 1992). Studies indicate that seroprevalence rates among minority gay males are particularly high. Injection drug users were also identified as being at high risk early in the epidemic. Seroprevalence rates as high as 50% have been found among this population in some cities.

As the epidemic continues, heterosexual women, who are often the sexual partners of male injection drug users, have emerged as a group at high risk. African Americans and Hispanics are disproportionately represented. The seriously mentally ill have also recently been identified as a group at high risk for HIV infection. A number of studies indicate that the seroprevalence rate of this group may be higher than that of the general population (Auerbach et al. 1994). The unique characteristics and special needs of these heterogeneous groups have significant implications with regard to the design and implementation of programs and services.

The Gay Male Community

By the beginning of the 1990s, the Centers for Disease Control (CDC) estimated that between 20% and 30% of gay men in the United States were infected with HIV (Hays et al. 1992), constituting a human disaster for a community whose right to exist publicly on the same basis as other communities within society had only recently been established. For some in the gay community in the early 1980s, sexual freedom had become an important symbolic representation of their community's human rights, so it is not surprising that there were those who initially responded to the need to reduce risky sexual behavior with denial (Shilts 1987). Overall, however, the level of risk reduction achieved within big-city gay communities in response to HIV's challenge to their very survival has been impressive; the more difficult challenge is to sustain such change. In the face of death and loss, renunciation of sexual pleasures with their life-affirming qualities can sometimes be all the more difficult. Thus, denial remains a challenge within gay communities, and safe-sex messages are likely to be most effective when they emphasize that risk reduction need not mean renouncing pleasure.

The impact of the AIDS epidemic on the gay community has been profound. Gay men have to cope not only with their own risk or HIV status, but with illness and death of their lovers and others in their social network. Many studies have revealed that gay men in AIDS epicenters report fairly high levels of distress (Hays et al. 1990, 1992). A literature has emerged that examines factors that predict or reduce psychological distress in this risk group. Much of the early behavioral research involved white, middle-class, urban, gay male volunteers who are active in gay organizations (Cvitanic 1990).

Chuang and associates (1989) compared the effects of various demographic, social network, and stressful life event variables on psychosocial distress in asymptomatic, HIV positive, and AIDS-diagnosed homosexual and bisexual patients. The first group consisted of 24 asymptomatic men; the second group of 22 exhibited some symptoms but had no systematic opportunistic infections; and the third group had been clinically diagnosed as having AIDS. The researchers found a high level of psychological distress in all three groups. Patients without full-blown AIDS (groups 1 and 2) exhibited significantly higher levels of depression, mood disturbance, and trait anxiety than those with full-blown AIDS. The authors suggest that the uncertainty prevalent in the early stages of the disease may be more emotionally taxing than coping with an actual diagnosis of AIDS (Chuang et al. 1989). Ostrow and colleagues (1989) studied 4,954 homosexual and bisexual men upon voluntary enrollment into the Multicenter AIDS Cohort Study (MACS) in 1984 and 1985. The purpose of the study was to examine the effects on depression of a variety of demographic and social support variables, self-reported HIV symptoms, and other physical health variables. The findings of this study support the findings by other researchers regarding the increased likelihood of depression by those with more physical symptoms and the decreased likelihood of depression in those who report having social support.

A 1990 study by Hays and associates compared help seeking, self-reported psychological distress, and AIDS-related worry among 530 gay men enrolled in the AIDS Behavioral Research Project. One subgroup included 30 men with a diagnosis of AIDS; subgroup two included 107 men who knew they were HIV positive; subgroup three included 149 men who knew they were HIV negative. The fourth subgroup included 244 men who had not been tested for HIV and thus were unaware of their HIV status. Respondents were asked to identify any sources from whom they had sought advice, including primary partner, friend, parents, siblings, counselor or psychologist, medical doctor, and clergy or spiritual leader. Findings indicated that there were no significant differences in psychological distress (anxiety and depression) among the groups, but that there were differences with regard to AIDS-related worry. Seropositive and AIDS-diagnosed men reported more worry than those who were seronegative or not yet tested. Similarly, a significantly higher percentage of seropositive and AIDS-diagnosed men sought help for these concerns. Further investigation revealed that subjects diagnosed with AIDS sought help from a significantly greater number of sources than did untested, seronegative, or seropositive subjects. The four groups of men did not seek help equally from all sources. Whereas AIDS-diagnosed men tended to seek help equally from various sources, the other three groups sought help most frequently from peers.

Peers were rated significantly more helpful than professional helpers, and professional helpers were rated as significantly more helpful than family members. These findings were true regardless of HIV status. The authors suggest that assisting peers to enhance their abilities as support providers, helping to prevent burnout, developing mutual support groups and buddy systems, and providing alternative sources of help for gay men whose supportive peer networks have been decimated are all strategies that mental health professionals can use to facilitate peer support within the gay community.

Injection Drug Users

The CDC reported that heterosexual injection drug users accounted for approximately 22% of AIDS cases diagnosed in the United States in 1992. By the 1990s, injection drug users (IDUs) accounted for the majority of new AIDS cases in New York and New Jersey (Batki 1990). In fact, HIV-infected drug users have been the primary bridge for introduction of HIV into the heterosexual population (Kelly & St. Lawrence 1988). This high-risk group poses significant challenges to the mental health system since drug abuse, psychiatric problems, and HIV disease often co-occur (Batki 1990). The needs, reactions to the disease, and other special issues of this population differ significantly from the predominantly white, middle- to upper-class, well-educated, gay male subjects examined in the studies described previously.

A disproportionate percentage of drug injectors are members of minority groups (Cvitanic 1990). New York and New Jersey have been major epicenters for IDU-associated AIDS. This group is characterized by low pre-diagnosis income, limited formal education, lack of insurance coverage, lack of preexisting relationships with health care providers, and other access barriers to the health and mental health system (Crystal 1992). Drug injectors have been reported to have high life-time prevalence of depression, anxiety, and other psychiatric diagnoses (Auerbach et al. 1994). Difficulty in accessing and identifying this population creates serious obstacles for researchers. Subjects were often those receiving treatment in methadone or drug detox centers and were usually long-term chronic injectors (Auerbach et al. 1994; Cvitanic 1990). Systematic information is scarce about addicts on the street, those who view themselves as recreational or occasional users, and younger, new injectors.

Tross and Hirsch (1988) and Batki (1990) suggested that a diagnosis of HIV could create a heightened stress response in IDUs that induces further substance abuse. Poor coping skills and ego deficits make these individuals more vulnerable to psychological distress, and a diagnosis of HIV may increase psychopathology. Psychiatric severity at intake into drug treatment was also found to be predictive of less successful outcomes. Batki (1990) reports that the presence of depression, hopelessness, and suicidality at treatment intake among HIV-infected patients was predictive of worse outcomes – as defined by heroin, cocaine, and injection drug use one year later.

Sharing of drug-injection equipment and unsafe sexual practices are the primary modes of transmission of HIV among this population. Batki (1990) suggests that drug-induced disinhibition of behavior, sex-for-drugs transactions, and the impairment of cell-mediated immunity as a result of drug use may all be significant factors in the transmission of the disease among this population.

Whereas behavioral research on the gay population often examined help-seeking behavior, the role of social support, and other factors that predict or reduce psychological distress, much current research regarding HIV-seropositive IDUs examines their access to health care services. Solomon and colleagues (1991) examined the relationship between health status and utilization of medical services among IDUs, as well as the role of health insurance in determining such utilization, in the AIDS Link to Intravenous Experience (ALIVE) study. The researchers examined independent impacts of health insurance, HIV serostatus, and AIDS-related symptoms on use of inpatient or outpatient care during a six-month period. The presence of two or more AIDS-related symptoms was found to be a significant predictor of both outpatient and inpatient services. In addition, health insurance was also found to be a significant predictor of service utilization, especially inpatient treatment. For IDUs with AIDS-related symptoms, utilization of inpatient service was less likely in the absence of insurance coverage. The study also found that asymptomatic HIV-seropositive IDUs were no more likely than HIV-seronegative IDUs to use services. Injection drug users often remain outside the health care system, frequenting emergency rooms on an as-needed basis. The authors suggest that characteristics inherent in drug use, such as the need to secure drugs daily, make it particularly difficult for active IDUs to schedule appointments or comply with treatment plans. They suggest that this should be considered in the development of services for this population.

Stein and colleagues (1991) analyzed self-reports of 880 outpatients with symptomatic HIV or AIDS from RWJ Foundation AIDS Health Services sites in nine cities to examine access to zidovudine (ZDV). There were 301 IDUs in the group, and 81% of them were offered ZDV as compared to 91% of non-IDUs. Mor and associates (1992) reported a mean of 6.72 outpatient medical visits in a three-month period for IDUs in a 1988–89 survey of RWJ-funded sites, compared with a mean of 8.13 visits for non-IDUs in the same study. The researchers also reported that IDUs tended to have more inpatient admissions and more emergency room visits than non-IDUs in the sample. Hospital stays for IDUs were longer. It has been suggested that this greater length of stay is due to lack of personal support networks and difficulties in finding suitable housing for this risk group.

A paper by Crystal (1992) examined data from a 1989–90 study of 107 persons with AIDS sampled from the New Jersey Department of Health AIDS Registry. Of the subjects, 65 were IDUs. The study found that availability of health insurance was a significant predictor of access to health services. This study also highlighted the important source of support that families provide for IDUs as well as the variety of barriers to adequate health care faced by IDUs, including lack of health insurance and other, more covert barriers such as negative attitudes of health care providers. In this study population, the proportion of IDUs receiving ZDV, the only antiviral then available for AIDS (also known as azidothymidine or AZT) differed significantly: 40% of IDUs received ZDV compared with 73% of infected gay men. Furthermore, IDUs tended to receive this treatment late in the course of the illness, beyond the point of its greatest effectiveness. Differences in access to antiviral treatment by IDUs during the first several years following the 1987 introduction of ZDV were also found in a larger study by Crystal, Sambamoorthi, and Merzel (1995).

Crystal (1992) suggested that including HIV-related medical care as a component of addiction treatment may be one method to address some of the unique access issues described here. Batki (1990) concurs that drug-abuse treatment can be an important avenue for providing needed services to HIV-infected IDUs. He suggests that psychiatric care, medical care, social services, and AIDS education can be incorporated into drug treatment programs. In order to adequately address the needs of former or current drug abusers with AIDS, treatment strategies are needed that address their intertwined drug treatment, HIV treatment, and mental health treatment needs within integrated clinical teams.

Women and HIV

By the 1990s, women accounted for an increasing number and percentage of AIDS cases in the United States. In fact, by 1987, AIDS had become the eighth leading cause of death in women between the ages of 15 and 44 in the United States and the leading cause of death in black women in the same age group in New York and New Jersey. Ellerbock and colleagues (1991) noted that over 50% of women with AIDS were infected via injection drug use and 29% were infected through heterosexual contact. The majority of these cases involved sexual contact with an IDU or a bisexual man. Most women with HIV were young (15–44), black or Hispanic, economically disadvantaged, and living on the Atlantic coast. Hanley and Lincoln (1992) hypothesized that as many as 80,000 women of reproductive age could be infected. Despite this number, the unique issues of women with HIV have received little attention.

Shaw (1987) noted that many women with HIV were single mothers primarily concerned with economic survival, and that the issue of AIDS may be low on their list of concerns. Wofsy (1988) noted that many asymptomatic women remained in denial of their illness. Ybarra (1991) pointed to the special needs that counselors should consider when working with women with AIDS. These include individual needs, relationship needs, and needs pertaining to mothering and pregnancy.

Anecdotal reports based on observations of HIV-infected women in therapeutic situations describe a number of common themes. Women have been reported to grieve the loss of their health, body image, sexuality, and childbearing potential. Some women must cope simultaneously with their own illness and the illness or death of a partner or child. Many women have experienced guilt, feelings of helplessness, and fear of abandonment. Other women, especially those who discover they contracted the disease from homosexual or bisexual men, experience feelings of betrayal, anger, and self-blame, and they often question their adequacy as women (Ybarra 1991). It has been noted that, in general, women at risk of HIV experience higher levels of social isolation with fewer readily identifiable sources of social support.

Worth (1990) noted that women's reactions to HIV often depend on their socio-cultural, sexual, and economic relationships. Many women perceive themselves as powerless over control of sexual encounters or use of contraceptives. Some women have been physically abused in response to requesting use of condoms. In some cultures, women who use condoms are considered to be "fast" or "easy." Some women perceive that they must make a choice between economic and emotional survival – between maintaining a relationship with a man and protecting themselves against HIV. This may be especially true of female IDUs whose partners support their drug habit or those who turn to prostitution to support their own habits (Worth 1990).

The important function that childbearing plays in the lives of many at-risk women often leads them to continue pregnancies after they discover their diagnosis. For many women, childbearing is a cultural expectation and a sign of their worth (Anastos & Palleja 1991). Thus, it has been found that knowledge of HIV status has little impact on reproductive decisions (King 1993). Those who forego childbearing often report a profound sense of loss (Ybarra 1991). Since 1994, it has been known that the risk of mother-to-child transmission of HIV can be reduced (from about 25% to 8% or lower, according to clinical trial results) through a regimen of ZDV treatment before, during, and (for the infant) after childbirth. Although use of this regimen has improved the odds of a successful outcome of pregnancy among HIV-positive women, there are still difficult choices to be faced concerning childbearing, and lack of prenatal care and other care barriers have made use of preventive treatment much less than universal.

The HIV-positive mother is confronted with myriad issues. Many women assume primary care for their children. Often they become too ill to continue this role, causing turmoil within the family (Wofsy 1988). Ybarra (1991) reports that many women blame themselves if their children contract the disease and experience guilt about leaving healthy children behind. Grieving for dying children, coping with one's own illness, and simultaneously planning for the care of surviving children is not uncommon. Some women have expressed strong desires to reestablish relationships with children before they die (Worth 1990).

In addition to the complex psychosocial issues just described, women generally have fewer economic and social resources (such as income or health insurance) to cover needed medical, mental health, or other HIV-related services. They also need concrete services to protect them against eviction and homelessness, loss of jobs, or loss of welfare or health benefits as a result of their own, their partners' or their children's diagnosis of HIV. Brown and Rundell (1990) conducted a study of 20 women who discovered they were HIV-positive as a result of mandatory screening by the United States Air Force. The authors indicated that the disease was transmitted to these women through heterosexual contact. None of the females were drug injectors. The authors found that 35% of the sample were assigned a DSM-III-R Axis I diagnosis, and over half received a diagnosis of hypoactive sexual desire disorder. Suicidal ideation was found to be rare among this sample (King 1993).

Other researchers have compared use of health services by women and men with HIV. Results have often conflicted, but several studies have documented indications of less adequate health care access for women. Stein and associates (1991), in an evaluation of the RWJ Foundation's AIDS health services program, found that males were more likely to be offered AZT than females. Hellinger (1993) also found that, even after being diagnosed and having accessed the medical care system, women received fewer services than men. Hellinger (1993) also compared the use of a variety of health services by men and women and found that an asymptomatic woman is 20% less likely to receive AZT than an asymptomatic man. Symptomatic women and women with AIDS were less likely than men to be hospitalized but more likely to make outpatient visits to emergency rooms, hospital or community clinics, or private doctors. Hellinger suggested that women may use fewer health services than men owing either to better health status or to greater discrimination as a result of HIV infection.

The Seriously Mentally Ill

The epidemiology of HIV in persons with serious mental illness has only recently begun to be explored. Concerns have been expressed that this population is at high risk of HIV. In the limited number of studies conducted by the mid-1990s, seroprevalence rates appeared to exceed those of the general population as well as those of various other groups. Many of the studies were conducted in New York City. Several authors suggested that increased prevalence may be due to more risk behavior, a greater likelihood of associating with other persons who engage in high-risk behaviors, and/or lack of knowledge about HIV transmission. It has also been suggested that mental illness may impair self-assessment of risk (Knox et al. 1994).

Most of the studies of this population examined knowledge of HIV or the risk behaviors of a sample of seriously mentally ill individuals. A limited number of other studies investigated whether knowledge about HIV transmission has an effect on risk behavior. Nearly all available information involved persons enrolled in inpatient or outpatient mental health services; information is lacking on seriously mentally ill individuals who are not in treatment. It has been suggested that mental health professionals must increase their awareness of HIV among those with serious mental illness – as well as their skills in assessing risk status and behaviors – in order to provide education, counseling, and referral to other services as needed (Carey, Weinhardt, and Carey 1995).

Katz, Watts, and Santman (1994) assessed AIDS knowledge, attitudes, and risk behaviors of 54 men and women at a drop-in center for mentally ill adults in Stockton, California. In terms of knowledge, 60% of respondents reported that AIDS could be contracted by giving blood, 30% reported that having sex was the only way one could contract AIDS, 42% were unaware that using injection drugs could spread the disease, and 30% reported that they could tell if someone had AIDS. When attitudes were assessed, 36% of the respondents indicated that it was acceptable to use injection drugs and 32% disagreed or had no opinion that sexually active individuals should wear condoms. With regard to actual behavior, 13% indicated that they had engaged in sex for money, drugs, or a place to stay; 15% stated that they had sex after using drugs or alcohol; and 7% said they had sex with a partner who used injection drugs. Finally, 61% (33) reported that they had been tested for HIV and 15% (5) tested positive (Katz et al. 1994).

Aruffo and associates (1990) compared 80 women (age 18–40) who were outpatients at a college-affiliated community psychiatric center with another 80 women attending medical clinics, matched for race and age. Findings indicated that the psychiatric outpatients, especially those with schizophrenia, had significantly lower levels of knowledge about HIV than women in the comparison group. With regard to high-risk behavior, although 73% of the psychiatric outpatients indicated that they were sexually active, only 53% indicated that they knew condoms could prevent transmission of HIV. Intravenous drug use was reported by 14% of the outpatient sample (King 1993).

Volavka and colleagues (1992) classified 52% of 476 psychiatric inpatients as being at high risk of HIV after analyzing responses to 13 questions regarding homosexual sex with men, sex with high-risk partners, and past use of intravenous drugs. Sacks and associates (1990) found that 42% of psychiatric inpatients reported a history of high-risk behaviors during the previous five years.

Knox and colleagues (1994) assessed HIV knowledge and risk behavior of 120 seriously mentally ill persons. Unlike the findings of Katz et al. (1994), the authors found that most subjects were able to correctly respond to most items regarding HIV and that subjects were generally able to identify the riskiest behaviors. Furthermore, 67% of the subjects were able to identify at least two prevention strategies. Despite this apparently high level of knowledge about HIV and AIDS, many engaged in high-risk behaviors: 40% reported having had multiple sex partners during the past year, 37% reported that they never used a condom, and only 15% reported using a condom every time they had sex. Also, 30% reported having sex while high on drugs or alcohol during the past year, 26% reported that they probably had sex with an IDU during the past year, and 17% reported using injection drugs at some time during the past ten years. Investigators categorized respondents by risk. They found that 21% were at no risk, 34% were at low risk, 33% were at medium risk, and 11% were at high risk. Subjects' perceptions of their risk differed markedly from investigators classifications, with most subjects underestimating their risk. The authors concluded that factual knowledge about HIV is not enough to prevent risky behavior.

Training and Support for Mental Health Professionals

Knox (1989) suggests that there are significant continuing education needs of mental health professionals in order to increase knowledge and clinical skills and to address attitudes and fears about HIV. Despite this need, training opportunities are often limited. Early research suggested that many mental health professionals were apprehensive about treating persons with HIV. Polan, Hellerstein, and Amchin (1985) reported that staff felt panicky, became openly hostile, and reported hypochondriacal fears when two patients with HIV and two patients who mistakenly believed they had the virus were admitted to an acute psychiatric facility in New York. Similarly, Rosse (1985) reported that staff became anxious and avoided an HIV-positive patient admitted to a psychiatric unit. Staff have reported fear of contamination and a reluctance to admit HIV-positive patients.

These attitudes may have resulted in discrimination in service delivery reported early in the epidemic. Further research is needed to determine whether staff attitudes in mental health treatment settings have improved over time. Ryan (1990) suggests that burnout is a common response of providers, especially in areas where a large number of patients with HIV are served. She recommends that, in these settings, support groups for providers are essential. These support groups give providers an opportunity to vent feelings and share resources.

Public policy statements have been issued by the American Medical Association, the American Psychological Association, the American Psychiatric Association, the American Nurses Association, and the National Association of Social Workers. These public policy statements provide guidelines for mental health professionals regarding many of the ethical challenges of the epidemic, including confidentiality, prolonging life in a technology dependent condition, duty to warn spouse or sexual partner, research with experimental drugs, and use of informed consent in HIV testing (Ryan 1990). These guidelines alone are not sufficient to address the many clinical, medical, legal, and ethical issues faced by those providing care to clients with HIV. Research has demonstrated that provider training to increase competence – which includes up-to-date information on diagnosis, treatment, infection control, mental health issues, and legal and ethical considerations – has served to improve comfort levels and attitudes in providing services to individuals with HIV.

Knox and Gaies (1990) describe a training program for mental health professionals developed at the University of South Florida. The program includes three constellations of topics to address the needs of mental health professionals: HIV prevention and treatment, clinical skills, and administrative and leadership skills. The authors note that the training includes a presentation on the role of community mental health in the AIDS crisis as well as up-to-date information on prevalence of HIV, routes of transmission, and prevention strategies. This information is followed by protocols for pre- and posttest counseling, descriptions of clinical manifestations, and early psychiatric and neurological presentations. Diagnosis and medical treatment strategies are also discussed. Specific methods for neuropsychological assessment, suicide risk and prevention, psychotherapeutic intervention strategies, and issues in serving terminally ill clients are addressed. The special needs of the seriously mentally ill, substance abusers, accessing support systems, and networking with other health care providers are included. Finally, legal and ethical issues, infection control guidelines, and discussion of staff attitudes are covered.

Ryan (1990) points out that gaps in professional education must also be addressed to improve appropriate clinical care. Many practitioners are reluctant to discuss sexuality. This may result in inadequate sexual history taking and may also limit a practitioner's effectiveness in assisting patients to identify high-risk sexual behaviors, grieve their loss, and replace them with low-risk activities. Ryan (1990) also notes that practitioners often need additional training to work with chemically dependent patients. She maintains that, although the length of time available and the resources to train staff may vary, essential components of HIV–AIDS training include: factual, scientific information on transmission; patient management and infection control; an emotional component to identify providers' feelings, fears, and biases; and an ethical component explaining providers' responsibilities in responding to the dilemmas introduced by the disease.

Current Program Models

Morrison (1993) discusses the critical need for continuity of care for persons living with HIV. He states that this concept of continuity includes three key elements: (1) clients with recurring and complex problems; (2) a comprehensive array of services, including health, mental health, personal care, and social services; and (3) an integrating mechanism. Morrison also suggests that case management is a strategy that shows great promise for promoting continuity of care. This strategy involves collaborative multidisciplinary care that includes assessment, community involvement, arranging and monitoring services, and education. Although it has been suggested that case management may reduce the cost of care for HIV or AIDS patients while concurrently enhancing their quality of life, empirical studies are lacking in this area.

Volunteer organizations have also emerged in response to the epidemic. Many provide peer support, advocacy, and companionship for persons with HIV. One well-known example has been the Shanti project, funded by the City of San Francisco to provide psychosocial services to persons with HIV and their families, friends, and loved ones. Shanti provided a practical support program and an emotional support program in addition to a residence and a counseling program at San Francisco General Hospital. Volunteers received a formal 40-hour training program (Batki 1990).

In addition to case management and other support interventions, investigators have examined the effects of various nonpharmacologic and cognitive behavioral interventions on psychological mood. In a controlled study, 50 men with AIDS were assigned either to a control group or to a cognitive–behavioral intervention that included training in stress management, relaxation, problem-solving skills, and coping styles. The men who participated in the cognitive–behavioral intervention reported greater reductions in anxiety and depression than those in the control group. In another study, 47 asymptomatic men were assigned randomly to stress management or to a measurement-only control group. Measurements were taken three days before and one week after notification. Seropositive subjects in the measurement-only group showed significant increases in depression and slight decreases in CD4 lymphocyte counts when comparing the three-days-before to the one-week-after measurements. The group who received stress management showed a buffering of both depression score and CD4 level decreases. Controlled studies of exercise and weight training also showed significant decreases in depression for those in the experimental groups (Chesney & Folkman 1994).

Chesney and Folkman (1994) reported the findings of a study of 24 HIV-positive and 20 HIV-negative men to evaluate the effects of a Coping Effectiveness Training (CET) intervention. The CET emphasizes fitting the coping strategy to the characterizations of each stress situation. This training included problem-focused and adaptive emotion-focused coping strategies. Individuals were trained to appraise situations and to use problem-focused coping when there are changeable aspects of the situation but adaptive emotion-focused coping for the unchangeable aspects of situations. Another aspect of CET was teaching participants to match the type of social support sought to the demands of the stressor and the resources of the provider of support. In this study, each subject was assigned to one of four groups: HIV-positive CET, HIV-positive waiting list, HIV-negative CET, or HIV-negative waiting list. Results indicate that CET is likely to be effective in improving coping, depression, and morale among both HIV-positive and HIV-negative subjects. The authors suggest that this was due to a reduction in self-blame coping in the treatment group (Chesney & Folkman 1994).

Although the development of ambulatory and community-based care has reduced the number and length of hospital stays (Morrison 1993), effective methods of treatment for inpatients are also being explored. Strain and Fulop (1990) describe AIDS cluster units and compare them to the "scatter bed" approach. Systematic studies are needed to evaluate the benefits and disadvantages of both approaches. Strain and Fulop (1990) indicate that cluster units offer psychosocial advantages and the organizational potential available in an inpatient psychiatric unit. These units can employ specially trained staff, emphasize biopsychosocial assessment, and offer ongoing specialized training; as a result, they can enhance the patients' quality of life during hospitalization. However, the cluster unit can also promote isolation, stigmatization, and exposure to fatal illness and death. The concept of an HIV–AIDS care team might enhance coordination of treatment among the various disciplines that provide care to such patients (Ostrow et al. 1990).

Morrison (1993) reminds us of the lack of data illuminating the care and service needs of individuals with HIV as they progress through the clinical course of the disease, or with respect to their unique cultural, geographic, economic, and social characteristics. Data are also lacking regarding the effectiveness of the types of services currently being offered or the systems and programs being developed. Given the lack of empirical knowledge and the limited and tenuous funding for which mental health needs compete with other needs as basic as housing, child care, and home care, it is likely that efforts to create a responsive system to address the psychosocial needs of individuals with HIV will pose a challenge to researchers, policy makers, and clinicians for quite some time.

Throughout the 1980s and the early 1990s, the HIV–AIDS epidemic in the United State represented a health-care problem that was, in important ways, new and sometimes unique, engendering a pattern of "AIDS particularism" in response to those needs. The rapid emergence and growth of the epidemic, the initial lack of medical knowledge about and treatments for the disease, its concentration among relatively young and active individuals, its association with emotionally charged sexual and drug-use behavior, and the almost uniquely stigmatizing impact of diagnosis in the epidemic's early years were among the factors that led to this pattern of particularism. In the late 1990s, as more effective treatments were introduced and public knowledge about HIV became more sophisticated, there was a trend toward "normalization" of AIDS with respect to policies, health-care delivery systems, and other aspects of care. In many respects, the mental health problems presented by HIV-affected individuals are similar to those of others with severe chronic illness and to those of others with similar social circumstances and comorbidities, which may include preexisting psychiatric conditions or substance abuse. Nevertheless, HIV–AIDS remains a distinctive challenge for mental health professionals who must assist HIV-affected persons to cope constructively with the distress of receiving what can be a devastating diagnosis; help them manage social stigma and strained relationships that remain significant risks; aid them in managing the periodic medical crises and decline in functional abilities, which continue to be prevalent although they may be long-delayed with effective therapy; and work with those who are stressed by HIV-related caregiving responsibilities. Despite medical progress in the war on AIDS, these will continue to be major challenges for human services workers for years to come.

30

Cultural Diversity and
Mental Health Treatment

David T. Takeuchi, Edwina Uehara,
& Gloria Maramba

This chapter examines cultural issues in the treatment of ethnic minorities who
have mental health problems. It presents data on the use of mental health services by ethnic minorities, including considerations of access to services, use of
services, and efforts to develop more culturally responsive services. Empirical
studies have found that ethnic and language match are related to a decrease in
dropout rate and an increase in utilization of services by ethnic minorities. The
authors describe a number of culturally competent programs and then, in the second part of the chapter, broaden the perspective to examine how recent trends
in mental health services can conflict with the goal of developing multicultural
mental health service systems. This conflict is attributed to three tendencies: (1)
endorsing etiologies of mental illness that stress biological over social and cultural
causes; (2) seeing culture as fixed, historical, and autonomous; and (3) overlook-
ing the substantial heterogeneity in socioeconomic status and stress-related life
experiences within specific ethnic groups. This chapter also discusses the societal functions of mental health services, contrasting the social control perspective
with views of mental health services either as complementary institutions to the
marketplace or as compensatory mechanisms for the distribution of resources.
Mental health services might accomplish all of these functions, but the question
of how to prioritize them is critical to social policy. Finally, the authors summarize three service models that emphasize different goals: the clinical services
model, the social welfare model, and the empowerment model. The juxtaposition of these models raises a fundamental question: How broadly is our society
willing to define the arena of public responsibility for mental health?

By the year 2025, it is expected that 35% of the U.S. adult population will be from
racial and ethnic minority groups. The percentage for children will be even higher:
racial and ethnic minorities will comprise 48% of all children residing in the United
States (Lewit & Baker 1994). Should these projections hold true, it will represent
a radical departure from the population characteristics of the early 1900s. At the
turn of the twentieth century and continuing until the 1950s, racial and ethnic minority groups (consisting primarily of African Americans) represented about 10%
of the adult and 12% of the child population. It should be noted that the white population was fairly diverse itself during this period, as 10% of the population was
foreign-born (U.S. Bureau of the Census 1975). Between 1950 and 1990, the U.S.
population became increasingly more racially and culturally diverse. By 1990, for
example, 31% of children and 23% of adults were from ethnic minority groups

(Hollman 1993). Although some of this increase can be attributed to the changes in the manner in which the U.S. Census defined racial categories (e.g., by creating "Hispanic" and "Asian/Pacific Islander" categories), the increase embodies a real and dramatic change in U.S. demography. In 1990, African Americans were still the largest ethnic minority category, but by 2025 they are projected to be only the second largest, after Latino Americans (Lewit & Baker 1994).

Immigration accounts for a large part of the demographic shift in the United States. Because of various changes in laws and policies over the past two decades, more than ten million people have come to the United States; an increase that matches the rise of immigrant population in the early part of this century. Of course, this figure does not include undocumented migrants, who could number about two million (Muller 1993). Approximately four out of five immigrants have settled in such large urban areas as Los Angeles, Boston, San Francisco, New York, Miami, and Washington, D.C. (Portes & Rumbaut 1990). A major difference between the rise in the immigrant population in the early 1900s and the current increase is the countries of origin. In the early part of the 1900s, most immigrants came from Europe and Canada; the recent immigration has come primarily from Asia and Latin America. Muller (1993) notes that this immigration has led to a level of change in the racial composition unseen since the late seventeenth century, when black slaves became part of the labor force in the South. This radical racial transformation has strong implications not only for the labor force, but also for how social services and health care are delivered to people who may be unaccustomed to Western methods of intervention.

This chapter will examine some attempts by service providers and researchers to examine cultural issues in the treatment of ethnic minorities who have mental health problems. It is unavoidable that the constructs of "race" and "class" come into play in discussions of cultural diversity (Omi & Winant 1994). However, we have attempted to keep most of our discussions about "culture" and treatment issues focused within the boundaries of this chapter. We begin the chapter with a review of the interventions for ethnic minorities that have been developed, what the empirical research suggests about these interventions, and some direction for future research. We conclude with a discussion about the perspectives that shape views about culture and mental health treatment.

Use of Mental Health Services

Access to Services

Statistics from mental hospitals and outpatient clinics have often been used to draw some conclusions pertinent to the access of mental health services among ethnic minorities. That is, the percentage of each group in the hospital or clinic was compared with the population in the United States or in a given community. A higher percentage in treatment was referred to as overrepresentation (sometimes overutilization); a lower percentage as underrepresentation (or underutilization). This use of treatment data has built-in biases such as the questionable assumption that all people who are mentally ill eventually end up in hospitals. However, these types of data analyses were common to assess problems that needed some attention, especially when community epidemiological survey data were not available.

In the early 1900s, African Americans were seen as overrepresented in mental hospitals. The reason for this overrepresentation was often debated, and the interpretation of these data was often shaped by the perspective one had about mental health services. We discuss more of this issue in our concluding section. Data on people admitted into mental hospitals were also used to conclude that immigrants, primarily from Europe, suffered from poorer mental health than native-born residents (Locke, Kramer, & Pasamanick 1960). Mental health hospital records confirmed early speculations that immigrants undergo social and psychological problems as they adapt to American society (Fabrega 1969). The reason for the higher rates ranged from the racist (i.e., ethnic minorities and immigrants were considered inferior) to the social (e.g., ethnic minorities and immigrants endured social problems that accrue because of discrimination in American society) (Wade 1993). A second prevailing theme was that mental health services were another form of a coercive social control agency that was quick to define ethnic minority behavior as deviant (Takeuchi, Bui, & Kim 1993).

Beginning in the 1940s, survey research methods became a more prominent means to collect community samples of treated and untreated respondents for the estimation of the prevalence of mental disorders (Dohrenwend & Dohrenwend 1974b), a trend that continues into the present. Results from community studies on immigrant status and mental health were not as consistently clear as findings from early studies using hospital records. In fact, some studies called into question whether ethnic minorities actually had higher rates of psychopathology than whites (Vega & Rumbaut 1991). On the other hand, community studies have been useful in demonstrating that ethnic minorities, even when the rates of psychopathology are comparable with whites, are often less likely to seek professional treatment for their problems.

People who suffer from some form of mental health problem, regardless of race or ethnicity, are unlikely to seek professional help (Link & Dohrenwend 1980a). When comparisons are made, however, ethnic minority group members are less likely to use mental health services than whites (Leaf et al. 1985). For example, the available evidence suggests that the use of mental health services is quite distinct for African Americans as compared with whites. Broman (1987) found that while African Americans and whites are equally likely to seek some source of professional help (e.g., social services, clergy, mental health services) for their emotional problems, whites are about one and a half times more likely than African Americans to contact a mental health resource.

In addition to a tendency not to seek professional care, ethnic minority groups may disproportionately belong to groups that have limited access to mental health services. Ethnic minorities are found to comprise a high proportion of these high-risk groups. Two examples are the homeless and people who are HIV-positive. Tessler and Dennis (1992) synthesized the results of studies from eight large U.S. cities and found that ethnic minorities were overrepresented in the homeless population. Regional studies tend to support this general finding. In a study of health services utilization of 832 homeless persons randomly selected from 16 homeless shelters in New York City, 71% were African-American, and 24.3% were Hispanic, Asian or Native American (Padgett, Struening, & Andrews 1990). Crystal and colleagues (1986) conducted a study at 14 New York City public shelters. Of the men and women who reported having psychological problems, 84% (6,363) were from ethnic minority groups. Of 248 homeless persons who were randomly selected from 13 emergency shelters in St. Louis, Missouri, 64.9% of the sample were ethnic minorities, all but two of whom were African-American (Morse & Calsyn 1986).

Regarding persons who are HIV-positive, the rates for African Americans and Alaskan Natives increased dramatically by 35% from 1990 to 1992 (Cummings & Dehart 1995). The rates for Hispanics during this time period, although stable, are high compared with whites. Based on a review of the literature, Lamping and Sewitch (1990) report that blacks and Hispanics are disproportionately HIV-infected, relative to their numbers in the general population. Blacks and Hispanics comprise about 40% of all persons with symptomatic HIV infection (Presidential Commission 1988).

In addition to being in high-risk groups, some ethnic minority groups may be severely constrained from seeking professional help. One such constraining factor in gaining needed care is limited (or nonexistent) health insurance coverage. The United States has the most costly health-care system among developed nations (Scheiber & Poullier 1991). A large segment of the American population has found quality health care to be unaffordable. Health insurance is intended to assist Americans in paying for health care, but it is estimated that 37 million Americans are not covered by public or private health insurance (Mechanic & Aiken 1989b). Ethnic minorities comprise a large segment of the uninsured. In a national survey sponsored by the Commonwealth Fund (1995), 14% of white adults reported no health insurance coverage. This proportion is lower than the uninsured rates for African Americans (26%), Latinos (38%), and Asian Americans (23%).

In summary, the rates of mental disorders have been generally used to indicate the need for professional care. Treatment studies tend to show that some ethnic minorities (e.g. African Americans) are overrepresented in mental health facilities and other groups (e.g. Asian Americans) are underrepresented. On the other hand, community studies generally provide a mixed assessment as to whether ethnic minorities are more in need of mental health services. Although these assessments have been inconclusive, community studies have typically found that ethnic minorities demonstrate a reluctance to use professional care. Finally, ethnic minorities may belong to special populations that are unable to access the mental health system or may be financially constrained by inadequate health insurance coverage.

Use of Services

Once ethnic minority consumers navigate the access barriers and enter hospitals or clinics, there is evidence that they receive differential clinical diagnoses. Misdiagnosis could result from mislabeling as "deviant" behavior what is normal in certain cultures. Lopez (1989) used the terms overpathologizing and underpathologizing to classify errors in diagnosis. It is difficult to determine when over- and underpathologizing occur, yet misdiagnoses are relevant to the extent that they determine the type of care received at a mental health facility (Neighbors et al. 1989; Pavkov et al. 1989). In fact, there is evidence that ethnic minority clients receive different types of care. Asian Americans stay in inpatient treatment longer than whites (Snowden & Cheung 1990). African Americans use emergency psychiatric services more than whites (Hu et al. 1991; Snowden & Holschul 1992) and are usually coercively referred (Rosenfield 1984).

That the mental health system may be incompatible with mental needs of ethnic minorities is evidenced by their high dropout rate from service (Sue & McKinney 1975). Dropout is still a good barometer of the responsiveness of mental health services (Sue, Zane, & Young 1994). Some studies have shown this to have diminished in the past decade (see e.g. O'Sullivan et al. 1989; Snowden, Storey, & Clancey 1989), whereas others have shown that a significant level of premature termination by ethnic minorities still exists (see e.g. Sue et al. 1991).

Disparate findings in utilization of services could be a function of regional differences. In an evaluation of two California counties, Hu and associates (1991) analyzed the records of 4,000 of the most severely disturbed and disabled clients. Multivariate models were employed to examine the use of vocational and socialization programs, residential care, partial hospitalization, medication, assessment, and group and individual therapy. The authors also examined psychiatric emergency care and hospitalization, two types of services that indicate a failure of support for the client in the community.

Variations in utilization were found across ethnic groups and across counties. In the first county, African Americans were more likely than whites to receive assessment and medication and were less likely to be hospitalized. In the other county, African Americans were more likely than whites to use emergency services and to be hospitalized. In one county, Asian-American clients participated in a wider range of programs than whites; Latino Americans received medication and individual psychotherapy more than whites; and whites used emergency room and inpatient care services more than Asian-American and Latino-American clients. In the other county, Asian-American and Latino-American clients were more likely than whites to be hospitalized; and Asian-American clients were less likely than whites to be assigned to assessment, partial hospitalization, and residential care.

Researchers and service planners have made recommendations and established many programs in the name of cultural competence. However, the elements of these programs that contribute to cultural competence have not been identified. For example, in a follow-up analysis of a study by Sue and McKinney (1975) that concluded that ethnic minorities were underutilizing community mental health services, O'Sullivan and colleagues (1989) found a significant decrease in the dropout rate of ethnic minorities from mental health clinics. This improvement was attributed to mental health clinics being more culturally responsive to the needs of its ethnic minority clients. However, there was no direct evidence to support this. The next section examines the issue of cultural responsiveness more closely.

Culturally Responsive Services

Spurred by the civil-rights movement of the 1960s and with a supportive federal government in the 1970s, many recommendations were advanced to meet the mental health needs of the ethnic minority community. Sue (1977) recommended a three-pronged approach: (1) within existing services, train mental health providers and hire ethnic specialists; (2) establish parallel services devoted specifically to ethnic minority clientele; and (3) establish nonparallel services specifically designed around the culture of ethnic minority clientele. Similarly, Uba (1982) discussed the pros and cons of training personnel within mainstream organizations, establishing a separate team within mainstream organizations for ethnic minority clients, and establishing physically separate facilities staffed by personnel trained in providing culturally sensitive services. Rogler and associates (1987) used a pyramid structure as a metaphor for necessary changes. At the base of the pyramid are changes involving linguistic accessibility, coordinating with the ethnic community, and creating an atmosphere open to the cultural values of the community. The second layer of the pyramid involves selecting mainstream treatments that fit the ethnic culture. Crowning the pyramid would be the creation of treatments specifically for the ethnic culture. Two themes emerge from these recommendations: (i) increasing cultural competence of mental health staff by training existing personnel or hiring ethnic minorities; and (ii) the need for culturally sensitive programs.

In line with the first theme, psychiatric clinics now employ more ethnic minority service providers. Wu and Windle (1980) found that this is related to an increase in ethnic minority clientele. The recommendation to hire more ethnic minority staff is based on the premise that their presence would facilitate the utilization of services by clients of similar backgrounds. Empirical studies have tested this notion by evaluating whether clients are more likely to use mental health services and experience improved outcome when matched with service providers of similar ethnicity and language ability.

O'Sullivan and Lasso (1992) analyzed records of 161 Hispanic clients in the Washington State Mental Health system. Hispanic clients who received services through an Hispanic community mental health center had a lower dropout rate and received more individual therapy sessions than those who did not receive services from Hispanic staff. Similarly, Blank and colleagues (1994) analyzed the records of 677 Caucasian and African-American clients of a rural community mental health center in Virginia and found that ethnic matching was related to a greater number of appointments made. However, in outcome studies of African Americans, no relationship was found between ethnic match and treatment outcome. Jones (1978, 1982) paired African-American and Caucasian clients with therapists of similar and different ethnicity. After analyzing the therapists' assessment of treatment outcome for all cases, it was determined that outcome did not differ as a function of client–therapist racial matching. Several studies on Asian Americans had similar results. Ethnic match and language match were related to decreased dropout after one session and an increase in the number of sessions, but for the most part ethnic and language match were not related to outcome (Flaskerud & Hu 1994; Flaskerud & Liu 1990, 1991; Fujino, Okazaki, & Young 1994; Ying & Hu 1994).

The largest study of ethnic and language match to date was conducted by Sue and associates (1991). It is an extensive analysis of data from the Los Angeles County outpatient mental health system. Information on over 13,000 African-American, Asian-American, Mexican-American, and Caucasian clients from a five-year period was analyzed. After controlling for sociodemographic and clinical variables, ethnic match and language match still predicted a decrease in dropout and an increase in number of sessions. For clients whose primary language was not English, ethnic match was an important predictor of dropout, number of sessions, and outcome.

In summary, empirical studies have found that ethnic and language match are related to a decrease in dropout rate and an increase in utilization of services by ethnic minorities. For non–English speaking clients, there is evidence that ethnic match is also predictive of improved outcome. These results are encouraging in that they indicate a way to provide services that benefit ethnic minorities. However, they still begged the question: Just what goes on between a client and a therapist of similar ethnicity or language that results in culturally responsive mental health services? Rogler and associates (1987: 566) call linguistic accessibility the "lowest common denominator of cultural sensitivity"; Bernal, Bonilla, and Bellido (1995: 73) describe language as the "carrier of the culture." Similarly, ethnic match facilitates mutual understanding, which is more likely to occur between people who are culturally similar (Rosenberg 1984). Thus, it seems that the traits of ethnicity and language ability are proxies for cultural characteristics. Therefore, matching a client with a service provider in language and ethnicity traits is related more to the complex issue of cultural similarity.

The mental health literature, especially in clinical psychology and psychiatry, presents a number of techniques that can be used by service providers working with ethnic minority consumers. These techniques are related to the second common theme found in recommendations for culturally competent services: the need for culturally competent programs. Some of these techniques are adaptations of Western modalities, others are indigenous techniques taken from ethnic minority cultures, and most fall somewhere in between.

Cuento therapy for Puerto Rican children is a storytelling therapeutic modality that involves the telling of folktales to children in which the characters are presented as peer models. Modeling exercises are then used to reinforce the beliefs, values, and behaviors of characters in the stories (Rogler, Malgady, & Rodriguez 1989). In working with African-American families, Stevenson and Renard (1993) recommend promoting the process of racial socialization in therapy. Racial socialization can be a tool for incorporating strengths of the African-American family into treatment. Examples of African-American family strengths are metaphorical parenting, spirituality, and ways to cope with racism. In overcoming issues of self-disclosure and trust with African Americans, Mehlman (1994) recommends appropriate self-disclosure by the therapist and attention to nonverbal communication.

The South Cove Community Mental Health Center modified Western techniques in recognition of client needs. South Cove was established in response to the lack of bilingual and culturally knowledgeable health and mental health providers in Boston's Chinatown–South Cove area. Form their experience with mostly Chinese-American clients, Western standard practice is modified to include: (1) restraint during intake and directly assigning clients to a therapist who would then take more detailed information from the client; (2) incorporating educational information early in treatment; (3) selectively involving family members in therapy; (4) using short-term therapy; and (5) a conservative use of pharmacotherapy (Lorenzo & Adler 1984). From his work with Asian-American clients, Hong (1988) describes a general family practitioner approach. With this approach, the psychologist provides services to a family in a way similar to that of a family doctor. The therapist is available to all members of the family, either individually or in a group, and is available as needed. Clients are not necessarily seen on a regular basis, and the concept of termination does not apply.

The foregoing examples are just some of the many techniques that have been documented. Although there is some evaluation of the effectiveness of these techniques (see e.g. Malgady, Rogler, & Constantino 1990), for the most part they have yet to be empirically tested. However, there is preliminary evidence that ethnic-specific mental health programs that develop and use culturally responsive techniques have been effective in increasing utilization among certain ethnic minority groups (Bestman 1986; Bobo et al. 1988; Owan 1981). After controlling for the effects of ethnic match and for sociodemographic and clinical variables, Takeuchi, Sue, and Yeh (1995) found that ethnic-specific programs reduced dropout rates and increased utilization of outpatient services among African Americans, Asian Americans, and Mexican Americans. Snowden, Hu, and Jerrel (1995, pers. commun.) also controlled for ethnic match, sociodemographic variables, and clinical variables in a study of African Americans, Asian Americans, and Latino Americans; the authors found that ethnic minority programs were effective in reducing the reliance on emergency services. They also noted that programs that mostly served ethnic minority clients provided more outpatient services but less case management services than programs primarily serving white clients.

Thus, empirical findings are beginning to document some improvement in the use of mental health services by ethnic minorities. Some studies have shown these improvements to be related to program factors other than ethnic and language match. The components of the programs, such as the techniques described here, that account for this improvement have been suggested but not evaluated.

Some scholars propose that the problems encountered by ethnic minority consumers in receiving appropriate care should be placed in a larger social context (Vega & Murphy 1990). For ethnic minority communities in particular, Chin (1993) suggests that the "standard practice" mental health service delivery does not account for world views of other cultures. As an alternative to current service models, Barrera (1982) suggests that priority be given to the social, economic, and political problems of the ethnic minority community rather than simply addressing the needs of the seriously mentally ill. Unfortunately, given the current tendency to reduce rather than increase public mental health services, providers are required to take the more limited view of mental health.

Conceptual Issues in Defining Culture and Mental Health Services

In the first part of this chapter, we selectively discussed some of the research conducted in the field of ethnic minority mental health services. We also examined attempts by mental health systems to analyze and respond to the needs of ethnic minorities. Although there are some outstanding examples of carefully conceptualized service models for specific ethnic groups (see e.g. Bestman 1986), much of the work in this area makes oversimplified assumptions about culture and about mental health services. When definitions for these terms are provided, they tend to be perfunctory in nature; moreover, assumptions about the fundamental purposes of services – for the individual, the community, and society – are rarely made explicit.

This lack of clarity and precision about the goals and purposes of multicultural mental health services has made it difficult to establish realistic service parameters and evaluation criteria (Vega & Murphy 1990: 9). Moreover, we suggest, it has failed to provide adequate guidance to advocates in analyzing the potential conflict between multicultural services and certain trends in the mainstream mental health service system. Thus, we begin this half of the chapter by summarizing trends in mental health services that, at some level, conflict with a commitment to develop multicultural mental health service systems. These trends include: (a) a tendency to favor etiological models of mental illness that stress common human biological causes over diverse cultural and social factors; (b) a tendency to reify the construct of "culture" – that is, to see culture as fixed, historical, and autonomous from social structure; and (c) a tendency to overlook the substantial heterogeneity in socioeconomic status and stress-related life experiences among specific ethnic groups in favor of amalgamating them under four large ethnic categories (i.e., African Americans, Asian Americans, American Indians and Alaskan Natives, and Latino Americans).

Conflicting Trends in Mental Health

Biological and Social Origins of Mental Illness. Psychiatrists have played a historically dominant role in setting the parameters of mental health as a subspecialty of medicine and defining the content of psychiatric disorders (Millon & Klerman 1986). As a result, mental health has been studied primarily from a nonnormative perspective. Marsella and colleagues (1985) note that there is a tendency in the mental health field to overlook variation in the expression of mental disorder when developing nosological categories. Early studies on minority mental health were derived primarily from clinically based studies and were rooted in a disease model (Fabrega 1990). More recently, a return to biological explanations of mental illness has further discouraged the search for social origins (Kleinman 1988).

In essence, the idea of a cross-cultural perspective on mental health services conflicts with the tendency in the field to adopt biological models of mental illness. The assumption underlying biological models is that concepts and measurement of mental health and illness are uniform from one cultural group to another. It is often assumed that psychiatric symptoms or syndromes are universally distributed and uniformly manifested. This assumption is unwarranted since groups vary in how they define such constructs as "distress," "normality," and "abnormality." These variations affect definitions of mental health and mental illness, expressions of psychopathology, and coping mechanisms (Marsella 1982). Without adequate attention to cultural variations in health and psychopathology, "multicultural" programs may be constrained in meeting the needs of minority communities. As Vega and Rumbaut (1991) suggest, the challenge for the mental health field is to understand how best to parcel out cultural influences to achieve more accurate measurement, understanding, and treatment of psychiatric problems.

Reification of "Culture." Westen (1985) focuses on the problematic nature of culture theory by differentiating between cognitive anthropologists, for

whom shared meaning systems are the essential elements of culture, and ecological anthropologists, for whom culture is firmly anchored in the material world of
social structures – including power and authority structures. The mental health
services field has tended to adopt the cognitive or "ideal" perspective, viewing
culture essentially as historically bound, autonomous from social structure, and
"located in the realm of expectations, values, ideas and belief systems" (Jayasuriya
1992: 41).

In many respects, a highly cognitive view of culture is both naive and static,
and it fails to capture the lived reality of culture as a form of cultural practice
(Westen 1985). As a system of symbolic meanings, culture is circumscribed by
social factors and institutional constraints, and it cannot be divorced from considerations of power (Jayasuriya 1992). From this perspective, the changing cultural
patterns of ethnic minority groups are inextricably linked to the structural limitations they encounter as the result of discrimination. Ethnic minorities are more
likely to face limited access to valued social roles and statuses and to face constraints on the successful fulfillment of ordinary role requirements such as that of
parent or spouse (Vega & Rumbaut 1991: 374). Within groups, cultural expressions of values and behavior will vary along status dimensions such as gender,
sexual orientation, and socioeconomic status. Clearly, mental health service programs that assume uniformity of cultural values and beliefs among the members
of ethnic minority communities run the risk of stereotyping consumers. Perhaps
even worse, programs that seek to address the cultural concerns of ethnic minority
communities – with*out* attending to issues of power, oppression, and discrimination – run the risk of trivializing key aspects of ethnic minority culture as its
participants live and experience it.

**Socioeconomic Status and Stress-Related Life Experiences of Ethnic
Groups.** Ethnic minority status has often been considered a general proxy for life
stress. Indeed, analysts often conceive of minority status itself as a stressor, independent of socioeconomic and demographic predictors of mental health problems
(Vega & Rumbaut 1991). Theoretically at least, stressors are important to mental
health because they increase the risk of experiencing certain psychiatric symptoms and disorders. As suggested earlier, however, differences across specific
ethnic groups in stress-related life conditions and experiences (such as poverty,
war-related physical and emotional trauma, and social role discontinuities) are
substantial, and they warrant more careful attention by service planners. Among
foreign-born members of ethnic groups, for example, a general distinction can be
made between "immigrants," who must cope with substantial life change upon
settling in a new country, and "refugees," who in addition tend to experience more
threat, more trauma, and less control over the circumstances surrounding their exit
from countries of origin. Such variations in life history imply substantially different mental health service needs (Vega & Rumbaut 1991).

Differences in the need for mental health services can be as striking *within* as they are across the four catchall ethnic minority categories. For example, the category, "Asian Americans" actually encompasses a number of specific ethnic groups, including native-born Chinese and Japanese, Chinese and Korean immigrants, and Cambodian and Hmong refugees. These groups differ substantially in levels of education and income, as well as in terms of their experiences of dislocation, trauma, and social role disruption. In tailoring services to the specific needs of ethnic minority clients, the utility of such general population categories as "Asians/ Pacific Islanders," "Latino Americans," "African Americans," and "Native Americans" must be carefully scrutinized. These categories may conceal more than they reveal.

Assumptions about the Goals and Purposes of Mental Health Programs

Potential conflicts between multicultural service goals and mainstream mental health trends continue at the level of service system assumptions. In this section, we review two basic dimensions along which such conflicts are possible: (1) assumptions about the essential societal functions of mental health services, and (2) assumptions about the basic purposes and scope of services for the individual.

In improving services for ethnic minority consumers, understanding how and what service elements contribute to specific outcomes for individuals is clearly important. While "services" and "programs" may be presumed to be the most important intervening variables that make a desired difference for clients, surprisingly little thought has gone into conceptualizing these elements. Few service models and evaluation studies of ethnic-specific services adopt a clear theoretical perspective for predicting "effective services" and explaining their effects on specific clients (Rosenfield 1992b). In mental health services research, for example, "service use" is often treated as a kind of theoretical black box. Investigators accept terms and definitions as they already exist in the service system's information system (e.g., total hours of individual treatment, group treatment, case management, crisis intervention), even though existing definitions are driven more by reimbursement and billing needs than by theoretical or clinical concerns. For advocates of culturally appropriate services, accepting "services" and "service units" as they are typically defined is problematic for a number of reasons. For example, this precludes the consideration of alternative (culturally appropriate) services and focuses attention on change strategies targeted to the individual rather than the environment.

Societal Functions of Mental Health Services. The importance of clarifying the basic purposes of mental health services in contemporary society is exemplified by the service use statistics presented earlier in this chapter: Is the relatively high use of mental health services by some ethnic minority groups an indicator of improved service access, of excessive social control, or of both? How such phenomena are appraised – indeed, just what constitutes "appropriate service use" and "positive" service use outcomes – is fundamentally shaped by our assumptions about the purposes or functions of mental health services in society. Clarity about these assumptions is necessary for appropriate service improvement and advocacy. The extent to which extensive service use is positive or negative is a particularly controversial subject with respect to ethnic minorities, where issues of discrimination and relative lack of political and economic power come into play.

One helpful way to examine this issue is through a political economy perspective. As the term implies, "political economy refers to the interplay between politics and economics – that is, how the institutions and transactions of each sphere impact on the other" (Rochefort 1987: 101). To take a political economy perspective means we view mental health services as an element in the social welfare system, and social welfare in turn is viewed as one of several major institutions within a market-centered society (Galper 1975; Martin & Zald 1981; Romanyshyn 1971). In addition, Rochefort (1987: 191) suggests that political economy analysts search for a "macro, holistic understanding of the welfare state that encompasses its organization, funding, and effects on the social order." Using a political economy framework is not new: a number of social scientists have conceptualized mental health services in such terms (see e.g. Aviram 1990; Gummer 1988; Rochefort 1987). For present purposes, however, the important point is to recognize that there are different political and theoretical stances that can be taken on the relationship between the market economy and mental health services. These perspectives in turn shape such critical factors as how "good" client and system outcomes are defined. Here, we address three of these perspectives.

We can view mental health services as essentially a means to control deviant groups (the poor, the chronically mentally ill, and ethnic or racial minorities). In this *social control* perspective, mental health services is one of several social institutions (including law enforcement) that operate to facilitate smoother running of the market, both by fostering and maintaining order and conformity (Aviram 1990: 83) and by creating and maintaining the secondary labor market. From this perspective, the most important outcomes of mental health services are those concerned with the containment of persons with mental illness – particularly those whose behavior has been deemed by "social control agents" to be dangerous, confrontative, or otherwise inappropriate. The social control perspective can be seen from two vantage points. It can be seen from the vantage of protecting society (conservative, status quo–oriented) or from a view of protecting the socially controlled (more reform- or change-oriented). From the first vantage point, major outcome questions include: Do services succeed at restraining or containing clients perceived as dangerous, disruptive, or otherwise offensive to the general public? Do services succeed at changing those offensive client behaviors and at socializing clients to conform to norms of public behavior? From the second view, major outcome questions revolve around issues of unjust treatment of clients – especially those who enter the mental health system through involuntary commitment or are served in relatively restricted settings.

A second view sees mental health services as an essentially *complementary* institution to the marketplace, one whose primary function is to improve people's ability to compete and perform adequately within the labor market. From this perspective, the most important outcomes of service are associated with improvements in clients' ability to compete and perform in the labor market and to become and remain as economically self-sufficient as possible. Have mental health services been effective at achieving such service objectives as improving client social and vocational skills? Increasing client wage levels? Moving clients from welfare dependency to independent work situations?

A third view proposes that services can serve as a *compensatory* mechanism for the distribution of resources. Contrary to the first two perspectives, we could view mental health services primarily as providing alternatives to market mechanisms for the distribution of resources (Gummer 1988: 263). From this perspective, the general criterion for service effectiveness is concerned with distributional equity and is relatively simple and straightforward (though interpretations of "equity" are anything but): Do mental health services "contribute to a more equal distribution of society's resources" (Gummer 1988: 263)? We should add that, in ethnic minority communities, the question of equity has often been viewed at the level of the individual consumer. In fact, much of the current debate about whether public mental health expenditures should be distributed on a "parity" or an "equity" basis uses the ethnic population or community as a unit of comparison.

In reality, mental health services are seen as means to accomplish some or all of these functions, and few would argue that one or another totally predominates (Aviram 1990). As Aviram suggests, it is probably unrealistic to assume that Americans would accept a service system that does not have some element of social control. Some tension between these functions is evident, however, and it is also unrealistic to presume that the mental health service system can simultaneously optimize all three. The question of how to prioritize these functions is thus paramount. This is particularly critical in the current climate of reduced public resources for community mental health services and a return to more narrowly circumscribed, medicalized models of practice (Aviram 1990).

Basic Purposes of Services vis-à-vis the Individual

The term "services" implies work performed and the application of some technology that is useful or beneficial to the client. However, just what constitutes a "benefit" – that is, what the desired goals and outcomes might be for the mental health client – is subject to some debate. At the risk of oversimplifying the distinctions among them, we summarize three service models that emphasize somewhat different goals: the clinical services model, the social welfare model, and the empowerment model. These are not necessarily mutually exclusive (e.g., the social welfare and empowerment models can encompass clinical services), but once again, differences among these models have important consequences for how mental health services are defined, planned, and evaluated.

Under the *clinical services* model, the primary purpose of mental health services is seen as alleviating the symptoms or causes of psychological or psychiatric distress experienced by the individual client or patient, reflecting what many analysts refer to as a "medical model" approach (see e.g. Aviram 1990). This model emphasizes the individual as the focus of service delivery and change, and it views psychiatric interventions as the major means of intervention. Services emphasized include: psychiatric assessments; symptom control through drug therapy; and individual, family, and group therapy.

Within the *social welfare* model, the problems that mental health services address – while encompassing clinical services – also include a broader range of such community living issues as poverty, homelessness and the lack of affordable housing, and inaccessibility to primary medical care. From the social welfare model, the majority of problems consumers experience are seen less in terms of individual-level causes and more as social structural in nature (Aviram 1990; Neighbors 1990).

From an *empowerment* model perspective, mental health services can best help consumers by addressing the psychological, economic, political, and social barriers that create conditions of relative powerlessness and that prevent individual and group empowerment (Rosenfield 1992b). Empowerment models can encompass elements of the clinical and social welfare models, yet they also attempt to increase control over services and provide the consumer with access to economic and other resources through consciousness raising, legislative advocacy, group and community organizing, program development, and administrative skills. This model also most closely fits with consumer-run mental health programs and alternative mental health systems (Chamberlin 1977).

The clinical, social welfare, and empowerment models differ in terms of the scope of desired goals and services, and their juxtaposition raises a fundamental question: As a society, how broadly are we willing to define the arena of public responsibility for mental health? This question is especially critical for members of ethnic minority communities, many of whom have few viable treatment alternatives to publicly funded services (Vega & Murphy 1990).

As Aviram (1990: 74) notes, the restricted focus of the clinical model fits well in many ways with contemporary U.S. welfare ideology, and there is a tendency in the United States to interpret the problems of those with mental illness in these terms. However, some analysts question the benefit of medicalized service approaches to ethnic minorities. For example, Neighbors (1990) points out that the narrower clinical approach is less appropriate for African Americans than wider approaches that address problems disproportionately shared by that group and stemming from social structural – and not individual pathological – causes. Vega and Murphy concur, noting that the community mental health services field has "returned to a very narrow disease model of mental illness at the very moment that social models of health are most needed" (Vega & Murphy 1990: 2).

Conclusion

As the United States enters a new decade and new century, tensions are likely to increase between the demands for meeting the social and health care needs of a changing population and the need to standardize care so that services become more efficient and cost-effective. Cultural factors are critical to understand access to mental health services, the proper screening and diagnoses that lead to treatment, and the actual effectiveness of treatment, but many of the relevant policy decisions will be based on the assumptions made about services and models of service delivery. Sociologists can play an important role in documenting how these tensions are resolved over time and whether cultural factors are ignored or incorporated into service delivery models.

31

Mental Health Systems in Cross-Cultural Context

Harriet P. Lefley

Whereas the previous chapter examined issues of culture within a predominately American framework, Lefley here focuses on issues of service delivery across countries. Concepts of mental health, distinctions between mental health and mental illness, and distinctions between mental and physical illness are highly variable across cultures. Lefley examines the cultural contexts that shape the definition of mental health and mental illness. She describes the relationship between culture and the experience of stress and a variety of culture-bound syndromes. The second part of the chapter turns to empirical findings from international research. The third part of the paper focuses on cultural diversity in mental health service systems, describing the important role of social stressors, ethnicity, and minority or refugee status. Traditional and biomedical healing systems are contrasted, and the Italian experiment to improve the quality of life of persons with mental illness is described. Self-help groups and the consumer movement have also emerged internationally. The chapter concludes by considering the future of mental health services as well as the merging of Western concepts with those of the developing world. What are some of the specific ways in which Western systems of care would benefit by incorporating alternative perspectives of mental health and care?

In this chapter we deal with culture as a major variable in the conceptualization, development, and administration of mental health systems. The study of culture has typically referred to the beliefs, values, symbolic meanings, and normative behavioral practices of a specific human group. But in social science research today, cultural groups are usually categorized and compared along axes such as Western versus non-Western or modern versus traditional. In recent years there has been increasing attention given to differentiating individualistic cultures, which give primacy to individual rights, from collectivist or sociocentric cultures, which focus on group loyalties and social role obligations (Triandis 1995). These respective modes of categorization in many ways tend to distinguish the wealthier, industrialized nations from the developing world. Thus they represent differences not only in world view and norms, but also in resources available for the provision and structure of health care. Within nation states, modal cultural attitudes and intergroup differences may shape the accessibility, appropriateness, and effectiveness of services for population subgroups such as racial or ethnic minorities (Takeuchi & Uehara 1996).

Cultural belief systems inform whether deviant behaviors are identified and classified as illness, the concepts of etiology and cure, and the designation of appropriate healers. In any cultural system, modal concepts of mental illness, help-seeking paths, and utilization patterns are intermeshed with the organization and structure of service delivery systems. Belief systems, value orientations, religious and medical practices, social organization, and family structure are related to the modes of developing and delivering services to persons identified as needing interventions. Additionally, a culture's assessed needs for social control and order, its prevailing political philosophies and legal protections, and its economic organization and resources all have had a significant impact on the structure of mental health service delivery systems (Lefley 1994).

Concepts of mental health, distinctions between mental health and mental illness, and distinctions between mental and physical illness are highly variable across cultures. These conceptualizations generally determine the nature of the resources devoted to their service. Almost all cultures in the world, from tribal units to nation states, recognize an officially sanctioned Western medical and mental health system. The people in these nations, and often the governments themselves, also support a variety of traditional healing systems. Most of these systems focus on the curing of illness or disability rather than on the diffuse concept of promoting mental health.

Cultural Context of Defining Mental Health

Psychiatrists associated with the Division of Mental Health of the World Health Organization (WHO) remind us that the WHO Constitution merges the definitions of health and mental health as "a state of complete physical, mental and social well-being, not merely the absence of disease" (Kuyken & Orley 1994: 3). Throughout the world, personal well-being is largely contingent on economic survival and on family and societal stability. Given these essentials, the source and expression of well-being are affected by the interactions of an individual's personal characteristics with at least three interrelated variables. These involve cultural norms and expectations, the status of the population subgroup of which an individual is a member, and the social stability of that subgroup within the dominant culture.

We have noted that cultures vary in individualism versus a sociocentric or collectivist orientation. These orientations also entail the extent to which individuals value personal autonomy and devalue dependency. Anthropologist Francis Hsu (1972) has referred to fear of dependency as the American core value. Cultural norms and social structures that promote values of independence versus interdependence, and that denigrate the status of dependency, have particular relevance to concepts of mental health and treatment of mental illness in any society.

In defining mental health, cultures have ideal role types as well as normative expectations that may generate a sense of well-being in very different individuals under very different conditions. Other things being equal, cultural norms determine whether the traits of submissiveness or assertiveness are likely to be linked with a sense of well-being in women. Men who are highly competitive may be revered in one setting and despised in another. There may be very different thresholds for physical well-being in agrarian versus industrial economies, for persons engaged in manual versus cognitive labor, or for cultures where somatization of emotional states is a normative pattern of behavior (Kleinman & Good 1985).

The Basic Behavioral Science Task Force of the National Advisory Mental Health Council (NAMHC 1996) has focused on these interactions of individual characteristics and cultural context. They note the important role of culture in grounding and identifying one's sense of self; in subjective interpretations of emotional states (including the experience and communication of symptoms of depression); in motivations for success (on behalf of self or for others); and in fundamental attributions, that is, ways of explaining the behavior of others. "Cross-cultural research has shown that in cultures that stress interdependence, people tend to explain others' actions in terms of situational factors rather than internal or personal factors" (NAMHC 1996: 724). This is a mode of externalizing the causes of unfortunate events or behaviors, rather than perceiving deficits in individuals. As we shall later see, cultural differences in attribution may have great power in explaining differential responses to mental illness, as well as different prognoses, in various parts of the world.

Individual characteristics also interact with social roles in particular cultural contexts. In the United States, a large literature suggests that the mental health of members of at least two subpopulations – minority groups and women – is affected by racism and sexism in the dominant culture (Willie et al. 1995). Throughout the world, characteristics such as socioeconomic status, gender, age, color, ethnicity, religion, sexual orientation, minority status – and, in some places, tribal or caste status or immigration status – affect not only role definitions but also self-evaluation, employment opportunities, and quality of life. These social perceptions are clearly interactive with the preexisting strains and stigmas of mental illness. In any culture and with most disorders, whether medical or psychiatric, insults to one's mental health may adversely affect an existing vulnerability or dysfunction.

Within the same cultural groups, mental health may also be related to levels of acculturation and family stability. A study of the Miccosukee and Seminole tribes of Florida, both of the same ethnolinguistic group, compared the psychological well-being of members distinguished by levels of acculturation (English speaking ability, years of formal education, maintenance of traditional religious rituals and traditional housing, etc.). Both mothers and children who were less acculturated showed healthier self-concept than their more acculturated counterparts. This finding was correlative with social disintegration in the more acculturated tribal group owing to loss of old norms and eroded family structure (Lefley 1982). Other studies have shown, however, that both low and high levels of acculturation are associated with poorer mental health, whereas the integration of traditional and acculturative skills yields maximum mental health benefits (Szapocznik et al. 1984).

The findings suggest that, with indigenous groups who have suffered culture loss, therapeutic interventions reaffirming traditional identity may be important. For all groups struggling to succeed in the mainstream society, there are strong indicators for bicultural effectiveness training (Szapocznik et al. 1984).

Cultural Context of Defining Mental Illness

There is now ample empirical evidence to go beyond earlier debates about the transcultural validity of mental illness as a construct (Gorenstein 1984). As Horwitz (1982a) has noted, every culture recognizes forms of negatively valued deviant behaviors that are distinguished from merely antisocial behaviors by their interpersonal incomprehensibility within that cultural idiom. The major issues are whether certain classes of deviant behaviors are manifested uniformly, with similar etiologies and comparable distributions across cultures, and whether they can be treated with the same technologies. To answer some of these questions, increasing attention is being devoted to epidemiology, to biological and genetic parameters, and to analysis of cultural factors in diagnosis and treatment (Al-Issa 1995; Jablensky et al. 1991; Mezzich et al. 1996; Sartorius et al. 1993).

Lin (1996) points out that anthropological research has disproved earlier speculations that psychotic conditions derive from the pressures of civilization and therefore are unlikely to be found among non-Western or more "primitive" populations. "Acute psychotic breakdowns as well as conditions characterized by chronic, often progressively deteriorating, nonorganic psychotic and asocial behavioral patterns have not only been identified in all contemporary Western and non-Western urban societies, but also in tribal villages . . . and among hunter-gatherer groups . . . living in remote mountainous areas . . . or on isolated Pacific islands" (1996: 50).

Universal prevalence of syndromes does not mean universal modes of recognition and labeling. The major mental illnesses are characterized by recognizable impairments of cognition and affect. Although they may not differ in biological substrates, symptoms may be manifested differently and evoke different social reactions. The syndromes may be recognized as disordered states beyond personal volition or control and yet evoke different interpretations of their meaning, source, temporal nature, and curability. Because schizophrenia is the most highly studied psychiatric disorder, the literature is filled with proliferating research findings from epidemiology, neuroradiology, neuropathology, neurochemistry, hematology, pharmacology, and genetics – all indicating biological parameters of what was once considered a psychogenic or sociogenic disorder (Hirsch & Weinberger 1996). Similar evidence is accumulating with respect to bipolar disorder, major endogenous depression, obsessive-compulsive disorders, and some other DSM-IV Axis I disorders as well (Tasman, Kay, & Lieberman 1997). These Axis I diagnoses may ultimately turn out to be heterogeneous syndromes rather than single disease entities, and their symptoms may vary in patterning and virulence as a function of environmental and cultural influences (Mezzich et al. 1996).

Despite the burgeoning biogenetic and epidemiological research findings, it is important to acknowledge the scope and variability of disorders found in our diagnostic and statistical manuals. Some social scientists still dispute the extent to which behavioral disorders are true disease entities or simply deviations from a cultural norm (Gaines 1992). They are concerned about the relationship of mental health to mental illness and whether these constructs refer to continuous or dichotomous variables – that is, whether *anyone* may decompensate given sufficient stress or whether a prior vulnerability for a specific mental disorder is required.

Culture and Stress

Many experts today tend to accept the diathesis–stress hypothesis in the case of major psychiatric diagnoses with known biological and genetic parameters, such as schizophrenia, bipolar disorder, or obsessive-compulsive disorder. That is, stressful environmental events are presumed to trigger a biological vulnerability to a specific condition. Nevertheless, many researchers claim that biological vulnerability alone is the first and only necessary cause for a neurodevelopmental disorder (Hirsch & Weinberger 1996). Moreover, if stress is involved in etiology then the stressful environment may be *in utero,* or in physical conditions that affect uterine development, rather than in the psychosocial environment or interpersonal interactions. There is ample presumptive evidence that war, famine, and flu virus may affect the fetal development of the person who in later years develops schizophrenia (Hirsch & Weinberger 1996; Tasman et al. 1997).

A major question today involves the interactions of the social and cultural environment with the expression of a biological vulnerability, and the contributions of these interactions to relapse (Warner 1994). To what extent do social pressures affect decompensation and hospitalization rates? Leff's (1988) overview of studies of Asian and West Indian immigrants to the United Kingdom concluded that both groups show above-average levels of admissions for schizophrenia to psychiatric hospitals. This is not reflected in higher prevalence data in the community nor in the home countries. "Hence, we have solid evidence that the high level of schizophrenia in Asian immigrants to the U.K. is not due to a constitutional liability to develop that condition. The alternative explanations, as with any immigrant group, are selective migration and the stress of living in an alien country" (Leff 1988: 205).

In the United States, on the other hand, the highest rates of psychiatric hospital admissions are found among the groups that have been in the country the longest – African Americans and American Indians (NIMH 1987). These groups have been subjected not to the strains of migration but instead to the stresses of long-term discrimination and forced culture loss imposed by the mainstream society. In contrast, there are relatively low rates of hospital admissions but longer duration of hospital stay for the two major immigrant groups – Hispanics and Asians (NIMH 1987). Among the explanations offered are discriminatory police and diagnostic practices that promote psychiatric labels for African Americans and American Indians. It has also been suggested that Asians and Hispanics may keep patients at home until they reach advanced stages of disability, hence their longer lengths of stay (Lefley 1990; Snowden & Cheung 1990).

For individuals with long-term mental illness, the role of stressful life events in relapse is still unclear. There is some international research suggesting that stressful life events are likely to precede acute episodes of schizophrenia (Day et al. 1987). However, the nature of the stress appears to be highly variable. Many stressors are idiosyncratic, and existential stressors such as economic problems or death of a loved one are usually not preventable. Other research has failed to confirm that life events triggered relapse in persons with long-term schizophrenia, whereas withdrawal from medication clearly did (Hirsch et al. 1996). Similarly, one prospective study indicated that life events stress had no effect on the recurrence of primary affective disorder (Pardoen et al. 1996). Another study of recurrent clinical depression showed that relapse occurred an average of seven months after the stressful life event (Monroe et al. 1996).

Culture-Bound Syndromes

In any discussion of epidemiology and culture, it is important to distinguish between (a) the universality of certain diagnostic syndromes demonstrated by cross-national studies and (b) the meanings attached to these syndromes by different populations (Gaine 1992; Mezzich et al. 1996). The cross-cultural literature has also reported seemingly unique syndromes, that is, patterned clusters of disordered or psychotic behaviors that seem to be found only in specific cultural settings (Hughes 1996). The following are examples of some of the better-known culture-bound syndromes, the population affected, and some of the hypotheses advanced regarding nosological characteristics and possible antecedents.

> *Koro* – Southern China, Southeast Asia, India. This is a mental disturbance characterized by a man's belief that his penis is shrinking into his abdomen. Now considered an acute anxiety state associated with sexual dysfunction.
>
> *Windigo psychosis* – Cree Eskimos and Ojibwa of Canada; characterized by cannibalistic delusions. Victim believes he has been transformed into a giant monster that eats human flesh. Delusion is possibly derived from tribal mythology reflecting survival struggle in Arctic.
>
> *Arctic hysteria* – Polar Eskimos. Person may scream for hours, imitating animal cry, thrashing about on snow nude or partially undresssed. Attributed by some to hypocalcemia or hypervitaminosis A.
>
> *Latah* – Southeast Asia; appears most commonly among women who break into obscenities and echolalia following an event that startles them. They may also follow commands automatically, or repetitively

imitate another person. It has been suggested that latah is an arousal state (possibly located in the amygdala) that may have developed as an adaptive response to snakes. This is a common precipitant of startle response in Malayan and Filipino cultures, where snakebite is a major cause of morbidity.

Susto or *espanto* – Latin-American Indians; a fear state or sudden fright attributed to loss of soul by the action of spirits, the evil eye, or sorcery. Symptoms include weakness, loss of appetite, sleeplessness, nightmares, and trembling, and their frequency in this population has sometimes been attributed to hypoglycemia. Susto may be diagnosed as a brief reactive dissociative disorder, but it cannot be healed by modern psychiatry. The cure for Susto requires a traditional healer whose ministrations will influence the spirits to release the soul and return it to the host body.

Culture-bound syndromes may either form a distinctive class of disordered behaviors or ultimately turn out to be local variants of known psychiatric diagnoses (Hughes 1996). As indicated, some may have biologically based parameters related to local diet, climate, or unique features of the physical environment.

Epidemiology, Diagnosis, and Treatment: Biological and Cultural Aspects

Official mental health systems throughout the world, despite their numerous local distinctions, all tend to honor the diagnostic categories found in the *Diagnostic and Statistical Manual* (DSM-IV) of the American Psychiatric Association (APA 1994), which is now the psychiatric component of the World Health Organization (WHO 1992) International Classification of Diseases (ICD-10). Although psychiatric nomenclature and some Western nosological categories continue to be questioned (Gaines 1992), numerous international studies show agreement on core symptom clusters and comparable incidence rates of major psychiatric disorders such as schizophrenia (Sartorius et al. 1993).

International research also informs us, however, that cultural variables may have a significant impact on the manifestations of psychopathology and the developmental course of illness. The same studies that informed us of panhuman incidence also informed us that the course of mental illness may vary greatly in different parts of the world (Jablensky et al. 1991).

Integrating the Findings of International Research

Most of our knowledge of genetic factors in schizophrenia has come from the Scandinavian countries, where national registers permit researchers to find and interview the biological relatives of adopted-away children whose parents were schizophrenic. "High-risk" studies (comparisons of these offspring with adopted counterparts of nonschizophrenic parents), twin studies (comparing monozygotic and dizygotic twins with concordant or discordant mental illness), and similar research has provided compelling evidence of a genetic factor in schizophrenia and major affective disorders, leading the way to further research on the still unknown mode of genetic transmission.

However, the research also indicates an interplay of epidemiology, genetics, and culture. Despite comparable distributions across nation states, some isolated populations with cultural barriers to intermarriage tend to show elevated levels of particular subtypes of schizophrenia (Goodman 1996) or major affective disorders (Egeland & Hostetter 1983). Cultural factors may also result in masking symptoms that affect the epidemiological picture. Egeland, Hostetter, and Eshleman (1983), for example, noted that – though most epidemiologic studies indicated a ratio of 4 : 1 for unipolar depression over manic depression – the ratio is closer to 1 : 1 in cultures that prohibit alcohol and severely sanction acting-out behaviors. This is because manic episodes in such cultures are easier to identify and less likely to be confused with antisocial or substance-induced behaviors.

The IPSS. The International Pilot Study of Schizophrenia (IPSS) was a WHO-sponsored transcultural investigation to determine whether the same symptom clusters would be similarly diagnosed in widely dispersed areas of the world. The initial research sites were in Colombia, Czechoslovakia, Denmark, India, Nigeria, Taiwan, the United Kingdom, the former Soviet Union, and the United States. Using the same interview tool with 1,202 first-contact patients, psychiatrists in different cultures generally agreed on the diagnostic screening criteria for schizophrenia, apparently confirming a universally recognized disease entity. The epidemiologic picture has been similarly comparable. In a 1990s report to the World Health Assembly, the WHO director-general stated that there were no demonstrable differences in the incidence and prevalence of schizophrenia between developing and developed countries. A uniform annual incidence rate of 0.1 per thousand and prevalence rates of 2 to 4 per thousand for schizophrenia have been reported (Sartorius et al. 1993).

Cultural differences, however, were found in follow-up studies two and five years later. The course of illness was significantly better in the developing world than in the more technologically advanced countries. Good outcome figures ranged from 58% in Nigeria and 51% in India to 7% in Moscow and 6% in Denmark (Sartorius et al. 1986). More current research on first-episode patients in ten countries found a continuing difference in outcome favoring the developing nations (Jablensky et al. 1991). Nearly two thirds (63%) of the patients in the developing world experienced a benign course and full remission, and only 16% suffered impaired social funtioning – compared with 37% remission and 42% functional impairment in the industrialized countries (Warner 1994).

Despite rigorous attempts at control, there is some debate about the equivalence of samples. For example, Warner (1992) has suggested that the IPSS incidence of cases with acute types of schizophrenia (no gradual onset, good premorbid adjustment) was four times as common in the developing-world samples (40% of cases) as in the developed countries (11%). Because acute cases are known to show better rates of recovery than those with slow insidious onset, this difference may indeed have accounted for the better prognosis. However, as the same author has elsewhere noted, the outcome in the developing-world subjects was better, regardless of whether they were acute or insidious in onset. "The general conclusion is unavoidable: . . . The majority of Third World schizophrenic people achieve a favorable outcome. The more urbanized and industrialized the setting, the more malignant becomes the illness" (Warner 1994: 157).

The literature interpreting the findings of more benign outcomes in developing countries postulates a hypothesis of relatively lower stress and higher social support. Common themes are that traditional cultures offer the following: (a) cultural belief systems that externalize causality, freeing the patient and family of blame; (b) greater opportunities for social reintegration and normalized work roles in agrarian economies; and (c) extended kinship networks to buffer the effects of illness on the patients and their caregivers (Leff 1988; Lefley 1990; Lin & Kleinman, 1988).

Different concepts of selfhood, of dependency and autonomy, and of obligations to kin are subsumed under some of these explanatory categories. Waxler (1979) has suggested that psychosis is seen in traditional nonindustrial cultures as a brief temporary aberration, with expectancies that the person will soon recover. In Western, individualistic cultures, even the first episode of mental illness connotes a depreciated personal identity, particularly if it involves psychiatric hospitalization (Estroff 1989). Patients are more likely to deny illness, reject medications, and fight the intrinsic dependency status of mental illness. Paternalistic control and loss of individual autonomy are less of a threat in traditional, family-oriented cultures. Lin and Kleinman (1988) suggest also that, in traditional collectivist cultures, there is less social isolation, a more tolerant family milieu, and extended human resources to buffer family burden as compared with the burdened nuclear family in Western societies. Leff (1988) speculates that such differences in family structure may explain the cultural differences found in another body of research, that on expressed emotion.

The Expressed Emotion (EE) Research.   Prior theoretical models suggesting that defective parenting or family interactions were significant factors in the etiology of schizophrenia have been discounted by the major schizophrenia researchers (see e.g. Hirsch & Weinberger 1996; Leff & Vaughn 1985). The EE research suggests, however, that familial and other interpersonal interactions may have a positive or negative effect on the course of illness. Expressed emotion, an empirical construct derived from the work of George Brown and his associates in London (Brown 1985), is essentially a test score that discriminates types of familial response associated with differential relapse rates for patients. These scores are derived primarily from three scales on the Camberwell Family Interview (Brown 1985): hostility toward the person rather than the behavior, critical comments, and emotional overinvolvement (self-sacrificing or overprotective concern). A cutoff point categorizes families as high or low EE. Numerous studies have demonstrated an association between high EE and shorter time to patient relapse (Lefley 1992). This has held not only for schizophrenia but for affective disorders and a variety of nonpsychiatric physical conditions as well (Leff 1990).

Low EE, on the other hand, seems to be a protective variable for patients with putatively the same level of psychopathology as those in high-EE families (a necessary control in assessing potential for relapse). Despite the emphasis on high EE among some clinicians, it is noteworthy that, in the international research literature, the majority of families of persons with schizophrenia manifest low EE, ranging from 77% in India to 52% in Great Britain (Jenkins & Karno 1992; Lefley 1992). Low EE seems to be normative in traditional cultures, including traditional ethnic groups in the United Kingdom and the United States.

Leff and Vaughn (1985) have described low-EE families as calm, empathic, respectful, and accepting. These characteristics tend to refute stereotypes that disturbed family systems cause schizophrenia and suggest that psychotic behaviors are found in even the most benign family environments. Overviews of research on psychoeducational interventions with families show that high EE may be fairly easily modified to low EE (Lefley 1992).

However, the most comprehensive overviews demonstrate that, regardless of EE levels, education and support for families are major factors in reducing relapse rates (Dixon & Lehman 1996). Also of considerable importance is the finding by McFarlane (1994) that psychoeducational multiple family groups are significantly more effective than single family interventions in deterring relapse. The investigators have attributed this to the sharing of sorrows, resources, and coping strategies, as well as the mutual support afforded by the group experience.

These findings are germane to Leff's (1988) explanation of the interrelationship between family structure and the IPSS and EE findings. In traditional cultures, the extended family offers an emotional and economic buffering mechanism and provides many people who can interact with and support the patient. In the Western nuclear family, there are at most two and often only one major caregiver to provide support, to negotiate the mental health, medical, welfare, and sometimes the criminal justice systems, and to balance the patient's needs against those of other family members. The stresses of caregiving have been well documented in the research on family burden (Greenley 1995; Lefley 1996b). Hostile criticism toward a patient refusing to take medications, or emotional overinvolvement with a depressed and defeated one, may indeed be more likely under these circumstances.

To EE dicoverer Brown (1985), these are normal family reactions. In contrast, the ability of an extended family to offer care with emotional distance, and to share responsibilities when burdens become too difficult, may indeed facilitate lower EE regardless of world view and other factors.

Family Education in Service Systems

In the United States, the majority of patients are discharged to their families (Goldman 1982), and about 40% of white American patients continue to share the same household. Co-residence figures and caregiving responsibilities are considerably higher among African-American, Hispanic, and Asian families (Guarnaccia & Parra 1996; Lefley 1996b). There is now a substantial research literature indicating that family psychoeducation is a powerful tool for alleviating family burden and deterring patient relapse (Dixon & Lehman 1996), particularly in the treatment of such major psychiatric disorders as schizophrenia and bipolar illness. In contrast to traditional family therapies that were based on a premise of family dysfunction, psychoeducational approaches are responsive to families' expressed needs for state-of-the-art information about the illnesses, empathic support, illness management techniques, and problem-solving strategies (McFarlane 1994).

These basics of psychoeducational interventions are now offered worldwide in a variety of settings, with the same salutary results. A psychoeducational program for families of patients with schizophrenia in five cities in China reduced relapse rates from 35% to 20% per year, and it also demonstrated reductions in patients' disability levels and in family burden (Zhang et al. 1993). Culturally responsive models of family psychoeducation have been developed in sites as diverse as Australia, India, and Sweden (see Hatfield 1994), as well as the models initially developed in the United Kingdom and the United States. Reports on psychoeducational models for ethnically diverse families in the United States point to differences in structure (individual families versus multifamily groups), length of treatment, focus of content, behavior of group leaders (authority relations, egalitarianism), community involvement, and other special cultural considerations (Jordan, Lewellen, & Vandiver 1995; McFarlane 1994).

Unfortunately, family psychoeducation is offered mostly in research projects. Despite the need and the powerful findings of effectiveness, most service delivery systems in the United States make little effort to offer family education and training for the caregiving role. Regardless of ethnicity and expectations of the system, most families continue to complain about lack of communication and information from mental health professionals (Guarnaccia & Parra 1996; Solomon 1994).

Cultural Diversity in Mental Health Service Systems

Despite long-term efforts of the World Health Organization to develop psychosocial community mental health initiatives in countries of the developing world (Sartorius & Harding 1983), it is primarily the richer countries that have been able to afford training and services oriented toward mental health as well as mental illness. In the United States and most European nations, clinical training in all core mental health professions has focused on psychotherapy, with psychopharmocology limited to those who are medical practitioners. The training in verbal therapies has largely targeted psychodynamic issues or techniques for effecting behavioral and cognitive change. The models frequently are oriented toward treating persons with ordinary problems in daily living or impediments to self-actualization. In many clinical training programs, there is a far greater emphasis on treating clientele with mental health problems than on treatment and rehabilitation of persons with severe and persistent mental illness (NIMH 1990).

The United States has developed networks of community mental health centers in response to federal legislation and funding initiated in 1963. Today, public mental health services are threatened by greatly reduced federal and state funding and by the constraints of managed care. In the industrialized world, however, many programs in both public and private sectors are still oriented toward serving the mental health needs of the general population. In countries with few resources, mental health systems inevitably are geared toward the most needful population – those with overt symptomatology who suffer from major psychiatric disorders. Most of the developing world is still dependent on a few large isolated mental hospitals, with short-term clinical care limited to major cities and few community-based resources such as halfway houses or psychosocial rehabilitation programs.

Paradoxically, however, the scarcer resources have necessitated creative approaches to service delivery that are sometimes superior to those in the West, such as the integration of mental health services with primary health care at the village level in India (Nagaswami 1990) and China (Yucun et al. 1990). The ARO village system is a model rehabilitation program found primarily in Nigeria, Senegal, and other African countries (Asuni 1990). Here, after treatment in a Western-style mental hospital or clinic, psychiatric patients live with a relative in a traditional village close to the mental health facility for several months to a year or longer. Patients are involved in household chores and other village community activities as their mental state improves. The relative is involved in treatment, is trained as a lifetime caregiver and support system, and may be paid to compensate for lost income during this period.

Although developing world nations may make creative attempts to deal with mental illness, most such countries harbor massive social stressors. The sequelae of colonialism, intertribal warfare, destabilization of once peaceful agrarian economies, and ravages of famine are some of the problems in the developing world that profoundly affect mental health. Industrial nations deal with fluctuating economies and numerous stressors linked to rapid culture change. Most Western nations are experiencing increasing racial and ethnic diversity, and there are numerous mental health problems related to the status of minority and immigrant populations.

Ethnicity, Minority, and Refugee Status

Research on culture and mental health in the United States has largely focused on two domains. One domain has involved differences in population characteristics that affect service utilization. These include cultural concepts of mental disorder, help-seeking patterns, modes of using services, and the use of alternative healing systems. The other, interrelated domain has targeted service system deficits such as accessibility barriers, diagnostic and treatment errors, and lack of culturally competent personnel. In addition, there is now a large clinical literature devoted to case studies and guidelines for working with different ethnic groups (e.g. Gaw 1993).

Over time, each service innovation has brought a discussion of cultural applications, such as ethnicity and family therapy (McGoldrick, Pearce, & Giordano 1995) or the cross-cultural practice of clinical case managment (Manoleas 1996). There are also models for restructuring the delivery system itself to respond to the cultural needs of specific ethnic groups, including community interventions to alleviate social stressors (Lefley & Bestman 1991). In most of these applications, the focus is on how best to help clients with existential problems in living. Typical problem areas include generational and marital conflict, substance-abusing youth, the oppression and rage of minority status, the translocations and loss of refugee status, adaptation to a foreign culture, and the like.

In modern industrial nations, members of ethnic minority groups are particularly vulnerable to the stresses of poverty, economically or politically forced migration, family disintegration, and the outrages of diminished status in mainstream society. The malaise engendered by feelings of oppression and loss – or the interpersonal conflicts generated by poverty, crowding, and family disruption – are often attributed to external malevolence. As in more traditional countries, these problems are frequently brought first to a religious practitioner or alternative healer rather than to a mental health professional.

Traditional and Biomedical Healing Systems

Distinctions between physical and mental illness, and the resources required to heal them, are based on a Cartesian mind–body dichotomy that is alien to most non-Western or traditional cultures (Gaines 1992). Symptoms of mental illness such as apathy and withdrawal, culturally atypical delusions or hallucinations, fluctuating mood states, and bizarre verbalizations are found throughout the world, but they are variously viewed as spiritual, psychological, or somatic in origin. Attention to these dimensions, characteristic of any experience of human malaise, may be split among different healing systems or incorporated in a holistic approach to treatment.

In many countries, parallel healing systems coexist, with reciprocal referrals. For example, in hospitals in the People's Republic of China, a pharmacopoeia of herbal remedies coexists with the latest in psychotropic medications. A building devoted to Ayurvedic medicine is found at the National Institute of Mental Health and Neuorsciences in Banagalore, India, a major center of psychiatric training and research. In many African countries, indigenous healing is integrated with modern psychiatry. In the ARO village system described previously, treatment typically combines native healing rituals with psychotropic medication and a type of milieu therapy in a traditional setting. In Asuni's (1990) description, relatives must live with their ill member in a compound of traditional healers in order to provide for the needs of the patient and to participate in the healing rituals. The treatment consists of administration of herbs, performance of rituals, and recitation of incantations.

Anthropologists generally agree that, in most non-Western societies, traditional healers are the first resort in mental health problems, and they continue to be used even after psychiatric services are enlisted (Jilek 1993). According to Jilek (1993), prohibitive restrictions on nonprofessional health care were largely imposed by European authorities in former colonial possessions. With the demise of colonialism, however, many developing nations have legalized the practice of traditional medicine. Officially sanctioned coexistence of traditional and modern medical systems is found in most African countries, Bangladesh, China, Korea, India, Nepal, Myanmar, Sri Lanka, and Thailand, to name a few. Countries that do not officially recognize but do not legally prohibit "nonscientific" medicine are Australia, Canada, Germany, most Latin American countries, the Netherlands, the Scandinavian countries, the United Kingdom, and the United States. Although some European countries have legal prohibitions, they are unlikely to proceed against non-European traditional healers practicing with immigrant compatriots (Jilek 1993).

In most traditional or folk healing systems, human behavior is mediated by multiple forces, both natural and supernatural. Diagnostic and treatment models are based on etiological concepts that typically involve some imbalance in life forces. The imbalance can be corrected only by invoking appropriate counterforces through ritualistic fulfillment of religious obligations. Most rituals require the intercession of supernatural powers, either directly or through the medium of a healer (Lefley, Sandoval, & Charles 1998).

Although cultures tend to distinguish between religious practitioners and herb doctors, in many traditional cultures the priest and healer are one. Both Western and traditional healers use medications and somatic therapies as needed. Some medications used by traditional healers have tranquilizing or antipsychotic properties; for example, extracts of the *rauwolfia serpentina* plant have been used to control psychotic symptoms in the ARO village programs and elsewhere in Africa and Asia.

When comparing Western psychiatry and traditional healing, it is evident that different etiological paradigms have generated different treatment modalities. Western healers have looked to psychodynamic issues or maladaptive behavioral patterns in fashioning cures, whereas ritual healers look to supernatural causality

or external malevolence. Traditional healing rituals may exorcise a curse, propi-
tiate gods, redress a wrong, or otherwise balance unequal forces. Through trance
possession, believers may become imbued with the power of a personal god to
control their malaise and improve their fortunes.

There are no adequately controlled studies comparing effectiveness of traditional and Western psychiatric healing interventions. An admittedly limited study
was reported by Koss (1987), in which 56 patients receiving either mental health
care or spiritist healing in Puerto Rico rated their therapist for symptom alleviation or problem resolution. Patients' outcome ratings were significantly better for
spiritists than for mental health professionals. Koss felt the difference could be accounted for by the higher expectations of spiritists' competency to control fate. She
also reported that spiritists' patients who had first encountered and then expressed
dissatisfaction with medical or psychiatric personnel were the most hopeful, because they viewed the traditional healer as a last resort. In most ethnographic
reports, however, many patients and families continue to use dual systems to serve
different needs (Bilu & Witzum 1993; Lefley et al. 1998; Weiss 1992).

Rehabilitation, Quality of Life, and the Self-Help Experience

Deinstitutionalization – the emptying of mental hospitals – is proceeding at an uneven pace throughout the world. Nevertheless, with the increasing availability of
antipsychotic medications, almost every culture has seen an increased emphasis
on community tenure and the need for rehabilitative services. In the international
mental health literature, there is an increasing emphasis on improving quality of
life (Kuyken & Orley 1994). One of the most important attempts to deinstitutionalize, rehabilitate, and improve the quality of life of persons with mental illness
has taken place in Italy.

Mental Health Systems and Outcomes: The Italian Experiment

In 1978, Italy passed Law 180, which banned all new admissions to public mental
hospitals and so set the stage for an allegedly more humane policy of deinstitutionalization and community tenure. Community mental health services have
subsequently developed very unevenly, with great disparity in the resources available in southern and northern Italy. An overview of studies of the Italian reform
movement found that in the South, community support services were virtually
nonexistent compared with other areas of the country (Bollini & Mollica 1989).
Others have reported that families are greatly burdened with a major caregiving
role and with totally inadequate clinical supports to deal with even floridly psychotic behavior (Jones & Poletti 1985).

A 15-year follow-up study looked at the long-term psychosocial outcome of
schizophrenic patients in southern Italy (Sardinia) who were discharged after the

1978 reform. The investigators found that 70% of the patients showed poor or very poor adjustment or severe maladjustment. Most were single and 85% were unemployed. Their treatment histories were marked by a large number of hospitalizations and rare or irregular outpatient contacts (Fariante et al. 1996).

The researchers noted that their 1996 study confirmed earlier findings that patients treated in areas where services are inadequate had the worst outcomes, whereas social performance improves when people with schizophrenia are treated in regions with appropriate rehabilitative services (Mignolli, Laccincani, & Platt 1991). In stark contrast to Sardinia, northern Italy has resources on the cutting edge of psychiatric rehabilitation. There are almost 100 cooperative industries that employ people with psychiatric disabilities. Marianne Farkas is an international trainer at Boston University's Center for Psychiatric Rehabilitation (Farkas & Anthony 1989). She frequently visits these industries and reports that their products are of excellent quality, with "gorgeous, Madison Avenue type publicity" and enthusiastic, often elite patronage (Farkas, pers. commun.). Examples are a fine costume jewelry shop, a leather handbag factory and boutique, and a moving company. There is a food division that has its own farm, food processing plant, grocery store, and four-star restaurant. An arts division has a radio station, video company, computer center, publishing house, and an industry that reconditions old manuscripts and books. The specialized industries are developed by experts and run jointly by patients and staff proficient in that industry. The radio station recruits top-flight people to donate one hour a month to these enterprises. From this outreach, they have developed a pool of expert consultants who help with product design, advertising, training, and marketing.

Several things are readily apparent in this northern Italian experiment. First, patients work in first-class industries of which they can be proud. There are no artificial work situations or demeaning entry-level jobs to erode an already diminished self-concept. Second, they work under conditions that are probably optimal for persons with a major mental illness. All businesses are small, with no more than 15–20 people. Research indicates that psychiatric patients have difficulty tolerating overstimulating, high-demand environments (see Lefley 1992). In these cooperatives, they can work without excessive interpersonal stimulation and at their own pace. The data on northern and southern Italy thus tell us much about the structure of good and bad mental health systems – and about the interaction of these systems with psychosocial outcomes and prognosis.

The Advocacy and Consumer Self-Help Movements

Probably the most notable development in mental health systems is the growth of advocacy and self-help movements throughout the world. At present at least 35 nations have organizations focusing on support and advocacy for persons with mental illness (Johnson 1995). These movements are largely composed of family members, but they also include many consumers (persons with mental illness who may be present or former psychiatric patients) and interested citizens. Major supportive resources have been developed by family organizations and even more by the various consumer movements. Since its inception in 1979, the American organization, the National Alliance for the Mentally Ill, has become a powerful political force at both national and state levels. Its primary focus is on public education, legislative initiatives to increase funding for research and services, and mutual support. The organization has helped develop private foundations for basic scientific research, has been influential in extending the Americans with Disabilities Act and obtaining insurance parity for persons with mental illness, and it is engaging the media in a massive antistigma campaign. State affiliates have also developed a range of rehabilitative facilities, including housing, employment opportunities, psychosocial rehabilitation programs, and clubhouses as adjuncts to the professional service delivery system.

Consumer organizations range from strictly nonpolitical self-help models to social action movements invested in political and legal change. In the United States, there are numerous self-help organizations for persons with psychiatric diagnoses ranging from agoraphobia and anxiety disorders to schizophrenia (White & Madara 1992). There are also general groups for persons recovering from mental illness, such as Recovery Inc. and Grow (which originated in Australia). Support groups are typically used in tandem with medication management, but they often replace the need for ancillary psychotherapy.

Internationally, we are beginning to see the emergence and expansion of networks of consumer organizations with the dual function of self-help and political advocacy. In the United States, these dual functions have been merged in numerous state consumer orgnizations and some national centers like the National Empowerment Center in Lawrence, Massachusetts, and the National Mental Health Consumer Self-Help Clearinghouse in Philadelphia. Both receive funding from the Substance Abuse and Mental Health Administration.

Today there are numerous consumer-operated enterprises serving persons with severe and persistent mental illness. These include housing and residential placement services, case management, peer counseling programs, social centers, employment services, crisis respite houses, and special programs for the homeless. Most of these enterprises were initiated with funding from the Community Support Program of the Substance Abuse and Mental Health Administration. Most state mental health administrations today have a Mental Health Consumer Affairs office, organized and staffed by one or more former psychiatric patients.

Judi Chamberlin, another consultant at the Boston University Center for Psychiatric Rehabilitation, has studied consumer organizations in Europe and other countries (Chamberlin, pers. commun.). A European network of consumer movements, based in Rotterdam, has held several large meetings with representatives from countries in Europe. Consumer groups are also found in Japan, Australia, and New Zealand, and they are beginning in Latin America. In Central Europe, some consumer groups are developing the types of consumer-run rehabilitative facilities that have already been implemented in other countries. In Slovenia, they are operating two halfway houses and a drop-in center and are working on sheltered employment. In Hungary, consumers have a radio program and are training people in the skill of bookbinding. Continental and world conferences facilitate cross-fertilization of ideas among these groups. International consumer organizations with a focus on social change include the World Federation of Psychiatric Survivors and Users (with offices in Aukland, New Zealand) and the Mental Disability Rights International (based in Washington, D.C.).

These self-help movements offer a forum for persons with psychiatric disabilities to utilize and refine their intelligence and skills in pursuit of a social agenda and a more meaningful life. Almost all the consumer movements offer knowledge dissemination and training for advocacy roles. They offer an understanding of shared experiences, mutual support, peer counseling, and role modeling. They have the capability for providing a new identity and revived strengths to persons whose mental health has been profoundly diminished by the social devaluation of their mental illness.

Conclusions

The mental health–mental illness distinction has particular relevance to the changing structure of services and training in the Western world. With the worldwide emergence of managed care systems, whether publicly or privately operated, mental health service providers are under increasing attack unless they can demonstrate a medical, illness-based rationale for their interventions. Insurers are increasingly unwilling to pay for psychotherapy addressed to psychological problem solving, personal growth, or self-actualization.

We are seeing a reorientation of disciplinary training and a restructuring of systems in advanced nations that paradoxically moves them more toward those of the developing world. Consider the anticipated future for psychiatry in the United States. The predictions are that psychiatrists will: (a) place increasingly greater emphasis on the major mental illnesses and neurobehavioral disorders than on psychological problems in living; (b) focus on psychosocial rehabilitation efforts for the disabled rather than on psychotherapy for the general population; and (c) deal more with the psychopathological aspects of general medical conditions, a move toward non-Cartesian concepts of health and illness (Lieberman & Rush 1996). Psychoanalysis, no longer reimbursed by insurance and increasingly viewed as a personal growth enhancer rather than a treatment modality, will continue to be utilized primarily by the educated few who comprehend its premises and can invest the time and money. The "refinement" of psychiatry – to a focus on biologically based disorders, the development of a seamless view of psyche and soma, and a retreat from psychotherapy – indeed moves us more toward the treatment systems of the developing world.

In many ways, also, Western concepts of mental illness are beginning to merge with those in the developing world. Western scientific thought and its correlative healing systems have been based on Descartes's mind–body dichotomy, which tended to separate medicine from psychological practice. For many years the conceptual basis and the behaviors of both mental health and mental illness were ascribed to psychogenic factors, or to psychogenic factors nested within sociogenic ones. The proliferation of research findings pointing to biogenensis of the major disorders has led to a more holistic view in which somatic vulnerabilities interact with psychosocial stressors that affect the course, if not the etiology, of the disorders. Mental illnesses generate a fragmented sense of self; they are intrinsically frightening, and the mode of social response determines the extent to which the individual will feel diminished and stigmatized or able to cope with a disability of cognition or affect.

Social scientists have turned their attention to the social meaning of illness and illness behaviors and their interactive effects. Cultural constructivists and symbolic interactionists remind us that all human behavior must be viewed in fluid interaction with ever-moving cultural currents. They note correctly that mental illness can be studied only as an interactive, constantly changing process within and among patients, families, healers, and other figures in the social environment (Gaines 1992). These interactive variables determine how a biologically based psychopathology is defined and experienced by individuals and their significant others. They also determine the societal architecture for diagnosis, treatment, and rehabilitation.

The cross-cultural literature tells us much about the architecture of healing. The findings from WHO research, and the preliminary findings of the Italian approaches to rehabilitation, suggest that culture can profoundly affect not only the experience of mental illness but also its course. This involves cultural acceptance, social support, and balanced expectations of persons with core cognitive and perceptual impairments. It also entails cultural mechanisms for meeting the needs of individuals at variable levels of functioning. The growth of consumer movements tells us that many persons once impaired enough to have been hospitalized are able to offer services, counseling, and role modeling to peers. As an embodiment of realized hope, recovered peers offer that which families and professionals cannot. We know that for many persons with mental illness, negative cultural attitudes lead to self-devaluation, abandonment of hope, and behavioral regression. Research in the years ahead may tell us whether members of the consumer movement, many of whom have triumphed over profound adversity, are able to counteract and change that social reflection.

References

Abrahamson, M. (1980). Sudden wealth, gratification and attainment: Durkheim's anomie of affluence reconsidered. *Amer. Sociological Rev.* 45: 49–57.

Abram, K. M. (1989). The effect of co-occurring disorders on criminal careers: Interaction of antisocial personality, alcohol and drug disorders. *Internat. J. Law & Psychiatry* 12: 133–48.

(1990). The problem of co-occurring disorders among jail detainees: Antisocial disorder, alcoholism, drug abuse, and depression. *Law & Human Behavior* 14: 333–45.

Abram, K. M., & L. A. Teplin (1991). Co-occurring disorders among mentally ill jail detainees. *Amer. Psychologist* 46: 1036–45.

Abramson, M. L. (1972). The criminalization of mentally disordered behavior: Possible side effects of a new mental health law. *Hospital & Community Psychiatry* 23: 101–5.

Achenbach, T. M. (1984). The status of research related to psychopathology. In A. W. Collins (Ed.), *Development during Middle Childhood: the Years from Six to Twelve*, pp. 370–97. Washington, DC: National Academy Press.

Acock, A. C., & J. S. Hurlbert (1993). Social networks, marital status, and well-being. *Social Networks* 15: 309–34.

Aday, L., R. Andersen, & G. V. Fleming (1980). *Health Care in the U.S. – Equitable for Whom?* Beverly Hills, CA: Sage.

Adelmann, P. K. (1994). Multiple roles and psychological well-being in a national sample of older adults. *J. Gerontology* 49: 277–85.

Adler, A. (1927). *The Practice and Theory of Individual Psychology.* New York: Harcourt, Brace, & World.

Adler, P. T. (1982). An analysis of the concept of competence in individuals and social systems. *Community Mental Health J.* 18: 34–45.

Advisory Commission on Intergovernmental Relations (1977). *Block Grants: A Comparative Analysis.* Washington, DC: U.S. GPO.

Agranoff, R. (1991). Human services integration: Past and present challenges in public administration. *Public Administration Rev.* 51: 533–42.

Agranoff, R., & L. S. Robins (1984). The politics and administration of intergovernmental relations in health. In T. J. Litman & L. S. Robins (Eds.), *Health Politics & Policy.* New York: Wiley.

Ahmed, P. I., & S. C. Plog (Eds.) (1976). *State Mental Hospitals: What Happens When They Close?* New York: Plenum.

Aiken, L., S. Somers, & M. Shore (1986). Private foundations in health affairs: A case study of a national initiative for the chronically mentally ill. *Amer. Psychologist* 41: 1290–5.

Ajzen, I., & M. Fishbein (1980). *Understanding Attitudes and Predicting Behavior.* Englewood Cliffs, NJ: Prentice-Hall.

Alberman, E. (1984). Low birthweight. In Bracken (1984: 86–98).

Albrecht, G., V. Walker, & J. Levy (1982). Social distance from the stigmatized: A test of two theories. *Social Science & Medicine* 16: 1319–27.

Alegría, M., R. Robles, D. H. Freeman, M. Vera, A. L. Jimenez, C. Rios, & R. Rios (1991). Patterns of mental health utilization among island Puerto Rican poor. *Amer. J. Public Health* 81: 875–9.

Alexander, J. F., A. Holtzworth-Munroe, & P. B. Jameson (1994). The process and outcome of marital and family therapy: Research review and evaluation. In Bergin & Garfield (1994: 595–630).

Ali, J., & W. R. Avison (1997). Employment transitions and psychological distress: The contrasting experiences of single and married mothers. *J. Health & Social Behavior* 38: 345–62.

Al-Issa, I. (1982). Gender and adult psychopathology. In I. Al-Issa (Ed.), *Gender and Psychopathology*, pp. 83–110. New York: Academic Press.

(Ed.) (1995). *Handbook of Culture and Mental Illness: An International Perspective*. Madison, CT: International Universities Press.

Allen, G. S., B. J. Burns, & W. A. Cook (1983). The provision of mental health services in the health care sector – United States. In C. A. Taube & S. A. Barrett (Eds.), *Mental Health, United States – 1983* (DHHS pub. no. ADM 83-1275). Rockville, MD: National Institute of Mental Health.

Allport, G. W. (1995). *Becoming*. New Haven, CT: Yale University Press.

Amaro, H., N. F. Russo, & J. Johnson (1987). Family and work predictors of psychological well-being among Hispanic women professionals. *Psychology Women Q.* 11: 505–21.

Amato, P. R., & B. Keith (1991). Parental divorce and the well-being of children: A meta-analysis. *Psychological Bull.* 110: 26–46.

American Bar Association Criminal Justice Standards Committee (1989). *American Bar Association Criminal Justice and Mental Health Standards*. Washington, DC: ABA.

American Hospital Association (1950, 1965). *Hospital Statistics*. Chicago: AHA.

Anastasi, A. (1988). *Psychological Testing*, 6th ed. New York: Macmillan.

Anastos, K., & S. M. Palleja (1991). Caring for women at risk of HIV infection. *J. General Internal Medicine* 6: S40–S46.

Andersen, R. (1968). A behavioral model of families' use of health services. Res. Ser. no. 25, Center for Health Administration Studies, University of Chicago.

(1995). Revisiting the behavioral model and access to care: Does it matter? *J. Health & Social Behavior* 36: 1–10.

Andersen, R., & J. Newman (1973). Societal and individual determinants of medical care utilization in the United States. *Milbank Q.* 51: 95–124.

Anderson, J., & S. Jay (1985). The diffusion of medical technology: Social network analysis and policy research. *Sociological Q.* 26: 49–64.

Anderson, M., & S. E. Feinberg (1995). Black, white, and shades of gray (and brown and yellow). *Chance* 8: 15–18.

Anderson, O. W., & R. Andersen (1972). Patterns of use of health services. In H. E. Freeman, S. Levine, & L. G. Reeder (Eds.), *Handbook of Medical Sociology*, 2nd ed., pp. 386–406. Englewood Cliffs, NJ: Prentice-Hall.

Andreasen, N. (1984). *The Broken Brain: The Biological Revolution in Psychiatry*. New York: Harper & Row.

Andreasen, N., & D. Black (1995). *Introductory Textbook of Psychiatry*. Washington, DC: American Psychiatric Press.

Andreasen, N., & V. Swayze (1989). Neuroimaging. In J. A. Silva & C. C. Nadelson (Eds.), *International Review of Psychiatry*, vol. 1, pp. 355–93. Washington, DC: American Psychiatric Press.

Andrews, G., C. Tennant, D. M. Hewson, & G. E. Valliant (1978). Life event stress, social support, coping style, and risk of psychological impairment. *J. Nervous & Mental Disease* 166: 307–16.

Aneshensel, C. S. (1985). The natural history of depressive symptoms: Implications for psychiatric epidemiology. *Res. in Community & Mental Health* 5: 45–75.

(1992). Social stress: Theory and research. *Annual Rev. Sociology* 18: 15–38.

(1996). Consequences of psychosocial stress. In Kaplan (1996b: 111–36).

Aneshensel, C. S., & R. R. Frerichs (1982). Stress, support, and depression: A longitudinal causal model. *J. Community Psychology* 10: 363–76.

Aneshensel, C. S., R. R. Frerichs, & G. J. Huba (1984). Depression and physical illness: A multiwave, nonrecursive causal model. *J. Health & Social Behavior* 25: 350–71.

Aneshensel, C. S., & G. J. Huba (1984). An integrative causal model of the antecedents and consequences of depression over one year. *Res. in Community & Mental Health* 4: 35–72.

Aneshensel, C. S., L. I. Pearlin, J. T. Mullan, S. Zarit, & C. Whitlatch (1995). *Profiles in Caregiving: The Unexpected Career.* New York: Academic Press.

Aneshensel, C. S., C. M. Rutter, & P. A. Lachenbruch (1991). Competing conceptual and analytic models: Social structure, stress, and mental health. *Amer. Sociological Rev.* 56: 166–78.

Aneshensel, C. S., & J. D. Stone (1982). Stress and depression: A test of the buffering model of social support. *Arch. General Psychiatry* 39: 1392–6.

Aneshensel, C. S., & C. A. Sucoff (1996a). The neighborhood context of adolescent mental health. *J. Health & Social Behavior* 37: 293–311.

(1996b). Macro and micro influences in the stress process. Paper presented at the American Sociological Association meetings (August 16–20), New York.

Anisman, H., & R. Zacharko (1982). Depression: The predisposing influence of stress. *Behavioral & Brain Sciences* 5: 89–137.

Anthony, J. C., M. Folstein, A. J. Romanoski, M. R. VonKorff, G. R. Nestadt, R. Chahal, A. Merchant, H. C. Brown, S. Shapiro, M. Kramer, & E. M. Gruenberg (1985). Comparison of the lay Diagnostic Interview Schedule and a standardized psychiatric diagnosis. Experience in Eastern Baltimore. *Arch. General Psychiatry* 42: 667–75.

Anthony, J. C., & K. R. Petronis (1991). Suspected risk factors for depression among adults 18–44 years old. *Epidemiology* 2: 123–32.

Anthony, W. A. (1993). Managed mental health care: Will it be rationed care or rational care? *Psychosocial Rehab. J.* 16: 120–3.

Anthony, W. A., M. Cohen, & M. A. Farkas (1990). *Psychiatric Rehabilitation.* Boston University Press.

Anthony, W. A., & M. A. Farkas (1982). A client outcome planning model for assessing psychiatric rehabilitation interventions. *Schizophrenia Bull.* 8: 13–38.

Anthony, W. A., & M. A. Jansen (1984). Predicting the vocational capacity of the chronically mentally ill. *Amer. Psychologist* 5: 537–49.

Anthony, W. A., & R. P. Liberman (1986). The practice of psychiatric rehabilitation: Historical, conceptual, and research base. *Schizophrenia Bull.* 12: 542–53.

Anton, T. J. (1989). *American Federalism and Public Policy.* New York: Random House.

(1997). New federalism and intergovernmental fiscal relationships: The implications for health policy. *J. Health Politics, Policy & Law* 22: 691–720.

Antonovsky, A. (1967). Social class, life expectancy and overall mortality. *Milbank Q.* 45: 31–73.

(1979). *Health, Stress, and Coping.* San Francisco: Jossey-Bass.

APA [American Psychiatric Association] (1980). *Diagnostic and Statistical Manual of Mental Disorders,* 3rd ed. Washington, DC: American Psychiatric Association.

(1987). *Diagnostic and Statistical Manual of Mental Disorders,* rev. 3rd ed. Washington, DC: American Psychiatric Association.

(1994). *Diagnostic and Statistical Manual of Mental Disorders,* 4th ed. Washington, DC: American Psychiatric Association.

Applebaum, P. (1994). *Almost a Revolution: Mental Health Law and the Limits of Change.* New York: Oxford University Press.

Apsler, R., & E. Rothman (1984). Correlates of compliance with psychoactive prescriptions. *J. Psychoactive Drugs* 16: 193–9.

Arana, J. D., B. Hastings, & E. Herron (1991). Continuous care teams in intensive outpatient treatment of chronically mentally ill patients. *Hospital & Community Psychiatry* 42: 503–8.

Arons, B. S., et al. (1994). Mental health and substance abuse coverage. *Health Affairs* 13: 192–205.

Aruffo, J. F., J. H. Cloverdale, R. C. Checko, & R. J. Dworkin (1990). Knowledge about AIDS among women psychiatric outpatients. *Hospital & Community Psychiatry* 41: 326–8.

Arvanites, T. M. (1988). The impact of state mental hospital deinstitutionalization on commitments for incompetency to stand trial. *Criminology* 26: 307–20.

Asuni, T. (1990). Nigeria: Report on the care, treatment, and rehabilitation of people with mental illness. *Psychosocial Rehab. J.* 14: 35–44.

Atkinson, J. H., & I. Grant (1994). Natural history of neuropsychiatric manifestations of HIV disease. *Psychiatric Clinics of North America* 17: 17–33.

Atkinson, T., R. Liem, & J. H. Liem (1986). The social costs of unemployment: Implications for social support. *J. Health & Social Behavior* 27: 317–31.

Attkisson, C., J. A. Cook, M. Karno, A. Lehman, T. H. McGlashan, H. Meltzer, M. O'Connor, D. Richardson, A. Rosenblatt, K. Wells, J. Williams, & A. A. Hohmann (1992). Clinical services research. *Schizophrenia Bull.* 18: 561–626.

Atwood, N. (1982). Professional prejudice and the psychotic patient. *Social Work* 27: 172–7.

Aubry, T., B. Tefft, & R. Currie (1995). Public attitudes and intentions regarding tenants of community mental health residences who are neighbours. *Community Mental Health J.* 31: 39–52.

Auerbach, J. D., C. Wypijewska, H. Keith, & H. Keith (Eds.) (1994). *AIDS and Behavior.* Washington, DC: National Academy Press.

Austin, M. J., S. R. Blum, & N. Murtaza (1995). Local–state government relations and the development of public sector managed mental health care systems. *Administration & Policy in Mental Health* 22: 203–15.

Ausubel, D. P. (1958). *Theory and Problems in Child Development.* New York: Grune & Stratton.

Aviram, U. (1990). Community care of the seriously mentally ill. *Community Mental Health J.* 26: 69–88.

Avison, W. R. (1995). Roles and resources: The effects of work and family context on women's psychosocial resources and psychological distress. In Greenley (1995: 233–56).

    (1997). Family structure and mental health. In A. C. Maney (Ed.), *The Social Contexts of Stress and Health.* Washington, DC: National Institute of Mental Health.

Avison, W. R., & I. H. Gotlib (Eds.) (1994). *Stress and Mental Health: Contemporary Issues and Prospects for the Future.* New York: Plenum.

Avison, W. R., & K. N. Speechley (1987). The discharged psychiatric patient: A review of social, social-psychological, and psychiatric correlates of outcome. *Amer. J. Psychiatry* 144: 10–18.

Avison, W. R., & R. J. Turner (1988). Stressful life events and depressive symptoms: Disaggregating the effects of acute stressors and chronic strains. *J. Health & Social Behavior* 29: 253–64.

Babcock, J. (1895). The colored insane. *Alienist & Neurologist* 16: 423–47.

Babigian, H., O. Mitchell, P. Marshall, & S. Reed (1992). A mental health capitation experiment: Evaluating the Monroe–Livingston experience. In R. Frank & W. G. Manning (Eds.), *Economics and Mental Health,* pp. 307–31. Baltimore: Johns Hopkins University Press.

Bachrach, L. L. (1976). *Deinistitutionalization: An Analytical Review and Sociological Perspective* (National Institute of Mental Health, Ser. D, no. 4; DHHS pub. no. ADM 79-351). Washington, DC: U.S. GPO.

    (1980). Overview: Model programs for chronic mental patients. *Amer. J. Psychiatry* 137: 1023–30.

Baker, N. Tish, & R. D. Seager (1991). A comparison of the psychosocial needs of hospice patients with AIDS and those with other diagnoses. *Hospice J.* 7: 61–9.

Baker, P. C., & F. L. Mott (1989). NLSY child handbook 1989: A guide and resource document for the National Longitudinal Study of Youth 1986 child data. Center for Human Resource Research, Ohio State University, Columbus.

Bakketeig, L. S., H. J. Hoffman, & A. R. Titmuss-Oakley (1984). Perinatal mortality. In Bracken (1984: 99–151).

Baltes, P. B., H. W. Reese, & L. P. Lipsitt (1980). Life-span developmental psychology. *Annual Rev. Psychology* 31: 65–110.

Bandura, A. (1969). *Principles of Behavior Modification.* New York: Holt, Rinehart, & Winston.

    (1986). *Social Foundations of Thought and Action.* Englewood Cliffs, NJ: Prentice-Hall.

Banfield, E. (1971). Revenue sharing in theory and practice. *Public Interest* 23: 33–44.

Bardach, E. (1977). *The Implementation Game.* Cambridge, MA: MIT Press.

Bar-Levav, R. (1976). The stigma of seeing a psychiatrist. *Amer. J. Psychotherapy* 30: 473–80.

Barnett, R. C., & G. K. Baruch (1987). Social roles, gender and psychological distress. In R. C. Barnett, L. Biener, & G. K. Baruch (Eds.), *Gender & Stress,* pp. 122–143. New York: Free Press.

Barnett, R. and N. L. Marshall (1991). The relationship between women's work and family roles and their subjective well-being and psychological distress. In Frankenhaueser et al. (1991: 111–36).

Barrera, M., Jr. (1981). Social support in the adjustment of pregnant adolescents. In Gottlieb (1981b: 69–96).

    (1982). Raza populations. In L. R. Snowden (Ed.), *Reaching the Underserved: Mental Health Needs of Neglected Populations,* pp. 119–42. Beverly Hills, CA: Sage.

(1986). Distinctions between social support concepts, measures and models. *Amer. J. Community Psychology* 14: 413–46.

Baruch, G. K., L. Biener, & R. Barnett (1987). Women and gender in research on work and family stress. *Amer. Psychologist* 42: 130–6.

Bassett, Ann. S., B. D. Jones, B. C. McGillivray, & J. T. Pantzar (1988). Partial trisomy chromosome 5 cosegregating with schizophrenia. *Lancet* 1: 799–801.

Bateson, G., D. D. Jackson, J. Haley, & J. Weakland (1956). Toward a theory of schizophrenia. *Behavioral Science* 1: 251–64.

Batki, S. L. (1990). Substance abuse and AIDS: The need for mental health services. *New Directions for Mental Health Services* 48: 66–7.

Baumheier, E. C. (1982). Services integration in the field of health and human services. In *Health Services Integration: Lessons for the 1980s,* vol. 4, pp. 1–36. Washington, DC: Institute of Medicine, National Academy of Sciences.

Baumgartner, F. R., & B. D. Jones (1993). *Agendas and Instability in American Politics.* University of Chicago Press.

Baumrind, D. (1971). Current patterns of parental authority. *Developmental Psychology Monograph* 4 (1, part 2, pp. 1–103).

Baumrind, D. (1991). Parenting styles and adolescent development. In J. Brooks-Gunn, R. Lerner, & A. C. Peterson (Eds.), *Encyclopedia of Adolescence,* pp. 746–58. New York: Garland.

Bayer, R. (1981). *Homosexuality and American Psychiatry: The Politics of Diagnosis.* New York: Basic Books.

Bayer, R., & R. Spitzer (1985). Neurosis, psychodynamics, and DSM-III: A history of the controversy. *Arch. General Psychiatry* 42: 187–96.

Bayley, M. (1991). Normalization or social role valorization: An adequate philosophy? In S. Baldwin & J. Hattersley (Eds.), *Mental Handicap: Social Science Perspectives,* pp. 87–99. New York: Routledge.

Bays, C. (1983). Patterns of hospital growth: The case of profit hospitals. *Medical Care* 21: 950–7.

Bazelon Center for Mental Health Law (1996). *Mental Health Managed Care Survey of the States.* Washington, DC: BCMHL.

Beachler, M. (1990). The mental health services program for youth. *J. Mental Health Admin.* 17: 115–21.

Beall, M. Ann (1992). Commissioner's guidance questionnaire: Survey results. Virginia Mental Health Consumers Association, Falls Church, VA.

Beard, J. H., R. N. Propst, & T. J. Malamud (1982). The Fountain House model of psychiatric rehabilitation. *Psychosocial Rehab. J.* 5: 47–54.

Beardslee, W. R., J. Bemporad, M. Keller, & G. Klerman (1983). Children of parents with major affective disorder: A review. *Amer. J. Psychiatry* 140: 825–32.

Bebbington, P. E. (1988). The social epidemiology of clinical depression. In A. S. Henderson & G. D. Burrows (Eds.), *Handbook of Social Psychiatry,* pp. 87–102. Amsterdam: Elsevier.

Beck, A. T., A. J. Rush, B. F. Shaw, & G. Emery (1979). *Cognitive Therapy of Depression.* New York: Guilford.

Becker, G. S. (1976). *The Economic Approach to Human Behavior.* University of Chicago Press.

Becker, H. S. (1973). *Outsiders: Studies in the Sociology of Deviance.* New York: Free Press.

Behar, L. (1988). An integrated state system of services for seriously disturbed children. In Looney (1988: 131–8).

Belcher, J. R. (1988). Are jails replacing the mental health system for the homeless mentally ill? *Community Mental Health J.* 24: 185–94.

Belkin, G. S., J. A. Fleishman, M. D. Stein, J. Piette, & V. Mor (1992). Physical symptoms and depressive symptoms among individuals with HIV infection. *Psychosomatics* 33: 416–26.

Bell, D. (1973). *The Coming of Post-Industrial Society: A Venture in Social Forecasting.* New York: Basic Books.

Bell, L. V. (1989a). From the asylum to the community in U.S. mental health care: A historical overview. In Rochefort (1989: 89–120).

Bell, M. D., R. M. Milstein, & P. H. Lysaker (1993). Pay as an incentive in work participation by patients with severe mental illness. *Psychiatric Services* 44: 684–6.

Bell, N. K. (1989b). AIDS and women: Remaining ethical issues. *AIDS Education & Prevention* 1: 22–9.

Belle, D. (1987). Gender differences in the social moderators of stress. In R. C. Barnett, L. Biener, & G. K. Baruch (Eds.), *Gender & Stress,* pp. 257–77. New York: Free Press.

Belsky, J., & D. Eggebeen (1991). Early and extensive maternal employment and young children's socioemotional development: Children of the national longitudinal survey of youth. *J. Marriage & the Family* 53: 1083–1110.

Bendix, R., & S. M. Lipset (1966). Karl Marx's theory of social classes. In R. Bendix & S. M. Lipset (Eds.), *Class, Status and Power,* 2nd ed., pp. 26–35. Glencoe, IL: Free Press.

Benford, R. D. (1993). Frame disputes within the nuclear disarmament movement. *Social Forces* 71: 677–701.

Bennett, N. S., C. W. Lidz, J. Monahan, E. P. Mulvey, S. K. Hoge, L. H. Roth, & W. Gardner (1993). Inclusion, motivation and good faith: The morality of coercion in mental hospital admission. *Behavioral Sciences & the Law* 11: 295–306.

Bentkover, J., P. Caper, M. Schlesinger, & J. Suldan (1988). Medicare's payment of hospitals. In D. Blumenthal, M. Schlesinger, & P. Brown-Drumheller (Eds.), *Renewing the Promise: Medicare and Its Reforms,* pp. 90–114. New York: Oxford University Press.

Bergin, A. E., & S. L. Garfield (Eds.) (1994). *Handbook of Psychotherapy and Behavior Change,* 4th ed. New York: Wiley.

Berk, R. A., & S. F. Berk (1979). *Labor and Leisure at Home: Content and Organization of the Household Day.* Beverly Hills, CA: Sage.

Berk, S. F. (1985). *The Gender Factory: The Apportionment of Work in American Households.* New York: Plenum.

Berkman, L. F., & L. Breslow (1983). *Health and Ways of Living: The Alameda County Study.* New York: Oxford University Press.

Bernal, G., J. Bonilla, & C. Bellido (1995). Ecological validity and cultural sensitivity for the cultural adaptation and development of psychosocial treatment with Hispanics. *J. Abnormal Child Psychology* 23: 67–82.

Bernheim, K. F. (1987). Family consumerism: Coping with the winds of change. In A. B. Hatfield & H. P. Lefley (Eds.), *Families of the Mentally Ill: Coping and Adaptation,* pp. 244–60. New York: Guilford.

Bestman, E. W. (1986). Cross-cultural approaches to service delivery to ethnic minorities: The Miami model. In M. Miranda & H. Kitano (Eds.), *Mental Health Research and Practice in Minority Communities: Development of Culturally Sensitive Training Programs,* pp. 199–226. Washington, DC: National Institute of Mental Health.

Beutler, L. E., M. Crago, & T. G. Arizmendi (1986). Research on therapist variables in psychotherapy. In Garfield & Bergin (1986: 257–310).

Bevilacqua, J. (1995). Why "states' embrace" may be premature. *Health Affairs* 14: 45–6.

Bianchi, S. (1995). Changing economic roles of women and men. In Farley (1995: 107–54).

Bianchi, S. M., & D. Spain (1986). *American Women in Transition.* New York: Russell Sage Foundation.

Bickman, L. (1996a). A continuum of care: More is not always better. *Amer. Psychologist* 51: 689–701.
    (1996b). Reinterpreting the Fort Bragg evaluation findings: The message does not change. *J. Mental Health Administration* 23: 137–45.

Bickman, L., P. Guthrie, E. Foster, W. Summerfelt, E. Lambert, C. Breda, & C. Heflinger (1995). *Evaluating Managed Mental Health Services: The Fort Bragg Experiment.* New York: Plenum.

Bieber, S. L., R. A. Pasewark, K. Bosten, & H. J. Steadman (1988). Predicting criminal recidivism of insanity acquittees. *Internat. J. Law & Psychiatry* 11: 105–12.

Bilder, R. M., L. Lipschutz-Bruch, G. Reiter, S. H. Geisler, D. I. Mayerhoff, & J. A. Lieberman (1992). Intellectual deficits in first-episode schizophrenia: Evidence for progressive deterioration. *Schizophrenia Bull.* 18: 437–48.

Billings, A. C., & R. H. Moos (1982). Stressful life events and symptoms: A longitudinal model. *Health Psychology* 1: 99–117.

Bilu, Y., & E. Witzum (1993). Working with Jewish ultra-Orthodox patients: Guidelines for a culturally sensitive therapy. *Culture, Medicine & Psychiatry* 17: 197–233.

Bird, C. E., & C. E. Ross (1993). Houseworkers and paid workers: Qualities of the work and effects on personal control. *J. Marriage & the Family* 55: 913–25.

Bittner, E. (1967). Police discretion in apprehension of mentally ill persons. *Social Problems* 14: 278–92.

Black, D. R., L. J. Gleser, & K. J. Kooyers (1990). A meta-analytic evaluation of couples weight-loss programs. *Health Psychology* 9: 330–47.

Blake, J. (1989). *Family Size and Achievement*. Berkeley: University of California Press.

Blanchard, E. B., L. C. Kolb, T. P. Pallmeyer, & R. J. Gerardi (1982). The development of a psychophysiological assessment procedure for posttraumatic stress disorder in Vietnam veterans. *Psychiatric Q.* 54: 220–9.

Blanche, A., & D. Penney (1995). "Identity politics" close to home. *Amer. Psychologist* 50: 49–50.

Bland, R. C., S. C. Newman, & H. Orn (1988a). Period prevalence of psychiatric disorders in Edmonton. *Acta Psychiatrica Scandinavica* 77: 33–42.

Bland, R. C., H. Orn, & S. C. Newman (1988b). Lifetime prevalence of psychiatric disorders in Edmonton. *Acta Psychiatrica Scandnavica* 77: 24–32.

Blaney, N. T., K. Goodkin, R. O. Morgan, D. Feaster, C. Millon, J. Szapocznik, & C. Eisdorfer (1991). A stress-moderator model of distress in early HIV-1 infection: Concurrent analysis of life events, hardiness and social support. *J. Psychomatic Res.* 35: 297–305.

Blank, M. B., F. L. Tetrick III, D. F. Brinkley, H. O. Smith, & V. Doheny (1994). Racial matching and service utilization among seriously mentally ill consumers in the rural south. *Community Mental Health J.* 30: 271–81.

Blashfield, R. K. (1991). An American view of the ICD-10 personality disorders. *Acta Psychiatrica Scandnavica* 82: 250–6.

Blau, P. M., & O. D. Duncan (1967). *The American Occupational Structure*. New York: Wiley.

Blauner, R. (1964). *Alienation and Freedom*. Berkeley: University of California Press.

Blazer, D. G., D. Hughes, L. K. George, M. Swartz, & R. Boyer (1991). Generalized anxiety disorder. In Robins & Regier (1991: 180–203).

Blendon, R. J., & K. Donnelan (1988). Discrimination against people with AIDS. *New England J. Medicine* 319: 1022–6.

Blood, R. O., & D. M. Wolfe (1966). *Husbands and Wives*. New York: Free Press.

Bloom, J. D., J. L. Rogers, S. M. Manson, & M. H. Williams (1986). Lifetime police contacts of discharged psychiatric security review board clients. *Internat. J. Law & Psychiatry* 8: 189–202.

Bloom, J. D., J. H. Shore, & B. Arvidson (1981). Local variations in arrests of psychiatric patients. *Bull. Amer. Acad. Psychiatry & Law* 9: 203–10.

Bloom, J. D., M. H. Williams, & D. A. Bigelow (1992). The involvement of schizophrenic insanity acquittees in the mental health and criminal justice systems. *Clinical Forensic Psychiatry* 15: 591–604.

Bloom, J. L., & J. D. Bloom (1981). Disposition of insanity defense cases in Oregon. *Bull. Amer. Acad. Psychiatry & Law* 9: 93–100.

Bobo, J. L., L. D. Gilchrist, G. T. Cvetkovich, J. E. Trimble, & S. P. Schinke (1988). Cross cultural service delivery to minority communities. *J. Community Psychology* 16: 263–72.

Bockoven, J. S. (1972). *Moral Treatment in Community Mental Health*. New York: Springer.

Bogerts, B., & J. Lieberman (1989). Neuropathology in the study of psychiatric disease. In J. A. Silva & C. C. Nadelson (Eds.), *International Review of Psychiatry*, vol. 1, pp. 515–55. Washington, DC: American Psychiatric Press.

Bolger, N., A. DeLongis, R. C. Kessler, & E. A. Schilling (1989). Effects of daily stress on negative mood. *J. Personality & Social Psychology* 57: 808–18.

Bollini, P., & R. Mollica (1989). Surviving without the asylum: An overview of the studies of the Italian reform movement. *J. Nervous & Mental Disease* 177: 607–15.

Bolton, B. A. (1974). A factor analysis of personal adjustment and vocational measures of client change. *Rehab. Counseling Bull.* 18: 99–103.

Bond, G. R., L. L. Dietzen, J. H. McGrew, & L. D. Miller (1995). Accelerating entry into supported employment for persons with severe psychiatric disabilities. *Rehab. Psychology* 40: 75–94.

Bond, G. R., J. Dincin, P. Setze, & T. Witheridge (1984). The effectiveness of psychiatric rehabilitation: A summary of research at thresholds. *Psychosocial Rehab. J.* 7: 6–22.

Bond, G. R., T. Witheridge, J. Dincin, D. Wasmer, D. Webb, & R. DeGraaf-Kaser (1990). Assertive community treatment for frequent users of psychiatric hospitals in a large city: A controlled study. *Amer. J. Community Psychology* 18: 865–91.

Bonovitz, J. C., & J. S. Bonovitz (1981). Diversion of the mentally ill into the criminal justice system: The police intervention perspective. *Amer. J. Psychiatry* 138: 973–6.

Bonovitz, J. C., & E. B. Guy (1979). Impact of restrictive civil commitment procedures on a prison psychiatric service. *Amer. J. Psychiatry* 136: 1045–8.

Borison, R. L., A. Pathiraja, B. Diamond, & R. Meibach (1992). Risperidone: Clinical safety and efficacy in schizophrenia. *Psychopharmacology Bull.* 28: 213–18.

Bourdon, K. H., D. S. Rae, B. Z. Locke, W. E. Narrow, & D. A. Regier (1992). Estimating the prevalence of mental disorders in U.S. adults from the Epidemiologic Catchment Area study. *Public Health Report* 107: 663–8.

Bowlby, J. (1969) *Attachment and Loss: Attachment,* vol. 1. London: Hogarth.
   (1973). *Attachment and Loss: Separation, Anxiety and Anger,* vol. 2. London: Hogarth.

Bowling, A. (1987). Mortality after bereavement: A review of the literature on survival periods and factors affecting survival. *Social Science & Medicine* 24: 117–24.

Bowling, A., & P. D. Browne (1991). Social networks, health, and emotional well-being among the oldest old in london. *J. Gerontology* 46: 20–32.

Bowman, A., & R. Kearney (1990). *State and Local Government.* Boston: Houghton Mifflin.

Boyd, J. H., & M. M. Weissman (1981). Epidemiology of affective disorders: A reexamination and future directions. *Arch. General Psychiatry* 38: 1039–46.

Boyer, C. A., & D. Mechanic (1994). Psychiatric reimbursement reform in New York State: Lessons in implementing change. *Milbank Q.* 72: 621–51.

Boyle, P., & D. Callahan (1995). Managed care in mental health: The ethical issues. *Health Affairs* 14: 7–22.

Bracken, M. B. (Ed.) (1984). *Perinatal Epidemiology.* New York: Oxford University Press.

Bradbury, T., & G. Miller (1985). Season of birth in schizophrenia: A review of evidence, methodology and etiology. *Psychological Bull.* 98: 569–94.

Bradley, R. H. (1985). The home inventory: Rationale and research. In J. Lachenmeyer & M. Gibbs (Eds.), *Recent Research in Developmental Psychopathology* (Book suppl. to *J. Child Psychology & Psychiatry*), pp. 191–201. New York: Gardner.

Bradley, R. H., & B. M. Caldwell (1984). The relation of infants' home environments to achievement test performance in first grade: A follow-up study. *Child Development* 55: 803–9.

Bradley, R. H., B. M. Caldwell, S. L. Rock, H. M. Hamrick, & P. Harris (1988). Home observation for measurement of the environment: Development of a home inventory for use with families having children 6 to 10 years old. *Contemporary Educational Psychology* 13: 58–71.

Braff, J., T. Arvinites, & H. J. Steadman (1983). Detention patterns of successful and unsuccessful insanity defendants. *Criminology* 21: 439–48.

Braginsky, B. M., D. D. Braginsky, & K. Ring (1969). *Methods of Madness: The Mental Hospital as a Last Resort.* New York: Holt, Rinehart & Winston.

Braithwaite, J. (1989). *Crime, Shame and Reintegration.* Cambridge University Press.

Brand, R. C., & W. L. Claiborn (1976). Two studies of comparative stigma. Employer attitudes and practices toward rehabilitated convicts, mental and tuberculosis patients. *Community Mental Health J.* 12: 168–75.

Bray, J. H. (1988). Children's development during early remarriage. In E. M. Hetherington & J. D. Aresteh (Eds.), *Impact of Divorce, Single Parenting, and Stepparenting on Children,* pp. 279–98. Hillsdale, NJ: Erlbaum.

Breggin, P. R. (1991). *Toxic Psychiatry. Why Therapy, Empathy, and Love Must Replace the Drugs, Electroshock, and Biochemical Theories of the New Psychiatry.* New York: St. Martin's.

Brenner, M. H. (1973). *Mental Illness and the Economy.* Cambridge, MA: Harvard University Press.
   (1987). Relation of economic change to Swedish health and social well-being 1950–1980. *Social Science & Medicine* 25: 183–95.

Breslau, N., & G. C. Davis (1985). DSM-III generalized anxiety disorder: An empirical investigation of more stringent criteria. *Psychiatry Res.* 15: 231.

Breslau, N., G. C. Davis, P. Andreski, & E. Peterson (1991). Traumatic events and posttraumatic stress disorder in an urban population of young adults. *Arch. General Psychiatry* 48: 216–22.

Brett, E. A., & R. Ostroff (1985). Imagery and posttraumatic stress disorder: An overview. *Amer. J. Psychiatry* 142: 417–24.

Briggs, J. L. (1970). *Never in Anger: Portrait of an Eskimo Family.* Cambridge, MA: Harvard University Press.

Broman, C. L. (1987). Race differences in professional help seeking. *Amer. J. Community Psychology* 4: 473–89.

Bromet, E. J., M. A. Dew, D. K. Parkinson, & H. C. Schulberg (1988). Predictive effects of occupational and marital stress on mental health of a male workforce. *J. Organizational Behavior* 9: 1–13.

Brooks-Gunn, Jeanne, G. J. Duncan, P. K. Klebanov, & N. Sealand (1993). Do neighborhoods influence child and adolescent development. *Amer. J. Sociology* 99: 353–95.

Brooks-Gunn, Jeanne, & A. C. Petersen (1991). Studying the emergence of depression and depressive symptoms during adolescence. *J. Youth & Adolescence* 20: 115–19.

Brooks-Gunn, Jeanne, & M. P. Warren (1989). Biological and social contributions to negative affect in young adolescent girls. *Child Development* 60: 40–55.

Brown, D. R., W. W. Eaton, & L. Sussman (1990). Racial differences in prevalence of phobic disorders. *J. Nervous & Mental Disease* 178: 434–41.

Brown, G. R., & J. R. Rundell (1990). Prospective study of psychiatric morbidity in HIV-seropositive women without AIDS. *General Hospital Psychiatry* 12: 30–5.

Brown, G. W. (1974). Meaning, measurement, and stress of life events. In Dohrenwend & Dohrenwend (1974a: 217–43).

(1985). The discovery of expressed emotion: Induction or deduction? In Leff & Vaughn (1985: 7–25).

(1986). Mental illness. In L. Aiken & D. Mechanic (Eds.), *Applications of Social Science to Clinical Medicine and Health Policy,* pp. 175–203. New Brunswick, NJ: Rutgers University Press.

Brown, G. W., B. Andrews, T. Harris, Z. Adler, & L. Bridge (1986a). Social support, self-esteem, and depression. *Psychological Medicine* 16: 813–31.

Brown, G. W., M. N. Bhrolchain, & T. Harris (1975). Social class and psychiatric disturbance among women in an urban population. *Sociology* 2: 225–54.

Brown, G. W., & T. O. Harris (1978). *Social Origins of Depression: A Study of Psychiatric Disorder in Women.* New York: Free Press.

(1989). *Life Events and Illness.* New York: Guilford.

Brown, G. W., T. Harris, & A. Bifulco (1986b). Long-term effects of early loss of parent. In M. Rutter, G. E. Izard, & P. B. Read (Eds.), *Depression in Young People,* pp. 251–96. New York: Guilford.

Brown, G. W., T. O. Harris, & C. Hepworth (1995). Loss, humiliation and entrapment among women developing depression: A patient and non-patient comparison. *Psychological Medicine* 25: 7–21.

Brown, G. W., & P. W. Moran (1997). Single mothers, poverty, and depression. *Psychological Medicine* 27: 21–4. Brown, L. (1983). *Politics and Health Care Organizations: HMOs as Federal Policy.* Washington, DC: Brookings.

Brown, P. (1985). *The Transfer of Care: Psychiatric Deinstitutionalization and Its Aftermath.* London: Routledge.

Brown, P. and E. Cooksey (1989). Mental health monopoly: Corporate trends in mental health services. *Social Science & Medicine* 28: 1129–39.

Bruce, M. L. and P. K. Leaf (1989). Psychiatric disorders and 15-month mortality in a community sample of older adults. *Amer. J. Public Health* 79: 727–30.

Bruce, M. L., D. T. Takeuchi, & P. J. Leaf (1991). Poverty and psychiatric status. *Arch. General Psychiatry* 48: 470–4.

Bryer, J. B., B. A. Nelson, J. B. Miller, & P. A. Krol (1987). Childhood sexual and physical abuse as factors in adult psychiatric illness. *Amer. J. Psychiatry* 144: 1426–30.

Bryk, A. S., & S. W. Raudenbush (1992). *Hierarchical Linear Models: Applications and Data Analysis Methods.* Newbury Park, CA: Sage.

Buchwald, D., S. M. Manson, N. G. Dinges, E. M. Keane, & J. D. Kinzie (1993). Prevalence of depressive symptoms among established Vietnamese refugees in the United States: Detection in a primary care setting. *J. General Internal Medicine* 8: 76–81.

Buckley, P., E. O'Callaghan, C. Larkin, & J. L. Waddington (1992). Schizophrenia research: The problem of controls. *Biological Psychiatry* 32: 215–17.

Bullard, R. D. (Ed.) (1993). *Confronting Environmental Racism: Voices from the Grassroots.* Boston: South End.

Bumpass, L. L., & J. A. Sweet (1989). Children's experience in single-parent families: Implications of cohabitation and marital transitions. *Family Planning Perspectives* 6: 256–60.

Burgess, A. W., & L. L. Holstrum (1974). The rape trauma syndrome. *Amer. J. Psychiatry* 131: 981–6.

Burnam, A., M. Karno, R. L. Hough, J. I. Escobar, & C. Telles (1987). Acculturation and lifetime prevalence of psychiatric disorders among Mexican Americans in Los Angeles. *J. Health & Social Behavior* 28: 89–92.

Burnam, A., J. A. Stein, J. M. Golding, J. M. Siegel, S. B. Sorenson, A. B. Forsythe, & C. A. Telles (1988). Sexual assault and mental disorders in a community population. *J. Consulting & Clinical Psychology* 56: 843–50.

Burt, R. S. (1987). A note on strangers, friends, and happiness. *Social Networks* 9: 311–32.

Burton, N. M., & H. J. Steadman (1978). Legal professionals' perceptions of the insanity defense. *J. Psychiatry & Law* 6: 173–87.

Busbin, J. (1993). Evolutionary changes in the marketing of mental health products to government, business and industry. *J. Nonprofit & Public Sector Marketing* 1: 107–26.

Cadoret, R. J. (1978). Evidence for genetic inheritance of primary affective disorder in adoptees. *Amer. J. Psychiatry* 133: 463–6.

(1991). Adoption studies in psychosocial epidemiology. In Tsuang et al. (1991: 33–46).

Cadoret, R., T. W. O'Gorman, E. Heywood, et al. (1985). Genetic and environmental factors in major depression. *J. Affective Disorders* 9: 155–64.

Callahan, J., et al. (1995). Mental health/substance abuse treatment in managed care: The Massachusetts Medicaid experience. *Health Affairs* 14: 173–84.

Callahan, L. A., C. Mayer, & H. J. Steadman (1987). Insanity defense reform in the United States – post Hinckley. *Mental & Physical Disability Law Reporter* 11: 54–9.

Callahan, L. A., M. A. McGreevy, C. Cirincione, & H. J. Steadman (1992). Measuring the effects of the guilty but mentally ill (GMBI) verdict: Georgia's 1982 GBMI reform. *Law & Human Behavior* 16: 447–62.

Callinicos, A., & C. Harman (1989). *The Changing Working Class*. Chicago: Bookmarks.

Campbell, A., P. E. Converse, & W. L. Rodgers (1976). *The Quality of American Life*. New York: Russell Sage Foundation.

Campbell, J., & R. Schraiber (1989). *The Well-Being Project: Mental Health Clients Speak for Themselves*. Sacramento, CA.: California Department of Mental Health.

Canino, G. J., H. R. Bird, M. Rubio-Stipic, & M. A. Woodbury (1987a). Reliability of child diagnosis in a Hispanic sample. *J. Amer. Acad. Child Psychiatry* 25: 254–9.

Canino, G. J., H. R. Bird, P. E. Shrout, M. B. Rubio-Stipec, M. Bravo, R. Martinez, M. Sesman, & L. M. Guevara (1987b). The prevalence of specific psychiatric disorders in Puerto Rico. *Arch. General Psychiatry* 44: 727–35.

Cannon, W. B. (1929). *Bodily Changes in Pain, Hunger, Fear and Rage,* 2nd ed. New York: Appleton.

Caras, S. (1994). ThisIsCrazy. Email to Sylvia Caras ⟨sylviac@netcom.com⟩.

Carey, M. P., L. S. Weinhardt, & K. B. Carey (1995). Prevalence of infection with HIV among the seriously mentally ill: A review of research and implications for practice. *Professional Psychology: Res. & Practice* 26: 262–8.

Carling, P. J. (1993). Housing and supports for persons with mental illness: Emerging approaches to research and practice. *Hospital & Community Psychiatry* 44: 439–49.

Carpenter, W. T., R. Conley, R. Buchanan, A. Breier, & C. A. Tammings (1995). Patient response and resource management: Another view of clozapine treatment of schizophrenia. *Amer. J. Psychiatry* 6: 827–32.

Caspi, A., & D. J. Bem (1990). Personality continuity and change across the life course. In L. A. Pervin (Ed.), *Handbook of Personality: Theory and Research*. New York: Guilford.

Caspi, A., G. H. Elder, Jr., & D. J. Bem (1988). Moving away from the world: Life course patterns of shy children. *Developmental Psychology* 24: 824–31.

Cassel, J. (1974). Psychosocial processes and "stress": Theoretical formulation. *Internat. J. Health Services* 4: 471–82.

(1976). The contribution of the social environment to host resistance. *Amer. J. Epidemiology* 14: 107–23.

Castonguay, L. G., & M. R. Goldfried (1994). Psychotherapy integration: An idea whose time has come. *Applied & Preventive Psychology* 3: 159–72.

Catalano, Ralph (1981). Contending with rival hypotheses in correlation of aggregate time series (CATS): An overview for community psychologists. *Amer. J. Community Psychology* 9: 667–79.

Catalano, R., & D. Dooley (1977). Economic predictors of depressed mood and stressful life events in a metropolitan community. *J. Health & Social Behavior* 18: 292–307.

(1983). The health effects of economic instability: A test of economic stress hypothesis. *J. Health & Social Behavior* 24: 46–60.

Catalano, Richard, D. Dooley, & R. Jackson (1981). Economic predictors of admissions to mental health facilities in a nonmetropolitan community. *J. Health & Social Behavior* 22: 284–97.

Cavalli-Sforza, L. L., P. Menozi, & A. Piazza (1994). *The History and Geography of Human Genes.* Princeton, NJ: Princeton University Press.

Cervantes, R. C., & W. Arroyo (1994). DSM-IV: Implications for Hispanic children and adolescents. *Hispanic J. Behavioral Sciences* 16: 8–27.

Chamberlin, J. (1977). *On Our Own. Patient-Controlled Alternatives to the Mental Health System.* New York: Hawthorn.

(1984). Speaking for ourselves: An overview of the ex-psychiatric inmates' movement. *Psychosocial Rehab. J.* 8: 56–63.

Chamberlin, J., & J. A. Rogers (1990). Planning a community-based mental health system: Perspectives of service recipients. *Amer. Psychologist* 45: 1241–4.

Chen, C., J. Wong, N. Lee, M. Chan-Ho, J. T. Lau, & M. Fung (1993). The Shatin community mental health survey in Hong Kong: II. Major findings. *Arch. General Psychiatry* 50: 125–33.

Cherlin, A. (1992). *Marriage, Divorce, Remarriage,* rev. ed. Cambridge, MA: Harvard University Press.

Cherlin, A. J., F. F. Furstenberg, Jr., P. L. Chase-Lansdale, K. E. Kiernan, P. K. Robins, D. R. Morrison, & J. O. Teitler (1991). Longitudinal studies of effects of divorce on children in Great Britain and the United States. *Science* 252: 1386–9.

Chesler, P. (1972). *Women and Madness.* New York: Doubleday.

Chesney, M., & S. Folkman (1994). Psychological impact of HIV disease and implications for intervention. *Psychiatric Clinics of North America* 17: 163–82.

Chin, J. L. (1993). Toward a psychology of difference: Psychotherapy for a culturally diverse population. In J. L. Chin (Ed.), *Diversity in Psychotherapy,* pp. 69–92. Westport, CT: Praeger.

Chodorow, N. (1974). Family structure and feminine personality. In M. Rosaldo & L. Lamphere (Eds.), *Women, Culture, and Society.* Stanford, CA: Stanford University Press.

(1978). *The Reproduction of Mothering.* Berkeley: University of California Press.

Choi, P. Y., & P. Salmon (1995). Stress responsivity in exercisers and non-exercisers during different phases of the menstrual cycle. *Social Science & Medicine* 41: 769–77.

Chomsky, N. (1989). *Necessary Illusions: Thought Control in Democratic Societies.* Boston: South End.

Christianson, J., et al. (1995). Utah's prepaid mental health plan: The first year. *Health Affairs* 14: 160–72.

Chu, F., & S. Trotter (1974). *The Madness Establishment.* New York: Grossman.

Chua, S. Eng, & P. J. McKenna (1995). Schizophrenia – A brain disease?: A critical review of structural and functional cerebral abnormality in the disorder. *Brit. J. Psychiatry* 166: 563–82.

Chuang, H. T., G. M. Devins, J. Hunsley, & M. J. Gill (1989). Psychosocial distress and well-being among gay and bisexual men with human immunodeficiency virus infection. *Amer. J. Psychiatry* 146: 876–9.

Cirincione, C., H. J. Steadman, P. C. Robbins, & J. Monahan (1994). Mental illness as a factor in criminality: A study of prisoners and mental patients. *Criminal Behavior & Mental Health* 4: 33–47.

Clancy, C. M., & H. Brody (1995). Managed care: Jekyll or Hyde? *J. Amer. Medical Assoc.* 273: 388–9.

Clausen, J. A. (1981). Stigma and mental disorder: Phenomena and terminology. *Psychiatry* 44: 287–96.

(1991). Adolescent competence and the shaping of the life course. *Amer. J. Sociology* 96: 805–42.

Clausen, J., & M. Yarrow (1955). Pathways to the mental hospital. *J. Social Issues* 11: 25–32.

Cleary, P. D. (1987). Gender differences in stress-related disorders. In R. C. Barnett, L. Biener, & G. K. Baruch (Eds.), *Gender and Stress,* pp. 144–56. New York: Free Press.

(1989) The need and demand for mental health services. In Taube et al. (1989: 161–84).

Clomipramine Collaborative Study Group (1991). Clomipramine in the treatment of patients with obsessive compulsive disorder. *Arch. General Psychiatry* 48: 730–8.

CMHS [Center for Mental Health Services] (1994a). Mental health systems improvement demonstration grants for consumer and family networks. Substance Abuse and Mental Health Services Administration, Department of Health and Human Services, Rockville, MD.

(1994b). Managed behavioral healthcare: History, models, key issues, and future course. Substance Abuse and Mental Health Services Administration, Department of Health and Human Services, Rockville, MD.

(1994c). The evolution and expansion of mental health care in the united states between 1955 and 1990. Mental Health Statistical Note no. 210, Substance Abuse and Mental Health Services Administration, U.S. Department of Health and Human Services, Washington, DC.

(1995). First year interim status report on the evaluation of access demonstration program. Substance Abuse and Mental Health Services Administration, Department of Health and Human Services, Rockville, MD.

Coates, T. J., L. Temoshok, & J. S. Mandel (1984). Psychosocial research is essential to understanding and treating AIDS. *Amer. Psychologist* 39: 1309–14.

Cobb, S. (1976). Social support as a moderator of life stress. *Psychosomatic Medicine* 38: 300–14.

(1979). Social support and health through the life course. In M. W. Riley (Ed.), *Aging from Birth to Death.* Boulder, CO: Westview.

Cockerham, W. C. (1990). A test of the relationship between race, socioeconomic status and psychological distress. *Social Science Medicine* 31: 1321–6.

Cohen, C. I., J. Teresi, & D. Holmes (1985). Social networks, stress, adaptation, and health. *Res. on Aging* 7: 409–31.

Cohen, N. L., & L. R. Marcos (1990). Law, policy and involuntary emergency room visits. *Psychiatric Q.* 63: 197–204.

Cohen, P., J. Johnson, S. A. Lewis, & J. S. Brook (1990). Single parenthood and employment: Double jeopardy? In J. Eckenrode & S. Gore (Eds.), *Stress between Work and Family,* pp. 117–32. New York: Plenum.

Cohen, P., E. L. Struening, G. L. Muhlin, et al. (1982). Community stressors, mediating conditions, and well-being in urban neighborhoods. *J. Community Psychology* 10: 377–91.

Cohen, S. (1992). Models of the support process. In Veil & Baumann (1992b: 109–24).

(1996). Psychological stress, immunity, and upper respiratory infections. *Current Directions in Psychological Science* 5: 86–90.

Cohen, S., & S. L. Syme (Eds.) (1985). *Social Support and Health.* New York: Academic Press.

Cohen, S., & G. M. Williamson (1991). Stress and infectious disease in humans. *Psychological Bull.* 109: 5–24.

Cohen, S., & T. A. Wills (1985). Stress, social support, and the buffering hypothesis. *Psychological Bull.* 98: 310–57.

Cole, J., & M. Pilisuk (1976). Differences in the provision of mental health services by race. *Amer. J. Orthopsychiatry* 46: 510–25.

Coleman, J. S. (1988). Social capital in the creation of human capital. *Amer. J. Sociology* 94: S95–S120.

Collins, J. G. (1988). Prevalence of selected chronic conditions, United States, 1983–85. *NCHS Advance Data* 155: 1–16.

Collins, J. J., & W. E. Schlenger (1983). The prevalence of psychiatric disorder among admissions to prisons. Paper presented at the annual meeting of the American Society of Criminology (November 9–13), Denver, CO.

Collins, R. (1994). *Four Sociological Traditions.* New York: Oxford University Press.

Coltrane, S. (1988). Father-child relationships and the status of women: A cross-cultural study. *Amer. J. Sociology* 93: 1060–95.

Commission on Lunacy (1855). *Report on Insanity and Idiocy in Massachusetts,* by E. Jarvis. Boston: Harvard University Press (reprinted 1971).

Commonwealth Fund (1995). *National Comparative Survey of Minority Health Care.* New York: Commonwealth Fund.

Comstock, G. W., & J. A. Tonascia (1977). Education and mortality in Washington County, Maryland. *J. Health & Social Behavior* 18: 54–60.

Conger, R. D., K. J. Conger, G. H. Elder, Jr., F. O. Lorenz, R. L. Simons, & L. B. Whitbeck (1992). A family process model of economic hardship and adjustment of early adolescent boys. *Child Development* 63: 526–41.

Conger, R. D., & G. H. Elder, Jr. (1994). *Families in Troubled Times: Adapting to Change in Rural America.* New York: de Gruyter.

Conger, R. D., G. H. Elder, Jr., F. O. Lorenz, K. J. Conger, R. L. Simons, L. B. Whitbeck, S. Huck, & J. N. Melby (1990). Linking economic hardship to marital quality and instability. *J. Marriage & the Family* 52: 643–56.

Conger, R. D., F. O. Lorenz, G. H. Elder, Jr., R. L. Simmons, & X. Ge (1993). Husband and wife differences in response to undesirable life events. *J. Health & Social Behavior* 34: 71–88.

Conger, J. J., W. Sawrey, & E. S. Turrell (1958). The role of social experience in the production of gastric ulcers in hooded rats placed in a conflict situation. *J. Abnormal Psychology* 57: 214–20.

Conlan, T. (1988). *New Federalism: Intergovernmental Reform from Nixon to Reagan.* Washington, DC: Brookings.

Consumer Managed Care Network (1996). *Platform for Action.* Washington, DC: CMCN.

Cook, J. A. (1988). Who "mothers" the chronically ill? *Family Relations* 37: 42–7.

(1994). Independent community living among women with mental illness: A comparison with outcomes among men. *J. Mental Health Administration* 21: 363–73.

(1995). Research on psychosocial rehabilitation services for persons with psychiatric disabilities. *Psychotherapy & Rehab. Res. Bull.* 4: 5–11.

Cook, J. A., K. Graham, & L. Razzano (1993). Psychosocial rehabilitation of persons who are deaf and mentally ill: A multivariate model of residential outcomes. *Rehab. Psychology* 38: 261–74.

Cook, J. A., & S. Hoffschmidt (1993). Comprehensive models of psychosocial rehabilitation. In R. W. Flexer & P. Solomon (Eds.), *Psychiatric Rehabilitation in Practice,* pp. 81–97. New York: Butterworth-Heinemann.

Cook, J. A., & J. A. Jonikas (1996). Outcomes of psychiatric rehabilitation service delivery. *New Directions in Mental Health Services* 71: 33–47.

Cook, J. A., J. A. Jonikas, & M. L. Solomon (1992). Models of vocational rehabilitation for youth and adults with severe mental illness. *Amer. Rehab.* 18: 6–11.

Cook, J. A., & L. Mock (1990). Minority issues in psychiatric rehabilitation. Thresholds National Research and Training Center, Chicago.

Cook, J. A., & S. A. Pickett (1995). Recent trends in vocational rehabilitation for people with psychiatric disability. *Amer. Rehab.* 20: 2–12.

Cook, J. A., S. A. Pickett, & J. Jonikas (1989). The community exploration program: Vocational laboratory experiences for psychiatrically disabled youth. Thresholds Research Institute, Chicago.

Cook, J. A., S. A. Pickett, L. Razzano, G. Fitzgibbon, J. A. Jonikas, & J. Cohler (1996). Rehabilitation services for persons with schizophrenia. *Psychiatric Ann.* 26: 97–104.

Cook, J. A., & L. Razzano (1992). Natural vocational supports for persons with severe mental illness. In L. Stein (Ed.), *Innovative Community Mental Health Programs,* pp. 23–41. San Francisco: Jossey-Bass.

Cook, J. A., & M. L. Solomon (1993). The community scholar program: An outcome study of supported education for students with severe mental illness. *Psychosocial Rehab. J.* 17: 84–97.

Cook, J. A., & E. R. Wright (1995). Medical sociology and the study of severe mental illness: Reflections on past accomplishments and directions for future research. *J. Health & Social Behavior* 36 (extra issue): 95–114.

Cooksey, E. C., E. G. Menaghan, & S. Jekielek (1997). Life course effects of work and family patterns on child well-being. *Social Forces* 76: 637–67.

Cooper, R. S., & R. David (1986). The biological concept of race and its application to public health and epidemiology. *J. Health & Politics, Policy & Law* 11: 97–116.

Corrado, R. R., D. Doherty, & W. Glackman (1989). A demonstration program for chronic recidivists of criminal justice, health and social service agencies. *Internat. J. Law & Psychiatry* 12: 211–30.

Costello, E. J. (1982). Locus of control and depression in students and psychiatric outpatients. *J. Clinical Psychology* 36: 661–7.

Coté, G., & S. Hodgins (1990). Co-occurring mental disorders among criminal offenders. *Bull. Amer. Acad. Psychiatry & Law* 18: 271–81.

(1992). The prevalence of major mental disorders among homicide offenders. *Internat. J. Law & Psychiatry* 15: 89–99.

Coulter, J. (1973). *Approaches to Insanity: A Philosophical and Sociological Study.* New York: Wiley.

Cox, G. L., & Merkel, W. T. (1989). A qualitative review of psychosocial treatments for bulimia. *J. Nervous & Mental Disease* 177: 77–84.

Coyne, J. C., & G. Downey (1991). Social factors and psychopathology: Stress, social support, and coping processes. *Annual Rev. Psychology* 42: 401–25.

Coyne, J. C., R. C. Kessler, M. Tal, J. Turnbull, C. B. Wortman, & J. F. Greden (1987). Living with a depressed person. *J. Consulting & Clinical Psychology* 55: 347–52.

Crespo, M. (1977). Deviance and aspirations in adolescence: The influence of school absenteeism, drug use, and mental disorder on educational and occupational aspirations. McGill University, Montreal.

Crocetti, G., H. Spiro, & I. Siassi (1971). Are the ranks closed? Attitudinal social distance and mental illness. *Amer. J. Psychiatry* 127: 41–7.

(1974). *Contemporary Attitudes Towards Mental Illness.* Pittsburgh, PA: University of Pittsburgh Press.

Crouter, A. C., J. Belsky, & G. B. Spanier (1984). The family context of child development: Divorce and maternal employment. In *Annals of Child Development,* vol. 1, pp. 201–38. Greenwich, CT: JAI.

Crouter, A. C., S. M. MacDermid, S. M. McHale, & M. Perry-Jenkins (1990). Parental monitoring and perceptions of children's school performance and conduct in dual and single-earner families. *Developmental Psychology* 26: 649–57.

Crow, T. (1994). Prenatal exposure to influenza as a cause of schizophrenia. *Brit. J. Psychiatry* 164: 588–92.

Crystal, S. (1992). Health care barriers and utilization patterns among intravenous-drug users with HIV disease. *AIDS & Public Policy J.* 7: 187–98.

Crystal, S., S. Bilder, U. Sambamoorthi, & C. Merzel (1993). Social support, coping and psychological distress among persons with HIV. Paper presented at the Ninth International Conference on AIDS, Berlin.

Crystal, S., and M. M. Jackson (1989). Psychosocial adaptation and economic circumstances of persons with AIDS and ARC. *Family & Community Health* 12: 77–88.

Crystal, S., S. Ladner, & R. Towber (1986). Multiple impairment patterns in the mentally ill homeless. *Internat. J. Mental Health* 14: 61–73.

Crystal, S., U. Sambamoorthi, & C. Merzel (1995). The diffusion of innovation in AIDS treatment: Zidovudine use in two New Jersey cohorts. *Health Services Res.* 30: 593–614.

Cuffel, B., L. Snowden, M. Masland, & G. Piccagli (1994). *Managed Health Care in the Public Sector.* Berkeley, CA: Institute for Mental Health Services Research.

Cumming, E., & J. Cumming (1957). *Closed Ranks: An Experiment in Mental Health Education.* Cambridge, MA: Harvard University Press.

Cumming, E., L. Edell, & I. Cumming (1965). Policeman as philosopher, guide and friend. *Social Problems* 12: 278–86.

Cumming, E., & C. Harrington (1963). Clergyman as counselor. *Amer. J. Sociology* 69: 234–43.

Cummings, C. M., & D. D. Dehart (1995). Ethnic minority physical health: Issues and interventions. In J. F. Aponte, R. Y. Rivers, & J. Wohl (Eds.), *Psychological Interventions and Cultural Diversity,* pp. 234–49. Boston: Allyn & Bacon.

Cutrano, C. E. (1986). Objective determinants of perceived social support. *J. Personality & Social Psychology* 50: 349–55.

Cvitanic, M. (1990). The use of mental health and social support services by people with AIDS. Ph.D. dissertation, Rand Graduate School of Policy Studies, Santa Monica, CA.

Davies, L., W. R. Avison, & D. D. McAlpine (1997). Significant life experiences and depression among single and married mothers. *J. Marriage & the Family* 59: 1–15.

Davis, J. M. (1975). Overview: Maintenance therapy in psychiatry: I. Schizophrenia.*Amer. J. Psychiatry* 132: 1237–45.

Davis, K., & W. Moore (1974). Some principles of stratification. In J. Lopreato & L. S. Lewis (Eds.), *Social Stratification: A Reader*, pp. 64–71. New York: Harper & Row.

Day, R., A. Nielsen, A. Korten, G. Ernberg, K. Dube, J. Gebhart, A. Jablensky, et al. (1987). Stressful life events preceding the acute onset of schizophrenia: A cross-national study from the World Health Organization. *Culture, Medicine & Psychiatry* 11: 123–205.

Deakin, J. F. W. (1996). Neurobiology of schizophrenia. *Current Opinion in Psychiatry* 9: 50–6.

Dean, A., & N. Lin (1977). The stress buffering role of social support. *J. Nervous & Mental Disease* 165: 403–17.

DeBruyn, L. M., K. Hymbaugh, & N. Valdez (1988). Helping communities address suicide and violence: The special initiatives team of the Indian Health Service. *American Indian & Alaska Native Mental Health Res.* 1: 56–65.

Deegan, P. E. (1993). Recovering our sense of value after being labeled. *J. Psychosocial Nursing* 31: 7–11.

de Girolamo, G., & J. H. Reich (1993). *Epidemiology of Mental Disorders and Psychosocial Problems: Personality Disorders*. Geneva: World Health Organization.

Dendron (1996). *Dendron News.* Eugene, OR: Clearinghouse on Human Rights and Psychiatry.

Desai, S., P. L. Chase-Lansdale, & R. T. Michael (1989). Mother or market? Effects of maternal employment on the intellectual ability of 4-year-old children. *Demography* 26: 545–61.

Dew, M. A., L. Penkower, & E. J. Bromet (1991). Effects of unemployment on mental health in the contemporary family. *Behavior Modification* 15: 501–44.

Dew, M. A., M. V. Ragni, & P. Nimorwicz (1990). Infection with human immunodeficiency virus and vulnerability to psychiatric distress. *Arch. General Psychiatry* 47: 737–44.

DeWitt, K. N. (1978). The effectiveness of family therapy: A review of outcome research. *Arch. General Psychiatry* 35: 549–61.

Dickey, W. (1980). Incompetency and the nondangerous mentally ill client. *Criminal Law Bull.* 16: 22–40.

Diehr, P., S. J. Williams, & D. P. Martin (1984). Ambulatory mental health services utilization in three provider plans. *Medical Care* 2: 1–13.

Dill, A., & D. Rochefort (1989). Coordination, continuity, and centralized control: A policy perspective on service strategies for the chronic mentally ill. *J. Social Issues* 45: 145–59.

Dilley, J. W., H. N. Ochitill, M. Perl, & P. A. Volberding. (1985). Findings in psychiatric consultations with patients with acquired immune deficiency syndrome. *Amer. J. Psychiatry* 142: 82–6.

Dimaggio, P., & H. K. Anheier (1990). The sociology of nonprofit organizations and sectors. *Ann. Rev. Sociology* 16: 137–59.

Dimaggio, P., and W. Powell (1983). The iron cage revisited: Institutional isomorphism and collective rationality in organizational fields. *Amer. Sociological Rev.* 48: 147–60.

Dincin, J. (1990). Speaking out. *Psychosocial Rehab. J.* 14: 83–5.

Dincin, J., & T. F. Witheridge (1982). Psychiatric rehabilitation as a deterrent to recidivism. *Hospital & Community Psychology* 33: 645–50.

Dion, G. L., & W. A. Anthony (1987). Research in psychiatric rehabilitation: A review of experimental and quasi-experimental studies. *Rehab. Counseling Bull.* 30: 177–203.

Dixon, L., & A. Lehman (1996). Family interventions for schizophrenia. *Schizophrenia Bull.* 21: 631–43.

Dodge, K. A. (1993). Social-cognitive mechanisms in the development of conduct disorder and depression. *Annual Rev. Psychology* 44: 559–84.

Dohrenwend, Barbara S., & Bruce P. Dohrenwend (Eds.) (1974a). *Stressful Life Events: Their Nature and Effects.* New York: Wiley.

Dohrenwend, B. S., L. Krasnoff, A. R. Askenasy, & B. P. Dohrenwend (1978a). Exemplification of a method for scaling life events: The PERI life events scale. *J. Health & Social Behavior* 19: 205–29.

Dohrenwend, Bruce P. (1990). Socioeconomic status (SES) and psychiatric disorders: Are the issues still compelling? *Social Psychiatry & Psychiatric Epidemiology* 25: 4–47.

(1995). The problem of validity in field studies of psychological disorders – revisited. In Tsuang et al. (1995: 3–22).

Dohrenwend, B. P., & B. S. Dohrenwend (1969). *Social Status and Psychological Disorder: A Casual Inquiry.* New York: Wiley.

(1974b). Social and cultural influences on psychopathology. *Annual Rev. Psychology* 25: 417–52.

(1982). Perspectives on the past and future of psychiatric epidemiology. *Amer. J. Public Health* 72: 1271–9.

Dohrenwend, B. P., B. S. Dohrenwend, M. Dodson, & P. E. Shrout (1984). Symptoms, hassles, social supports, and life events: The problem of confounded measures. *J. Abnormal Psychology* 93: 222–30.

Dohrenwend, B. P., B. S. Dohrenwend, M. S. Gould, B. Link, R. Neugebauer, & R. Wunsch-Hitzig (1980). *Mental Illness in the United States: Epidemiological Estimates.* New York: Praeger.

Dohrenwend, B. P., I. Levav, P. E. Shrout, S. Schwartz, G. Naveh, B. G. Link, A. E. Skodol, & A. Stueve (1992). Socioeconomic status and psychiatric disorders: The causation–selection issue. *Science* 255: 946–52.

Dohrenwend, B. P., & E. Chin Shong (1967). Social status and attitudes towards psychological disorder: The problem of tolerance of deviance. *Amer. Sociological Rev.* 32: 417–33.

Dohrenwend, B. P., T. J. Yager, G. Egri, & F. S. Mendelsohn (1978b). The psychiatric status schedule (PSS) as a measure of dimensions of psychopathology in the general population. *Arch. General Psychiatry* 35: 731–9.

Donald, C. A., & J. E. Ware (1982). *The Quantification of Social Contacts and Resources.* Santa Monica, CA: Rand.

Dooley, D., & Ralph Catalano (1979). Economic, life, and disorder changes: Time-series analyses. *Amer. J. Community Psychology* 7: 381–96.

(1984a). The epidemiology of economic stress. *Amer. J. Community Psychology* 12: 387–409.

(1988). Recent research on the psychological effects of unemployment. *J. Social Issues* 44: 1–12.

Dooley, D., R. Catalano, & K. Rook (1988). Personal and aggregate unemployment and psychological symptoms. *J. Social Issues* 44: 107–23.

Dooley, D., R. Catalano, & G. Wilson (1994). Depression and unemployment: Panel findings from the Epidemiologic Catchment Area study. *Amer. J. Community Psychology* 22: 742–65.

Dooley, D., & Richard Catalano (1984b). Why the economy predicts help-seeking: A test of competing explanations. *J. Health & Social Behavior* 25: 160–76.

Dorwart, R., et al. (1991). A national study of psychiatric hospital care. *Amer. J. Psychiatry* 148: 204–10.

(1992). A national study of psychiatrists' professional activities. *Amer. J. Psychiatry* 149: 1499–1505.

Dorwart, R., & S. Epstein (1991). Issues in psychiatric hospital care. *Current Opinion in Psychiatry* 4: 789–93.

Dorwart, R., & M. Schlesinger (1988). Privatization of psychiatric services. *Amer. J. Psychiatry* 145: 543–53.

Dowdall, G. (1996). *The Eclipse of the State Mental Hospital: Policy, Stigma, and Organization.* Albany, NY: SUNY Press.

Dowell, D., & J. A. Ciarlo (1989). An evaluative overview of the community mental health centers program. In Rochefort (1989: 195–236).

Downey, G., & J. C. Coyne (1990). Children of depressed parents: An integrative review. *Psychological Bull.* 108: 50–76.

Draguns, J. G. (1984). Assessing mental disorder across cultures. In Pederson et al. (1984: 31–58).

Draine, J., & P. Solomon (1992). Comparison of seriously mentally ill case management clients with and without arrest histories. *J. Psychiatry & Law* 20: 335–49.

(1994). Jail recidivism and the intensity of case management services among homeless persons with mental illness leaving jail. *J. Psychiatry & Law* 22: 245–61.

Draine, J., P. Solomon, & A. T. Meyerson (1994). Predictors of reincarceration among patients who received psychiatric services in jail. *Hospital & Community Psychiatry* 45: 163–7.

Dranove, D., A. Drake, & M. Shanley (1996). Are multihospital systems more efficient? *Health Affairs* 15: 100–4.

Dranove, D., & M. Shanley (1995). Cost reductions or reputation enhancement as motives for mergers: The logic of multihospital systems. *Strategic Management J.* 16: 55–74.

Drehmer, D. E., & J. E. Bordieri (1985). Hiring decisions for disabled workers: The hidden bias. *Rehab. Psychology* 30: 157–64.

Dressler, W. W. (1985). Extended family relationships, social support, and mental health in a southern black community. *J. Health & Social Behavior* 26: 39–48.

Drillien, C. M. (1964). *The Growth and Development of the Prematurely Born Infant*. Baltimore: Williams & Wilkins.

Dunham, H. W. (1959). *Sociological Theory and Mental Disorder*. Detroit: Wayne State University Press.

Dunn, R. L., & Schwebel, A. I. (1995). Meta-analytic review of marital therapy outcome research. *J. Family Psychology* 9: 58–68.

Durham, M. L. (1994). Healthcare's great challenge: Providing services for people with severe mental illness in managed care. *Behavioral Sciences & the Law* 12: 331–49.

(1995). Can HMOs manage the mental health benefit? *Health Affairs* 14: 116–22.

Durham, M. L., H. D. Carr, & G. L. Pierce (1984). Police involvement in involuntary civil commitment. *Hospital & Community Psychiatry* 35: 580–4.

Durkheim, E. (1897). *Suicide: A Study in Sociology*. New York: Free Press (reprinted 1951).

Dvoskin, J. A., & H. J. Steadman (1989). Chronically mentally ill inmates: The wrong concept for the right services. *Internat. J. Law & Psychiatry* 12: 203–11.

(1994). Using intensive case management to reduce violence by mentally ill persons in the community. *Hospital & Community Psychiatry* 45: 679–84.

Dwork, A. (1996). Recent progress and future directions for neuropathologic studies of schizophrenia. In Kauffmann & Gorman (1996: 63–78).

Dykstra, P. (1990). *Next of (Non)Kin: The Importance of Primary Relationships for Older Adults' Well-Being*. Amsterdam: Swets & Zeitlinger.

Eaton, W. W. (1974). Residence, social class, and schizophrenia. *J. Health & Social Behavior* 15: 289–99.

(1978). Life events, social supports, and psychiatric symptoms: A re-analysis of the New Haven data. *J. Health & Social Behavior* 19: 230–4.

(1985). The epidemiology of schizophrenia. *Epidemiologic Rev.* 7: 105–26.

Eaton, W. W., J. C. Anthony, J. Gallo, G. Cai, A. Tien, A. Romanoski, C. Lyketsos, & L.-S. Chen (1997). Natural history of DIS/DSM major depression: The Baltimore ECA Followup. *Arch. General Psychiatry* 54: 993–9.

Eaton, W. W., A. Dryman, & M. M. Weissman (1991). Panic and phobia. In Robins & Regier (1991: 155-79).

Eaton, W. W., & L. G. Kessler (1981). Rates of symptoms of depression in a national sample. *Amer. J. Epidemiology* 114: 528–38.

(Eds.) (1985). *Epidemiologic Field Methods in Psychiatry: The NIMH Epidemiologic Catchment Area Program*. Orlando, FL: Academic Press.

Eaton, W. W., & P. M. Keyl (1990). Risk factors for the onset of DIS/DSM-III agoraphobia in a prospective, population-based study. *Arch. General Psychiatry* 47: 819–24.

Eaton, W. W., & J.-C. Lasry (1978). Mental health and occupational mobility in a group of immigrants. *Social Science & Medicine* 12: 53–8.

Eaton, W. W., D. A. Regier, B. Z. Locke, & C. A. Taube (1981). The Epidemiologic Catchment Area program of the National Institute of Mental Health. *Public Health Report* 96: 319–25.

Edwards, R. (1979). *Contested Terrain: The Transformation of the Workplace in the Twentieth Century*. New York: Basic Books.

Egeland, J. A., & A. Hostetter (1983). Amish study I: Affective disorders among the Amish. *Amer. J. Psychiatry* 140: 56–61.

Egeland, J. A., A. Hostetter, & S. K. Eshleman (1983). Amish study III: The impact of cultural factors in the diagnosis of bipolar illness. *Amer. J. Psychiatry* 140: 67–71.

Egendorf, A., C. Kashudin, R. S. Laufer, G. Rothbart, & L. Sloan (1981). *Legacies of Vietnam: Comparative Adjustment of Veterans and Their Peers*. New York: Center for Policy Research.

Eisenberg, L. (1995). The social construction of the human brain. *Amer. J. Psychiatry* 152: 1563–75.

Eisenberg, P., & P. F. Lazarsfeld (1938). The psychological effects of unemployment. *Psychological Bull.* 35: 358–90.

Elardo, R. D., & R. H. Bradley (1981). The Home Observation for Measurement of the Environment (HOME) Scale: A review of research. *Developmental Rev.* 1: 113–45.

Elias, E., & M. Navon (1995). The Massachusetts experience with managed mental health care and Medicaid. *Health Affairs* 14: 46–9.

Elder, G. H., Jr. (1974). Children of the great depression: Social change in life experience. University of Chicago Press (reprinted 1977).

Elder, G. H., Jr., & A. Caspi (1988a). Human development and social change: An emerging perspective on the life course. In N. Bolger, A. Caspi, G. Downey, & M. Moorehouse (Eds.), *Persons in Context: Developmental Processes,* pp. 77–113. Cambridge University Press.

  (1988b). Economic stress in lives: Developmental perspectives. *J. Social Issues* 44: 25–45.

Elder, G. H. Jr., L. K. George, & M. J. Shanahan (1996). Psychosocial stress over the life course. In Kaplan (1996b: 247–92).

Elder, G. H. Jr., T. V. Nguyen, & A. Caspi (1985). Linking family hardship to children's lives. *Child Development* 56: 361–75.

Elkin, I., M. T. Shea, J. T. Watkins, S. D. Imber, S. M. Sotaky, J. F. Collins, D. R. Glass, P. A. Pilkonis, W. R. Leber, J. P. Docherty, S. J. Fiester, & M. B. Parloff (1989). NIMH treatment of depression collaborative research program: General effectiveness of programs. *Arch. General Psychiatry* 46: 971–82.

Ellenberger, H. F. (1970). *The Discovery of the Unconscious.* New York: Basic Books.

Ellerbock, T. V., T. J. Bush, M. E. Chamberland, & M. J. Oxtoby (1991). Epidemiology of women with AIDS in the United States, 1981 through 1990. *J. Amer. Medical Assoc.* 265: 2971–5.

Ellis, A. (1962). *Reason and Emotion in Psychotherapy.* New York: Stuart.

Emanuel, E. J., & N. N. Dubler (1995). Preserving the physician–patient relationship in the era of managed care. *J. Amer. Medical Assoc.* 273: 323–9.

Emerick, R. E. (1989). Group demographics in the mental patients movement. *Community Mental Health J.* 25: 227–300.

Emmelkamp, P. M. G. (1994). Behavior therapy with adults. In Bergin & Garfield (1994: 379–427).

Emmons, D., & A. Chawla (1991). Physician perceptions of the intrusiveness of utilization review. In *Socioeconomic Characteristics of Medical Practice,* pp. 3–8. Chicago: American Medical Association.

Engel, G. L. (1980). The clinical application of the biopsychosocial model. *Amer. J. Psychiatry* 137: 535–44.

Engels, F. (1958). *The Condition of the Working Class in England,* Trans. by O. W. Henderson and W. H. Chalones. Stanford, CA: Stanford University Press.

Engels, G. I., N. Garnefski, & R. F. W. Diekstra (1993). Efficacy of rational-emotive therapy: A quantitative analysis. *J. Consulting & Clinical Psychology* 61: 1083–90.

Englund, M. (1994). From fee-for-service to accountable health plans. In Schreter et al. (1994b: 3–10).

Ensel, W. M., & N. Lin (1991). The life stress paradigm and psychological distress. *J. Health & Social Behavior* 32: 321–41.

Eraker, S. A., J. P. Kirscht, & M. H. Becker (1984). Understanding and improving patient compliance. *Ann. Internal Medicine* 2: 1–13.

Erikson, E. (1950). *Childhood and Society.* New York: Norton (reprinted 1963).

Erikson, K. T. (1976). Loss of community at Buffalo Creek. *Amer. J. Psychiatry* 133: 302–5.

  (1986). On work and alienation. *Amer. Sociological Rev.* 51: 1–8.

Erikson, R. E., & J. H. Goldthrope (1993). *The Constant Flux. A Study of Class Mobility in Industrial Societies.* Oxford: Clarendon.

Ermann, D. (1988). Hospital utilization review: Past experience, future directions. *J. Health Politics, Policy & Law* 13: 683–704.

Ernst, C., & J. Angst (1992). The Zurich study XII. Sex difference in depression. Evidence from longitudinal epidemiological data.*European Arch. Psychiatry & Clinical Neuroscience* 241: 222–30.

Essed, P. (1990). *Everyday Racism: Reports from Women of Two Cultures.* Alameda, CA: Hunter House.

  (1991). *Understanding Everyday Racism.* Newbury Park, CA: Sage.

Essock, S. M., & H. H. Goldman (1995). State's embrace of managed mental health care. *Health Affairs* 14: 35–44.

Estrada, P., W. F. Arsenio, R. D. Hess, & S. D. Holloway (1987). Affective quality of the mother–child relationship: Longitudinal consequences for children's school-relevant cognitive functioning. *Developmental Psychology* 23: 210–15.

Estroff, S. E. (1989). Self, identity, and subjective experiences of schizophrenia: In search of the subject. *Schizophrenia Bull.* 15: 189–96.

Estroff, S. E., W. S. Lachincotte, L. C. Illingworth, & A. Johnston (1991). Everybody's got a little mental illness: Accounts of illness and self among people with severe, persistent mental illness. *Medical Anthropology Q.* 5: 331–69.

Fabrega, H. (1969). Social psychiatric aspects of acculturation and migration: A general statement. *Comprehensive Psychiatry* 10: 314–92.

(1990). Hispanic mental health research: A case for cultural psychiatry. *Hispanic J. Behavioral Sciences* 23: 339–65.

Fairweather, G. W. (1980). *New Directions for Mental Health Services: The Fairweather Lodge: A Twenty-five Year Retrospective.* San Francisco: Jossey-Bass.

Faraone, S., & S. Santangelo (1992). Methods in genetic epidemiology. In M. Fava & J. F. Rosenbaum (Eds.), *Research Designs and Methods in Psychiatry,* pp. 93–118. Amsterdam: Elsevier.

Faraone, S., & M. T. Tsuang (1995). Methods in psychiatric genetics. In Tsuang et al. (1995: 81–133).

Fariante, C. M., P. Salis, P. Dazzan, M. G. Carta, & B. Carpiniello (1996). Outcome of patients after reform in Italy. *Psychiatric Services* 47: 1266–7.

Farina, A., J. Allen, & B. Saul (1968). The role of the stigmatized person in effecting social relationships. *J. Personality* 36: 169–82.

Farina, A., & R. D. Felner (1973). Employment interviewer reactions to former mental patients. *J. Abnormal Psychology* 82: 268–72.

Farina, A., D. Gliha, L. Boudreau, J. Allen, & M. Sherman (1971). Mental illness and the impact of believing others know about it. *J. Abnormal Psychology* 77: 1–5.

Faris, R. E. L., & H. W. Dunham (1939). *Mental Disorders in Urban Areas: An Ecological Study of Schizophrenia and Other Psychoses.* University of Chicago Press.

Farkas, M., & W. Anthony (1989). *Psychiatric Rehabilitation.* Baltimore: Johns Hopkins University Press.

Farley, J. E. (1994). *Sociology,* 3rd ed. Englewood Cliffs, NJ: Prentice-Hall.

(Ed.) (1995). *State of the Union: America in the 1990s,* vol. I (Economic Trends). New York: Russell Sage Foundation.

Faulstich, M. F. (1987). Psychiatric aspects of AIDS. *Amer. J. Psychiatry* 144: 551–6.

Feagin, J. R. (1991). The continuing significance of race: Anti-Black discrimination in public places. *Amer. Sociological Rev.* 56: 101–16.

Feder, L. (1991). A comparison of the community adjustment of mentally ill offenders with those from the general population: An 18 month followup. *Law & Human Behavior* 15: 477–94.

(1994). Psychiatric hospitalization history and parole decisions. *Law & Human Behavior* 18: 395–410.

Federal Task Force on Homelessness and Severe Mental Illness (1992). *Outcasts on Main Street.* Washington, DC: Interagency Council on the Homeless.

Fennell, M., & R. Warnecke (1988). *The Diffusion of Medical Innovations: An Applied Network Analysis.* New York: Plenum.

Fenwick, R., & M. Tausig (1994). The macroeconomic context of job stress. *J. Health & Social Behavior* 35: 266–82.

Ferree, M. Max, & F. D. Miller (1985). Mobilization and meaning: Toward an integration of social psychological and resource perspective on social movements. *Sociological Inquiry* 55: 38–61.

Ferguson, T. (1995). *Golden Rule: The Investment Theory of Party Competition and the Logic of Money-Driven Political Systems.* University of Chicago Press.

Festinger, L. (1957). *A Theory of Cognitive Dissonance.* Evanston, IL: Row, Peterson.

Finn, P. E., & M. Sullivan (1988). Police respond to special populations. *NIJ Reports* 209: 2–8.

Fischer, J. (1969). Negroes and whites and rates of mental illness: Reconsideration of a myth. *Psychiatry* 32: 428–46.

Fischer, P. J. (1988). Criminal activity among the homeless: A study of arrests in Baltimore. *Hospital & Community Psychiatry* 39: 46–51.

Fisher, D. B. (1994). A new vision of healing as constructed by people with psychiatric disabilities working as mental health providers. *Psychosocial Rehab. J.* 17: 67–81.

———— (1996). *Newsletter.* Lawrence, MA: National Empowerment Center.

Fisher, J. D. (1988). Possible effects of reference group-based social influence on AIDS-risk behavior and AIDS prevention. *Amer. Psychologist* 43: 914–20.

Flaherty, J. A., & R. Meagher (1980). Measuring racial bias in inpatient treatment. *Amer. J. Psychiatry* 137: 679–82.

Flaherty, J. A., & J. A. Richman (1986). Effects of childhood relationships on the adult's capacity to form social supports. *Amer. J. Psychiatry* 59: 143–53.

Flanagan, J. G. (1989). Hierarchy in simple egalitarian societies. *Annual Rev. Anthropology* 18: 245–66.

Flaskerud, J. H., & L.-T. Hu (1992). Relationship of ethnicity to psychiatric diagnosis. *J. Nervous & Mental Disease* 180: 296–303.

———— (1994). Participation in and outcome of treatment for major depression among low income Asian-Americans. *Psychiatry Res.* 53: 289–300.

Flaskerud, J. H., & P. Y. Liu (1990). Influence of therapist ethnicity and language on therapy outcome of Southeast Asian clients. *Internat. J. Social Psychiatry* 36: 18–29.

———— (1991). Effects of Asian client–therapist ethnicity and gender match on utilization and outcome of therapy. *Community Mental Health J.* 27: 31–42.

Fleishman, J. A., & B. Fogel (1994). Coping and depressive symptoms and people with AIDS. *Health Psychology* 13: 156–69.

Flynn, L. (1994). Managed care and mental illness. In Schreter et al. (1994b: 203–12).

Folkman, S. (1984). Personal control and stress and coping processes: A theoretical analysis. *J. Personality & Social Psychology* 46: 839–52.

Folkman, S., & R. S. Lazarus (1980). An analysis of coping in a middle-aged community sample. *J. Health & Social Behavior* 21: 219–39.

Forsyth, B. H., & J. T. Lessler (1991). Cognitive laboratory methods: A taxonomy. In P. P. Biemer, R. M. Groves, L. E. Lyberg, N. A. Mathiowetz, & S. Sudman (Eds.), *Measurement Errors in Surveys,* pp. 393–418. New York: Wiley.

Forthofer, M. S., R. C. Kessler, A. L. Story, & I. H. Gotlib (1996). The effects of psychiatric disorders on the probability and timing of first marriage. *J. Health & Social Behavior* 37: 121–32.

Foucault, M. (1965). *Madness and Civilization: A History of Insanity in the Age of Reason.* New York: Random House.

———— (1975). *Discipline & Punish: The Birth of the Clinic.* New York: Vintage Books.

Fountain House (1985). Evaluation of clubhouse model community-based psychiatric rehabilitation: Final report. National Institute of Handicapped Research, Washington, DC.

Fox, J. W. (1980). Gove's specific sex-role theory of mental illness: A research note. *J. Health & Social Behavior* 21: 260–6.

Frances, A. J., T. A. Widiger, & M. R. Fyer (1990). The influence of classification methods on comorbidity. In J. D. Maser & C. R. Cloninger (Eds.), *Comorbidity of Mood and Anxiety Disorders,* pp. 41–59. Washington, DC: American Psychiatric Press.

Frank, E., & B. P. Anderson (1987). Psychiatric disorders in rape victims: Past history and current symptomatology. *Comprehensive Psychiatry* 28: 77–82.

Frank, E., D. Kupfer, & J. Perel (1989). Early recurrence in unipolar depression. *Arch. General Psychiatry* 46: 397–400.

Frank, R., et al. (1991). A new look at rising mental health insurance costs. *Health Affairs* 10: 116–23.

Frank, R. G., C. Koyanagi, & T. G. McGuire (1997). The politics and economics of mental health "parity" laws. *Health Affairs* 16: 108–20.

Frank, R., & T. McGuire (1995). Estimating costs of mental health and substance abuse coverage. *Health Affairs* 14: 102–15.

Frank, R., T. McGuire, & J. Newhouse (1995). Risk contracts in managed mental health care. *Health Affairs* 14: 50–64.

Frank, R. G., T. G. McGuire, D. A. Regier, R. W. Manderscheid, & A. Woodward (1994). Paying for mental health and substance abuse care. *Health Affairs* 1: 337–42.

Frank, R., & L. Morlock (1997). *Managing Fragmented Public Mental Health Services*. New York: Milbank Memorial Fund.

Frankenhaeuser, M. (1991). The psychophysiology of sex differences as related to occupational status. In Frankenhaeuser et al. (1991: 39–61).

Frankenhaeuser Marianne, U. Lundberg, & M. Chesney (Eds.) (1991). *Women, Work and Health: Stress and Opportunities*. New York: Plenum.

Frankl, V. E. (1975). Paradoxical intention and dereflection. *Psychotherapy: Theory, Res., & Practice* 12: 226–37.

Freed, E. X. (1978). Alcohol and mood: An updated review. *Internat. J. Addictions* 13: 173–200.

Freeman, M. A., & T. Trabin (1994). *Managed Behavioral Healthcare: History, Models, Key Issues, and Future Course*. Rockville, MD: U.S. Center for Mental Health Services.

Freeman, R. J., & R. Roesch (1989). Mental disorder and the criminal justice system: A review. *Internat. J. Law & Psychiatry* 12: 105–16.

Freidson, E. (1970a). *Profession of Medicine*. New York: Dodd Mead.

(1970b). *Professional Dominance*. Chicago: Aldine.

Frerichs, R., C. Aneshensel, & V. Clark (1981). Prevalence of depression in Los Angeles County. *Amer. J. Epidemiology* 113: 691–9.

Frese M., & D. Zapf (1989). Methodological issues in the study of work stress: Objective vs. subjective measurement of work stress and the question of longitudinal studies. In C. L. Cooper & R. Payne (Eds.), *Causes, Coping and Consequences of Stress at Work*, pp. 375–411. New York: Wiley.

Freud, A. (1937). *The Ego and the Mechanisms of Defense*. London: Hogarth.

Freud, S. (1900). *The Interpretation of Dreams* (Standard Edition, vol. 4). London: Hogarth.

(1919). *Introduction to the Psychology of the War Neuroses* (Standard Edition, vol. 18). London: Hogarth.

(1930). *Civilization and Its Discontents* (Standard Edition, vol. 21). London: Hogarth.

(1949). An example of psycho-analytic work. In *An Outline of Psychoanalysis*. New York: Norton.

(1950). *Project for a Scientific Psychology* (Standard Edition, vol. 1). London: Hogarth.

(1959a). Some psychological consequences of the anatomical distinction between the sexes. In *Collected Papers*, vol. 5. New York: Basic Books.

(1959b). Female sexuality. In *Collected Papers*, vol. 5. New York: Basic Books.

(1959c). The passing of the Oedipus complex. In *Collected Papers*, vol. 2. New York: Basic Books

(1966a). Femininity. In *The Complete Introductory Lectures on Psychoanalysis*. New York: Norton.

(1966b). Anxiety and instinctual life. In *New Introductory Lectures*. New York: Norton.

Freund, D., & R. Hurley (1995). Medicaid managed care: Contributions to issues of health reform. *Annual Rev. Public Health* 16: 473–95.

Friedson, E. (1988). *The Profession of Medicine*, 2nd ed. University of Chicago Press.

Frisman, L. K., & T. G. McGuire (1989). The economics of long-term care for the mentally ill. *Social Issues* 45: 119–30.

Fromm, E. (1941). *Escape from Freedom*. New York: Holt.

(1947). *Man for Himself*. New York: Rinehart.

Fujino, D. C., S. Okazaki, & K. Young (1994). Asian-American women in the mental health system: An examination of ethnic and gender match between therapist and client. *J. Community Psychology* 22: 164–76.

Funch, D. P., & C. Mettlin (1982). The role of support in relation to recovery from breast surgery. *Social Science & Medicine* 16: 91–8.

Furnham, A., & S. Shiekh (1993). Gender, generational and social support correlates of mental health in Asian immigrants. *Internat. J. Social Psychiatry* 39: 22–33.

Furstenberg, F. F., & J. Brooks-Gunn (1986). Teenage childbearing: Causes, consequences, and remedies. In L. Aiken & D. Mechanic (Eds.), *Applications of Social Science to Clinical Medicine and Health Policy*, pp. 307–34. New Brunswick, NJ: Rutgers University Press.

Furstenberg, F. F., & A. J. Cherlin (1991). *Divided Families: What Happens to Children When Parents Part*. Cambridge, MA: Harvard University Press.

Gaines, A. D. (Ed.) (1992). *Ethnopsychiatry: The Cultural Construction of Professional and Folk Psychiatrists*. Albany, NY: SUNY Press.

Gala, C., G. C. Pergami, J. Catalan, M. Riccio, F. Durbano, M. Musicco, T. Baldeweg, & G. Invernizzi (1992). Risk of deliberate self-harm and factors associated with suicidal behavior among asymptomatic individuals with human immunodeficiency virus infection. *Acta Psychiatrica Scandinavica* 86: 70–5.

Gallagher, E. B., D. J. Levinson, & I. Erlich (1957). Some sociopsychological characteristics of patients and their relevance for psychiatric treatment. In M. Greenblatt, D. Levinson, & R. H. Williams (Eds.), *The Patient and the Mental Hospital,* pp. 357–79. Glencoe, IL: Free Press.

Galper, J. H. (1975). *The Politics of Social Services.* Englewood Cliffs, NJ: Prentice-Hall.

Ganster, D. C. (1989). Work control and well-being: A review of research in the workplace. In S. L. Sauter, J. J. Hurrell, & C. L. Cooper (Eds.), *Job Control and Worker Health,* pp. 2–23. New York: Wiley.

Gardner, H. (1985). *The Mind's New Science: A History of the Cognitive Revolution.* New York: Basic Books.

Gardner, W., S. K. Hoge, N. S. Bennett, L. H. Roth, C. W. Lidz, J. Monahan, & E. P. Mulvey (1993). Two scales for measuring patients' perceptions of coercion during mental hospital admission. *Behavioral Sciences & the Law* 11: 307–22.

Garfield, S. L., & A. E. Bergin (Eds.) (1986). *Handbook of Psychotherapy and Behavior Change,* 3rd ed. New York: Wiley.

Gaw, A. C. (Ed.) (1993). *Culture, Ethnicity, and Mental Illness.* Washington, DC: American Psychiatric Press.

Ge, X., R. D. Conger, F. O. Lorenz, & R. L. Simons (1994). Parents' stressful life events and adolescent depressed mood. *J. Health & Social Behavior* 35: 28–44.

Gecas, V. (1989). The social psychology of self-efficacy. *Annual Rev. Sociology* 15: 291–316.

Geertsen, R., M. R. Klauper, M. Rindflesh, R. L. Kane, & R. Gray (1975). A re-examination of Suchman's views on social factors in health care utilization. *J. Health & Social Behavior* 16: 226–37.

Geller, J. L., & E. D. Lister (1978). The process of criminal commitment for pretrial psychiatric examination: An evaluation. *Amer. J. Psychiatry* 135: 53–60.

Gelles, R. J., & J. R. Conte (1990). Domestic violence and sexual abuse of children: A review of research in the eighties. *J. Marriage & the Family* 52: 1045–58.

George, L. K. (1996). Social factors and illness. In R. K. Binstock & L. K. George (Eds.), *Handbook of Aging and the Social Sciences,* pp. 229–53. San Diego, CA: Academic Press.

George, L. K., D. G. Blazer, D. C. Hughes, & N. Fowler (1989). Social support and the outcome of major depression. *Brit. J. Psychiatry* 154: 478–85.

Gerbner, G., L. Gross, M. Morgan, & N. Signorielli (1981). Health and medicine on television. *New England J. Medicine* 305: 901–4.

Gershon, E., J. Hamovit, J. Guroff, et al. (1982). A family study of schizoaffective bipolar I, bipolar II, unipolar and normal control probands. *Arch. General Psychiatry* 39: 1157–67.

Gershon, E., A. Mark, N. Cohen, et al. (1975). Transmitted factors in the morbid risk of affective disorders: A controlled study. *J. Psychiatric Res.* 12: 283–99.

Gershon, E., & J. I. Nurnberger (1995). Bipolar illness. In J. Oldham & M. B. Riba (Eds.), *Review of Psychiatry,* vol. 14, pp. 339–423. Washington, DC: American Psychiatric Press.

Gershon, E., S. Targum, S. Matthysse, et al. (1979). Color blindness not closely linked to bipolar illness: Report of a new pedigree series. *Arch. General Psychiatry* 36: 1423–30.

Gerstein, D. R., & H. J. Harwood (Eds.) (1990). *Treating Drug Problems.* Washington, DC: National Academy Press.

Gerstel, N. (1988). Divorce and kin ties: The importance of gender. *J. Marriage & the Family* 50: 209–19.

Gerstel, N., & C. K. Reisman (1984). Marital Dissolution and health: Do males or females have greater risk? *Social Science & Medicine* 20: 627–35.

Gerstel, N., C. K. Riessman, & S. Rosenfield (1985). Explaining the symptomatology of separated and divorced women and men: The role of material conditions and social networks. *Social Forces* 64: 84–101.

Gersten, J. C., T. S. Langner, J. C. Eisenberg, & L. Orzek (1974). Child behavior and life events: Undesirable change or change per se? In Dohrenwend & Dohrenwend (1974a: 159–70).

Giaconia, R. M., H. Z. Reinherz, A. B. Silverman, B. Pakiz, A. K. Frost, & E. Cohen (1994). Ages of onset of psychiatric disorders in a community population of older adolescents. *J. Amer. Acad. Child Adolescent Psychiatry* 33: 706–17.

Giele, J. Z. (1988). Gender and sex roles. In N. J. Smelser (Ed.), *Handbook of Sociology,* pp. 291–323. Newbury Park, CA: Sage.

Gilbert, P. (1992). *Depression: The Evolution of Powerlessness.* New York: Guilford.

Gittleman, M. B., & D. R. Howell (1995). Changes in the structure and quality of jobs in the United States: Effects by race and gender, 1973–1990. *Industrial & Labor Relations Rev.* 48: 420–40.

Glenn, N., & K. Kramer (1985). The psychological well-being of adult children of divorce. *J. Marriage & the Family* 47: 905–11.

Goffman, E. (1961). *Asylums.* New York: Anchor.

——— (1974). *Frame Analysis: An Essay on the Organization of Experience.* New York: Harper & Row.

Gold, M., et al. (1995). *Arrangements between Managed Care Plans and Physicians: Results from a 1994 Survey of Managed Care Plans* (Selected External Research Series, no. 3). Washington, DC: Physician Payment Review Commission.

Gold, P., F. Goodwin, & G. Chrousos (1988a). Clinical and biochemical manifestations of depression: Relation to the neurobiology of stress, part I. *New England J. Medicine* 319: 348–53.

——— (1988b). Clinical and biochemical manifestations of depression: Relation to the neurobiology of stress, part II. *New England J. Medicine* 319: 413–20.

Goldberg, E. L., & G. W. Comstock (1980). Epidemiology of life events: Frequency in general populations. *Amer. J. Epidemiology* 111: 736–52.

Goldberg, E. M., & S. L. Morrison (1963). Schizophrenia and social class. *Brit. J. Psychiatry* 109: 785–802.

Goldberger, L., & S. Breznitz (Eds.) (1993). *Handbook of Stress: Theoretical and Clinical Aspects,* 2nd ed. New York: Free Press / Macmillan.

Golding, S. L., D. Eaves, & A. M. Kowaz (1989). The assessment, treatment and community outcome of insanity acquittees: Forensic history and response to treatment. *Internat. J. Law & Psychiatry* 12: 149–79.

Goldman, H. (1982). Mental illness and family burden: A public health perspective. *Hospital & Community Psychiatry* 33: 557–60.

Goldman, H. H., R. G. Frank, & M. S. Gaynor (1995). What level of government? Balancing the interests of the state and the local community. *Administration & Policy in Mental Health* 23: 127–35.

Goldman, H. H., & A. A. Gattozzi (1988). Murder in the cathedral revisited: President Reagan and the mentally disabled. *Hospital & Community Psychiatry* 39: 505–9.

Goldman, H., A. Lehman, J. Morrissey, S. Newman, R. Frank, & D. Steinwachs (1990a). Design for the national evaluation of the Robert Wood Johnson Foundation program on chronic mental illness. *Hospital & Community Psychiatry* 41: 1217–21.

Goldman, H., & J. Morrissey (1985). The alchemy of mental health policy: Homelessness and the fourth cycle of reform. *Amer. J. Public Health* 75: 727–31.

Goldman, H., J. Morrissey, & M. Ridgely (1990b). Form and function of mental health authorities at RWJ Foundation program sites: Preliminary observations. *Hospital & Community Psychiatry* 41: 1222–30.

——— (1994). Evaluating the Robert Wood Johnson Foundation program on chronic mental illness. *Milbank Q.* 72: 37–47.

Goldman, H., & C. Taube (1989). State strategies to restructure psychiatric hospitals: A selective review. *Inquiry* 26: 146–57.

Goldsmith, H. F., D. J. Jackson, & R. Hough (1988). Process model of seeking mental health services: Proposed framework for organizing the literature on help-seeking. In H. F. Goldsmith, E. Lin, & R. A. Bell (Eds.), *Needs Assessment: Its Future* (DHHS pub. no. ADM 88-1550), pp. 49–64. Washington, DC: U.S. GPO.

Goldsmith, M. F. (1983). From mental hospitals to jails: The pendulum swings. *J. Amer. Medical Assoc.* 250: 3017–18.

Goodman, A. B. (1996). Medical conditions in Ashkenazi schizophrenic pedigrees. *Schizophrenia Bull.* 20: 507–17.

Gorenstein, E. E. (1984). Debating mental illness: Implications for science, medicine, and social policy. *Amer. Psychologist* 39: 50–6.

Gotkin, J., & P. Gotkin (1975). *Too Much Anger, Too Many Tears. A Personal Triumph over Psychiatry.* New York: Quadrangle.

Gotlib, Ian. H., & C. L. Hammen (1992). *Psychological Aspects of Depression: Toward a Cognitive-Interpersonal Integration*. Chichester, NY: Wiley.

Gottlieb, B. H. (1981a). Social networks and social support in community mental health. In Gottlieb (1981b: 11–42).

(Ed.) (1981b). *Social Networks and Social Support*. Beverly Hills, CA: Sage.

(1983). *Social Support Strategies: Guidelines for Mental Health Practice*. Beverly Hills, CA: Sage.

Gottlieb, P., G. Gabrielsen, & P. Kramp (1987). Psychotic homicides in Copenhagen from 1959–1988. *Acta Psychiatrica Scandinavica* 76: 285–92.

Gove, W. R. (1970). Societal reaction as an explanation of mental illness: An evaluation. *Amer. Sociological Rev.* 35: 873–84.

(1975). *The Labeling of Deviance: Evaluating a Perspective*. New York: Sage.

(1978). Sex differences in mental illness among adult men and women: An evaluation of four questions raised regarding the evidence on the higher rates of women. *Social Science & Medicine* 12B: 187–98.

(1980). Labeling and mental illness: A critique. In W. R. Gove (Ed.), *Labeling Deviant Behavior*, pp. 53–109. Beverly Hills, CA: Sage.

(1982). The current status of the labeling theory of mental illness. In W. R. Gove (Ed.), *Deviance and Mental Illness*, pp. 273–300. Beverly Hills, CA: Sage.

(1984). Gender differences in mental and pychiatric illness: The effects of fixed roles and nurturant roles. *Social Science & Medicine* 19: 77–91.

Gove, W. R., & T. Fain (1973). The stigma of mental hospitalization: An attempt to evaluate its consequences. *Arch. General Psychiatry* 29: 494–500.

Gove, W. R., & M. R. Geerken (1977). The effect of children and employment on the mental health of married men and women. *Social Forces* 56: 66–76.

Gove, W. R., M. Hughes, & C. Briggs Style (1984). Does marriage have positive effects on the psychological well-being of the individual? *J. Health & Social Behavior* 24: 122–31.

Gove, W. R., S. T. Ortega, & C. B. Style (1989). The maturational and role perspectives on aging and self through the adult years: An empirical evaluation. *Amer. J. Sociology* 94: 1117–45.

Gove, W. R., & J. Tudor (1973). Adult sex roles and mental illness. *Amer. J. Sociology* 78: 812–35.

Granovetter, M. (1973). The strength of weak ties. *Amer. J. Sociology* 78: 1360–80.

(1995). *Getting a Job. A Study of Contacts and Careers*. University of Chicago Press.

Gray, B. (1991). *The Profit Motive and Patient Care: The Changing Accountability of Doctors and Hospitals*. Cambridge, MA: Harvard University Press.

Gray, B., & M. Field (1989). *Controlling Costs and Changing Patient Care? The Role of Utilization Management*. Washington, DC: National Academy Press.

Greden, J. F., R. Gardner, D. King, L. Grunhaus, B. Carroll, & Z. Kronfol (1983). Dexamethasone suppression tests in antidepressant treatment of melancholia: The process of normalization and test–retest reproducibility. *Arch. General Psychiatry* 40: 493–500.

Green, B. L., M. C. Grace, & G. C. Gleser (1985). Identifying survivors at risk: Long-term impairment following the Beverly Hills Supper Club fire. *J. Consulting & Clinical Psychology* 53: 672–8.

Greenberg, J. R., & S. A. Mitchell (1983). *Object Relations in Psychoanalytic Theory*. Cambridge, MA: Harvard University Press.

Greenberg, L. S., R. K. Elliott, & G. Lietar (1994). Research on experiential psychotherapies. In Bergin & Garfield (1994: 509–39).

Greenhouse, L. (1996). Power of states is high on agenda of Supreme Court. *New York Times* (October 7): A1.

Greenley, J. R. (1992). Neglected organization and management issues in mental health systems development. *Community Mental Health J.* 28: 371–84.

(Ed.) (1995). *Research in Community and Mental Health*, vol. 8: *The Family and Mental Illness*. Greenwich, CT: JAI.

Greenley, J. R., & D. Mechanic (1976). Social selection in seeking help for psychological problems. *J. Health & Social Behavior* 17: 249–62.

Greenley, J. R., D. Mechanic, & P. D. Cleary (1987). Seeking help for psychological problems. *Medical Care* 25: 1113–28.

Grinker, R., & J. P. Spiegel (1945). *Men under Stress*. Philadelphia: Blakiston.

Grisso, T., & P. S. Appelbaum (1995). The MacArthur treatment competence study: III. Abilities of patients to consent to psychiatric and medical treatment.*Law & Human Behavior* 19: 149–74.

Grob, G. N. (1971). Introduction. In Commission on Lunacy (1855).

(1973). *Mental Institutions in America: Social Policy to 1875.* New York: Free Press.

(1983). *Mental Illness and American Society: 1875–1940.* Princeton, NJ: Princeton University Press.

(1987). Mental health policy in post–World War II America. In D. Mechanic (Ed.), *Improving Mental Health Services: What the Social Sciences Can Tell Us* (New Directions for Mental Health Services, no. 36), pp. 15–32. San Francisco: Jossey-Bass.

(1991). *From Asylum to Community.* Princeton, NJ: Princeton University Press.

(1994a). *The Mad among Us: A History of the Care of America's Mentally Ill.* New York: Free Press.

(1994b). Government and mental health policy: A structural analysis. *Milbank Q.* 72: 471–98.

Gronfein, W. (1985a). Incentives and intentions in mental health policy: A comparison of the medicaid and community mental health programs. *J. Health & Social Behavior* 26: 192–206.

(1985b). Psychotropic drugs and the origins of deinstitutionalization. *Social Problems* 32: 437–55.

Growick, B. S. (1979). Another look at the relationship between vocational and nonvocational client change. *Rehab. Counseling Bull.* 23: 136–9.

Guarnaccia, P. J. (1992). Ataques de nervios in Puerto Rico: Culture-bound syndrome or popular illness. *Medical Anthropology* 15: 1–14.

Guarnaccia, P. J., & P. Parra (1996). Ethnicity, social status, and families' experiences of caring for a mentally ill family member. *Community Mental Health J.* 32: 243–60.

Gudeman, J. E. (1988). The evolution of a public psychiatric hospital and its system of care. In M. F. Shore & J. E. Gudeman (Eds.), *Serving the Chronically Mentally Ill in an Urban Setting* (New Directions for Mental Health Services, no. 39), pp. 25–32. San Francisco: Jossey-Bass.

Gueron, J. M., & E. Pauly (1991). *From Welfare to Work.* New York: Russell Sage Foundation.

Gummer, B. (1988). Competing perspectives on the concept of "effectiveness" in the analysis of social services. *Administration in Social Work* 11: 257–70.

Guralnik, J. M., & G. A. Kaplan (1989). Predictors of healthy aging: Prospective evidence from the Alameda County study. *Amer. J. Public Health* 79: 703–8.

Gurin, G., Joseph Veroff, & S. Feld (1960). *Americans View Their Mental Health: A Nationwide Survey.* New York: Basic Books.

Haberman, P. (1976). Psychiatric symptoms among Puerto Ricans in Puerto Rico and New York City. *Ethnicity* 3: 133–44.

Hafferty, F., & F. Wolinsky (1991). Conflicting characterizations of professional dominance. *Current Res. Occupations & Professions* 6: 225–49.

Hafner, H., & W. Boker (1982). *Crimes of Violence by Mentally Abnormal Offenders,* Trans. by H. Marshall. Cambridge University Press.

Haines, V. A., & J. S. Hurlbert (1992). Network range and health. *J. Health & Social Behavior* 33: 254–66.

Halaby, C. N., & D. L. Weakliem (1989). Worker control and attachment to the firm. *Amer. J. Sociology* 95: 549–91.

(1993). Ownership and authority in the earnings function: Nonnested tests of alternative specifications. *Amer. Sociological Rev.* 58: 16–30.

Haley, J. (1973). *Uncommon Therapy: The Psychiatric Techniques of Milton H. Erickson, M.D.* New York: Norton.

(1976). *Problem-Solving Therapy.* San Francisco: Jossey-Bass (reprinted 1987).

Hall, B. A. (1992). Overcoming stigmatization: Social and personal implications of the human immunodeficiency virus diagnosis. *Arch. Psychiatric Nursing* 6: 189–94.

Hall, P., I. F. Brockington, J. Levings, & C. Murphy (1993). A comparison of responses to the mentally ill in two communities. *Brit. J. Psychiatry* 162: 99–108.

Hallmayer, J., W. Maier, M. Ackenheil, et al. (1992). Evidence against linkage of schizophrenia to chromosome Sq11-q13 markers in systematically ascertained families. *Biological Psychiatry* 31: 83–94.

Halpern, J., K. L. Sackett, P. R. Binner, & C. B. Mohr (1980). *The Myths of Deinstitutionalization: Policies for the Mentally Disabled.* Boulder, CO: Westview.

Hamilton, S., M. Rothbart, & R. M. Dawes (1986). Sex bias, diagnosis and DSM-III. *Sex Roles* 15: 269–74.

Hamilton, V. L., C. L. Broman, W. S. Hoffman, & D. S. Renner (1990). Hard times and vulnerable people: Initial effects of plant closing on autoworkers' health. *J. Health & Social Behavior* 31: 23–40.

Hammen, C. L. (1982). Gender and depression. In I. Al-Issa (Ed.), *Gender and Psychopathology,* pp. 133–52. New York: Academic Press.

Hammen, C. L., A. Mayol, R. deMayo, & T. Marks (1986). Initial symptom levels and the life-event-depression relationship. *J. Abnormal Psychology* 95: 114–22.

Hammer, M., S. Makiesky-Barrow, & L. Gutwirth (1978). Social networks and schizophrenia. *Schizophrenia Bull.* 4: 522–45.

Hanley, E., & P. Lincoln (1992). HIV infection in women. *Nursing Clinics of North America* 27: 925–36.

Hans, V. P. (1986). An analysis of public attitudes toward the insanity defense. *Criminology* 4: 393–415.

Hansell, S., & D. Mechanic (1991). Introspectiveness in adolescence. In R. M. Lerner, A. C. Peterson, & J. Brooks-Gunn (Eds.), *The Encyclopedia of Adolescence,* pp. 560–4. New York: Garland.

Harlow, H. E. (1959). Love in infant monkeys. *Scientific Amer.* 200: 68–74.

Harris, G. T., M. E. Rice, & C. A. Cormier (1991). Psychopathy and violent recidivism. *Law & Human Behavior* 15: 625–38.

Harris, M., & H. C. Bergman (1987). Case management with the chronically mentally ill: A clinical perspective. *Amer. J. Orthopsychiatry* 57: 296–302.

Harris, M. J., R. Millich, E. M. Johnston, & D. W. Hoover (1990). Effects of expectancies on children's social interactions. *J. Experimental Social Psychology* 26: 1–12.

Harry, B., & H. J. Steadman (1988). Arrest rates of patients treated at a community mental health center. *Hospital & Community Psychiatry* 39: 862–6.

Hartlage, L. C., & P. E. Roland (1971). Attitudes of employers toward different types of handicapped workers. *J. Applied Rehab. Counseling* 2: 115–20.

Hartmann, H. (1939). *Ego Psychology and the Problem of Adaptation.* New York: International Universities Press.

Hartunian, N. S., C. N. Smart, & M. S. Thompson (1981). *The Incidence and Economic Costs of Major Health Impairments: A Comparative Analysis of Cancer, Motor Vehicle Injuries, Coronary Heart Disease, and Stroke.* Lexington, MA: Lexington Books.

Hatfield, A. B. (Ed.) (1994). *Family Interventions in Mental Illness* (New Directions in Mental Health Services, no. 62). San Francisco: Jossey-Bass.

Haug, M., & B. Lavin (1983). Utilization models: A review. Paper presented at the annual meeting of the American Sociological Association, Detroit.

Haveman, R., B. L. Wolfe, & J. Spaulding (1991). Educational achievement and childhood events and circumstances. *Demography* 28: 133–57.

Hawkins, J. D., & Richard F. Catalano (1990). Broadening the vision of education: Schools as health promoting environments. *J. School Health* 60: 178–81.

Hays, R. B., J. A. Catania, L. McCusick, & T. J. Coates (1990). Help-seeking for AIDS-related concerns: A comparison of gay men with various HIV diagnoses. *Amer. J. Community Psychology* 18: 743–55.

Hays, R. B., H. Turner, & T. J. Coates (1992). Social support, AIDS-related symptoms and depression among gay men. *J. Consulting & Clinical Psychology* 60: 463–9.

Hayward, C., J. D. Killen, & C. B. Taylor (1989). Panic attacks in young adolescents. *Amer. J. Psychiatry* 146: 1061–2.

Heath, D. B. (1989). American Indians and alcohol: Epidemiological and sociocultural relevance. In *Alcohol Use among Ethnic Minorities* (NIAAA Research Monograph no. 18; DHHS pub. no. ADM 87-1435). Washington, DC: U.S. GPO.

Heider, F. (1958). *The Psychology of Interpersonal Relations.* New York: Wiley.

Heilbrun, K., & P. A. Griffin (1993). Community based forensic treatment of insanity acquittees. *Internat. J. Law & Psychiatry* 16: 133–50.

Heinrichs, R. W. (1993). Schizophrenia and the brain: Conditions for a neuropsychology of madness. *Amer. Psychologist* 48: 221–33.

Heller, K. (1979). The effects of social support: Prevention and treatment implications. In A. P. Goldstein & F. H. Kanfer (Eds.), *Maximizing Treatment Gains: Transfer Enhancement in Psychotherapy.* New York: Academic Press.

Hellinger, F. J. (1993). The use of health services by women with HIV infection. *Health Services Res.* 28: 543–61.

Helzer, J. E., A. Burnam, & L. T. McEvoy (1991). Alcohol abuse and dependence. In Robins & Regier (1991: 81–115).

Helzer, J. E., R. K. Stoltzman, A. Farmer, I. F. Brockington, D. Plesons, B. Singerman, & J. Works (1985). Comparing the DIS with a DIS/DSM-III-based physician reevaluation. In Eaton & Kessler (1985: 285–308).

Henderson, A. S. (1992). Social support and depression. In Veil & Baumann (1992b: 85–92).

Henderson, S. (1977). The social network, support and neurosis: The functions of attachment in adult life. *Brit. J. Psychiatry* 131: 185–91.

Henry, J. P., & J. C. Cassel (1969). Psychological factors in essential hypertension. *J. Epidemiology* 90: 171–200.

Henry, William P., H. H. Strupp, T. E. Schacht, & L. Gaston (1994). Psychodynamic approaches. In Bergin & Garfield (1994: 467–508).

Herman, N., & C. Miall (1990). The positive consequences of stigma: Two case studies in mental and physical disability. *Qualitative Sociology* 13: 251–69.

Heston, L. L. (1966). Psychiatric disorders in foster home reared children of schizophrenic mothers. *Brit. J. Psychiatry* 112: 819–25.

(1992). *Mending Minds: A Guide to the New Psychiatry of Depression, Anxiety and Other Serious Mental Disorders.* New York: Freeman.

Hetherington, E. M., M. Cox, & R. Cox (1978). The aftermath of divorce. In J. H. Stevens, Jr.& M. Matthews (Eds.), *Mother/Child Father/Child Relationships,* pp. 149–76. Washington, DC: National Association for the Education of Young Children.

Hiday, V. A. (1988). Civil commitment: A review of empirical research. *Behavioral Sciences & the Law* 6: 15–43.

(1990). Dangerousness of civil commitment candidates: A six months followup. *Law & Human Behavior* 14: 551–67.

(1991). Hospitals to jails: Arrests and incarceration of civil commitment candidates. *Hospital & Community Psychiatry* 42: 729–34.

(1992a). Coercion in civil commitment: Process, preferences and outcome. *Internat. J. Law & Psychiatry* 15: 359–77.

(1992b). Civil committment and arrests: An investigation of the criminalization thesis. *J. Nervous & Mental Disease* 180: 184–91.

(1995). The social context of mental illness and violence. *J. Health & Social Behavior* 36: 122–37.

Hiday, V. A., & S. J. Markell (1981). Components of dangerousness: Legal standards in civil commitment. *Internat. J. Law & Psychiatry* 3: 405–19.

Hiday, V. A., & L. N. Smith (1987). Effects of the dangerousness standard in civil commitment. *J. Psychiatry & Law* 15: 433–54.

Hinkle, L. (1987). Stress and disease: The concept after 50 years. *Social Science & Medicine* 25: 561–7.

Hiroto, D. S. (1974). Locus of control and learned helplessness. *J. Experimental Psychology* 102: 187–93.

Hirsch, B. (1980). Natural support systems and coping with major life changes. *Amer. J. Community Psychology* 8: 159–72.

Hirsch, Sherry, J. K. Adams, L. R. Frank, W. Hudson, R. Keene, G. Krawitz-Keene, D. Richman, & R. Roth (1974). *Madness Network News Reader.* San Francisco: Glide Publications.

Hirsch, Steven, J. Bowen, J. Emami, P. Cramer, A. Jolley, C. Haw, & M. Dickinson (1996). A one year prospective study of the effect of life events and medication in the aetiology of schizophrenic relapse. *Brit. J. Psychiatry* 168: 49–56.

Hirsch, Steven, & D. Weinberger (Eds.) (1996). *Schizophrenia.* Oxford: Blackwell.

Hirschi, T., & M. Gottfredson (1983). Age and the explanation of crime. *Amer. J. Sociology* 89: 552–84.

Hochschild, A. R. (1979). Emotion work, feeling rules, and social structure. *Amer. J. Sociology* 85: 551–75.

Hochschild, A., & A. Machung (1989). *The Second Shift: Working Parents and the Revolution at Home.* New York: Academic Press.

Hochschild, J. L. (1995). *Facing Up to the American Dream.* Princeton, NJ: Princeton University Press.

Hodgins, S. (1992). Mental disorder, intellectual deficiency and crime: Evidence from a birth cohort. *Arch. General Psychiatry* 49: 476–83.

Hodgins, S. (1993). *Mental Disorder and Crime.* London: Sage.

(1995). Assessing mental disorder in the criminal justice system: Feasibility versus clinical accuracy. *Internat. J. Law & Psychiatry* 18: 15–28.

Hoffman, F. L., & X. Mastrianni (1993). The role of supported education in the inpatient treatment of young adults: A two-site comparison. *Psychosocial Rehab. J.* 17: 109–19.

Hoffman, M. S. (Ed.) (1991). *The World Almanac and Book of Facts.* New York: Pharos.

Hogan, D. P. (1978). The variable order of events in the life course. *Amer. Sociological Rev.* 43: 573–86.

Hoge, M., L. Davidson, E. Griffith, W. Sledge, & R. Howensteine (1994). Defining managed care in public-sector psychiatry. *Hospital & Community Psychiatry* 45: 1085–9.

Holahan, C. J., & R. H. Moos (1994). Life stressors and mental health. In Avison & Gotlib (1994: 213–38).

Holahan, J., et al. (1995). Insuring the poor through Medicaid 1115 waivers. *Health Affairs* 14: 200–16.

Holcomb, W. R., & P. R. Ahr (1988). Arrest rates among young adult psychiatric patients treated in inpatient and outpatient settings. *Hospital & Community Psychiatry* 39: 52–7.

Holland, J. C., & S. Tross (1985). The psychosocial and neuropsychiatric sequelae of the acquired immunodeficiency syndrome and related disorders. *Ann. Internal Medicine* 103: 760–4.

Hollingshead, A. (1961). Some issues in the epidemiology of schizophrenia. *Amer. Sociological Rev.* 26: 5–13.

Hollingshead, A. B., & F. C. Redlich (1958). *Social Class and Mental Illness.* New York: Wiley.

Hollman, F. W. (1993). *U.S. Population Estimates by Age, Sex, Race, and Hispanic Origin: 1980–1990* (Current Population Report, Ser. P-25, no. 1095). Washington, DC: U.S. GPO.

Hollon, S. D., & A. T. Beck (1994). Cognitive and cognitive-behavioral therapies. In Bergin & Garfield (1994: 428–66).

Holmes, T. H., & M. Masuda (1974). Life change and illness susceptibility. In Dohrenwend & Dohrenwend (1974a: 45–72).

Holmes, T. H., & R. H. Rahe (1967). The Social Readjustment Rating Scale. *J. Psychosomatic Res.* 11: 213–18.

Holstein, J. A. (1993). *Court-ordered insanity: Interpretive practice and involuntary commitment.* Hawthorne, NY: de Gruyter.

Holzer, C. E. III, B. M. Shea, J. W. Swanson, P. J. Leaf, J. K. Myers, L. George, M. M. Weissman, & P. Bednarski (1986). The increased risk for specific psychiatric disorders among persons of low socioeconomic status: Evidence from the Epidemiologic Catchment Area surveys. *Amer. J. Social Psychiatry* 6: 259–71.

Hong, G. K. (1988). A general family practitioner approach for Asian-American mental health services. *Professional Psychology: Res. & Practice* 19: 600–5.

Horgan, C. M. (1984). *Demand for Ambulatory Mental Health Services from Specialty Providers.* Rockville, MD: National Center for Health Services Research.

Horney, K. (1926). *Feminine Psychology.* New York: Norton (reprinted 1967).

(1937). *Neurotic Personality of Our Times.* New York: Norton.

Horwath, E., & M. M. Weissman (1995). Epidemiology of depression and anxiety disorders. In Tsuang et al. (1995: 317–44).

Horwitz, A. V. (1977a). Social networks and pathways to psychiatric treatment. *Social Forces* 56: 86–105.

(1977b). The pathways into psychiatric treatment: Some difference between men and women. *J. Health & Social Behavior* 18: 169–78.

(1982a). *The Social Control of Mental Illness.* New York: Academic Press.

(1982b). Sex role expectations, power, and psychological distress. *Sex Roles* 8: 607–23.

(1984). The economy and social pathology. *Annual Rev. Sociology* 10: 95–119.

Horwitz, A. V., & H. R. White (1991). Marital status, depression, and alcohol problems among young adults. *J. Health & Social Behavior* 32: 221–37.

Horwitz, A. V., H. R. White, & S. Howell-White (1996a). Becoming married and mental health: A longitudinal study of a cohort of young adults. *J. Marriage & the Family* 58: 895–907.

(1996b). The use of multiple outcomes in stress research: A case study of gender differences in responses to marital dissolution. *J. Health & Social Behavior* 37: 278–91.

Hough, R. L., J. A. Landsverk, M. Karno, A. Burnam, D. M. Timbers, & J. I. Escobar (1978). Utilization of health and mental health services by Los Angeles Mexican Americans and non-Hispanic whites. *Arch. General Psychiatry* 44: 702–9.

House, J. S. (1981). *Work Stress and Social Support*. Reading, MA: Addison-Wesley.

(1987). Social support and social structure. *Sociological Forum* 2: 135–46.

House, J. S., & C. Robbins (1983). Age, psychosocial stress, and health. In M. W. Riley, B. B. Hess, & K. Bond (Eds.), *Aging and Society: Selected Reviews and Recent Research,* pp. 175–97. Hillsdale, NJ: Erlbaum.

House, J. S., D. Umberson, & K. R. Landis (1988). Structures and processes of social support. *Annual Rev. Sociology* 14: 293–318.

Howes, C. (1988). Relations between early child care and schooling. *Developmental Psychology* 24: 53–7.

Hoy, E., R. Curtis, & T. Rice (1991). Change and growth in managed care. *Health Affairs* 10: 18–36.

Hsu, F. L. K. (1972). American core value and national character. In F. L. K. Hsu (Ed.), *Psychological Anthropology.* Cambridge, MA: Schenkman.

Hu, T.-W., L. R. Snowden, J. M. Jerrell, & T. D. Nguyen (1991). Ethnic populations in public mental health: Services choice and level of use. *Amer. J. Public Health* 81: 1429–34.

Hudson, C. G., & J. DeVito (1994). Mental health under national health care reform. *Health & Social Work* 19: 279–87.

Hughes, C. C. (1996). The culture-bound syndromes and psychiatric diagnosis. In Mezzich et al. (1996: 289–312).

Hughes, M., & W. R. Gove (1981). Living alone, social integration and mental health. *Amer. J. Sociology* 87: 48–74.

Husaini, B. A., J. A. Neff, J. R. Newbrough, & M. C. Moore (1982). The stress-buffering role of social support and personal competence among the rural married. *J. Community Psychology* 10: 409–26.

Hwu, H. G., E. K. Yeh, & L. Y. Chang (1989). Prevalence of psychiatric disorders in Taiwan defined by the Chinese Diagnostic Interview Schedule. *Acta Psychiatrica Scandinavica* 79: 136–47.

Iglehart, J. K. (1995). Medicaid and managed care. *New England J. Medicine* 332: 1727–31.

(1996). Managed care and mental health. *New England J. Medicine* 334: 131–5.

Ingleby, D. (1982). The social construction of mental illness. In P. Wright & A. Treacher (Eds.), *The Problem of Medical Knowledge: Examining the Social Construction of Medicine,* pp. 123–43. Edinburgh University Press.

Institute of Medicine (1989). *Controlling Costs and Changing Patient Care? The Role of Utilization Management*. Washington, DC: National Academy Press.

(1994). *Reducing Risks for Mental Disorders: Frontiers for Preventive Intervention Research*. Washington, DC: National Academy Press.

(1997). *Managing Managed Care: Quality Improvement in Behavioral Medicine*. Washington, DC: National Academy Press.

Israel, B. A., & T. C. Antonucci (1987). Social network characteristics and psychological well-being: A replication and extension. *Health Education Q.* 14: 461–81.

Jablensky, A., N. Sartorius, G. Ernberg, M. Anker, A. Korten, J. E. Cooper, R. Day, & A. Bertlesen (1991). Schizophrenia: Manifestations, incidence, and course in different cultures. World Health Organization ten country study. *Psychological Medicine* (monograph suppl.) 20.

Jackson, J. S., T. N. Brown, D. R. Williams, et al. (1996). Racism and the physical and mental health status of African Americans: A thirteen year national panel study. *Ethnicity & Disease* 6: 132–47.

Jaco, E. G. (1960). *The Social Epidemiology of Mental Disorders.* New York: Russell Sage Foundation.

Jacobson, N. S., & M. E. Addis (1993). Research on couples and couple therapy: What do we know? Where are we going? *J. Consulting & Clinical Psychology* 61: 85–93.

Jacobson, Neil. S., A. Holtzworth-Munroe, & K. B. Schmaling (1989). Marital therapy and spouse involvement in the treatment of depression, agoraphobia, and alcoholism. *J. Consulting & Clinical Psychology* 57: 5–10.

Jahoda, M. (1958). *Current Concepts of Positive Mental Health.* New York: Basic Books.

   (1982). *Employment and Unemployment: A Social Psychological Analysis.* Cambridge University Press.

James, F., D. Gregory, & R. K. Jones (1980). Psychiatric morbidity in prisons. *Hospital & Community Psychiatry* 140: 674–7.

Janzen, J. M. (1978). *The Quest for Therapy in Lower Zaire.* Berkeley: University of California Press.

Jayasuriya, L. (1992). The problematic of culture and identity in social functioning. *J. Multicultural Social Work* 2: 37–58.

Jencks, C. (1980). Heredity, environment, and public policy reconsidered. *Amer. Sociological Rev.* 45: 723–36.

Jenkins, J., & M. Karno (1992). The meaning of expressed emotion: Theoretical issues raised by cross-cultural research. *Amer. J. Psychiatry* 149: 9–21.

Jensen, A. R. (1969). How much can we boost IQ and scholastic achievement? *Harvard Educational Rev.* 39: 1–123.

Jeste, D. V., J. B. Lohr, & F. Goodwin (1988). Neuroanatomical studies of major affective disorders: A review and suggestions for further research. *Brit. J. Psychiatry* 153: 444–59.

Jilek, W. G. (1993). Traditional medicine relevant to psychiatry. In Sartorius et al. (1993: 341–83).

Johnson, Dale (1995). Families and psychiatric rehabilitation. *Internat. J. Mental Health* 24: 47–58.

Johnson, Donald (1994). Stress, depression, substance abuse, and racism. *American Indian & Alaska Native Mental Health Res.* 6: 29–33.

Johnson, H., & D. S. Broder (1996). *The System.* Boston: Little, Brown.

Johnson, J. V., & E. M. Hall (1988). Job strain, work place social support, and cardiovascular disease: A cross-sectional study of a random sample of the Swedish working population. *Amer. J. Public Health* 78: 1336–42.

Johnson, J. V., W. Stewart, & E. M. Hall (1996). Long-term psychosocial work environment and cardiovascular mortality among Swedish men. *Amer. J. Public Health* 86: 324–31.

Jones, Edward E., A. Farina, A. H. Hastorf, H. Markus, D. T. Miller, & R. A. Scott (1984). *Social Stigma: The Psychology of Marked Relationships.* New York: Freeman.

Jones, Enrico E. (1978). Effects of race on psychotherapy process and outcome: An exploratory investigation. *Psychotherapy: Theory, Res. & Practice* 15: 226–36.

   (1982). Psychotherapists' impressions of treatment outcome as a function of race. *J. Clinical Psychology* 38: 722–31.

Jones, K., & A. Poletti (1985). The Italian transformation of the asylum. *Internat. J. Mental Health* 13: 210–15.

Jonikas, J. A., & J. A. Cook (1993). Safe, secure, and street-smart: Empowering women with mental illness to achieve greater independence in the community. Thresholds National Research and Training Center, Chicago.

Jordan, B. K., W. E. Schlenger, J. A. Fairbank, & J. M. Caddell (1996). Prevalence of psychiatric disorders among incarcerated women II. Convicted women felons entering prison. *Arch. General Psychiatry* 53: 513–19.

Jordan, C., A. Lewellen, & V. Vandiver (1995). Psychoeducation for minority families: A social work perspective. *Internat. J. Mental Health* 23: 27–43.

Jordan, J., A. Kaplan, J. B. Miller, I. Stiver, & J. Surrey (1991). *Women's Growth in Connection: Writings from the Stone Center.* New York: Guilford.

Jung, C. G. (1924). *Psychological Types.* New York: Random House.

Kadushin, C. (1966). The friends and supporters of psychotherapy: On social circles in urban life. *Amer. Sociological Rev.* 31: 786–802.

   (1969). *Why People Go to Psychiatrists.* New York: Atherton.

   (1982). Social density and mental health. In P. V. Marsden & N. Lin (Eds.), *Social Structure and Network Analysis,* pp. 147–58. Beverly Hills, CA: Sage.

   (1983). Mental health and the interpersonal environment: A reexamination of some effects of social structure on mental health. *Amer. Sociological Rev.* 48: 188–98.

Kagan, S. (1993). *Integrating Services for Children and Families*. New Haven, CT: Yale University Press.

Kahn, A. J., & S. B. Kammerman (1992). Integrating services integration: An overview of initiatives, issues and possibilities. National Center for Children in Poverty, Columbia University School of Public Health, New York.

Kahn, R. L. (1981). *Work and Health*. New York: Wiley.

Kalleberg, A. L., & K. A. Loscocco (1983). Aging, values, and rewards: Explaining age differences in job satisfaction. *Amer. Sociological Rev.* 48: 78–90.

Kandel, D. (1966). Status homophily, social context, and participation in psychotherapy. *Amer. J. Sociology* 71: 640–50.

Kane, J., G. Honigfeld, J. Singer, H. Meltzer, & the Clozaril Collaborative Study Group (1988). Clozapine for the treatment-resistant schizophrenic: A double-blind comparison with chlorpromazine. *Arch. General Psychiatry* 45: 789–96.

Kanner, A. D., J. C. Coyne, C. Schaefer, & R. S. Lazarus (1981). Comparison of two modes of stress measurement: Daily hassles and uplifts versus major life events. *J. Behavioral Medicine* 4: 1–39.

Kaplan, G. A., & J. E. McNeil (1993). Socioeconomic factors and cardiovascular disease: A review of the literature. *Circulation* 88 (4, part I): 1973–98.

Kaplan, Harold, B. J. Sadock, & J. A. Grebb (1994). *Kaplan and Sadock's Synopsis of Psychiatry: Behavioral Sciences, Clinical Psychiatry*. Baltimore: Williams & Wilkins.

Kaplan, Howard H. (Ed.) (1983). *Psychosocial Stress: Trends in Theory and Research*. New York: Academic Press.

(1996a). Themes, lacunae, and directions in research in psychosocial stress. In Kaplan (1996b: 369–403).

(Ed.) (1996b). *Psychosocial Stress: Perspectives on Structure, Theory, Life-Course, and Methods*. New York: Academic Press

Kaplan, H., & R. H. Bohr (1976). Change in the mental health field? *Community Mental Health J.* 12: 244–51.

Kaprio, J., M. Koskenuo, & H. Rita (1987). Mortality after bereavement: A prospective study of 95,647 widowed persons. *Amer. J. Public Health* 77: 283–7.

Karasek, R. (1979). Job demands, job decision latitude, and mental strain: Implications for job redesign. *Administrative Science Q.* 24: 285–308.

Karasek, R., B. Gardell, & J. Windell (1987). Work and nonwork correlates of illness and behaviour in male and female Swedish white-collar workers. *J. Occupational Behavior* 8: 87–207.

Karasek, R., & T. Theorell (1990). *Healthy Work: Stress, Productivity, and the Reconstruction of Working Life*. New York: Basic Books.

Karasek, R., T. Theorell, J. Schwartz, P. Schnall, C. Pieper, & J. Michela (1988). Job characteristics in relation to the prevalence of myocardial infarction in the U.S. HES and HANES. *Amer. J. Public Health* 78: 910–18.

Kasarda, J. D. (1995). Industrial restructuring and the changing location of jobs. In Farley (1995: 215–67).

Kasl, S. V. (1982). Strategies of research on economic instability and health. *Psychological Medicine* 12: 637–49.

(1989). An epidemiological perspective on the role of control in health. In S. L. Sauter, J. J. Hurrell, & C. L. Cooper (Eds.), *Job Control and Worker Health*, pp. 161–89. New York: Wiley.

Kasl, S. V., & S. Cobb (1979). Some mental health consequences of plant closing and job loss. In L. Ferman & J. Gordus (Eds.), *Mental Health and the Economy*, pp. 255–300. Kalamazoo, MI: Upjohn Institute for Employment Research.

Kass, F. (1985). Scaled ratings of DSM-III personality disorders. *Amer. J. Psychiatry* 142: 627–30.

Katz, R. C., C. Watts, & J. Santman (1994). AIDS knowledge and high risk behaviors in the chronically mentally ill. *Community Mental Health J.* 30: 395–402.

Katz, S. J., R. C. Kessler, R. G. Frank, P. Leaf, & E. Lin (in press). Mental health care use, morbidity, and socioeconomic status in the United States and Ontario. *Inquiry*.

Katzper, M., & R. W. Manderscheid (1984). Applications of systems analysis to national data on the mental health service delivery system. *Psychiatric Ann.* 14: 596–607.

Kauffmann, C. A., & J. M. Gorman (Eds.) (1996). *Schizophrenia: New Directions for Clinical Research and Treatment.* New York: M.A. Liebert.

Kaufmann, C. L., P. D. Freund, & J. Wilson (1989). Self-help in the mental health system: A model for consumer-provider collaboration. *Psychosocial Rehab. J.* 13: 5–21.

Kaufmann, C. L., C. Ward-Colasante, & J. Farmer (1993). Development and evaluation of consumer-run drop-in centers. *Hospital & Community Psychiatry* [now *Psychiatric Services*] 33: 678–83.

Keane, T. M., P. F. Malloy, & J. A. Fairbank (1984). Empirical development of an MMPI sub-scale for the assessment of combat-related posttraumatic stress disorder. *J. Consulting & Clinical Psychology* 52: 888–91.

Keilitz, I. (1987). Researching and reforming the insanity defense. *Rutgers Law Rev.* 39: 289–322.

Keith, S. J., D. A. Regier, & D. S. Rae (1991). Schizophrenic disorders. In Robins & Regier (1991: 33–52).

Kellam, S. G., C. H. Brown, B. R. Rubin, & M. E. Ensminger (1983). Paths leading to teenage psychiatric symptoms: Developmental epidemiological studies in Woodlawn. In S. N. Guze, F. J. Earls, & J. W. Barrett (Eds.), *Childhood Psychopathology and Development.* New York: Raven.

Kelly, G. A. (1955). *The Psychology of Personal Constructs.* New York: Norton.

Kelly, J., J. Lawrence, S. Smith, H. Hook, & D. Cook (1987). Stigmatization of AIDS patients by physicians. *Amer. J. Public Health* 77: 789–91.

Kelly, J. A., & D. A. Murphy (1992). Psychological interventions with AIDS and HIV: Prevention and treatment. *J. Consulting & Clinical Psychology* 60: 576–85.

Kelly, J. A., & J. S. St. Lawrence (1988). AIDS prevention and treatment: Psychology's role in the health crisis. *Clinical Psychology Rev.* 8: 255–84.

Kendall-Tackett, K. A., L. M. Williams, & D. Finkelhor (1993). Impact of sexual abuse on children: A review and synthesis of recent and empirical studies. *Psychological Bull.* 113: 164–80.

Kendler, K. (1983). Overview: A current perspective on twin studies of schizophrenia. *Amer. J. Psychiatry* 140: 1413–25.

—— (1988). Familial aggregation of schizophrenia and schizophrenia spectrum disorders. Evaluation of conflicting results. *Arch. General Psychiatry* 45: 377–83.

Kendler, K. S., R. C. Kessler, E. E. Walters, C. MacLean, M. C. Neale, A. C. Heath, & L. J. Eaves (1995). Stressful life events, genetic liability, and onset of an episode of major depression in women. *Amer. J. Psychiatry* 152: 833–42.

Kendler, K. S., T. J. Gallagher, J. M. Abelson, & R. C. Kessler (1996). Lifetime prevalence, demographic risk factors and diagnostic validity of nonaffective psychosis as assessed in a U.S. community sample: The National Comorbidity Survey. *Arch. General Psychiatry* 53: 1022–31.

Kendler, K., A. Heath, M. Neale, R. Kessler, & L. Eaves (1993a). Alcoholism and major depression in women. A twin study of the causes of comorbidity. *Arch. General Psychiatry* 50: 690–8.

Kendler, K., R. Kessler, A. Heath, M. Neale, & L. Eaves (1991a). Coping: A genetic epidemiological investigation. *Psychological Medicine* 21: 337–46.

Kendler, K., M. Lyons, & M. T. Tsuang (1991b). Introduction. In Tsuang et al. (1991: 1–11).

Kendler, K. S., M. C. Neale, R. C. Kessler, A. C. Heath, & L. J. Eaves (1992a). A population based twin study of major depression in women: The impact of varying definitions of illness. *Arch. General Psychiatry* 49: 257–66.

Kendler, K., M. Neale, R. Kessler, A. Heath, & L. Eaves (1992b). Childhood parental loss and adult psychopathology in women: A twin study perspective. *Arch. General Psychiatry* 49: 109–16.

Kendler, K., M. Neale, R. Kessler, A. Heath, & L. Eaves (1993b). A twin study of recent life events and difficulties. *Arch. General Psychiatry* 50: 789–96.

Kennedy, J. L., L. A. Giuffra, H. W. Moises, L. L. Cavalli-Sforza, A. J. Pakstis, J. R. Kidd, C. M. Castiglione, B. Sigren, L. Wettenberg, & K. K. Kidd (1988). Evidence against linkage of schizophrenia to markers on chromosome 5 in a northern Swedish pedigree. *Nature* 336: 167–70.

Kessler, R. C. (1979). Stress, social status, and psychological distress. *J. Health & Social Behavior* 20: 259–72.

—— (1982). A disaggregation of the relationship between socioeconomic status and psychological distress. *Amer. Sociological Rev.* 47: 752–64.

—— (1993). The National Comorbidity Study. Paper presented to the American Sociological Association, Miami Beach, FL.

(1995). The epidemiology of psychiatric comorbidity. In Tsuang et al. (1995: 179–97).

Kessler, R. C., P. A. Berglund, P. J. Leaf, A. C. Kouzis, M. L. Bruce, R. M. Friedman, R. C. Grosser, C. Kennedy, T. G. Kuehnel, E. M. Laska, R. W. Manderscheid, W. Narrow, R. A. Rosenheck, T. W. Santoni, & M. Schneier (1995a). Estimation of the 12-month prevalence of serious mental illness (SMI). NCS working paper no. 8, Institute for Social Research, University of Michigan, Ann Arbor.

Kessler, R. C., R. L. Brown, & C. L. Broman (1981). Sex differences in psychiatric help-seeking: Evidence from four large scale surveys. *J. Health & Social Behavior* 22: 49–64.

Kessler, R. C., & P. D. Cleary (1980). Social class and psychological distress. *Amer. Sociological Rev.* 45: 463–78.

Kessler, R. C., & M. Essex (1982). Marital status and depression: The importance of coping resources. *Social Forces* 61: 484–507.

Kessler, R. C., C. L. Foster, W. B. Saunders, & P. E. Stang (1995b). Social consequences of psychiatric disorders, I. Educational attainment.*Amer. J. Psychiatry* 152: 1026–32.

Kessler, R. C., J. S. House, R. Anspach, & D. R. Williams (1995c). Social psychology and health. In K. S. Cook, G. A. Fine, & J. S. House (Eds.), *Sociological Perspectives on Social Psychology,* pp. 548–70. Boston: Allyn & Bacon.

Kessler, R. C., J. S. House, & J. B. Turner (1987). Unemployment and health in a community sample. *J. Health & Social Behavior* 28: 51–9.

Kessler, R. C., & W. J. Magee (1993). Childhood adversities and adult depression: Basic patterns of association in a U.S. national survey. *Psychological Medicine* 23: 679–90.

(1994a). Childhood family violence and adult recurrent depression. *J. Health & Social Behavior* 35: 13–27.

(1994b). The disaggregation of vulnerability to depression as a function of the determinants of onset and recurrence. In Avison & Gotlib (1994: 239–58).

Kessler, R. C., K. A. McGonagle, K. B. Carnelley, C. B. Nelson, M. Farmer, & D. A. Regier (in press a). Comorbidity of mental disorders and substance use disorders: A review and agenda for future research. In P. J. Leaf (Ed.), *Research in Community and Mental Health.* Greenwich, CT: JAI.

Kessler, R. C., K. A. McGonagle, M. Swartz, D. G. Blazer, & C. B. Nelson (1993). Sex and depression in the National Comorbidity Survey I: Lifetime prevalence, chronicity and recurrence. *J. Affective Disorders* 29: 85–96.

Kessler, R. C., K. A. McGonagle, S. Zhao, C. B. Nelson, M. Hughes, S. Eshleman, H.-U. Wittchen, & K. S. Kendler (1994). Lifetime and 12-month prevalence of DSM-III-R psychiatric disorders in the United States: Results from the National Comorbidity Survey. *Arch. General Psychiatry* 51: 8–19.

Kessler, R. C., & J. D. McLeod (1984). Sex differences in vulnerability to undesirable life events. *Amer. Sociological Rev.* 49: 620–31.

(1985). Social support and mental health in community samples. In Cohen & Syme (1985: 219–40).

Kessler, R. C., J. D. McLeod, & E. Wethington (1985a). The costs of caring: A perspective on the relationship between sex and psychological distress. In Sarason & Sarason (1985: 491–506).

Kessler, R. C., & J. A. McRae (1982). The effect of wives' employment on the mental health of married men and women. *Amer. Sociological Rev.* 47: 216–27.

Kessler, R. C., D. K. Mroczek, & R. F. Belli (in press b). Retrospective adult assessment of childhood psychopathology. In D. Shaffer & J. Richters (Eds.), *Assessment in Childhood Psychopathology.* New York: Guilford.

Kessler, R. C., & H. W. Neighbors (1986). A new perspective on the relationships among race, social class, and psychological distress. *J. Health & Social Behavior* 27: 107–15.

Kessler, R. C., C. B. Nelson, K. A. McGonagle, M. J. Edlund, R. G. Frank, & P. J. Leaf (1996). The epidemiology of co-occurring addictive and mental disorders: Implications for prevention and service utilization. *Amer. J. Orthopsychiatry* 66: 17–31.

Kessler, R. C., & R. H. Price (1993). Primary prevention of secondary disorders: A proposal and agenda. *Amer. J. Community Psychology* 21: 607–34.

Kessler, R. C., R. H. Price, & C. B. Wortman (1985b). Social factors in psychopathology: Stress, social support, and coping processes. *Annual Rev. Psychology* 36: 531–72.

Kessler, R. C., A. Sonnega, E. Bromet, M. Hughes, & C. B. Nelson (1995d). Posttraumatic stress disorder in the National Comorbidity Survey. *Arch. General Psychiatry* 52: 1048–60.

Kessler, R. C., J. B. Turner, & J. S. House (1989). Unemployment, reemployment and emotional functioning in a community sample. *Amer. Sociological Rev.* 54: 648–57.

Kettle, P., & E. O. Bixler (1993). Alcohol and suicide in Alaska Natives. *American Indian & Alaska Native Mental Health Res.* 5: 34–45.

Kety, S. (1986). The interface between neuroscience and psychiatry. In R. Rosenberg, F. Schulsinger, & E. Stromgren (Eds.), *Psychiatry and Its Related Disciplines.* Copenhagen: World Psychiatric Association.

Kety, S. S., D. Rosenthal, P. H. Wender, F. Schulsinger, & B. Jacobsen (1975). Mental illness in the biological and adoptive families of adopted individuals who have become schizophrenic. In R. R. Fieve, D. Rosenthal, & H. Brill (Eds.), *Genetic Research in Psychiatry.* Baltimore: Johns Hopkins University Press.

Keyl, P. M., & W. W. Eaton (1990). Risk factors for the onset of panic attacks and panic disorder. *Amer. J. Epidemiology* 131: 301–11.

Kibria, N., R. C. Barnett, G. K. Baruch, N. L. Marshall, & J. H. Pleck (1990). Homemaking-role quality and the psychological well-being and distress of married women. *Sex Roles* 22: 327–47.

Kiesler, C. A., & A. E. Sibulkin (1987). *Mental Hospitalization: Myths and Facts about a National Crisis.* Newbury Park, CA: Sage.

Kihlstrom, L. C. (1997). Characteristics and growth of managed behavioral health care firms. *Health Affairs* 16: 127–30.

Kilbourne, B. Stanek, P. England, G. Farkas, K. Brown, & D. Weir (1994). Returns to skill, compensating differentials, and gender bias: Effects of white women and men. *Amer. J. Sociology* 100: 689–719.

Kilpatrick, D. G., & H. S. Resnick (1992). Posttraumatic stress disorder associated with exposure to criminal victimization in clinical and community populations. In J. R. T. Davidson & E. B. Foa (Eds.), *Posttraumatic Stress Disorder: DSM-IV and Beyond.* Washington, DC: American Psychiatric Press.

Kilpatrick, D. G., B. E. Saunders, L. J. Veronen, C. L. Best, & J. M. Von (1987). Criminal victimization: Lifetime prevalence, reporting to police, and psychological impact. *Crime & Delinquency* 33: 479–89.

Kim, P. Suk, & G. B. Lewis (1994). Asian Americans in the public service: Success, diversity and discrimination. *Public Administration Rev.* 54: 285–90.

King, M. B. (1993). *AIDS, HIV and Mental Health.* Cambridge University Press.

Kinon, B., & J. Lieberman (1996). Mechanisms of action of atypical antipsychotic drugs: A critical analysis. *Psychopharmacology* 124: 2–34.

Kinzie, D. J., J. K. Boehnlein, P. K. Leung, L. J. Moore, C. Riley, & D. Smith (1990). The prevalence of posttraumatic stress disorder and its clinical significance among Southeast Asian refugees. *Amer. J. Psychiatry* 147: 913–17.

Kinzie, D. J., J. K. Boehnlein, J. Matsunaga, D. Johnson, S. Manson, S. Shore, J. Heinz, & M. Williams (1992). Psychiatric epidemiology of an Indian village, a 19-year replication study. *J. Nervous & Mental Disease* 180: 33–9.

Kirk, S. A., & H. Kutchins (1988). Deliberate misdiagnosis in mental health practice. *Social Service Rev.* 62: 225–37.

(1992). *The Selling of DSM: The Rhetoric of Science in Psychiatry.* New York: de Gruyter.

(1994). Is bad writing a mental disorder? *New York Times* (June 20): A17.

Kirk, S. A., & M. E. Therrien (1975). Community mental health myths and the fate of former hospitalized patients. *Psychiatry* 38: 209–17.

Kitagawa, E. M., & P. M. Hauser (1973). *Differential Mortality in the United States.* Cambridge, MA: Harvard University Press.

Kitson, G. C., & W. M. Holmes (1992). *Portrait of Divorce: Adjustment to Marital Breakdown.* New York: Guilford.

Kittrie, N. N. (1971). *The Right to Be Different.* Baltimore: Johns Hopkins University Press.

Klein, D. F. (1978). A proposed definition of mental illness. In R. L. Spitzer & D. F. Klein (Eds.), *Critical Issues in Psychiatric Diagnosis,* pp. 41–71. New York: Raven.

Klein, D., & P. Wender (1993). *Understanding Depression: A Complete Guide to Its Diagnosis and Treatment.* New York: Oxford University Press.

Kleinman, A. (1980). *Patients and Healers in the Context of Culture.* Berkeley: University of California Press.

—— (1988). *Rethinking Psychiatry: From Cultural Category to Personal Experience.* New York: Free Press.

Kleinman, A., & B. Good (Eds.) (1985). *Culture and Depression.* Berkeley: University of California Press.

Klerman, G. L. (1988). The current age of youthful melancholia: Evidence for increases in depression among adolescents and young adults. *Brit. J. Psychiatry* 152: 4–14.

Kneebone, P., J. Rogers, & R. J. Hafner (1995). Characteristics of police referrals to a psychiatric emergency unit in Australia. *Psychiatric Services* 46: 620–2.

Knitzer, J. (1982). *Unclaimed Children.* Washington, DC: Children's Defense Fund.

Knowledge Exchange Network (1997). Nation's mental health groups joining forces to change attitudes about mental illness. Press release (October 7), Center for Mental Health Services, Substance Abuse and Mental Health Services Administration, U.S. Department of Health and Human Services, Washington, DC.

Knox, M. D. (1989). Community mental health's role in the AIDS crisis. *Community Mental Health J.* 25: 185–96.

Knox, M. D., T. L. Boaz, M. A. Friedrich, & M. G. Dow (1994). HIV risk factors for persons with serious mental illness. *Community Mental Health J.* 30: 551–63.

Knox, M. D., & J. S. Gaies (1990). The HIV clinical tutorial for community mental health professionals. *Community Mental Health J.* 26: 559–63.

Kobasa, S. C., S. R. Maddi, & S. Kahn (1982). Hardiness and health: A prospective study. *J. Personality & Social Psychology* 42: 168–72.

Kohlberg, L. (1969). Continuities and discontinuities in child and adult moral development. *Human Development* 12: 93–120.

Kohn, M. L. (1968). Social class and schizophrenia: A critical review. *J. Psychiatric Res.* 6 (suppl.): 155–73.

—— (1977). *Class and Conformity,* 2nd ed. University of Chicago Press.

Kohn, M. L., A. Naoi, C. Schoenbach, C. Schooler, & K. M. Slomczynski (1990). Position in the class structure and psychological functioning in the United States, Japan, and Poland. *Amer. J. Sociology* 95: 964–1008.

Kohn, M. L., & C. Schooler (1982). Job conditions and personality: A longitudinal assessment of their reciprocal effects. *Amer. J. Sociology* 87: 1257–86.

—— (Eds.) (1983). *Work and Personality: An Inquiry into the Impact of Social Stratification.* Norwood, NJ: Ablex.

Kohn, M. L., & K. M. Slomczynski (1990). *Social Structure and Self-Direction: A Comparative Analysis of the United States and Poland.* Cambridge: Blackwell.

Koss, J. (1987). Expectations and outcomes for patients given mental health care or spiritist healing in Puerto Rico. *Amer. J. Psychiatry* 144: 56–61.

Kotler, P., & D. L. Wingard (1989). The effect of occupational, marital and parental roles on mortality: The Alameda County study. *Amer. J. Public Health* 79: 607–12.

Koyanagi, C., & H. H. Goldman (1991). *Inching Forward: A Report on Progress in Federal Mental Health Policy in the 1980s.* Alexandria, VA: National Mental Health Association.

Kramer, P. D. (1993). *Listening to Prozac.* New York: Penguin.

Krieger, N. (1987). Shades of difference: Theoretical underpinnings of the medical controversy on black/white differences in the United States, 1830–1870. *Internat. J. Health Services* 17: 259–78.

—— (1990). Racial and gender discrimination: Risk factors for high blood pressure? *Social Science & Medicine* 30: 1273–81.

Krieger, N., D. L. Rowley, A. A. Herman, B. Avery, & M. T. Phillips (1993). Racism, sexism, and social class: Implications for studies of health, disease, and well-being. *Amer. J. Preventive Medicine* 9 (suppl.): 82–122.

Krieger, N., D. R. Williams, & N. Moss (1997). Measuring social class in U.S. public health research: Concepts, methodologies, and guidelines. *Annual Rev. Public Health* 18: 341–78.

Kropp, P. R., D. N. Cox, R. Roesch, & D. Eaves (1989). The perceptions of correctional officers toward mentally disordered offenders. *Internat. J. Law & Psychiatry* 12: 181–8.

Kulka, R. A., W. E. Schlenger, J. A. Fairbank, R. L. Hough, K. B. Jordan, C. R. Marmar, & D. S. Weiss (1990). *Trauma and the Vietnam War Generation.* New York: Brunner/Mazel.

Kulka, R., Joseph Veroff, & E. Douvan (1979). Social class and the use of professional help for personal problems: 1957–1976. *J. Health & Social Behavior* 20: 2–17.

Kusserow, R. (1991). *Services Integration: A Twenty-Year Retrospective.* Washington, DC: Department of Health and Human Services, Office of the Inspector General.

Kuo, W. H. (1984). Prevalence of depression among Asian Americans. *J. Nervous & Mental Disorders* 172: 449–57.

——— (1995). Coping with racial discrimination: The case of Asian Americans. *Ethnic & Racial Studies* 18: 109–27.

Kupfer, D., E. Frank, & J. Perel (1989). The advantage of early treatment intervention in recurrent depression. *Arch. General Psychiatry* 46: 771–5.

Kuyken, W., & J. Orley (1994). Quality of life assessment: Cross-cultural issues – 1. *Internat. J. Mental Health* 23: 3–96.

Ladd, E. C. (1993). *The American Polity,* 5th ed. New York: Norton.

Lafond, J. Q., & M. L. Durham (1992). *Back to the Asylum.* New York: Oxford University Press.

Lagos, J. M., K. Perlmutter, & H. Huefinger (1977). Fear of the mentally ill: Empirical support for the common man's response. *Amer. J. Psychiatry* 134: 1134–7.

Laing, R. D. (1959). *The Divided Self.* London: Tavistock.

Lakey, B., & P. B. Cassady (1990). Cognitive processes in perceived social support. *J. Personality & Social Psychology* 59: 337–48.

Lakey, B., & L. G. Dickinson (1994). Antecedents of perceived support: Is perceived family environment generalized to new social relationships? *Cognitive Therapy & Res.* 18: 39–53.

Lamb, H. R., & R. W. Grant (1982). The mentally ill in a urban county jail. *Arch. General Psychiatry* 39: 17–22.

——— (1983). Mentally ill women in a county jail. *Arch. General Psychiatry* 40: 363–8.

Lamb, H. R., R. Shaner, D. M. Elliott, W. J. De Cuir, & J. T. Foltz (1995). Outcome for psychiatric emergency patients seen by an outreach police–mental health team. *Psychiatric Services* 46: 1267–71.

Lamb, H. R., L. E. Weinberger, & B. H. Gross (1988). Court mandated outpatient treatment for persons found NGRI: A 5 year follow-up. *Amer. J. Psychiatry* 145: 450–6.

Lambert, M. J., & A. E. Bergin (1994). The effectiveness of psychotherapy. In Bergin & Garfield (1994: 143–89).

Lamborn, S., N. Mounts, & L. Steinberg (1991). Patterns of competence and adjustment among adolescents from authoritative, authoritarian, indulgent, and neglectful homes. *Child Development* 62: 1049–65.

Lamping, D. L., & M. Sewitch (1990). *Review of the Literature on HIV Infection and Mental Health.* Toronto: Minister of Supply and Services.

Lamy, R. E. (1966). Social consequences of mental illness. *J. Counseling & Clinical Psychology* 30: 450–5.

Landes, R. G. (1987). *The Canadian Polity: A Comparative Introduction,* 2nd ed. Scarborough, Ontario: Prentice-Hall.

Lang, C. L. (1981). Good cases–bad cases: Client selection and professional prerogative in a community mental health center. *Urban Life* 10: 289–309.

Langner, T. S. (1962). A twenty-two item screening score of psychiatric symptoms indicating impairment. *J. Health & Human Behavior* 3: 269–76.

Langner, T. S., & S. T. Michael (1963). *Life Stress and Mental Health.* New York: Free Press.

Laosa, L. (1981). Maternal behavior: Sociocultural diversity in modes of interaction. In R. W. Henderson (Ed.), *Parent–Child Interaction: Theory, Research and Prospects,* pp. 125–67. New York: Plenum.

La Rocco, J. M., J. S. House, & J. R. P. French, Jr. (1980). Social support, occupational stress, and health. *J. Health & Social Behavior* 21: 202–28.

Larson, D. B., A. A. Hohmann, L. G. Kessler, K. G. Meador, J. H. Boyd, & E. McSherry (1988). The couch and the cloth: The need for linkage. *Hospital & Community Psychiatry* 39: 1064–9.

Laufer, R. S., M. S. Gallops, & E. Frey-Wouters (1984). War stress and trauma: The Vietnam veteran experience. *J. Health & Social Behavior* 25: 65–85.

Laurin-Frenette, N. (1976). *Functionalist Theories of Social Class: Sociology and Bourgeois Ideology*. Paris: Editions Anthropos.

Lave, J. R., et al. (1988). The early effects of Medicare's prospective payment system on psychiatry. *Inquiry* 25: 354–63.

Lave, J. R., & H. H. Goldman (1990). Medicare financing for mental health care. *Health Affairs* 9: 19–30.

Lazarus, R. S. (1966). *Psychological Stress and the Coping Process*. New York: McGraw-Hill.

Lazarus, R. S., & S. Folkman (1984). *Stress, Appraisal, and Coping*. New York: Springer.

Leaf, P. J., & M. L. Bruce (1987). Gender differences in the use of mental health-related services: A re-examination. *J. Health & Social Behavior* 28: 171–83.

Leaf, P. J., J. K. Myers, & L. T. McEvoy (1991). Procedures used in the Epidemiologic Catchment Area study. In Robins & Regier (1991: 11–32).

Leaf, P. J., M. M. Livingston, G. L. Tischler, M. M. Weissman, C. E. Holzer II, & J. Myers (1985). Contact with health professionals for the treatment of psychological and emotional problems. *Medical Care* 23: 1322–37.

Leavy, R. L. (1983). Social support and psychological disorder: A review. *J. Consulting & Clinical Psychology* 54: 438–46.

Lebow, J. L., & A. S. Gurman (1995). Research assessing couple and family therapy. *Annual Rev. Psychology* 46: 27–57.

Leete, E. (1988). The role of the consumer movement and persons with mental illness. Paper presented at conference entitled "Rehabilitation support services for persons with long-term mental illness: Preparing for the next decade" (Mary Switzer Memorial Seminar), Washington, DC.

Leff, J. (1988). *Psychiatry around the Globe: A Transcultural View*, 2nd ed. London: Gaskell.

(1990). Expressed emotion and psychoeducation: An update. *Tie-Lines* 7: 1–2.

Leff, J., & C. Vaughn (1985). *Expressed Emotion in Families*. New York: Guilford.

Lefley, H. P. (1982). Self-perception and primary prevention for American Indians. In S. Manson (Ed.), *New Directions in Prevention among American Indian & Alaska Native Communities*, pp. 65–89. Portland: Oregon Health Sciences University.

(1984). Delivering mental health services across cultures. In Pederson et al. (1984: 135–71).

(1990). Culture and chronic mental illness. *Hospital & Community Psychiatry* 41: 277–85.

(1992). Expressed emotion: Conceptual, clinical, and social policy issues. *Hospital & Community Psychiatry* 43: 591–8.

(1994). Mental health treatment and service delivery in cross-cultural perspective. In L. L. Adler & U. Gielen (Eds.), *Cross-Cultural Topics in Psychology*, pp. 179–200. New York: Praeger.

(1996a). Impact of consumer and family advocacy movements on mental health services. In Levin & Petrila (1996: 81–96).

(1996b). *Family Caregiving in Mental Illness*. Thousand Oaks, CA: Sage.

Lefley, H. P., & E. W. Bestman (1991). Public–academic linkages for culturally sensitive community mental health. *Community Mental Health J.* 27: 473–88.

Lefley, H. P., M. Sandoval, & C. Charles (1998). Traditional healing systems in a multi-cultural setting. In S. Okpaku (Ed.), *Clinical Methods in Transcultural Psychiatry*. Washington, DC: American Psychiatric Press.

Lefton, M. (1966). Former mental patients and their neighbors: A comparison of performance levels. *J. Health & Human Behavior* 7: 107–13.

Lehman, A. (1983). The well-being of chronic mental patients: Assessing their quality of life. *Arch. General Psychiatry* 40: 369–73.

Lehman, A., L. Postrado, D. Roth, S. McNary, & H. Goldman (1994). An evaluation of continuity of care, case management, and client outcomes in the Robert Wood Johnson program on chronic mental illness. *Milbank Q.* 72: 105–22.

Leigh, J. P. (1983). Direct and indirect effects of education on health. *Social Science & Medicine* 17: 227–34.

Leighton, A. H. (1959). *My Name Is Legion*. New York: Basic Books.

Lemert, E. M. (1951). *Social Pathology*. New York: McGraw-Hill.

Lennon, M. C. (1987). Sex difference in distress: The impact of gender and work roles. *J. Health & Social Behavior* 28: 290–305.

(1994). Women, work, and well-being: The importance of work conditions. *J. Health & Social Behavior* 35: 235–47.

(1998). Domestic arrangements and depression: An examination of household labor. In B. P. Dohrenwend (Ed.), *Adversity, Stress, and Psychopathology,* pp. 409–21. New York: Oxford University Press.

Lennon, M. C., & S. Rosenfield (1992). Women and mental health: The interaction of work and family conditions. *J. Health & Social Behavior* 33: 316–27.

(1994). Relative fairness and the division of housework: The importance of options. *Amer. J. Sociology* 100: 506–31.

Lenzenweger, M. F., A. W. Loranger, L. Korfine, & C. Neff (1997). Detecting personality disorders in a non-clinical population: Application of a two-stage procedure for case identification. *Archives of General Psychiatry* 54: 345–51.

Lester, N., L. E. Nebel, & A. Baum (1994). Psychophysiological and behavioral measurement of stress: Applications to mental health. In Avison & Gotlib (1994: 291–314).

Levin, B. L., & J. Petrila (1996). *Mental Health Services: A Public Health Perspective.* New York: Oxford University Press.

Levine, M. (1981). *The History and Politics of Community Mental Health.* New York: Oxford University Press.

Levy, F. (1995). Incomes and income inequality. In Farley (1995: 1–57).

Lewinsohn, P. M., H. Hops, R. E. Roberts, J. R. Seeley, & J. A. Andrews (1993). Adolescent psychopathology: I. Prevalence and incidence of depression and other DSM-III-R disorders in high school students. *J. Abnormal Psychology* 102: 133–44.

Lewis, S. (1990). Computerized tomography in schizophrenia 15 years on. *Brit. J. Psychiatry* 157: 16–24.

Lewit, E. M., & L. Baker (1994). Race and ethnicity: Changes for children. *The Future of Children* 4: 134–44.

Lewontin, R. C. (1972). The apportionment of human diversity. In T. Dobzhansky, M. K. Hecht, & W. C. Steere (Eds.), *Evolutionary Biology,* vol. 6, pp. 381–6. New York: Appleton-Century-Crofts.

Lewontin, R. C., S. Rose, & L. Kamin (1984). *Not in Our Genes: Biology, Ideology, and Human Nature.* New York: Pantheon.

Liberatos, P., B. G. Link, & J. L. Kelsey (1988). The measurement of social class in epidemiology. *Epidemiologic Rev.* 10: 87–121.

Liberman, R. P., C. J. Wallace, G. Blackwell, T. A. Eckman, J. V. Vaccaro, & T. G. Kuehnel (1993). Innovations in skills training for the seriously mentally ill: The UCLA social and independent living skills modules. *Innovations & Res.* 2: 43–59.

Lickey, M. E., & B. Gordon (1991). *Medicine and Mental Illness: The Use of Drugs in Psychiatry.* New York: Freeman.

Liddell, H. S. (1950). Some specific factors that modify tolerance for environmental stress. In H. G. Wolff, S. Wolf, & C. Hare (Eds.), *Life Stress and Bodily Disease,* pp. 155–71. Baltimore: William & Wilkins.

Lidz, C. W., E. P. Mulvey, & W. P. Gardner (1993). The accuracy of predictions of violence to others. *J. Amer. Medical Assoc.* 269: 1007–11.

Lidz, C. W., E. P. Mulvey, W. P. Gardner, & E. C. Shaw (1996). Conditional clinical predictions of violence: The condition of alcohol use. *Law & Human Behavior* 20: 35–48.

Lidz, T. (1975). *The Origin and Treatment of Schizophrenic Disorders.* London: Hutchinson.

Lidz, T., S. Fleck, & A. Cornelison (1965). *Schizophrenia and the Family.* New York: International Universities Press.

Lieberman, J., A. Brown, & J. Gorman (1994). Schizophrenia. In *Review of Psychiatry,* vol. 13. Washington, DC: American Psychiatric Press.

Lieberman, J. A., & A. J. Rush (1996). Redefining the role of psychiatry in medicine. *Amer. J. Psychiatry* 153: 1388–97.

Liem, R., & J. H. Liem (1978). Social class and mental illness reconsidered: The role of economic stress and social support. *J. Health & Social Behavior* 19: 139–56.

(1988). Psychological effects of unemployment on workers and their families. *J. Social Issues* 44: 87–105.

Light, D., & S. Levine (1988). The changing character of the medical profession: A theoretical overview. *Milbank Q.* 66 (suppl. 2): 10–32.

Lin, K.-M. (1996). Cultural influences on the diagnosis of psychotic and organic disorders. In Mezzich et al. (1996: 49–62).

Lin, K.-M., & A. Kleinman (1988). Psychopathology and clinical course of schizophrenia: A cross-cultural perspective. *Schizophrenia Bull.* 14: 555–67.

Lin, N. (1982). Social resources and instrumental action. In P. V. Marsden & N. Lin (Eds.), *Social Structure and Network Analysis,* pp. 131–45. Beverly Hills, CA: Sage.

(1986). Conceptualizing social support. In Lin et al. (1986a: 17–30).

Lin, N., A. Dean, & W. Ensel (Eds.) (1986a). *Social Support, Life Events, and Depression.* Orlando, FL: Academic Press.

Lin, N., M. Y. Dumin, & M. Woelfel (1986b). Measuring community and network support. In Lin et al. (1986a: 153–72).

Lin, N., & W. M. Ensel (1989). Life stress and health: Stressors and resources. *Amer. Sociological Rev.* 54: 382–99.

Lin, N., R. S. Simeone, W. M. Ensel, & W. Kuo (1979). Social support, stressful life events, and illness: A model and an empirical test. *J. Health & Social Behavior* 20: 108–19.

Lin, N., M. Woelfel, & S. C. Light (1986c). Buffering the impact of the most important life event. In Lin et al. (1986a: 307–32).

Lind, J. (1914). The color complex in the Negro. *Psychoanalytic Rev.* 1: 404–14.

Link, B. G. (1982). Mental patient status, work, and income: An examination of the effects of a psychiatric label. *Amer. Sociological Rev.* 47: 202–15.

(1983). The reward system of psychotherapy: Implications for inequities in service delivery. *J. Health & Social Behavior* 24: 61–9.

(1987). Understanding labeling effects in the area of mental disorders: An assessment of the effects of expectations of rejection. *Amer. Sociological Rev.* 52: 96–112.

Link, B. G., H. Andrews, & F. T. Cullen (1992). The violent and illegal behavior of mental patients reconsidered. *Amer. Sociological Rev.* 57: 275–92.

Link, B. G., & F. T. Cullen (1983). Reconsidering the social rejection of ex-mental patients: Levels of attitudinal response. *Amer. J. Community Psychology* 11: 261–73.

(1990). The labeling theory of mental disorder: A review of the evidence. *Res. in Community & Mental Health* 6: 75–105.

Link, B. G., F. T. Cullen, J. Frank, & J. F. Wozniak (1987). The social rejection of former mental patients: Understanding why labels matter. *Amer. J. Sociology* 92: 1461–1500.

Link, B. G., F. T. Cullen, E. Struening, P. Shrout, & B. P. Dohrenwend (1989). A modified labeling theory approach in the area of the mental disorders: An empirical assessment. *Amer. Sociological Rev.* 54: 400–23.

Link, B. G., & B. P. Dohrenwend (1980a). Formulation of hypotheses about the true relevance of demoralization in the United States. In Dohrenwend et al. (1980: 114–32).

(1980b). Hypotheses concerning the relationship of treated to true rates of psychological disorder. In Dohrenwend et al. (1980: 133–49).

Link, B. G., B. P. Dohrenwend, & A. E. Skodol (1986). Socio-economic status and schizophrenia: Noisome occupational characteristics as a risk factor. *Amer. Sociological Rev.* 51: 242–58.

Link, B. G., M. C. Lennon, & B. P. Dohrenwend (1993). Socioeconomic status and depression: The role of occupations involving direction, control and planning. *Amer. J. Sociology* 98: 1351–87.

Link, B. G., & B. Milcarek (1980). Selection factors in the dispensation of therapy: The Matthew effect in the allocation of mental health resources. *J. Health & Social Behavior* 21: 279–90.

Link, B. G., J. Mirotznik, & F. T. Cullen (1991). The effectiveness of stigma coping orientations: Can negative consequences of mental illness labeling be avoided. *J. Health & Social Behavior* 32: 302–20.

Link, B. G., & J. Phelan (1995). Social conditions as fundamental causes of disease. *J. Health & Social Behavior* (special issue): 80–94.

Link, B. G., & A. Stueve (1994). Psychotic symptoms and the violent/illegal behavior of mental patients compared to community controls. In J. Monahan & H. J. Steadman (Eds.), *Violence and Mental Disorder,* pp. 137–60. University of Chicago Press.

Link, B. G., E. Struening, M. Rahav, J. C. Phelan, & L. Nuttbrock (1997). On stigma and its conse-quences: Evidence from a longitudinal study of men with dual diagnoses of mental illness and substance abuse. *J. Health & Social Behavior* 38: 177–90.

Linn, J. G., & D. A. McGranahan (1980). Personal disruptions, social integration, subjective well-being, and predisposition toward the use of counseling services. *Amer. J. Community Psychology* 8: 87–100.

Linsky, A. S., J. P. Colby, Jr., & M. A. Straus (1987). Social stress, normative constraints, and alcohol problems in American states. *Social Science & Medicine* 24: 875–83.

Lion, J. R., W. Snyder, & G. L. Merrill (1981). Under reporting of assaults on staff in a state hospital. *Hospital & Community Psychiatry* 32: 497–8.

Lipman, E. L., D. R. Offord, & M. H. Boyle (1997). Sociodemographic, physical, and mental health characteristics of single mothers in Ontario: Results from the Ontario health supplement. *Cana-dian Medical Assoc. J.* 156: 639–45.

Lipsey, M. W., & D. B. Wilson (1993). The efficacy of psychological, educational, and behavioral treatment: Confirmation from meta-analysis. *Amer. Psychologist* 48: 1181–1209.

Little, D. (1991). *Varieties of Social Explanation: An Introduction to the Philosophy of Social Science.* Boulder, CO: Westview.

Litwack, E., & P. Messeri (1989). Organizational theory, social supports, and mortality rates: A theo-retical convergence. *Amer. Sociological Rev.* 54: 49–66.

Locke, B., M. Kramer, & B. Pasamanick (1960). Immigration and insanity. *Public Health Reports* 75: 301–6.

Loo, C., B. Tong, & R. True (1989). A bitter bean: Mental health status and attitudes in Chinatown. *J. Community Psychology* 17: 283–96.

Looney, J. (1988). *Chronic Mental Illness in Children and Adolescents.* Washington, DC: American Psychiatric Press.

Lopez, S. R. (1989). Patient variable biases in clinical judgment: Conceptual overview and method-ological considerations. *Psychological Bull.* 106: 184–203.

Loranger, A. W., N. Sartorius, & A. Janca (Eds.) (1996). *Assessment and Diagnosis of Personality Disorders: The International Personality Disorder Examination (IPDE).* Cambridge University Press.

Lorenzo, M. K., & D. A. Adler (1984). Mental health services for Chinese in a community health center. *J. Contemporary Social Work* 65: 600–9.

Loring, M., & B. Powell (1988). Gender, race, and DSM-III: A study of the objectivity of psychiatric behavior. *J. Health & Social Behavior* 29: 1–22.

Lubchansky, I., G. Egri, & J. Stokes (1970). Puerto Rican spiritualists view mental illness: The faith healer as paraprofessional. *Amer. J. Psychiatry* 127: 88–97.

Luborsky, L. (1984). *Principles of Psychoanalytic Psychotherapy.* New York: Basic Books.

Ludwig, E. V. (1991). The mentally ill homeless: Evolving involuntary commitment issues. *Villanova Law Rev.* 36: 1085–1111.

Luft, H. (1981). *Health Maintenance Organizations: Dimensions of Performance.* New York: Wiley.

Lui, W. T., & E. Yu (1985). Asian/Pacific American elderly: Mortality differentials, health status and use of health services. *J. Applied Gerontology* 4: 35–63.

Lum, O. M. (1995). Health status of Asians and Pacific Islanders. *Ethnogeriatrics* 11: 53–67.

Luster, T., K. Rhoades, & B. Haas (1989). The relation between parental values and parenting behavior: A test of the Kohn hypothesis. *J. Marriage & the Family* 51: 139–47.

Lutz, S. (1994). NME to pay fine of $379 million. *Modern Healthcare* (July 4): 2.

Lynch, J. (1977). *The Broken Heart.* New York: Basic Books.

Lyons, M., K. Kendler, A. G. Provet, & M. T. Tsuang (1991). The genetics of schizophrenia. In Tsuang et al. (1991: 119–52).

Maccoby, E. E. (1984). Middle childhood in the context of the family. In A. W. Collins (Ed.), *Devel-opment during Middle Childhood: The Years from Six to Twelve,* pp. 184–239. Washington, DC: National Academy Press.

Madakasira, S., & K. F. O'Brien (1987). Acute posttraumatic stress disorder in victims of a natural disaster. *J. Nervous Mental Disease* 53: 672–8.

Magee, W. J. (1993). Psychosocial predictors of agoraphobia, simple phobia, and social phobia onset in a U.S. national sample. Dissertation, Department of Sociology, University of Michigan, Ann Arbor.

Mahoney, M. J. (1974). *Cognition and Behavior Modification.* Cambridge, MA: Ballinger.

Mail, P. D. (1989). American Indians, stress, and alcohol. *American Indian & Alaska Native Mental Health Res.* 3: 7–26.

Mail, P. D., & S. Johnson (1993). Boozing, sniffing, and toking: An overview of the past, present, and future of substance use by American Indians. *American Indian & Alaska Native Mental Health Res.* 5: 1–33.

Malaspina, D., L. Kegeles, & R. V. Heertum (1996). Brain imaging in schizophrenia. In Kauffmann & Gorman (1996: 35–61).

Malgady, R. G., L. H. Rogler, & G. Constantino (1990). Culturally sensitive psychotherapy for Puerto Rican children and adolescents: A program of treatment outcome research. *J. Consulting & Clinical Psychology* 58: 704–12.

Malzberg, B. (1944). Mental disease among American Negroes: A statistical analysis. In O. Klineberg (Ed.), *Characteristics of the American Negro,* pp. 373–402. New York: Harper.

Manderscheid, R. W., & Henderson, M. J. (1996). The growth and direction of managed care. In Manderscheid & Sonnenschein (1996: 17–26).

Manderscheid, R. W., D. S. Rae, W. E. Narrow, B. Z. Locke, & D. A. Regier (1993). Congruence of service utilization estimates from the Epidemiologic Catchment Area project and other sources. *Arch. General Psychiatry* 50: 108–14.

Manderscheid, R. W., & M. A. Sonnenschein (Eds.) (1994). *Mental Health, United States – 1994* (DHHS pub. no. SMA 94-3000). Washington, DC: U.S. GPO.

(1996). *Mental Health, United States – 1996* (DHHS pub. no. SMA 96-3098). Washington, DC: U.S. GPO.

Manderscheid, R. W., M. J. Witkin, M. J. Rosenstein, & R. D. Bass (1986). The national reporting program for mental health statistics: History and findings. *Public Health Reports* 101: 532–9.

Manning, W., T. Stoner, N. Lurie, J. B. Christianson, D. Z. Gray, & M. Popkin. (1993). Outcomes for Medicaid beneficiaries with schizophrenia in the first year of the Utah prepaid mental health plan. Paper presented at the annual meeting of the American Public Health Association, San Francisco.

Manoleas, P. (Ed.) (1996). *The Cross-Cultural Practice of Clinical Case Management in Mental Health.* New York: Haworth.

Manson, S. (1995). Culture and major depression. *Psychiatric Clinics of North America* 18: 487–501.

Manson, S., D. Walker, & D. R. Kivlahan (1987). Psychiatric assessment and treatment of American Indians and Alaska Natives. *Hospital Community Psychiatry* 38: 165–73.

March, J. S. (1992). What constitutes a stressor? The "criterion A" issue. In J. R. T. Davidson & E. B. Foa (Eds.), *Posttraumatic Stress Disorder: DSM-IV and Beyond.* Washington, DC: American Psychiatric Press.

Marks, N. F., & S. S. McLanahan (1993). Gender, family structure, and social support among parents. *J. Marriage & the Family* 55: 481–93.

Marmor, T. R., & K. C. Gill (1989). The political and economic context of mental health care in the United States. *J. Health Politics, Policy & Law* 14: 459–75.

Marmor, T., M. Schlesinger, & R. Smithey (1986). A new look at nonprofits: Health care policy in a competitive age. *Yale J. Regulation* 3: 313–49.

Marmot, M. G., & E. M. A. Koveginas (1987). Social/economic status and disease. *Annual Rev. Public Health* 8: 111–35.

Marques, J. K., R. L. Haynes, & C. Nelson (1993). Forensic treatment at Atascadero State Hospital. *Internat. J. Law & Psychiatry* 16: 57–70.

Marsella, A. J. (1982). Culture and mental health: An overview. In A. J. Marsella & G. M. White (Eds.), *Cultural Conceptions of Mental Health and Therapy,* pp. 359–88. Boston: Reidel.

Marsella, A. J., N. Sartorius, A. Jablensky, & F. R. Fenton (1985). Cross-cultural studies of depressive disorders: An overview. In Kleinman & Good (1985: 299–324).

Martell, D. A., R. Rosner, & R. B. Harmon (1995). Base-rate estimates of criminal behavior by homeless mentally ill persons in New York City. *Psychiatric Services* 46: 596–601.

Martin, G. T., Jr., & M. N. Zald (Eds.) (1981). *Social Welfare in Society.* New York: Columbia University Press.

Marx, K. (1967). *Capital: A Critique of Political Economy.* New York: International.

Marzuk, P. M., H. Tierney, K. Tardiff, E. M. Gross, E. B. Morgan, M.-A. Hsu, & J. J. Mann (1988). Increased risk of suicide in persons with AIDS. *J. Amer. Medical Assoc.* 259: 1333–7.

Maslow, A. H. (1954). *Motivation and Personality.* New York: Harper (reprinted 1970).

(1966). *The Psychology of Science: A Reconnaissance.* New York: Harper & Row.

Massey, O. T., & L. Wu (1993). Service delivery and community housing: Perspectives of consumers, family members and case managers. *Innovation & Res.* 2: 9–15.

Mastekaasa, A. (1992). Marriage and psychological well-being: Some evidence on selection into marriage. *J. Marriage & the Family* 54: 901–11.

Matras, J. (1984). *Social Inequality, Stratification, and Mobility,* 2nd ed. Englewood Cliffs, NJ: Prentice-Hall.

Matthews, A. R. (1970). Observations on policy, policing and procedures for emergency detention of the mentally ill. *J. Criminal Law, Criminology & Police Science* 61: 283–95.

Mattlin, J. A., E. Wethington, & R. C. Kessler (1990). Situational determinants of coping and coping effectiveness. *J. Health & Social Behavior* 31: 103–22.

Matza, D. (1967). The disreputable poor. In R. Bendix & S. M. Lipset (Eds.), *Class, Status, and Power.* London: Routledge & Kegan-Paul.

McAuliffe, W. (1990). Health policy issues in the drug abuser treatment field. *J. Health Politics, Policy & Law* 15: 357–86.

McCarthy, J. D., & W. L. Yancey (1971). Uncle Tom and Mr. Charlie: Metaphysical pathos in the study of racism and personal disorganization. *Amer. J. Sociology* 76: 648–72.

McCarthy, J., & M. Zald (1977). Resource mobilization and social movements: A partial theory. *Amer. J. Sociology* 82: 1212–41.

McCue, M., & J. Clement (1992). Relative performance of for-profit psychiatric hospitals in investor-owned systems and nonprofit psychiatric hospitals. *Amer. J. Psychiatry* 150: 77–82.

McCue, M., J. Clement, & T. Heorger (1993). The association of ownership and system affiliation with the financial performance of inpatient psychiatric hospitals. *Inquiry* 30: 306–17.

McCusick, L. (Ed.) (1986). *What to Do about AIDS.* Berkeley: University of California Press.

McEwen, S. B., & S. Mendelson (1993). Effects of stress on the neurochemistry and morphology of the brain: Counterregulation versus damage. In Goldberger & Breznitz (1993: 101–26).

McFarland, B., et al. (1995). A capitated payment system for involuntary mental health clients. *Health Affairs* 14: 185–96.

McFarland, B. H., L. R. Faulkner, J. D. Bloom, R. Hallaux, & J. D. Bray (1989). Chronic mental illness and the criminal justice system. *Hospital & Community Psychiatry* 40: 718–23.

McFarland, D. (1969). Measuring the permeability of occupational structures: An information-theoretic approach. *Amer. J. Sociology* 75: 41–61.

McFarlane, W. (1994). Families, patients, and clinicians as partners: Clinical strategies and researching outcomes in single and multiple-family psychoeducation. In H. P. Lefley & M. Wasow (Eds.), *Helping Families Cope with Mental Illness,* pp. 195–222. Newark, NJ: Harwood.

McGhie, A., & J. Chapman (1961). Disorders of attention and perception in early schizophrenia. *Brit. J. Medical Psychology* 34: 103–16.

McGoldrick, M., J. Pearce, & J. Giordano (1995). *Ethnicity and Family Therapy,* rev. ed. New York: Guilford.

McGraw, S. A., J. B. Kimley, S. L. Crawford, & L. A. Costa (1992). Health survey methods with minority populations: Some lessons from recent experience. *Ethnicity & Disease* 2: 273–87.

McGuffin, P., P. Asherson, M. Own, & A. Farmer (1994). The strength of the genetic effect: Is there room for an environmental influence in the aetiology of schizophrenia? *Brit. J. Psychiatry* 164: 593–9.

McKinlay, J. B. (1972). Some approaches and problems in the study of the use of services – An overview. *J. Health & Social Behavior* 13: 115–52.

McKusick, V. A. (1967). The ethnic distribution of disease in the United States. *J. Chronic Disease* 20: 115–18.

McLanahan, S. S. (1983). Family structure and stress: A longitudinal comparison of two-parent and female-headed families. *J. Marriage & the Family* 45: 347–57.

(1985). Single mothers and psychological well-being: A test of the stress and vulnerability hypotheses. In J. R. Greenley (Ed.), *Research in Community and Mental Health,* vol. 5, pp. 253–66. Greenwich, CT: JAI.

McLanahan, S. S., & J. Adams (1987). Parenthood and psychological well-being. *Annual Rev. Sociology* 5: 237–57.

McLanahan, S., & K. Booth (1989). Mother-only families: Problems, prospects, and politics. *J. Marriage & the Family* 51: 557–80.

McLanahan, S. S., & L. L. Bumpass (1988). Intergenerational consequences of family disruption. *Amer. J. Sociology* 94: 130–52.

McLanahan, S., & L. Casper (1995). Growing diversity and inequality in the American family. In R. Farley (Ed.), *State of the Union: America in the 1990s,* vol. II (Social Trends), pp. 1–45. New York: Russell Sage Foundation.

McLanahan, S. S., & G. Sandefur (1994). *Growing Up with a Single Parent: What Hurts, What Helps.* Cambridge, MA: Harvard University Press.

McLean, A. (1990). Contradictions in the production of clinical knowledge: The case of schizophrenia. *Social Science & Medicine* 30: 969–85.

McLean, D., & B. G. Link (1994). Unraveling complexity: Strategies to refine concepts, measures and research designs in the study of life events and mental health. In Avison & Gotlib (1994: 15–42).

McLeod, J. D. (1991). Childhood parental loss and adult depression. *J. Health & Social Behavior* 32: 205–20.

McLeod, J. D., & R. C. Kessler (1990). Socioeconomic status differences in vulnerability to undesirable life events. *J. Health & Social Behavior* 31: 162–72.

McLeod, J. D., R. C. Kessler, & K. R. Landis (1992). Speed of recovery from major depressive episodes in a community sample of married men and women. *J. Abnormal Psychology* 101: 277–86.

McLeod, J. D., & M. J. Shanahan (1993). Poverty, parenting, and children's mental health. *J. Health & Social Behavior* 58: 351–66.

McLoyd, V. C. (1989). Socialization and development in a changing economy. *Amer. Psychologist* 44: 293–302.

McLoyd V. C., T. E. Jayaratne, R. Ceballo, & J. Borquez (1994). Unemployment and work interruption among African American single mothers: Effects on parenting and adolescent socioemotional functioning. *Child Development* 65: 562–89.

McMain, S., C. D. Webster, & R. J. Menzies (1989). The postassessment careers of mentally disordered offenders. *Internat. J. Law & Psychiatry* 12: 189–201.

McNiel, D. E., & R. L. Binder (1987). Predictive validity of judgments of dangerousness in emergency civil commitment. *Amer. J. Psychiatry* 144: 197–200.

(1994). The relationship between acute psychiatric symptoms, diagnosis and short-term risk of violence. *Hospital & Community Psychiatry* 45: 133–7.

McNiel, D. E., C. Hatcher, H. Zeiner, H. L. Wolfe, & R. S. Myers (1991). Characteristics of persons referred by police to the psychiatric emergency room. *Hospital & Community Psychiatry* 42: 425–7.

McQuillan, K. F. (1992). Falling behind: The income of lone-mother families, 1970–1985. *Canadian Rev. Sociology & Anthropology* 29: 511–23.

Mead, G. H. (1934). *Mind, Self, and Society.* University of Chicago Press.

Mechanic, D. (1975). Sociocultural and social-psychological factors affecting personal responses to psychological disorder. *J. Health & Social Behavior* 16: 393–404.

(1978). *Medical Sociology,* 2nd ed. New York: Free Press.

(1986). The challenge of chronic mental illness: A retrospective and prospective view. *Hospital & Community Psychiatry* 37: 891–6.

(1989). *Mental Health and Social Policy,* 3rd ed. Englewood Cliffs, NJ: Prentice-Hall.

(1991). Strategies for integrating public mental health services. *Hospital & Community Psychiatry* 42: 797–801.

(1994). Establishing mental health priorities. *Milibank Q.* 72: 501–14.

(1996). Emerging issues in international mental health services research. *Psychiatric Services* 47: 371–5.

(1999). *Mental Health and Social Policy: The Emergence of Managed Care,* 4th ed. Boston: Allyn & Bacon.

Mechanic, D., & L. Aiken (Eds.) (1989a). *Integrating Mental Health Care Services through Capitation.* San Francisco: Jossey-Bass.

Mechanic, D., & L. Aiken (1989b). Capitation in mental health: Potentials and cautions. *New Directions in Mental Health* 43: 1–16.

Mechanic, D., R. Angel, & L. Davies (1991). Risk and selection processes between the general and the specialty mental health sectors. *J. Health & Social Behavior* 32: 49–64.

Mechanic, D., & D. A. Rochefort (1990). Deinstitutionalization: An appraisal of reform. *Annual Rev. Sociology* 16: 301–27.

(1992). A policy of inclusion for the mentally ill. *Health Affairs* 11: 128–50.

Mechanic, D., & M. Schlesinger (1996). The impact of managed care on patients' trust in medical care and their physicians. *J. Amer. Medical Assoc.* 275: 1693–7.

Mechanic, D., M. Schlesinger, & D. McAlpine (1995). Management of mental health and substance abuse services: State of the art and early results. *Millbank Q.* 73: 19–55.

Mehlman, E. (1994). Enhancing self-disclosure of the African-American college student in therapy with the Caucasian therapist. *J. College Student Psychotherapy* 9: 3–20.

Mehta, Sheila, & A. Farina (in press). Destigmatizing mental "illness": Medical versus psychosocial models of mental disorder. *Journal of Social and Clinical Psychology.*

Meichenbaum, D. (1977). *Cognitive Behavior-Modification: An Integrative Approach.* New York: Plenum.

Melick, M. E., H. J. Steadman, & J. J. Cocozza (1979). The medicalization of criminal behavior among mental patients. *J. Health & Social Behavior* 20: 228–37.

Meltzer, H. Y. (1995). Clozapine: Is another view valid? *Amer. J. Psychiatry* 152: 821–5.

Meltzoff, J., & M. Kornreich (1970). *Research in Psychotherapy.* New York: Atherton.

Menaghan, E. G. (1983). Individual coping efforts: Moderators of the relationship between life stress and mental health outcomes. In Kaplan (1983: 157–91).

(1991). Work experiences and family interaction processes: The long reach of the job? *Annual Rev. Sociology* 17: 419–44.

Menaghan, E. G., L. Kowaleski-Jones, & F. L. Mott (1997). The intergenerational costs of parental social stressors: Academic and social difficulties in early adolescence for children of young mothers. *J. Health & Social Behavior* 38: 72–86.

Menaghan, E. G., & M. A. Lieberman (1986). Changes in depression following divorce: A panel study. *J. Marriage & the Family* 48: 319–28.

Menaghan, E. G., & T. L. Parcel (1991). Determining children's home environments: The impact of maternal characteristics and current occupational and family conditions. *J. Marriage & the Family* 53: 417–31.

(1995). Social sources of change in children's home environments: Effects of parental occupational experiences and family conditions over time. *J. Marriage & the Family* 57: 69–84.

Mendlewicz, J., & J. D. Rainer (1977). Adoption study supporting genetic transmission in manic-depressive illness. *Nature* 268–329.

Mental Health Report (1997). Experts address privacy issue at Rosalynn Carter symposium. *Mental Health Report* 21: 23.

Menzies, R. J. (1987). Cycles of control: The transcarceral careers of forensic patients. *Internat. J. Law & Psychiatry* 10: 233–49.

Menzies, R. J., C. D. Webster, S. McMain, S. Staley, & R. Scaglione (1994). The dimensions of dangerousness revisited: Assessing forensic predictions about violence. *Law & Human Behavior* 18: 1–28.

Mercy, J., A., & L. C. Steelman (1982). Familial influence on the intellectual attainment of children. *Amer. Sociological Rev.* 47: 532–42.

Merikangas, K. R. (1989). Epidemiology of DSM-III personality disorders. In R. Michels, et al. (Eds.), *Psychiatry,* vol. 3, pp. 1–16. Philadelphia: Lippincott.

Merton, R. K. (1938). Social structure and anomie. In Merton (1956/1968: 185–214).

(1956). *Social Theory and Social Structure.* New York: Free Press (3rd ed., 1968).

(1957). The role fit: Problems in sociological theory. *Brit. J. Sociology* 8: 106–20.

Meyer, A., & J. Goes (1988). Organizational assimilation of innovations: A multilevel contextual analysis. *Acad. Management J.* 31: 897–923.

Meyerson, A. (1994). Hospital chain sets guilty plea: Kickbacks, bribes paid for referrals. *New York Times* (June 29): D1.

Mezzich, J. E., A. Kleinman, H. Fabrega, & D. L. Parron (1996). *Culture and Psychiatric Diagnosis: A DSM-IV Perspective.* Washington, DC: American Psychiatric Press.

Michels, R., & P. M. Marzuk (1993). Progress in psychiatry: Part I. *New England J. Medicine* 329: 552–60.

Mignolli, G., C. Laccincani, & S. Platt (1991). Psychopathology and social performance in a cohort of patients with schizophrenic psychoses: A seven-year follow-up study. *Psychological Medicine* (monograph suppl.) 19: 17–26.

Miller, D. (1990). Psychological problems in HIV. In Ostrow (1990: 187–204).

Miller, J., C. Schooler, M. L. Kohn, & K. A. Miller (1979). Women and work: The psychological effects of occupational conditions. *Amer. J. Sociology* 85: 66–94.

Miller, R. D. (1987). *Involuntary Civil Commitment of the Mentally Ill in the Post-Reform Era.* Springfield, IL: Charles Thomas.

  (1988). Outpatient civil commitment of the mentally ill: An overview and update. *Behavioral Science & the Law* 6: 99–118.

Millon, T., & J. G. Klerman (Eds.) (1986). *Contemporary Directions in Psychopathology: Toward the DSM-IV.* New York: Guilford.

Mills, C. W. (1956). *The Power Elite.* New York: Oxford University Press.

Minuchin, S. (1974). *Families and Family Therapy.* Cambridge, MA: Harvard University Press.

Mirowsky, J. (1985). Depression and marital power: An equity model. *Amer. J. Sociology* 91: 557–92.

  (1995). Age and the sense of control. *Social Psychology Q.* 58: 31–43.

Mirowsky, J., & P. N. Hu (1996). Physical impairment and the diminishing effects of income. *Social Forces* 74: 1073–96.

Mirowsky, J., & C. E. Ross (1983). Paranoia and the structure of powerlessness. *Amer. Sociological Rev.* 48: 228–39.

  (1984). Mexican culture and its emotional contradictions. *J. Health & Social Behavior* 25: 2–13.

  (1986). Social patterns of distress. *Annual Rev. Sociology* 12: 23–45.

  (1988). Child care and emotional adjustment to wives' employment. *J. Health & Social Behavior* 29: 127–38.

  (1989a). Psychiatric diagnosis as reified measurement. *J. Health & Social Behavior* 30: 11–25.

  (1989b). *Social Causes of Psychological Distress.* New York: de Gruyter.

  (1990). Control or defense? Depression and the sense of control over good and bad outcomes. *J. Health & Social Behavior* 31: 71–86.

  (1991). Eliminating defense and agreement bias from measures of the sense of control: A 2×2 index. *Social Psychology Q.* 54: 127–45.

  (1992). Age and depression. *J. Health & Social Behavior* 33: 187–205.

  (1995). Sex differences in distress: Real or artifact? *Amer. Sociological Rev.* 60: 449–68.

Mischel, W., E. B. Ebbesen, & A. R. Zeiss (1973). Selective attention to the self: Situational and dispositional determinants. *J. Personality & Social Psychology* 27: 129–42.

Modern Healthcare (1995). Former Charter exec sentenced to prison term. *Modern Healthcare* (February 13): 32.

Moen, P., D. Dempster-McClain, & R. M. Williams, Jr. (1989). Social integration and longevity: An event history analysis of women's roles and resilience. *Amer. Sociological Rev.* 54: 635–47.

Mollica, R. F., K. Donelan, S. Tor, J. Lavelle, C. Elias, M. Frankel, & R. J. Blendon (1993). The effect of trauma and confinement on functional health and mental health status of Cambodians living in Thailand–Cambodia border camps. *J. Amer. Medical Assoc.* 270: 581–6.

Monahan, J. (1992). Mental disorder and violent behavior: Perceptions and evidence. *Amer. Psychologist* 47: 511–21.

Monahan, J., C. Caldeira, & H. D. Friedlander (1979). Police and the mentally ill: A comparison of committed and arrested persons. *Internat. J. Law & Psychiatry* 2: 509–18.

Monahan, J., & H. J. Steadman (1982). Crime and mental disorder: An epidemiological approach. In M. Tonry & N. Morris (Eds.), *Crime and Justice: An Annual Review of Research,* vol. 4, pp. 145–89. University of Chicago Press.

Monroe, S. M., et al. (1996). Life stress and treatment course of recurrent depression. II.*J. Consulting & Clinical Psychology* 105: 313–28.

Monroe, S. M., D. F. Imhoff, B. D. Wise, & J. E. Harris (1983). Prediction of psychological symptoms under high-risk psychosocial circumstances. *J. Abnormal Psychology* 92: 338–50.

Monroe, S. M., & J. R. McQuaid (1994). Measuring life stress and assessing its impact on mental health. In Avison & Gotlib (1994: 43–73).

Montagu, A. (1965). *The Concept of Race.* New York: Free Press.

Moore, K. A., & N. O. Snyder (1991). Cognitive attainment among firstborn children of adolescent mothers. *Amer. Sociological Rev.* 56: 612–24.

Mor, V., J. A. Fleishman, M. Dresser, & J. Piette (1992). Variations in health services use among HIV-infected patients. *Medical Care* 30: 17–29.

Morey, L. C. (1988). Personality disorders in DSM-III and DSM-III-R: Convergence, coverage and internal consistency. *Amer. J. Psychiatry* 145: 573–7.

Morlock, L. L. (1989). Recognition and treatment of mental health problems in the general health sector. In Taube et al. (1989: 39–61).

Morris, R., & I. Hirsch-Lescohier (1978). Service integration: Real vs. illusory solutions to welfare dilemmas. In R. Sarri & Y. Hassenfeld (Eds.), *The Management of Human Services.* New York: Columbia University Press.

Morrison, C. (1993). Delivery systems for the care of persons with HIV infection and AIDS. *Nursing Clinics of North America* 28: 317–33.

Morrissey, J. P. (1982). Deinstitutionalizing the mentally ill. In W. R. Gove (Ed.), *Deviance and Mental Illness,* vol. 6, pp. 147–78. Beverly Hills, CA: Sage.

Morrissey, J. P., M. Calloway, W. T. Bartko, M. S. Ridgeley, H. H. Goldman, & R. J. Paulson (1994). Local mental health authorities and service system change: Evidence from the Robert Wood Johnson program on chronic mental illness. *Milbank Q.* 72: 49–80.

Morrissey, J. P., M. O. Calloway, M. C. Johnsen, & M. D. Ullman (1997). Service system performance and integration: A baseline profile of the ACCESS demonstration sites. *Psychiatric Services* 48: 374–80.

Morrissey, J. P., & H. H. Goldman (1984). Cycles of reform in the care of chronically mentally ill. *Hospital & Community Psychiatry* 35: 785–93.

(1986). Care and treatment of the mentally ill in the United States: Historical developments and reforms. *Ann. Amer. Acad. Political & Social Science* 484: 12–27.

Morrissey, J. P., H. H. Goldman, & L. V. Klerman (1980). *The Enduring Asylum.* New York: Grune & Stratton.

Morrissey, J., & M. Lindsey (1987). *Organizational Structure and Continuity of Care: A Study of Community Health Centers.* Albany: New York State Office of Mental Health.

Morrissey, J. P., M. Tausig, & M. Lindsey (1984). Interorganizational networks in mental health systems: Assessing community support programs for the chronically mentally ill. Paper presented at the workshop sponsored by NIMH on Organizations and Mental Health (September 17–18), Rockville, MD.

Morse, G. A., & R. J. Calsyn (1986). Care and treatment of the mentally ill in the United States: Historical developments and reforms. *Ann. Amer. Acad. Political & Social Science* 484: 12–27.

Morse, N., & R. S. Weiss (1955). The function and meaning of work. *Amer. Sociological Rev.* 20: 191–8.

Morse, S. J. (1985). Excusing the crazy: The insanity defense reconsidered. *Southern California Law Rev.* 58: 777–836.

Moscicki, E. E., B. Locke, D. S. Rar, & J. H. Boyd (1989). Depressive symptoms among Mexican Americans: The Hispanic health and nutrition examination survey. *Amer. J. Epidemiology* 130: 348–60.

Moscovice, I., N. Lurie, J. B. Christianson, M. Finch, M. R. Atchtar, & M. Popkin (1993). Access of use of health services by chronically mentally ill Medicaid beneficiaries. *Health Care Financing Rev.* 14: 75–87.

Mott, F. L. (1991). Developmental effects of infant care: Mediating role of gender and health. *J. Social Issues* 47: 139–58.

(1992). The impact of father's absence from the home on subsequent development of younger children: Linkages between socio-emotional and cognitive well-being. Paper presented at the annual meeting of the American Sociological Association, Pittsburgh.

(1993). *Absent Fathers and Child Development* (Monograph prepared for the National Institute of Child Health and Human Development). Columbus, OH: Center for Human Resource Research.

(1994). Sons, daughter, and fathers' absence: Differentials in father-leaving probabilities and in home environments. *J. Family Issues* 15: 97–128.

Mott, F. L., L. Kowaleski-Jones, & E. G. Menaghan (1997). Paternal absence and child behavior: Does a child's gender make a difference? *J. Marriage & the Family* 59: 103–18.

Mowbray, C. T., D. Oyserman, J. Zemencuk, & S. Ross (1995). Motherhood for women with serious mental illness: Pregnancy, childbirth, and the postpartum period. *Amer. J. Orthopsychiatry* 65: 21–38.

Mowbray, C. T., & C. Tan (1992). Evaluation of an innovative consumer-run service model: The drop-in center. *Innovations & Res.* 1: 19–23.

Mrazek, P. J., and R. J. Haggerty (Eds.) (1994). *Ruducing Risks for Mental Disorders.* Washington, DC: National Academy Press.

Muchtler, J. E., & J. A. Burr (1991). Racial differences in health and health service utilization in later life: The effect of SES. *J. Health & Social Behavior* 32: 342–56.

Mukherjee, S., S. Shukls, J. Woodle, A. M. Rosen, & S. Olarte (1983). Misdiagnosis of schizophrenia in bipolar patients: A multiethnic comparison. *Amer. J. Psychiatry* 14: 1571–4.

Mulkern, V. (1995). The community support program: A model for federal–state partnership. Mental Health Policy Resource Center, Cambridge, MA.

Mullan, J. T. (1992). The bereaved caregiver: A prospective study of changes in well-being. *Gerontologist* 32: 673–83.

Muller, T. (1993). *Immigrants and the American City.* New York University Press.

Mulvey, E. P., W. Gardner, C. W. Lidz, J. Graus, & E. C. Shaw (1996). Symptomatology and violence among mental patients. Unpublished manuscript, Western Psychiatric Institute, Pittsburgh, PA.

Mulvey, E. P., J. L. Gelber, & L. H. Roth (1987). The promise and peril of involuntary outpatient commitment. *Amer. Psychologist* 42: 571–84.

Muntaner, C., & W. W. Eaton (1996). Psychosocial and organizational factors. Chronic outcomes: Mental illness. In J. Stellman (Ed.), *ILO Encyclopedia of Occupational Health and Safety,* pp. 137–40. Geneva: International Labor Office.

Muntaner, C., A. Y. Tien, W. W. Eaton, & R. Garrison (1991). Occupational characteristics and the occurrence of psychotic disorders. *Social Psychiatry & Psychiatric Epidemiology* 26: 273–80.

Murphy, J. M. (1976). Psychiatric labeling in a cross-cultural perspective. *Science* 191: 1019–28.

Myers, J. K., J. J. Lindenthal, & M. P. Pepper (1975). Life events, social integration and psychiatric symptomatology. *J. Health & Social Behavior* 16: 421–7.

Nagaswami, V. (1990). Integration of psychosocial rehabilitation in national health care programmes. *Psychosocial Rehab. J.* 14: 53–65.

Naidu, G., & C. Naryana (1991). How marketing oriented are hospitals in a declining market? *J. Health Care Marketing* 11: 23–30.

Nakao, K., L. J. Milazzo-Sayre, M. J. Rosenstein, & R.W. Manderscheid (1986). Referral patterns to and from inpatient psychiatric services: A social network approach. *Public Health Reports* 76: 755–60.

NAMHC [National Advisory Mental Health Council], Basic Behavioral Task Force (1996). Basic behavioral science research for mental health: Sociocultural and environmental processes. *Amer. Psychologist* 51: 722–31.

Namir, S., D. L. Wolcott, F. I. Fawzy, & M. J. Alumbaugh (1987). Coping with AIDS: Psychological and health implications. *J. Applied Social Psychology* 17: 309–28.

Napholz, L. (1994). Mental health and American Indian women's multiple roles. *American Indian & Alaska Native Mental Health Res.* 6: 57–75.

Narrow, W. E., D. Rea, E. K. Moscicki, B. Z. Locke, & D. A. Reiger (1991). Depression among Cuban Americans: The Hispanic health and nutrition examination survey. *Social Psychology & Psychiatric Epidemiology* 25: 260–8.

Nathan, K. I., & A. F. Schatzberg (1994). Mood disorders. In J. Oldham & M. B. Riba (Eds.), *Review of Psychiatry,* vol. 13. Washington, DC: American Psychiatric Press.

Nathan, R. P., F. C. Dolittle, et al. (1987). *Reagan and the States.* Princeton, NJ: Princeton University Press.

National Advisory Mental Health Council (1993). Health care reform for Americans with severe mental illness. *Amer. J. Psychiatry* 150: 1447–65.

National Center for Health Statistics (1990). Advance report of final mortality statistics, 1988. *Monthly Vital Statistics Report* 39: 1–47.

National Health Policy Forum (1995). Exploring the impact of Medicaid block grants and spending caps. Issue brief no. 672, George Washington University, Washington, DC.

National Mental Health Consumer Self-Help Clearinghouse (1998). The key. Philadelphia.

National Research Council, Commission on Behavioral and Social Sciences and Education (1983). *Losing Generations: Adolescents in High Risk Settings.* Washington, DC: National Academy Press.

Navarro, V. (1994). The politics of health policy. In *The U.S. Reforms, 1980–1994.* Boston: Blackwell.

Needleman, H. L. (1995). Behavioral toxiocology. *Environmental Health Perspectives* 103 (suppl.): 77–9.

Needleman, H. L., & D. Bellinger (1991). The health effects of low level exposure to lead. *Annual Rev. Public Health* 12: 111–40.

Neff, J. A. (1985). Race and vulnerability to stress: An examination of differential vulnerability. *J. Personality & Social Psychology* 49: 481–91.

Neighbors, H. W. (1984). The distribution of psychiatric morbidity in black Americans. *Community Mental Health J.* 20: 169–81.

(1990). The prevention of psychopathology in African Americans: An epidemiological perspective. *Community Mental Health J.* 26: 167–79.

Neighbors, H. W., R. Bashshur, R. Price, S. Selig, A. Donabedian, & G. Shannon (1992). Ethnic minority mental health service delivery: A review of the literature. *Res. in Community Mental Health* 7: 53–69.

Neighbors, H. W., J. S. Jackson, L. Campbell, & D. Williams (1989). The influence of racial factors on psychiatric diagnosis: A review and suggestions for research. *Community Mental Health J.* 25: 301–11.

Newhill, C. E., E. P. Mulvey, & C. W. Lidz (1995). Characteristics of violence in the community by female patients seen in a psychiatric emergency service. *Psychiatric Services* 46: 785–9.

Newman, K. S. (1993). Declining fortunes: The withering of the American dream. New York: Basic Books.

Newmann, J. P. (1986). Gender, life strains, and depression. *J. Health & Social Behavior* 27: 161–78.

Nicholas, H. G. (1986). *The Nature of American Politics,* 2nd ed. Oxford University Press.

Nielsen, S. L., C. K. Petito, C. D. Urmacher, et al. (1984). Subacute encephalitis in acquired immune deficiency syndrome: A postmortem study. *Amer. J. Clinical Pathology* 82: 678–82.

NIMH [National Institute of Mental Health] (1987). *Mental Health, United States – 1987.* Washington, DC: U.S. GPO.

(1990). *Clinical Training in Serious Mental Illness,* Ed. by H. P. Lefley (DHHS pub. no. ADM 90-1679). Washington, DC: U.S. GPO.

Nolan, W. J. (1917). Occupational and dementia praecox. *State Hospitals Q.* 3: 127–54.

Nolen-Hoeksema, S. (1987). Sex differences in unipolar depression: Evidence and theory. *Psychological Bull.* 101: 259–82.

Norman, R. M. G., & A. K. Malla (1983). Adolescents' attitudes towards mental illness: Relationships between components and sex differences. *Social Psychiatry* 18: 45–50.

Norquist, G. S., & K. B. Wells (1991). How do HMOs reduce outpaient mental health care costs? *Amer. J. Psychiatry* 148: 96–101.

Norris, F. H. (1992). Epidemiology of trauma: frequency and impact of different potentially traumatic evens on different demographic groups. *J. Consulting & Clinical Psychology* 60: 409–18.

Nunnally, J. C. (1961). *Popular Conceptions of Mental Health.* New York: Holt, Rinehart, & Winston.

Oakley, A. (1974). *The Sociology of Housework.* New York: Pantheon.

Oats, D. (1992). Psychiatric survivors and allies hold counter-conference and protests across the street from American Psychiatric Association huge annual meeting. *Dendron,* pp. 27–9.

O'Dowd, M. A., & F. P. McKegney (1990). AIDS patients compared with others in psychiatric consultation. *General Hospital Psychiatry* 12: 50–5.

O'Farrell, T. J. (1989). Marital and family therapy in alcoholism treatment. *J. Substance Abuse Treatment* 6: 23–9.

Ogloff, J. R. P. (1991). A comparison of insanity defense standards on juror decision making. *Law & Human Behavior* 15: 509–32.

Okun, M. A., J. F. Melichar, & M. D. Hill (1990). Negative daily events, positive and negative social ties, and psychological distress among older adults. *Gerontologist* 30: 193–9.

Olfson, M. (1990). Assertive community treatment: An evaluation of the experimental evidence. *Hospital & Community Psychiatry* 41: 634–41.

Omer, H. (1993). The integrative focus: Coordinating symptom- and person-oriented perspectives in therapy. *Amer. J. Psychotherapy* 47: 283–95.

Omi, M., & H. Winant (1994). *Racial Formation in the United States: From the 1960s to the 1990s,* 2nd ed. New York: Routledge.

Ommundsen, R., & T.-J. Ekeland (1978). Psychiatric labeling and social perception. *Scandinavian J. Psychology* 19: 193–7.

Ortega, S. T., & J. Corzine (1990). Socioeconomic status and mental disorders. In J. R. Greenley (Ed.), *Research in Community and Mental Health,* vol. 6: *Mental Disorder in Social Context,* pp. 149–82. Greenwich, CT: JAI.

Ostrow, D. G. (Ed.) (1990). *Behavioral Aspects of AIDS.* New York: Plenum.

Ostrow, D. G., J. H. Atkinson III, & I. Grant (1990). The management of the HIV-positive patient with neuropsychiatric impairment. In Ostrow (1990: 171–86).

Ostrow, D. G., A. Monjan, J. Joseph, M. VanRaden, R. Fox, L. Kingsley, J. Dudley, & J. Phair (1989). HIV-related symptoms and psychological functioning in a cohort of homosexual men. *Amer. J. Psychiatry* 146: 737–42.

O'Sullivan, M. J., & B. Lasso (1992). Community mental health services for Hispanics: A test of the culture compatibility hypothesis. *Hispanic J. Behavioral Sciences* 14: 455–68.

O'Sullivan, M. J., P. D. Peterson, G. B. Cox, & J. Kirkeby (1989). Ethnic populations: Community mental health services ten years later. *Amer. J. Community Psychology* 47: 17–30.

Ouellette, S. C. (1993). Inquiries into hardiness. In Goldberger & Breznitz (1993: 77–100).

Owan, T. (1981). Neighborhood-based mental health: An approach to overcome inequities in mental health services delivery to racial and ethnic minorities. In D. D. Biegal & A. J. Naparstek (Eds.), *Community Support Systems and Mental Health: Practice, Policy, and Research,* pp. 282–300. New York: Springer.

Oxford Illustrated Dictionary, 2nd ed. (1975). Oxford: Clarendon.

Padgett, D. K., C. Patrick, B. J. Burns, & H. J. Schlesinger (1994). Ethnicity and the use of outpatient mental health services in a national insured population. *Amer. J. Public Health* 84: 222–6.

Padgett, D., E. L. Struening, & H. Andrews (1990). Factors affecting the use of medical, mental health, alcohol, and drug treatment services by homeless adults. *Medical Care* 28: 805–21.

Page, S. (1977). Effects of the mental illness label in attempts to obtain accommodation. *Canadian J. Behavioral Science* 9: 85–90.

Pagel, M. D., W. W. Erdly, & J. Becker (1987). Social networks: We get by with (and in spite of) a little help from our friends. *J. Personality & Social Psychology* 53: 793–804.

Paikoff, R. L., J. Brooks-Gunn, & M. P. Warren (1991). Effects of girls' hormonal status on depressive and aggressive symptoms over the course of one year. *J. Youth & Adolescence* 20: 191–215.

Paley, W. D. (1993). Overview of the HMO movement. *Psychiatric Q.* 64: 5–12.

Parcel, T. L., & E. G. Menaghan (1990). Maternal working conditions and child verbal facility: Studying the intergenerational transmission of inequality from mothers to young children. *Social Psychology Q.* 53: 132–47.

(1994). *Parents' Jobs and Children's Lives.* New York: de Gruyter.

Pardoen, D., et al. (1996). Life events and primary affective disorders: A one year prospective study. *Brit. J. Psychiatry* 169: 160–6.

Parker, G. (1987). Editorial: Are the lifetime prevalence estimates in the ECA study accurate? *Psychological Medicine* 17: 275–82.

Parker, J. G., & S. R. Asher (1987). Peer relations and later personal adjustment: Are low-accepted children at risk? *Psychological Bull.* 102: 357–89.

Parker, S., & R. J. Kleiner (1966). *Mental Illness in the Urban Negro Community.* New York: Free Press.

Parsons, T. (1951). *The Social System.* Glencoe, IL: Free Press.

Pasamanick, B. (1963). Some misconceptions concerning differences in the racial prevalence of mental disease. *Amer. J. Orthopsychiatry* 33: 72–86.

Pasamanick, B., & H. Knobloch (1961). Epidemiologic studies on the complications of pregnancy and birth process. In G. Caplan (Ed.), *Prevention of Mental Disorders in Children,* pp. 74–94. New York: Basic Books.

Pasewark, R. A., & M. L. Pantle (1979). Insanity plea: Legislator's view. *Amer. J. Psychiatry* 136: 222–3.

Pasewark, R. A., M. L. Pantle, & H. J. Steadman (1982). Detention and rearrest rates of persons found not guilty by reason of insanity and convicted felons. *Amer. J. Psychiatry* 139: 892–7.

Pasewark, R. A., & D. Seidenzahl (1979). Opinions concerning the insanity plea and criminality among mental patients. *Bull. Amer. Acad. Psychiatry & Law* 7: 199–202.

Patel, V., & M. Winston (1994). "Universality of mental illness" revisited: Assumptions, artefacts and new directions. *Brit. J. Psychiatry* 165: 437–9.

Patterson, G. R. (1988). Family process: Loops, levels, and linkages. In N. Bolger, A. Caspi, G. Downey, & M. Moorehouse (Eds.), *Persons in Context: Developmental Processes,* pp. 114–51. Cambridge University Press.

Patterson, G., & L. Bank (1989). Some amplifying mechanisms for pathologic processes in families. In M. R. Gunnar & E. Thelen (Eds.), *Systems and Development* (Minnesota Symposia on Child Psychology, vol. 22), pp. 167–209. Hillsdale, NJ: Erlbaum.

Patterson, G. R., B. D. DeBaryshe, & E. Ramsey (1989). A developmental perspective on antisocial behavior. *Amer. Psychologist* 44: 329–35.

Patterson, J. T. (1986). *America's Struggle against Poverty, 1900–1985.* Cambridge, MA: Harvard University Press.

Pavkov, T. W., D. A. Lewis, & J. S. Lyons (1989). Psychiatric diagnoses and racial bias: An empirical investigation. *Professional Psychology: Res. & Practice* 20: 364–8.

Payer, L. (1988). *Medicine and Culture: Varieties of Treatment in the United States, England, West Germany and France.* New York: Holt.

Paykel, E. S. (1978). Contribution of life events to causation of psychiatric illness. *Psychological Medicine* 8: 245–53.

Pear, R. (1996a). Clinton to sign welfare bill that ends U.S. aid guarantee and gives states broad power.*New York Times* (August 1): A1.

    (1996b). Experts foresee health plan shift for mental care. *New York Times* (September 21): A1.

Pearlin, L. I. (1975). Sex roles and depression. In N. Datan & L. Ginsberg (Eds.), *Lifespan Developmental Psychology: Normative Life Crises,* pp. 191–202. New York: Academic Press.

    (1983). Role strains and personal stress. In Kaplan (1983: 3–32).

    (1989). The sociological study of stress. *J. Health & Social Behavior* 30: 241–56.

Pearlin, L. I., C. S. Aneshensel, J. T. Mullan, & C. Whitlatch (1995). Social support and the stress process: The case of family caregiving. In R. H. Binstock & L. K. George (Eds.), *Handbook of Aging and the Social Sciences,* 4th ed., pp. 283–302. Orlando, FL: Academic Press.

Pearlin, L. I., & J. C. Johnson (1977). Marital status, life strains, and depression. *Amer. Sociological Rev.* 42: 704–15.

Pearlin, L. I., & M. A. Lieberman (1979). Social sources of emotional stress. In R. Simmons (Ed.), *Research in Community and Mental Health,* pp. 217–48. Greenwich, CT: JAI.

Pearlin, L. I., M. A. Lieberman, E. G. Menaghan, & J. T. Mullan (1981). The stress process. *J. Health & Social Behavior* 22: 337–56.

Pearlin, L. I., J. T. Mullan, S. J. Semple, & M. M. Skaff (1990). Caregiving and the stress process: An overview of concepts and their measures. *Gerontologist* 30: 583–94.

Pearlin, L. I., & C. W. Radabaugh (1976). Economic strains and the coping functions of alcohol. *Amer. J. Sociology* 82: 652–63.

    (1985). Age and stress: Perspectives and problems. In B. H. Hess & E. W. Markson (Eds.), *Growing Old in America,* 3rd ed., pp. 293–308. New Brunswick, NJ: Transaction.

Pearlin, L. I., & C. Schooler (1978). The structure of coping. *J. Health & Social Behavior* 19: 2–21.

Pearlin, L. I., & M. M. Skaff (1995). Stressors and adaptation in late life. In M. Gatz (Ed.), *Mental Health and Aging,* pp. 97–123. Washington, DC: American Psychological Association.

Pearlin, L. I., & H. A. Turner (1987). The family as a context of the stress process. In S. V. Kasl & C. L. Cooper (Eds.), *Stress and Health: Issues in Research Methodology,* pp. 143–65. New York: Wiley.

Pederson, P. B., N. Sartorius, & A. J. Marsell (Eds.) (1984). *Mental Health Services: The Cross-Cultural Context.* Beverly Hills, CA: Sage.

Peek, M. K. (1996). Social networks in the life stress process. Dissertation, Duke University, Durham, NC.

Penkower, L., E. J. Bromet, & M. A. Dew (1988). Husband's layoff and wives mental health. *Arch. General Psychiatry* 45: 994–1000.

Penn, D. L., K. Guynan, T. Daily, W. Spaulding, C. Garbin, & M. Sullivan (1994). Dispelling the stigma of schizophrenia: What sort of information is best. *Schizophrenia Bull.* 20: 567–77.

Penn, D. L., S. Kommana, M. Mansfield, & B. G. Link (1998). Dispelling the stigma of schizophrenia: The impact of information on dangerousness. *Schizophrenia Bull.*

Perelberg, R. J. (1983). Mental illness, family and networks in a London borough. *Social Science & Medicine* 17: 481–91.

Perrow, C., & M. F. Guillén (1990). *The AIDS Disaster.* New Haven, CT: Yale University Press.

Perrucci, C. C., R. Perrucci, D. B. Targ, & H. R. Targ (1988). *Plant Closings: Interactional Context and Social Costs.* New York: de Gruyter.

Perrucci, R., & C. Perrucci (1990). Unemployment and mental health: Research and policy implications. In J. R. Greenley (Ed.), *Research in Community and Mental Health: Mental Disorder in Social Context,* pp. 237–64. Greenwich, CT: JAI.

Perrucci, R., & D. B. Targ (1982). Network structure and reactions to primary deviance of mental patients. *J. Health & Social Behavior* 23: 2–17.

Perry, J. C. (1992). Problems and considerations in the valid assessment of personality disorders. *Amer. J. Psychiatry* 149: 1645–53.

Perry, S., B. Fishman, L. Jacobsberg, J. Young, & A. Frances (1991). Effectiveness of psychoeducational interventions in reducing emotional distress after human immunodeficiency virus antibody testing. *Arch. General Psychiatry* 48: 143–7.

Perry, S., L. B. Jacobsberg, B. Fishman, P. H. Weiler, J. W. M. Gold, & A. J. Frances (1990). Psychological responses to serological testing for HIV. *AIDS* 4: 145–52.

Perry, S., & P. Jacobsen (1986). Neuropsychiatric manifestations of AIDS-spectrum disorders. *Hospital & Community Psychiatry* 37: 135–42.

Persons, J. B. (1986). The advantages of studying psychological phenomena rather than psychiatric diagnoses. *Amer. Psychologist* 41: 1252–60.

(1991). Illness careers and network ties: A conceptual model of utilization and compliance. In G. Albrecht & J. Levy (Eds.), *Advances in Medical Sociology,* vol. 2, pp. 164–81. Greenwich, CT: JAI.

(1992). Beyond rational choice: The social dynamics of how people seek help. *Amer. J. Sociology* 97: 1096–1138.

(1996). Bringing the "community" into utilization models: How social networks link individuals to changing systems of care. In J. J. Kronenfeld (Ed.), *Research in the Sociology of Health Care,* pp. 171–98. Greenwich, CT: JAI.

(1997). Bringing people back in: Why social networks matter in treatment effectiveness. Unpublished manuscript.

Pescosolido, B. A., C. B. Gardner, & K. Lubell (1995). Choice, coercion and "muddling through": Accounts of help-seeking from first-timers. Paper presented at the NIMH conference on mental health services research (September), Washington, DC.

Pescosolido, B. A., & J. J. Kronenfeld (1995). Health, illness and healing in an uncertain era: Challenges from and for medical sociology. *J. Health & Social Behavior* 36 (extra issue): 5–33.

Pescosolido, B. A., E. Wright, M. Alegría, & M. Vera (1996a). Social networks and patterns of use among the poor with mental health problems in Puerto Rico. Paper presented at the annual meeting of the American Public Health Association.

Pescosolido, B. A., E. R. Wright, & W. P. Sullivan (1996b). Communities of care: A theoretical perspective on case management models in mental health. In G. Albrecht (Ed.), *Advances in Medical Sociology,* vol. 6. Greenwich, CT: JAI.

Peters, M., & G. C. Massey (1983). Mundane extreme environmental stress in family stress theories: The case of black families in white America. *Marriage & Family Rev.* 6: 193–218.

Petersen, A. C., B. Compas, J. Brooks-Gunn, M. Stemmler, S. Ey, & K. E. Grant (in press). Depression in adolescence. *American Psychology.*

Peterson, C. (1992). *Personality,* 2nd ed. Fort Worth, TX: Harcourt Brace.

(1996). *The Psychology of Abnormality.* Fort Worth, TX: Harcourt Brace.

Pfefferbaum, A., K. Lim, M. Rosenbloom, & R. B. Zipursky (1990). Brain magnetic resonance imaging: Approaches for investigating schizophrenia. *Schizophrenia Bull.* 16: 452–76.

Phelan, J. C., & B. G. Link (1995). How far can we see from the shelter door? A comparison of demographic and disability profiles of currently and formerly homeless people. Paper presented at the annual meeting of the Society for the Study of Social Problems, Washington, DC.

Phelan, J. C., B. G. Link, A. Stueve, & B. Pescosolido (1996). Have public conceptions of mental health changed over the past half century? Does it matter? Paper presented at the annual meeting of the American Public Health Association, New York.

Pierce, A. (1967). Economic cycle and the social suicide rate. *Amer. Sociological Rev.* 32: 457–62.

Pierce, G. R., B. R. Sarason, I. G. Sarason, H. J. Joseph, & C. A. Henderson (1996). Conceptualizing and assessing social support in the context of the family. In G. R. Pierce, B. R. Sarason, & I. G. Sarason (Eds.), *Handbook of Social Support and the Family,* pp. 3–24. New York: Plenum.

Pilkonis, P. A., C. L. Heape, J. M. Proiette, S. W. Clark, J. D. McDavid, & T. E. Pitts (1995). The reliability and validity of two structured diagnostic interviews for personality disorders. *Arch. General Psychiatry* 52: 1025–33.

Pinderhughes, E. B. (1983). Empowerment for our clients and for ourselves. *Social Casework* 64: 331–8.

Piotrkowski, C. S., R. N. Rapoport, & R. Rapoport (1987). Families and work. In M. B. Sussman & S. K. Steinmetz (Eds.), *Handbook of Marriage and the Family,* pp. 251–83. New York: Plenum.

Pleck, J. (1985). *Working Wives, Working Husbands.* Beverly Hills, Ca.: Sage

Plomin, R. (1990). *Nature and Nurture: An Introduction to Human Behavioral Genetics.* Pacific Grove, CA: Brooks/Cole.

Plotnik, R. (1993). *Introduction to Psychology.* Pacific Grove, CA: Brooks/Cole.

Polan, J., D. Hellerstein, & J. Amchin (1985). Impact of AIDS-related cases in an inpatient therapeutic milieu. *Hospital & Community Psychiatry* 36: 173–6.

Pollack, D., B. H. McFarland, R. A. George, and R. H. Angell (1994). Prioritization of mental health services in Oregon. *Milibank Q.* 72: 515–50.

Porporino, F. J., & L. L. Motiuk (1995). The prison careers of mentally disordered offenders. *Internat. J. Law & Psychiatry* 18: 29–44.

Portes, A., D. Kyle, & W. W. Eaton (1992). Mental illness and help-seeking behavior among Mariel Cuban and Haitian refugees in South Florida. *J. Health & Social Behavior* 33: 283–98.

Portes, A., & R. G. Rumbaut (1990). *Immigrant America: A Portrait.* Berkeley: University of California Press.

Powell, W. (1991). Expanding the scope of institutional analysis. In Powell & Dimaggio (1991b: 337–60).

Powell, W., & P. Dimaggio (1991a). Introduction. In Powell & Dimaggio (1991b: 1–40).

(Eds.) (1991b). The New Institutionalism in Organizational Analysis, University of Chicago Press.

Powers, R. J., & I. L. Kutash (1985). Stress and alcohol. *Internat. J. Addictions* 20: 461–82.

Presidential Commission (1988). *Report of the Presidential Commission on the Human Immunodeficiency Virus Epidemic.* Washington, DC: U.S. GPO.

President's Commission on Mental Health and Illness (1978). *Report to the President from the President's Commission on Mental Health,* vol. 1. Washington, DC: U.S. GPO.

Price, R. H., E. L. Cowen, R. P. Lorion, & J. Ramos-McKay (Eds.) (1988). *14 Ounces of Prevention.* Washington, DC: American Psychological Association.

Prien, R., D. Kupfer, P. Mansky, J. Small, V. Tuason, C. Voss, & W. Johnson (1984). Drug therapy in prevention of recurrences in unipolar and bipolar affective disorders. *Arch. General Psychiatry* 41: 1096–1104.

Psychiatric News (1995). Violence among mentally ill found to be concentrated among those with comorbid substance abuse disorders. *Psychiatric News* (December 2): 8.

Pugh, R. L., B. J. Ackerman, E. B. McColgan, P. B. de Mesquite, P. J. Worley, & N. J. Goodman (1994). Attitudes of adolescents toward adolescent psychiatric treatment. *J. Child & Family Studies* 3: 351–63.

Pugliesi, K. (1995). Work and well-being: Gender differences in the psychological consequences of employment. *J. Health & Social Behavior* 36: 57–71.

Putnam, F. W., J. J. Guroff, E. K. Silberman, L. Barban, & R. M. Post (1986). The clinical phenomenology of multiple personality disorder: Review of 100 recent cases. *J. Clinical Psychiatry* 47: 285–93.

Pynoos, R. S., & K. Nader (1988). Children who witness the sexual assaults of their mothers. *J. Amer. Acad. Child & Adolescent Psychiatry* 27: 567–72.

Rabkin, J. G. (1972). Opinions about mental illness: A review of the literature. *Psychological Bull.* 77: 153–71.

(1979). Criminal behavior of discharged mental patients: A critical appraisal of the research. *Psychological Bull.* 86: 1–27.

(1984). Community attitudes and local psychiatric facilities. In J. Talbott (Ed.), *The Chronic Mental Patient: Five Years Later,* pp. 325–35. New York: Grune & Stratton.

(1993). Stress and psychiatric disorders. In Goldberger & Breznitz (1993: 477–510).

Rabkin, J. G., & E. L. Struening (1976). Life events, stress, and illness. *Science* 194: 1013–20.

Rachlin, S., A. Pam, & J. Milton (1975). Civil liberties versus involuntary hospitalization. *Amer. J. Psychiatry* 132: 189–92.

Radloff, L. (1975). Sex differences in depression: The effects of occupational and marital status. *Sex Roles* 1: 249–65.

(1977). The CES-D scale: A self-report depression scale for research in the general population. *Applied Psychological Measurement* 1: 385–401.

Randolph, F. (1995). Improving service systems through systems integration: The ACCESS program. *Amer. Rehab.* 21: 36–8.

Randolph, F., M. Blasinsky, W. Leginski, L. Parker, & H. Goldman (1997). Creating integrated service systems for homeless persons with mental illness: The ACCESS program. *Psychiatric Services* 48: 369–73.

Rapaport, D. (1959). The structure of psychoanalytic theory: A systematizing attempt. In S. Koch (Ed.), *Psychology: A Study of a Science,* vol. 1. New York: McGraw-Hill.

Ray, C., & M. Oss (1993). Community mental health and managed care. In W. Goldman & S. Feldman (Eds.), *Managed Mental Health Care. New Directions in Mental Health Services,* pp. 89–98. San Francisco: Jossey-Bass.

Raz, S., & N. Raz (1990). Structural brain abnormalities in the major psychoses: A quantitative review of the evidence from computerized imaging. *Psychological Bull.* 16: 391–402.

Razzano, L., S. A. Pickett, & B. M. Astrachan (in press). Psychiatric rehabilitation. In B. Shahani, B. J. deLateur, & M. Erlich (Eds.), *Principles and Practice of Rehabilitation.* Baltimore: Williams & Wilkins.

Reamer, F. G. (1989). The contemporary mental health system: Facilities, services, personnel, and finances. In Rochefort (1989: 21–42).

Redick, R. W., R. W. Manderscheid, M. J. Witkin, & M. J. Rosenstein (1983). *A History of the U.S. National Reporting Program for Mental Health Statistics – 1840–1983* (National Institute of Mental Health, Ser. HN, no. 3; DHHS pub. no. ADM 83-1296). Washington, DC: U.S. GPO.

Regier, D. A., M. E. Farmer, D. S. Rae, B. Z. Locke, B. J. Keith, L. L. Judd, & F. K. Goodwin (1990). Comorbidity of mental health disorders with alcohol and other drug abuse. *J. Amer. Medical Assoc.* 264: 2511–18.

Regier, D. A., L. G. Kessler, B. J. Burns, & I. D. Goldberg (1979). The need for a psychosocial classification system in primary care settings. *Internat. J. Mental Health* 8: 16–29.

Regier, D. A., J. K. Myers, M. Kramer, L. N. Robins, D. G. Blazer, R. L. Hough, W. W. Eaton, & B. Z. Locke (1984). The NIMH Epidemiologic Catchment Area (ECA) program: Historical context, major objectives, and study population characteristics. *Arch. General Psychiatry* 41: 934–41.

Regier, D. A., W. E. Narrow, D. S. Rae, R. W. Manderscheid, B. Z. Locke, & F. K. Goodwin (1993). The de facto U.S. mental and addictive disorders service system: Epidemiologic Catchment Area prospective 1-year prevalence rates of disorders and services. *Arch. General Psychiatry* 50: 85–94.

Reisner, R. (1985). *Law and the Mental Health System* (American Casebook Series). St. Paul, MN: West.

Reiss, D., R. Plomin, & E. M. Hetherington (1991). Genetics and psychiatry: An unheralded window on the environment. *Amer. J. Psychiatry* 148: 283–91.

Resnick, H. S., D. G. Kilpatrick, B. S. Dansky, B. E. Saunders, & C. L. Best (1993). Prevalence of civilian trauma and posttraumatic stress disorder in a representative national sample of women. *J. Consulting & Clinical Psychology* 61: 984–91.

Reynolds, S., & P. Gilbert (1991). Psychological impact of unemployment: Interactive effects of vulnerability and protective factors on depression. *J. Counseling Psychology* 38: 76–84.

Rice, M., & G. T. Harris (1992). A comparison of criminal recidivism among schizophrenic and non-schizophrenic offenders. *Internat. J. Law & Psychiatry* 15: 397–408.

(1995). Psychopathy, schizophrenia, alcohol abuse and violent recidivism. *Internat. J. Law & Psychiatry* 18: 249–63.

Richman, J., & K. Rospenda (1991). Gender roles and alcohol abuse: Costs of noncaring. Paper presented at the Society for the Study of Social Problems, Washington, DC.

Rickel, A. U., & T. S. Langner (1985). Short-term and long-term effects of marital disruption on children. *Amer. J. Community Psychology* 13: 599–611.

Ridley, C. R. (1984). Clinical treatment of the non-disclosing black client: A therapeutic paradox. *Amer. Psychologist* 39: 1234–44.

Riley, M. W., M. E. Johnson, & A. Foner (1972). *Aging and Society: III. A Sociology of Age Stratification.* New York: Russell Sage Foundation.

Risch, N. (1991). Genetic linkage studies in psychiatry: Theoretical aspects. In Tsuang et al. (1991: 71–93).

Riskind, J., & O. Wahl (1992). Moving makes it worse: The role of rapid movement in fear of psychiatric patients. *J. Social & Clinical Psychology* 11: 349–64.

Ritzer, G., & W. Walczak (1988). Rationalization and the deprofessionalization of physicians. *Social Forces* 67: 1–22.

Roberts, B. L., R. Dunkle, & M. Haug (1994). Physical, psychological, and social resources as moderators of the relationship of stress to mental health of the very old. *J. Gerontology* 49: 35–43.

Roberts, R. E. (1980). Prevalence of psychological distress among Mexican Americans. *J. Health & Social Behavior* 21: 134–45.

Robins, E., & S. Guze (1970). Establishment of diagnostic validity in psychiatric illness: Its application to schizophrenia. *Amer. J. Psychiatry* 126: 983–7.

Robins, L. N. (1966). *Deviant Children Grown Up.* Baltimore: Williams & Wilkins.

(1975). Alcoholism and labeling theory. In Gove (1975: 21–33).

(1979). Follow-up studies. In H. C. Quay & J. S. Werry (Eds.), *Psychopathological Disorders of Childhood,* 2nd ed., pp. 483–513. New York: Wiley.

(1985). Epidemiology: Reflections on testing the validity of psychiatric interview. *Arch. General Psychiatry* 42: 918–24.

(1993). Childhood conduct problems, adult psychopathology and crime. In Hodgins (1993: 173–93).

Robins, L. N., J. E. Helzer, J. Croughan, & K. S. Ratcliff (1981). The NIMH Diagnostic Interview Schedule: Its history, characteristics and validity. *Arch. General Psychiatry* 28: 381–9.

Robins, L. N., J. E. Helzer, H. Orvaschel, J. C. Anthony, D. G. Blazer, A. Burnam, & J. D. Burke, Jr. (1985). The diagnostic interview schedule. In Eaton & Kessler (1985: 143–70).

Robins, L. N., J. E. Helzer, M. M. Weissman, H. Orvaschel, E. Gruenberg, J. D. Burke, Jr., & D. A. Regier (1984). Lifetime prevalence of specfic psychiatric disorders in three sites. *Arch. General Psychiatry* 41: 949–56.

Robins, L. N., B. Z. Locke, & D. A. Regier (1991). An overview of psychiatric disorders in America. In Robins & Regier (1991: 328–66).

Robins, L. N., & D. A. Regier (Eds.) (1991). *Psychiatric Disorders in America: The Epidemiological Catchment Area Study.* New York: Free Press.

Robins, L. N., J. Wing, H.-U. Wittchen, J. E. Helzer, T. F. Babor, J. D. Burke, A. Farmer, A. Jablenski, R. Pickens, D. A. Regier, N. Sartorius, & L. H. Towle (1988). The Composite International Diagnostic Interview: An epidemiologic instrument suitable for use in conjunction with different diagnostic systems and in different cultures. *Arch. General Psychiatry* 45: 1069–77.

Robins, P. K., R. G. Spiegelman, S. Weiner, & J. G. Bell (Eds.) (1980). *A Guaranteed Annual Income.* New York: Academic Press.

Robinson, L. A., J. S. Berman, & R. A. Neimeyer (1990). Psychotherapy for the treatment of depression: A comprehensive review of controlled outcome research. *Psychological Bull.* 108: 30–49.

Robinson, R. V., & J. Kelley (1990). Class as conceived by Marx and Dahrendorf: Effects on income inequality, class consciousness, and class conflit in the U.S. and Great Britain. *Amer. Sociological Rev.* 55: 827–41.

Rochefort, D. A. (1987). The political context of mental health care. In D. Mechanic (Ed.), *Improving Mental Health Services: What the Social Sciences Can Tell Us* (New Directions for Mental Health Services, no. 36), pp. 93–106. San Francisco: Jossey-Bass.

(Ed.) (1989). *Handbook on Mental Health Policy in the United States.* New York: Greenwood.

(1993). *From Poorhouses to Homelessness: Policy Analysis and Mental Health Care.* Westport, CT: Auburn House.

Rodin, J. (1986a). Aging and health: Effects of the sense of control. *Science* 233: 1271–6.

(1986b). Health, control, and aging. In M. M. Baltes & P. B. Baltes (Eds.), *The Psychology of Control and Aging,* pp. 139–65. Hillsdale, NJ: Erlbaum.

(1990). Control by any other name: Definitions, concepts and processes. In J. Rodin, C. Schooler, & K. W. Schaie (Eds.), *Self-Directedness: Causes and Effects throughout the Life Course,* pp. 1–18. Hillsdale, NJ: Erlbaum.

Rodin, J., & P. Salovey (1989). Health psychology. *Annual Rev. Psychology* 40: 533–79.

Roesch, R., & R. Corrado (1983). Criminal justice system interventions. In E. Seidman (Ed.), *Handbook of Social Intervention,* pp. 385–407. Beverly Hills, CA: Sage.

Roesch, R., & S. L. Golding (1980). *Competency to Stand Trial.* Urbana: University of Illinois Press.

(1985). The impact of deinstitutionalization. In D. P. Farrington & J. Gunn (Eds.), *Aggression and Dangerousness,* pp. 209–39. New York: Wiley.

Roesch, R., J. R. P. Ogloff, & D. Eaves (1995). Mental health research in the criminal justice system: The need for common approaches and international perspective. *Internat. J. Laws & Psychiatry* 18: 1–14.

Rogers, C. R. (1942). *Counseling and Psychotherapy: Newer Concepts in Practice.* Boston: Houghton Mifflin.

(1951). *Client-Centered Therapy: Its Current Practice, Implications, and Theory.* Boston: Houghton Mifflin.

(1961). *On Becoming a Person.* Boston: Houghton Mifflin.

Rogers, Carl R., E. T. Gendlin, D. V. Kiesler, & C. B. Truax (1967). *The Therapeutic Relationship and Its Impact: A Study of Psychotherapy with Schizophrenics.* Madison: University of Wisconsin Press.

Rogers, E. (1995a). *Diffusion of Innovations,* 4th ed. New York: Free Press.

Rogers, E. S., W. A. Anthony, J. Toole, & M. A. Brown (1991a). Vocational outcomes following psychosocial rehabilitation: A longitudinal study of three programs. *J. Vocational Rehab.* 1: 21–9.

Rogers, Jeffrey L., J. D. Bloom, & S. M. Manson (1984). The first five years of the psychiatric security review board. *Bull. Amer. Acad. Psychiatry & Law* 12: 383–403.

Rogers, Joseph A. (1995b). Community organizing: Self-help and providing mental health services. *J. California Alliance for the Mentally Ill* 6: 41–3.

Rogers, Stacy, T. L. Parcel, & E. G. Menaghan (1991b). The effects of maternal working conditions and mastery on children's behavior problems: Studying the intergenerational transmission of social control. *J. Health & Social Behavior* 32: 145–64.

Rogers, Susan (1987). The self-help alternative. Mental health bulletin no. 99-87-05, Department of Public Welfare, Harrisburg, PA.

Rogler, L. H. (1989). The meaning of culturally sensitive research in mental health: Issues of memory in the Diagnostic Interview Schedule. *J. Nervous & Mental Disease* 146: 296–303.

Rogler, L. H., & D. E. Cortes (1993). Help-seeking pathways: A unifying concept in mental health care. *Amer. J. Psychiatry* 150: 554–61.

Rogler, L. H., D. E. Cortes, & R. G. Malgady (1991). Acculturation and mental health status among Hispanics. *Amer. Psychologist* 46: 585–97.

Rogler, L. H., & A. Hollingshead (1961). The Puerto Rican spiritualist as psychiatrist. *Amer. J. Sociology* 67: 17–21.

Rogler, L. H., R. G. Malgady, G. Constantino, & R. Blumenthal (1987). What do culturally sensitive mental health services mean? *Amer. Psychologist* 42: 565–70.

Rogler, L. H., R. G. Malgady, & O. Rodriguez (1989). *Hispanic Mental Health: A Framework for Research.* Malabar, FL: Eriger.

Rogler, L. H., R. G. Malgady, & W. W. Tyron (1992). Evaluation of mental health: Issues of memory in the Diagnostic Interview Schedule. *J. Nervous & Mental Disease* 180: 215–22.

Rollins, B. C., & D. L. Thomas (1979). Parental support, power, and control techniques in the socialization of children. In W. R. Burr, R. Hill, F. I. Nye, & I. L. Reiss (Eds.), *Contemporary Theories about the Family,* vol. I. New York: Free Press.

Roman, P., & T. Blum (1992). Drugs, the workplace and employee-oriented programming. In D. Gerstein & H. Harwood (Eds.), *Treating Drug Problems,* vol. 2, pp. 197–244. Washington, DC: National Academy Press.

Romanucci-Ross, L. (1977). The hierarchy of resort in curative practices: The Admiralty Islands, Melanesia. In D. Landy (Ed.), *Culture, Disease and Healing,* pp. 481–6. New York: Macmillan.

Romanyshyn, J. M. (1971). *Social Welfare: Charity to Justice.* New York: Random House.

Rook, K. S. (1984). The negative side of social interaction: Impact on psychological well-being. *J. Personality & Social Psychology* 46: 1097–1108.

Rose, R. (1991). Twin studies and psychosocial epidemiology. In Tsuang et al. (1991: 12–32).

Rose, S. P., & B. L. Black (1985). *Advocacy and Empowerment: Mental Health Care in the Community.* Boston: Routledge.

Rosen, G. (1968). *Madness in Society.* University of Chicago Press.

Rosenbaum, J. Leslie, & L. Prinsky (1991). The presumption of influence: Recent responses to popular music subcultures. *Crime & Delinquency* 37: 528–35.

Rosenberg, M. (1965). *Society and Adolescent Self-Image.* Princeton, NJ: Princeton University Press.

(1979). The self concept: Source, product and social force. In M. Rosenberg & R. H. Turner (Eds.), *Social Psychology: Sociological Perspectives.* New York: Basic Books.

(1984). A symbolic interactionist view of psychosis. *J. Health & Social Behavior* 25: 289–302.

(1985). Self-concept and psychological well-being in adolescence. In R. L. Leahy (Ed.), *Development of the Self,* pp. 205–56. Orlando, FL: Academic Press.

(1992). *The Unread Mind.* New York: Lexington.

Rosenberg, M., & L. I. Pearlin (1978). Social class and self-esteem among children and adults. *Amer. J. Sociology* 84: 53–77.

Rosenberger, J. (1990). Central mental health authorities: Politically flawed? *Hospital & Community Psychiatry* 41: 1171.

Rosenblatt, A., & C. Attkisson (1993). Assessing outcomes for sufferers of severe mental disorder: A conceptual framework and review. *Evaluation & Program Planning* 16: 347–63.

Rosenfield, S. (1980). Sex differences in depression: Do women always have higher rates? *J. Health & Social Behavior* 21: 33–42.

(1984). Race differences in involuntary hospitalization: Psychiatric vs. Labeling perspectives. *J. Health & Social Behavior* 25: 14–23.

(1989). The effects of women's employment: Personal control and sex differences in mental health. *J. Health & Social Behavior* 30: 77–91.

(1991). Homelessness and rehospitalization: The importance of housing for the chronically mentally ill. *J. Community Psychology* 19: 60–9.

(1992a). The costs of sharing: Wives' employment and husbands' mental health. *J. Health & Social Behavior* 33: 213–25.

(1992b). Factors contributing to the subjective quality of life of the chronically mentally ill. *J. Health & Social Behavior* 33: 299–315.

(1995). Gender stratification, stress, and mental illness. Paper presented at the workshop sponsored by NIMH on Social Structure, Stress, and Mental Illness (August), Washington, DC.

Rosenfield, S., & S. Neese-Todd (1993). Elements of a psychosocial rehabilitation clubhouse associated with a satisfying quality of life. *Hospital & Community Psychiatry* 44: 76–8.

Rosenfield, S., & S. Wenzel (1996). Social support and chronic mental illness: A test of four hypotheses. Paper presented for the Society for the Study of Social Problems, Cincinnati, OH.

Rosenheck, R., & J. A. Lam (1997). Client and site characteristics as barriers to service use by homeless persons with serious mental illness. *Psychiatric Services* 48: 387–92.

Rosenhan, D. (1973). On being sane in insane places. *Science* 179: 250–8.

Rosenstock, I. M. (1966). Why people use health services. *Milbank Q.* 44: 94–106.

Rosenthal, D. (1970). *Genetic Theory and Abnormal Behavior.* New York: McGraw-Hill.

Ross, C. E. (1995). Reconceptualizing marital status as a continuum of social attachment. *J. Marriage & the Family* 57: 129–40.

Ross, C. E., & C. E. Bird (1994). Sex stratification and health lifestyle: Consequences for men's and women's perceived health. *J. Health & Social Behavior* 35: 161–78.

Ross, C. E., & J. Huber (1985). Hardship and depression. *J. Health & Social Behavior* 26: 312–27.

Ross, C. E., & J. Mirowsky (1979). A comparison of life event weighting schemes: Change, undesirability, and effect-proportional indices. *J. Health & Social Behavior* 20: 166–77.

(1987). Normlessness, powerlessness, and trouble with the law. *Criminology* 25: 257–78.

(1988). Child care and emotional adjustment to wives' employment. *J. Health & Social Behavior* 29: 127–38.

(1989). Explaining the social patterns of depression: control and problem solving-or support and talking? *J. Health & Social Behavior* 30: 206–19.

(1992). Households, employment, and the sense of control. *Social Psychology Q.* 55: 217–35.

(1995a). Sex differences in distress. *Amer. Sociological Rev.* 60: 450–68.

(1995b). Does employment affect health? *J. Health & Social Behavior* 36: 230–43.

Ross, C. E., J. Mirowsky, & K. Goldsteen (1990). The impact of the family on health: The decade in review. *J. Marriage & the Family* 52: 1059–78.

Ross, C. E., J. Mirowsky, & J. Huber (1983). Dividing work, sharing work, and in-between: Marriage patterns and depression. *Amer. Sociological Rev.* 48: 809–23.

Ross, C. E., & C.-L. Wu (1995). The links between education and health. *Amer. Sociological Rev.* 60: 719–45.

Rosse, R. B. (1985). Reactions of psychiatric staff to an AIDS patient. *Amer. J. Psychiatry* 142: 523.

Roszell, P. (1996). A life course perspective on the implications of stress exposure. Ph.D. dissertation, University of Toronto, Ontario, Canada.

Roth, J. A. (1963). *Timetables.* Indianapolis, IN: Bobbs-Merrill.

Rothaus, P., P. G. Hanson, S. E. Cleveland, & D. L. Johnson (1963). Describing psychiatric hospitalization: A dilemma. *Amer. Psychologist* 18: 85–8.

Rotter, J. B. (1966). Generalized expectancies for internal versus external control of reinforcement. *Psychological Monographs* 80: 1–28.

Rowe, J. W., & R. J. Kahn (1987). Human aging: Usual and successful. *Science* 143: 143–9.

Roxburgh, S. (1996). Gender differences in work and well-being: Effects of exposure and vulnerability. *J. Health & Social Behavior* 37: 265–77.

Ruesch, J. (1949). Social techniques, social status and social change. In C. Kluckhohn & H. A. Murray (Eds.), *Personality in Nature, Society and Culture,* pp. 117–30. New York: Knopf.

Rush, A. J., A. T. Beck, M. Kovacs, & S. D. Hollon (1977). Comparative efficacy of cognitive therapy and imipramine in the treatment of depressed outpatients. *Cognitive Therapy & Res.* 1: 17–37.

Rushing, W. (1978). Status resources, societal reactions, and type of mental hospital admission. *Amer. Sociological Rev.* 43: 521–33.

Russell, L. (1989). *Medicare's New Hospital Payment System: Is It Working?* Washington, DC: Brookings.

Rutter, M. (1970). Sex differences in children's responses to family stress. In E. J. Anthony & C. Koupernik (Eds.), *The Child in His Family,* pp. 165–96. New York: Wiley.

Ryan, C. C. (1990). The training and support of health care professionals dealing with the psychiatric aspects of AIDS. In Ostrow (1990: 355–91).

Ryff, C. D. (1989). Happiness is everything, or is it? Explorations on the meaning of psychological well-being. *J. Personality & Social Psychology* 57: 1069–81.

Sacks, M. H., S. Perry, R. Graver, R. Schindledecker, & S. Hall (1990). Self-reported HIV-related risk behaviors in acute psychiatric inpatients: A pilot study. *Hospital & Community Psychiatry* 41: 1253–5.

Sagan, L. A. (1987). *The Health of Nations: True Causes of Sickness and Well-Being.* New York: Basic Books.

Saler, L. (1992). Childhood parental death and depression in adulthood: Roles of surviving parent and family environment. *Amer. J. Orthopsychiatry* 62: 504–16.

Sales, B., & T. Hafemeister (1984). Empiricism and legal policy on the insanity defense. In Teplin (1984b: 253–78).

Sales, G. N. (1991). A comparison of referrals by police and other sources to a psychiatric emergency service. *Hospital & Community Psychiatry* 42: 950–2.

Salgado de Snyder, V. N. (1987). Factors associated with acculturative stress and depressive symptomatology among married Mexican immigrant women. *Psychology Women Q.* 11: 475–88.

Salloway, J. C., & P. B. Dillon (1973). A comparison of family networks and friend networks in health care utilization. *J. Comparative Family Studies* 4: 140–8.

Sampson, H., S. Messinger, & R. Towne (1964). *Schizophrenic Women: Studies in Marital Crisis.* New York: Atherton.

Santos, A., S. Henggeler, B. Burns, G. Arana, & N. Meisler (1995). Research on field-based services: Models for reform in the delivery of mental health care to populations with complex clinical problems. *Amer. J. Psychiatry* 152: 1111–23.

Sapolsky, R. M. (1994). *Why Zebras Don't Get Ulcers: Guide to Stress, Stress-Related Diseases and Coping.* New York: Freeman.

Sarason, B. R., G. R. Pierce, & I. G. Sarason (1990a). Social support: The sense of acceptance and the role of relationships. In B. R. Sarason, I. G. Sarason, & G. R. Pierce (Eds.), *Social Support: An Interactional View,* pp. 97–129. New York: Wiley.

Sarason, B. R., I. G. Sarason, & G. R. Pierce (1990b). Traditional views of social support and their impact on assessment. In B. R. Sarason, I. G. Sarason, & G. R. Pierce (Eds.), *Social Support: An Interactional View,* pp. 9–25. New York: Wiley.

Sarason, I. G., & B. R. Sarason (Eds.) (1985). *Social Support: Theory, Research, and Applications.* Boston: Martinus Nijhoff.

Sarason, I. G., B. R. Sarason, & E. N. Shearin (1986). Social support as an individual difference variable: Its instability, origins, and relational aspects. *J. Personality & Social Psychology* 50: 845–55.

Sartorius, N., G. de Girolamo, G. Andrews, G. A. German, & L. Eisenberg (1993). *Treatment of Mental Disorders: A Review of Effectiveness.* (Published on behalf of the World Health Organization.) Washington, DC: American Psychiatric Press.

Sartorius, N., & T. W. Harding (1983). The WHO collaborative study on strategies for extending mental health care. *Amer. J. Psychiatry* 140: 1470–3.

Sartorius, N., A. Jablensky, A. Korten, et al. (1986). Early manifestations and first contact incidence of schizophrenia in different cultures. *Psychological Medicine* 16: 909–28.

Scallet, L. J., & J. T. Havel (1994). Reflections on the mental health community's experience in the health care reform debate. *Hospital & Community Psychiatry* 45: 916–19.

Scarr, S., & K. McCartney (1983). How people make their own environments: A theory of genotype environmental effects. *Child Development* 54: 424–35.

Schaefer, C., J. C. Coyne, & R. S. Lazarus (1981). The health-related functions of social support. *J. Behavioral Medicine* 4: 381–406.

Schaie, K. W. (1983). The Seattle longitudinal study: A 21-year exploration of psychometric intelligence in adulthood. In K. W. Schaie (Ed.), *Longitudinal Studies of Adult Psychological Development,* pp. 64–135. New York: Guilford.

Scheff, T. J. (1966a). *Being Mentally Ill: A Sociological Theory.* Chicago: Aldine (reprinted 1984).
 (1996b). Users and nonusers of a student psychiatric clinic. *J. Health & Social Behavior* 7: 114–21.

Scheffler, R., et al. (1991). The impact of Blue Cross/Blue Shield plan utilization management programs, 1980–88. *Inquiry* 28: 263–75.

Scheffler, R., C. Grogan, B. Cuffel, & S. Penner (1993). A specialized mental health plan for persons with severe mental illness under managed competition. *Hospital & Community Psychiatry* 41: 937–42.

Scheffler, R. M., & A. G. Miller (1989). Demand analysis of mental health service use among ethnic subpopulations. *Inquiry* 26: 202–15.

Scheiber, G. J., & J.-P. Poullier (1991). International health spending: Issues and trends. *Health Affairs* 10: 106–16.

Scheid, T. L., & C. Anderson (1995). Living with chronic mental illness: Understanding the role of work. *Community Mental Health J.* 31: 163–76.

Schlesinger, M. (1986). On the limits of expanding health care reform: Chronic care in prepaid settings. *Milbank Q.* 64: 189–215.

(1989). Some potential pitfalls of capitation. In Mechanic & Aiken (1989a: 97–115).

(1995). Ethical issues in policy advocacy. *Health Affairs* 14: 23–9.

Schlesinger, M., et al. (1997a). Competition and access to hospital services: Evidence from psychiatric hospitals. *Medical Care* 35: 974–92.

Schlesinger, M., et al. (1997b). The determinants of dumping: A national study of economically motivated transfers involving mental health care. *J. Health Services Res.* 32: 561–90.

Schlesinger, M., J. Bentkover, D. Blumenthal, R. Musacchio, & J. Willer (1987). The privatization of health care and physicians' perceptions of access to hospital services. *Milbank Q.* 65: 25–58.

Schlesinger, M., & R. Dorwart (1984). Ownership and mental-health services: A reappraisal of the shift toward privately owned facilities. *New England J. Medicine* 311: 959–65.

(1992). Falling between the cracks: Failing national strategies for the treatment of substance abuse. *Daedelus* 121: 195–237.

Schlesinger, M., R. Dorwart, & S. Epstein (1996a). Managed care constraints on psychiatrists' hospital practices: Bargaining power and professional autonomy. *Amer. J. Psychiatry* 153: 256–60.

Schlesinger, M., B. Gray, & E. Bradley (1996b). Charity and community: The role of nonprofit ownership in a managed health care system. *J. Health Politics, Policy & Law* 21: 697–752.

Schofield, W. (1964). *Psychotherapy: The Purchase of Friendship.* Englewood Cliffs, NJ: Prentice-Hall.

Schooler, C. (1987). Psychological effects of complex environments during the life span: A review and theory. In C. Schooler & K. W. Schaie (Eds.), *Cognitive Functioning and Social Structure over the Life Course,* pp. 24–49. Norwood, NJ: Ablex.

Schooler, C., M. L. Kohn, K. A. Miller, & J. Miller (1983). Housework as work. In Kohn & Schooler (1983: 242–60).

Schreter, R., S. Sharfstein, & C. Schreter (1994a). Introduction. In Schreter et al. (1994b: 3–10).

(Eds.) (1994b). *Allies and Adversaries: The Impact of Managed Care on Mental Health Services.* Washington, DC: American Psychiatric Press.

Schuerman, L. A., & S. Kobrin (1984). Exposure of community mental health clients to the criminal justice system: Client/criminal or patient/prisoner. In Teplin (1984b: 87–118).

Schulberg, H. C., & M. Killilea (1982a). Community mental health in transition. In Schulberg & Killilea (1982b: 40–94).

(Eds.) (1982b). *The Modern Practice of Community Mental Health.* San Francisco: Jossey-Bass.

Schulberg, H. C., & R. W. Manderscheid (1989). The changing network of mental health service delivery. In Taube et al. (1989: 11–22).

Schwalbe, M. L. (1985). Autonomy in work and self-esteem. *Sociological Q.* 26: 519–35.

Schwartz, B. (1984). *Psychology of Learning and Behavior,* 2nd ed. New York: Norton.

Schwartz, R. A., & I. K. Schwartz (1977). Reducing the stigma of mental illness. *Diseases of the Nervous System* 38: 101–3.

Schwartz, S. (1991). Women and depresson: A Durkheimian perspective. *Social Science & Medicine* 32: 127–40.

Scott, R. W., & J. C. Lammers (1985). Trends in occupations in the medical care and mental health sectors. *Medical Care Rev.* 42: 37–76.

Scott, R., & J. Meyer (1991). The organization of societal sectors: Propositions and early evidence. In Powell & Dimaggio (1991b: 108–42).

Scull, A. (1977). *Decarceration: Community Treatment and the Deviant.* Engelwood Cliffs, NJ: Prentice-Hall.

Seeman, M. (1959). On the meaning of alienation. *Amer. Sociological Rev.* 24: 783–91.

(1983). Alienation motifs in contemporary theorizing. *Social Psychology Q.* 46: 171–84.

Seeman, T. E., & L. F. Berkman (1988). Structural characteristics of social networks and their relationship with social support in the elderly: Who provides support. *Social Science & Medicine* 27: 737–49.

Seeman, T. E., M. L. Bruce, & G. J. McAvay (1996). Social network characteristics and onset of ADL disability: MacArthur studies of successful aging. *J. Gerontology* (Social Sciences) 51B: S191–S200.

Segal, S. P., C. Silverman, & T. Temkin (1995a). Characteristics and service use of long-term members of self-help agencies for mental health clients. *Psychiatric Services* 46: 269–74.

(1995b). Measuring empowerment in client-run self-help agencies. *Community Mental Health J.* 31: 215–27.

Seligman, M. E. P. (1975). *Helplessness: On Depression, Development, and Death.* San Francisco: Freeman.

Selye, H. (1936). A syndrome produced by divers nocuous agents. *Nature* 138: 32.

——— (1956). *The Stress of Life.* New York: McGraw-Hill.

——— (1993). History of the stress concept. In Goldberger & Breznitz (1993: 7–17).

Semmer, N. (1982). Stress at work, stress in private life and psychological well-being. In W. Bachmann & I. Udris (Eds.), *Mental Load and Stress in Activity: European Approaches.* New York: Elsevier.

Sewell, W. H., A. O. Haller, & G. W. Ohlendorf (1970). The educational and early occupational status attainment process: Replication and revision. *Amer. Sociological Rev.* 35: 1014–27.

Shadish, W. R., A. J. Lurigio, & D. A. Lewis (1989). After deinstitutionalization: The present and future of mental health long-term policy. *J. Social Issues* 45: 1–15.

Shapiro, S., E. Skinner, L. Kessler, M. V. Korff, P. German, G. Tischler, P. Leaf, L. Benham, L. Cottler, & D. Regier (1984). Utilization of health and mental health services: Three Epidemiologic Catchment Area sites. *Arch. General Psychiatry* 41: 971–8.

Shapiro, S., E. A. Skinner, M. Kramer, D. M. Steinwachs, & D. A. Regier (1985). Measuring need for mental health services in a general population. *Medical Care* 23: 1033–43.

Sharfstein, S. (1982). Medicaid cutbacks and block grants: Crisis or opportunity for community mental health. *Amer. J. Psychiatry* 139: 466–70.

Sharif, Z. (1996). Neurochemistry of schizophrenia. In Kauffmann & Gorman (1996: 79–103).

Shaw, N. (1987). AIDS: Special concerns for women. In M. Helmquist (Ed.), *Working with AIDS.* San Francisco: University of California Regents.

Shephard, R. L. (1987). *Physical Activity and Aging,* 2nd ed. Rockville, MD: Aspen.

Sheridan, K., T. J. Coates, M. A. Chesney, G. Beck, & P. J. Morokoff (1989). Health psychology and AIDS. *Health Psychology* 8: 761–5.

Sheridan, K., & E. P. Sheridan (1988). Psychological consultations to persons with AIDS. *Professional Psychology: Res. & Practice* 19: 532–5.

Sherman, P., & C. Kaufmann (1995). A compilation of the literature on what consumers what from mental health services. *Report Prepared for the Mental Health Statistics Improvement Project Phase II Task Force on the Design Mental Health Component: A Mental Health Report Card.* Cambridge, MA: Evaluation Center@HSRI.

Shern, D., N. Wilson, A. S. Coen, D. Patrick, M. Foster, & D. Bartsch (1994). Client outcomes II: Longitudinal client data from the Colorado treatment outcome study. *Milbank Q.* 72: 123–48.

Sherrington, R., J. Bynjolfsson, H. Petursson, et al. (1988). Localization of a susceptibility locus for schizophrenia on chromosome 5. *Nature* 336: 164–9.

Shilts, R. (1987). *And the Band Played On: Politics, People and the AIDS Epidemic.* New York: St. Martin's.

Shlay, A. B., & P. H. Rossi (1992). Social science research and contemporary studies of homelessness. *Annual Rev. Sociology* 18: 129–60.

Shore, J. M. (1987). A pilot study of depression among American Indian patients with research diagnostic criteria. *American Indian & Alaska Native Mental Health Res.* 1: 4–15.

Shore, Martin F., & M. D. Cohen (1990). The Robert Wood Johnson Foundation program on chronic mental illness: An overview. *Hospital and Community Psychiatry* 41: 1212–16.

Shore, Miles F., & A. Biegel (1996). The challenges posed by managed behavioral health care. *New England J. Medicine* 334: 116–18.

Sibicky, M., & J. F. Dovidio (1986). Stigma of psychological therapy: Stereotypes, interpersonal reactions, and the self-fulfilling prophecy. *J. Consulting & Clinical Psychology* 33: 148–54.

Siegal, M. (1984). Economic deprivation and the quality of parent–child relations: A trickle-down framework. *J. Applied Developmental Psychology* 5: 127–44.

Siegel, K., V. Ravies, & D. Karus (1994). Psychological well-being of gay men with AIDS: Contribution of positive and negative illness-related network interactions to depressive mood. *Social Science & Medicine* 39: 1555–63.

Signorelli, N. (1989). The stigma of mental illness on television. *J. Broadcasting & Electronic Media* 33: 325–31.

Silk-Walker, P., R. D. Walker, & D. Kiivlahan (1988). Alcoholism, alcohol abuse, and health in American Indians and Alaska Natives. *American Indian and Alaska Native Mental Health Research* 1 (monograph 1): 65–83.

Silver, E. (1995). Punishment or treatment? Comparing the lengths of confinement of successful and unsuccessful insanity defendants. *Law & Human Behavior* 19: 375–88.

Silver, E., C. Cirincione, & H. J. Steadman (1994). Demythologizing inaccurate perceptions of the insanity defense. *Law & Human Behavior* 18: 63–70.

Simon, J., & J. Zusman (1983). The effect of contextual factors on psychiatrists' perception of illness: A case study. *J. Health & Social Behavior* 24: 186–98.

Simon, R. (1995). Gender, multiple roles, role meaning, and mental health. *J. Health & Social Behavior* 36: 182–94.

Simons, R. L., J. Beaman, R. D. Conger, & W. Chao (1993). Stress, support, and antisocial behavior trait as determinants of emotional well-being and parenting practices among single mothers. *J. Marriage & the Family* 55: 385–98.

Skaff, M. M., L. I. Pearlin, & J. T. Mullan (1996). Transitions in the caregiving career: Effects on sense of mastery. *Psychology & Aging* 11: 247–57.

Skinner, L. J., K. K. Berry, S. E. Griffith, & B. Byers (1995). Generalizability and specificity of the stigma associated with the mental illness label: A reconsideration twenty-five years later. *J. Community Psychology* 23: 3–17.

Smith, B. (1968). Competence and socialization. In J. A. Clausen (Ed.), *Socialization and Society,* pp. 270–320. Boston: Little, Brown.

Smith, D. (1978). K is mentally ill. *Sociology* 12: 23–53.

Smith, M. L., G. Glass, & T. Miller (1980). *The Benefits of Psychotherapy.* Baltimore: Johns Hopkins University Press.

Smith, M. R. (1990). What is new in new structuralist analyses of earnings? *Amer. Sociological Rev.* 55: 827–41.

Smith, W. K. (1987). The stress analogy. *Schizophrenia Bull.* 13 : 215–20.

Snider, W. D., D. M. Simpson, S. Nielsen, et al. (1983). Neurological complications of acquired immune deficiency syndrome: Analysis of 50 patients. *Ann. Neurology* 14: 403–18.

Snow, D. A., S. G. Baker, L. Anderson, & M. Martin (1986). The myth of pervasive mental illness among the homeless. *Social Problems* 33: 407–23.

Snowden, L. R., & F. K. Cheung (1990). Use of inpatient mental health services by members of ethnic minority groups. *Amer. Psychologist* 45: 347–55.

Snowden, L. R., & J. Holschuh (1992). Ethnic differences in emergency psychiatric care and hospitalization in a program for the severely mentally ill. *Community Mental Health J.* 28: 281–91.

Snowden, L. R., T.-W. Hu, & J. M. Jerrel (1995). Emergency care avoidance: Ethnic matching and participation in minority-serving programs. *Community Mental Health J.* 31: 463–73.

Snowden, L. R., C. Storey, & T. Clancey (1989). Ethnicity and continuation in treatment at a black community mental health center. *J. Community Psychology* 17: 111–18.

Solomon, L., R. Frank, D. Vlahov, & J. Astermborski (1991). Utilization of health services in a cohort of intravenous drug users with known HIV-1 serostatus. *Amer. J. Public Health* 81: 1285–90.

Solomon, P. (1994). Families' views of service delivery: An empirical assessment. In H. P. Lefley & M. Wasow (Eds.), *Helping Families Cope with Mental Illness,* pp. 259–74. Newark, NJ: Harwood.

Somervell, P. D., B. H. Kaplan, G. Heiss, H. A. Tyroler, D. G. Kleinbaum, & P. A. Oberist (1989). Psychological distress as a predictor of mortality. *Amer. J. Epidemiology* 130: 1013–23.

Sorlie, P. D., E. Backlund, & J. B. Keller (1995). U.S. Mortality by economic, demographic and social characteristics: The national longitudinal mortality study. *Amer. J. Public Health* 85: 903–5.

Sosowsky, L. (1980). Explaining the increased arrest rate among mental patients: A cautionary note. *Amer. J. Psychiatry* 137: 1602–5.

Spade, J. Z. (1991). Occupational structure and men's and women's parental values. *J. Family Issues* 12: 343–60.

Spector, P. E. (1986). Perceived control by employees: A meta-analysis of studies concerning autonomy and participation at work. *Human Relations* 39: 1005–16.

Spitz, R. A. (1946). Anaclitic depression: An inquiry into the genesis of psychiatric conditions in early childhood II. *Psychoanalytic Study of the Child* 2: 313–42.

Spitzer, R. L., & J. Endicott (1978). Medical and mental disorder: Proposed definition and criteria. In R. L. Spitzer & D. F. Klein (Eds.), *Critical Issues in Psychiatric Diagnosis*, pp. 15–39. New York: Raven.

Spitzer, R. L., & J. B. W. Williams (1982). The definition and diagnosis of mental disorder. In W. R. Gove (Ed.), *Deviance and Mental Illness*, pp. 15–31. Beverly Hills, CA: Sage.

Spitzer, R. L., J. B. W. Williams, M. Gibbon, & M. B. First (1990). *Structured Clinical Interview for DSM-III-R, Patient Edition (SCID-P)*, ver.1.0. Washington, DC: American Psychiatric Press.

Srole, L., T. S. Langner, S. T. Michael, P. Kirkpatrick, M. K. Opler, & T. A. C. Rennie (1962). *The Midtown Manhattan Study.* New York: McGraw-Hill (reprinted 1978).

——— (1975). *Mental Health in the Metropolis (Midtown I)*, rev. ed., Ed. by L. Srole & A. Fischer. University of New York Press.

Srole, L., T. S. Langer, S. T. Michael, K. Opler, & T. A. C. Rennie (1961). *Mental Health in the Metropolis*, vol. I (Thomas A. C. Rennie Series in Social Psychology). New York: McGraw-Hill.

Stanton, M. D. (1981). Strategic approaches to family therapy. In A. S. Gurman & D. P. Kniskern (Eds.), *Handbook of Family Therapy*. New York: Brunner/Mazel.

Steadman, H. J., & J. J. Cocozza (1978). Selective reporting and the public's misconceptions of the criminally insane. *Public Opinion Q.* 42: 523–33.

Steadman, H. J., J. J. Cocozza, & M. E. Melick (1978). Explaining the increased crime rate of mental patients: The changes in clientele of state hospitals. *Amer. J. Psychiatry* 135: 816–20.

Steadman, H. J., S. Fabisiak, J. Dvoskin, & E. J. Holohean (1987). A survey of mental disability among state prison inmates. *Hospital & Community Psychiatry* 38: 1086–90.

Steadman, H. J., D. W. McCarty, & J. P. Morrissey (1989). *The Mentally Ill in Jail: Planning for Essential Services.* New York: Guilford.

Steadman, H. J., M. A. McGreevy, J. Morrissey, L. A. Callahan, P. C. Robbins, & C. Cirincione. (1993). *Before and After Hinkley: Evaluating Insanity Defense Reform.* New York: Guilford.

Steadman, H. J., J. Monahan, B. Duffee, E. Hartstone, & P. C. Robbins (1984). The impact of state mental hospital deinstitutionalization on U.S. prison populations, 1968–1978. *J. Criminal Law & Criminology* 75: 474–90.

Steadman, H. J., S. M. Morris, & D. L. Dennis (1995). The diversion of mentally ill persons from jails to community based services: A profile of programs. *Amer. J. Public Health* 85: 1630–5.

Steadman, H. J., & J. P. Morrissey (1982). Predicting violent behavior: A note on a cross-validation study. *Social Forces* 61: 475–83.

——— (1987). The impact of deinstitutionalization on the criminal justice system: Implications for understanding changing modes of social control. In J. Lawman, R. J. Menzies, & T. S. Palys (Eds.), *Transcarceration: Essays in the Sociology of Social Control*, pp. 227–48. Aldershot, UK: Gower.

Steadman, H. J., J. P. Morrissey, J. Braff, & J. Monahan (1986). Psychiatric evaluations of police referrals in a general hospital emergency room. *Internat. J. Law & Psychiatry* 8: 39–47.

Steele, C., & J. Aronson (1995). Stereotype threat and the intellectual test performance of African Americans. *J. Personality & Social Psychology* 69: 797–811.

Steelman, L. C., & B. Powell (1991). Sponsoring the next generation: Parental willingness to pay for higher education. *Amer. J. Sociology* 96: 1505–29.

Stein, L., & L. Ganser (1983). Wisconsin's system for funding mental health services. In J. Talbott (Ed.), *Unified Mental Health Systems: Utopia Unrealized.* San Francisco: Jossey-Bass.

Stein, L. I., & M. A. Test (1980). An alternative to mental hospital treatment: I. Conceptual model, treatment program, and clinical evaluation. *Arch. General Psychiatry* 37: 409–12.

——— (1985). The evolution of the training in community living model. *New Directions for Mental Health Services* 26: 7–16.

Stein, M., & A. H. Miller (1993). Stress, the immune system, and health and illness. In Goldberger & Breznitz (1993: 127–41).

Stein, M. D., J. Piette, V. Mor, et al. (1991). Differences in access to zidovudine among symptomatic HIV-infected persons. *J. General Internal Medicine* 6: 35–41.

Steinberg, L., S. D. Lamborn, S. M. Dornbusch, & N. Darling (1992). Impact of parenting practices on adolescent achievement: Authoritative parenting, school involvement, and encouragement to succeed. *Child Development* 63: 1266–81.

Steinberg, R. (1992). The market for drug treatment. In *Treating Drug Problems,* vol. 2, pp. 245–88. Washington, DC: National Academy Press.

Steinwald, B., & D. Neuhauser (1970). The role of the proprietary hospital. *J. Law & Contemporary Problems* 35: 817–38.

Stelovich, S. (1979). From the hospital to the prison: A step forward in deinstitutionalization? *Hospital & Community Psychiatry* 30: 618–20.

Stern, D. (1985). *The Interpersonal World of the Infant.* New York: Basic Books.

Stern, R., & K. Minkoff (1979). Paradoxes in programming for chronic patients in a community clinic. *Hospital & Community Psychiatry* 30: 613–17.

Sternberg, R. J. (1995). For whom the bell curve tolls: A review of the bell curve. *Psychological Science* 6: 257–61.

Steury, E. H., & M. Choinski (1995). "Normal" crimes and mental disorder: A two-group comparison of deadly and dangerous felonies. *Internat. J. Law & Psychiatry* 18: 183–207.

Stevenson, H. C., & G. Renard (1993). Trusting ole' wise owls: Therapeutic use of cultural strengths in African-American families. *Professional Psychology: Res. & Practice* 24: 433–42.

Steward, J. (1986). *Clinical Anatomy and Physiology.* Miami, FL: MedMaster.

Stiffman, A. R., & L. E. Davies (Eds.) (1990). *Ethnic Issues in Adolescent Mental Health.* Newbury Park, CA: Sage.

Stone, Allen A. (1975). *Mental Health and Law: A System in Transition.* Washington, DC: Department of Health, Education, and Welfare.

Stone, Arthur A., & J. M. Neale (1984). Effects of daily events on mood. *J. Personality & Social Psychology* 46: 137–44.

Strain, J. J., & G. Fulop (1990). Mental health service delivery issues. In Ostrow (1990: 305–20).

Strobino, D. M., M. E. Ensminger, Y. J. Kim, & J. Nanda (1995). Mechanisms for maternal age differences in birth weight. *Amer. J. Epidemiology* 142: 504–14.

Stroul, B., & R. Friedman (1986). *A System of Care for Severely Emotionally Disturbed Children and Youth.* Washington, DC: Georgetown University Child Development Center, CASSP Technical Assistance Center.

Stroup, T. S., & R. A. Dorwart (1995). Impact of a managed mental health program on Medicaid recipients with severe mental illness. *Psychiatric Services* 46: 885–9.

Sturm, R., C. A. Jackson, L. S. Meredith, W. Yip, W. G. Manning, W. H. Rogers, & K. B. Wells (1995). Mental health care utilization in prepaid and fee-for-service plans among depressed patients in the medical outcomes study. *Health Services Res.* 30: 319–40.

Substance Abuse and Mental Health Service Administration (1993). Final notice establishing definitions for (1) Children with a serious emotional disturbance, and (2) Adults with a serious mental illness. *Federal Register* 58: 29422–5.

Suchman, E. (1964). Sociomedical variation among ethnic groups. *Amer. J. Sociology* 70: 319–31.

Sue, S. (1977). Community mental health services to minority groups. *Amer. Psychologist* 32: 616–24.

Sue, S., D. C. Fujino, L.-T. Hu, D. T. Takeuchi, & N. W. S. Zane (1991). Community mental health services for ethnic minority groups: A test of the cultural responsiveness hypothesis. *J. Consulting & Clinical Psychology* 59: 533–40.

Sue, S., & H. L. McKinney (1975). Asian Americans in the community mental health care system. *Amer. J. Orthopsychiatry* 45: 111–18.

Sue, S., W. S. Zane, & K. Young (1994). Research on psychotherapy with culturally diverse populations. In Bergin & Garfield (1994: 783–817).

Sue, S., D. W. Sue, L. Sue, & D. T. Takeuchi (1995). Psychopathology among Asian Americans: A model minority? *Cultural Diversity & Mental Health* 1: 39–51.

Sullivan, H. S. (1947). *Conceptions of Modern Psychiatry.* Washington, DC: W.A. White Psychiatric Foundation.

Summers, F. (1981). The effects of aftercare after one year. *J. Psychiatric Treatment & Evaluations* 3: 405–9.

Surtees, P. G., & J. G. Ingham (1980). Life stress and depressive outcome: Application of a dissipation model of life events. *Social Psychiatry* 15: 21–31.

Susko, M. (1991). *Cry of the Invisible: Writings from the Homeless and Survivors of Psychiatric Hospitals.* Baltimore: Conservatory Press.

Susser, E., & S. P. Lin (1992). Schizophrenia after prenatal exposure to the Dutch hunger winter of 1944–1945. *Arch. General Psychiatry* 49: 983–8.

Susser, M. W., W. Watson, & K. Hopper (1985). *Sociology in Medicine,* 3rd ed. Oxford University Press.

Sussman, L. K., L. N. Robins, & F. Earls (1987). Treatment-seeking for depression by black and white Americans. *Social Science & Medicine* 24: 187–96.

Swank, G. E., & D. Winer (1976). Occurrence of psychiatric disorder in a county jail population. *Amer. J. Psychiatry* 133: 1331–3.

Swanson, J. W. (1994). Mental disorder, substance abuse and community violence: An epidemiological approach. In J. Monahan & H. J. Steadman (Eds.), *Violence and Mental Disorder,* pp. 101–36. University of Chicago Press.

Swanson, J. W., R. Borum, J. Monahan, & M. Swartz (1996). Psychotic symptoms and the risk of violent behavior: Evidence from the Epidemiologic Catchment Area surveys. *Criminal Behavior & Mental Health* 6: 309–29.

Swanson, J. W., C. K. Holzer, V. K. Ganju, & R. T. Jono (1990). Violence and psychiatric disorder in the community: Evidence from the Epidemiologic Catchment Area surveys. *Hospital & Community Psychiatry* 41: 761–70.

Sweet, A. A., & A. L. Loizeaux (1991). Behavioral and cognitive treatment methods: A critical comparative review. *J. Behavior Therapy & Experimental Psychiatry* 22: 159–85.

Sweet, J. A., L. Bumpass, & V. Call (1988). The design and content of the National Survey of Families and Households. Working paper no. NSFH-1, Center for Demography and Ecology, University of Wisconsin, Madison.

Swinnerton, K. A., & H. Wial (1995). Is job stability declining in the U.S. economy? *Industrial & Labor Relations Rev.* 48: 293–304.

Symonds, P. (1939). *The Psychology of Parent–Child Relationships.* New York: Appleton-Century-Crofts.

Szapocznik, J., D. Santiesteban, W. Kurtines, A. Perez-Vidal, & O. Hervis (1984). Bicultural effectiveness training. *Hispanic J. Behavioral Sciences* 6: 317–44.

Szasz, T. S. (1961). *The Myth of Mental Illness: Foundations of a Theory of Personal Conduct.* New York: Harper & Row (rev. ed. 1974).

    (1963). *Law, Liberty, and Psychiatry: An Inquiry into the Social Use of Mental Health Practices.* New York: Macmillan.

    (1984). *The Therapeutic State: Psychiatry in the Mirror of Current Events.* Buffalo, NY: Prometheus.

Takeuchi, D., K.-V. T. Bui, & L. Kim (1993). The referral of minority adolescents to community mental health centers. *J. Health & Social Behavior* 34: 153–64.

Takeuchi, D. T., S. Sue, & M. Yeh (1995). Return rates and outcomes from ethnicity-specific mental health programs in Los Angeles. *Amer. J. Public Health* 85: 638–43.

Takeuchi, D. T., & E. Uehara (1996). Ethnic minority mental health services: Current research and future conceptual directions. In Levin & Petrila (1996: 63–80).

Tanaka, H. T. (1983). Psychosocial rehabilitation: Future trends and directions. *Psychosocial Rehab. J.* 6: 7–12.

Tanzman, B. (1993). An overview of surveys of mental health consumers' preferences for housing and support services. *Hospital & Community Psychiatry* 44: 450–5.

Tasman, A., J. Kay, & J. A. Lieberman (1997). *Psychiatry,* 2 vols. Philadelphia: Saunders.

Taube, C. A., H. H. Goldman, & D. Salkever (1990). Medicaid coverage for mental illness: Balancing access and costs. *Health Affairs* 9: 5–18.

Taube, C. A., D. Mechanic, & A. A. Hohmann (1989). *The Future of Mental Health Services Research* (DHHS pub. no. ADM 89-1600). Washington, DC: U.S. GPO.

Tausig, M. (1992). Caregiver network structure, support and caregiver distress. *Amer. J. Community Psychology* 20: 81–96.

Tavris, C. (1992). *The Mismeasure of Woman.* New York: Simon & Schuster.

Taylor, J., & B. Jackson (1990). Factors affecting alcohol consumption in black women, part II. *Internat. J. Addictions* 25: 1415–27.

(1991). Evaluation of a holistic model of mental health symptoms in African American women. *J. Black Psychology* 18: 19–45.

Taylor, S. E. (1981). The interface of cognitive and social psychology. In J. Harvey (Ed.), *Cognition, Social Behavior, and the Environment.* Hillsdale, NJ: Erlbaum.

Taylor, S. E. (1989). *Positive Illusions.* New York: Basic Books.

Telles, E. E., & E. Murgia (1990). Phenotypic discrimination and income differences among Mexican Americans. *Social Science Q.* 71: 682–97.

Temerlin, M. (1968). Suggestion effects in psychiatric diagnosis. *J. Nervous & Mental Disease* 147: 349–53.

Teplin, L. A. (1983). The criminalization of the mentally ill: Speculation in search of data. *Psychological Bull.* 94: 54–67.

(1984a). Criminalizing mental disorder: The comparative arrest rate of the mentally ill. *Amer. Psychologist* 39: 794–803.

(1984b). *Mental Health and Criminal Justice.* Beverly Hills, CA: Sage.

(1985). The criminality of the mentally ill: A dangerous misconception. *Amer. J. Psychiatry* 142: 593–9.

(1990a). The prevalence of severe mental disorder among male urban jail detainees: Comparison with the Epidemiologic Catchment Area program. *Amer. J. Public Health* 80: 1–7.

(1990b). Detecting disorder: The treatment of mental illness among jail detainees. *J. Consulting & Clinical Psychology* 58: 233–6.

(1994). Psychiatric and substance abuse disorders among male urban jail detainees. *Amer. J. Public Health* 84: 290–3.

Teplin, L. A., K. M. Abram, & G. M. McClelland (1994). Does psychiatric disorder predict violent crime among released jail detainees? A six-year longitudinal study. *Amer. Psychologist* 49: 335–42.

(1996). Prevalence of psychistric disorders among incarcerated women. *Arch. General Psychiatry* 53: 505–12.

Teplin, L. A., W. J. Filstead, G. M. Hefler, & E. P. Sheridan (1980). Police involvement with the psychiatric emergency patient. *Psychiatric Ann.* 10: 46–54.

Teplin, L. A., G. M. McClelland, & K. M. Abram (1993). The role of mental disorder and substance abuse in predicting violent crime among released offenders. In Hodgins (1993: 86–103).

Teplin, L. A., & N. S. Pruett (1992). Police as street corner psychiatrists: Managing the mentally ill. *Internat. J. Law & Psychiatry* 15: 157–70.

Terr, L. C. (1991). Childhood traumas: An outline and overview. *Amer. J. Psychiatry* 148: 10–20.

Tessler, R. C., & D. L. Dennis (1992). Mental illness among homeless adults: A synthesis of recent NIMH-funded research. *Res. in Community & Mental Health* 7: 3–53.

Tessler, R., & H. Goldman (1982). *The Chronically Mentally Ill: Assessing Community Support Programs.* Cambridge, MA: Ballinger.

Tessler, R., & R. Manderscheid (1982). Factors affecting adjustment to community living. *Hospital & Community Psychiatry* 33: 203–7.

Test, M. A., & L. I. Stein (1980). Alternative to mental hospital treatment: III. Social cost.*Arch. General Psychiatry* 37: 400–5.

Theorell, T., & R. A. Karasek (1996). Current issues relating to psychosocial job strain and cardiovascular disease research. *J. Occupational Health Psychology* 1: 9–26.

Thoits, P. A. (1982a). Longitudinal effects of income maintenance upon psychological distress: Four waves of analysis. *Social Science Forum* 4: 38–57.

(1982b). Life stress, social support, and psychological vulnerability: Epidemiological considerations. *J. Community Psychology* 10: 341–62.

(1983). Dimensions of life events that influence psychological distress: An evaluation and synthesis of the literature. In Kaplan (1983: 33–103).

(1984). Coping, social support, and psychological outcomes: The central role of emotion. In *Review of Personality and Social Psychology,* vol. 5, pp. 219–38. Beverly Hills, CA: Sage.

(1985). Self-labeling processes in mental illness: The role of emotional deviance. *Amer. J. Sociology* 91: 221–49.

(1987). Gender and marital status differences in control and distress: Common stress versus unique stress explanations. *J. Health & Social Behavior* 28: 7–22.

(1992). Identity structures and psychological well-being: Gender and marital status comparisons. *Social Psychology Q.* 55: 236–56.

(1995a). Stress, coping, and social support processes: Where are we? What next? *J. Health & Social Behavior* (extra issue): 53–79.

(1995b). Identity-relevant events and psychological symptoms: A cautionary tale. *J. Health & Social Behavior* 36: 72–82.

Thomas, W. I., & D. S. Thomas (1928). *The Child in America: Behavior Problems and Programs.* New York: Knopf.

Thompson, C. (1942). Cultural pressures on the psychology of women. In C. Zanardi (Ed.), *Essential Papers on the Psychology of Women.* New York University Press (reprinted 1990).

Tijhuis, M. (1994). *Social Networks and Health.* Utrecht: Nivel.

Torrey, E. F. (1992). Are we overestimating the genetic contribution to schizophrenia? *Schizophrenia Bull.* 18: 159–70.

(1995). Jails and prisons – America's new mental hospitals. *Amer. J. Public Health* 85: 1611–13.

Torrey, E. F., A. E. Bowler, E. H. Taylor, & I. I. Gottesman (1994). *Schizophrenia and Manic-Depressive Disorder.* New York: Basic Books.

Torrey, E. F., S. M. Wolfe, & L. Flynn (1988). *Care of the Seriously Mentally Ill: A Rating of State Programs,* 2nd ed. Washington, DC / Arlington, VA: Public Citizen Health Research Group / National Alliance for the Mentally Ill.

Triandis, H. C. (1995). *Individualism and Collectivism.* San Francisco: Westview.

Tringo, J. (1970). The hierarchy of preference toward disability groups. *J. Special Education* 4: 295–306.

Trochim, W., J. Dumont, & J. Campbell (1993). Mapping mental health outcomes from the perspective of consumer/survivors: A report for the state mental health agency profiling system. National Association of State Mental Health Program Directors Research Institute, Arlington, VA.

Tross, S., & D. A. Hirsch (1988). Psychological distress and neuropsychological complications of HIV infection and AIDS. *Amer. Psychologist* 43: 929–34.

Tsuang, M. T., & S. Faraone (1990). *The Genetics of Mood Disorders.* Baltimore: Johns Hopkins University Press.

Tsuang, M. T., S. Faraone, & M. Lyons (1989). Advances in psychiatric genetics. In J. A. C. Silva & C. C. Nadelson (Eds.), *International Review of Psychiatry,* vol. 1, pp. 395–439. Washington, DC: American Psychiatric Press.

Tsuang, M. T., K. S. Kendler, & M. J. Lyons (Eds.) (1991). *Genetic Issues in Psychosocial Epidemiology.* New Brunswick, NJ: Rutgers University Press.

Tsuang, M. T., M. Tohen, & G. E. P. Zahner (Eds.) (1995). *Textbook in Psychiatric Epidemiology.* New York: Wiley.

Tsuang, M. T., G. Winokur, & R. R. Crowe (1980). Morbidity risks of schizophrenia and affective disorders among first-degree relatives of patients with schizophrenia, mania, depression, and surgical conditions. *Brit. J. Psychiatry* 137: 497–504.

Tucker, C., R. McKay, B. Kojetin, R. Harrison, M. de la Puente, L. Stinson, & E. Robison (1996). Testing methods of collecting racial and ethnic information: Results of the current population survey supplement on race and ethnicity. *Bureau of Labor Statistical Notes* 40: 1–149.

Tucker, L., et al. (1992). Looking at innovative multihospital systems: How marketing differs. *J. Health Care Marketing* 12: 8–21.

Tucker, W. H. (1994). *The Science and Politics of Racial Research.* Urbana: University of Illinois Press.

Turner, B. J. (1995). Economic context and the health effects of unemployment. *J. Health & Social Behavior* 36: 213–29.

Turner, B. S. (1987). *Medical Power and Social Knowledge.* London: Sage.

Turner, H. A. (1994). Gender and social support: Taking the bad with the good? *Sex Roles* 30: 521–41.

Turner, R. Jay (1981). Social support as a contingency in psychological well-being. *J. Health & Social Behavior* 22: 357–67.

(1983). Direct, indirect and moderating effects of social support upon psychological distress and associated conditions. In Kaplan (1983: 105–55).

Turner, R. Jay, & W. R. Avison (1989). Gender and depression: Assessing exposure and vulnerability to life events in a chronically strained population. *J. Nervous & Mental Disease* 177: 443–55.

Turner, R. J., B. G. Frankel, & D. M. Levin (1983). Social support: Conceptualization, measurement and implications for mental health. In J. R. Greeley (Ed.), *Research in Community and Mental Health,* vol. 3. Greenwich, CT: JAI.

Turner, R. Jay, C. F. Grindstaff, & N. Phillips (1990). Social support and outcome in teenage pregnancy. *J. Health & Social Behavior* 31: 43–57.

Turner, R. Jay, & F. Marino (1994). Social support and social structure: A descriptive epidemiology. *J. Health & Social Behavior* 35: 193–212.

Turner, R. Jay, & S. Noh (1983). Class and psychological vulnerability among women: The significance of social support and personal control. *J. Health & Social Behavior* 24: 2–15.

Turner, R. Jay, & P. Roszell (1994). Psychosocial resources and the stress process. In Avison & Gotlib (1994: 179–210).

Turner, R. J., & W. TenHoor (1978). The NIMH community support program: Pilot approach to a needed social reform. *Schizophrenia Bull.* 4: 319–408.

Turner, R. Jay, & M. O. Wagenfeld (1967). Occupational mobility and schizophrenia. *Amer. Sociological Rev.* 32: 104–13.

Turner, R. Jay, B. Wheaton, & D. A. Lloyd (1995). The epidemiology of social stress. *Amer. Sociological Rev.* 60: 104–25.

Twaddle, A. C., & R. M. Hessler (1977). *A Sociology of Health.* St. Louis, MO: Mosby.

Tyrer, P., P. Casey, & B. Ferguson (1991). Personality disorder in perspective. *Brit. J. Psychiatry* 159: 463–71.

Uba, L. (1982). Meeting the mental health needs of Asian Americans: Mainstream or segregated services. *Professional Psychology* 13: 215–21.

Ulbrich, P., G. J. Warheit, & R. Zimmerman (1989). Race, socioeconomic status and psychological distress. *J. Health & Social Behavior* 30: 131–46.

Umberson, D. (1987). Family status and health behaviors: Social control as a dimension of social integration. *J. Health & Social Behavior* 28: 306–19.

Unger, K. V. (1994). Access to educational programs and its effect on employability. *Psychosocial Rehab. J.* 17: 117–26.

Unger, K. V., W. A. Anthony, K. Sciarappa, & E. S. Rogers (1991). A supported education program for young adults with long-term mental illness. *Hospital & Community Psychiatry* 42: 838–42.

Urban, H. B. (1983). Phenomenological-humanistic approaches. In M. Hersen, A. E. Kazdin, & A. S. Bellack (Eds.), *The Clinical Psychology Handbook.* New York: Pergamon.

U.S. Bureau of the Census (1975). *Historical Statistics of the United States: Colonial Times to 1970* (Bicentennial Edition, Part 1, Ser.119–134). Washington, DC: U.S. GPO.

   (1989). *Money Income and Poverty Status in the United States: 1988* (Current Population Reports, Ser. P-60, no. 166). Washington, DC: U.S. GPO.

   (1991a). *The Hispanic Population in the United States: March 1991* (Current Population Reports, Ser. P-20, no. 455). Washington, DC: U.S. GPO.

   (1991b). *Household and Family Characteristics: March 1989 and 1990* (Current Population Reports, Ser. P-20, no. 477). Washington, DC: U.S. GPO.

   (1996). *Statistical Abstract of the United States,* 116th ed. Washington, DC: U.S. GPO.

U.S. Congress, Congressional Budget Office (1990). *Sources of Support for Adolescent Mothers.* Washington, DC: CBO.

U.S. Congress, Office of Technology Assessment (1992). *The Biology of Mental Disorders* (OTA-BA-538). Washington, DC: U.S. GPO.

U.S. Department of Commerce, Office of Management and Budget (1978). Race and ethnic standards for federal statistics and administrative reporting. Directive no. 15, Office of Federal Statistical Policy and Standards, Washington, DC.

U.S. Department of Labor (1995). *Report on the American Workforce.* Washington, DC: U.S. GPO.

U.S. News & World Report (May 16): 91.

Vaillant, G. E. (1977). *Adaptation to Life.* Boston: Little, Brown.

Valdiserri, E. B., K. R. Carroll, & A. J. Hart (1986). A study of offenses committed by psychotic inmates in a county jail. *Hospital & Community Psychiatry* 37: 163–6.

Van Tosh, L., & P. Del Vecchio (1998). Consumer-operated self-help programs: A technical report. Center for Mental Health Services, Rockville, MD.

Vaux, A. (1988). *Social Support: Theory, Research, and Intervention.* New York: Praeger.

Vega, W. A., & J. W. Murphy (1990). *Culture and the Restructuring of Community Mental Health.* Westport, CT: Greenwood.

Vega, W. A., & R. G. Rumbaut (1991). Ethnic minorities and mental health. *Annual Rev. Sociology* 17: 351–83.

Veil, H. O. F., & U. Baumann (1992a). The many meanings of social support. In Veil & Baumann (1992b: 1–7).

(Eds.) (1992b). *The Meaning and Measurement of Social Support.* New York: Hemisphere.

Vernon, S. W., & R. E. Roberts (1982). Prevalence of treated and untreated psychiatric disorders in three ethnic groups. *Social Science in Medicine* 16: 1575–82.

Veroff, Joanne B. (1981). The dynamics of help-seeking in men and women: A national survey study. *Psychiatry* 44: 189–200.

Veroff, Joseph B., R. A. Kulka, & E. Douvan (1981). *Mental Health in America.* New York: Basic Books.

Vinokur, A., Y. Schul, & R. D. Caplan (1987). Determinants of perceived social support: Interpersonal transactions, personal outlook, and transient affect states. *J. Personality & Social Psychiatry* 53: 1137–45.

Vitalo, R. L. (1971). Teaching improved interpersonal functioning as a preferred model of treatment. *J. Clinical Psychology* 27: 166–71.

Vladeck, B. (1980). *Unloving Care: The Nursing Home Tragedy.* New York: Basic Books.

Volavka, J. A. C., J. O'Donnell, R. Douyon, C. Evangelista, & P. Czobor (1992). Assessment of risk behaviors for HIV infection among psychiatric patients. *Hospital & Community Psychiatry* 43: 482–5.

von Knorring, A.-L., R. Cloninger, M. Bohman, & S. Sigvadsson (1983). An adoption study of depressive disorders and substance abuse. *Arch. General Psychiatry* 40: 943–50.

Voydanoff, P. (1987). *Work and Family Life.* Beverly Hills, CA: Sage.

(1990). Economic distress and family relations: A review of the eighties. *J. Marriage & the Family* 52: 1099–1115.

Wack, R. C. (1993). Treatment services at Kirby forensic psychiatric center. *Internat. J. Law & Psychiatry* 16: 83–104.

Wade, J. C. (1993). Institutional racism: An analysis of the mental health system. *Amer. J. Orthopsychiatry* 63: 536–44.

Wahl, O. (1995). *Media Madness: Public Images of Mental Illness.* New Brunswick, NJ: Rutgers University Press.

Waite, L. J. (1995). Does marriage matter? *Demography* 32: 483–501.

Wakefield, J. C. (1992a). The concept of mental disorder: On the boundary between biological facts and social values. *Amer. Psychologist* 47: 373–88.

(1992b). Disorder as harmful dysfunction: A conceptual critique of DSM-III-R's definition of mental disorder. *Psychological Rev.* 99: 232–47.

(1993). Limits of operationalization: A critique of Spitzer and Endicott's (1978) proposed operational criteria for mental disorder. *J. Abnormal Psychology* 102: 160–72.

(1996). DSM-IV: Are we making diagnostic progress? *Contemporary Psychology* 41: 646–52.

(in press). Meaning and melancholia: Why DSM cannot (entirely) ignore the patient's intentional system. In J. W. Barron (Ed.), *Making Diagnosis Meaningful: New Psychological Perspectives.* Washington, DC: American Psychological Association.

Waldron, I. (1983). Sex differences in illness incidence, prognosis and mortality: Issues and evidence. *Social Science & Medicine* 17: 1107–23.

Waldron, I., & J. A. Jacobs (1988). Effects of labor force participation on women's health: New evidence from a longitudinal study. *J. Occupational Medicine* 30: 977–83.

Walker, D. B. (1995). *The Rebirth of Federalism.* Chatham, NJ: Chatham House.

Walker, P. S., & D. Kiivlahan (1993). Treatment implications of comorbid psychopathology in American Indians and Alaska natives. *Culture, Medicine & Psychiatry* 16: 555–72.

Wallace, C. J. (1995). Social skills rehabilitation services. *Psychotherapy & Rehab. Res. Bull.* 4: 17–22.

Wallace, P. M., & I. H. Gotlib (1990). Marital adjustment during the transition to parenthood: Stability and predictors of change. *J. Marriage & the Family* 52: 21–9.

Wallerstein, J. S. (1984). Children of divorce: Preliminary report of a ten-year follow up of young children. *Amer. J. Orthopsychiatry* 54: 444–58.

Wallerstein, J. S., & S. Blakeslee (1989). *Second Chances: Men, Women and Children a Decade After Divorce.* New York: Ticknor & Fields.

Ward, K. B., & C. W. Mueller (1985). Sex differences in earnings: The influence of industrial sector, authority hierarchy, and human capital variables. *Work & Occupations* 12: 437–63.

Ware, J. E., W. G. Manning, N. Duan, K. B. Wells, & J. P. Newhouse (1984). Health status and the use of outpatient mental health services. *Amer. Psychologist* 39: 1090–1100.

Warheit, G. J. (1979). Life events, coping, stress, and depressive symptomatology. *Amer. J. Psychiatry* 136: 502–7.

Warner, R. (1992). Commentary on Cohen. Prognosis for schizophrenia in the Third World. *Culture, Medicine & Psychiatry* 16: 85–8.

  (1994). *Recovery from Schizophrenia: Psychiatry and Political Economy,* 2nd ed. London: Routledge.

Warr, P., & P. Jackson (1985). Factors influencing the psychological impact of prolonged unemployment and of re-employment. *Social Science & Medicine* 15: 795–807.

Warr, P., P. Jackson, & M. Banks (1988). Unemployment and mental health: Some British studies. *J. Social Issue* 44: 47–68.

Warren, C. A. B. (1977). Involuntary commitment for mental disorder: The application of California's Lanterman–Petris–Short Act. *Law & Society Rev.* 11: 629–50.

  (1982). *Court of Last Resort: Judicial Review of Involuntary Civil Commitment in California.* University of Chicago Press.

Warren, R. (1973). Comprehensive planning and coordination: Some functional aspects. *Social Problems* 20: 355–64.

Washington, P., & R. J. Diamond (1985). Prevalence of mental illness among women incarcerated in five California county jails. *Res. in Community Mental Health* 5: 33–41.

Waxler, N. (1979). Is outcome for schizophrenia better in nonindustrial societies? The case of Sri Lanka. *J. Nervous & Mental Disease* 167: 144–58.

Way, B., M. E. Evans, & S. M. Banks (1993). An analysis of police referrals to 10 psychiatric emergency rooms. *Bull. Amer. Acad. Psychiatry & Law* 21: 389–97.

Webster, P., T. L. Orbuch, & J. S. House (1995). Effects of childhood family background on adult marital quality and perceived stability. *Amer. J. Sociology* 101: 404–32.

Weinstein, N. D. (1993). Testing four competing theories of health protective behavior. *Health Psychology* 12: 325–33.

Weinstein, R. (1979). Patient attitudes toward mental hospitalization: A review of quantitative research. *J. Health & Social Behavior* 20: 237–58.

  (1983). Labeling theory and the attitudes of mental patients: A review. *J. Health & Social Behavior* 24: 70–84.

Weiss, C. I. (1992). Controlling domestic life and mental illness: Spiritual and aftercare resources used by Dominican New Yorkers. *Culture, Medicine & Psychiatry* 16: 237–71.

Weiss, M. F. (1986). Children's attitudes toward the mentally ill: A developmental analysis. *Psychological Reports* 58: 11–20.

Weiss, M. G., R. Raguram, & S. M. Channabasavanna (1995). Cultural dimensions of psychiatric diagnosis. A comparison of DSM-III-R and illness explanatory models in South India. *Brit. J. Psychiatry* 166: 353–9.

Weiss, R. (1974). The provisions of social relationship. In Z. Rubin (Ed.), *Doing unto Others.* Englewood Cliffs, NJ: Prentice-Hall.

Weiss, R. S. (1975). *Marital Separation.* New York: Basic Books.

Weissman, M. M. (1993). The epidemiology of personality disorders: A 1990 update. *J. Personality Disorders* 7: 44–62.

Weissman, M. M., R. Bland, P. R. Joyce, S. Newman, E. J. Wells, & H.-U. Wittchen (1993). Sex differences in rates of depression: Cross-national perspectives. *J. Affective Disorders* 29: 77–84.

Weissman, M. M., M. L. Bruce, P. J. Leaf, L. P. Florio, & C. Holzer III (1991). Affective disorders. In Robins & Regier (1991: 53–80).

Weissman, M., E. Gershon, & K. Kidd (1984). Psychiatric disorders in the relatives of probands with affective disorders: The Yale–NIMH collaborative family study. *Arch. General Psychiatry* 41: 13–21.

Weissman, M., R. Jarret, & J. Rush (1987a). Psychotherapy and its relevance to the pharmacotherapy of major depression: A decade later (1976–1985). In H. Y. Meltzer (Ed.), *Psychopharmacology: The Third Generation of Progress,* pp. 1059–69. New York: Raven.

Weissman, M. M., & G. L. Klerman (1985). Gender and depression. *Trends in Neurosciences* 8: 416–20.

(1992). Depression: Current understanding and changing trends. *Annual Rev. Public Health* 13: 319–39.

Weissman, M. M., P. S. Leaf, & M. L. Bruce (1987b). Single parent women. *Social Psychiatry* 22: 29–36.

Weissman, M. M., & J. K. Myers (1978). Affective disorders in a U.S. urban community. *Arch. General Psychiatry* 35: 1304–11.

Weissman, M. M., J. K. Myers, & C. E. Ross (1986). *Community Surveys of Mental Disorders* (Series in Epidemiology). New Brunswick, NJ: Rutgers University Press.

Weisz, J., & B. Weiss (1993). *Effects of Psychotherapy with Children and Adolescents.* Newbury Park, CA: Sage.

Weithorn, L. (1988). Mental hospitalization of troublesome youth: An analysis of skyrocketing admission rates. *Stanford Law Rev.* 40: 773–838.

Weitz, R. (1991). *Living with AIDS.* New Brunswick, NJ: Rutgers University Press.

Wellman, B. (1981). Applying network analysis to the study of support. In Gottlieb (1981b: 171–200).

(1990). The place of kinfolk in personal community networks. *Marriage & Family Rev.* 15: 195–227.

Wellman, B., & S. Wortley (1989). Brother's keepers: Situating kin relations in broader networks of social support. *Sociological Perspectives* 32: 273–306.

Wells, J. E., J. A. Bushnell, A. R. Hornblow, P. R. Joyce, & M. A. Oakley-Browne (1989a). Christchurch psychiatric epidemiology study, part I: Methodology and lifetime prevalence for specific psychiatric disorders. *Australian–New Zealand J. Psychiatry* 23: 315–26.

Wells, J. C., A. Y. Tien, R. Garrison, & W. W. Eaton (1994). Risk factors for the incidence of social phobia as determined by the Diagnostic Interview Schedule according to DSM-III in a population-based study. *Acta Psychiatrica Scandinavica* 90: 84–90.

Wells, K. B., B. M. Astrachnon, G. T. Tischerler, & J. Unutzer (1995). Issues and approaches in evaluating managed mental health care. *Millbank Q.* 73: 57–74.

Wells, K. B., J. M. Golding, R. L. Hough, A. Burnam, & M. Karno (1988). Factors affecting the probability of use of general and medical health and social/community services for Mexican Americans and non-Hispanic whites. *Medical Care* 26: 441–52.

Wells, K. B., W. G. Manning, N. Duan, J. P. Newhouse, & J. E. Ware (1986). Sociodemographic factors and the use of outpatient mental health services. *Medical Care* 24: 75–85.

Wells, K. B., A. Stewart, R. D. Hays, A. Burnam, W. Rogers, M. Daniels, S. Berry, S. Greenfield, & J. Ware (1989b). The functioning and well-being of depressed patients: Results from the medical outcomes study. *J. Amer. Medical Assoc.* 262: 914–19.

Wells, K., & R. Sturm (1995). Care for depression in a changing environment. *Health Affairs* 14: 78–89.

Wender, P., S. Kety, D. Rosenthal, et al. (1986). Psychiatric disorders in the biological and adoptive families of adopted individuals with affective disorders. *Arch. General Psychiatry* 43: 923–9.

Wender, P., D. Rosenthal, K. Seymour, F. Schulsinger, & J. Welner (1974). Cross-fostering: A research strategy for clarifying the role of genetic and experimental factors in the etiology of schizophrenia. *Arch. General Psychiatry* 30: 121–8.

Werner, P. D., J. A. Yesavage, J. M. T. Becker, D. W. Brunsting, & J. Issacs (1983). Hostile words and assaultive behavior on an acute inpatient unit. *J. Nervous & Mental Disease* 171: 385–7.

Wertlieb, D. (1991). Children and divorce: Stress and coping in developmental perspective. In J. Echenroche (Ed.), *The Social Context of Coping,* pp. 31–54. New York: Plenum.

Westen, D. (1985). *Self and Society.* Cambridge University Press.

Western, M., & E. O. Wright (1994). The permeability of class boundaries to intergenerational mobility among men in the United States, Canada, Norway and Sweden. *Amer. Sociological Rev.* 59: 606–29.

Wethington, E., G. W. Brown, & R. C. Kessler (1995). Interview measurement of stressful life events. In S. Cohen, R. C. Kessler, & L. U. Gordon (Eds.), *Measuring Stress: A Guide for Health and Social Scientists,* pp. 59–79. New York: Oxford University Press.

Wethington, E., & R. Kessler (1986). Perceived support, received support, and adjustment to stressful life events. *J. Health & Social Behavior* 27: 78–89.

Wetzel, J. R. (1995). Labor force, unemployment, and earnings. In Farley (1995: 59–105).

Wexler, D. B. (1981). *Mental Health Law.* New York: Plenum.

Wheaton, B. (1978). The sociogenesis of psychological disorder: Reexamining the causal issues with longitudinal data. *Amer. Sociological Rev.* 43: 383–403.

(1980). The sociogenesis of psychological disorder: An attributional theory. *J. Health & Social Behavior* 21: 100–24.

(1982). A comparison of the moderating effects of personal coping resources on the impact of exposure to stress in two groups. *J. Community Psychology* 10: 293–311.

(1983). Stress, personal coping resources, and psychiatric symptoms: An investigation of interactive models. *J. Health & Social Behavior* 24: 208–29.

(1985). Models for the stress-buffering functions of coping resources. *J. Health & Social Behavior* 26: 352–64.

(1990). Life transitions, role histories, and mental health. *Amer. Sociological Rev.* 55: 209–23.

(1991). Chronic stress: Models and measurement. Paper presented at the Society for Social Problems meetings (August 19–21), Cincinnati, OH.

(1994). Sampling the stress universe. In Avison & Gotlib (1994: 77–114).

(1996). The domains and boundaries of stress concepts. In Kaplan (1996b: 29–70).

(1997). The nature of chronic stress. In B. H. Gottlieb (Ed.), *Coping with Chronic Stress,* pp. 43–73. New York: Plenum.

Wheaton, B., P. Roszell, & K. Hall (1997). The impact of twenty childhood and adult traumatic stressors on the risk of psychiatric disorder. In I. Gotlib & B. Wheaton (Eds.), *Stress and Adversity over the Life Course: Trajectories and Turning Points,* pp. 50–72. New York: Cambridge University Press.

Wheeler, D. S. (1989). Disease or childhood history: Social consequences of the perceived nature of mental disorders. Ph.D. dissertation, University of Connecticut, Storrs.

Whitaker, R. E. D., & D. G. Ostrow (1991). Psychiatric and psychopharmacologic problems in HIV-1 infection. *Hospital Formulary* 26: 948–59.

White, B. J., & E. Madara (1992). *The Self-Help Sourcebook,* 4th ed. Denville, NJ: American Self-Help Clearinghouse.

White, R. W. (1959). Motivation reconsidered: The concept of competence. *Psychological Rev.* 66: 297–333.

WHO [World Health Organization] (1977). *Manual of the International Statistical Classification of Diseases, Injuries, and Causes of Death,* 9th rev. Geneva: WHO.

(1990). *Composite International Diagnostic Interview* (CIDI, ver.1.0). Geneva: WHO.

(1992). *The ICD-10 Classification of Mental and Behavioral Disorders* (International Classification of Diseases), 10th ed. Geneva: WHO.

Wickizer, T., D. Lessler, & K. Travis (1996). Controlling inpatient psychiatric utilization through managed care. *Amer. J. Psychiatry* 53: 339–45.

Wilcox, B. L. (1981a). Social support in adjusting to marital disruption: A network analysis. In Gottlieb (1981b: 97–116).

(1981b). Social support, life stress, and psychological adjustment: A test of the buffering hypothesis. *Amer. J. Community Psychology* 9: 371–86.

Wilhelm, K., & G. Parker (1989). Is sex necessarily a risk factor to depression? *Psychological Medicine* 19: 401–13.

Wilkinson, C. B. (1983). Aftermath of a disaster: The collapse of the Hyatt Regency Hotel skywalks. *Amer. J. Psychiatry* 140: 1134–9.

Williams, A. W., J. W. Ware, & C. A. Donald (1981). A model of mental health, life events, and social support applicable to general populations. *J. Health & Social Behavior* 22: 324–36.

Williams, David R. (1990). Socioeconomic differentials in health: A review and redirection. *Social Psychology Q.* 53: 81–99.

(1996a). Race/ethnicity and socioeconomic status: Measurement and methodological issues. *Internat. J. Health Services* 26: 483–505.

(1996b). Racism and health: A research agenda. *Ethnicity & Disease* 6: 1–6.

(1997). Race and health: Basic questions, emerging directions. *Ann. Epidemiology* 7: 322–33.

(in press). Race, stress and mental health. In C. Hogue, M. Hargraves, & K. Collins (Eds.), *Minority Health in America.* Baltimore: Johns Hopkins University Press.

Williams, D. R., & A.-M. Chung (in press). Racism and health. In R. Gibson & J. S. Jackson (Eds.), *Health in Black America.* Thousand Oaks, CA: Sage.

Williams, D. R., & C. Collins (1995). U.S. socioeconomic and racial differences in health.*Annual Rev. Sociology* 21: 349–86.

Williams, D. R., & B. Fenton (1994). The mental health of African Americans: Findings, questions, and directions. In I. L. Livingston (Ed.), *Handbook of Black American Health: The Mosaic of Conditions, Issues, Policies, and Prospects,* pp. 253–68. Westport, CT: Greenwood.

Williams, D. R., R. Lavizzo-Mourey, & R. C. Warren (1994). The concept of race and health status in America. *Public Health Reports* 109: 26–41.

Williams, D. R., D. T. Takeuchi, & R. K. Adair (1992a). Socioeconomic status and psychiatric disorder among blacks and whites. *Social Forces* 71: 179–94.

(1992b). Marital status and psychiatric disorders among blacks and whites. *J. Health & Social Behavior* 33: 140–58.

Williams, D. R., Y. Yu, J. S. Jackson, & N. B. Anderson (1997). Racial differences in physical and mental health: Socioeconomic status, stress, and discrimination. *J. Health & Psychology* 2: 335–51.

Williams, Donald (1986). The epidemiology of mental illness in Afro Americans. *Hospital & Community Psychiatry* 37: 42–9.

Williams, D. H., E. C. Bells, & S. W. Wellington (1980). Deinstitutionalization and social policy: Historical perspectives and present dilemmas. *Amer. J. Orthopsychiatry* 50: 54–64.

Williams, R. H. (1995). Constructing the public good: Social movements and cultural resources. *Social Problems* 42: 124–44.

Williams, S. (1987). Goffman, interactionism, and the management of stigma in everyday life. In G. Scambler (Ed.), *Sociological Theory and Medical Sociology,* pp. 135–64. London: Tavistock.

Williams-Morris, R. (1996). Racism and children's health: Issues in development. *Ethnicity & Disease* 6: 69–82.

Willie, C. W., P. Rieker, B. Kramer, & B. Brown (Eds.) (1995). *Mental Health, Racism, and Sexism.* Pittsburgh, PA: University of Pittsburgh Press.

Wilson, C., D. Civic, & D. Glass (1994). Prevalence and correlates of depressive syndromes among adults visiting an Indian health service primary care clinic. *American Indian & Alaska Native Mental Health Res.* 6: 1–12.

Wilson, D., G. Tien, & D. Eaves (1995). Increasing the community tenure of mentally disordered offenders: An assertive case management program. *Internat. J. Law & Psychiatry* 18: 61–70.

Wilson, H. S. (1982). *Deinstitutionaled Residential Care for the Mentally Disordered.* New York: Greene & Strath.

Wilson, M. (1993). DSM-III and the transformation of American psychiatry. *Amer. J. Psychiatry* 150: 399–410.

Wilson, W. J. (1985). Urban poverty. *Annual Rev. Sociology* 11: 231–58.

Windle, C., & D. Scully (1974). Community mental health centers and the decreasing use of state mental hospitals. *Community Mental Health J.* 12: 239–43.

Wittchen, H.-U. (1994). Reliability and validity studies of the WHO–Composite International Diagnostic Interview (CIDI): A critical review. *J. Psychiatric Res.* 28: 57–84.

Wofsy, C. B. (1988). Women and the acquired immunodeficiency syndrome: An interview. *Western J. Medicine* 149: 687–90.

Wolcott, D. L., F. I. Fawzy, & R. O. Pasnau (1985). Acquired immune deficiency syndrome (AIDS) and consultation–liaison psychiatry. *General Hospital Psychiatry* 7: 280–92.

Wolcott, D. L., S. Namir, F. I. Fawzy, M. S. Gottlieb, & R. T. Mitsuyasu (1986). Illness concerns, attitudes towards homosexuality and social support in gay men with AIDS. *General Hospital Psychiatry* 8: 395–403.

Wolf, T. M., P. M. Balson, E. V. Morse, P. M. Simon, R. H. Gaumer, P. W. Dralle, & M. H. Williams (1991). Relationship of coping style to affective state and perceived social support in asymptomatic and symptomatic HIV-infected persons: Implications for clinical management. *J. Clinical Psychiatry* 52: 171–3.

Wolff, E. N. (1995). *Top Heavy: A Study of Wealth Inequality in America*. New York: Twentieth Century Fund.

Wolff, N. (1989). Professional uncertainty and physician medical decision-making in a multiple treatment framework. *Social Sciences & Medicine* 28: 99–107.

Wolff, N., M. Schlesinger, & F. Vajhe (1997). Professional responsibilities and advocacy for patients: The impact of managed care. Working paper, Institute for Health, Health Care Policy and Aging Research, Rutgers University, New Brunswick, NJ.

Wolinsky, F. D., & C. L. Arnold (1986). A different perspective on health and health service utilization. *Annual Rev. Gerontology & Geriatrics* 8: 71–101.

Wolpe, J. (1958). *Psychotherapy by Reciprocal Inhibition*. Stanford, CA: Stanford University Press.

Woods, W. J. (1985). A comparison study of psychological status of AIDS-associated Kaposi's sarcoma patients, acute leukemia patients and healthy gay and heterosexual men. Ph.D. dissertation, Ohio State University, Columbus.

Worth, D. (1990). Women at high risk of HIV infection: Behavioral, prevention, and intervention aspects. In Ostrow (1990: 101–17).

Worthington, C. (1992). An examination of factors influencing the diagnosis and treatment of black patients in the mental health system. *Arch. Psychiatric Nursing* 6: 195–204.

Wright, E. (1994). Caring for those who "can't": Gender, network structure, and the burden of caring for people with mental illness. Ph.D. dissertation, Department of Sociology, Indiana University, Bloomington.

Wright, E. O. (1979). *Class Structure and Income Determination*. New York: Academic Press.

(1985). *Classes*. London: Verso.

(1993). Typologies, scales, and class analysis: A comment on Halaby and Weakliem. *Amer. Sociological Rev.* 58: 31–4.

Wu, I.-H., & C. W. Windle (1980). Ethnic specificity in the relative minority use and staffing of community mental health centers. *Community Mental Health J.* 16: 156–68.

Wurtzel, E. (1995). *Prozac Nation*. New York: Riverhead.

Yarrow, M. R., C. G. Schwartz, H. S. Murphy, & L. C. Deasy (1955). The psychological meaning of mental illness in the family. *J. Social Issues* 11: 12–24.

Ybarra, S. (1991). Women and AIDS: Implications for counseling. *J. Counseling & Development* 69: 285–97.

Yesavage, J. A., P. D. Werner, J. M. T. Becker, & M. J. Mills (1982). Short-term civil commitment and the violent patient: A study of legal status and inpatient behavior. *Amer. J. Psychiatry* 139: 1145–9.

Ying, Y.-W., & L.-T. Hu (1994). Public outpatient mental health services: Use and outcome among Asian Americans. *Amer. J. Orthopsychiatry* 64: 448–55.

Young, J. C. (1981). *Medical Choices in a Mexican Village*. New Brunswick, NJ: Rutgers University Press.

Young, K., & D. T. Takeuchi (1998). Racism. In L. C. Lee & N. W. S. Zane (Eds.), *Handbook of Asian American Psychology*. Thousand Oaks, CA: Sage.

Young, M. (1994). *The Rise of the Meritocracy* (with a new Introduction by the author). New Brunswick, NJ: Transaction.

Young, M. A., L. F. Fogg, W. A. Scheftner, M. B. Keller, & J. A. Fawcett (1990). Sex differences in the lifetime prevalence of depression. *J. Affective Disorders* 18: 187–92.

Yucun, S., C. Changhui, Z. Esixi, X. Tingming, & T. Yunhua (1990). An example of community-based health/home care programme. *Psychosocial Rehab. J.* 14: 29–34.

Zajonc, R. B. (1976). Family configuration and intelligence. *Science* 192: 227–36.

Zald, M., & J. McCarthy (1987). *Social Movements in an Organizational Society*. New Brunswick, NJ: Transaction.

Zaslow, M., B. Rabinovich, & J. T. D. Suwalsky (1991). From maternal employment to child outcomes: Preexisting group differences and moderating variables. In J. V. Lerner & N. Galambos (Eds.), *Employed Mothers and Their Children*, pp. 237–82. New York: Garland.

Zeifert, P., M. Leary, & A. A. Boccellari (1995). AIDS and the impact of cognitive impairment. AIDS Health Project, University of California, San Francisco.

Zhang, M. Y., H. Yan, et al. (1993). Effectiveness of psychoeducation of relatives of schizophrenic patients: A prospective cohort study in five cities in China. *Internat. J. Mental Health* 22: 47–57.

Zich, J., & L. Temoshok (1987). Perceptions of social support in men with AIDS and ARC: Relationships with distress and hardiness. *J. Applied Social Psychology* 17: 193–215.

Zimmerman, M. (1994). Diagnosing personality disorders: A review of issues and research methods. *Arch. General Psychiatry* 51: 225–45.

Zinman, S., Howie the Harp, & S. Budd (1987). Reaching across: Mental health clients helping each other. California Network of Mental Health Clients, Riverside.

Zuravin, S. J. (1988). Effects of fertility patterns on child abuse and neglect. *J. Marriage & the Family* 50: 983–94.

Name Index

Subject Index

Email
-or-
30 College Ave.
Green Victorian
Ham. & College Ave